Social Research Methods

Second Edition

Edited by
Maggie Walter

Social Research Methods

Second Edition

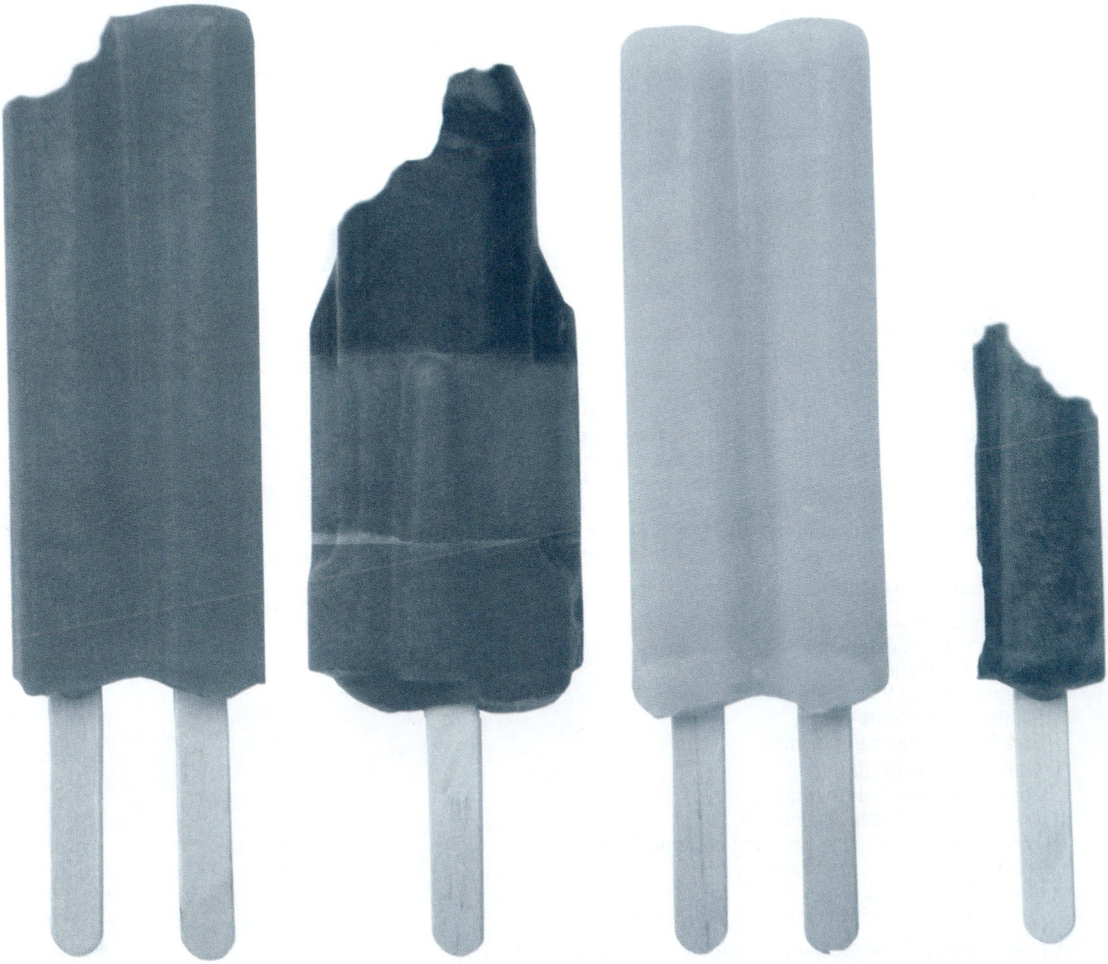

OXFORD
UNIVERSITY PRESS
AUSTRALIA & NEW ZEALAND

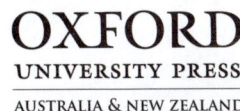

OXFORD
UNIVERSITY PRESS

Oxford University Press is a department of the University of Oxford.
It furthers the University's objective of excellence in research,
scholarship, and education by publishing worldwide. Oxford is a registered
trademark of Oxford University Press in the UK and in certain other
countries.

Published in Australia by
Oxford University Press
253 Normanby Road, South Melbourne, Victoria 3205, Australia

© Maggie Walter 2010

The moral rights of the author have been asserted.

First published 2006
Second edition published 2010
Reprinted 2010, 2011 (twice), 2012

All rights reserved. No part of this publication may be reproduced, stored in a retrieval system, or transmitted, in any form or by any means, without the prior permission in writing of Oxford University Press, or as expressly permitted by law, by licence, or under terms agreed with the reprographics rights organisation. Enquiries concerning reproduction outside the scope of the above should be sent to the Rights Department, Oxford University Press, at the address above.

You must not circulate this work in any other form and you must impose this same condition on any acquirer.

National Library of Australia Cataloguing-in-Publication data

Social research methods / edited by Maggie Walter.
2nd edn

978 0 19 556283 5 (pbk)
Bibliography.
Includes index.

Social sciences—Research—Australia.
Social sciences—Australia—Statistical methods.

Walter, Maggie.

300.72

Reproduction and communication for educational purposes
The Australian *Copyright Act 1968* (the Act) allows a maximum of one chapter or 10% of the pages of this work, whichever is the greater, to be reproduced and/or communicated by any educational institution for its educational purposes provided that the educational institution (or the body that administers it) has given a remuneration notice to Copyright Agency Limited (CAL) under the Act.

For details of the CAL licence for educational institutions contact:

Copyright Agency Limited
Level 15, 233 Castlereagh Street
Sydney NSW 2000
Telephone: (02) 9394 7600
Facsimile: (02) 9394 7601
Email: info@copyright.com.au

Edited by Bruce Gillespie
Cover design by Josh Durham
Text design by Caitlin Ziegler
Typeset by Kerry Cooke, eggplant communications
Proofread by Elaine Cochrane
Indexed by Karen Gillen
Printed in China by Sheck Wah Tong Printing Press Ltd

Links to third party websites are provided by Oxford in good faith and for information only.
Oxford disclaims any responsibility for the materials contained in any third party website referenced in this work.

Brief Contents

Contributors	xiii
Acknowledgments	xvi
Preface	xvii
A Note for Lecturers in Social Research Methods	xx
A Note for Students of Social Research Methods	xxiii

Part 1: The Foundations of Good Social Science Research — 1

Chapter 1: The Nature of Social Science Research — 3

Chapter 2: Research Design — 31

Chapter 3: The Research Process — 61

Chapter 4: Ethics and Social Research — 89

Chapter 5: Sampling — 123

Part 2: Quantitative Methods and the Power of the Numbers — 149

Chapter 6: Surveys — 151

Chapter 7: Population-level Analysis — 183

Chapter 8: Analysing Quantitative Data — 217

Chapter 9: Using SPSS for Quantitative Analysis — 243

Part 3: Qualitative Methods and Meaning-making — 285

Chapter 10: Qualitative Interviewing Methods — 287

Chapter 11: Content Analysis — 323

Chapter 12: Discourse Analysis — 351

Chapter 13: Doing Evaluation Research — 377

Chapter 14: Analysing Qualitative Data — 407

Part 4: Writing Up Our Research for Dissemination — 437

Chapter 15: Writing Up Research — 439

Glossary	472
Index	502

Social Research Methods

Extended Contents

Contributors	xiii
Acknowledgments	xvi
Preface	xvii
A Note for Lecturers in Social Research Methods	xx
A Note for Students of Social Research Methods	xxiii

Part 1: The Foundations of Good Social Science Research — 1

Chapter 1: The Nature of Social Science Research — 3
Maggie Walter

What is social research?	4
The 'science' in social science	8
Social patterns and social meanings	9
Social research: Why do we do it?	10
The language of social science	12
Method and methodology: Understanding the difference	12
What goes into making a methodology?	13
Voices in the field: Karen Martin	23
Voices in the field: Virginia Watson	24
From method to practice	25
Conclusion	28

Chapter 2: Research Design — 31
Kristin Natalier

Introduction	32
Research questions	32
Research aims	35
Literature review	36
Methods	44
Voices in the field: Trisch Short	46
Definition and measurement decisions	47
The theoretical direction: Deductive or inductive?	49
Timelines	50
Resources	52
Design in practice: The research proposal	52
From method to practice	55
Conclusion	58

Chapter 3: The Research Process — 61
Douglas Ezzy

Introduction	62
The process of social research	63

Ten issues for social researchers — 64
Voices in the field: Sarah Wendt — 77
From method to practice — 79
A qualitative interview study of teenage Witchcraft — 81
A discourse analysis of racism in newspapers — 83
Conclusion — 85

Chapter 4: Ethics and Social Research — 89
Daphne Habibis

Introduction — 90
Why is ethics an issue in social research? — 90
The history of ethics and research — 92
The history of ethics and research in Australia — 94
When is ethical review needed? — 95
Protecting participants — 96
Data management — 103
Data storage — 103
Safety — 104
Research merit — 105
Vulnerable participant groups — 105
Ethics and the researcher — 108
Ethics and the organisation — 110
Everyday ethical dilemmas — 111
Can the ends justify the means? Covert research — 112
Voices in the field: Hannah Graham — 114
From method to practice — 115
Conclusion — 116

Chapter 5: Sampling — 123
Bruce Tranter

Why we sample — 124
Defining the population — 124
Selecting our sampling method — 125
Probability sampling — 126
Sample non-response — 134
Non-probability sampling — 137
Selecting sampling size for non-probability sampling — 140
Voices in the field: Wally Karnilowicz — 143
From method to practice — 144
Conclusion — 146

Part 2: Quantitative Methods and the Power of the Numbers 149

Chapter 6: Surveys 151
Maggie Walter

Introduction	152
Choosing a survey as your social research method	152
Advantages of surveys	152
Disadvantages of surveys	154
Common types of survey design	155
The process of survey research	156
Voices in the field: Allan Welch	175
From method to practice	176
Conclusion	179

Chapter 7: Population-level Analysis 183
Natalie Jackson

Introduction	184
What is population-level data analysis?	185
Differences between population-level data and survey data	186
Uses of population-level analysis	187
Strengths and weaknesses of population-level analysis	188
Analytical issues	190
Analytical complexities	194
Intra-collection discontinuities	194
Inter-collection discontinuities	195
Useful techniques	197
Standardisation	203
Voices in the field: Honours student to practitioner	211
From method to practice	212
Conclusion	214

Chapter 8: Analysing Quantitative Data 217
Tim Phillips

Introduction: The lure of quantitative data and analysis	218
What is quantitative data, and why do we analyse it?	219
How to do quantitative data analysis	220
A mini-quantitative analysis	223
Beginning the analysis: Locating appropriate data	225
Choosing appropriate techniques in quantitative data analysis	234
Doing quantitative data analysis well: Imagination and devotion	236
Voices in the field: Joanna Sikora and Lawrence J. Saha	238
From method to practice	239
Conclusion	240

Chapter 9: Using SPSS for Quantitative Analysis — 243
Phillip Patman

Introduction: Our SPSS dataset	244
Coding your data into the SPSS file	244
Data analysis in SPSS	256
Recoding data	270
Transforming data	273
Saving data	276
Exporting data	276
Voices in the field: Kate Warner	279
From method to practice	280
Conclusion	281

Part 3: Qualitative Methods and Meaning-making — 285

Chapter 10: Qualitative Interviewing Methods — 287
Max Travers

Introduction	288
What is a qualitative interview?	289
The importance of meaning	290
How to conduct an in-depth interview	291
Choosing a topic	293
How many interviews?	294
Recruiting interviewees	296
Approaching the interview	298
Interviewing techniques	303
Recording your data	307
Beyond interviewing	309
From method to practice	312
Voices in the field: Margaret Alston	313
Focus groups	314
Voices in the field: Tim Marjoribanks	316
Conclusion	319

Chapter 11: Content Analysis — 323
Warren Sproule

Introduction	324
What is content analysis?	324
Explicit and implicit coding	325
Types of content analysis	327
Conducting a content analysis	332
Voices in the field: Adrian Franklin	344
From method to practice	344
Conclusion	347

Chapter 12: Discourse Analysis — 351
Keith Jacobs

Introduction	352
The background to discourse analysis	353
Advantages of discourse analysis as a method of social research	354
Key terms and concepts in discourse analysis	354
Critical discourse analysis	356
Foucauldian-inspired analysis	357
Challenges associated with discourse analysis	360
Undertaking a critical discourse analysis	363
Foucauldian-inspired analysis	366
Voices in the field: Brendan Churchill	370
From method to practice	371
Conclusion	372

Chapter 13: Doing Evaluation Research — 377
Rob White

Introduction	378
The unique aspects of evaluation research	378
Purposes of evaluation	379
Undertaking an evaluation	380
Preparing the report	394
Limitations of evaluation	395
Voices in the field: Diane Heckenberg	399
From method to practice	400
Conclusion	404

Chapter 14: Analysing Qualitative Data — 407
Karen Willis

Introduction	408
Creating meaning: The vital ingredients	409
Organising our data	415
Approaches to analysis	418
Commencing analysis	418
Exploring relationships between categories	421
Discrepancies and deviant cases	421
Explaining what is going on: Themes	422
Grounded theory	423
Narrative analysis and life histories	424
Extending the analytical challenge: Analysing focus groups	427
Voices in the field: Jane Maree Maher	429
Voices in the field: Fiona Gill	430
From method to practice	431
Conclusion	432

Part 4: Writing Up Our Research for Dissemination — 437

Chapter 15: Writing Up Research — 439
Michelle Gabriel

Introduction	440
Discovery through writing	440
Writing style	442
Writing a research plan or proposal	445
Writing a research report	447
Presentation of quantitative data	452
Presentation of qualitative data	453
Final statement	456
Writing strategies	457
Editing and revising	459
Voices in the field: Evan Willis	463
Dissemination	464
From method to practice	465
Conclusion	468

Glossary	472
Index	502

Contributors

All chapter contributors are academics, teaching and researching in the School of Sociology and Social Work at the University of Tasmania.

Douglas Ezzy

Douglas Ezzy's research is driven by a fascination with how people make meaningful and dignified lives. His most recent publication is the book *Teenage Witches* (Rutgers 2007), which is an international study of teenage Witchcraft with Helen Berger (West Chester University). His other books include: *Qualitative Analysis*, *Narrating Unemployment* and *Practising the Witch's Craft*.

Michelle Gabriel

Michelle Gabriel is a postdoctoral research fellow with the Housing and Community Research Unit (HACRU) at the University of Tasmania, part of a consortium of housing researchers within the Australian Housing and Research Institute's (AHURI) Southern Research Centre. Michelle researches and publishes on a wide variety of housing-related issues, including housing affordability and changing housing careers.

Daphne Habibis

Daphne Habibis' research interests include mental health, with a focus on people living with a serious mental illness and housing. She has also been a member of the University of Tasmania's Ethics (Human Experimentation) Committee, and chaired its Northern Campus subcommittee. Her most recent publication is *Social Inequality in Australia: Discourses, Realities and Futures* (Oxford University Press 2008) with Maggie Walter.

Natalie Jackson

Natalie Jackson has published extensively on population–ageing issues in both Australia and New Zealand. Her main areas of research are the political–economic implications of the different rates of population ageing unfolding across Australia's states, territories, and local government areas; and whether Australia's baby boomers will change their retirement intentions in line with government thinking on the issue.

Keith Jacobs

Keith Jacobs' teaching focus is urban sociology. His major areas of research interest are housing policy, migration and urban politics. He has published widely on housing policy.

Recent work includes *The Dynamics of Local Housing Policy* (1999) and *Social Constructionism in Housing Research* (2004) edited with Jim Kemeny and Tony Manzi. Both books are published by Ashgate Press.

Kristin Natalier

Kristin Natalier is a qualitative researcher, working within an interpretive frame to discover how people make sense of the challenges they face in their day-to-day lives. In particular, she studies how people experience families and housing. Her current work centres on an Australian Housing and Research Institute's (AHURI) funded project investigating the links between state care and young people's housing circumstances. She is also writes on issues surrounding child support and parenting apart.

Phillip Patman

Phillip Patman works in a statistical and quantitative support role for postgraduate candidates and staff across the Faculties of Arts and Humanities, and also tutors in social research and quantitative methods. He has been using statistical software including SPSS and SAS since such programs first became available.

Tim Phillips

Tim Phillips teaches in the areas of social theory and research methods. His research interests include Australian society, research methods, culture and identity, and deviance. He is currently undertaking a nationwide survey on experiences of rude and inconsiderate behaviour in everyday life.

Warren Sproule

Warren Sproule currently teaches in the areas of the sociology of underdevelopment, and mass media and contemporary society. His research interests include poststructural theory, neoanarchist social movements, globalisation and the sociology of war.

Bruce Tranter

Bruce Tranter teaches social research methods at the University of Tasmania. His research interests include national identity, social movements, political attitudes, and behaviour and postmaterial values, and he is a Principal Investigator for the Australian Survey of Social Attitudes (AuSSA) 2007.

Max Travers

Max Travers teaches qualitative research and sociological theory. He has published in the areas of sociology of law, criminology and qualitative research methods. His previous publications include *Qualitative Research Through Case Studies* (Sage 2001). His current projects include the impact of quality assurance on public sector work; and sentencing in children's courts.

Maggie Walter

Maggie Walter teaches social research methods at the undergraduate and postgraduate level, and in the areas of social policy and Indigenous issues. Her research interests centre on the impact of social policy. She is passionate about the interaction of policy and inequality, the family and Indigenous lives, and has recently published *Social Inequality in Australia: Discourses, Realities and Futures* (Oxford University Press 2008) with Daphne Habibis.

Rob White

Rob White has research and scholarly interests in criminology, youth studies and public policy, with a special interest in green or environmental criminology. Among his recent publications are *Crimes Against Nature: Environmental Criminology and Ecological Justice*; *Environmental Crime: A Reader*; *Crime Prevention: Principles, Perspectives and Practices* (with Adam Sutton and Adrian Cherney); *Controversies in Environmental Sociology*; *Youth and Society* (with Johanna Wyn); and *Crime and Criminology* (with Fiona Haines).

Karen Willis

Karen Willis is a Senior Lecturer in Sociology at UTAS and an Adjunct Senior Lecturer at Mother and Child Health Research at La Trobe University. She has a particular interest in the use of qualitative methods to achieve best evidence in health policy and practice, and has published widely on this topic. She is currently researching the ways that qualitative research methods can inform complex interventions in health care.

Acknowledgments

After beginning life as an in-house social research methods guide for our undergraduate and honours students, this text has now been used by several thousand Australian social research students. I know; I have taught around 500 of them. This achievement, along with the publication of this second edition, is a credit to the chapter contributors. These contributors, most of whom are academic staff from the University of Tasmania, are exemplars of collegial virtue. Their on-going support of the project, and their willingness to update their chapters competently and creatively, meet the additional criteria and complete on time, made the task of editing not only rewarding but enjoyable. A special mention is deserved by the authors of the new topics—research design, sampling and measurement, and SPSS—who delivered full chapter drafts in the same, relatively short, time period as those with revisions. The generous contribution of social researchers around Australia of vignettes and overviews of their research projects and enthusiasms also invaluably strengthens the real research context of the different chapters.

My appreciation also continues for the students of our HGA 203/303 Social and Political Research unit, who provide irreplaceable frontline, timely and often frank feedback on different aspects and features of the text, especially the in-class exercises.

I would also like to thank the reviewers of the first edition, who provided constructive suggestions on how to improve the text for social research methods lecturers who teach the subject and for the students who study it. The additional chapters, as well as other 'new features' of the book, are based on that advice.

To our publishers, Oxford University Press, especially Rachel Saffer and Katie Ridsdale, your enthusiasm for the text, encouragement of its concepts and aims, and support during the often arduous process of turning a good idea and basic materials into an operational text is warmly recognised.

Finally, I am grateful to those publishers and authors who kindly gave permission for us to reproduce their copyright material. The targeted use of their work in the various chapters contributes to the research practice orientation of the text. Every effort has been made to trace the original source of material contained in this book. Where the attempt has been unsuccessful the publisher would be pleased to hear from the author or publisher to rectify the omission.

Maggie Walter
2009

Preface

This text is designed for students at the beginning of their journey in social research. Our aim is to provide an accessible, practically orientated and Australian-focused introduction to social research methods. Within this, we seek to develop students' awareness and appreciation of the very wide range of research methods and practices available, and the unique value and limitations of each. Essentially, each chapter presents a succinct 'what is' introduction, followed by practical 'how to' instruction, plus a concise explanation of the topic's major strengths or weaknesses. Each chapter also has the critical added benefit of being written by an active research practitioner, experienced in the particular social science method or practice.

In developing the text, our intention is not to be tied too rigidly to the traditional offerings of social research methods texts. Without losing the essential base of the social research process, the research methods included in this book are selected on the basis of their relevance to contemporary Australian social research practice. Recent Australian case studies are used liberally within the text to provide direct examples of how the methods are actually employed within the social sciences.

As an introductory undergraduate social research text, our goal is not to fully equip students as social researchers in any specific method or technique. Rather, our aim is to inspire students to continue their engagement with social research by presenting the requisite introductory skills within a framework of exciting, up-to-date, relevant Australian research. A broad and comparative understanding of the major contemporary Australian social research methods is a vital prerequisite for beginner social scientists. This text aims to provide that prerequisite.

What's new in this edition?

The additions, revisions and new features of this second edition are outlined in detail in the following section for lecturers and course coordinators. In summary, however, there are four major areas of change:

1. All first edition chapters are updated and revised to maximise their relevancy and strengthen links between the chapters. To improve usability for students, key social science terms are now defined where they appear in the text as well as in the glossary. The text has also been segmented into four coherent subgroupings, and the progression line reorganised to reflect the new structure. The four segments are:

    Part 1   The Foundations of Good Social Science Research

    Part 2   Quantitative Methods and the Power of the Numbers

Part 3   Qualitative Methods and Meaning-making
   Part 4   Writing Up Our Research for Dissemination.
2 Again based on feedback, three additional chapters are included: one details the research design process and practice; another expands the techniques, types and theories of sampling into its own chapter; plus a new chapter, quantitative analysis using SPSS.
3 All chapters, new and existing, have added: 'Voices in the field' and 'From method to practice' sections. 'Voices in the field' are vignettes from Australian social scientists outlining relevant aspects of their research practice. The 'From method to practice' sections provide real-world descriptions of applying the method within a research project.
4 The online resources are substantially increased, and now provide: additional material relating to social research methods not included in the text; two extension chapters on quantitative analysis using SPSS; a set of frequently asked questions and interviews with text authors; a range of additional method modules, including chapters on Indigenous methodologies; conversation analysis, narrative methods, experiments, ethnography and memory work. These are available at <**www.oup.com.au/orc/walter**>. In addition, support material is included. For the quantitative methods and analysis section, this includes a subset of 50 variables from the 2007 Australian Survey of Social Attitudes (AuSSA) and, for use with the qualitative sections, a set of five transcripts of in-depth interviews on the topic of national identity.

The structure of the book

Part 1 is the largest section, containing five chapters, which set the social science research context for the method chapters in parts 2 and 3. The first of these, the nature of social research, outlines what social research actually is. In particular, this chapter stresses the difference between a method and a methodology, and defines the different aspects of a research methodology. Chapter 2 builds on this foundation by focusing on the key aspects of designing a social research project, including the centrality of the research question, theoretical and conceptual elements, and the research proposal. Chapter 3 develops the pragmatic elements of research design into the larger picture of the research process, emphasising the interconnectedness of each phase and how they fit together. Chapter 4 is a comprehensive discussion of the purpose of ethics within social research, and its place as a fundamental determinant in the design, development and implementation of all social research projects alongside its practical embodiment in the research process. In chapter 5, the core facets of sampling and measurement, probability and non-probability, are explained and demonstrated.

Part 2 concentrates on research methods and analysis associated with quantitative research. The quantitative chapters are deliberately placed before the qualitative chapters to try to engage students in what they often consider is the 'harder' methods early in their learning. As social research lecturers know, teaching bivariate analysis in week 11 of a semester can be an unrewarding task. The qualitative section begins a concise but thorough overview of the key aspects of survey research in chapter 6. In chapter 7, the use of quantitative methods is expanded into the increasingly influential field of demographic research. This chapter provides a practical hands-on introduction to population data and population-level analysis. The next two chapters deal with the analysis and interpretation of quantitative data (chapter 8) and how to conduct quantitative data analyses using SPSS (chapter 9). Directly applicable univariate and bivariate quantitative techniques are explored, explained and demonstrated.

Part 3 contains qualitative research methods. In chapter 10 the basic imperatives of in-depth qualitative interviewing are developed, along with an outline of focus group processes and practice. Chapter 11 follows a case study through the different stages of content analysis, and develops the basics skills required for this research method. The importance of language and meaning to social enquiry is expanded in the chapter on discourse analysis (chapter 11), where the variety of approaches is discussed along with the key practices. An area of rising prominence within social research, evaluation research, is the subject of chapter 12. While evaluation research and content analysis do not fall neatly into the qualitative camp, their focus on meaning leads to their more appropriate placement in this section. Chapter 14 provides a functional introduction to analysing qualitative social research data, focusing on the thematic or narrative analysis of in-depth interviews and focus group sessions.

Part 4 contains only one chapter, chapter 15, a user-friendly and practical guide to the essential—but in other social research texts often neglected—skills needed for the effective write-up of social science research to allow for dissemination.

Finally, while we have divided our text into succinct parts and chapters, each addressing a different fact of social research and a different social research method, the skills and understanding included in each chapter are applicable across the general field of social science research. A central message of this text is that social research is a process and a practice that legitimately and effectively uses a very wide range of social research methods.

A Note for Lecturers in Social Research Methods

The rationale for the text

The impetus for the first edition of this book emerged from a number of coalescing sources and these remain valid for this second edition. The primary motivation was the frustration that I, and colleagues as lecturers in undergraduate and postgraduate social research methods units, felt at the dearth of well-written, concise, practically orientated, and, most importantly, Australian, introductory social research texts. We continued, like many other Australian tertiary institutions, to 'make do' with American- or British-based texts, trying to overcome their deficits by supplying an Australian context and Australian examples through our lectures.

The second impetus was the feeling that while the books we were currently using, as mostly one-author texts, tended to do well in some areas of social research methods, in others, the author's lack of practical experience and expertise was obvious. Given that a major aim of our introductory social research unit is to develop students' awareness and appreciation of the very wide range of methods available to social researchers, and the unique value of each, this deficit was particularly problematic. As a result we were only using the prescribed texts selectively as core reading and substituting our own material for the chapters we deemed lacking.

The third source for this book was the realisation that our own school contained a highly skilled social research methods resource. Whether by good luck or good management we had assembled as colleagues a group of social researchers with skills and experience across a diverse and comprehensive range of the major social research methods. Why not, we thought, bring these skills and expertise together in our own social research methods, Australian-orientated text? In this edition we have built on this resource, bringing in other colleagues for the new chapters and expanding beyond the boundaries of the University of Tasmania to include the research voices and stories of social science researchers from a variety of disciplines across Australia.

And while most, but not all, of the contributors to this book are sociologists, the material is purposefully generic to the social sciences. The unit for which this text was originally designed contains students from a wide variety of disciplines and the class is strongly encouraged, or in some cases mandated, as a central part of a variety of undergraduate courses.

Finally, our key rationale and determinant of the book's shape and direction is our desire to provide students with the skills and knowledge base needed to select the most appropriate social research methods and methodologies for their own future research projects.

Features of the text

As lecturers in social science research methods our role is to bring social research alive for our students and to engage them in the thrill of the research process. As we know, this can be a formidable task. Not only are social science students often wary of anything that includes terms such as 'statistics' or 'analysis', but our classes are often very large. We must also somehow manage to fit the basics of the huge topic of social research into a 13-week semester.

With the first edition in 2006 we began the design process by specifying the key dimensions of the sort of text we would like to use. The results were that the text should be: user-friendly (for both students and lecturers); Australian in its focus; have a strong practical orientation; and be accessible in its language and presentation. To meet these criteria each chapter in the text included:

- numerous Australian examples and case studies
- summary boxes of key points
- explicit, but concise, 'how to' instructions on different techniques
- highlighting of key terms throughout and at the end of the chapter, plus a combined glossary of all terms and definitions at the end the book
- topic exercises in each chapter
- a main points summary at the end of each chapter.

Again, the exercises are a special feature of the design. Each is developed to allow students to gain hands-on practice in different elements of the social research process. These exercises can be used in a number of ways: as a material resource for tutorials; as within-lecture exercises to engage students directly in important aspects of social research methods and process; or as take-home exercises to reinforce classroom learning. They have all been trialled successfully within our own units over the last few years. Their placement within the text also saves having to reproduce multiple copies and allows students to prepare for tutorial sessions.

These features have been expanded in this edition. We have updated the features from the first edition and added the following sections:

- **Voices in the field**
  Each chapter now contains a vignette from a prominent Australian social science researcher (and in some, two researchers) on aspects of their practice. These provide insight into the work currently being done in the field, and add detail on what social science looks like and feels like outside of a textbook.

- **From method to practice**
  Each chapter also now contains a section on the direct practice of the method. Again the purpose is to provide students with a more grounded understanding of the social science research process and its real-world practice.
- **In-text definitions**
  As well as being collated in the glossary, key social science terms and concepts are now also succinctly defined where they appear within the chapters.

Online features

For this edition, the online resources have also been substantially expanded. These are designed to be easily accessible and usable for students and lecturers to support and enhance in-text material and exercises. These now include:

- additional chapter material on common Australian usage of social research methods. Conversational analysis, Participatory action research; Ethnographic research and case study methods; Memory work and life histories are all outlined in separate online chapters, as is a new outline of the key aspects of Indigenous methodologies. Extension chapters on quantitative analysis are also included
- a subset of 50 variables from the 2007 *Australian Survey of Social Attitudes* (AuSSA) for use with the chapters on quantitative methods and analysis, including SPSS
- a set of five transcripts of in-depth interviews on the topic of national identity for use in the qualitative analysis and interviewing methods chapters
- a set of frequently asked questions (and answers)
- interviews with the editor and some of the chapter contributors.

We formally express our thanks here to the researchers on the *Australian Survey of Social Attitudes* (AuSSA) for making available a subset of variables from their 2007 survey. Also thanks to those students who volunteered to be respondents for our qualitative example in-depth interviews and transcripts.

Online resources are available at <www.oup.com.au/orc/walter>.

We hope this updated, extra-feature second edition provides a solid base for your teaching in social research methods. We are also always open to suggestions for improvements, additions or changes.

A Note for Students of Social Research Methods

The thrill of social research

Students beginning their study social science research methods tend to have two basic expectations: that the unit will be hard and/or boring. Or possibly both. As a former social science research beginner, I understand completely how students are feeling. But, as an enthusiastic social science research practitioner, I can assure students reading this text that learning about social research need be neither hard nor boring.

Let's deal with the boring bit first. Social science research is what makes social science come alive. While learning some of the theory and practices associated with research can sometimes be a hard slog, it is the skills and understandings you acquire here that allow you to move from being a social science student to a social science practitioner. Research skills are the bridge between passive study of what others have done and active participation in finding social answers. Essentially, research is the creative part of being a social scientist, the adventurous part, and the part where what you do can actually make a difference. Gaining a grasp of basic social science research skills is like moving from a student learner status to your social science researcher P plates. While you still need guidance and support, you are able to head out in a research direction of choice, under your own steam— and that is exciting.

More pragmatically, your social research abilities will prove an ongoing, highly regarded, marketable set of skills across your academic and professional life. A core understanding of social research methods gives you practical, hands-on research skills. Whether you plan to enter the workforce after your undergraduate degree or go on to postgraduate studies, these skills provide a base for you to:

- undertake your own research projects
- interpret and apply the social research findings of others
- critically analyse contemporary social research literature and findings.

Social research methods skills are increasingly required and valued by business and government agencies, and can be directly marketed to your future employers. Past students have used their social science research skills to support their employment aims and are now working across a wide variety of realms; including as a policy officer with a state department of economic development; with the Australian Bureau of Statistics; with community welfare agencies as research officers; as graduate trainees with the Commonwealth and state public service and with market research companies.

Now let's turn to hard. Learning about social research methods is not harder than other social science units, but it does differ in the construction of the task and the way it needs to be undertaken. Here I am reminded of my own undergraduate experience of vainly trying to master introductory quantitative statistics. My study partner, with a background in physics and no doubt tired of my grumbling, picked up my text and turned it back to page 1. 'It's simple', he said, 'read page 1 and when you understand it, read page 2. When you understand page 2, read page 3 and so on.' This is a lesson I have never forgotten—to gain a clear understanding of social research skills, you need to take a sequential approach, mastering one aspect of the subject before you move on to the next. So, as opposed to, say, studying the sociology of crime, where you concentrate on understanding the links between core concepts, empirical data and theoretical arguments, often dipping in and out of the reading at different points, the study of research skills requires a more structured approach.

Additionally, you are likely to find that social research is both simpler and more complex than you imagined. Simpler, in that many of the methods or analysis techniques you might perceive as difficult are actually straightforward when examined closely. More complex, in that the amount of planning, preparation and awareness of the nature of social research processes and practices needed to undertake a social research project are likely to be significantly more than you anticipated. Good research relies on rigorous theoretical, conceptual and practical preparation. Although good research results can be obtained from using straightforward research processes and methods, good research cannot be done on the run. The results of research directly reflect the level of planning, preparation and attention to the process of research steps. Research undertaken without adequate preparation leads to unreliable results; and poor research is worse than none at all.

Most importantly, social research is a thrilling endeavour. The power to ask your own social questions, explore social phenomena from your own perspective and seek the social answers for yourself, rather than relying always on the work of 'expert' others, cannot be underestimated.

The excitement of social discovery is also addictive. Once you begin the process of active research, it is hard to stop. Be warned: you are likely to start seeing social questions and potential social research projects everywhere. Moreover, the skills acquired and the social research perspective have almost unlimited applications. You can use them formally within the academy but also in other aspects of daily life. Finally, I hope your study of this subject will impart to you some of the thrill of the research process and the enthusiasm for social research that so engages myself and the other contributors to this text.

Using this book to begin the journey

This text does not expect students to have an existing knowledge set of social research methods or techniques. Rather, the key objectives are to enable you to develop a clear understanding of the nature and processes of social science research; gain an appreciation of the wide range of methods available to social researchers; and develop a set of basic practical research skills. While the methods included are limited by what can feasibly be covered within a one-semester unit, these 15 chapters provide a broad coverage of the major qualitative and quantitative social research methods in current Australian usage. Their presentation is organised along categorical lines, moving from the backbone of social science research practice to quantitative methods and qualitative methods from data collection to data analysis. While the chapters are practically orientated, each also stresses that social research is fundamentally a dedicated curiosity about our social world rather than just the application of techniques and processes. In addition, each chapter is written by a social scientist with broad experience in the research process, method or type of analysis detailed in his or her chapter.

While each chapter presents a different method or analysis process, a core message of this text is that all established social research methods have value. There is no such thing as a 'better' method. Rather, some research methods are better for investigating particular types of social research questions. Your selection of a research method should depend on the research question your project seeks to investigate, not the other way around. This text also does not seek to make you an expert in any of the methods discussed. Our aim is to provide you with a key understanding of a range of social science research methods to a level where you can knowledgably select an appropriate research method for your particular research project. The resource lists at the end of each chapter are included to allow new researchers to further develop their knowledge in those methods or topics.

1
The Foundations of Good Social Science Research

Social research is an exciting active endeavour and, for me, the thrill of seeing a set of my data for the first time is right up there in the list of life's good moments. For most new social researchers, and a good many old ones, our enthusiasm at the start of a new research project can be almost overwhelming. The impetus to get out there and start the 'real research', that is, collecting and analysing our data, is very strong.

But social science research is a process and a practice that involves much more than data collection and analysis. To achieve the results we want and to ensure that our first forays into our data are thrilling, not devastating, all elements of that process and practice need to be fully understood and embedded into the research project in a coherent and structured way. For most projects, data collection and analysis will come towards the end of the research project, not at the start. Good quality data, of whatever type, can only be collected from a strong foundation. This is where most of the real research work of any project is actually done.

This foundation is made up of: a solid theoretical and personal understanding of the process of social science research; a dedication to thorough preparation and planning within that process; an awareness and a commitment to addressing the moral and ethical dimensions of our research; an extensive and critical review of the empirical and theoretical literature around our topic; and ensuring we have the technical and theoretical expertise to undertake all aspects of the research process in a competent and rigorous way. While figurative outlines of this process tend to be linked linear boxes, I prefer a more metaphorical vision of these aspects as a nest, supporting, enveloping and nurturing the data and its analysis and interpretation. It is these foundational elements of social science research that are covered in this first section.

The opening five chapters set the context for the next 10 chapters. Each details a different core element of good social science research. Chapters 1 to 4, on the nature of, the design of, and the process of social science research are individually focused, but work together to set out, in practical terms, the whats, whys and hows of developing a quality social science research project; one that is methodologically clear, theoretically informed and empirically and conceptually rigorous. It is at this developmental stage that the ethical and moral dimensions of the research must be addressed. The foregrounding of what makes research practice ethical into this first section is purposeful. Because most of our research concerns people, ethics sits at the core of social science research. And ethical research goes further than ensuring we do not expose our respondents, wittingly or unwittingly, to harm. Ethical research is also research that is diligent in its accuracy of results, acknowledgment of sources and the inputs of others. Finally, chapter 5 in this section addresses the key, all-research method: theoretical, empirical and technical skills needed for quality and robust sampling and measuring.

For impatient personalities, such as myself, the large body of preparatory and foundational work required before the data phase can be daunting. But I also know such work is critical to good research, and there is no point doing research that is not good. To remind myself to always take the time to ensure thoroughness of process and practice I have framed the following anonymous maxim on the importance of planning. It reads:

> The really nice thing about not planning is that failure comes as a complete surprise and is not preceded by long periods of worry and depression.

As you get started on your journey into social research, remember that, while social research is an exciting, even adventurous undertaking, it is also an expensive undertaking, in time, money and personal commitment, from ourselves, our institution and, more importantly, our respondents. We cannot just do it again if we make a mistake. So, engage with these first five chapters and ensure that you are never surprised.

Chapter 1

The Nature of Social Science Research

Maggie Walter

Asking social questions, seeking social answers

Information and communication technologies (ICTs), such as internet sites, email and mobile telecommunications, influence nearly all aspects of our lives. Not only do we use such technology for communicating in social and employment contexts, increasingly ICTs are a presence in our personal lives. Do such cyber possibilities change the way we approach and understand personal relationships? Seeking answers to the question, 'What types of dating activity or relationships are mediated or sustained by such technologies; and do online dating technologies transform that nature of intimacy?', Barraket and Henry-Waring (2008) conducted 23 in-depth interviews with people (5 men and 18 women) who self-identified as having used online dating services. Defining online dating as purposeful 'meeting of people through specifically designed internet sites' (p. 149), the researchers sought to gain a deeper understanding of the motivations for online dating, the way respondents represented themselves online and how they experienced online dating and online technology more generally. Barraket and Henry-Waring's study found that, although their participants used online dating as a way of moving outside their current social networks, they were still looking for relationships with people who lived geographically close and who matched 'their own communities of characteristic and interest' (pp. 158–9). Although different formats for meeting and interacting with others were used, such as a shared etiquette around the pace of electronic communication and the sharing of personal information, these tended to mirror existing gendered patterns of dating protocols. An examination of dating sites found that the language used and site functions tended to promote traditional, gendered romantic ideals. The authors conclude therefore that, despite some changes, at its base online dating tends to extend traditional patterns of intimate interpersonal connections rather than transforming them.

Key terms

- axiology
- descriptive research
- empirical data
- epistemology
- explanatory research
- exploratory research
- method
- methodology
- ontology
- paradigm
- quantitative–qualitative debate
- research question
- scientific method
- social aggregates
- social meanings
- social patterns
- social theory
- standpoint
- triangulation

What is social research?

> **Language:** A performative activity encompassing words, texts and other expressive behaviours.
>
> **Social research:** The systematic study of society, the patterns in it and the processes that shape what people do.

The term 'research' has bad press. With its popular imagery as a scholarly endeavour pursued using complicated formulas, and uninterpretable **language** and techniques, research seems far removed from our everyday lives and our social world. But appearances here are deceptive. **Social research** makes the social world go around. Research, and especially social research, is everywhere, and touches many aspects of our social lives. Essentially, social research is about investigating and seeking answers to the social questions that we and others ask about our social world. 'Investigation' is the key word here. To be good social researchers, we need to be keen social investigators, or even social sleuths. The constantly changing nature of our social world means that we will never run out of social questions to ask or social issues and phenomena to investigate. For example, results from the current *Growing Up in Australia*, the Longitudinal Study of Australian Children (AIFS 2002) being conducted by the Department of Family and Community Services, is already adding immeasurably to our understanding of contemporary childhood in Australia. This research influences government policy decisions around families and children, and some of the results are publicly disseminated through the documentaries *Life at One* and *Life at Three*, shown on ABC television in 2006 and 2008. Similarly the Longitudinal Study of Indigenous Children, the *Footsteps in Time* project, also currently under way, will show how Indigenous children in Australia grow up strong. These two projects demonstrate the components of good social research: an important social question; a well thought out and theoretically informed research plan; the use of appropriate research **methods** rigorously applied; valid analysis and interpretation; and broad dissemination of results and findings.

> **Method:** The research technique or practice used to gather and analyse the research data.

Researching the social

As social scientists, we compare ourselves directly with other scientists, often using many of the same methods and techniques. Yet researching the social world is often more complicated than researching the physical world. Social science research is research on, and with, real people in the real world, and this aspect of social research is one of its exciting elements. The social experience and understanding we bring to our research as members of our society are also important ingredients of the research process.

The social nature of our field of study also means that much social research involves direct communication with our research respondents. This essential difference between social science and other science research, such as physics, biology or geology, is not given the emphasis it deserves. Effective people skills, that is, a genuine liking of interacting with others, ease in verbal and written communication, and perhaps most importantly, listening skills, are vital but often underrated attributes for good social research. In a hypothetical example, does it matter to an amoeba, or the research project, if the physical scientist investigating its properties cannot hold a coherent conversation with another human being to save herself? Probably not. Would the outcome be the same if a social science researcher were afflicted with the same deficit in the social skills department? How effective would that researcher be in conducting an unstructured, **in-depth interview**, or facilitating a **focus group**, or even designing an effective survey? Crucially, not only can the lack of appropriate people skills reduce the value of **data** gathered by whatever social research method, but poor people skills can also jeopardise the social research project itself.

As shown in box 1.1, the human facet of social research can act as both an aid and a barrier to social research. On the one hand, our personal lived experience combined with our education and training as social scientists allows us to bring to our research a complex understanding of our social world. On the other hand, the fact that we are enmeshed in our social world means that we can often fail to see the social and cultural assumptions that inform our own worldviews, through which we perceive social questions and social issues.

In-depth interview: In-depth interviews are guided by general themes rather than pre-set questions. They are also less formal than structured interviews, exploring issues as the interviewee raises them.

Focus group: A research method that involves encouraging a group of people to discuss some social or political issue.

Data: The information we collect and analyse to answer our research question. Data come in all manner of forms, such as survey forms, documents and secondary data.

Box 1.1: Researching the social: A complex process

The human aspect of social research adds to not only the excitement but also to the complexity of our research endeavour.

Ethics

We cannot research people or societies the way we study inanimate objects such as minerals or energy waves, no matter how useful that might be to our research. As detailed in chapter 3, ethical constraints, from a moral perspective, and increasingly from formal **ethics** bodies, such as **human research ethics committees (HRECs)**, set boundaries and limitations on how we approach and undertake our research. These are important to protect our human subjects from us as researchers, and perhaps as enthusiastic social researchers, to protect us from ourselves.

Ethics: The establishment of a set of moral standards that govern behaviour in a particular setting or for a particular group.

Human research ethics committee (HREC): A committee established by an institution or organisation for the task of viewing research proposals and monitoring ongoing investigations with the aim of protecting the welfare and rights of participants in research.

Human ambiguity, irrationality and social awareness

People and society are not always rational or predictable. The motives and rationales of people are not always clear, sometimes not even to themselves. This means that,

Maggie Walter

although we can ask the questions, the answers we obtain from our respondents cannot necessarily be regarded as 'fact' or unambiguous. Our social awareness also means that we are not always prepared to be frank in our discussions of our behaviour, attitudes and belief systems. For example, we would not be surprised if a study of weight-loss program participants found a discrepancy between the self-reported eating behaviour of the respondents and the associated weekly weight loss. As researchers, we must recognise the essential subjectivity of much of our data, but not be paralysed by it.

Social and personal change

People and societies are not static. Social and personal change are the norm, not the exception, and this is an important consideration in social research. While our research might provide a plausible explanation for today's social phenomena, this does not mean these same explanations can be directly applied to the social phenomena of tomorrow. For example, research on the career aspirations of married women in 1980 would no doubt produce very different results to a similar study carried out in 2010.

Cultural factors and assumptions

Cultural factors and assumptions, our own rather than those of our respondents, can operate to blind us both to some social questions and to some social answers. For example, until very recently most social researchers operated under the unquestioned assumption of Western science and Western society as the norm. Inherent, but undeclared, in this were gendered and culturally exclusive perspectives. More recently, other ways of knowing, such as Indigenous and feminist research paradigms, have successfully challenged these assumptions and shown that there are other ways of being and making meaning of the social world. Social research has become a richer and more valid enterprise because of these.

Hawthorne effect

The humanness of our research subjects can lead to particular social research dangers around validity. We need to be very careful to ensure that what we think we are measuring is what we are actually measuring. In some cases, research results can be affected by the subject's interpretation of what the research is about—the Hawthorne effect. The Hawthorne effect was first identified in a study undertaken in the 1930s by Elton May at a Western Electrics Plant in Hawthorne, USA. The research was aimed at establishing if different independent working environments—related variables, such as lighting, meal break lengths and how the workers were paid—would have an effect on the dependent variable, the worker's productivity. The problem was that every independent variable had a positive effect on productivity (to the initial delight of the researchers), but so also did a return to the original working conditions. The researchers finally concluded that the workers at the plant were interested in the research, enjoyed participating, and so tried to ensure that the researchers achieved the effects they were looking for. As noted by the Hawthorne investigator, unlike inanimate objects, people tend to 'notice that they are being studied and form feelings and attitudes about being studied, which may in turn influence the outcome of the research' (Dooley 1990:212).

The complicating social context

As social scientists, we use social theories to explain the phenomena we observe in the social world. This seems a fairly straightforward exercise, but we need to remember that social phenomena are not stand-alone items. Social phenomena are entwined within political and moral belief systems or ideologies, and this complexity leads to social research often having a political dimension. For example, social research that seeks to explore and explain rising rates of sole parenthood in Australia, as a social phenomenon, can clash with the belief systems that view marriage and two-parent families as the only legitimate form of family.

Alternatively, the presence of the political or ideological dimension of social phenomena can result in different social researchers coming up with very different theoretical explanations or interpretations of exactly the same data, as shown in case study 1.1.

Case study 1.1: Who and what is poor?

Social research into poverty in Australia has, in recent years, been mired in a sometimes acrimonious debate about how poverty should be measured. This argument is more than just a contestation about where the poverty line should be set or how poverty should be defined. Different ways of measuring poverty deliver very different results. As outlined below, the preferred models of different groups tend to reflect differing ideological stances on whether poverty is a growing problem in contemporary Australian society.

In 2001, a study commissioned by the Smith Family, *Financial Disadvantage in Australia: 1990–2000*, was published. The main findings were that:

- Poverty had increased steadily from 11 to 13 per cent of the population.
- Unemployment was the key generator of poverty.

Maggie Walter

- Having a job was no longer always an effective protector against poverty, with the risk of poverty for those in part-time jobs rising.

This report's findings were immediately challenged by the Centre for Independent Studies (CIS). CIS argued that the study exaggerated the extent and nature of poverty in Australia. The major problem, argued CIS, was that the Smith Family study had used the **mean** (average) income rather than the less volatile median as the base for its poverty line measure. Also, the CIS countered, the Smith Family study confused poverty and inequality. Rising inequality does not automatically increase poverty. In the CIS's own estimates, only around 5 per cent of the Australian population were living in 'chronic' poverty in 2000.

Source: Senate Community Affairs References Committee 2004:35–40

> **Mean:** The average score for a set of cases.

The 'science' in social science

Because our social world is all around us, it is often assumed that explaining social phenomena is just a matter of common sense. Yet being a member of a society definitely does not equate to an automatic understanding of our social reality. Indeed, as outlined in the previous paragraph on cultural factors and assumptions, being a member of society can, and does, act as a impediment to understanding or even asking some social questions. What sets social science apart from social commentary or opinion is our use of **scientific method**. Scientific method is traditionally defined as being about observation, classification and interpretation. As Karl Pearson (1900) stated: 'The man who classifies facts of any kind, who sees their mutual relation and describes their sequences, is applying the scientific fact and is a man of science' (cited in Mann 1985:19).

> **Scientific method:** Planned methodical research based around observing, analysing and interpreting our research data, conducted with professionalism and ethical integrity, and transparent and rigorous in its approach.

While today we would most definitely quarrel with Pearson's presumption of a social scientist as male, and substitute the term 'analysis' for 'classification', we recognise the essential sequence of tasks involved in social science research. Just as a geologist might explore rock formations, analyse what is found, and then theorise, based on this analysis, that the area was previously the site of volcanic activity, so social science researchers follow their social observations, whether they be 'hard' quantitative data or 'softer' qualitative research material, with analysis and theoretical interpretations of those social phenomena. Social science research is a planned methodical activity built around a solid, well-formulated research design.

Scientific method is also about the way we conduct our research. Neuman explains that scientific method is not just one thing, but 'refers to the ideas, rules, techniques and approaches that the scientific community uses' (2004:8). These include professionalism, ethical integrity in how we go about the social research process, plus ensuring that the social research we conduct is rigorous in method and techniques as well as transparent in research methods and interpretation. These aspects of scientific method mean that we endeavour to conduct our research, through all its phases, in a professional manner that abides by ethical principles. 'Transparency and rigour' refer to making explicit, at all stages of the research, the specific research method we use, the reasons for our choice and how we use our data to develop our theory or interpretations. The strength of these standards on how we conduct our social science research is that they are shared. Acceptance of, and adherence to, these standards within our research practice is a central element of being an active social science researcher, and a core defining element that sets social science apart from everyday thinking or other ways of knowing about our social world.

As social scientists, one of the key ways we ensure professionalism, integrity and transparency is by making our research public. As expanded in chapter 15, publication of our results, usually in a recognised journal, makes our research open to public scrutiny. As an additional safeguard, most published research is subjected to a peer review process, where anonymous social scientists review the research before it is published.

Social patterns and social meanings

Put into simple terms, our primary aim in social research is to identify, investigate and seek to understand **social patterns** and **social meanings**. It is the persistent patterns in social life, as well as the social meanings inherent in these, that we are endeavouring to uncover. By social patterns, we mean those phenomena that occur repeatedly in social life. For example, research data finding that Australians with strong religious beliefs are consistently underrepresented among those who reside in a cohabiting relationship (Dempsey & de Vaus 2003) demonstrate an enduring social pattern. By social meanings, we mean how people make sense of aspects of their social lives and the understandings they make of these. For example, Natalier (2001) interviewed motorcycle riders to try to develop an understanding of the social meanings of motorcycling risk. Her results suggest bike riders downplay their risk by aligning adverse events of others and themselves with lack of technique rather than inherent risk in riding a motorcycle.

> **Social patterns:** Persistent patterns in social phenomena that occur repeatedly in the social world.
>
> **Social meanings:** How people(s) make sense of aspects of their social lives and the understandings that they develop of these.

In its analysis of social patterns and social meaning, social research also has a debunking role, testing the veracity and sometimes exposing the inaccuracy of our everyday assumptions about our social world. When we test these beliefs empirically using scientific method, we often find that the social reality and the social belief are not a good match. Health is a good

Maggie Walter

example here. As Australia is an egalitarian and wealthy society, our health is generally perceived as essentially an individual aspect of our lives. Yet, analysis of health data shows that in Australia, as in other Western countries, health is not shared equally. Social research consistently finds that health status and socioeconomic status are strongly linked, and that there is a clear and widening health gap between low-income and higher-income groups. The poorer you are, the more likely you are to both get sick and die at a younger age, and this applies right along the social gradient, rather than just to those at the extremes (Walker 2000).

'But', you'll always hear someone say if you discuss the social gradient of health, 'I know somebody who came from a very poor family who lived till 105 and was never sick a day in her life'. The question here is whether an exception such as this challenges the **social theory** we have developed from our identification of social patterns or meanings, as those pointing them out often assume they do. The answer is a huge no. Exceptions, and there are always exceptions, are not a threat to social science findings or, indeed, unexpected. Our interpretations or theories of social phenomena are not predicting what every single outcome for every single person within a society will be. Rather, as social scientists we deal with **social aggregates**, that is, the 'collective actions of and situations of many individuals' (Babbie 2002:12); so richer Australians, in aggregate, will have better health than poorer Australians, in aggregate. For social scientists, a single case, or even a group of cases, is just that until shown by rigorous analysis that a group of cases actually forms a social pattern. But once we have established that a social pattern exists, we need to look for a social explanation for that pattern: a theory of why and how this pattern manifests itself.

> **Social theory:** An idea or a set of ideas that explain social phenomena.
>
> **Social aggregates:** The collective, aggregate social outcomes or circumstances of individuals or groups.

Social patterns also alter along with social life. For example, if you are researching the family in Australia, one of the first things you will find is that the picture is one of continual change. The average age at first marriage, the likely number of children a couple will have, and the social meanings that are ascribed to marriage and children have changed repeatedly over time. Critically, you can expect that such changes in social patterns and social meanings will continue.

Social research: Why do we do it?

Why do we do social research? We do it because we want to know, and because knowing is important. For our social world to function well we need to understand it, and social research is the way we gain social understandings. The level of understandings we seek will vary according to our question. Three core levels of social research are commonly identified (see, for example, Babbie 2002:83–5; Glicken 2003:14–15; Neuman 2004:15).

These are:

- **exploratory research**
- **descriptive research**
- **explanatory research**.

In reality, social research often does not fall neatly into one category of research or another. Rather, exploratory research can also be used to describe the social phenomena under investigation, and may also develop at least tentative explanations for what is found.

> **Exploratory research**: Research undertaken to explore or open up new areas of social enquiry.
>
> **Descriptive research**: Research that has as its major purpose to describe social phenomena.
>
> **Explanatory research**: Research that seeks to provide or develop explanation of the social world or social phenomena.

Exercise 1.1 Exploring charity

Consider the following hypothetical research scenario.

You have been asked to be a research assistant in a project that has as its research focus the giving of donations to charity as a social behaviour. The respondents will be adults (those aged 18 years and above) living in a certain capital city. Although still in the development phase, the initial aims of the project are:

- to examine actual charity behaviour
- to explore the social meanings that individuals ascribe to the making of a charity donation.

The research method for the project plans to use a two-phase data collection. In the first phase, a telephone survey will collect the data from a random representative **sample** of residents. In the second phase, a series of in-depth interviews will be undertaken with 25 individual respondents.

> **Sample**: A sample is a set of cases or elements that are selected from a population.
>
> **Ambiguity**: Vague or imprecise terms that have more than one meaning.

Your task

Answer the following questions, either as individuals or in groups.

1. Which aspects of charity giving might you want to investigate? As an example, you might want to determine the influence of peer pressure on giving behaviour. List five dimensions of this social phenomenon that you think would be interesting to explore.
2. How would your own experience of charity giving influence how you went about your task of determining what aspects of the topic to investigate?
3. Can you think of any immediate ethical concerns that might limit or constrain the way you conduct the research?
4. What factors around **ambiguity** and social awareness would you need to keep in mind when designing the study?

Maggie Walter

5. How might external events affect your study? Would a study that occurred before a series of documentaries about homelessness on current affairs shows have different outcomes from one undertaken immediately following their screening?

The language of social science

Like other scientific endeavours, social research uses a set of key terms and concepts. Many of these are unfamiliar or have meanings that differ from their everyday usage, but they are not inherently difficult. Rather, they form part of the language of social research, and most are just shorthand for broader ideas. The meaning of commonly used social science terms and concepts are highlighted and defined throughout each chapter, and set out as a combined set in the book's glossary.

Method and methodology: Understanding the difference

The previous sections emphasised the scientific, methodical aspects of social science research. Our approach, as social scientists, is clear, scientific and objective—or at least this is the way social science research is often presented. But if social science is neutral, how and why are some social research projects prioritised over others? And why do different researchers interpret social phenomena so differently?

Our methodology is at least a part explanation of this complex and sometimes ambiguous terrain.

Method: The research technique or practice used to gather and analyse the research data.

Methodology: Methodology is the theoretical lens through which the research is designed and conducted.

The distinction between **method** and **methodology** is an important one, and one that is often misunderstood. Very often the term methodology is used when people really mean the method. But the difference is an essential element of understanding social research. Put simply, method refers to a technique for gathering information, such as an interview, questionnaire or documentary analysis, and methodology is the theoretical and worldview lens through which the research is understood, designed and conducted. Our methodology includes our method, but the method is a component of our methodology and not the most important one.

Understanding the difference between a method and a methodology is important in understanding research for three reasons.
1. It allows us to see where values, theories and worldviews interact with social research.
2. It allows us to understand how specific methodologies emerge and why understanding our methodology is vital to our research practice.

3   It allows us to view methods as tools, tried and tested ways and techniques for gathering our data, rather than the research itself.

What goes into making a methodology?

Understanding methodology as the lens through which we view, undertake and translate our research provides some level of explanation, but in my experience fails to convey adequately what a methodology actually is. Yes, our methodology has multiple components, method among them, but what else is included? How do we recognise one? The specifics of methodology are less straightforward and more debated than method. My own definition is that methodology is the worldview lens through which the **research question** and the core concepts are viewed and translated into the research approach we take to the research. I include the following as core components. In practice, these elements are often inextricably entwined, but it is helpful to clarify each separately.

- our standpoint
- our theoretical **conceptual framework** and **paradigm**
- our method.

> **Research question**: Research questions state the major aim of the research in question form, specifying the key idea that the research seeks to investigate and/or explain and also identifying the key concepts of the research.
>
> **Conceptual framework**: The theoretical frame that we use to conceptualise the collection, and analyse and interpret our data.
>
> **Paradigm**: A shared framework of viewing and approaching the investigation and research of social phenomena.
>
> **Standpoint**: The way we see the world and our position in it in relation to others and society. Our standpoint recognises the filters and frames that have an impact on our approach to our research.

Our standpoint

Our **standpoint** is the most important aspect in defining our methodology, because it influences all other components. But it is also an aspect that in most social research is poorly addressed. Our standpoint is basically our own position, who we are and how we see ourselves in relation to others and in relation to society. This means understanding that the position of the researcher is highly relevant to the way he or she approaches and understands the research. How we see the world is not a neutral, objective understanding, but is inevitably influenced by the filters and frames of our life experiences and circumstances and our social, cultural, economic and personal identity location. This means that female researchers will have a different worldview on many topics than their male colleagues; younger people will likely see the social landscape differently to older people; and an Aboriginal researcher will see society and social research in very different terms to a non-Indigenous researcher. Our standpoint, who we are socially, economically, culturally and even politically, underpins the questions we see, the answers we seek, the way we go about seeking those answers and the interpretation we make, the theoretical paradigms that make 'sense' to us. Our standpoint is theoretically summarised

Maggie Walter

as the way research is guided by researchers' epistemological, axiological and ontological frameworks.

- epistemology: theory of knowledge
- axiology: theory of values
- ontology: theory of being.

Epistemology

> **Epistemology:** Theory of knowledge concerned with understanding how knowledge is defined, valued and prioritised.

What we regard as 'knowledge' has a strong value and cultural component. This concept is encapsulated by the term **epistemology**, which refers to a theory of knowledge—ways of knowing. Epistemology is concerned with understanding how the (mostly unwritten) rules about what is counted as knowledge are set; that is, what is defined as knowledge, who can and cannot be 'knowledgeable', and which 'knowledges' are valued over others (Dooley 1990). Like social assumptions, dominant ways of knowing and the dominance of some knowers over others are embedded into our society. Social research is conducted against a background of these dominant 'ways of knowing'.

Gender provides a good example of how our epistemology is influenced by our social location. Feminist social epistemology challenges the assumed objectivity and rationality of traditional ways of designating and valuing knowledge. This epistemology seeks to understand how the social relations of gender shape knowledge in our societies and investigates how socially constructed norms of gender and gendered experiences influence the production of knowledge and valid knowers. A feminist social epistemology also challenges the abstract individualism of social theories and theorists. Until the 1970s, most social theories and theorists were uncritically perceived as universal: a positioning that ignored that these knowledges were essentially all produced by white middle and upper class European or North American males. A feminist social epistemology illuminates that the experiential differences of knowers leads to differences in perspective, and that these differences have epistemic consequences. Therefore the knowledges produced and the valuing of those knowledges become entwined with and influenced by the identities, social positions and social locations linked to the attributes of the knowledge producers (Stanford Encyclopedia of Philosophy 2006).

For example, Marx's theories of capitalism essentially relate to men's experience of the system, and the inequality and exploitation he exposes is also that of men. Women's position and experience are not considered, except in their role as producers of the next generation of workers or as a reserve army of labour for the bourgeoisie to exploit. Yet, women's experience of the capitalist system is very different to men's, and much of that difference in both experience and consequent knowledge is based on gender.

Additionally, institutions of knowledge production, such as the stock market, the judicial system or even universities, can be dominated by the perspective of one 'type' of knower without that perspective being recognised (Stanford Encyclopedia of Philosophy 2006). Underrepresentation of women, younger people or non-Whites, or an over-representation of those from the upper and upper middle classes, means that knowledge is likely to be shaped by the epistemological perspective of that group, perhaps even positioning such a perspective as the only way of knowing. The judiciary provides a clear example. With older, white Anglo-heritage upper-class males dominating nearly all influential positions, the perspectives of those from non-English speaking backgrounds, the poor, women and Indigenous peoples are only reflected in rulings as they are understood by those in positions of power. This is not to suggest that the judiciary is biased, but that without lived experience of the social location of migrants, Indigenous people, poorer people and women, such understandings are inevitably limited and incomplete.

Axiology

Axiology refers the theory of values, extrinsic and intrinsic. Applying this concept to social research and seeing how it fits within our methodology means that we need to understand our own value systems and those of the groups and institutions that have an impact on and are intertwined within our research approach.

> **Axiology:** The theory of values that inform how we see the world and the value judgments we make within our research.

This link between a researcher's axiological position and his or her research raises the contested issue of values in research. A traditional perspective holds that researchers must aim to produce value-neutral knowledge based on observed objective facts. The feasibility and desirability of such an aim has been substantially challenged, and is mostly rejected by contemporary social science researchers. The stronger argument in current social research debates is that social research cannot be value free. The reasoning here relates to two key aspects of the social **context** of social research.

> **Context:** The settings in which texts are situated.

1 **Social science is part of the social world**
   Social phenomena occur in the real world, where moral, political and cultural values are an integral but often unseen part of the social landscape. This social context of our field of study means that being value free is next to impossible, and claiming a value-free perspective is just another value statement.

2 **Social context is central to our social science**
   The specific social, cultural, personal and moral milieus of the social phenomena we study are inextricably entwined in those social phenomena. For a social researcher to ignore the social context of the research is similar to a physical scientist ignoring the

laws of physics: you might still generate results and theories, but the value of these are highly suspect.

To gain some insight into our own axiological framework, we need to ask ourselves some reflexive questions. These can include:

- Why have we chosen the topic we have?
- What is our particular research question, and why have we settled on that aspect?
- How did we decide that topic was worth researching—as opposed to others?

The critical point is that the questions we ask and the research decisions we make are not innate. Social scientists are embedded members of society too, and the non-acknowledgment of personal and/or social and institution values in the research does not equate to value-free or objective research. Rather, social research is about the real world in which moral, political and cultural values are central to the things we examine. Therefore being value free is impossible, and those who say this are kidding themselves or disingenuous.

Acknowledging our axiological frame does not mean that it is valid to try to make our research deliver particular results. The research project relies on open and professional practice. We must always adhere to research rigour and the scientific process and not to do so renders our research invalid, if not fraudulent. Rather, understanding our own axiology and recognising that values are implicitly, at least, embedded in all research allows us to read our own research and that of others with an eye to the values informing it. Indeed, in some research, such as discourse analysis (see chapter 12), unearthing explicit and implicit values is the core focus of study.

Ontology

Ontology can be defined as theories related to the nature of being. Therefore, our ontological framework refers to our understanding of what constitutes reality; how we perceive the world around us. At its most concentrated it is about how the world is understood; what is reality.

> **Ontology:** The understandings of reality and the nature of being that inform our view of the world.

Like axiology and standpoint, ontology tends to be little discussed, mostly because the nature of reality tends to be taken for granted, especially within predominantly Western cultures such as Australia. But as social scientists we know that 'reality' is not quite as concrete and immutable as we might usually think. As demonstrated in the classic Australian film *The Castle*, the meaning and reality of a house is very different if you are the home-owner as opposed to being the engineer planning a runway extension in your area. Similarly, perceptions and understanding of time change completely if we are talking about our own activities, lifetimes, specific events or the theory of relativity. From inside a Western framework, with its taken-for-granted assumptions of reality, it can be hard to come to grips with ontology. But for other cultures, which hold different understanding of reality, ontological frameworks are very clear because of the likelihood of a clash between their own ontology and dominant Western understandings. As with epistemology and axiology, it is easier to perceive ontological differences from outside the dominant culture.

In Australia and New Zealand, this is most clearly seen in the ontological positions of Indigenous peoples. Aboriginal people, Torres Strait Islander people and Māori hold ontological understandings of the nature of reality that differ from Western norms. While unique to each Indigenous people, these ontologies tend to be more holistic in the way they view reality and less wedded to the Western presumption of humans as separate from other life and the earth itself. Scholar Karen Martin demonstrates this when she talks about her own Aboriginal people's ontology of relatedness. In Quandamoopa ontology, all experiences are anchored to relatedness, which is the set of conditions, processes and practices that occur among all entities, human, animal, spiritual and ancestral and all aspects of nature, animate and inanimate. In Martin's words, 'relatedness occurs across context and is maintained within conditions that are: physical, spiritual, political, geographical, intellectual, emotional, social, historical, sensory, instinctive and intuitive' (2008: 69). The core message is that all social science researchers, whether from the dominant or another culture, must try to recognise the ontological assumptions that frame their research topic and practice.

As case study 1.2 shows, undertaking research developed from one culture's perspective can be an activity fraught with danger.

Case study 1.2: **When systems collide**

Australia's five-yearly census asks about 40 questions on items such as household composition, cultural background and key demographic details. From a mainstream Australian perspective, the questions appear clear, unambiguous and basically value free. Such assumptions come seriously unstuck when such 'straightforward' questions are asked outside their cultural frame.

Observations of the conduct of the 2001 census at an Aboriginal settlement in the Northern Territory highlight some of the pitfalls. Morphy (2002:40) reports that both the Aboriginal interviewers and interviewees found the process strange—'they were Indigenous actors in a non-Indigenous scenario'. More critically, the quality of the data was compromised by the 'mainstream' cultural assumptions of the questions and the corresponding Indigenous lack of understanding of the mainstream culture and the intent of the census.

Maggie Walter

Examples of particular problems included:

- How old are you?
  - **Almost no one knew how old they were by the exact date or year of birth. Rather, local terms are used which designate degrees of maturity or stages of life, such as baby, child, circumcised boy, pubescent girl, young man. While there are clinical records for some of the younger people, for many older people dates of birth are guesstimates, and often use 1 January or 1 July for official documents.**
- Place of residence
  - **'Place' was interpreted to mean 'community' rather than 'dwelling'. The community is seen as home, and the answers reflected identity rather than physical presence. Most answered 'Yes' to the question of whether they lived there most of the time, even if they were highly mobile. 'Staying' and 'Living' were viewed differently.**
- What is a household?
  - **Community residents saw themselves as part of a family, but this family rarely mirrored the nuclear model of parents and children, and was often spread across more than one dwelling. Kinship relationships within households also did not fit the mainstream Australian model, and could not be adapted to the census questions around relationships.**

Overall, the Aboriginal interviewers took the task very seriously and endeavoured to complete the forms as best they could, but the quality of the data collected was doubtful. For a significant number of questions, Morphy (2002:40) notes that a jocular approach was taken to ease the awkwardness, with 'jokes made at the expense of white people for wanting to know these things'.

Theoretical foundations

In acquiring social research skills, the concentration on research methods and the collection of data means that it is easy to forget that social research involves two core elements. These are:

1 **Empirical data**
2 **Social theory**.

Empirical data: Pieces of information that are the result of observing and/or measuring social phenomena.

Social theory: An idea or a set of ideas that explain social phenomena.

Social theory and empirical data have separate but interdependent roles. Each is an essential aspect of social research, and each is relatively useless on its own. For example, while data finding a low rate of breast screening/mammograms among Aboriginal women are informative, alone these data are relatively meaningless. They lack a theoretical framework in which they can be understood. Alternatively, proposing that Aboriginal women are disempowered by the medical model and are reluctant to seek non-urgent medical care is an interesting theory. However, without empirical supporting data, it is essentially an unproven speculation. There is no way to tell whether the theory is correct or not. Put the empirical data and the social theory together, however, and what we have is social research.

Theoretical conceptual framework

This theoretical terrain is our conceptual framework. A conceptual framework is just that: a theoretical map for how we will conceptualise our data, its analysis and its interpretation to answer our research question. The conceptual framework is the theory(s) that will guide our analysis and understanding of the empirical data. Which theory, or more often theories, we will use to provide this map emerges from our literature review. What theories have others used, or developed, when researching our or an aligned topic? Do they make sense to us and do they meet the requirements of our research question? An example helps illustrate what many new researchers find a challenging task. In my honours research I was interested in the topic of child support, and decided to focus on private collection, that is, collection of child support monies directly arranged between the separated parents, rather than by the Child Support Agency. My question was: how satisfied are payee parents with their private child support collection arrangements? (Walter 2002). The topic and developing a clear research question was relatively unproblematic, but I struggled with defining my theoretical conceptual framework. My area was (then) new, and there was little existing literature, or theories, around the topic. After much reading I finally realised that feminist theories around the delegation of the family to the private sphere in social policy and family discourse were theoretically central to the topic and the question.

I am also often asked whether a theoretical conceptual framework is always necessary in social research. Can't we just identify the issue, such as low rates of take-up of breast screening services by Aboriginal women, then move straight into developing strategies to address the problem? The answer is most strongly no. As Babbie (2002) points out, no matter how practical or idealistic our aims, unless we have a theoretical understanding of the social terrain we are traversing, our research is likely doomed to failure. Even worse, the lack of an acknowledged theoretical base can disguise the unacknowledged concepts and understandings that inform our work. Operating without a clearly established conceptual framework significantly constrains the value of our work and undermines its validity and its rigour.

Theoretical paradigms

Our conceptual framework is likely to be made up of a number of theories that influence our understanding of the topic. These individual theories can also often be aligned with a

Maggie Walter

larger theoretical category, or paradigm, which encompasses a broad theoretical field that emerges from the same perspective. A paradigm is essentially a macro theoretical frame of reference. For example, in my honours research noted above, the theories I used fit within a feminist paradigm.

Within the social sciences, a set of established paradigms exists, within which individual social theories are often drawn and developed. A range of these are outlined below, but this is by no means an exhaustive list. Nor is it fixed. Social science paradigms are an evolving, developing landscape with new paradigms emerging, or re-emerging in their influence, or fading in impact. You should refer to your social theory texts for a broader explanation of the key social theories that inform and influence social science research.

Functionalist perspective

Functionalism was the dominant sociological paradigm through the mid twentieth century. Associated with the work of Emile Durkheim (1858–1917) and later developed by American sociologist Talcott Parsons, functionalism starts with a basic question of 'how is social order possible?', and sees the answers in terms of stability, social order and consensus. The organic analogy, developed by Durkheim, is used to explain how society works by comparing the social world to a biological entity where all parts are separate but interdependent. If one part is not functioning well, it affects the operation of the others and, therefore, the well-being of the whole social system. With its emphasis on the objective nature of social norms and values, functionalism in social research is associated with the social science research conducted within objective scientific frameworks.

Conflict perspective

From a conflict perspective, social relations are based on exploitation, oppression and conflict. The work of Karl Marx (1818–83), who focused on the struggle of the economic classes, especially the exploitation of the working classes or proletariat by the capitalist classes, forms the basis of conflict perspective. However, the application of a conflict paradigm now encompasses more than just economic oppression, and is used in examining social struggles based around class and ethnic divisions or wherever a conflict of interest occurs among different social groups (Babbie 2002:30). A conflict perspective begins from the notion of society as inherently unequal, and engaged in ongoing conflict around the competing interests of different social groups. It is this conflict and the consequent relations of power that exist between different groups that determine a society's social arrangements and drive social change. Social research framed or developed within a conflict paradigm tends to examine social phenomena in terms of the question of 'who benefits?' from this set of social arrangements or this social change, and who is disadvantaged. A conflict perspective provides a big-picture, macro perspective of society or larger social groups. Research using a conflict perspective frame, therefore, tends to be associated with large-scale, often quantitative, research methods, such as surveys (see chapter 8).

Interpretivist paradigm

An interpretivist paradigm concentrates on social agency, and is concerned with the way we, as social beings, interrelate and interact in society. Developed initially from the work of Max Weber (1864–1920), the interpretivist perspective emphasises the meanings individual actors give to social interactions, and the use of symbols, such as language, in the creation of that meaning. From an interpretivist perspective, the human world is a world of meaning in which our actions take place on the basis of shared understandings. To understand society, we need to understand people's motives and interpretations of the world. The meanings actors give to their circumstances are the explanation of what they do. The micro-level emphasis of the interpretivist paradigm and its focus on the role of meanings in how individuals interpret social life mean that the interpretivist paradigm is fundamentally associated with qualitative social research methods, such as in-depth interviews (see chapter 4).

Feminist paradigms

Feminist paradigms are developed by feminist scholars to counteract what has been an overwhelming male-centric approach to the study of our social world. Until relatively recent times, women were largely ignored in the social sciences, both as researchers and as social subjects. Women's differing experiences of social reality were essentially invisible in mainstream social science research and theory. Although feminist paradigms see gender as a fundamental social division and signifier of life chances, there exist a number of feminist paradigms rather than a single perspective. Thus, there is no single feminist approach to social research, and feminist paradigms have been used as the theoretical frame for a diverse range of social research methods and projects. Rather, a feminist perspective is more likely to inform the social question that is posed and how the topic is defined. However, because of the feminist challenge to traditional social research paradigm claims of objectivity and reason, feminist paradigms are often associated with qualitative research methods such as **ethnography**, life histories and **memory work**.

> **Ethnography**: A research method that involves conducting ethnographic fieldwork.
>
> **Memory work**: Memory work is a collaborative technique used to generate stories that are based on personal memories among a group of co-researchers. Also see *triggers*.

Indigenous paradigm

Here, the theoretical framework that directs the questions, the choice of methods, the way of studying and what is valued as knowledge is determined from an Indigenous perspective.

Maggie Walter

> **Outcomes**: The specific consequences of a particular course of action.
>
> **Participatory action research**: A cyclical research process aimed at providing feedback into a cycle for problem solving. It is a practical research method that requires an equal and open collaboration between the researcher and the research community.

The Indigenous paradigm, therefore, directly challenges many of the traditional Western ways of thinking about and approaching social research, what the research process should look like and what the research **outcomes** should be. The research techniques used within an Indigenous research paradigm have generally been those that can more easily admit Indigenous agendas and Indigenous community interests to their purpose and practice (Tuhiwai Smith 1999). The applied research framework of **participatory action research** (see online module), which emphasises the relocation of the power in the research relationship from the researcher to the researched, means that this social research method is frequently employed by researchers approaching their work from an Indigenous paradigm (see online chapter on Indigenous methodologies).

Postmodernism

The postmodernist paradigm has had a strong influence on the social sciences in recent years. Associated with the work of French philosophers such as Jean-François Lyotard and Jean Baudrillard, from a postmodern perspective, reality is always a subjective experience and essentially constructed. Rather than observable social phenomena, social reality is fragmented and diverse, and all human knowledge and experience is relative. Therefore, there are no absolute values or truths, and it becomes impossible to study objective realities. While a postmodernist paradigm brings into sharp relief many of the unsupported assumptions of a positivistic model, such as the 'provability' of an **hypothesis** about the social world or the objectivity of social data, it also raises a social research dilemma. If all reality, or social phenomena, are fundamentally subjective, then, from a postmodern paradigm, what is the point of undertaking any social research at all?

> **Hypothesis**: Hypotheses are prescriptive forms of research question that state a particular scenario that the research will confirm or refute.

Method

The final component of your methodology is the research method you choose; the core topic of this book. As stated, our research method is the technique or practice we use to gather our research data, such as an in-depth interview, survey or discourse analysis. Indeed, social science researchers are spoilt for choice in their selection of a social research method. This book, and the online chapters, cover a wide selection of the methods in common use by Australian social science researchers, but this range is by no means complete. How to go about selecting your research method is covered in the next chapter, but it is important to remember two key premises in relation to method selection:

- The method must suit the research topic and question, not the other way around.
- All methods have strengths and weaknesses. There are no such things as good methods, bad methods or even methods that cannot be used within particular types of research.

Voices in the field

Karen Martin

Karen Martin is an Associate Professor in the Education Faculty at the Southern Cross University. The following paragraphs outline how she developed an Indigenous methodology for her now completed doctoral research:

'My professional background is in early childhood education, particularly Aboriginal education. It is through my teaching that a keen interest in knowledge acquisition and transfer occurs in Aboriginal teaching–learning contexts (in homes and classrooms). It is through the experiences of a Native Title application that procedures for research caught my attention, particularly in the way the knowledge and realities of Aboriginal people were represented, misrepresented, distorted and stolen. Thus began a journey of understanding research and how this misrepresentation occurs, but equally how it could be different and have better outcomes for Aboriginal people.

'I theorised an Indigenist research methodology informed by Aboriginal worldview, knowledge and ethics. Underpinning this methodology is relatedness, an essential and core condition by which Aboriginal people have lived, do and will continue to live. This is articulated within the research through the use of "traditional devices" whereby Aboriginal ways of knowing, ways of being and ways of doing are centred and strengthened.

'This Indigenist research methodology was used in a PhD study regarding the regulation of outsiders by Rainforest Aboriginal peoples of Far North Queensland. The findings reveal the multiple forms of agency used to regulate outsiders occurring from the past, to the present and for the future. Therefore, the necessity for researchers to regulate their own behaviours in respect of and in accordance with Aboriginal terms of reference and in relatedness is paramount. When research is regarded as an interface of Aboriginal people, research and researchers, Aboriginal voices are not erased, silenced or diminished. This research is a vehicle for getting our Stories back.'

Maggie Walter

Voices in the field

Virginia Watson

Virginia Watson is an academic at the University of Technology, Sydney, where she teaches across the disciplines of sociology, history and political and cultural studies. Her research, which covers Australian history, politics and public policy with a specific focus on Indigenous affairs, is similarly cross-disciplinary in approach. She is especially interested in using political theory to examine and explain the relationships between ideas and political and social institutions with a view to better understanding public policy and its effects. This has resulted in several academic articles and a book: *Mining Australia's Northern Frontier: Government, Development and Indigenous People*.

Another aspect of Virginia's research has involved her in some work being undertaken by two Aboriginal Land Councils and a non-government organisation that looks at the provision of telecommunications services to remote Indigenous communities. This research has involved fieldwork across some of those communities to ascertain the viewpoints, ideas and understandings of community residents. It has been centrally informed by the research method, ethnographic action research. You can read more about this work in an edited collection, *Communication for Social Change and Development*.

Virginia's current research has taken her to state and Commonwealth archives and is for a book tentatively titled, *Mining Culture: Land Nation and Identity in Australian history*.

Quantitative and qualitative methodologies

In a return to the first message of this section, qualitative or quantitative methods are not the same as qualitative or quantitative methodologies, although we will almost certainly use a qualitative method within a qualitative methodology and a quantitative method within a quantitative methodology. Also remember that there are many more social research methods available to you than those listed in this text. Social research methods are a dynamic field and new methods are emerging, and others wax and wane in their use, within this field. The accompanying website to this text <www.oup.com.au/orc/walter> provides core information on a range of other methods. On quantitative methods, the website contains a module on experiments plus two extension segments, quantitative analysis using SPSS 1: correlations and quantitative analysis using SPSS 2: comparison of means. Qualitative modules include:

conversation analysis; action research; narrative research; ethnographic research; Indigenous methodologies (which can be qualitative or quantitative); memory work and the emerging field of sensory and visual research methods.

Quantitative methodology

Quantitative research involves the collection and analysis of data that can be presented numerically or codified and subjected to statistical testing. Its primary role is to allow the collection, analysis and development of understandings and interpretations of data on social phenomena from large groups or large data sources. Quantitative research is commonly associated with standard Western research scientific method, but this association is limited to the shared usage of statistical analysis to demonstrate and measure associations between different concepts. Quantitative methods can be incorporated into a range of methodologies. Major quantitative methods include gathering data through surveys, questionnaires and structured interviews.

Qualitative methodology

The key task of qualitative research, on the other hand, is meaning making, and this process does not usually require statistics or large-scale data. Instead, the key focus in qualitative

---

From method to practice

To understand what a research methodology is, we must recognise that all research and all researchers are embedded in our cultural milieu and steeped in particular standpoints. Does the cultural relativity of our own 'ways of knowing', the acknowledgment of the influence of our value system and our understandings of the nature of reality leave us, as social researchers, in a quandary about the worth of our research? Not really. We just need to understand and acknowledge that our research process, our research findings and the theories we develop are not core truths, but shaped and influenced by our rather particular values and understandings.

From this perspective, all research is a cultural product. And as you will have gathered from the preceding sections, the combination of standpoint, conceptual framework, theoretical paradigm and method are unique to the individual researcher. But this does not mean that methodologies are a random combination, or that there are as many methodologies as there are researchers. Rather, there tend to be similarities across key underpinnings that shape our methodologies as well as the need for scholarly rigour, the need to open our research process and practice and the need for incorporating research ethics (see chapter 4). This means that we can usually categorise individual frames of research reference into umbrella types of methodologies, such a feminist or Indigenous methodologies. However, the most basic way of delineating methodological categories is into qualitative or quantitative approaches.

Maggie Walter

research tends to be on smaller units of people and society, with the method and analyses drawing out the meanings, perceptions and understandings that individuals and groups attach to behaviours, experiences and social phenomena. Qualitative research methodology is adaptable to a broad range of methods and data sources. It is a subjective approach whereby the researcher aims to understand and interpret experiences by viewing the world through the eyes of the individuals being studied. Methods include the various forms of observation, focus groups and unstructured interviews.

The qualitative–quantitative debate

At the centre of this point is what is commonly known as the **quantitative–qualitative debate**. In this somewhat vexed and pointless argument, sides are taken as to whether quantitative methods (that is, methods that produce data relating to social phenomena that are amenable to statistical analysis) or qualitative methods (methods that concentrate on drawing on the detail and social meaning of social phenomena) are 'superior'. The origins of the debate are buried in the times when the dominant use of quantitative, statistically based social science was challenged by emerging qualitative methodologies and approaches. This debate is now past its use-by date, with the place of qualitative research within the social sciences firmly established. Rather, qualitative and quantitative research methods are now regarded as forming different, but equally vital, aspects of the social science research endeavour. Each methodological approach is just an element of the same whole: research. This debate also demonstrates the misunderstanding between method and methodology. Methodology is the approach, not the methods used. Many research designs now combine quantitative methods, which provide reliable results that can be generalised to the wider population under study, with qualitative methods to produce results that are rich in meaning and understanding of social processes **(triangulation).** However, neither the addition nor subtraction of one method or another determines the methodology.

Quantitative–qualitative debate: Debate in which sides are taken by researchers as to whether quantitative methods (that is, methods that produce data relating to social phenomena that are amenable to statistical analysis) or qualitative methods (that is, methods that concentrate on drawing on the detail and social meaning of social phenomena) are 'superior'.

Triangulation: Triangulation describes the combining of different research methods. The value of this practice is that the researcher can gain the advantages of each method used while also reducing the limitations of a single method.

Exercise 1.2: Food in prison

In 2006, Di Heckenberg and Dannielle Cody undertook a study of food in prison. The research was triggered by a seige at the prison the year before, when a central demand was the delivery of 15 pizzas and strong protests at new processes and practices around prison food. The research question was: what is the place and meaning of food in the prison experience of inmates? To answer this question, the researchers conducted semistructured interviews with six ex-inmates. The interviews revealed concerns about the following areas:

- the closure of mess rooms
- being expected to eat in cells
- re-heating food that had been prepared earlier
- the move to plastic utensils and foil containers rather than plates and cutlery
- the replacement of hot week-day lunches with sandwiches.

Respondents also tended to reflect positively of the 'old days'. One ex-inmate said:

Years ago, I used to look forward to our food. What I mean, it was, it wasn't anything spectacular, but there was plenty of it. Back then, you could always get extras and that, like they used to bring down whatever was left from the kitchen, they would bring it down on plates—just say you had a steak for tea, whatever steak was left in the kitchen they would just bring it—divide it around the yards—that was back then.

Your task

1. What explanations (theories) can you think of that might explain why the changes around food have been so unpopular with prisoners?
2. Based on your social understanding of the meanings we make of food, theorise why food might be such a significant topic for inmates that they would riot over changes.
3. How might we interpret the data around the unpopularity of the closure of the mess rooms and having to eat their meals in their cells?
4. Why do you think prison authorities made the described changes to the food regime in this prison?

Maggie Walter

Conclusion

The key message of this first chapter is that social research is a very broad undertaking. Good social science research is based on a sound understanding of the scientific method, the specific complexities of studying the social realm, and the key interrelationship between data and theory. From this base, there is an endless number of social questions to be asked and social phenomena to be studied, and many different methods and frameworks for conducting the social research questions we pursue. To be an effective and enthralled social researcher, you need a core familiarity and understanding of a wide range of these methods. The specific research method you select for your social research project is dependent on the topic of your study, the methodological framework from which you are approaching your topic, the specific research question that you ask, and the practical and resource constraints.

Main points

> Social research is about investigating the social questions we have about our social world.

> The humanness of social research means that social research is often a more complicated endeavour than other scientific research.

> Social science research is distinguished from social commentary or opinion by its use of scientific method.

> The primary aim of social research is to identify, investigate and try to understand social patterns and social meanings.

> The social context of social phenomena is an essential element of social science research.

> Social scientists deal in social aggregates, and individual exceptions do not challenge social findings or explanatory theories.

> The two core elements of social science research are empirical data and social theory.

> Social science research is informed and influenced by our worldviews and perspectives. In social science terms, these can be classified as our standpoint, our epistemologies, axiologies and ontologies.

> Methodologies are made up of these, as well as our method and theoretical framework.

Further reading

There are many social research books available, varying in quality, depth, level of coverage and accessibility. Your library should contain a wide variety of such texts. For more detail on the process of research, the following Australian text is useful.

Bouma, G. D. and Ling, R. (2004). *The Research Process*, 5th edn. South Melbourne: Oxford University Press.

References

Australian Institute of Family Studies (2002). *Introducing the Longitudinal Study of Australian Children. Longitudinal Study of Australian Children.* Discussion Paper No 1. Melbourne: Australian Institute of Family Studies.

Barraket, J. and Henry-Waring, M. (2008) 'Getting It On(Line): Sociological Perspectives on E-Dating', *Journal of Sociology*, 44 (2): 149–66.

Babbie, E. (2002). *The Basics of Social Research*, 2nd edn. Southbank: Thomson Wadsworth.

Dempsey, K. and de Vaus, D. (2003). 'Who Cohabits in 2001? The Significance of Age, Gender, Religion and Ethnicity', *Journal of Sociology*, 40 (1): 157–78.

Dooley, D. (1990). *Social Research Methods*, 2nd edn. Englewood Cliffs, NJ: Prentice-Hall.

Glicken, M. D. (2003). *Social Research: A Simple Guide.* Boston: Pearson Education.

Heckenberg, D. and Cody, D. (2006). *Food Matters: Issues Surrounding Food in Prison*. Criminology Research Unit, Occasional Paper No 3. Hobart: School of Sociology and Social Work, University of Tasmania.

Mann, P. H. (1985). *Methods of Social Investigation.* New York: Basil Blackwell Inc.

Martin, K. (2008). *Please Knock Before You Enter: Aboriginal Regulation of Outsiders and the Implications for Researchers.* Teneriffe QLD: Post Press.

Morphy, F. (2002). 'When Systems Collide: The 2001 Census at a Northern Territory Outstation', in Martin, D. F., Morphy, F., Sanders, W. G. and Taylor, J. (eds), *Making Sense of the Census: Observations of the 2001 Enumeration in Remote Australia.* CAEPR Research Monograph No 22. Canberra: Centre for Aboriginal Economic Policy Research, Australian National University: 29–73.

Natalier, K. (2001). 'Motorcyclists' Interpretations of Risk and Hazard', *Journal of Sociology*, 37 (1): 65–80.

Maggie Walter

Neuman, W. L. (2004). *Basics of Social Research: Qualitative and Quantitative Approaches.* Boston: Pearson Education.

Senate Community Affairs References Committee (2004). *A Hand Up Not a Hand Out: Renewing the Fight Against Poverty.* Canberra: Commonwealth of Australia.

Stanford Encyclopedia of Philosophy (2006). Stanford, CA: Stanford University Center for the Study of Language and Information.

Tuhiwai Smith, L. I. (1999). *Decolonizing Methodologies: Research and Indigenous Peoples.* London and New York: Zed Books Ltd.

Walker, A. (2000). *Measuring the Health Gap Between Low Income and Other Australians, 1977 to 1995: Methodological Issues.* Discussion Paper No 50. Canberra: National Centre for Social and Economic Modelling, University of Canberra.

Walter, M. (2002). 'Private Collection of Child Support: Back to the Future', *Just Policy*, 26:18–27.

Chapter 2
Research Design

Kristin Natalier

The research question: The heart of the research design

The research question is the defining aspect of the research process. Once you know precisely what it is that you want your research to achieve, designing the rest of the research project can be relatively straightforward. From a well-defined, clearly articulated and well-thought-out research question, the best way to approach the topic, the most appropriate data collection method and the most effective analysis techniques are likely to suggest themselves.

Research questions come in different shapes and sizes. Some are simple and open in terms of what findings they can generate. For example, one recent project was guided by this research question: 'Why do people take out private health insurance?' (Natalier & Willis 2008). Others specify a more bounded focus, such as another project where our question was 'How does the payment and receipt of child support, along with the receipt of government income and housing assistance, affect the housing outcomes of parents apart (both resident and non-resident parents)'? (Natalier et al. 2008). Some questions incorporate concepts that will need to be further defined. All specify exactly what the particular study is investigating and specify it in question form. The research question sits at the heart of research design.

Key terms

conceptualisation	method	research proposal
deductive theory	methodology	research questions
inductive theory	nominal definition	theory
literature review	operationalisation	
measurement	research design	

Introduction

Research design: The thorough planning process that develops an outline of all aspects of the research project and how they will fit together to result in rigorous research.

Research question: Research questions state the major aim of the research in question form, specifying the key idea that the research seeks to investigate and/or explain and also identifying the key concepts of the research.

Conceptualisation: The process of developing concepts that focus on the research question.

Operationalisation: The process of defining how concepts will be measured.

Measurement: How we are going to measure our key concepts. How we measure and what we measure differs between quantitative and qualitative methodologies.

Research proposal: A formal written document that fully details all aspects of the research we intend to undertake. A research proposal is usually required before academic research can proceed.

Method: The research technique or practice used to gather and analyse the research data.

Research design is the first, necessary step in undertaking a research project. It is essentially about planning: first, what it is you want to know, and second, devising the best way of finding out. Research design is a comprehensive task that draws together all aspects of the research, the topic, initial question and aims, through to deciding how to collect your data. Without a strong research design, your research is likely to be swamped by choices and options that are difficult to respond to consistently within the research process.

In practice, the amount of detail in a research design partially depends on your initial approach. Some qualitative work can unfold over time and in response to questions and themes that emerge through the collection and analysis of data. In contrast, quantitative work requires a prestructured approach to the specification of **research questions**, and the **conceptualisation, operationalisation** and **measurement** of variables. But even researchers who plan to stay open to where the data lead them need clear statements about the basis of their project and how decisions will be made.

The process of research design usually results in a formal document, the **research proposal**, which specifies and justifies the research plan and is reviewed before the researcher can begin the data collection. Even when a research proposal is not required, thinking through the design is a vital prerequisite for a successful project.

This chapter details the central aspects of how to design a social science research project through to the research proposal stage. Emphasis is given to the core components of a thorough research proposal: the importance of the research question and project aims; the design task of a comprehensive literature review; deciding the most appropriate research **method**; defining and measuring the key concepts; along with the pragmatic prerequisites of developing a time line and a resource budget.

Research questions

Developing good research questions is hard work. It is also highly creative work. You have to think really hard, apply conceptual skills and give the process sufficient time.

Given the effort required, perhaps it is not surprising that it is also a step that is often missed, as people move straight from the research focus to research method selection. Can you spot the perhaps fatal flaw in this process? The research question will shape every other component of the project. A research question places boundaries on a project, giving it coherence and direction. It will determine which methods are appropriate, the focus of analysis and the framework for writing up research. In short, a research question keeps a researcher focused. It is important to get it right, and to see the development of a research question not as wasted time (so few words for so much effort!) but as the necessary foundation of a final successful outcome. At the end of the process, our research might have generated many interesting findings, but without a clearly articulated research question, these are likely to just wander around the topic rather than form a coherent social analysis.

Bouma and Ling (2004:14) specify two properties of strong questions. First, they are limited in scope (even though any research question is part of a broader issue). No one project can address every dimension of a topic. Second, research questions are related to an empirical phenomenon; that is, they can be answered through studying observable and tangible things. Therefore, metaphysical questions such as 'Does God exist?' or moral questions such as 'Is terrorism ever justified?', while important, are not questions social scientists seek to answer through their research.

Generating research questions

As Robson (1993:25) notes, there is no guaranteed way of generating good research questions. Sometimes, our research question(s) is reasonably clearcut, arising cleanly from our research focus and our review of the existing literature and background of the topic. More often, however, formulating our precise research question is a more difficult task. There are so many aspects of so many social issues that we could explore or investigate. Selecting one aspect necessarily excludes others, but a decision has to be made. As detailed in chapter 1, such decisions are not only dictated by our interests but also influenced by how we see the world and our values.

The dos of research question generation

When it comes to developing a research question, here are some useful strategies:

- **Read.** Questions rarely emerge from our thoughts fully formed. Through reading, we refine what we want to know, or what is yet to be known about a topic.
- **Think in terms of concepts, not just topics.** A topic may be very broad (for example, finances in couple households), but exploring it through the lens of a particular concept (such as individualisation or gender) can help focus on what it is we want to ask.

Kristin Natalier

- **Identify puzzles.** Through the literature review (discussed in more detail, below), we can often identify contradictions in the existing research. These contradictions may inform our own research question.
- **Identify existing gaps and limitations.** There may be particular groups that have not been studied in relation to our topic, either because their conceptual significance was not recognised or because previous samples did not include them. We might also develop a project that responds to the limits of previous studies. For example, we might develop a question that requires a quantitative study to explore the statistical relationships between variables within a topic that has only previously been studied through small-scale qualitative studies.
- **Acknowledge feedback loops.** David Silverman (2005:90) points out that the move from research questions to findings is not always one way, and emergent findings may shape research questions. But it is a balancing act. While we always aim for a tight focus we do not want a question that is unyielding to important emerging issues. Nor do we want a question that is so unfocused that it leads us chasing down every potential issue at the expense of following through analysis and conclusions.
- **Write a question.** Rather than making a statement (for example, 'I will be exploring what activities divorced fathers do with their children'), actually shape your focus into a question form, something that ends with a question mark ('What activities do divorced fathers do with their children?').

The don'ts of research question generation

There are also some things to avoid when developing research questions.

- **Avoid rushing to your research question**. A good research question requires critical and creative skills, and takes time and work to get right.
- **Avoid problems of misinterpretation, by conceptualising all of the core concepts** contained in your research question unambiguously. This will militate against questions that are too broad or vague (for example, those dealing with 'poverty' or 'social problems').
- **Avoid posing long and complicated research questions**. Our research question should be clearly and simply articulated. Use subquestions (also clearly and simply articulated) to include the other important facets of your research question.
- **Avoid basing or tying your research question to a particular method**. The research question should always be the precursor to your selection of a research method—not the other way around.

- **Avoid asking questions that have already been answered.** Replicating a research study or question to verify a finding or to test if it is applicable in a different social context is different from being ignorant of previous studies in your field (Robson 1993:28).

Exercise 2.1: Developing research questions

Below are listed three current social issues:

1   High school truancy in regional towns
2   Housing affordability for Generation Y
3   Ageing population and the labour market.

Develop a research question for each of them. Then check to see if you have inadvertently done any of the things you should avoid.

Research aims

When we develop a research question, we do so for a reason. That reason is described in our research **aims**. Research aims explain why we have chosen to pursue a particular issue; what is our motivation for undertaking the study? Another way of thinking about it is to ask: what do we hope will be the outcomes of the study? Most obviously, we hope to find an answer to the research question we have posed, but beyond that, a good research design is clear about why we are seeking that answer.

> **Aims**: What we want to achieve by our research; for example, an understanding of how year 8 students use mobile phones.

Researchers pursue many different aims. These may include a contribution to social scientific knowledge (testing a **theory** or exploring an underresearched phenomenon), a wish to inform public policy (developing more effective ways of addressing a social issue) or a desire to improve practices in a particular field (helping people understand the social world and respond to it). We may have only one aim for our study or we may be driven by multiple motivations. But as with the research question, it is best to keep our aims modest, so that they can be met.

> **Theory**: A record of previous thinking about the important processes that shape social patterns.

Box 2.1: An example of clear research aims

It can be difficult to find a clear statement of aims even in the work of experienced researchers. Often, aims are a rewording of the research question. Others are clearer in specifying what they are trying to do with their work. In a piece of research

Kristin Natalier

conducted for the Australian Housing and Urban Research Institute, Birdsall-Jones and Shaw (2008) listed two aims, the first of which was a contribution to knowledge, the second was a contribution to practice:

> Identify and address unmet housing needs of Indigenous people through the identification of paths to and from homelessness; and Improve the capacity of Indigenous community housing organisations in planning and service delivery of housing needs through the acquisition of an analytical understanding of Indigenous homeless that takes into account the multiple facets of regional, cultural and environmental variation in the situation of Indigenous homeless people.

Literature review

A literature review is a vital early step in any project (with the exception of projects adopting a pure grounded theory approach). When we conduct a literature review we find out what is and is not known, how it has been studied, and the key questions, debates, concepts and any tensions and gaps in existing knowledge; it should be, in the words of Neuman (2006:123), 'comprehensive, [but] selective, current and critical'.

Using these goals as a guide, a comprehensive literature review shows familiarity with existing knowledge and establishes your credibility as a researcher in the field. Rather than just reviewing everything related to your topic, in your literature review you need to be selective in your focus on literature that links the proposed research with previous work. Being current is also important, because this helps the reader and researcher make sense of what is known. Our literature review must also be critical. It must be more than a report of previous theories and empirical findings; it must critically analyse these in relation to the topic. Finally, it should also provide the rationale for our study, either by identifying gaps in the literature or by demonstrating that a new or different approach is needed on an existing topic.

Reviewing the literature

It can feel quite daunting when we approach a literature review for a new project. After all, there is so much information. The key is to draw boundaries around the mass of material by thinking very clearly about what it is you want to do, therefore what it is you need to read and comment on. Some people may begin a literature review with a clearly defined research question, but as a literature review will stimulate new ideas, your question needs to be flexible enough to change as you read. Others will develop a question only after a lot of reading. Regardless, you will need well-developed information literacy and retrieval skills.

Literature search skills have two dimensions. The first is ensuring familiarity with generic search procedures. Most institutions run short workshops on how to use the library, databases and the internet, and the few hours of instruction can in the end save a great deal of time and annoyance. The second is developing your search strategies for your own topic. Sometimes you will be working in a field that has been well researched, but other topics may be relatively new or underresearched. Regardless of whether you are facing too much or too little information, you will need to be creative in your exploration of existing information. It is useful to consider the following:

- What disciplinary boundaries are you working in? If there is too much information, can you narrow your search to just sociology or criminology, at least as you begin your reading (your final review may broaden the discussion)? Alternatively, it may be that a topic with no profile in sociology may have received considerable attention in sociolegal research.
- How are you conceptualising key issues in your topic? This requires some higher level thinking than a simple topic area. It may be that you are using your topic as a way of thinking about higher order concepts, or that those concepts will give you an insight into the empirical issue.
- Identify the key works. As you begin reading, you will quickly find that the same monographs and articles are cited again and again. Focus on these, at least to begin with, as they form the basis of your field. Also refer to the reference lists of the works you are reading.
- Look in journals. When even sophisticated searching turns up little of relevance, sit down with a journal in the field and start to flip through the abstracts. You may find previously unconsidered synonyms or conceptualisations that point you in the direction of existing research.

Case study 2.1: Finding the right literature

My PhD thesis explored the gendered dimensions of housework in shared households. An initial search turned up almost no literature, but once I broadened my thinking and my search terms, there was a lot of relevant material. I wasn't interested in shared households so much as I was interested in the gendered dimensions of housework. Shared households were a subset of non-traditional household structures in which housework was (not) done. When I thought about the topic in this light, I found relevant studies among the old communal living literature (largely from the 1970s), as well as more recent work on gay and lesbian relationships, couples who are separated

Kristin Natalier

and those who are cohabiting. This work, as well as studies on gender and housework in marital households, formed the basis of my literature review.

Other researchers may need to narrow the literature available to them. When starting her PhD, Dr Emily Bishop wanted to look at young people's sexual practices. This is an issue that has been framed up as a social, policy and theoretical problem, and Emily was faced with masses of studies. But when she thought carefully about where her interests lay, she realised she wanted to explore how young people made sense of their sexual practices and, in particular, how they understood 'risk'; she also focused on rural youth. Clarifying what it was she wanted to research helped her limit what she needed to read.

A range of key social science databases is listed in box 2.2. These databases can be located directly on the web, or via the university library website. The university library is also the best resource for learning more about literature searches and accessing databases. Often, university libraries will have already collated relevant resources in subject-specific guides and indexes, and these can provide a good starting point.

Box 2.2: Relevant databases

Multidisciplinary databases
- Web of Science
- Current Contents Connect
- ProQuest
- Ingenta
- Australia/New Zealand Reference Centre.

Social scientific databases
- IBSS: International Bibliography of the Social Sciences
- Project Muse
- FAMILY: Australian Family and Society abstracts
- APAIS: Australian Public Affairs Information Service
- ATSIhealth: Aboriginal and Torres Strait Islander Health bibliography
- Gender Studies Database
- Sociological Abstracts.

Evaluating sources

When you conduct a literature review, you will be faced with an array of sources of information. Depending on the topic, some are likely to be more useful than others, but you should try to ensure that you have not missed any major sources. Each brings something different to your literature review, and a review based on one source only is likely to be both bland and limited.

Peer reviewed articles in scholarly journals

These are research articles that have been read and commented on by other academics—they have been 'quality controlled'. They provide full details of the research, including the methods and research questions as well as findings and conclusions. They are an important resource for students because they present legitimate research and discussion on how to interpret that research. However, the length of the peer review process and publishing schedules mean that data and social problems can sometimes be a little out of date.

Conference proceedings

These are a bit like edited books, created from papers presented at gatherings of academics (in the main). Many conference proceedings are peer reviewed, and published in conjunction with, or soon after, the conference. They can include new research, but may not be easily accessible.

Monographs and edited books

In this context, monographs are scholarly books on a particular issue; edited books consist of chapters by a number of different authors. They are sometimes, but not always, peer reviewed. Again, they can be a useful source of information and analysis, but are not always completely up to date.

Textbooks

These are written with the aim of making information accessible to people who are learning about a subject. Writers develop summarised and simplified accounts of research, which may be incomplete or lack the nuance of the original report.

Research reports

Not all research is conducted by academics in universities, and not all research is reported in books and articles. Other institutions also conduct and report on research. Some have strong links to academics and subject reports to peer review—the Australian Housing and Urban Research Institute is one example of this. Research reports are also produced by government departments, and are subject to internal review processes (for example, the Australian Institute of Health and Welfare or the Australian Bureau of Statistics). Market researchers may also report research on the web; some of this work is very strong, but some

Kristin Natalier

should be read with caution. Some social organisations also have research arms; Anglicare and the Brotherhood of St Laurence are examples of these. Finally, 'think tanks' such as the Australia Institute or the Melbourne Institute produce reports. The quality and rigour of all of these sources varies, as does the extent of their bias in conceptualising, conducting and reporting on research. Traditionally, these have not played a large role in literature reviews, but their increased dissemination and political relevance in recent years means they are becoming a very visible element in the research landscape.

Media pieces

This includes a broad array of materials, including articles, opinion pieces and editorials, interviews, and radio and television reports. None of these is peer reviewed, and many offer an intelligent layperson's account of social and policy issues. However, media often discuss legitimate research, and can be used to locate a more academic account of a topic. They also provide a current and often informative social context for your topic.

Internet sites

There is a broad array of sources on the internet. This information is accessible, and often reports on very recent issues. Some sites are simply electronic versions of social scientific research (for example, the ABS or journal sites) but others—for example, interest groups, blogs, discussion forums or online journalism—are not subject to peer review, and the information they provide should be treated with caution. Some present personal opinion, and others can report on research that has not necessarily been conducted rigorously.

Box 2.3: Useful internet sites

There are thousands of research-orientated internet sites that may be useful for you as a student. Here are some Australian sites to help you begin your searches:

- Australian Policy Online ‹www.apo.org.au›. A useful collection point for new Australian research, but be aware not all of the reports are peer reviewed, and some are more rigorous than others.
- Australian Institute of Family Studies ‹www.aifs.gov.au›. Families and relationships research from Australia.
- Australian Institute of Health and Welfare ‹www.aihw.gov.au›. Data and discussion papers on health and some social services.
- Australian Institute of Criminology ‹www.aic.gov.au›. Data and discussion on crime and criminal justice issues.
- Australian Bureau of Statistics ‹www.abs.gov.au›. Statistics on almost every component of life in Australia.

- Australian Housing and Urban Research Institute <www.ahuri.edu.au>. Peer-reviewed research on housing and urban planning issues.

Evaluating available literature is an important task, but one that has few clear rules. It is not possible to say 'you can always rely on peer reviewed articles' or 'think tank reports can never be trusted'. You will find this yourself as you read 'legitimate' research that doesn't seem to be very rigorous, or find an internet site that is full of relevant information and carefully designed research projects. So, rather than following hard and fast rules, it can be useful to consider these questions:

- Is the work peer reviewed? This process is an important part of ensuring the rigour of the research.
- Who is the author of the work? Is the author known in your field? What are his or her institutional affiliations? What are the aims of, and who are the personnel in, the institution or organisation? Organisations vary in their motivations for conducting research, and this will shape what is studied, how it is studied and what claims are made of the findings. You need to think about the implications of such differences (but not prejudge the research on the basis of them).
- Who is the author writing for? Consider how the audience may have shaped the project design and interpretation of findings.
- What is the research design? Is it clear from the report? Are the methods and methodologies consistent, and do they generate the kind of data necessary to answer the research questions? What are the assumptions informing the research? What are the limitations and strengths of the research? (But remember, no piece of research is perfect.) How have the research questions and aims, methods and analysis shaped the findings? Are findings and conclusions based in the data?
- Has the author used a bibliography and references? Do they show an understanding of the broader context within which their work is located? (The ways in which these are used will differ according to the type of report. A technical report by the Australian Bureau of Statistics (ABS) will use references very differently from the way a monograph uses them.)
- Is the material dated? This doesn't necessarily mean that the report is no good, but you must consider the implications of using old data.
- Can the data presented be corroborated? Are they comparable to other data on the issue? Research won't generate exactly the same findings, because each project is going to be different, but there should be comparable results from comparable studies.

Kristin Natalier

Exercise 2.2: Evaluating sources

Find an example of each of the sources described previously. Subject each to the questions listed above.

1   Can you think of other indicators that can be used to evaluate research?
2   What sources are most appropriate for your own research purposes?

Managing your review

Writing a literature review will be vastly easier if you have systematically managed your information, right from the very first search. Programs such as Endnote offer a huge range of options for retrieving and managing your reference database, but they are not necessary. It can be just as effective to develop a simple template. Regardless of which option you choose, you need to have some discipline and diligence, and make a commitment to yourself to record as you go, every single time.

Ideally, you will keep a record of the following types of information:

1   the key search terms you've used, so that you don't repeat them
2   the full bibliographic details of each work you read
3   the details of each work, including key words, abstract, research questions, problems and aims, methods, key findings, arguments, conclusions
4   a list of works that look relevant, and that you plan to track down.

This information should be recorded with a view to its use in your literature review. If you make a habit of noting the page numbers on which you found not only relevant quotes, but any type of key information, this will help you reference appropriately when you are writing a literature review, and it will assist you in revisiting an author's ideas. As you read, make notes, but limit the quotes you transcribe. Importantly, insert your own thoughts and responses to what you read: describe what you think about the claims made for the research, its limitations and its significance within the discipline and for your own research project. To differentiate your responses from the piece you are reading, divide each note page in two, with one side used for notes and the other as a space for your own voice.

Actually read the work: don't simply skim the work, highlight almost everything, or copy out entire passages. The main purpose of reading is to identify the key points in the piece. In my own work I always try to summarise these and my own responses to the work on the front of each (photocopied) source. Finally, you should make the time to review your notes on the day after, so that the issues are more likely to become embedded in your memory, and linked with other ideas.

The decision on when to stop reading can be a difficult one. You are not required to read and report on everything written on your topic—you are creating a context, not a catalogue. As a rule of thumb, when your reading is revealing nothing new in terms of general findings, discussion or conclusions, then it is time to end the literature search and begin writing in earnest.

Writing the literature review

By the time you come to write your **literature review**, you should already have a lot of words and thoughts that can form the basis of your written material. You need to be selective in terms of what you write about and how you write about it. When weighing what to include, ask yourself, 'Does the reader need to know this to appreciate my own research plan?' You are aiming to demonstrate your knowledge of an area by identifying relevant information, then synthesising and evaluating it.

> **Literature review:** A critical analysis of the existing research literature, theoretical and empirical, related to our research topic. It informs us of what is known and not known about our topic.

Crucially, a literature review is about critical quality rather than simple quantity.

You cannot present a critical discussion of the literature by only describing books and articles. A good literature review teases out the key themes and issues within a body of literature. To do this you must organise information in ways that relate to your own research question, critically evaluate what is and is not known about an issue (which will include empirical data and the core methods, and methodological, conceptual and theoretical approaches) and explore any issues of controversy or gaps in the literature. Your literature review should also be organised into an argument, so that the reader is in no doubt over where you are heading in the discussion and why you have included the issues and references you have. By the end, the reader should have a strong sense of how the area as a whole fits together, and where your proposed research fits within it.

Your ideas should be expressed in your own words. Too much quoting suggests you are not confident enough in your understanding of the issue. Sometimes people write something so well it can be hard to think about how to put it better, but the point is to let the reader know how you are interpreting a study—both its findings and its meanings—for your own research project.

Your ideas should also be presented in a respectful tone, even when you disagree with an author's conclusions or are not convinced of the rigour of their work. It is also wise to avoid qualifying statements (for example, 'it may be the case', 'probably') and emotive language (for example, 'this is a shocking and outrageous misinterpretation'). Also, avoid oversimplification. Most social science topics are complex, and a review will often reveal contradictory literature. Findings or theories that do not agree provide critical diversity within a literature review.

Kristin Natalier

A word on plagiarism: don't do it. Appropriate and accurate referencing is an expected academic practice. You must acknowledge others' work—not just their exact words but their ideas as well. It is unprofessional and dishonest to present their ideas and words out of context. Make sure you understand the expectations and style of your institution.

Methods

Once you have decided on what you are studying and why, your attention should turn to the how. This involves decisions about the methodological basis of your study, and the methods you will use. Methodological issues are covered in chapter 1, and for the purposes of this discussion it is important to remember that your methods need to fit into the methodological framework you have adopted.

Selecting a research method

So how does a budding social scientist go about selecting his or her research method? There are three key points to be made here:

1 Understand a wide range of social research methods

Just as in a restaurant, where to select the dish of your preference you first need to know what is on the menu, so it is with selecting a social research method: to be able to effectively select an appropriate research method, you first need to have a good understanding of the range of social research methods available and the key elements that they can bring to your research project. Otherwise, you might select a method that, while adequate for your research purposes, is not the method you would have chosen if you were aware of other, perhaps more appropriate, choices.

Again using our restaurant menu analogy, you might just keep on selecting the same dish or research method every time because you know about it, without considering whether another might suit you better. While such an attitude might produce reasonable quality research, you might never know what it is that you are missing from a research perspective. This point does not mean you need to be an expert in all research methods, but you should hold a basic working knowledge of a broad range of research methods: the key objective of this text.

2 Acknowledge that all research methods have strengths and weaknesses

All social science research methods are valid—all have strengths and all have value. As importantly, all social science research methods have weaknesses. Simply, there is no best method, or even best category of method. And while we will all develop preferences, it is important not to be partisan about 'our' method, or 'our' type of method. As noted in the previous chapter, triangulation of methods, often combining qualitative and quantitative method, is increasingly used in the social sciences.

3   Select the research method to suit the research project

The third important point to emphasise is that we must select the research method for the social science research project, not adjust our research project or question to suit a selected method. Fundamentally, the research method is just a tool of the social research project. Remembering this key point helps us avoid the trap of basing our research project around a method, or more problematically, seeing the research method as the research project. Using our selected research method to collect our data is just one part of the overall research endeavour.

Moving from your research question to the research method

As shown in figure 2.1, the starting point in selecting our method is the research question. Our choice is guided by the essential aim of selecting the best research method to answer the question we are asking. However, there are several other considerations that

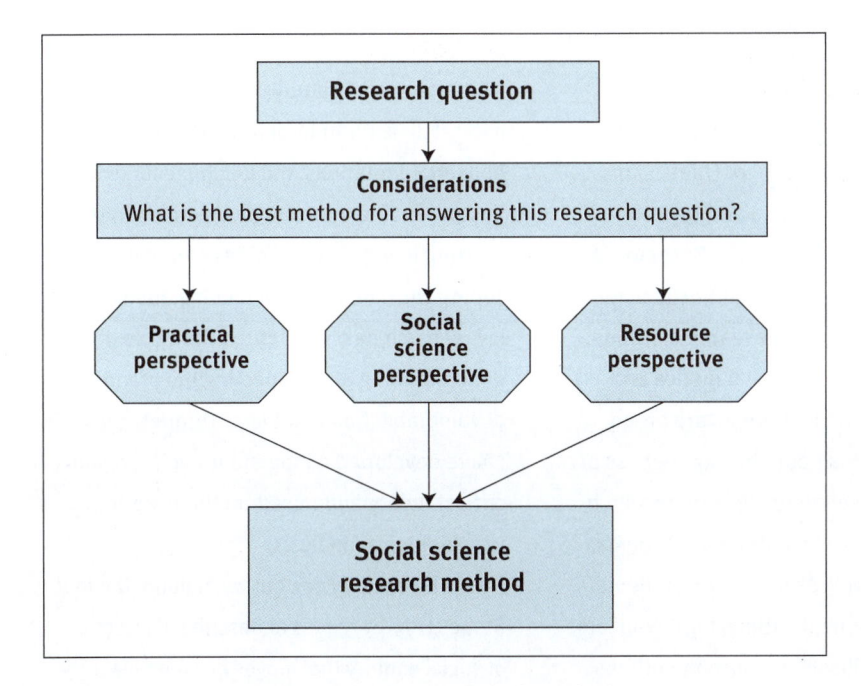

Figure 2.1: Selecting your social science research method

Kristin Natalier

mediate this process. In selecting the best method for our research question, we should also consider:

- **Practicability considerations**: Which research methods are feasible for this particular research question and also for ourselves as the researcher?
- **Social science considerations:** Which methods will provide the most rigorous and valid way of answering this research question from a social science perspective?
- **Resource considerations:** Which research methods are the most cost-effective in terms of time, for both the researcher and respondents and also in terms of finances, to answer this research question?

Remember also the wide range of social research methods available and that modules on additional qualitative and quantitative methods are included on this book's website at <www.oup.com.au/orc/walter>.

Voices in the field

Trisch Short

Patricia Short is a Lecturer in Sociology at the University of Queensland, and Director of the Bachelor of Social Science and Master of Social Science programs. She teaches research methods, applied research, and social justice and health. Her research interests are broad ranging, but focus upon the experiences of vulnerable householders. Recent research (Short et al. 2008) includes a study of *Risk-Assessment Practices in the Private Rental Sector* and their implications for low-income renters. The following paragraph outlines Patricia's perspective on how the inclusion of a range of methods (mixed methods) in social research design adds depth and richness.

'From large-scale study of the impacts of natural disaster to in-depth analysis of household relations and kinship economies to studies of low-income households in the housing market, and families of inmates coping with the cycles of criminal justice, my research has highlighted the value of understanding and respecting the standpoints of vulnerable householders. Through my work, I have developed a long-standing interest in critical theory and mixed-methods approaches to sociological analysis.

'The analogy of a hot-air balloon ride that Stones (1996:77) uses to describe a process of social enquiry that moves between macro (and necessarily more abstract) and micro-level (closely contextualised) views of the social world, rings true for me for it draws attention to how we might gain different perspectives on the same subject by employing a range of research methods and also to the connectedness among them. Like the hot-air balloon ride, a journey of social enquiry requires expert preparation; it demands well-informed, astute decision-making along the way, and a reflexive awareness of one's position in relation to others and the context of the journey. Moreover, to persuade onlookers that either journey is worthwhile, we would need to document our path, assure them of our competence and the reliability of our mode of travel, recount the experience in detail, and provide snapshots to demonstrate the insights the journey affords.

'Imagining a hot-air balloon ride provides a way of understanding the value of both viewing the social world from afar (as we do when using large-scale, quantitative methods of analysis and statistical theory to describe our subjects) and moving in close to take in sights, sounds, and odours, conversations and stories, and emotions "on the ground" (as we do when adopting smaller-scale, qualitative, interpretive approaches). Mixed-methods approaches can reveal how patterns we observe from afar are produced by people who animate them, how the experiences that motivate (or constrain) people to persist with, preserve, change, abandon or succumb to their everyday/night worlds constitute such patterns. In the broader view, we may see the sum total; in close up, what is rendered invisible from afar can be brought into the picture.'

Definition and measurement decisions

The focus of our research is clarified not only through a research question, but by defining what it is exactly that we are going to study, and what is the best way to measure that concept or variable. This process is generally known as conceptualisation and measuring or operationalisation.

Conceptualisation

Conceptualisation means the clear and unambiguous definition of the key concepts in our research. Through this process, we develop a **nominal definition** of exactly what we mean by the particular concepts we are using. Concepts are constructs that do not have an intrinsic or fixed meaning. This can sometimes be difficult to remember, particularly if you are using terms that are part of our everyday language (like 'poverty', for example, or 'gender' or 'housework'). But as we become more familiar with our topic, it becomes clear that social scientists have differing takes on how to define almost any element of social life. The important aspect is to be absolutely clear what it is you mean by a particular concept for this particular piece of research.

Conceptualisation: The process of developing concepts that focus on the research question.

Nominal definition: A definition of exactly what we mean by the particular concepts we are using.

Kristin Natalier

Conceptualising something often entails breaking it down into elements, which are called dimensions. De Vaus (2001:25) suggests three steps for arriving at a nominal definition. First, gather a range of definitions in the course of your literature review. Second, adopt a definition or draw together elements from various existing definitions. Third, delineate the dimensions and think about which are relevant to the current study.

The place to start conceptualising is defining the key concepts in our research question. For example, if our research question is 'Is smoking during pregnancy more common among teenage than older mothers?', we need to first define what we mean by our key terms. In this case, the key terms are 'smoking during pregnancy', 'teenage mothers' and 'older mothers'. 'Smoking' we can define as smoking cigarettes on a regular basis throughout the pregnancy. But what is a 'regular basis'? Based on our literature review we might decide that this means smoking more than five cigarettes in a week for at least half of the pregnancy. 'Teenage mothers' is also pretty straightforward: mothers aged from 13 years to 19 years inclusive. But as pregnancy is a nine-month process, what happens if they are 19 when they become pregnant but are 20 years old when they have their baby? 'Older mothers' is more problematic. We know this comparative group will be older than teenagers, but how much older? The answer depends on what we decide it should be, based on our literature review, other studies and conventions. If we found that other comparative motherhood studies with an age dimension tended to class 'older' mothers as 30 years and above, this might be a good definition to adopt. We need to also keep in mind conventions of data sources, such as that of the Australian Bureau of Statistics to report data in five-year age groups, such as '19–24 years' and '25–29 years'. For the purposes of our project, we decide that 'older mothers' means 'aged 30 years or more at the time of their baby's birth'. So, to summarise, our core concepts are conceptualised as:

- 'smoking during pregnancy': smoked five cigarettes or more per week for at least half of the pregnancy
- 'teenage mothers': mothers aged below 20 years at the birth of their child
- 'older mothers': mothers aged 30 years and above at the birth of their child.

Operationalisation, or measuring

Operationalisation (the term most used in quantitative research) or measuring (the term most used in qualitative research) is about deciding how we will measure or identify our concept, and the means we will use to determine its presence or its absence. How we operationalise depends again on the type of study we are undertaking. In quantitative work conceptualisation, operationalisation and applying the measures while collecting data are strictly applied, and are guided by rules specifying how data can be measured and how they are linked to concepts. The process is necessary for each variable. But in qualitative work, decisions may be made about operationalising the different concepts as they emerge during in-depth interviews.

As with all elements of the research process, deciding how to measure is a creative enterprise. Sometimes you will create your own indicators, and sometimes you will use pre-existing ones. The tack you take will depend on your research question and the existing body of knowledge. On the one hand, adopting existing indicators can be very useful: there is no point reinventing the wheel, and using agreed-upon indicators means your research can be compared to that of others. But if the topic has been understudied, or studied through different methods, if you have identified significant weaknesses in existing approaches or your data set does not have the variables you need to adopt existing definitions, then you may need to develop your own indicators.

Regardless of your approach, you need to fit your measure to the conceptual definition you have adopted. In the example above, we were to answer our research question by surveying all new mothers at a busy maternity ward over a period of 12 months. We would operationalise our concepts by dividing the mothers into two groups by age, as per our conceptualisation, and then count them as either smokers or non-smokers during pregnancy, again according to our conceptualisation of that concept. To answer our research question, we would then compare the number of smokers among our group of teenage mothers with the number of smokers among the older mothers. Similarly, if we were to conduct a follow-up qualitative study to try to gain an understanding of why some women continue to smoke during pregnancy and others do not, in our interviews with new mothers we would still need to classify their level of smoking activity (perhaps in this case conceptualising only those who were smokers pre-pregnancy, then measure these by dividing mothers into stopped-smoking or continued-to-smoke groups) before asking more in-depth questions about how they made sense of their smoking or non-smoking decisions and behaviours.

The theoretical direction: Deductive or inductive?

As detailed in chapter 1, thinking through the place of theory in your research project is important to the overall design, and your aims and research questions. In some cases, the theory is developed first, and the researcher then collects empirical data to test if the evidence supports the theory. This order of theory then data is referred to as a **deductive theory** (see definition on page 50) development. For example, a social scientist might deduce from a

Kristin Natalier

Deductive theory: Deductive theory is a way of developing theory that begins with the idea (theory) and proceeds to collect data to test the validity of the theory.

Inductive theory: Inductive theory is a way of developing theory that begins with the identification of a pattern in a social phenomenon and then proceeds to the development of a theory to explain that pattern.

theoretical study of the class system that children of working-class parents are less likely to attend university than those of the middle class. The researcher would then undertake an analysis of the parental background of university students to test the veracity of this theory.

In other cases, and perhaps more commonly, it works the other way: first a pattern in social phenomena is identified, and a theory is then developed to explain that pattern. This order of empirical data to theory is referred to as **inductive theory** development. Using the same example, an analysis of the demographic background of university students might reveal that students from families where the father has a blue-collar occupation are significantly underrepresented within the university's undergraduate population. A theory is then developed to explain this social phenomenon.

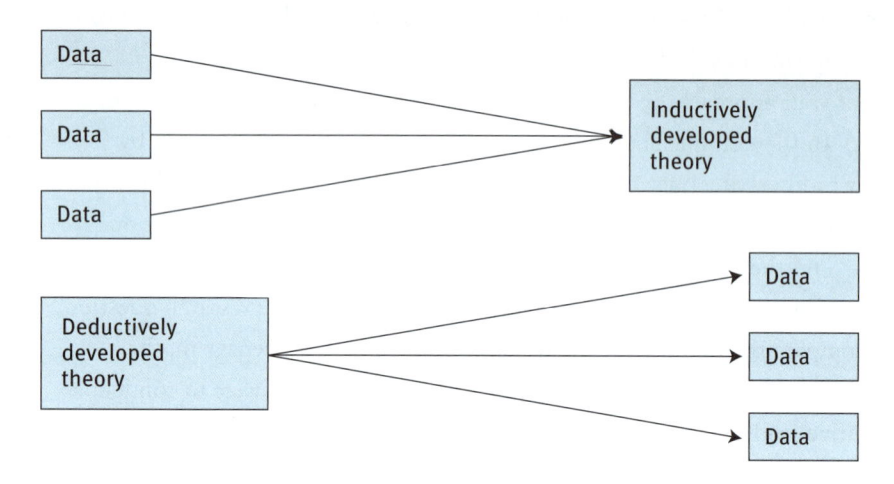

Figure 2.3: Developing theory: inductive or deductive

In the real research world, the trajectory does not always follow the precise, preset path of models. Rather, the sequencing is often neither definitively inductive nor deductive, tending to a more circular process. Theory development leads to empirical data collection, which in turn leads to a redefinition or refinement of the original theory, which often again leads to more data collection, and so on.

Timelines

Research, like most other activities in our lives, operates within time periods. Whether you are an honours student, a PhD candidate or an internationally recognised expert in your field, your research will always need to be planned, implemented and completed within a set period of time. In many cases, that period of time is strictly regulated. The research must be completed and the final thesis or report submitted by the deadline. To manage your research within the time allowed, you need a thought-through, tightly organised but feasible, timeline. Developing timelines requires breaking down the research into discrete tasks, which can in turn give a sense of exactly what needs to be done and if the project can be completed in the time available. It will also help to plan for upcoming tasks, and gives an early indication if things aren't going according to plan. If working in a team or with a supervisor, a shared timeline lets people know what to expect and when they need to make time available to the project.

Case study 2.2: An example of a timeline

The following timeline was developed for a funded project that investigated the relationship between the payment and receipt of child support and housing outcomes of resident and non-resident parents. In this project, the initial work around aims, research questions and methods had been completed for the funding application. In the end, recruiting participants took far longer than the research team envisaged and a contract extension was needed because the extra time needed for data collection bumped out all the tasks that relied on the data.

Figure 2.4: An example of a timeline

Task	2006										2007	
	M	A	M	J	J	A	S	O	N	D	J	F
Literature review												
Positioning paper												
Statistical data analysis												
Develop interview schedule												
Ethics clearance												
Pilot interviews												
Project status report												
Recruitment and interviews												
Transcription												
Analyse interview data												
Final report												
Research bulletin												

Kristin Natalier

Students should also remember to check that their own timetable matches the availability and expectations of their supervisors. Acknowledge that some elements of the process are out of your control, and build in some leeway; in my own experience, recruitment and analysis can be unexpectedly time consuming. Making changes to ethics applications also bites into the time available, especially if you are required to resubmit the application to a committee that only meets once a month, for example. Do not plan to have everything finished on the last day: leave time for editing, last-minute changes and space for things that do not run according to your schedule.

Resources

As with timelines, developing a budget can be crucial. For academics and professional researchers, budgets are a required element of research projects. Funding contracts are negotiated in accordance with institutional costs, industry standards and competitiveness in mind. This level of detail is not necessary for students, but estimating the cost of the project is still vital. Knowing likely costs in advance will help you decide if your plan is doable or if it will need to be changed to conform to the resource constraints you are working under. It may be that, in the end, it will cost too much to travel to 30 interview sites and then have the interviews professionally transcribed, but you may be able to afford to do 20. Such calculations require a back and forth between practical considerations and the aims and logic of the project. It may be that conducting fewer interviews means you can't answer your research question, in which case you may have to alter your aims, or alternatively, find a less expensive way of getting interview data (telephone rather than face-to-face interviews, for example, or doing your own transcribing).

As with timetables, talk about your costs with people who have worked in comparable projects, as well as your supervisor or lecturer. List all of the project elements, and be realistic about what they cost and if you can afford to meet those costs. Also make sure you are familiar with the resources available to you as a student: it might be the institution covers photocopying or telephone calls or travel, all of which can affect what you can cover in your project.

Design in practice: The research proposal

Research proposal: A formal written document that fully details all aspects of the research we intend to undertake. A research proposal is usually required before academic research can proceed.

A **research proposal** is when the process of research design is pulled together. It is a substantial written document that details and justifies the proposed research project, and it is usually submitted for academic review and approval. It is a requirement of honours and research higher degree level study, and forms the basis of most applications for research grants. A research proposal can take a lot of time, both in terms of thinking about the necessary issues and then writing and revising the document. However, research proposals are more than red tape. They require you to set down a clear statement of your proposed research and your plan for proceeding. They clarify points you might have taken for granted and show up any 'gray areas or loose thinking' (Kelly 1998:114). Well-written proposals ensure the whole project hangs together. They also act as a road map, and remind you what you are trying to achieve when you get lost in the fog of data collection or analysis. In short, research proposals are as important as generating and analysing data and reporting findings.

Getting started

First, take note of the institutional requirements for the research proposal: the word-length limitations, necessary documentation and due dates. Also take note of where the relevant people will be when the proposal is due—it can be a nerve-wracking experience to chase a signature when no one knows where your supervisor is. This information will help you timetable your work plan for this initial component of your research, and ensure your project is not rejected because you did not cross your t's and dot your i's. It can also be useful to read other research proposals, to get a sense of the language used, and what format and level of detail is required.

General principles

The structure of a research proposal and the information it includes will differ according to institutional requirements and level of study. However, a set of general considerations is relevant regardless of the context. It is important to provide as much clear and detailed information as you can. Regardless of the headings you are required to work under, Silverman (2005:144) uses Marshall and Rossman (1989:2) to describe the questions a research proposal must answer:

- What is the research about and what is it trying to achieve? A proposal must clearly state parameters of the project by specifying the research questions, problems and hypotheses (if relevant). It needs to specify its aims.
- Why should anyone be interested in the research? The research proposal must justify the time, effort and other resources that will be expended on the project. It needs to be clear that the research has a relevance and importance beyond the immediate interest of the researcher.
- Is the research design credible, achievable and carefully explained? The proposal must show that the project is coherent and the elements are logically related. It must also

Kristin Natalier

> **Methodology:** Methodology is the theoretical lens through which the research is designed and conducted.

provide detail on the methods and **methodology** that informs the project: are they appropriate and are they realistic?
- Is the researcher capable of doing the research? A researcher does not necessarily need to have existing expertise in the proposed methods, and the project might offer a valued opportunity to develop the relevant skills. But it should be clear from the proposal that the researcher has a full understanding of the implications of undertaking the project.

Write clearly, avoid jargon and try to avoid presumptions about what your readership 'should' know. The proposal may be judged by people who are not experts in your field. This does not mean they are not able to critically and usefully judge your research plan and offer insights, but it does mean you should not take their understanding of key issues for granted. (This is not a bad thing, as it militates against your own presumptions undermining the rigour of the research.)

Be honest and realistic about the scope of your project and the issues it raises. The research proposal is not the blueprint of a perfect study. It is written to clarify the project and show that the researcher will be able to carry out the project. Every piece of research has its strengths and weaknesses—being clear about the limits of your own proposed research indicates you have thought carefully about what you plan to do, and why; avoiding the issues may be read as a failure to understand the implications of your approach.

'Selling' your project is also important. A research proposal should be more than a statement about what you are going to do. Be persuasive about the value of the proposed research; our chosen research topic often comes to mean a great deal to us, but we cannot assume that it is self-evidently relevant and exciting. You need to make an argument to convince the reader that your project is worthwhile and doable. This is most obviously the purpose of any discussion justifying 'why'—why this question or why these methods?—but it should also be evident in the insight you show throughout the research proposal, and in the way it hangs together.

While usually set out under headings, the proposal should be approached as a coherent whole. The sections should relate to each other and to an overarching argument about the value of the proposed research. There should be no repetition, and you should make your points in a logical order. Your proposal should be a stand-alone document, one that can be read without the need to clarify points with the author or refer to previous research reports you might have produced.

Structure of the research proposal

Research proposal formats and headings are not consistent across institutions, but all will have some combination of the following (not necessarily in the following order):

Title

The title should succinctly and clearly sum up the project so that its focus is evident to a non-expert reader. Avoid puns, jargon and very long titles. In the words of Punch (2000:69), it 'should convey as much information as possible in as few words as possible'.

Introduction

This is a preview of the key issues of the research project. Write the introduction to be appealing to the reader, to spark his or her interest. You need to capture the attention of people who might not know a lot about the area or be particularly interested in the topic generally. However, don't oversell and don't be defensive about the value of the project.

Research questions and aims

The research questions should be stated near the beginning of the proposal, so that the readers know exactly what you are proposing to do, and can read the document with this in mind. There should be no mystery or confusion in the mind of readers. It can be helpful to explicitly introduce the research questions and aims, along the lines of: 'This project explores the following research questions: ...', and 'This project has the following aims ...'

Remember, the research questions and aims need to be fully justified so that the question 'Why should we care about this issue?' is answered, either explicitly or implicitly. Marshall and Rossman (1989) suggest three types of significance: contribution to knowledge, to policy considerations or to practitioners. Some proposals also require a separate statement of significance, so that it is easy to remember to argue the case. But even if this is not required, your literature review and/or background discussion should contribute to the justification. You may find it useful to explain clearly the importance of your project, using wording such as 'This research is significant because ...'

Literature review and/or background to the issue

Punch (2000:43–4) suggests three questions when determining the scope of the literature review:

> What literature is relevant to the project?
> What is the relationship of the literature to the proposed study?
> How will the literature be used in the proposal?

Kristin Natalier

When answering these questions, you should remember that the literature review makes a case for the study's relevance, and it should be clear how the questions, problems and methods arise out of the literature.

Methodology and conceptual framework

A proposal should include a statement of your methodology and theoretical conceptual framework and how these are related. These should be justified, rather than merely stated, but any justification needs to be brief and written in plain English. On your statement of methodology: this is not the time to develop an extended response to methodological debates. Rather, the aim of this section is to make your starting point clear, so that the reader can judge how your initial stance shapes your project.

Methods

You should provide a lot of detail in your methods discussion. You must do more than state, for example, you are doing semistructured in-depth interviews or bivariate analysis. Rather, you need to be specific on how the methods will be used in this particular piece of research. You should be clear about your sample and recruitment processes, conceptualisation, operationalisation and variables (where relevant), instruments and data collection processes, and analysis. The implications of these decisions for generalisability and rigour should be discussed, remembering that all projects have their limitations, and it is best to present an informed discussion about what you can and cannot do with your sample and methods.

Qualitative proposals often involve evolving procedures, questions, theories, operationalisation and conceptualisation, as themes emerge through the data. This is acceptable when it is part of the logic of the research design (rather than evidently arising through sloppy thinking and planning) and in these instances, it is important to explain the basis of the flexibility, and how decisions will be made as the study evolves.

Ethics

Institutions will often ask that you acknowledge ethical implications of the research. Some projects may give rise to difficult ethical issues, but this does not mean they will be rejected out of hand. Rather, the researcher should be open about potential issues and their strategies for dealing with them. This clarity shows that you have thought seriously about the issues and ways of protecting participants in the research. Trying to hide ethical challenges by failing to acknowledge them is likely to be read as a lack of both understanding and competence to undertake the research properly.

Timetable

Be realistic with key deliverables or accomplishments, and focus on what can actually be done in the time, rather than trying to impress the reader with promises of delivering so much for so little. This is an important piece of information for people assessing your research proposal, because it helps them judge if the project is doable.

Budget

Students are likely to be dealing with very limited budgets. However, the resource implications may still be used to judge if the project is workable.

Dissemination of results

Be clear about how you are going to share your findings. In some projects it may be relevant to explore the possibility of communicating results to the people who took part in a study.

Reference list

This is often an afterthought, popped in at the last minute. But it is important to remember that referencing is an expected part of academic practice, and that a research proposal is an academic document. Referencing allows the reader to return to your sources to make up their own mind, and gives an appropriate acknowledgment to other authors when you work with their ideas.

In sum, when you are writing your research proposal, you need to be:

> succinct
> detailed
> honest
> logical
> justified.

Kristin Natalier

Conclusion

Research design is essential for research that is rigorous and relevant. It can be confusing to think your way through a new topic before you have actually done the research, but doing this groundwork will guide your research project and your own development as a competent researcher. This chapter cannot properly convey the iterative nature of research design. In a book, one topic follows another in a linear fashion, but in real life, things are messier. You will find yourself going back and forth between your research question, conceptualisation and operationalisation, methods and literature. You may start with a clear question that does not change throughout the research design process, but it is just as likely you will rethink what you want to know, what you need to know and what you can know as you read existing research and come to some hard decisions about the methods you can use. The key is to accept this back-and-forth process, and to give yourself time to do it, balancing flexibility with the need for some structure and boundaries as you develop and then do your research. You will also learn how to balance your intellectual curiosity with practical constraints. These are skills that aren't easily taught in a textbook—they require judgment, confidence and a willingness to learn from your mistakes; and we all make mistakes, even the most seasoned researchers.

Main points

> - The process of research design in a necessary foundation for successful research outcomes.
> - Research design involves generating research questions and aims, undertaking a literature review, conceptualising and operationalising key terms, and specifying methodologies and methods.
> - Designing research properly allows the project to 'hang together', so that each element of the research is informed by the others.
> - Research questions form the basis of a project. They need to be limited in scope and answerable empirically.
> - Conceptualising and operationalising key terms assists in clarifying what exactly is being studied and how it will be identified in the data collected.
> - A literature review provides the context for the proposed study. It should synthesise rather than describe relevant literature.

> Methods should be chosen with a view to answering the research question. For the purposes of research design they should be as detailed as possible, but it is also important to remember that there will sometimes be a need to be flexible once the research begins.

> A research proposal is a document that clearly explains and justifies the research project.

Further reading

de Vaus, D. (2001). *Research Design in Social Research*. London: Sage.

Fink, A. (2005). *Conducting Research Literature Reviews: From the Internet to Paper*. Thousand Oaks, CA: Sage.

Punch, K. F. (2000). *Developing Effective Research Proposals*. London: Sage.

References

Birdsall-Jones, C. and Shaw, W. (2008). *Indigenous Homelessness: Place, House and Home. Positioning Paper*. Melbourne: Australian Housing and Urban Research Institute.

Bouma, G. D. and Ling, R. (2004). *The Research Process*. South Melbourne: Oxford University Press.

de Vaus, D. (2001). *Research Design in Social Research*. London: Sage.

Kelly, M. (1998). 'Writing a Research Proposal', in Seale, C., *Researching Society and Culture*. London: Sage: 111–22.

Marshall, C. and Rossman, G. (1989). *Designing Qualitative Research*. Newbury Park, CA: Sage.

Natalier, K., Walter, M., Wulff, M., Reynolds, M. and Hewitt, B. (2008). *Child Support and Housing Outcomes: Final Report*. Melbourne: Australian Housing and Urban Research Institute.

Natalier, K. and Willis, K. (2008). 'Taking Responsibility or Averting Risk? A Socio-cultural Approach to Risk and Trust in Private Health Insurance Decisions', *Health, Risk and Society*, 10(4), 399–411.

Neuman, W. L. (2006). *Social Research Methods. Qualitative and Quantitative Approaches*. Boston: Pearson.

Kristin Natalier

Punch, K. F. (2000). *Developing Effective Research Proposals*. London: Sage.

Robson, C. (1993). *Real World Research: A Resource for Social Scientists and Practitioner-researchers*. Oxford: Blackwell Publishers.

Short P, Seelig, T., Warren, C. M. J., Susilawati, C. and Thompson, A. (2008). *Risk Assessment Practices in the Private Rental Sector: Implications for Low-Income Renters*. Final Report No. 117. Melbourne: Australian Housing and Urban Research Institute.

Sidhu, R. and Taylor, S. (2007). 'Educational Provision for Refugee Youth in Australia: Left to Chance?', *Journal of Sociology*, 43(3), 283–300.

Silverman, D. (2005). *Doing Qualitative Research*. London: Sage.

Stones, R. (1996). *Sociological Reasoning: Towards a Past-modern Sociology*. Houndmills, Basingstoke: Macmillan.

Chapter 3
The Research Process

Douglas Ezzy

Testing the traditional and questioning the accepted

I want to know if men are better leaders than women. What do you think? Men are more often chosen as leaders. Men are more likely than women to be ministers in parliament, leaders in business or senior academics, and to hold many other leadership positions (Moon & Fountain 1997; Pini 2002, 2005; White 2003). Is this because men are better at being leaders than women, or is there some other process at work here?

One way of answering this question would be to appeal to an authority, or tradition. Some people believe that 'a woman's place is in the home'. Indeed, for much of the twentieth century, Australian society was organised around a family structure in which the father worked and the woman stayed at home and cared for the children. Until 1966, married women were not allowed to work in the public service in Australia (Probert 1980). Traditional answers to questions like this are often based on moral or religious beliefs. However, if women are limited to roles in 'the home', this denies women the right to participate more broadly in society, which has negative consequences both for women and for the rest of society. On a more pragmatic level, one problem with the idea that 'a woman's place is in the home' is that few families can now afford for women to stay at home (McDonald 1998). More and more women are delaying having children so they can build their careers, and when they do have children, they are choosing to stay in employment. In other words, men used to be in positions of leadership because most women stayed at home to look after the children, but now women are staying at work, so why are there still more men than women in positions of leadership?

The question of whether men or women are better leaders, therefore, has to be answered in terms of social process and cultural assumptions. We cannot understand the question, let alone answer it, unless we consider both the social context and the influence of social processes on our assumptions about the topic. And it is the research process that ensures that we understand both what it is we are examining and the contexts in which these social phenomena occur, as we investigate the social question.

Key terms

concept	qualitative research	textual analysis
conceptualisation	quantitative research	theory
ideology	reductionism	units of analysis
interpretations	reliability	validity
measurement	sample	variables
population	sampling frame	

Introduction

A key role of social research is to investigate what is actually going on in our social world. As discussed already in chapters 1 and 2, social investigation requires rigorous, innovative, scientific and questioning research activity, and it needs to be undertaken in such a way as to ensure that it meets these prerequisites. Just as the research design allowed us to develop a map of our research project, the research process provides a map for how social research, in general, needs to be undertaken.

In its questioning role, social research looks anew at social phenomena rather than relying on tradition, or accepting social assumptions or beliefs. In the introductory box, social researchers have looked at some of the social processes involved in determining why there are fewer female than male leaders in our society. Others have taken this question further, asking, 'What evidence is there that women perform better or worse as leaders?'. For example, Kabakoff (2002) conducted a study of 172 American corporate managers, asking all their employees to rate these managers on their effectiveness as leaders. He found that there was no difference in the ratings for male and female leaders. Similarly, Eagly and associates (1995) reviewed a wide range of psychological studies of leadership and found that there was no overall difference in the effectiveness of male and female leaders. In other words, social research results indicate that female leaders are just as good as male leaders.

If women are just as good leaders as men, why are there still more male leaders? Pini (2002:45) studied women in leadership in the sugar industry in Australia, finding that elected leaders of the sugar industry claimed that the election process was 'open, objective and gender neutral'. However, when Pini studied how these same leaders described their own success, they described a system that was closed, subjective and clearly biased against women. In other words, Pini argues, there are more men in leadership because the system is biased against women.

The question 'What is a "better" leader?' is also important. Studies suggest differences in the leadership style of men and women (Rosser 2003). How do you measure 'better'? Is a leader of a church with more people a 'better' leader? Is it more important that church leaders are trustworthy and compassionate? Is a manager who looks after the welfare of his or her workers a 'better' manager, or is it more important that the company makes a high profit? What if the company happens to sell chemicals that make people sick when they use them, such as cigarette companies? Does this make the manager better or worse? The choice about how to define 'better' must, eventually, appeal to some sort of ethical criteria as well as the conceptual criteria aligned with our research (see section on conceptualisation).

The process of social research

Social sciences, like sociology, politics or anthropology, involve social research. Social research is the process of examining social life to obtain a better understanding of what people are doing and why they are doing it. Before an engineer builds a dam, he or she first examines the rocks and geology of the area in which the dam is to be built. Similarly, it makes sense that before a politician introduces a new program to, say, prevent the spread of HIV/AIDS, that she or he finds out what people are doing and why they are doing it. It doesn't make much sense to have a television advertising campaign aimed at heterosexuals in the general population, as the early Australian AIDS programs were, when the people most at risk are gay men, injecting drug users and prostitutes.

Many of the more pressing world problems include a significant social dimension, and require social solutions. For example, global warming will not be solved by new technology alone. Changes in patterns of behaviour and in cultural beliefs are also required. Zero-emission cars, for example, will only be developed and sold widely if policy-makers and the general population believe that they are required, and start purchasing such cars. These changes in beliefs and patterns of buying are cultural and social changes. HIV/AIDS will not be cured by medical advances alone. Policy-makers and people need to change their willingness to talk about safe sex, and condom use in particular. This is very difficult in cultures where talk about sex is taboo. Violent conflict associated with terrorism will not be resolved by military power alone. Rather, an examination of the cultural beliefs and social conditions, including economic and political contexts, that lead people to be willing to participate in terrorism is required. A more sophisticated understanding of social and cultural conditions that generate terrorism may help to prevent the development of terrorism in the first place, rather than trying to crush it once it has arisen.

These issues require social research. Why is it that men are still more likely to be leaders? Why is it that many people still think that global warming is not an important issue? How can we encourage people to practise safer sex and safer injecting practices to minimise the spread of HIV/AIDS? Why do people become terrorists, and what social, political and economic changes might lead them to choose differently? These are the sorts of questions that social researchers ask.

This chapter has two parts. In the first, a set of issues that all researchers must address as part of the process of social research is explored. The second half examines the research process in action through an analysis of these core steps in three recent social research projects. These are: a survey of who does housework in Australia; a qualitative interview study of teenage Witches; and a discourse analysis of racism in newspapers.

Douglas Ezzy

Ten issues for social researchers

The process of social research can be usefully divided into ten key issues. These are:

1. Identifying the topic.
2. Focusing on a research question.
3. Specifying the theoretical framework that will inform the research.
4. Developing a research methodology.
5. Delineating the main **variables** or processes.
6. Defining and measuring.
7. Selecting a research sample and collecting data.
8. Addressing the political and ethical dimensions of the research.
9. Analysis of data and interpretation of results.
10. Writing up the results.

Variable: A characteristic of data that has more than one category. A variable varies between different values, and is measured in social research; for example, the variable gender has two categories: male and female.

These steps are sequential and interrelated, with decisions and developments in one task leading on to and informing the next step. Because the practice of social research is a very varied one, not all researchers will need to address all these steps to the same degree or in the same order. However, while there is variation in how a social researcher addresses each step of the research, skipping or ignoring a step can jeopardise the validity of the whole research project. Some of these steps have already been touched on in the first two chapters. The focus of this chapter is the critical importance of how these elements operate as a process, rather than as individual aspects; they all work together to create valid and rigorous social research. This sequential nature of the research process is demonstrated in figure 3.1.

Identifying the topic
↓
The research question
↓
Theoretical frame
↓
Research methodology
↓
Delineating variables and processes
↓
Defining and measuring
↓
Selecting a sample and collecting data
↓
Political and ethical dimensions
↓
Analysis and interpretation
↓
Writing up and communication of results

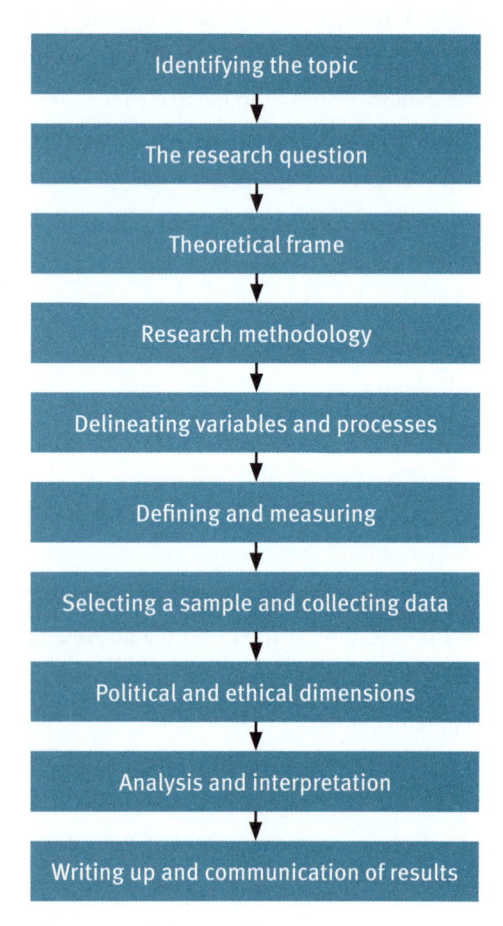

Figure 3.1: The research process

1 Identifying the topic

Most research begins with a topic deemed important and the research question, as outlined in chapter 2, flows from the activities undertaken during the design process. Others have a topic, but may not fully articulate the research question until some way into their research. This is a product of the different reasons for conducting social research. When research is funded by an organisation with a specific concern, then clearly the topic is already given. For example, in 2006 WorkCover Tasmania approached myself and Dr Maggie Walter with the topic 'The outcomes for longer-term workers compensation claims in Tasmania'. We began with a scoping study of the research problem, and from this developed the research question related to the claimants' longer-term health, social and economic outcomes. This larger project is currently under way. In contrast, some research is motivated by fascination. When I began my PhD research, for example, I was fascinated with the topic of the meaning of life. It was only after quite a bit of thinking and writing that I narrowed my research down to a question concerning how people make meaning of their lives when they become unemployed.

The topic of a research project should be clear enough to specify exactly what it is that you wish to research. This specification is an essential part of developing your specific research question. 'Injecting drug users' would be too vague and general. Although it might serve as a starting point, it requires further clarification. 'Dental hygiene and the health of injecting drug users' is probably too specific, although in certain circumstances it may be appropriate. This is not to minimise the significance of this issue, but the health of injecting drug users is shaped by many factors other than dental care, and narrowing the question to this one aspect may limit the usefulness of the research. Similarly, a topic like 'global warming' is too broad, and requires more specification. A more realistic topic is probably something like: 'Representations of global warming in newspapers'. In turn, this specification will lead directly to the development of your research question. In this case, this might be: 'How is global warming represented in mainstream Australian newspapers?'

2 Focusing on a research question

As already outlined in chapter 2, clearly specifying the research question takes the researcher beyond the topic of interest to 'nailing down' *exactly* what it is that he or she wants to know. Specifying the research question can avoid many problems later in the research. Research questions that are too general or vague can be very difficult to answer, and research projects easily become bogged down when the topic is not translated into a clearly defined research question. For example, a recent PhD student in Sociology at the University of Tasmania began her PhD research with the topic, 'What is a good life?' (Verdouw 2008). This is a good sociological research question, but it proved to be a very 'big' question, which was not

Douglas Ezzy

focused enough. She embarked on a qualitative study of the topic, interviewing 41 young adults about what they understood to be a good life. However, as she began to analyse her data, Verdouw identified many different aspects of the 'good life' and found it difficult to try to discuss them all. She eventually decided to narrow her question down to the role of money in the 'good life'. Her specific research question was: 'How do the orientations of 41 young adults towards what is "good" in life shape their money meanings, and consequently their motives, values, behaviours and social interactions?' (Verdouw 2008:8). This research question still allowed Verdouw to examine her more general topic of 'the good life', but it provided a narrower focus that was manageable and practical for a PhD project.

Research questions relate closely to the theory (step 3) and the methodology (step 4) of the research. It is often useful to move back and forth between these steps to ensure that the research question, theory and methodology are compatible. Research questions that focus on meanings and experience are typically best studied using qualitative methodologies and interpretive theory. Research questions that ask 'how many?' type questions are best studied with quantitative research methodologies, perhaps using a survey.

3 Specifying the theoretical framework that will inform the research

Research is like a conversation. The researcher 'talks' to what is happening 'out there' in society, and 'listens' to what is said in reply. A researcher might wonder if newspapers are accurately representing what scientists say about global warming. When she or he does some research on this, the research 'talks back' to her or him about what newspapers say about global warming. Theory, therefore, can be thought of as a record of previous conversations on the same topic. Research brings the ideas from these previous conversations and uses them to shape the way research is conducted.

As outlined in chapter 1, the theory or paradigm that a researcher uses will shape the way in which he or she understands the research topic. Marxist theory, which is associated with a conflict perspective, for example, argues that the primary inequalities in society are a product of economic processes. Marxist-influenced studies of global warming argue that coal and oil companies are using their influence on governments and policy-makers to ensure that global warming is not taken seriously as an issue (Newell & Paterson 1998). In a fascinating study of global warming sceptics, Jacques and colleagues (2008) found that 92 per cent of global warming sceptic books published were linked to conservative 'think tanks', which have a clear political agenda that serves the interests of the elite and wealthy. If a social researcher were to study newspaper representations of global warming from a Marxist or conflict perspective, she or he would probably point out that the leaders of big business own most newspapers, and that it is in the short-term interests of the wealthy and powerful to ignore the issue of global warming.

Theory is an essential part of all social research, but theories can be, and are, changed and developed as a consequence of research. Marx, for example, began with a model of two classes in society: those who own factories, and those who work in them. However, later in his life, after he had 'researched' these issues in more detail, he developed a more complex model that included other classes, such as people who inherit wealth and people who we would now describe as the middle class.

Also, as detailed in chapter 2, the placement of theory within social research can vary. Deductively conducted research begins with theories. For example, Newell and Paterson (1998) deductively develop a Marxist theory that the coal and oil industries have influenced government policy to protect their own interests. They then go on to test this theory empirically by examining oil and coal lobbying strategies, and how these have shaped particular government decisions. Inductively conducted research, on the other hand, begins with data. For example, I developed an inductive analysis of environmental change by examining four popular journals (two from business and two from science) and comparing the way they described climate change (Ezzy 2001). I found that the business journals were not worried about climate change, because the writers seemed confident that science would solve any problem that arose. In contrast, the science journals were worried about climate change because they did not think that human science would be able to stop global warming once it was started. My analysis started from the data and built up to the theory, whereas Newell and Paterson started with a theory, then tested it against some data. Although one side is usually emphasised, all research contains both deductive and inductive elements.

4 Developing a research methodology

Research methodology is the frame of reference for social research. As previously outlined in chapter 1, this frame is influenced by our worldview (standpoint), and the paradigm in which our theoretical perspective is placed or developed. Methodologies are broad ranging, but at their basic level, research methodologies can be categorised into one of two main types: quantitative (or statistical) research and qualitative (or interpretative) research.

In **quantitative statistical research**, the main research questions are 'what?' and 'how many?' questions. A quantitative methodology perceives that we can best understand the world, or the particular research question being asked about an aspect of the world, by using statistical methods. The focus of statistical research is measuring or counting.

> **Quantitative research**: The study of social processes through the collection of data that is amenable to statistical analysis. Quantitative research is often used to identify and establish relationships between research variables. Major quantitative social research methods include surveys, structured interviewing and secondary data analysis.

Douglas Ezzy

Knowing the answer to 'what?' and 'how many?' questions can explain a lot about how or why people do things. Quantitative methodologies tend to examine social issues from a 'big picture' perspective, gathering larger-scale data that can then be analysed using statistical techniques to establish patterns. For example, in the workers' compensation research discussed in the last section, we surveyed a representative sample of longer-term workers' compensation claimants to establish the parameters of their current and previous financial, social and health status.

> **Qualitative research:** Qualitative research is concerned with exploring the understandings, meanings and interpretations that people or other groups attribute to their social world. Major qualitative methods include participant observation studies and in-depth interviews.

In **qualitative research**, the main research questions are 'what meaning?' questions. The focus is on how people think about and interpret what they are doing. Knowing the answers that people give to 'what meaning?' questions can explain a great deal about how or why they do what they do. For example, in the second phase of the workers' compensation research we conducted in-depth interviews with 20 longer-term claimants to delve into the meanings and understandings they had of their experience of the workers' compensation process. A qualitative methodology tends to investigate social issues from a more micro perspective, concentrating on individual experiences or those of a small group, involving interviews and thematic analysis.

Research methodologies, such as quantitative or qualitative, are the theories, or general research paradigms, that justify the particular research method chosen. If the research question is 'At what age do women have their first child?', then it probably makes most sense to use statistical methods to study this question. However, if you want to know why women are having their first child at an older age than was previously the case, this question could be examined using either quantitative or qualitative methods. Statistics may reveal that more women are working than ever before, and qualitative interviews would reveal the meanings that women are giving to having children. It is important to match the research question correctly with the appropriate method and methodology.

Although 'quantitative' and 'qualitative' are the two main categories of methodology, there are a variety of other methodologies and methods, some discussed in this book—either within the text or on the accompanying website: <www.oup.com.au/orc/walter>—that do not fit neatly into this distinction. These include discourse analysis, semiotics and some forms of content analysis. Further, the distinction between these two types of research is in many ways an oversimplification. It is possible to construct statistical surveys that provide answers to questions about 'what meanings' people give to things. It is also possible that some qualitative research can answer 'how many?' questions, particularly if the group being studied is a small one. Nonetheless, the distinction between statistical and qualitative research is a useful way to begin thinking about research methodology.

5 Delineating the main variables or processes

Once the research topic, question and methodology are identified, the next question to ask is 'What are the main dimensions of the topic?' The key point is that the identification of the dimensions of the research topic is closely related to the choice of research method and methodology, and that these three aspects need to be considered together. For example, a study of the health needs of injecting drug users (IDUs) could focus on how many IDUs have particular sorts of medical conditions. The main dimensions would be variables that measure the particular medical conditions IDUs have. One way to examine these sorts of variables would be through a survey distributed to IDUs or to medical practitioners involved with IDUs. For example, Bammer and associates (2002) report HIV status from a survey of injecting drug users who attend needle-exchange clinics. Here, the key variable is whether a person attending a needle exchange is HIV positive or not. In this case, IDUs are either HIV positive or HIV negative. Counting up the results from recording this variable, Bammer and associates found that 3 per cent were HIV positive and 97 per cent were HIV negative. Such a finding allows a larger picture of the level of HIV infection among IDUs to be developed.

In contrast, other researchers have examined the social processes that generate these sorts of health issues. Why is it, for example, that some IDUs use clean injecting equipment, or take medication for medical conditions such as HIV, when other IDUs don't maintain their health in these ways? Such research could be conducted qualitatively, with long interviews with a smaller number of IDUs. For example, Demas and associates (1995) interviewed 15 injecting drug users with HIV to try to identify what motivated, or prevented, them taking their HIV treatments. They found that social factors such as stigma, uncertainty and social support, among other factors, influenced their actions. These social factors could be measured as variables. The degree of social support could be measured, for example, and examined through a statistical survey. However, the main point of the study is not to measure social factors, but to show how the experience of social support, as a social process, influences the way that people with HIV feel about taking their medication, and therefore changes their behaviour. Increased social support, reduced stigma and increased certainty shape the way IDUs feel about themselves, and this in turn increases the likelihood of them taking their medication. The focus of this qualitative study is on social processes. The research is not a 'how many?' question, but a question about 'what meaning' people give to their actions. Why do some IDUs take HIV medications when others do not, and what meanings and understandings shape these decisions?

In summary, the dimensions of a research project can be variables that can be measured statistically through surveys. They can also be social processes that are usually described

Douglas Ezzy

qualitatively through interviews. Social researchers also use a variety of other research methodologies, such as content analysis and discourse analysis, to examine dimensions and variables. The important point is that the dimensions of the research are worked out in conjunction with the research topic and the methodology.

Case study 3.1: Shoplifting

Cameron (1964) conducted an inductive qualitative study to identify what meanings people gave to being caught shoplifting. She conducted her research in a large department store, observing the way that different people responded when they were caught by store detectives. From her observations, she inductively identified two main types of shoplifters: pilferers and professional thieves.

1. Pilferers are people who have typically never been caught shoplifting before. Therefore, they do not think of themselves as thieves. When they are arrested, they are told that they could go to court and to jail, and this forces them to realise that they are a thief and typically results in emotional outbursts. Pilferers are also very concerned about what their family and friends will say and think once they find out, fearing they will be ashamed and disgraced.

2. In contrast, the professional thief is someone who has stolen before and knows the risks. Professionals already think of themselves as thieves, and while they may be frustrated at being arrested, they are typically not overly disturbed by the arrest. They are also not worried about the reactions of their friends, who already know about their shoplifting, and they may already have contacts with a lawyer who acts for them.

The main dimensions that Cameron identifies in this study are the differences between first-time offenders, or pilferers, and professional thieves.

6 Defining, measuring and observing

Conceptualisation: The process of developing concepts that focus on the research question.

Concepts: Concepts are components of theories that can be drawn from theory, or developed through induction from the data. They describe key aspects of the processes or patterns examined in the research.

Once the main dimensions are identified, the next step is to determine how to define, measure and observe the variables or processes. As outlined already in chapter 2, defining, also called **conceptualisation**, involves carefully and unambiguously defining research variables or processes. This specification of **concepts** is important for both quantitative (statistical) and qualitative (meaning-orientated) research. Much confusion arises in social research, of various types, because researchers do not clearly define the concepts they are using, then how they are measuring or observing these concepts.

For quantitative researchers, once terms have been conceptualised, these concepts are operationalised through survey questions. Two key terms here are **validity** and **reliability**. The general health questionnaire (GHQ), for example, has been established as a valid and reliable set of questions that measure a person's mental health (Ezzy 1993). To say that a measure is 'valid' means that it actually measures what it is supposed to measure. If a person has a high score on the GHQ, this probably means that she or he has some mental health issues. However, the GHQ might not be a valid measure of whether people are delusional or not. Someone who is delusional might think that everything is wonderful. The GHQ is also a reliable measure. This means that the GHQ consistently provides similar results for people with similar sorts of mental health conditions. People who are healthy, for example, consistently score well on the GHQ. Questions of validity and reliability are clearly central to the 'how many?' questions that quantitative researchers typically ask.

> **Validity**: Validity is the extent to which our data or results measure what we intended them to measure.
>
> **Reliability**: Reliability is the consistency of our data or results. If we repeated the data collection or analysis, will we consistently get the same results?

Qualitative researchers prefer to use the term rigour instead of 'validity' and 'reliability' (Ezzy 2002). Meanings and **interpretations** are often complex and historically and socially located. The aim of the qualitative research is to provide a rich and nuanced description of the meanings that people give to their experiences. 'Rigour' refers to the methods that qualitative researchers have developed for ensuring that they faithfully represent the stories and experiences of the people being studied. Elements of rigour include: close scrutiny of the detail of the lives of the people being studied, 'thick description', a focus on process and subjective meanings, and a tolerance for complex and nuanced explanations (Ezzy 2002:54). Selecting concepts that represent people's experiences and meanings adequately is central to conducting 'rigorous' qualitative research.

> **Interpretation**: Data analysis results must be interpreted in light of our conceptual frame; that is, not only what our results indicate, but what they mean in the context of our topic.

Each of the strategies for measuring or observing has advantages and disadvantages. The important thing is to ensure that the correct approaches are used for the methods, methodology and research questions for the study.

Case study 3.2: Working sole mothers

> Maggie Walter (2002) conducted a quantitative statistical study to examine if Australian sole mothers were better off when they were on welfare or when they obtained work. Walter conceptualises 'better off' as 'material well-being', focusing on economic issues. She then identifies three measures, or ways of operationalising, material well-being. I will discuss the first two measures.

Douglas Ezzy

The first measure examines the respondents' earnings from employment. Clearly, this improves if someone obtains paid work when she previously had not had any paid work, although Walter points out that this is not a very good measure of material well-being.

Second is a measure of the annual total household income, including government benefits. Walter shows that if a sole parent obtains part-time work in a lowly paid job, such as in sales or a manual occupation, her total household income does not improve. This is a consequence of the loss of various government benefits, and the additional costs, such as child care, that the sole parent has to pay. Household income only improves if the person can obtain higher-paid work, such as professional or administrative work.

The important point here is to see that different ways of measuring, or operationalising, variables have a significant influence on the results of a study. Walter uses the results of a large survey to test whether sole mothers are indeed better off, as measured by these two indicators.

7 Selecting a research sample

A **sample** is a subset of the **population** or range of elements that you wish to study. To choose a sample, the research must first choose who or what is to be observed; your **units of analysis**.

In Nissani's study of global warming, for example, the units of analysis are newspaper stories (see box 3.1 for more detail on units of analysis).

There are many different ways of sampling, and they have different justifications. This topic is detailed in chapter 5, and is overviewed here to make sense of how sampling fits within the research process. Quantitative or statistical research typically seeks to find a representative sample. A statistically representative sample should have the same make-up as the population from which it is drawn. For example, Gurlich and associates (2003) conducted a survey of Australians about their sexual and drug-use practices. The sampling method was to dial telephone numbers randomly and interview a preset number of respondents over the phone. Random digit dialling includes people with silent numbers that would be missed if the phone book were used as the **sampling frame**. While the researchers recognised the problems inherent in this method—for example, it excludes people without phones—they considered that this was a better way to conduct their survey than other sampling alternatives. They argue that random digit dialling gives a reasonably representative sample of the Australian population with minimum of bias. On the basis of this study, Gurlich

Sample: A sample is a set of cases or elements that are selected from a population.

Population: The collection of all the units that we want to study.

Unit of analysis: A particular instance of what or who we are researching. A unit of analysis can include individuals, groups, social artefacts such as newspaper articles or policy documents, or anything related to social life that can be investigated.

Sampling frame: A list that represents as closely as possible an abstract population; the researcher uses this list to draw a probability sample.

and associates (2003:245) found that 4 per cent of men and 1.8 per cent of women in their survey reported ever having injected drugs; more than twice as many men as women. As the sample was representative of the Australian population, the results can answer quantitative questions about the population from which they are drawn. Therefore, the authors can be confident that when 4 per cent of men in the survey say they have ever injected drugs, that this is also the case for the Australian population as a whole.

Other strategies can also be used to gain a representative sample. For example, there is no list anywhere of the people in Australia who are injecting drug users (IDUs), but as most IDUs in Australia attend needle exchanges to obtain clean injecting equipment, sampling people who attend needle exchanges provides a reasonable indicator of the health of IDUs in Australia. Of course, it excludes those who do not attend needle exchanges. This is not ideal, but this group of people is even harder to access, and researchers try to take this bias into account in interpreting their results.

The aim of qualitative research is to be representative of the processes that are studied. There are a number of ways to do this (Rice & Ezzy 1999). Cases may be selected that are 'typical' and studied in depth. Alternatively, extreme cases may be selected to provide the greatest range. For example, Vincent (2004), in his qualitative study of the health needs of IDUs, selected 'typical' injectors who attended a needle exchange. His study included equal numbers of men and women. This was because he wanted to see if the same social processes were at work for men and women who inject drugs. Vincent does not identify any major differences between the way men and women talk about risk, and this suggests that similar social processes are operating in both groups. One of Vincent's most interesting findings is that when people who inject drugs become socially isolated and depressed, they are unable to look after their health.

Samples that are representative of processes are used to answer 'what meaning?' questions. Vincent wanted to know 'what meanings' IDUs give to the risks they face and health issues they deal with. Because Vincent studied 'typical' injecting drug users, the processes he describes are likely to be similar for many other IDUs; that is, lack of social support and higher social isolation can lead IDUs to ignore basic health issues such as eating well, exercise and dental hygiene.

Sampling techniques sometimes involve more impressionistic justifications. Nissani (1999), for example, in her study of American newspapers, selected four newspapers that she argues are typical of American newspapers. She then found all the news stories that mentioned 'global warming' and analysed these stories. In this case, while the units of analysis are news stories, the sampling technique involved selecting representative newspapers. Nissani's argument for the representativeness of these newspapers is not statistical, but rather is justified on the grounds

Douglas Ezzy

that they are typical of American newspapers. For a range of common sampling techniques used in qualitative research projects, see the section in chapter 5 relating to non-probability sampling.

8 Addressing the political and ethical dimensions of the research

Social researchers, and the research reports they produce, are part of political processes. Research is inherently, and unavoidably, political in nature, and with ethical dimensions. Research about IDUs can help or harm the lives of IDUs. Research about global warming will involve the researcher in an ongoing political debate about how to respond to this issue.

Even how a research topic or question is framed has political and ethical implications. For example, a research topic might examine 'the frequency of dangerous injecting practices' by measuring how often IDUs share injecting equipment. This may be useful information to have. However, such a research topic begs the question: are IDUs sharing needles because they are ignoring advice? Or is it because it is difficult to obtain clean injecting equipment, as is the case in the United States? It is important to design research in which all aspects of an issue are examined. While the research might be technically correct, with a representative sample and well-constructed questions, it has been designed to examine only a limited part of the issue, and as such is ethically suspect. Some politicians and policy-makers often selectively use research to justify reducing the public resources spent on minority groups such as IDUs. However, if the research also examined the availability and obstacles to access to clean injecting equipment, then the research could also examine what social policies and organisational practices help or hinder safer injecting practices. Service providers and advocates of minority groups have used such arguments to advocate for services that improve the lives of members of these minority groups.

As detailed in chapter 4, social researchers are routinely required to obtain ethics approval for their research from ethics committees. Many large institutions involved with research, such as universities and hospitals, have ethics committees. Some of the key concerns of ethics committees are that the people who participate in research know what they are participating in (this is called informed consent), that they remain anonymous and that people are not harmed by participating. Most surveys are anonymous, and people can choose to participate or not. However, many qualitative studies are more detailed, and ethics committees typically require that the participant be provided with an information sheet about the research and sign a statement of informed consent.

9 Analysis of data and interpretation of results

Data analysis is the process of analysing the evidence that is produced from the research. In quantitative research, this involves various statistical techniques, some as simple as counting the number of responses and calculating **percentages**. In qualitative research, this involves identifying patterns of meanings and interpretations. Methods and techniques for data analysis vary hugely, and more detailed discussions of qualitative and quantitative analysis are provided in chapters 8 and 14, respectively.

> **Percentage**: A number expressed as a proportion of 100.

Data analysis can be one of the most exciting parts of the research. Analysis can reveal surprising findings that contradict expectations and shed new understandings on your research topic. Cameron's (1964) realisation that there were two types of shoplifters is like this. It might seem obvious once you discuss it, but only good social research can provide this sort of insight. Similarly, data analysis can be socially valuable, when it is demonstrated, for example, that there is little economic incentive for Australian sole mothers to obtain part-time poorly paid employment (Walter 2002). Methods of data analysis vary considerably, depending on the research methodology, and this is discussed in detail in various chapters later in the book.

It is not enough, however, to analyse data and obtain results. This is only part of the task, and not necessarily the most important aspect. The real question is: what do these results mean? It is the theoretical and contextual interpretation of the results that provides this information, and it is this interpretation that sits at the heart of the research process. And it is here that all the elements of the research process come together. When the data have been collected, by the most appropriate method, and analysed in the most rigorous and relevant way, these results must be interpreted within their social and political context using the theoretical framework. It is only when the results are analysed against and within your theoretical base, and the political and ethical context taken into account, that their meaning can be assessed and formulated. It is here that we use our theoretical base to move from the 'what?' to the 'why?' or 'how?' and to theorise our findings. For example, it is not enough to say longer-term workers' compensation claimants have poorer social outcomes post injury or illness, although this is a very important finding in itself. Rather, using our theoretical framework relating to stigma and primary role disruption, we can theorise that aspects of a longer-term involvement in the workers' compensation system can operate to negatively affect injured workers' relationships and marginalise them from previous support networks.

Box 3.1: Understanding units of analysis

Units of analysis

Our unit of analysis is what or who we are researching. While much social research uses the individual respondent as the unit of analysis, our unit of analysis can be much wider. Households, organisations such as universities, social artefacts such as

Douglas Ezzy

newspaper articles or policy documents, or indeed anything related to social life that can be investigated can be our unit of analysis for social research. Correctly specifying our unit of analysis is important if we want to avoid two common errors in social research: the ecological fallacy and reductionism.

The ecological fallacy

The ecological fallacy occurs when we incorrectly draw conclusions about one unit of analysis from social research conducted with a different unit of analysis. Primarily, the problem occurs when we move findings from an aggregate unit of analysis, such as a group or an organisation, to the level of the individual. For example, if we were to investigate the entertainment venues in the inner city (the aggregated unit of analysis) and were to find that for most the average age of patrons is 20 years younger (25 years) than that of suburban venues (45 years), and also that inner-city entertainment venues sell proportionately far more peanuts as bar snacks than do suburban venues, we might conclude that younger patrons like peanuts more than do older patrons. Such a conclusion could be an ecological fallacy, because we cannot make a conclusion about any link between the two disaggregated variables (patron age and level of peanut consumption) from data from an aggregate unit of analysis (entertainment venues). We do not know, from our unit of analysis, which patrons are eating the most peanuts, and there are likely to be many other explanations for this phenomenon. What other explanations can you think of?

Reductionism

Reductionism is also related to an incorrect use of the unit of analysis, but the mismatch occurs in the other direction. That is, data from disaggregated units of analysis are used to make inferences about aggregated units of analysis. The result is the reduction of a complex social issue or phenomenon to a specific explanation. For example, while research on unemployed young people (the disaggregated unit of analysis) might find many are ill prepared for the workforce in terms of job skills, we cannot then claim that the cause of youth unemployment (the aggregate unit of analysis) is poor labour market skills. This is reductionism, in that the complex issue of unemployment has been reduced to a single cause from findings that related to individual unemployed youth. The tendency to reductionism can derive from our worldview. For example, under the **ideology** of economic rationalism, social behaviour tends to be explained in exclusively economic terms (economic reductionism). As social scientists, we must try to ensure that we do not commit the error of social reductionism.

> **Reductionism:** Reducing complex arguments to simplistic assertions.
>
> **Ideology:** Shared values held by groups and societies.

10 Writing up the results

The final stage of the research process involves writing up the results and communicating the results of the research. Again, this aspect of the process is the subject of a separate chapter (chapter 15), but is overviewed here to place it into research process context. Most researchers advise that writing should begin as early as possible in the research process, and continue throughout the research. It is much easier to write up your findings if you have a collection of notes and ideas that you have already begun to write (Ezzy 2002).

Writing is the act that brings a research project together as a whole. Research reports include discussions of the whole research process, from the topic and research question, through the theory, method and methodology to the ethics and political significance of the findings. One of the most difficult skills to acquire as a social researcher is that of clear expression. Writing with clarity and precision demonstrates respect for both the reader and those who have participated in the research.

It is also important to identify the audience for which you are writing. The writing style for an academic journal article is different to that of a popular book, which is different again for a report for a business, government adviser or community lobby group.

Voices in the field

Sarah Wendt

Dr Sarah Wendt is an academic at the University of South Australia in the School of Social Work and Social Policy. She has researched how local cultures in rural communities have an impact on women's experiences and men's perpetration of domestic violence. She used a qualitative methodology that involved conducting in-depth semistructured interviews with key community informants, human service workers and women who had experienced domestic violence, as well as content analysis of local texts, such as newspapers and tourist booklets. Her research was informed by feminist and poststructural ideas, which guided a discourse analysis of the interview data. She found that several local cultural discourses can bear on the issue of domestic violence, including self-reliance, pride, privacy, belonging and closeness, family and Christianity. The power and influence of these discourses made it difficult to name and challenge domestic violence. The significance of Sarah's research is that it recognises the complexity and diversity of rural women and men's values, beliefs and experiences. The stories told can inform the development of

Douglas Ezzy

effective and appropriate responses to rural domestic violence. The finding of Sarah's research shows that it is imperative to learn about local cultures and dynamics from rural communities with respect, openness and willingness so that the discourses that have power and strength within a community can be identified. By including the community and their stories there is more opportunity to create alternative discourses that confront domestic violence and build local solutions to addressing abuse.

Exercise 3.1: The research process

1. Identify an issue on which you would be interested to conduct some social research. Make sure you specify your topic clearly.
2. What is it, specifically, that you want to know about this topic? What is your research question?
3. What theory do you think might inform your research? Some examples of theoretical traditions include feminism, Marxism, functionalism and symbolic interactionism. (Refer back to chapter 1 if you are unsure of the main features of these traditional theoretical social science paradigms.)
4. What sort of research methodology is best suited to answer this question? Are you interested in 'how many' questions, or are you interested in finding 'what meaning' questions? Is your question best answered by conducting a survey, or focus groups, or perhaps a **textual analysis** of newspapers or television programs?
5. What are the main variables or processes that you are interested in? Try to identify at least two of the key dimensions of your research topic.
6. How would you conceptualise and operationalise these variables or processes? What sorts of questions would you ask?
7. What are your units of analysis: people, stories, organisations or events? How would you sample these? Would your sample be statistically representative, or representative of processes?
8. What political and ethical issues might come up in the research? Do you think your participants might become distressed while participating in your research?
9. Would the analysis involve statistical methods, or would it utilise qualitative techniques that look for patterns of meaning and interpretation? How would you use your theoretical frame to interpret your results?
10. How would you communicate the findings of your research? Would you write a policy document for government advisers or business leaders, or would you write an academic journal article or book?

> **Textual analysis:** Analysis of the vocabulary, grammar, cohesion and structure within a text.

The research process in practice

The following three studies provide examples of how the research process has been worked out in practice. They are chosen because they provide examples of three very different types of research. At the end of each case study, I provide a list of how they have addressed the ten issues discussed in exercise 3.1.

A survey of who does housework in Australia

Are married men doing more of the housework than they used to a few decades ago? What do you think? Do you think your father does more housework than your grandfather? Do you think your mother does less housework than your grandmother?

> Feminist reformers in the 1960s and 1970s were optimistic that changes in the labour force participation rates for married women, in combination with increased awareness of the value of women's unpaid work in the home, would lead to an increased involvement of men in domestic labour and a more equal domestic division of labour between men and women (Baxter 2002:400).

How do we find out if there has been some change in who does the housework?

The way to answer this question is through research. Janeen Baxter examined three Australian national surveys from 1986, 1993 and 1997, which included questions about the amount of housework performed by the men and women living in the household. Each of these surveys was designed to be representative. This means that even though they only asked questions of a thousand or so people, we can be confident that their responses are very similar to the responses of the general population (see the later chapter on sampling for more detail). Baxter's research question is well defined. Has the gender distribution of housework changed in recent decades? This is clearly a 'how many?' question, and, as such, a quantitative statistical analysis of survey data is appropriate.

The results of her analysis are fascinating. There is almost no change in the distribution of child care tasks. For example, in answer to questions about who has responsibility for getting children to bed, on average men had responsibility for this 43 per cent of the time in both 1986 and in 1997. Women had responsibility for getting the children to bed 68 per cent of the time in 1986 and 62 per cent of the time in 1997 (the numbers add up to more than 100 per cent because of the particular method of calculation used by Baxter). The difference between 68 per cent and 62 per cent was not large enough to be statistically significant. In other words, there is no significant change in who puts the children to bed. In the past it was mostly done by women, and this has not changed.

Douglas Ezzy

There were some significant changes, however, in the hours spent on housework. For example, with respect to the number of hours spent on preparing meals and cleaning up afterwards, on average men spent 7 hours a week in 1986 and 5 hours a week in 1997. Women, on the other hand, on average spent 14 hours a week in 1986 and 10 hours a week in 1997. Both of these changes were statistically significant. In other words, both men and women are spending less time on food preparation. Baxter suggests that this is probably a result of people making greater use of takeaway and pre-prepared food. There are similar patterns in a variety of other household tasks. For example, when asked about the hours spent on cleaning the house and washing, on average men spent 3 hours a week in both 1986 and 1997. Women, on the other hand, on average spent 10 hours a week in 1986 and 8 hours a week in 1997. The change in hours for women is statistically significant. In summary, men are not spending any extra time doing household duties, but women are spending less time on them. There are a number of possible reasons for this, but one might simply be that less housework is being done. Perhaps we don't iron so many clothes or vacuum the floors as much as was done in the past.

Baxter (2002:401) identifies two possible theories: that of the economic exchange model 'that argues that women perform housework in exchange for economic support', and a feminist perspective, that emphasises 'power differences' and gender roles. Using a statistical regression analysis to assess the level and type of change in housework activity across time and gender, Baxter (2002:419) interprets these against her theoretical framework to conclude that both the economic exchange model and the feminist analysis of gender roles are important for explaining patterns of housework in Australia.

The interesting thing about Baxter's findings is that it does show a change in housework, but not in the way that was expected. As Baxter (2002: 420) puts it: 'The gender gap in domestic labour involvement is getting smaller, but mainly because women are doing much less, rather than men doing much more.' The ethical and political dimensions of Baxter's research are not explicitly discussed by Baxter. The research findings clearly do have political and ethical import. If aspects of both the economic exchange model and the feminist model are correct, then equality in the home will not be achieved simply by women entering the labour market and becoming economically independent. Rather, if household duties are to be distributed equally between men and women, then changes will also be required in attitudes towards gender roles.

Box 3.1: The research process: A survey of who does housework in Australia

1 Topic and question	Gender distribution of housework in Australia
2 Question	Has gender distribution of housework changed 1986–1997?
3 Theoretical framework	Economic exchange model and feminist theory
4 Research method	Secondary analysis of survey data
5 Main variables or processes	Gender, and amount of housework
6 Defining and measuring	Concepts derived from pre-existing research and theory
	'How many hours per week do you do housework duties?'
7 Sampling	Representative national sample
8 Ethics and politics	Feminist perspective identifies private and political dimensions
9 Analysis and interpretation	Quantitative analysis and interpretation of results against theories
10 Writing up	Journal article

A qualitative interview study of teenage Witchcraft

Witchcraft is a contemporary Pagan religion that began in Britain in the 1940s and in Australia in the 1970s (Hume 1997). Witchcraft focuses on venerating the earth and nature as sacred. In the 1990s large numbers of teenagers became interested in Witchcraft around the same time as the release of movies such as *The Craft* and television shows such as *Buffy* and *Charmed*, and popular 'how to' books on Witchcraft became available in mainstream bookstores (Berger & Ezzy 2007). Why are young people so interested in Witchcraft? 'What meanings' and interpretations lead young people to become Witches?

Helen Berger and Douglas Ezzy (2007) interviewed 90 young Witches, 30 each from Australia, the United States and Britain. The questions Berger and Ezzy asked were not 'how many?' questions, so we did not use a survey. Rather, we studied the meanings and interpretations of the young Witches. In order to do this, we interviewed the young Witches for approximately an hour each about their practice and experience of Witchcraft.

Unlike Baxter's research on housework, Berger and Ezzy do not examine variables, such as gender, hours in child care or food preparation. Rather, we examine the meanings or social processes that lead young people to become Witches. We utilised the method of long qualitative interviews with young Witches to examine the meanings and interpretations that people give to Witchcraft. In particular, we were interested in how Witchcraft related to

Douglas Ezzy

their sense of self-identity. A survey would not have given us as close an understanding of why people participate in Witchcraft.

The theories that inform our research are drawn from sociology, anthropology and religious studies. For example, in our discussion of Witchcraft and self-identity, we draw on the sociological theory of Anthony Giddens (1991). He discusses the centrality reflexivity to contemporary identity. We show how young Witches are reflexive about their spirituality. They had often spent substantial time researching various religions and reflexively thought through the appropriateness of Witchcraft as a religion for them.

Qualitative researchers aim to tell a good story about what is going on. If you do not know much about the teenage Witches, when you hear a bit of their story it might feel like walking in on a movie when it is half way through. News reports about teenage Witches are somewhat like events in those movies that don't make sense because the background information is missing. However, if you have read the book behind the movie, or if you borrow the DVD or download it and see the first half of the movie, then the meaning of the events may become clear. In the same way, qualitative research aims to tell the whole story about why people do things. If the researcher does his or her job well enough, then the actions of the people being studied will make sense, because the ethnographer has clearly told the story of what is going on.

Meanings cannot be measured. Rather, they are stories to be heard, and retold by the researcher. Through our research, we recorded the stories of young Witches. The central skill of the qualitative researcher is to be able to step inside the skin of the people they are studying, so that he or she can genuinely listen to the stories, and make sense of the meanings the participants give to their actions.

Berger and Ezzy's sampling method was to advertise for participants on various Internet forums and through newsletters and other established networks of Witches. The sampling logic here is not statistical, because the questions are not 'how many?' questions. Rather, the sampling logic is one of significance. Our interviews with young Witches provide a clear picture of the meanings and significance of Witchcraft for young people.

The politics of our research is not explicitly stated, but is still discernible. We are arguing that the religion of Witchcraft is typically a positive and life-affirming practice for young people. We describes how young people choose Witchcraft as a way of reflexively helping themselves deal with the challenges of contemporary life. Even this short quote from one of the young Witches we interviewed may seem like coming in halfway through a movie, but it gives you a taste of our argument:

> Probably the main reason why I like being Pagan [a Witch] is it's equal. It's got Gods and Goddesses ... It's not male dominated or anything ... And you can be yourself ... You don't

have to believe in this, this, and this, and you don't have to go to church on this day, or you don't have to do this ritual in this way. I like being an individual [laughs]… The essence of Witchcraft? For me, it's just being myself (Berger & Ezzy 2007:19).

Box 3.2: The research process: A qualitative interview study of teenage Witchcraft

1 Topic and question	Teenage Witches and identity
2 Question	How do young people become witches?
3 Theoretical frame	Sociological identity theory
4 Research method	Long qualitative interviews
5 Main variables or processes	Meanings and interpretations of young Witches
6 Defining and measuring	Inductively derived concepts
	Telling the participants' stories
7 Sampling	Self-selected sample in response to advertisements
8 Ethics and politics	Witchcraft is portrayed as a valid religion
9 Analysis and interpretation	Thematic analysis and Interpretation using identity theory
10 Writing up	Book

A discourse analysis of racism in newspapers

On 29 April 1996, *The Australian* newspaper proclaimed the headline '33 slain in our worst massacre'. *The Australian* went on to report on the Port Arthur massacre by Martin Bryant, saying: 'The Tasmanian massacre surpasses any other documented in Australia's history, and is believed to be one of the worst mass shootings of all time' (Banerjee & Osuri 2000:268). These few lines of text, and those from the headlines of a few other newspapers, form the basis of Banerjee and Osuri's research. They ask a simple question of these headlines, that could also be a description of their research topic: 'Why … was this event termed the worst massacre in Australian history when the Australian nation seemed to have been founded on a history of [Aboriginal] massacres?' (Banerjee & Osuri 2000:264). The difference between Banerjee and Osuri's research and that of Berger and Ezzy is not simply in the very small piece of empirical evidence that Banerjee and Osuri examine. It is also that they are as much interested in what the text does *not* say as they are in what the text does say. The main dimension of Banerjee and Osuri's research is the endemic racism in Australian news, and they use these few headlines as a way of further examining this issue.

Theory is central to their research question, and in fact theoretical argument takes up the bulk of their article. They are particularly interested in theories of racism; for example, drawing on Stuart Hall's distinction between overt racism, which does not apply to the Port Arthur massacre news reports, and 'inferential racism', which can be applied to the news reports. In particular, they argue that the news reports implied that 'the history of Australia is the history of Anglo-Celtic Australians ... [and] that the histories of Aboriginal peoples are not a part of Australian national history' (Banerjee & Osuri 2000:272).

Ethics and politics are central to this form of research. This is because research like Banerjee and Osuri's often aims to use social research to demonstrate that politics and power are central parts of social life. Cultural studies research is often informed by theories that explicitly incorporate political dimensions, such as feminism, socialism or race relations theory. Banerjee and Osuri (2000:279) refer to Foucault, arguing that their research aims to 'unmask the power relations behind knowledge production'.

Sampling and **measurement**, or observation, are not central issues to this sort of research. Some cultural studies reports do not provide any justification for the texts they analyse, while others use more systematic methods for selecting their sample.

> **Measurement**: How we are going to measure our key concepts. How we measure and what we measure differs between quantitative and qualitative methodologies.

Box 3.3: The research process: Discourse analysis of racism in newspapers

1 Topic	Racism in newspapers
2 Question	Why are massacres of Aboriginal people silenced?
3 Theoretical frame	Theories of racism and power
4 Research method	Cultural textual analysis
5 Main variables or processes	Derived from analysis of inferential racism
6 Defining and measuring	Deductively derived concepts
	Examination of language, presence and absence
7 Sampling	Case study
8 Ethics and politics	Politics of Indigenous history as 'invisible'
9 Analysis and interpretation	Discourse analysis and interpretation
10 Writing up	Journal article

Conclusion

This chapter builds on the material discussed in chapters 1 and 2 to provide a solid foundation of the why, what, how, where and when of contemporary social research. Within this, the importance of good social research to our lives and our society has been stressed. Social issues are some of the most pressing and difficult issues that confront contemporary society. Many of our major problems, such as global warming, terrorism, pollution, mental health and the spread of HIV/AIDS, are primarily social issues, requiring responses from policy-makers that address the social dimensions of these issues. Social research provides essential background information so that policy-makers can respond appropriately to such issues. But good policy responses rely on solid research evidence. And well-constructed, valid and rigorous social research follows a process. This research process guides researchers, and ensures that each vital step is undertaken, to the right depth and at the right time for the specific research project. In this chapter, ten key steps have been identified and explained. Understanding and using the research process allows us to have confidence in both our research and ourselves as researchers.

Main points

> Social research includes a variety of different types of research.

> Social research methodologies can be categorised into two main groups: quantitative and qualitative.

> Quantitative, or statistical, research primarily aims to examine 'how many' questions. More complex forms of statistical research can be used to examine questions of causality.

> Qualitative, or interpretative, research is used to examine 'what meaning' questions that focus on interpretations and understandings.

> There are a variety of other forms of research that do not fit into either of these categories.

> This chapter has identified ten key issues that social researchers must address.

> Social researchers aim to provide a better understanding of what is happening in the social world.

> Many of the biggest challenges faced in contemporary society are primarily social issues.

> Social researchers cannot escape from issues of ethics and politics.

Douglas Ezzy

> Social researchers hope that their research will provide a better understanding of social processes so that policymakers and political leaders can make better policy decisions to benefit society.

Further reading

If you want to learn more about social research, the following books are recommended:

Bouma, G. and Ling, R. (2004). *The Research Process*, 5th edn. South Melbourne: Oxford University Press.

Kellehear, A. (1993). *The Unobtrusive Researcher: A Guide to Methods*. Sydney: Allen & Unwin.

May, T. (1997). *Social Research: Issues, Methods and Process*. Buckingham: Open University Press.

References

Bammer, G., Hall, W., Hamilton, M. and Ali, R. (2002). 'Harm Minimization in a Prohibition Context', *Annals of the American Academy of Political and Social Science*, 582 (1): 80–93.

Banerjee, S. and Osuri G. (2000). 'Silences of the Media: Whiting Out Aboriginality in Making News and Making History', *Media, Culture and Society*, 22 (3): 263–84.

Baxter, J. (2002). 'Patterns of Change and Stability in the Gender Division of Household Labour in Australia, 1986–1997', *Journal of Sociology*, 38 (4): 399–424.

Berger, H. and Ezzy, D. (2007). *Teenage Witches*. Piscataway, NJ: Rutgers University Press.

Cameron, M. (1964). 'Identity and the Shoplifter', in *The Booster and the Snitch*. New York: Free Press.

Demas, P., Schoenbaum, E., Wills, T., Doll, L. and Klein, R. (1995). 'Stress, Coping, and Attitudes toward HIV Treatment in Injecting Drug Users: A Qualitative Study', *AIDS Education and Prevention*, 7 (5): 429–42.

Eagly, A., Karau, S., and Makhijani, M. (1995). 'Gender and the Effectiveness of Leaders: A Meta-analysis', *Psychological Bulletin*, 117 (1): 125–45.

Ezzy, D. (1993). 'Unemployment and Mental Health: A Critical Review', *Social Science and Medicine*, 37 (11): 41–52.

Ezzy, D. (2001). 'Reading for the Plot, and Not Hearing the Story: Ecological Tragedy and Heroic Capitalism', in Mills, A. and Smith, J. (eds), *Utter Silence: Voicing the Unspeakable*. New York: Peter Lang.

Ezzy, D. (2002). *Qualitative Analysis.* Sydney: Allen & Unwin.

Gurlich, A., de Visser, R., Smith, A., Rissel, C. and Richters, J. (2003). 'Injecting and Sexual Risk Behaviour in a Representative Sample of Adults', *Australian and New Zealand Journal of Public Health,* 27 (2): 242–50.

Giddens, A. (1991). *Modernity and Self-Identity.* Stanford: Stanford University Press.

Hume, L. (1997). *Witchcraft and Paganism in Australia.* Melbourne: Melbourne University Press.

Jacques, P., Dunlap, R. and Freeman, M. (2008). 'The Organisation of Denial: Conservative Think Tanks and Environmental Scepticism', *Environmental Politics,* 17 (3): 349–85.

Kabakoff, R. (2002). 'Gender and Leadership in the Corporate Boardroom' <www.mrg.com/Publications/articles/APA2000.pdf>.

McDonald, P. (1998). 'Contemporary Fertility Patterns in Australia', *People and Place,* 6 (1): 1–13.

Moon, J. and Fountain, I. (1997). 'Keeping the Gates? Women as Ministers in Australia, 1970–96', *Australian Journal of Political Science,* 32 (3): 455–66.

Newell, P. and Paterson, W. (1998). 'A Climate for Business: Global Warming, the State and Capital', *Review of International Political Economy,* 5 (4): 679–703.

Nissani, M. (1999). 'Media Coverage of the Greenhouse Effect', *Population and Environment,* 21 (1): 27–43.

Pini, B. (2002). 'Gender and Power: The Exclusion of Women from Agri Political Leadership: A Case Study of the Australian Sugar Industry', *Sociologia Ruralis,* 42 (1): 45–60.

Pini, B. (2005) 'The Third Sex: Women Leaders in Australian Agriculture', *Gender, Work and Organization,* 12 (1): 73–88.

Probert, B. (1980). *Working Life.* Melbourne: McPhee Gribble.

Rice, P. and Ezzy, D. (1999). *Qualitative Research Methods.* Melbourne: Oxford University Press.

Robinson, A. and Robinson, Z. (1997). 'Science Has Spoken: Global Warming Is a Myth', *Wall Street Journal,* 4 December, 1.

Rosser, V. (2003). 'Faculty and Staff Members' Perceptions of Effective Leadership: Are There Differences Between Women and Men Leaders?', *Equity and Excellence in Education,* 36 (1): 71–81.

Sarantakos, S. (1993). *Social Research.* South Melbourne: Macmillan Education.

Sony (2004). *EverQuest* <http://eqlive.station.sony.com/library/faqs/faq_pop.jsp>.

Vincent, A. (2004). Health, Risk, and Injecting Drugs. Honours thesis, School of Sociology, Social Work and Tourism, University of Tasmania.

Verdouw, J. (2008) For the Love of Money. Unpublished PhD thesis, Hobart: School of Sociology, University of Tasmania.

Walter, M. (2002). 'Working their Way out of Poverty? Sole Motherhood, Work, Welfare and Material Well-being', *Journal of Sociology*, 38 (4): 361–80.

White, K. (2003). 'Women and Leadership in Higher Education in Australia', *Tertiary Education and Management*, 9 (1): 45–60.

Chapter 4
Ethics and Social Research

Daphne Habibis

The Carnegie Mellon study on cyber porn

In 1995, a Carnegie Mellon University student, Martin Rimm, gathered data on the reading habits of 4227 users of a university computer system's newsgroup service (Usenet) (Rimm 1995). The controversial finding was that 83.5 per cent of the 900,000 images accessed by the Usenet groups were pornographic. The paper implied that those individuals who used blocking software to screen their internet use from surveillance could be paedophiles.

The results were published as the cover story in *Time* magazine (Elmer-Dewitt 1995), unleashing a storm of public controversy about the moral values of American society. There were also concerns about Rimm's methodology and ethical issues of informed consent and invasion of privacy (Thomas 1995). These included:

- accessing personal information about the university's internet users, including their names, age, sex, nationality, marital status and employment
- misrepresentation of data
- the unsubstantiated imputed allegation that those using blocking software were paedophiles
- the probable use of covert methods to obtain the data
- the publication of potentially identifying information such as the names of the cities from which the user called, including small cities.

Source: Thomas 1995

Key terms

academic fraud	ethics	informed consent
anonymity	experimental	longitudinal study
confidentiality	human research ethics	low-risk research
covert research	committees (HRECs)	plagiarism
ethical research	information sheet	

Introduction

Ethics is concerned with the establishment of a set of moral standards that govern behaviour in a particular setting or for a particular group. **Ethical research** is therefore concerned with ensuring that ethical principles and values always govern research involving humans. John Barnes explains that ethical decisions in research are those decisions that arise when we try to decide between one course of action and another, not in terms of expediency or efficiency, but by reference to standards of what is morally right or wrong (Barnes 1979:16).

> **Ethics:** The establishment of a set of moral standards that govern behaviour in a particular setting or for a particular group.
>
> **Ethical research:** Ensuring that ethical principles and values always govern research involving humans.

Whereas in every other aspect of research the core focus is on the project and the requirements flowing from the research questions, when it comes to ethical issues, the focus shifts from the needs of the project to those of the key stakeholders: the participants, the researcher, the research organisation and the scientific community, as well as the broader public.

Why is ethics an issue in social research?

Public outcry and academic debate about studies that violated the human rights of participants led to the requirement that all social research conducted by government organisations be first submitted for approval to a human research ethics committee (HREC) before being funded. The vulnerability of many research participants is at the centre of this concern, with the power of the medical profession in its guise of researchers especially significant (Willis 1989).

Understanding the power of the researcher over the researched is critical to understanding the ethical concerns that accompany social research. Undertaking research carries a certain mystique and prestige. To be a researcher implies the possession of expert knowledge and the discovery of 'truth'. There is even a glamour associated with the role, because of the cultural value attributed to scientific knowledge as well as the qualifications and high status of researchers. Researchers belong to the 'new' middle class. Most enjoy secure, well-paid jobs with considerable autonomy in the workplace. As producers of knowledge, they influence the public sphere. Through their contribution to public debates and social policy, researchers possess significant social and cultural capital.

The power and influence of researchers often contrasts with that of their study population. In its concern with social problems and policies, social science has a particularly intense gaze on vulnerable populations, such as young people, criminals, women, ethnic minorities and the sick. Researchers 'use' participants with a particular objective in mind, but participants may have only partial understanding of this. With important exceptions, such as action research and some feminist research, it is the researcher who controls the production of knowledge, including the design, data collection, interpretation and reporting of the project. Participants may or may not agree with this interpretation, yet once published, they can do little to alter its content.

Different methodologies place different emphases on the level of involvement of participants. In general, interpretative methodologies give more space to the participants' views than do quantitative approaches. But, in most cases, it is the researcher who sets the agenda. Feminist theorists argue that the relationship between researcher and researched is fundamentally exploitative because, at a personal level, the researcher's career benefits from the research (Oakley 1981). The direct benefits received by participants are generally slight and usually limited to some small financial recompense. Yet this is rarely acknowledged; instead, the research is justified in terms of its contribution to knowledge, and its anticipated benefits to the population group to which participants belong.

Box 4.1: Areas of potential conflict between the researcher and the researched

The needs of the researcher	The needs of the researched
Inexpensive and fast data collection	Protection from exploitation through HREC approval prior to commencement
	Adequate information and time to make an informed decision about participation
High response rate	The right to refuse participation
Low attrition rate	The right to withdraw participation at any time
Minimal missing data	The right to refuse any question
Use of a wide choice of methods, including covert investigation	Protection from methods that potentially violate rights, such as informed consent
	Protection from acts that might cause harm or discomfort beyond what is normally experienced in everyday life
Freedom to use the findings in the most effective way, including informing other studies	Protection of anonymity and confidentiality
Speedy data analysis and the freedom to interpret the data	Control over how the individual contribution to data is used through access to draft publications and the right to withdraw contribution
Speedy and widespread dissemination of findings	Control over who receives copies of the report and where it is published

Daphne Habibis

There are many examples where researchers have threatened the safety of participants or abused their trust in some way (see case study 4.1). The reasons researchers may disregard the rights and needs of participants are influenced by the institutional context within which research takes place. Far from being disinterested observers motivated by 'pure' considerations of knowledge, researchers have careers to which successful research is central. Paying careful attention to the moral and ethical requirements of research can get in the way of speedy and successful projects (see box 4.1).

Feminist research and some types of action research try to overcome what they see as the inherently exploitative nature of research by involving participants in some or all stages of the research process (Wadsworth 1997). This may include establishing a reference group, involving participants in data collection, and giving them control over what and how the results are reported.

Ultimately, the most important mechanism to ensure ethical research is the researcher's own sense of integrity and moral values. The solitary and autonomous nature of most research means that ultimately the researcher must be responsible for the ethical conduct of his or her projects. The relative rarity of reported abuses suggests that most researchers are committed to ensuring the well-being of their participants.

Exercise 4.1: Empowering participants

Think about the respective roles of the researcher and the researched, and answer the following questions:

1   What measures can researchers put in place to empower participants?
2   What are the methodological advantages and disadvantages of bringing participants into the research process?

The history of ethics and research

Contemporary approaches to ethical issues in research can be dated back to the Second World War and the appalling abuses perpetrated by physicians and scientists on Jewish and other inmates of Nazi concentration camps in the name of scientific investigation. This led to the Nuremberg Code (1949) (see box 4.2), which set out what were to become the basic principles for ethical research on human beings.

Box 4.2: The Nuremberg Code: Directives for human experimentation

1. The voluntary consent of the human subject is absolutely essential. This means that the person involved should have legal capacity to give consent; should be so situated as to be able to exercise free power of choice, without the intervention of any element of force, fraud, deceit, duress, overreaching or other ulterior form of constraint or coercion; and should have sufficient knowledge and comprehension of the elements of the subject matter involved as to enable him to make an understanding and enlightened decision. This latter element requires that before the acceptance of an affirmative decision by the experimental subject, there should be made known to him the nature, duration and purpose of the experiment; the method and means by which it is to be conducted; all inconveniences and hazards reasonably to be expected; and the effects upon his health or person which may possibly come from his participation in the experiment.

   The duty and responsibility for ascertaining the quality of the consent rests upon each individual who initiates, directs or engages in the experiment. It is a personal duty and responsibility, which may not be delegated to another with impunity.

2. The **experiment** should be such as to yield fruitful results for the good of society, unprocurable by other methods or means of study, and not random and unnecessary in nature.

3. The experiment should be so designed and based on the results of animal experimentation and a knowledge of the natural history of the disease or other problem under study that the anticipated results will justify the performance of the experiment.

4. The experiment should be so conducted as to avoid all unnecessary physical and mental suffering and injury.

5. No experiment should be conducted where there is an a priori reason to believe that death or disabling injury will occur; except, perhaps, in those experiments where the experimental physicians also serve as subjects.

6. The degree of risk to be taken should never exceed that determined by the humanitarian importance of the problem to be solved by the experiment.

7. Proper preparations should be made and adequate facilities provided to protect the experimental subject against even remote possibilities of injury, disability or death.

> **Experiment:** A research method in which pretest measurements are taken of a target group or area, before the implementation of an experimental intervention (introduction of a particular program, strategy or project), followed by post-test measurements after the intervention has had time to take effect.

Daphne Habibis

8   The experiment should be conducted only by scientifically qualified persons. The highest degree of skill and care should be required through all stages of the experiment of those who conduct or engage in the experiment.

9   During the course of the experiment the human subject should be at liberty to bring the experiment to an end if he has reached the physical or mental state where continuation of the experiment seems to him to be impossible.

10 During the course of the experiment the scientist in charge must be prepared to terminate the experiment at any stage, if he has probable cause to believe, in the exercise of the good faith, superior skill and careful judgment required of him that a continuation of the experiment is likely to result in injury, disability, or death to the experimental subject.

These principles were enshrined in the World Medical Assembly's Declaration of Helsinki in 1965.

> Source: Reprinted from *Trials of War Criminals before the Nuremberg Military Tribunals under Control Council Law*, No 10, vol. 2:181–2. Washington, DC: US Government Printing Office, 1949

The history of ethics and research in Australia

In Australia, a Statement on Human Experimentation was produced initially by the National Health and Medical Research Council (NHMRC) in 1966, based on the Declaration of Helsinki. The application of these principles was initially left to researchers, but reports of abuses led to the external surveillance of research by **human research ethics committees (HRECs)**. In 1973, the NHMRC made it a requirement that all grant applications must have received ethical approval from a human research ethics committee (Loblay & Chalmers 1999:9).

Human research ethics committee (HREC): A committee established by an institution or organisation for the task of viewing research proposals and monitoring ongoing investigations with the aim of protecting the welfare and rights of participants in research.

In 1992, the NHMRC released the *National Statement on Ethical Conduct in Research Involving Humans*, in accordance with the NHMRC Act of that year. This established the NHMRC as a statutory body with functions, powers and obligations to issue human research guidelines as developed by the Australian Health Ethics Committee. This is regularly updated in a process of community consultation, with the current statement being released in 2007 (see box 4.3) (NHMRC 2007). All human research undertaken within a government organisation that involves the potential risk of harm or inconvenience to humans must receive ethical approval before it can be conducted. Professional organisations such as the Australian Sociological Association (TASA), the Sociological Association of Aotearoa New Zealand (SAANZ), and the Australian Association of Social Workers (AASW) include sections requiring their members to conform to the standards established by the NHMRC.

Case study 4.1: An ethically controversial research study

Humphreys' tearoom trade

Humphreys' study of casual homosexual encounters caused considerable debate about whether the ends can ever justify the means. This influential study was conducted in the late 1960s, and employed a **covert research** methodology to discover the social background of men who engage in homosexual acts (Humphreys 1970). Humphreys' method involved observing homosexual encounters in public places including truckstop restaurants (tearooms). Having gained the trust of the unwitting participants, Humphreys acted as their lookout—the 'watchqueen'. In this role he was able to make a note of their car registration numbers. A year later, he used this information to track down the addresses of the 'participants'. Under the guise of collecting data for another study, he then visited the men and obtained detailed information about their socioeconomic background. His key finding was that the men were quite 'ordinary' citizens. Many were married and many held 'respectable' jobs.

> **Covert research:** The inclusion of respondents in a research project without their awareness and/or agreement to their participation.

Humphreys' study challenged negative stereotypes about gay men and so made an important contribution to the destigmatisation of homosexuality. However, its violation of fundamental ethical principles, such as informed consent, the safety of participants and the use of deception, compromised its validity within the academic community. Although Humphreys had been careful to disguise who his participants were, and kept details of their identities under lock and key, he was criticised for his invasion of their privacy and the possibility that the information might fall into the public arena (Warwick 1982). However, he defended his methods on the grounds that the study demystified a critical social issue and that it was only through covert techniques that the knowledge would have become available.

When is ethical review needed?

Research that involves **negligible risk** to humans may be exempt from submission to an HREC. This research must carry no foreseeable risk of harm or discomfort, and any foreseeable risk should be no more than inconvenience. The use of existing data or records that contain only non-identifiable data, and which are publicly accessible, is an example of research that would meet this criterion.

> **Negligible risk research:** Research that carries no foreseeable risk of harm or discomfort to respondents.

Daphne Habibis

> **Low-risk research:** Research where the only foreseeable risk to respondents is one of discomfort. Low-risk research may involve a lower level of scrutiny by HRECs.

Research that is of low risk may be reviewed under expedited processes involving a lower level of scrutiny by the HREC or others familiar with the legislation on ethical research. Research is low risk where the only foreseeable risk is one of discomfort. **Low-risk research** may involve a lower level of scrutiny by HRECs. To be designated low risk, the project must not involve:

- deception of participants
- participation of people without their prior consent
- withholding from one group treatment or methods of learning from which they may benefit
- access or use of medical records where participants can be identified or linked to their records
- the use of personal data obtained from a Commonwealth or state government department without the consent of the participants
- potential disclosure of illegal activities or criminal behaviour
- specific targeting of vulnerable population groups, such as children and young people, Indigenous peoples and people unable to give **informed consent** because of difficulties in understanding an information sheet
- socially or emotionally sensitive topics such as ethnic identity, eating disorders, parenting practices, personal issues, suicide, grief and substance abuse
- risk to the researcher
- politically sensitive information.

> **Informed consent:** A document or agreement that ensures, first, that research respondents are fully informed about what the research is about and what participation will involve, and second, that they make the decision to participate without any formal or informal coercion.

Protecting participants

The *National Statement on Ethical Conduct in Research Involving Humans* (Section 1) (NHMRC 2007) identifies four values that govern research involving humans. These are research merit and integrity, justice, beneficence and respect.

Research merit and integrity

Unless research has merit through its potential benefit and is carried out with integrity and honesty, then the involvement of participants cannot be justified ethically.

Justice

This involves a regard for the human sameness that each person shares with every other and requires distributive and procedural justice. Distributive justice is expressed in the fair distribution of the benefits and burdens of research; procedural justice involves 'fair treatment' in the recruitment of participants and the review of research.

Beneficence

This requires researchers to assess and take account of the risks of harm and the potential benefits of research to participants and to the wider community; to be sensitive to the welfare and interests of people involved in their research, and to reflect on its social and cultural implications.

Respect for human beings

This value binds the three values of research merit and integrity, justice and beneficence. Recognition of the intrinsic value of human beings through respectful treatment underpins the ethics framework. This means having due regard for the welfare, beliefs, perceptions, customs and cultural heritage of those involved in research.

Implicit in these values are the principles of:

- informed consent
- anonymity
- confidentiality
- protection from harm.

Box 4.3: Excerpt from the *National Statement on Ethical Conduct in Research Involving Humans*

> The relationship between researchers and research participants is the ground on which human research is conducted. The values set out in this section—respect for human beings, research merit and integrity, justice and beneficence—help to shape that relationship as one of trust, mutual responsibility and ethical equality. For this reason, the National Statement speaks of research 'participants' rather than 'subjects' ...
>
> The values of respect, research merit and integrity, justice and beneficence have become prominent in the ethics of human research in the past six decades, and they provide a substantial and flexible framework for principles to guide the design, review and conduct of such research. This National Statement is organised around these values ...
>
> Among these values, respect is central. It involves recognising that each human being has value in himself or herself, and that this value must inform all interaction between people. Such respect includes recognising the value of human autonomy ... It also involves providing for the protection of those with diminished or no autonomy ... Reference to these values throughout the National Statement serves as a constant reminder that, at all stages, human research requires ethical reflection that is informed by them.

Daphne Habibis

Informed consent

The principle of informed consent requires ensuring that participants:

- are fully informed about what the research is about and what participation will involve
- make the decision to participate without any formal or informal coercion.

> **Information sheet**: A short written document that provides respondents with a summary of key aspects of the research for the purposes of informed consent. This includes what the research is about, what participation involves and any potential risks arising from participation.

The main mechanism used to ensure that potential participants are fully informed is the **information sheet** (see box 4.4). This is usually a single A4 document, written in plain English, that outlines:

- what the research is about and its objectives
- the characteristics of the desired research participants; for example, women aged 35 to 55 who have experienced domestic violence
- what involvement in the research will mean for them; for example, how much time participation will involve
- any risks or potential harms associated with the research
- what will happen to the data collected
- whether and how they can access the findings and results.

Consent may be expressed orally, in writing or by other means, such as return of a survey or conduct implying consent, depending on:

- the nature, complexity and level of risk involved in the research
- the participant's personal and cultural circumstances.

Box 4.4: Information sheet

The role of spirituality in the recreation of self-identity after experience of mental illness

Researcher: Dr Noel Edge.

What is the study about?
This study seeks to examine the role that spirituality plays in the life of people who have had a mental illness. It aims to explore how people who have had psychotic experiences use spirituality to make sense of them. It is especially concerned with the role that a person's spirituality may play in helping the person to accommodate these experiences into his or her sense of who he or she is—the person's sense of self-identity. The study hopes to give people who have had psychosis the opportunity to describe the positive role that spirituality has played in their lives. It also seeks to shed light on the relationship between spirituality and recovery from mental illness.

Who would we like to contribute to it?
We would like to talk to men and women aged 18-plus years who have been diagnosed with schizophrenia for at least one year, and who feel that their spirituality has played an important role in helping them get, or stay, better.

What's involved if I agree to participate?
If you agree to participate, you will be asked to agree to be interviewed on one or two occasions for about 1–2 hours each time. The interview will involve talking about your experience of your illness and the role that spirituality has played in helping you adjust to it. With your agreement, the interview will be audiotaped and then transcribed. The interview can take place in your home or in any other mutually agreed location.

Will I be reimbursed for any expenses?
Because being involved in the study may involve some inconvenience and expense, such as travel or arranging child care, you will be offered $30 if you agree to participate.

Are there any possible risks?
Although we will do our best to deal with all matters sensitively and in confidence, it is possible that talking about your experience of mental illness will cause you some emotional distress. If this does happen, the interviewer will give you the opportunity to stop discussing that topic and also to consider stopping the interview at that stage.

Will the interview be confidential?
Every effort will be made to ensure that any personally identifying information you provide will be treated confidentially. We will use a pseudonym to record your contribution and will also change any details that could be used to identify you. Your contact details will be kept in a locked filing cabinet separate from the interview material.

Am I able to refuse or withdraw at any time?
Participation in the research is voluntary, and you can choose to stop the interview at any time without giving a reason. You can also refuse to answer specific questions. The research is not connected with any treatment service, and being involved, or withdrawing at any time, won't affect any treatment services you receive.

People to contact for information, counselling or for concerns or complaints
If you have any questions about the study, you can contact the researcher, Dr Noel Edge, on (03) 8026 09 3946.

If, as a result of the interview, you are distressed in any way and would like to speak to a counsellor, please contact Ms S. Counsellor, who is an experienced, qualified social worker, on (01) 07 253900.

Daphne Habibis

This study has been approved by the Southern Banksville Social Sciences Human Research Ethics Committee. If you have any concerns or complaints about the conduct of this study, please contact the Executive Officer or Chair of the Southern Banksville Social Sciences Human Research Ethics Committee, Professor Inn Vestigator (Chair): Tel.: 209 3576; or Mr Fin Dings (Executive Officer): Tel.: 8026 2790.

The research project has received ethical approval from the University Human Research Ethics Committee.

Can I find out the results of the research?

Let the interviewer know if you would like a summary of the results of the project when it is completed and we will arrange for it to be sent to you.

Thank you for taking the time to hear about this study. Please keep a copy of this sheet and the accompanying Statement of Informed Consent.

Having read the Information Sheet, potential participants are asked to read and sign a Statement of Informed Consent (see box 4.5). This explains that participants are under no obligation to participate in the study, and can withdraw consent at any time. In many areas of social science, for example, health research, participants may be recruited through a service they are receiving. In this case, participants should be informed that whether they agree to participate or not will not affect any services they receive now or in the future. Both the researcher and the participant sign this document, and a copy of the Information Sheet and **consent form** is given to the participant to keep.

Consent form: A short, written statement that respondents are asked to read and sign before participation in an investigation. It states that respondents have been fully informed about the study and that their participation is voluntary.

Box 4.5: Statement of Informed Consent

Title of Project: The role of spirituality in the recreation of self-identity after experience of mental illness

1. I have read and understood the Information Sheet for this project.
2. The nature and possible effects of the study have been explained to me.
3. I understand that the study involves a one-hour interview about the role that spirituality has played in my life following experience of mental illness.
4. I understand that participation in the study may cause me some emotional discomfort and that if this happens I will be given the opportunity to stop discussing the topic or to cease participation in the study.
5. I understand that all research data will be securely stored on the University premises for at least five years and will be destroyed when no longer required.

6   Any questions that I have asked have been answered to my satisfaction.
7   I agree that research data gathered from me for the study may be published provided that I cannot be identified as a participant.
8   I understand that the researchers will maintain my identity confidential and that any information I supply to the researcher(s) will be used only for the purposes of the research.
9   I agree to participate in this investigation and understand that I may withdraw at any time without any effect, and if I so wish, may request that any data I have supplied to date be withdrawn from the research.

Name of participant: _____

Signature: _____ Date: _____

I have explained the project and the implications of participation in it to this volunteer and I believe that the consent is informed and that he/she understands the implications of participation.

Name of investigator:_____

Signature of investigator:_____

Date:_____

There are some circumstances in which written consent is not required, for example where it is not practicable, as in telephone surveys or where the level of intrusion is minimal. In a study on the introduction of a community mental health team, I made contact with potential participants at the time that they were experiencing a psychotic episode (Habibis et al. 2002). Some participants were willing to participate in the study and understood what this would entail, but were reluctant to sign a document. Rather than pressing them for their signature, their verbal agreement was noted on the form, and wherever possible this was also witnessed by a third party.

Anonymity

Anonymity refers to the protection of participants from identification as participants in the research. This ensures their rights to privacy are respected and that any information they provide cannot be used to identify them. The most effective way of ensuring anonymity is not to collect identifying data. This is easily achieved in some cross-sectional studies, such as mail-out surveys, and whenever it is not necessary to record personal information such as names or addresses.

Anonymity: The protection of respondents from identification as participants in the research.

Daphne Habibis

There are many investigations where this is not possible. For example, the method of recruitment may require researchers to have access to the contact details and names of participants. The usual method of preserving anonymity in these circumstances is to use a pseudonym for the participant and to keep the 'code-breaker' in a secure place, such as a filing cabinet, separate from the collected data. The same technique may be used in **longitudinal studies** when participants are recontacted at intervals.

> **Longitudinal study:** A study that collects data on the same phenomena over an extended period of time.

There are some studies where anonymity is difficult or impossible to achieve. Studies of small towns close to where the researcher lives may be difficult to disguise. The normal practice is to change the name of the town and to deliberately change any potentially identifying information. This technique was employed by Dempsey in *Smalltown* (1990).

There are other circumstances in which the ethical requirement for anonymity may be breached; for example, if there is a legal or moral requirement for identification of participants, as in cases of child abuse, or sexual assault.

Anonymity can also be compromised once it enters the public domain. This is especially when there is of intense public interest and the issue is politically contentious (Warwick & Pettigrew 1983). There have been cases where the government has demanded researchers name participants. In the 1950s, the US State Department and the FBI requested the research records on individuals who participated in the Kinsey sex study. The Kinsey Sex Institute refused, and eventually the government agencies backed down, but the issue presented a moral dilemma for the researchers and for sociologists in general (Diener & Crandall 1978:70).

Confidentiality

> **Confidentiality:** The principle of ensuring that the specific contribution of respondents cannot be identified.

The principle of **confidentiality** overlaps with that of anonymity, since both are concerned with maintaining the privacy of participants. Anonymity is concerned with the identification of individual participants, while confidentiality is concerned with ensuring the information they provide cannot be linked directly to them. Even if the participants in a study are identified, the principle of confidentiality means their specific contribution cannot be identified.

The most common method of ensuring confidentiality is to aggregate the data by grouping it into categories such as percentages or themes.

There are a number of ways in which confidentiality may be breached. As well as the immediate data collector, a number of people on the research team and administrative staff may see their information. Those in authority over participants may only consent to research taking place within their organisation if they have access to the data. In this case, the researcher needs to negotiate what information will be made available and whether it will be provided in a way that identifies individual participants. Potential participants must be informed of this arrangement.

There are situations where participants wish their contribution to be recognised. This is most likely to occur in types of qualitative research such as ethnographic, action, or feminist research where the aim is to give a voice to participants. In *Sidewalk* (1999), Duneier used ethnography, including **participant observation**, to provide a richly detailed account of the ways in which race and class intersect in the lives of mainly homeless, African-American, male street vendors living around New York's Greenwich Village. Identifying participants gave them a public voice otherwise denied them. (This observation and the example of Duneier's study was made by an anonymous reviewer of this book.)

> **Participant observation**: The main data-collecting technique used by ethnographers. It involves the researcher observing first hand in the research setting. The researcher is free to be an active participant in the normal routines of the research.

Exercise 4.2: Writing an information sheet

> Imagine you are a researcher seeking to undertake a qualitative investigation of intravenous drug use among young people using in-depth interviews as your research method. Think about the following:
>
> - What are the ethical issues you will face?
> - How would you deal with them?
>
> Now write an Information Sheet to accompany your application to an HREC. You can use the example in box 4.4 as a guide.

Data management

The principles of anonymity and confidentiality also have implications for the way data are recorded and stored. In addition to keeping identifying information such as contact details separate from the **raw data**, researchers need to be sensitive to their use by third parties, either legally or illegally. For example, the Australian Research Council requires recipients of its grants to deposit their data in an archive that is accessible to other researchers, such as the Australian Social Science Data Archive (ASSDA). This raises questions of informed consent, confidentiality and ownership of material (Richardson & Godfrey 2003), as well as how long the original researcher must keep the data.

> **Raw data**: Numeric data in a crude, unanalysed form.

Data storage

According to the NHMRC *National Statement on Ethical Conduct in Research Involving Humans*, researchers should:

- remove identifying material from records at the earliest possible time

- only collect personal information where it is absolutely necessary for the research
- use coding procedures
- store separately any data containing personal information
- not store personal information on their hard disk
- dispose of personal information as soon as possible; for example, destroy contact information once data collection is complete.

Safety

Issues of participant safety are especially relevant to medical research, which may involve placing research participants in situations that carry some physical risk. Some forms of psychological research, particularly experimental psychology, where participants may be deliberately placed in stressful situations in order to see how they behave, also have a safety aspect. The most famous example of this is Milgram's study on authority. One group of participants took on the role of 'teacher' and were asked to apply what they incorrectly believed were potentially lethal electrical shocks to 'pupils' if they failed to answer questions 'correctly' (Milgram 1963, 1974). The 'pupils' were another group of participants who had been instructed to fake signs of physical distress when the 'shock treatment' was applied. Despite the apparent distress of the 'pupils', most 'teachers' continued to apply the shock treatment. The study provided important insight into how perceptions of authority can lead 'ordinary' people to physically harm others, but also became an example of the unethical use of deception. The study's use of covert research techniques placed the 'teachers' in a situation of moral discomfort that could have caused ongoing distress.

Most social research does not expose participants to the risk of physical or psychological harm, but it may cause potential psychological discomfort by, for example, asking them to recall past or current experiences about which they have strong feelings, such as personal relationships or their experience of illness. Some research may also uncover information among a network of people that could be disruptive to their relationships.

Safety also relates to protection from legal harm, and researchers must take care not to place participants in legal jeopardy. If participants are asked to disclose involvement in illegal behaviour, such as illegal drug-taking or motor vehicle theft, researchers need to take special care to protect their anonymity and the confidentiality of any information provided. There have been cases in the USA where legal authorities have required researchers to provide their data as evidence for the prosecution (Hallowell in Neuman 1991:443).

To prevent this, participants should be warned not to provide information about illegal activity that has not been dealt with by the judicial system.

Qualitative methodologies tend to involve greater ethical dilemmas than quantitative methodologies (Hopf 2004). Field research in particular can lead to difficult legal issues. A researcher may unintentionally observe criminal behaviour, making him or her liable to becoming a witness in criminal proceedings. Or researchers may place themselves in situations where they deliberately witness criminal activity. Stephen Tomsen's research on the relationship between alcohol and violence in public places involved participant observation in pubs and clubs, some of which were chosen because of their reputation for violent fights (Tomsen 1997). Tomsen was a witness to the violence, and sometimes had limited contact with perpetrators, victims and others at the scene.

Had someone been seriously injured, Tomsen could have found himself being subpoenaed as a witness and his research notes treated as legal evidence.

Research merit

When potential participants are invited to participate in a research project, the request is justified through its potential benefits to society. Ethical guidelines therefore require the research design and methodology to meet discipline standards and be acceptable for publication in a peer-reviewed academic journal. It should also avoid researching a topic where there already exists a strong knowledge base.

Vulnerable participant groups

Incidences of abuse of some study populations, such as prisoners or children with a disability, by medical researchers has led to National Statement guidelines that specifically protect vulnerable populations. Vulnerable populations include:
- children and young people
- people in dependent or unequal relationships including:
    - carers and people with chronic conditions or disabilities
    - health care professionals and their patients or clients
    - teachers and their students
    - prison authorities and prisoners
    - governmental authorities and refugees
    - service providers and especially vulnerable communities
    - employers and employees

Daphne Habibis

- Aboriginal and Torres Strait Islander people
- people highly dependent on medical care
- people with an intellectual or mental disability
- people who may be involved in illegal activities.

All vulnerable groups, such as the elderly or those in ill health or on low incomes, should be treated with special sensitivity by the social researcher. Special care is required to ensure that requirements such as informed consent are observed. For example, in my research on people receiving treatment in an acute psychiatric ward, obtaining informed consent was difficult, because potential respondents were often quite unwell and their medication sometimes meant they did not understand what they were being invited to be involved in. Special protocols were established through the HREC to work with psychiatric staff on when and how to approach them.

Aboriginal and Torres Strait Islander people

Submissions and personal representations from Indigenous peoples and health and research organisations to the Australian Health Ethics Committee in the mid 1990s led to ethical guidelines for health research with and by Aboriginal and Torres Strait Islander people (NHMRC 2002; NHMRC 2003, 2004). These introduce additional requirements to develop and conduct research in a manner that is respectful and inclusive of Aboriginal and Torres Strait Islander values and cultures (see box 4.6). A key message to researchers is that there is a great diversity across the many Aboriginal and Torres Strait Islander cultures and societies. Although there is a set of common values shared, each society has the right to express how these common values and their own unique values should be addressed in research (NHMRC 2007).

Box 4.6: NHMRC *National Statement Guidelines on Research with Aboriginal and Torres Strait Islander Peoples*

Research with Aboriginal and Torres Strait Islander peoples should:

- be conducted in a way that reflects the six core values of reciprocity, respect, equality, responsibility, survival and protection, spirit and integrity, identified as being important to Aboriginal and Torres Strait Islander Peoples
- provide evidence of support from relevant Indigenous communities
- ensure that its methods provide for mutually agreed mechanisms for such matters as appropriate recruitment techniques; suitable information about the research; notification of participants' consent and research progress; final reporting

- identify any potential negative consequences of the proposed research, to design processes to monitor them and to advise steps for minimising them
- adopt methods and processes that provide opportunities to develop trust and a sense of equal research partnerships
- provide fair opportunity for involvement of Aboriginal and Torres Strait Islander Peoples
- ensure that benefits include the enhancement or establishment of capabilities, opportunities or research outcomes that advance the interests of Aboriginal and Torres Strait Islander Peoples, that these should have been discussed with them, and that any realisable benefits should be distributed in a way that is agreed to and considered fair by these participants
- should demonstrate evidence of respectful engagement with Aboriginal and Torres Strait Islander Peoples and that the research approach should value and create opportunities to draw on their knowledge and wisdom through their active engagement, including interpretation of the research data
- that national or multicentre research should take care to gain local level support for research methods that risk not respecting cultural and language protocols.

Source: NHMRC 2007:69–71

Māori people

In New Zealand, the Māori Health Committee of the Health Research Council of New Zealand has produced guidelines that all researchers are required to meet when conducting research projects on a topic relevant to a Māori health issue or Māori are to be involved as participants. This has developed against a background in which some Māori communities and groups have felt overresearched and disempowered, and have received few benefits from participation in the research. The key requirements are that (Health Research Council of New Zealand 2008):

- the objectives of the research should address the significant differences in Māori and non-Māori health status
- the research should be a collaborative process between researchers and Māori
- it should involve full, ongoing and sincere consultation with Māori at every stage, including research design, data collection, analysis and dissemination. Research that breaches Māori culture will not be supported by the Māori Health Council, unless it is supported by local Māori communities and organisations
- informed consent may be required from both individuals and organisations
- where possible, a process of mutual mentoring should occur in which Māori have the opportunity to develop their skills and knowledge of research processes and researchers develop their cross-cultural skills as well as the possibility of new methodologies.

Daphne Habibis

Ethics and the researcher

The second stakeholder in any research project is the researcher, and there are a number of areas where ethical issues are important. These include:

- personal safety
- truthful reporting
- acknowledgment of sources (as opposed to **plagiarism**).

Plagiarism: The unacknowledged use of the work of another person so that the ideas or information appear to be one's own.

Personal safety

Personal safety of researchers is regarded by the NHMRC as an ethical issue (for example, see Collyer 2004:18–19). Concerns include:

- safety of interviewing in participants' homes
- 'cold' interviewing (that is, with no formal introductory process), especially in settings that may be unsafe, such as nightclubs
- observation of, or involvement in, illegal activities
- the psychological impact of researching sensitive issues.

Truthful reporting

That findings should be truthfully reported is axiomatic in social research. Yet bias in the reporting of results can be introduced because of attachment to a particular view. As discussed in chapter 1, researchers do not undertake their work in a social vacuum, but with a particular set of beliefs and assumptions that influence what they choose to study and how they go about their work, including the interpretation of their findings. There is always the possibility that attachment to a particular perspective will lead to judgmental attitudes towards the social group under investigation, thereby introducing bias into the study. The need to guard against such value bias is acknowledged in the Australian Sociological Association's *Code of Ethics*. Article 10 states:

> Members have a responsibility to consider the interests of those involved in their research, those affected by their work, and those utilising their findings. This broad responsibility implies that in conducting research, and presenting the results, due consideration is given to the plurality of the social world, the diversity of beliefs and values, especially in the context of culture, age, gender and other aspects of social complexity, and to the requirements set out in affirmative action and anti-discrimination legislation and policies (TASA 2008).

Some researchers deal with this issue by being explicit about their own values in the write-up of the research so that the research community can assess their contribution in an informed way.

Academic fraud is another aspect of truthful reporting. Most professional ethical codes within the social sciences include a statement about the unacceptability of presenting false or misleading results. Any researcher found to have engaged in **academic fraud** faces severe disciplining, professional ostracism and probable loss of employment. While blatant fabrication of findings is rare in social research, it does occur. An Australian example is the case of William McBride. William McBride achieved fame for being the person who first publicly identified the link between the drug thalidomide and the occurrence of birth defects in babies. In a development quite unrelated to this he was later accused of systematically falsifying data in a paper published in the *Australian Journal of Biological Sciences*. An inquiry by his university confirmed that this had taken place. Despite this, he was permitted to return to the board of the foundation that had conducted the research; however, his academic reputation was irredeemably tarnished.

> **Academic fraud:** The misrepresentation or falsification of research findings by the researcher.

Less obvious and understood are more subtle modifications of findings such as the 'tweaking' of responses to fit an anticipated pattern or the misleading interpretation of findings. Diener and Crandall (in Homan 1991:8) suggest it is possible that 'a sizable proportion of published findings may be based on quicksand'.

Acknowledgment of authorship

Authorship or ownership of research also have ethical dimensions. This is especially so when the research and ownership is embedded in the relationship between academics and honours and postgraduate students. What are the implications for authorship of the contribution supervisors make to their student's production of knowledge? How this is acknowledged in any publications will vary depending on the extent of the supervisor's contribution, with possibilities ranging from no acknowledgment to the supervisor being first author. Most research institutions and professional codes have guidelines on how the contribution of students and supervisors should be reflected in authorship.

Box 4.7: Guidelines on authorship of publications (University of Tasmania 2006:31)

The Statement and Guidelines on Research Practice addresses the related area of authorship of publications. Each person who has made a substantial contribution to the research leading to a publication must be given the opportunity to be included as an author. Someone who has not participated in conceiving, executing or interpreting at least part of the relevant research should not be included as an author. This may be a sensitive issue when the contributions of a candidate and his or her supervisors are

Daphne Habibis

considered in determining authorship and the order in which the authors' names are listed. Some candidates are disinclined to acknowledge any contributions made by their supervisor, just as some supervisors are inclined to claim a result as theirs alone even though their last real contribution was two years ago. The question of authorship should be discussed at the earliest possible stage in a research project, and reviewed whenever there are changes in participation.

Candidates are encouraged to publish their research findings, if appropriate, throughout candidature. The Board strongly advises candidates, in consultation with their supervisors, to prepare a statement of authorship at the time each paper is submitted for publication. This statement should provide the details of the contribution of the candidate, the proportionate authorship of each of the coauthors and, where practical, should be endorsed by all of the coauthors. These statements should be kept on file in the school. If co-authored papers are to be included in the thesis, these statements will be needed to verify authorship.

Ethics and the organisation

Social research is usually practised within an organisation, with more than one organisation often carrying some responsibility for the research. Most university research is funded by an external body, such as the federal government-funded Australian Research Council or a private charitable or industry organisation. There are a number of ethical issues affecting the funding source of research activity.

Disclosure of funding sources

How social research is funded raises ethical issues because of the potential for research bias in favour of the interests of the funding source, whether government or private. The potential for bias in biomedical research is an area of current debate, because of the potential profits and large financial investment in research and development by biomedical companies. Pharmaceutical companies in particular have a documented history of ethical violations in medical research (Braithwaite 1985).

Although less common in the social sciences than in medical research, there have been cases where sponsors have compromised the independence of researchers (Blumer 1967), in the social sciences. however, it is more likely to be ideological rather than commercial interests that threaten the requirement for honesty in the conduct of social research. The role of social research in informing social policy means that findings often have implications for government support for the funding body or for the population under investigation, raising potential ethical dilemmas about the reporting of findings. The political nature of research is also apparent in debates about what projects public money should support, with claims sometimes being made that some projects were not sufficiently in line with the nation's strategic goals, and were therefore a waste of public money. One of the ways in which governments seek to prevent such criticisms is to ensure that researchers identify how their research contributes to identified national objectives. For example, the Australian Research Council requires all research proposals to classify their research under one of four socioeconomic objectives: defence; economic development; society; and environment. 'Society' covers 'research and development directed towards individual and community well-being or towards general social development', and has three subdivisions: health; education and training; and social development and community services (ABS 1998).

For these reasons, ethical guidelines for research invariably carry a statement that all publications should acknowledge who has provided funding and how much it amounts to. In addition, they should declare any affiliation with the sponsor as well as any financial interest.

Everyday ethical dilemmas

Ethical dilemmas are routinely experienced, and the researcher must assess what is the appropriate course of action to achieve the research goals without compromising ethical standards.

Volunteers

The ideal of 'voluntary participation' sounds straightforward, but in practice there are many ways in which individuals may be subtly encouraged or manipulated into participation. A doctor asking a hospital patient to complete a consent form for participation in a research project may state that participation is voluntary, but the setting and the relationship may cause the patient to feel an obligation to agree. One way of ensuring potential participants are not coerced to participate in any way is for contact with the researcher to be instigated by the participant rather than the other way round. This usually means reliance on the dissemination of information about the project through the media, posters in strategic locations, postal surveys and the use of a third party.

This can work well; for example, postal surveys rely on participants to complete the form and mail it back to the researcher. But there are many projects where reliance on participants to contact researchers is not realistic. This is especially true of many qualitative data collection methods, where the populations being researched are often small and difficult to locate.

Some population groups are also unlikely to contact researchers. This is especially true of those drawn from disempowered social groups. Participants may find the idea of

Daphne Habibis

participation in research unfamiliar, unnecessary and uncomfortable, and so be unwilling to engage in it. Some low-income groups and groups experiencing ill health, legal problems or disabilities may see involvement in a research project as just another demand, with no obvious benefit. From the researcher's perspective, the best way of reaching participants is to contact them to explain what the project is about and to discuss their possible involvement in it. This can be achieved indirectly through use of a third party, such as a service used by the research population. An employee of the service can be approached and asked to make the initial contact, and to provide the potential participant with an information sheet and a brief outline of what the research project is about and what involvement would mean. If a person expresses interest in participation, he or she can then be asked if he or she is willing for the researcher to be given the contact details or if the participant can be given the contact details of the researcher.

Payments to research subjects

When research subjects agree to participate in a research project, they are donating their time as well as their knowledge and experiences. They may also incur expenses, such as travel to and from a focus group, arranging child care or taking time off work. It is reasonable that they should receive some financial remuneration for the inconvenience. This payment needs to be made in the context of an understanding that payment can also be a form of coercion or inducement that transgresses the principle of voluntary consent. For this reason, HRECs provide guidelines on payments to research volunteers.

Can the ends justify the means? Covert research

Covert research: The inclusion of respondents in a research project without their awareness and/or agreement to their participation.

One of the ways in which codes of ethics work is to prevent ethically dubious projects from ever going beyond the stage of the researcher's imagination. One contentious methodology is **covert research**, which is the inclusion of subjects in a research project without their awareness of, and/or agreement to, their participation. It usually involves a qualitative methodology, including the use of some kind of direct observation, especially participant observation.

Political involvement in marginal political organisations is one of a number of sensitive topics that can be difficult to investigate with the full knowledge of participants. Other areas include sexual behaviour, membership of marginal religious organisations, criminal involvement, and violent behaviour. There is a long tradition of studies using covert techniques (see case studies 4.2 and 4.3), which in itself suggests that covert methodologies are not always unethical. Deliberate deception of participants in ways that place them at risk is clearly in a different category from the unobtrusive observation conducted by Tomsen.

Case studies 4.2 and 4.3: Studies using covert methodologies

Case study 4.2: Fiddling and pilferage in a bread factory

Paul Ditton was a PhD student who had experienced employment in a factory. His study in industrial relations was investigating whether there is a difference in the output of workers according to whether they are paid by piecework or by the hour. He returned to the factory as a worker without revealing to the organisation or his co-workers that he was using this as an opportunity to collect data. Working 12-hour shifts, he used the breaks to write up his observations of his co-workers' behaviour. The title of his book, *Part-time Crime: An Ethnography of Fiddling and Pilferage* (1977) proclaims his main findings. It is likely that Ditton's co-workers would not have cooperated with the research if they had been given the choice. On the other hand, the extent of 'fiddling' in the factory would not have been revealed by conventional techniques.

Case study 4.3: A top night out

Stephen Tomsen was interested in the relationship between crime and masculinities, and decided to explore this by looking at pub violence (Tomsen 1997). This involved spending time in pubs with a reputation for violent confrontations between customers. He never revealed his identity to customers or staff, but appeared as a paying customer. He witnessed a number of fights between customers and between customers and bouncers.

In addition to violating the principle of informed consent, covert techniques may also:

- violate the personal liberty of the unwitting informants
- betray their trust
- contaminate the research environment for subsequent researchers
- discriminate against the defenceless and powerless
- damage the behaviour or interests of subjects
- become a habitual technique of particular researchers, with the risk that lying to participants becomes a habit that undermines democratic principles of openness and fair treatment
- influence the behaviour of the unwitting participants and thereby undermine the integrity of research findings (Homan 1991:108–12).

The general consensus among social scientists today is that covert research should generally not be used, but that partial disclosure may be considered in circumstances where it will not cause harm to participants, the value of the research justifies it and there is no

Daphne Habibis

alternative. There is a cost to this consensus, and that is that important topics remain underinvestigated. Balancing the rights of participants against the rights of the public to know therefore remains an important conundrum for the social researcher.

Voices in the field

Hannah Graham

Hannah Graham is a PhD candidate at the University of Tasmania, and is conducting research in the complex area of mental health. The following paragraphs outline the clashes of ethical interest that can occur when working with what are defined as 'vulnerable groups' such as those with a mental illness.

'In 2007, I conducted a preliminary evaluation of a mental health court pilot for the Magistrates Court of Tasmania. Research participants included practitioners and offenders with a mental illness. Safeguards were adopted, including: anonymity, confidentiality, informed consent, advanced verbal notice of the research to defendants from forensic mental health staff, opportunities for feedback and verbal clarification of consent in court.

'Permission from the Human Research Ethics Committee (HREC) of Tasmania was obtained. One stipulation by the committee, however, ignited joint opposition from myself, the magistrate, lawyers and forensic mental health workers. All defendants were required to read a detailed information briefing and sign a consent form to simply allow me to observe this open court. This yielded little sensitive information because the media could attend, and the names and charges of defendants were made public in court lists on the internet. The Ethics Committee rejected the request for verbal consent instead.

'I perceived their requirement as problematic because it was difficult to orchestrate graciously in the crowded court foyer 15 minutes beforehand. I had to approach every person to ask if he or she were appearing in this court. Defendants were often anxious, and did not want to be seen filling out the forms, because it publicly identified them as 'mentally ill'. Common questions included: 'Is it legally binding?', 'Is this part of the court process?' or 'I want to do it but I don't want forms'. Added confusion arose because of low literacy or, for those with paranoid psychosis, suspicion about signing things. Family members or lawyers often assisted, expressing support for my research but anger at the paperwork. Overall, the research progressed well with full defendant participation. However, complex issues like these do raise the question of 'ethical according to whom?'

Ethics in practice

In its 2006 Report to the federal government on challenging issues in contemporary social research (2006) the National Health and Medical Research Council (NHMRC) described research involving interviews with mental health professionals and their patients. The objective of the research was to discover how commonplace 'dual relationships' were in rural communities where everyone knows everyone else socially as well as professionally. An incident occurred during the investigation, in which a patient interviewee told the interviewer that one of the psychiatrists had raped her during her consultation and wanted to know what the researcher was going to do about it. There were a number of ethical dilemmas posed by this. The respondent was from a vulnerable population, but the researcher's role did not include responsibility to provide assistance. They were from a small community with few qualified persons available to investigate the allegation. It was not clear that the participant wanted the researcher to report the alleged incident.

The HREC decided that, in the event of such a disclosure or allegation emerging during an interview, the researcher should inform the interviewee of their rights in relation to reporting the matter to the appropriate authorities, but refrain from taking any further action on the interviewee's behalf. However, some members of the HREC were uneasy about this advice because they felt that vulnerable people were less likely to report sexual misconduct than the population generally, and that some further support or follow-up would have been desirable.

Source: NHMRC 2006:7–8

Question:

Do you agree with the HREC's decision? Why or why not?

Exercise 4.3: Assessing the ethical dimensions

Imagine that you are a member of a human research ethics committee (HREC) that has received an application from a social scientist seeking to use covert methods to examine the treatment of refugees in detention centres. Answer the following questions on how you might go about determining the ethical dimensions of this project.
- What criteria would you use to assess the research project application?
- What politicolegal considerations might influence your decision?
- What conditions would you require to be met before you would be willing to consider approving the proposal?

Daphne Habibis

Conclusion

Attention to ethical considerations at all stages of the research process is an essential component of professional research. Because social research has an impact on people, both directly and indirectly, the potential for social harm needs to be consciously addressed. This potential extends beyond research subjects, and includes the population group to which they belong, funding bodies, the research profession and anyone involved in the investigation, including the researchers themselves. Because researchers lead the investigation and control most aspects of it, they have a direct responsibility to minimise the potential for harm to their participants, especially if they are drawn from a vulnerable social groups. They need to operate with an awareness that their interests and those of their participants do not always coincide, and that all research must be bounded by ethical practice. Without ethical guidelines and ethical practice as an integral part of the research process, abuse and breach of the participants' trust can occur. Ethical considerations also vary by the research method used. Ethical concerns particular to individual methods are noted within each methods chapter in the text (chapters 6–14) and also in the 10 other methods modules that are available at <www.oup.com.au/orc/walter>.

Main points

> Ethics is concerned with the establishment of a set of moral standards that govern behaviour in a particular setting or for a particular group.

> Ethical research is concerned with ensuring that ethical principles and values always govern research involving humans.

> There are many stakeholders involved in research, including the participant, the researcher, the funding organisation and the researcher's employer.

> One of the main reasons why guidelines for ethical standards in research are necessary is because of the power imbalance between the researcher and the researched.

> Different methodologies place different emphasis on the level of involvement of participants. In general, interpretative methodologies give space to participants' views while quantitative approaches do not.

> Researchers are not disinterested observers motivated by 'pure' considerations of knowledge, but have careers in which the success of their investigations is central. Paying careful attention to the moral and ethical requirements of research can get in the way of speedy and successful projects.

- Feminist research and some types of action research try to overcome what they see as the inherently exploitative nature of research by involving participants in some or all stages of the research process.
- Any research undertaken or funded by a government organisation must receive ethical approval from a human research ethics committee (HREC) before it can be conducted.
- The key Australian document identifying the principles for ethical research on humans is the *National Statement on Ethical Conduct in Research Involving Humans* (Section 1).
- The principles most concerned with the protection of participants are the principles of informed consent, anonymity, confidentiality and protection from harm.
- The principle of informed consent is concerned with ensuring that:
    - research participants are fully informed about what the research is about and what participation will involve
    - they make the decision to participate without any formal or informal coercion.
- The main mechanisms used to ensure that potential participants are fully informed and that participation is voluntary are the information sheet and consent form.
- Anonymity refers to the protection of participants from identification as participants in the research.
- Confidentiality is concerned with ensuring that the information provided by participants cannot be linked back to them.
- Qualitative methodologies give rise to more ethical dilemmas than quantitative methodologies.
- Researchers need to take special care not to abuse the human rights of vulnerable groups, such as children or prisoners.
- Ethical considerations relating to the researcher are ensuring their personal safety; truthful reporting; and accurate acknowledgment of sources.
- Researchers should always disclose the funding sources of their research.
- Covert research is the inclusion of subjects in a research project without their awareness of, and/or agreement to, their participation.

Daphne Habibis

Further reading

American Association of University Professors (2004). *Protecting Human Beings: Institutional Review Boards and Social Science Research* <www.aaup.org/statements/redbook/repirb.htm>. First published in 1999 and 2000.

Australian Association of Social Workers (2004). *Code of Ethics* <www.aasw.asn.au/adobe/about/AASW_Code_of_Ethics-2004.pdf>. Accessed 14 May 2004.

Australian Sociological Association (2008). *Code of Ethics* <www.tasa.org.au/ethical-guidelines>. Accessed 31 October 2008.

Grieg, A., Taylor, J. and MacKay, T. (2007). *Doing Research with Children*. London: Sage.

Homan, R. (1991). *The Ethics of Social Research*. London: Longman.

Israel, M. and Hay, I. (2006). *Research Ethics for Social Scientists: Between Ethical Conduct and Regulatory Compliance*. London: Sage.

Lee, R. (1993). *Doing Research on Sensitive Topics*. London: Sage.

Mills, G. E. (2007). *Action Research: A Guide for the Teacher Researcher*. Upper Saddle River, NJ: Pearson Merrill/Prentice Hall.

National Health and Medical Research Council (2007). *National Statement on Ethical Conduct in Human Research*. <www.nhmrc.gov.au/PUBLICATIONS/synopses/e72syn.htm>. Accessed 31 October 2008.

References

Australian Bureau of Statistics (1998). Australian Standard Research Classification Cat. No. 1297.0 <www.abs.gov.au/Ausstats/abs@.nsf/0/43FB5359D374B8D1CA25697E0018FB82?opendocument>. Accessed 31 October 2008.

Australian Sociological Association (TASA) (2008). *Code of Ethics* <www.tasa.org.au/ethical-guidelines>. Accessed 31 October 2008.

Barnes, J. (1979). *Who Should Know What?* Harmondsworth: Penguin.

Blumer, H. (1967). 'Threats from Agency-Determined Research: The Case of Camelot', in Horowitz, I. (ed.), *The Rise and Fall of Project Camelot: Studies in the Relationship between Social Science and Practical Politics*. London: MIT.

Braithwaite, J. (1985). *Corporate Crime in the Pharmaceutical Industry*. Canberra: Australian Institute of Criminology.

Christensen, P. and Prout, A. (2002). 'Working with Ethical Symmetry in Social Research with Children', *Childhood*, 9 (4): 477–97.

Collyer, F. (2004). 'Ethics and Institutional Reform', *Nexus* 16 (2): 18–19.

Craig, G., Corden, A. and Thornton, P. (2001). 'Safety in Social Research', *Social Research Update*, 29 <www.soc.surrey.ac.uk/sru/SRU29.html>. Accessed 28 February 2005.

Dempsey, K. (1990). *Smalltown: A Study of Social Inequality, Cohesion and Belonging*. Melbourne: Oxford University Press.

Diener, E. and Crandall, R. (1978). *Ethics in Social and Behavioral Research*. Chicago: University of Chicago Press.

Ditton, J. (1977). *Part-time Crime: An Ethnography of Fiddling and Pilferage*. London: Macmillan.

Duneier, M. (1999). *Sidewalk*. New York: Farrar, Straus & Giroux.

Elmer-Dewitt, P. (1995). 'On a Screen Near You: Cyberporn', *Time*, 3 July, 38–45.

Habibis, D., Hazelton, M., Schneider, R., Davidson, J. and Bowling, A. (2002). 'A Comparison of Patient Psychiatric and Social Outcomes before and after the Introduction of an Extended-hours Community Mental Health Team', *Australian and New Zealand Journal of Psychiatry*, 36 (3): 392–8.

Health Research Council of New Zealand (2008). *Guidelines for Researchers on Health Research Involving Māori*. Health Research Council of New Zealand, Auckland <www.hrc.govt.nz/assets/pdfs/publications/MHGuidelines%202008%20FINAL.pdf>. Accessed 31 October 2008.

Homan, R. (1991). *The Ethics of Social Research*. London: Longman.

Hopf, C. (2004). 'Research Ethics and Qualitative Research', in Flick, U., von Kardorff, E. and Steinke, I. K., *A Companion to Qualitative Research*. London: Sage.

Humphreys, L. (1970). *Tearoom Trade: Impersonal Sex in Public Places*. Chicago: Aldine.

Jones, D. G. (1990). 'Contemporary Medical Scandals: A Challenge to Ethical Codes and Ethical Principles', *Perspectives on Science and Christian Faith*, 42: 2–14 <www.asa3.org/ASA/PSCF/1990/PSCF3-90Jones.html>. Accessed 14 May 2005.

Loblay, R. H. and Chalmers, D. (1999). 'Ethics Committees: Is Reform in Order?', *Medical Journal of Australia*, 170 (1): 9–10.

Mackintosh, N. (ed.) (1995). *Cyril Burt: Fraud or Framed?* Oxford: Oxford University Press.

McCosker, H., Barnard, A. and Gerber, R. (2001). 'Undertaking Sensitive Research: Issues and Strategies for Meeting the Safety Needs of All Participants', *Qualitative Social Research*, 2 (1): <http://qualitative-research.net/fqs/fqs-eng.htm>. Accessed 18 November 2004.

Daphne Habibis

Milgram, S. (1963). 'Behavioral Study of Obedience', *Journal of Abnormal and Social Psychology*, 67: 371–8.

Milgram, S. (1974). *Obedience to Authority: An Experimental View.* New York: Harper & Row.

National Health and Medical Research Council (NHMRC) (2002). *The NHMRC Road Map: A Strategic Framework for Improving Aboriginal and Torres Strait Islander Health through Research* <www.nhmrc.gov.au/research/srdc/indigen.htm>. Accessed 2 February 2005.

National Health and Medical Research Council (NHMRC) (2003). *Values and Ethics: Guidelines for Ethical Conduct in Aboriginal and Torres Strait Islander Health Research* <www.nhmrc.gov.au/publications/synopses/e52syn.htm>. Accessed 2 February 2005.

National Health and Medical Research Council (NHMRC) (2004). Community Guide to the Ethics of Health Research, Unreleased draft V. Canberra: Commonwealth of Australia.

National Health and Medical Research Council (NHMRC) (2006). *Challenging Ethical Issues in Contemporary Research on Human Beings.* Commonwealth of Australia <www.nhmrc.gov.au/PUBLICATIONS/synopses/e73syn.htm>. Accessed 31 October 2008.

National Health and Medical Research Council (NHMRC) (2007). *National Statement on Ethical Conduct in Human Research* <www.nhmrc.gov.au/PUBLICATIONS/synopses/e72syn.htm>. Accessed 31 October 2008.

Neuman, W. H. (1991). *Social Research Methods.* Sydney: Allyn & Bacon.

Oakley, A. (1981). 'Interviewing Women: A Contradiction in Terms', in Roberts, H. (ed.), *Doing Feminist Research.* London: Routledge & Kegan Paul: 30–61.

Richardson, J. C. and Godfrey, B. (2003). 'Towards Ethical Practice in the Use of Archived Transcripted Interviews', *International Journal of Social Research Methodology*, 6 (4): 347–55.

Rimm, M. (1995). 'Marketing Pornography on the Information Superhighway', *Georgetown Law Journal*, 83: 1849–1934.

Thomas, J. (1995). *The Ethics of Carnegie Mellon's Cyberporn Study* <http://sun.soci.niu.edu/~jthomas/ethics.cmu>.

Tomsen, S. (1997). 'A Top Night: Social Protest, Masculinity and the Culture of Drinking Violence', *British Journal of Criminology*, 37 (1): 90–103.

University of Tasmania, Board of Graduate Research (2006). *Graduate Research Resource Book* <www.research.utas.edu.au/gr/docs/resource_book.pdf>. Accessed 31 October 2008.

Wadsworth, Y. (1997). *Do It Yourself Social Research.* Sydney: Allen & Unwin.

Warwick, D. and Pettigrew, T. (1983). 'Towards Ethical Guidelines for Social Science Research in Public Policy', in Callahan, D. and Jennings, B. (eds), *Ethics, the Social Sciences and Policy Analysis.* London: Plenum.

Warwick, D. P. (1982). 'Tearoom Trade: Means and Ends in Social Research', in Bulmer, M., *Social Research Ethics: An Examination of the Merits of Covert Participation*. London: Macmillan.

Willis, E. (1989). *Medical Dominance*. Sydney: Allen & Unwin.

Chapter 5

Sampling

Bruce Tranter

A population study: Acupuncture in Australian general practice: practitioner characteristics

While the focus here is sampling, on occasion it is possible to conduct research based upon the whole population the researcher wants to study. A research project (Easthope et al. 1998) to examine the provision of acupuncture by Australian general practitioners provides an example of this approach. In this study the researchers were interested in the proportion of medical practitioners who provided acupuncture and the characteristics of the general practitioners (GPs) who provided acupuncture.

Acupuncture performed by a medical practitioner had its own Medicare item number in the Medicare Benefits Schedule. The researchers were able to access Medicare data for all acupuncture services claimed by Australian GPs in 1996. They also had access to data on their sex and age group, and an index that measured socioeconomic disadvantage, based upon the postcode of the doctors' practice and the country where they gained their original medical qualification.

Using a multivariate approach called logistic regression analysis, Easthope and colleagues (1998) found that female doctors, those aged between 35 and 54 and doctors who trained overseas were most likely to administer acupuncture to their patients, although there was no clear difference according to the socioeconomic status of the area in which the practice was located.

Importantly, because they had access to the complete set of data for the provision of acupuncture recorded on the Medicare database, Easthope and colleagues' (1998) research was a population study. The results were not estimates of population characteristics based upon a sample, but were the actual population values (parameters).

Key terms

- confidence intervals
- confidence levels
- convenience sampling
- non-probability sampling
- population
- probability sampling
- purposive sampling
- quota sampling
- sample non-response
- sample
- sampling error
- sampling frame
- self-selected sampling
- simple random sampling
- snowball sampling
- stratified sampling
- systematic sampling

Why we sample

Probability sampling: Samples selected in accordance with probability theory. Probability sampling relies on (a) that we have a list of all elements or cases in the population we are studying; and (b) that we are able to randomly select elements or cases from this list and that all cases or elements have an equal chance of being selected.

Confidence: The quantitative researcher is, more often than not, very interested in specifying the level of certainty with which a relationship between variables within a data set can be generalised beyond the confines of a specific sample to some wider population.

Non-probability sampling: A sampling process that does not use probability sampling techniques to select a sample. Examples include convenience sampling, snowball sampling and self-selected sampling.

Representativeness: What quantitative researchers want their sample to achieve with respect to a population of interest.

The case study above of population based research raises the inevitable question: 'Why do we sample?' Sampling is the process by which researchers usually select their unit of analysis (see chapter 3), and there are four main reasons we draw samples rather than survey or interview a whole research population. The first two are more applicable to quantitative research, and the final two are more relevant to qualitative research.

1. It is generally not practicable to survey all members of a given group. For example, if we wanted to find out how satisfied Australians were with the federal government's responses to climate change, it would not be feasible to survey all Australians. Even if we limited the study to only those people living in one Australian state, the number of potential respondents would still be unfeasibly large.
2. If we select our sample using **probability sampling** techniques (as explained below), we will be able to draw inferences that apply to the whole population of interest. Using a well-designed sampling strategy and a sample of sufficient size means we can make general statements about our population with a known degree of **confidence** about how accurate our results are. So, drawing upon the tenets of probability theory, there is no need to survey the entire population.
3. In qualitative research, there is no need to work with the whole group, because we are interested in meanings and understandings, not in statistics. In such work, more is not necessarily better, and a **non-probability sample** (see below) of 10, 20, 30 (the number chosen will depend on the research question) will likely provide all the rich detail and nuanced understandings required.
4. For many units of analysis there is simply no complete list of subjects, so it is impossible to work with a whole population. A sample of a particular group, or particular artefact, such as film posters, is the only option, even though **representativeness** cannot be established.

Defining the population

Samples are selected from our population of interest. In this context, the meaning of the term 'population' differs from its everyday use. For research purposes, a population is the collection of all the units we want to study, and it is important that we are able to delineate precisely and unambiguously who or what comprises the population. For example, if we aim to investigate the proportion of workers who plan to stay in the workforce past 65 years of age, we need to decide whether to include all adult workers in our study, or to limit the definition of our target **population** to older workers, say those aged 50 and older. There are also other considerations in determining our target population. Given that the literature suggests retirement decisions are often influenced by the retirement plans of a spouse, do we interview couples, or individual workers? Making these sorts of decisions is usually relatively straightforward, and guided by both our research question and our resources. The important thing is to define our population clearly and unambiguously, before we begin selecting our sample.

> **Population**: The collection of all the units that we want to study.

Selecting our sampling method

There are two main types of sampling:

- probability sampling
- non-probability sampling.

Probability sampling is exclusively connected to quantitative research methodologies, although some qualitative studies do incorporate an element of representativeness is their sampling. Surveys (chapter 6) mostly use probability sampling and quantitative analysis techniques as outlined in chapters 8 and 9. These chapters, as well as the quantitative analysis extension modules on the website, include a presumption of probability sampling. Non-probability sampling is mostly associated with qualitative methodologies, but can be utilised in quantitative projects (usually with conditions attached) if a probability sample is not feasible. In this text, methods where non-probability sampling would be used include in-depth interviews (chapter 10) and discourse analysis (chapter 12). Also, narrative research, conversation analysis memory work and sensory and visual methods are detailed in the online modules available at <www.oup.com.au/orc/walter>.Because of their alignment to different methodological categories, these two sampling methods are discussed separately in this chapter, but you should also remember the possibility of crossover utilisation.

Box 5.1: Some sampling definitions

- **Sample**: A set of cases or elements selected from a population.
- **Population**: The total collection of all the cases or elements that we want to study (such as Australians aged 18 and over).
- **Study population**: The finite set of individuals (or other unit of analysis) that we intend to study, such as Australians aged 18 and over registered on the Australian electoral roll as at 1 October 2008.

Bruce Tranter

- **Population parameter**: An aspect of our population that we want to measure or estimate (such as the actual proportion of Australian adults who voted for the Greens at the 2007 federal election).
- **Sample statistic**: Used in probability sampling, and is an estimate of a population parameter generated from sample data (such as an *estimate* of the proportion of Australian adults who voted for the Greens at the 2007 federal election).
- **Sampling frame**: The list of all of the cases or sampling units from which we will select our sample, such as the Australian electoral roll.

Probability sampling

In probability sampling, samples are selected in accordance with probability theory, using a procedure that gives every member of the population a known probability of selection (Maisel & Persell 1996:5). Probability sampling is an extremely powerful technique, and is the primary method of selecting large, representative (and 'representative' is the key word) samples for social and political research. Probability sampling allows researchers to use comparatively small samples to draw accurate inferences about a large population. This is especially useful in cases where the population is too large to be observed directly, such as the population of Australian voters or the population of Vietnam War veterans. Another advantage of probability sampling is that it prevents the researcher from consciously or unconsciously choosing a sample in a biased way.

Probability sampling relies on two core assumptions. First, we need a list of all of the elements in the population that we want to study: our **sampling frame**. For example, in order to survey Melbourne high school students we would need a list of all high school students in Melbourne. But such lists are rarely complete. Some students may have left school, changed schools or changed their address, while others may have commenced studying in the time between the preparation of the sampling frame and the administration of the survey to students. Such situations, while imperfect from an absolute accuracy perspective, still fulfil our requirement for a list of all elements in our population. By definition populations that are social, whether people or other social artefacts, are never static. The result is a slightly imperfect sampling frame, a usually unavoidable reality of selecting probability samples.

Sampling frame: A list that represents as closely as possible an abstract population; the researcher uses this list to draw a probability sample.

Second, probability sampling assumes that we are able to randomly select elements from our sampling frame according to probability theory. This means that each element of the sample has a known chance of being selected in the sample, independent of any other event in the selection process. Probability sampling has a mathematical justification in probability theory, and allows us to determine how accurately our sample characteristics (sample statistics) estimate our population characteristics (population parameters) by quantifying the degree of sampling error (see box 5.2 for an explanation of sampling error).

Simple random sampling

Simple random sampling (SRS) is the sampling strategy upon which probability sampling theory and inferential statistics are based. SRS requires an accurate sampling frame, in other words, a complete list of all of the elements from which the sample will be drawn. The basic idea here is that a sample will be drawn from the population at random, free from any bias or pattern in the selection process. In the past, SRS was accomplished using the tedious process of selection using tables of random numbers. Luckily, many databases and other computer programs will draw samples at random, again assuming the researcher has access to an appropriate list of sampling elements. Computer programs can be used to assign numbers to the sampling elements, and then draw a sample of the required size at random from the sampling frame. For example, if we know that all Tasmanian private telephone numbers fall between 6200 0000 and 6499 9999, we could program a computer to randomly dial from this number range to select a sample. SRS can generate unbiased estimates of population parameters when a complete list of the sampling elements is available, although in practice systematic sampling will produce samples of similar quality, which also enables researchers to calculate inferential statistics.

> **Simple random sampling:** Sampling randomly using probability, but with no additional techniques such as stratification.

Systematic sampling

While SRS seems like a relative straightforward approach to probability sampling, in practice many researchers tend to employ **systematic sampling**. Like SRS, systematic sampling is a probability sampling approach. It allows the calculation of sampling error, and therefore also enables the researcher to make inferential claims about the population based upon the sample from which it was drawn.

> **Systematic sampling:** A probability sampling approach that uses a sampling fraction to determine the system of drawing a random sample.

To draw a sample systematically, the researcher first needs to decide on an appropriate sample size. Once again, in systematic sampling it is necessary to have an accurate list of sampling elements of a known size. Next, the researcher divides the number of elements in the sampling frame by the required sample size. This provides the 'sampling fraction' (de Vaus 2002:72). For example, if the sampling frame comprised 200,000 cases and we require a sample of 1000, we would have a sampling interval of 200 (that is, 200,000 ÷ 1000 = 200). The next step is to take a random starting point and select every 200th case from the sampling frame until a sample of 1000 cases is drawn.

Systematic sampling is an efficient, relatively straightforward method of sampling so long as the sampling frame is not ordered in a way that is at all cyclical. For example,

Bruce Tranter

assume we wanted to systematically sample houses from streets in a particular suburb. We have a list of the street addresses of the houses, and in our list the houses are listed as odd number, even number, odd number, and so on. After taking a random start, for example on an odd street number, then selecting every tenth house, we would end up with a sample that consisted of all odd numbers. Odd and even numbers usually coincide with a particular side of a street, so we would end up with a sample that contained houses from one side of the street only. In some suburbs, houses on the upper side of hilly streets tend to have better views, and therefore may be more expensive than those on the lower side. In such a case, our systematic sample could result in sample bias by selecting higher-income households.

The problem of selecting a biased sample from a sampling frame that is itself cyclically ordered can be avoided by using a computer program to first randomise the elements in the sampling frame, then systematically sampling from the randomised list of elements. Alternatively, the fact that the sampling frame is ordered cyclically or stratified can be used to the researcher's advantage if we want to capture a particular subsample, such as those living on the upper sides of streets.

Stratified sampling

Stratified sampling: Often used with probability sampling to ensure that certain subgroups (such as an equal number from each state) are included at an appropriate level within the sample.

Stratified sampling is not a probability sampling method, but can be used in conjunction with probability sampling to enhance the representativeness of a sample. Stratified sampling is an attempt to reduce the level of sampling error, by splitting the population into subgroups or 'strata', and then drawing a sample using a probability selection process such as SRS or systematic sampling from within the strata. The example in case study 5.1 below demonstrates how stratified sampling is often used in Australia to make sure that a large enough sample is obtained from each state and territory to allow comparisons to be made.

Case study 5.1: Disproportionate and proportionate stratified sampling

In 1999 a group of political scientists conducted the national Australian Constitutional Referendum Survey (ACRS), a mail out, mail back administration with the sample drawn from the Australian electoral roll. The referendum asked Australians if they should change their head of state from a constitutional monarchy to a president appointed by the parliament, and also asked whether the preamble to the Australian constitution should be altered.

The sample was stratified on the basis of the states and territories. However, a random or systematic sample drawn from the electoral roll would tend to include more people from the most populous states such as New South Wales and Victoria, and very few from Tasmania and the territories. As the researchers wanted to make comparisons between the states with large enough subsamples for meaningful statistical analysis, they sent 1000 questionnaires to potential respondents in each of the states. This is known as a disproportionately stratified sample, as the smaller states were deliberately 'oversampled' as a proportion of the population of Australian adults.

The table below is reproduced from the ACRS codebook. It shows the population in each state in thousands, the size of the sample drawn, the numbers in 'In scope' which is the number of surveys sent after refusals and return to sender questionnaires are removed, the actual number of responses and the response rate for each state and territory.

State	Population (000s)	Sample size	In scope	Response number	Response rate
New South Wales	4133	1000	948	507	53.5
Victoria	3161	1000	941	557	59.2
Queensland	2222	1000	926	517	55.8
Western Australia	1172	1000	944	548	58.1
South Australia	1028	1000	945	607	64.2
Tasmania	326	1000	949	588	62.0
Australian Capital Territory	212	100	95	57	60.0
Northern Territory	108	50	45	22	48.9
Unknown			28	28	—
Total	12362	6150	5821	3431	58.9

Source: Adapted from Gow et al. (2000)

Sampling error, confidence levels and confidence intervals

The use of a sample instead of the whole population usually involves a degree of error. In practice, the true value may vary by a few percentage points, above or below, our sample statistic. To work out how much our sample value varies from the whole population value, we need to determine our sampling error, confidence levels and confidence intervals.

Sampling error

In probability sampling, the **sampling error** is the measurement error or difference between a sample statistic and the actual population parameter it represents. The method for calculating sampling error is outlined in box 5.2. For the main purposes of this chapter, just be

Sampling error: The error in sampling statistics caused by the difference between a sample and its population.

Bruce Tranter

aware that in all studies undertaken using probability sampling there will usually be some degree of difference between the sample estimate and the population value. The sampling error allows us estimate the size of that difference.

Confidence levels

Confidence level: Tells us how confident we can be that our population parameter lies within a given confidence interval.

All such studies are also conducted with a certain **confidence level**. The confidence level refers to the degree of confidence that the researcher can have when making claims about his or her statistical estimates—in this case, predicting an election outcome. This level of confidence is expressed as a percentage or a probability (for example, the 95 per cent level corresponds to a probability or 'p' value of .05). Social scientists often use the 95 per cent or 99 per cent confidence levels (also referred to respectively in relation to the .05 and .01 probability or 'p' values). For example, if we choose the 95 confidence level and calculate statistics based upon a probability sample, we can be 95 per cent confident that our sample estimate will hold in the population. This essentially means that, while we are 95 per cent confident, we also consider that our sample estimates could be wrong 5 per cent of the time. Most social science research uses a confidence level of 95 per cent.

Confidence interval

Confidence interval: The statistical range (interval) of our results within which we estimate the true population figure lies.

Next, combining the confidence level and the sample error we are able to estimate the **confidence interval** for our results. The confidence interval refers to the range, usually expressed in percentage points above and below, our sample result, where we estimate that the true population value actually lies. So it is the interval associated with a particular confidence level that encompasses the true population parameter we are seeking to estimate.

An example

Let's assume that a political scientist collected a sample of voters and asked questions about who they would vote for in the Australian House of Representatives if a federal election were to be held next Saturday. The political researcher draws a random sample from the most recent Australian electoral roll, and estimates the proportion of people who said they would vote for the Labor Party, and the proportion who claimed they would vote for the Coalition (Liberal and National) parties. In this hypothetical example, 54 per cent said they would vote Labor and 46 per cent for the Coalition (voting for other political parties is excluded here). But this result is from a sample, and we know the sample usually varies at least a little from the whole population. Working through this result from a sampling error, confidence level and confidence interval base allows us to estimate from this sample result what are the parameters of the actual or 'true' two-party voting intentions are in the population of Australian voters.

First the researcher needs to calculate the sampling error for this binomial voting variable (that is the variable where voters are counted as indicating whether they would vote Labour or Coalition). The sampling error in this case is calculated to be 1.8 percentage points. Without engaging in a detailed explanation of statistical concepts such as Z cores and the standard normal distribution, suffice to say the researcher then draws upon probability theory to calculate the confidence interval, or the range that encompasses the 'true' intended vote among our population of Australian voters. To construct a confidence interval for these proportion, with 95 per cent level of confidence, probability theory suggests that we multiply the sampling error by 1.96 (corresponding to a Z score of 1.96). The researcher then subtracts this result from the sample statistic (the estimated Labor vote of 54 per cent) to calculate the lower bound of the confidence interval (54 − [1.8 * 1.96] = 50.47), and add it to the sample statistic to calculate the upper bound (54 + [1.8 * 1.96] = 57.53).

So, as the Labor vote is estimated at 54 per cent, and the sample error at 1.8, at the 95 per cent confidence level, the confidence interval for the Labor vote is 54% ± approximately 3.5 percentage points, or between 50.5 and 57.5 percentage points. The 95 per cent confidence interval for the Coalition vote is 42.5 to 49.5 percentage points, so that the upper bound for the Coalition is less than the lower bound for Labor. As the confidence intervals for the two parties do not overlap, the researcher can say with 95 per cent confidence that the 'true' Labor vote in the population is somewhere between 50.5 and 57.5 per cent (that is, the lower bound is just over the magic 50 per cent), and therefore we could predict that Labor would win an election based upon these results.

The confidence level chosen by the researcher also has an impact upon the confidence intervals. If our political scientist wanted to be even more certain of the election outcome, the confidence level could be increased to 99 per cent. However, for a given sample error, if the confidence level is increased the confidence interval will widen, because, according to probability theory, at the 99 per cent level of confidence the sampling error should be multiplied by 2.58 (that is, by a Z score of 2.58).

At the 99 per cent confidence level, the confidence interval for Labor increases to 54 per cent ±4.6 percentage points, or between 49.4 to 58.6, and the Coalition between 41.4 and 50.6, so that the intervals for the parties now overlap. In other words, the researcher would not be able to predict with 99 per cent confidence that the Australian Labor Party would win the election, based on these results. In order to make a more accurate prediction of the intended vote at the 99 per cent level, the researcher would need a larger sample in order to reduce the size of the sampling error.

Bruce Tranter

Box 5.2: Sampling error

In the social sciences we are often interested in measuring variables that are categorical (nominal or ordinal level variables), such as the percentage of Australians who are in favour of Australia changing from a constitutional monarchy to a republic, how many consider themselves to be middle class, or participate in voluntary community organisations.

It is therefore useful to consider how to calculate standard errors (that is, sampling error) for proportions, and to construct a confidence interval around the proportion that encompasses the true population value (parameter) at a certain level of confidence. In statistical jargon, the standard error we are calculating is called the standard error for binomial variables.

$$SE = \sqrt{\frac{p \times q}{n}}$$

- *SE* is the standard error for the binomial distribution
- *p* is the percentage of the category of the variable we are interested in
- *q* is the percentage for the remaining category or categories of the variable of interest
- *n* is the sample size.

If we work though this simple formula we can see the importance of the heterogeneity or homogeneity of the variable in question and the size of the sample in the calculation of the standard error for proportions. For example, we have some data from the Australian Survey of Social Attitudes suggesting that the proportion of Australians who view climate change as an urgent environmental issue is approximately 82 per cent and the number of valid cases (sample size) is 2637.

We can use this information in our estimation of the standard error. With a sample size of 2637, the standard error would be the sqrt([82 * 18] ÷ 2,637) = 0.75 rounded. If, however, we had no idea of the proportion in the population we were interested in, we would assume a 50/50 split on the variable of interest, so that the standard error would increase in size to sqrt([50 * 50] ÷ 2,637) = 0.97.

While there is always some error associated with estimates of population parameters based on sample data, we can use the standard error (sampling error) to create confidence intervals around our estimates. Confidence intervals are statistics that can be used to make inferential claims about a population. Based on these environmental attitudes from the AuSSA data, we can be 95 per cent confident that concern over the urgency of climate change in the population of Australian adults is between 80.5 and 83.5 percentage points.

Probability sampling: Deciding on an appropriate sample size

The question everyone asks at some stage is: how many cases do we need in our sample? The answer is unsatisfying: it depends. While a detailed discussion of the calculation of sample size is beyond the scope of this chapter, the necessary probability sample size for any project is basically determined according to four factors: the amount of variation in key variables in the population; the confidence level set by the researcher; the amount of sampling error the researcher is prepared to tolerate; and the population size. There are formulas available for calculating suitable sample size based on these contingencies.

Other things being equal, larger samples produce smaller standard errors, and therefore provide us with more accurate estimates of our population parameters. As a rule of thumb, to reduce sampling error by half it is necessary to quadruple the sample size. For example, randomly drawing a sample of 100 university students to examine their attitudes toward an increase in student course fees would allow us to collect data on this topic, but the sampling error might be too large to allow us to make accurate estimates. Therefore, if our budget allows for the collection of a larger sample, it may be reasonable to increase the sample size to 400 cases. This would halve the sampling error.

Yet there is also a point where increasing sample size to reduce sampling error will provide diminishing returns. Other things being equal, a sample of 2500 has a sampling error of approximately ±2 percentage points. To reduce the sample error to ±1 percentage point would require a sample of 10,000 cases: a large increase in sample numbers for not much change in sampling error. Social researchers are usually prepared to tolerate sampling error of ±2 to 3 percentage points. This is why many academic researchers and public opinion pollsters tend to draw samples of between 1000 and 2000 cases; for example, the 2007 Australian Election Survey has 1783 cases. The confidence level also plays a role. Being able to claim with 95 per cent confidence that the 'true' population value (parameter) lies within our confidence intervals is generally acceptable. Being 99 per cent confident is more accurate, but the cost of increasing our sample size to achieve this level often may not be judged to be worth the additional expense.

The homogeneity or heterogeneity of a sample, in other words the amount of variation in key variables, is also an important consideration. For example, because of the way sampling error is calculated (see box 5.2), opinion pollsters who attempt to estimate voting intentions during a close election campaign where voting intention is assumed to be a homogeneous variable—when two parties each appear close to achieving 50 per cent of the vote—will require a relatively large sample to differentiate between the parties. Alternatively, when there is a lot of variation in a variable of interest (heterogeneity), such as the proportion of Australian adults who join environmental groups (around 7 per cent of

Bruce Tranter

Australian adults, according to the 2007 Australian Election Study), smaller samples can be used. Again, other things being equal, the more variation in the variables we are interested in studying, the smaller the required sample size.

Sample non-response

Sample non-response: The number of sample respondents who do not participate in the research.

A particular problem faced by survey researchers is referred to as **sample non-response**. This term covers the number of sample respondents, who, for whatever reasons, decide not to participate. (This topic is discussed in relation to surveys in chapter 6). Survey response rates have been declining in many countries (Porter 2004). In Australia, for example, the Australian Election Study has shown a decline in recent years. Large falls in response rates may dramatically increase the costs of conducting a survey. As response rates decrease, it is necessary to make more calls before securing each telephone interview and to send out larger numbers of surveys in the mail to achieve a sample of the desired size.

To calculate response rates, the sample size is reduced by the number of potential respondents who were either ineligible (did not complete the survey correctly or did not meet sample criteria) or who were unreachable (phone number disconnected or survey returned undelivered). This number is then used to divide the number of completed surveys and multiplied by 100 to attain a percentage. The formula is:

$$\text{Response rate} = \frac{\text{Number of surveys completed}}{\text{N in sample} - (\text{ineligible and unreachable})} \times 100$$

Sample non-response of itself is not necessarily an issue, but becomes a problem when non-respondents differ from respondents in a non-random manner. In studies of the general population, people who are unlikely to participate in surveys tend to be older and to have low levels of formal education (de Vaus 2002). The problem is that this introduces sampling bias, as samples drawn from the general population will be more highly educated and younger than the population from which they are drawn. Given that age and education are associated with many of the phenomena that survey researchers are typically interested in studying, such as social and political attitudes, the potential arises for estimates based upon such samples to be biased.

Weighting to adjust for sample non-response?

Weighting the responses is one possible action. Weighting is most often done to adjust the sample to be proportionately representative, such as for the whole of Australia, with correspondingly adjusted weighted responses for each state. For example, weighting was used in the data gathered in case study 5.1 to adjust between state and national level analyses. It is also possible to statistically adjust for sampling non-response by 'weighting' the sample. That is, we can adjust our data by multiplying the categories of particular variables by a factor so that the sample proportions for a given variable are the same as the proportions of the population parameter. This approach requires the researcher to select some key variables that are not representative of the population parameters; for example, demographic variables such as age, sex and education level can be compared with their respective parameters in the population from which the sample was drawn. Then variables are created to adjust the sample statistics so that they resemble the population parameters. As an example, we calculate from the 2006 Australian census data that the proportion of women aged 18 and over in Australia is 51.27 per cent and the percentage of adult men is 48.73 per cent. However, let's assume we have drawn a sample where 56 per cent of respondents are women and 44 per cent are men. Clearly, women are over-represented and men under-represented in our sample compared to the population.

Given that the 2006 census is population data, we can adjust our sample data by multiplying the proportion of men and women by a factor so the sample proportions for a given variable are the same as the proportions in the population. To do so, we divide the population proportions for men and women by the sample proportions for men and women as in table 5.1, to create a weight variable, then, using a statistical package such as SPSS, statistically adjust our sample estimates. In this example, we would reduce the proportion of women and increase the proportion of men in our sample so they resemble the population.

Weighting our sample according to key variables such as age, sex and education is particularly useful when our aim is to estimate summary statistics. As an illustration, to estimate the median income of Australians involved in paid work from a labour force participation survey, it would be important to first check the age, sex and education profile of our sample, because all of these variables have an influence upon income. On average, men tend to receive higher incomes than women, tertiary graduates earn more than non-graduates, and very young or old people are less likely to be involved in paid work and therefore to be on lower incomes. We could therefore weight your sample to reflect the age, sex and education profile of all Australian adults before estimating the median income.

Table 5.1: Calculation of simple weight variable for sex

Variable attribute	Population per cent	Sample per cent	Weight = (population % ÷ sample %)	Multiply sample proportion by weight	Weighted sample per cent
Women	51.27	56	0.9155	56 * 0.9155	51.27
Men	48.73	44	1.1075	44 * 1.1075	48.73

Bruce Tranter

Case study 5.2: Declining response rate in a mail survey: The Australian Election Study, 1987 to 2007

The longest running and most important academic social and political survey in Australia is the Australian Election Study (AES) series. The first academic attitudinal surveys in Australia, and precursors to the AES, were the Australian National Political Attitude surveys administered by Don Aitkin in 1967, 1969 and 1979. The AES has been administered as a self-completion mail out, mail back survey from the Australian National University by political scientists such as Roger Jones, and in more recent years, the team of Ian McAllister, Clive Bean, David Gow and their collaborators as the Principal Investigators.

The AES has been administered in a relatively consistent format at the time of every federal election since 1987, and contains a range of consistently worded behavioural and attitudinal questions on topics such as voting behaviour, election issues, environmental concerns and value orientations. By asking questions in an identical format at each election, researchers are able to examine changes in attitudes and behaviours over time; for example, how has the proportion of Australian adults who agree that abortion should be widely available changed between 1987 and 2007, or to what extent has the percentage of Australians who identify with a particular political party declined over time?

The AES formerly achieved impressive response rates, particularly for a mail survey, as the researchers have adopted a set of strategies in order to maximise responses. Samples were drawn systematically from the Australian Electoral Roll by the Australian Electoral Commission. Individually addressed envelopes containing questionnaires were sent to respondents on the Monday following each election, which is always held on a Saturday. The letters also contain a signed letter explaining the study, guaranteeing confidentiality for participants and a return envelope with postage paid. After one week a follow-up 'thank you/reminder' postcard was sent by letter, then after three weeks a second questionnaire, letter and return postpaid envelope were mailed to those who had not responded or had not asked to be excluded from the study (McAllister & Clark 2007:74).

In recent years, however, the response rate to the AES has declined quite sharply (see table 5.2). From high points of 63 per cent in 1987 and 1993, the response rate has declined since the late 1990s, dropping markedly from 55 per cent in 2001 to 45 per cent in 2004 and 40 per cent in 2007. While we can only speculate as to the reasons for the decline, it seems likely that the increase in telephone marketing and the plethora of surveys employed by commercially orientated social researchers have had an impact on the response rate of surveys such as the AES.

Table 5.2: Australian Election Study response rates

	1987	1990	1993	1996	1998	2001	2004	2007
Response rate per cent	62.8	58.0	62.8	61.8	57.7	55.4	44.5	40.2
Sample size	(1,825)	(2,020)	(3,023)	(1,795)	(1,896)	(2,010)	(1,769)	(1,873)

Sources: Australian Election Surveys (1987–2007)

Non-probability sampling

Despite its many advantages, probability sampling is not always possible, or necessary, for social research. For example, for research with victims of domestic violence, how would you access a random sample? Although domestic violence crisis centres might have lists of people who have been involved in domestic violence, the lists won't be close to being complete, and there is no feasible way of developing a complete list. People who mark their ballot invalid in elections is another example. In such circumstances, we can, and do, use non-probability sampling techniques; that is, select a sample without reference to probability theory. The most commonly used non-probability sampling methods are:

- convenience sampling
- purposive sampling
- snowball sampling
- quota sampling
- self-selected sampling.

Convenience sampling

Babbie (2005:189) refers to this method as 'reliance on available subjects'. It is also known as haphazard or opportunity sampling. **Convenience sampling** refers to sampling those who are easy to locate. Sampling the people you know, such as friends or relatives, or your classmates, are examples of convenience sampling. Conducting a vox pop by standing on street corner and asking anyone who passes by if you can interview that person is another. The popularity of this approach is related to the ease and inexpensive nature of data collection. However, these advantages are outweighed by the likelihood that the sample will be extremely unrepresentative. For example, we tend to know and mix with people like ourselves, while standing on a street corner will only allow you to meet people who happen to be walking past on that particular street at the time you are standing there. While convenience sample is an easy way of finding respondents for a research project, its lack of representativeness constrains the validity of the results.

> **Convenience sampling:** Convenience sampling is making up your sample of respondents from people who are easy to locate, such as your friends, family, students or classmates.

Bruce Tranter

Purposive sampling

Purposive sampling: Purposive sampling is selecting a sample in a systematic or purposive way, based on what we know about our target population and the purpose of our study.

In **purposive sampling**, the sample is selected based on what we know about the target population and the purpose of the study. The researcher exercises his or her judgment or knowledge of a population and the aims of the research to select a sample. For example, if we wanted to conduct a study of why people own firearms but do not have access to the government register of firearm owners, we could make a list of gun clubs. We could then approach each club and ask if we can interview their members. While a purposive sample of firearms owners may be more representative than a convenience sample of firearms owners, neither convenience nor purposive sampling would allow us to generalise our results to the wider population of gun owners. This is because we simply do not know how representative our sample is. However, purposive sampling is useful for certain applications. For example, in pilot testing of survey questions you may decide to select a wide range of respondents to test a new questionnaire (Babbie 2005:189). In such a case the representativeness of the sample is not an important consideration.

Snowball sampling

Snowball sampling: Used to access respondents from hard-to-reach groups by asking respondents to suggest other prospective respondents to the researcher.

Snowball sampling makes use of the respondents we do have to find other potential respondents. Snowball sampling is so called because, after making initial contact with participants referred to as 'informants' or 'gatekeepers', each respondent is asked to suggest other respondents, so that the sample grows like a snowball that expands in size as it rolls down a mountain. The technique is most appropriate when the aim is to collect data on a small number of respondents from difficult-to-reach groups where a sampling frame does not exist or the researcher does not have access to one. For example, in the author's honours research on environmental leaders in Tasmania (see 'From method to practice'), environmental activists who held positions in prominent environmental organisations were contacted initially as 'gatekeepers'. These gatekeepers then provided the author with the names of people who they identified as influential in the Tasmanian environmental movement. These leaders were subsequently interviewed and provided the names of other leaders, until considerable overlap occurred in the names that emerged and a sample was obtained (Tranter 1995). Snowball sampling will, by its nature, be unrepresentative of the population. However, as the technique is often used to locate members of a specific subgroup, sample representativeness is often not of primary concern.

Quota sampling

As in probability sampling, the aim in **quota sampling** is to attempt to draw a sample that is representative of the population we wish to study. Rather than using probability theory, however, quota sampling is an attempt to draw a representative sample on the basis of information about key variables in the population. The variables of interest in the population, such as gender, age or education, are defined, and a table or matrix is constructed based on the proportions for each of the categories of each key variable (for example, sex * age * education). Data are then collected, for example by ensuring interviewers fill the quotas for the proportions for each key variable (Barnett 1974). A big problem with quota sampling is that in many cases the population parameters are not known. However, even if accurate population data are available, selection bias can still occur. This is a potential problem in face-to-face interviewing, where interviewers are required to approach individual dwellings to interview the occupants, then use a quota system to sample those with particular characteristics. For example, the interviewer may need to interview 30 females aged between 18 and 30 to fulfil a quota, although bias may occur in the selection of households that are difficult to reach, or where the interviewer is concerned about his or her safety (Babbie 2002:196).

> **Quota sampling**: The development of a sample that is representative of a population by drawing a sample on the basis of population estimations of factors such as gender, age and education level.

Self-selected sampling

Self-selected sampling is where people are requested to make contact with the researchers to participate in a study. People self-select into the study. For example, television programs or newspapers that survey their audience by asking them to phone in or send SMS messages to express an opinion on a particular topic are self-selected samples (Maisel & Persell 1996:5). For more specific target populations, researchers might use newspaper advertisements or articles, or advertise on websites requesting that people who fulfil the criteria of the target population make contact with the researchers. The major limitation of self-selected sampling is the high potential for sample bias. Those people with a strong interest in the topic are most likely to self-select. For example, in a recent qualitative study of longer-term workers' compensation claimants' experiences (Welch et al. 2009), respondents self-selected into the study by answering newspaper advertisements. This sampling technique was successful in garnering a good number of willing respondents, but it also ensured that those interviewed tended to have strong feelings about different aspects of the workers' compensation process.

> **Self-selected sampling**: Where people self-select into a survey or study by making contact with a researcher or by choosing to respond to questions, such as in television programs or newspaper polls that ask people to register their opinion or vote.

Bruce Tranter

Case study 5.3: Child support and housing

A recent research project (Natalier et al. 2008) exploring how the payment or receipt of child support related to housing outcomes posed some interesting non-probability sampling issues. Semistructured in-depth interviews were conducted with 33 resident Parents Apart (those living with their children) and 27 non-resident Parents Apart (those living apart from their children). Respondents were sought from two states, Tasmania and Queensland, and concentrated in Brisbane. Participants were recruited through snowball sampling, posting flyers (self-selected sampling), and through contact with support groups (purposive sampling), who advertised the study to their members via email lists, mailouts and websites.

While the requisite Tasmanian sample was recruited relatively easily, the sample of parents from the Brisbane area was much harder to find. The researchers put the difference in ease of participant recruitment down to the more open social networks in the smaller towns and cities of Tasmania, where people are more likely to know each other, as opposed to the thinner social networks of a large city like Brisbane. The sampling was not designed to be representative of the broader population, but did reflect the broad array of social demographic and housing characteristics. The majority of respondents are concentrated in the 30–39 and 40–49 age categories, and most of the resident Parents Apart were female, while the majority of non-resident Parents Apart were male. It was also harder to recruit male respondents to the study than female respondents. Because the study sought to understand the meanings that resident and non-resident parents made of the relationship between paying or receiving child support to their housing, it was important that the numbers be relatively balanced.

Selecting sampling size for non-probability sampling

Deciding the appropriate sample size for non-probability sampling is both easier and harder than the same task in probability sampling. Unlike probability sampling, there is no formula to calculate the right size, and no 'right' answer to the 'how many?' question. In qualitative research, as outlined in chapter 10, sample sizes can legitimately vary from 100 or more respondents to just one.

Again, how many depends on the project question; your budget and time limits, and interviewing resources. For example, an honours student undertaking qualitative interviewing would probably interview between 8 and 15 respondents, whereas a PhD candidate might interview 40 or more. The 'right' number also depends on the saturation point for your key concepts. Saturation point is when the interviews or other data collection method you are undertaking are no longer revealing new information on meanings or understandings. When this point is reached depends on the question and concepts. Achieving saturation is the main idea in deciding what size sample you need for qualitative research. Remember that more is not necessarily better, and indeed may actually be worse. This is because qualitative data such as interview transcripts tend to be quite long (about 40 pages for an hour-long interview) and require intensive analysis (see chapter 14). The quality and rigour of your research is likely increased by analysing a smaller number of interviews thoroughly than a larger number but with less attention to detail.

When making this decision, it is often helpful to look at other research that has a similar methodology and topic or field as a guide of what an appropriate size sample would be.

Exercise 5.1: Sampling strategies

Imagine the following scenario:

You work as the manager of a community health centre in a regional area of 70,000 people. Your service employs two doctors full time and two nurses full time, with one focusing on diabetes and hypertension management and the other on general nursing work. Your service also provides regular access to a range of other services, including social work (two days per week), dentistry (one week per month), and podiatry (two days per month). Additionally, there is yourself as manager, one administrative staff member, and the receptionist. The hours of the centre are 9 a.m. to 5 p.m. Monday to Friday.

Your service is open to all members of your local community, and has been up and running for three years. The feedback you get from the community is mostly positive, although lately you have heard a few complaints, usually secondhand, about waiting times for some services, attitudes of some staff (but no specific instances) and the location of your service, which is in a suburban setting. You decide to try to evaluate how satisfied your clients are with the health centre so that you can gain a fuller picture of how your services are meeting the health needs of your community. You are considering whether a survey will be the most appropriate research method for this topic.

Bruce Tranter

Your research question

How satisfied are our patients with the health services they receive at the community health centre?

Obtaining a sample

You have now decided that the best way to gather the information you need to assess how satisfied your patients are with the health services they receive is to conduct a survey of your patients. The patient database at the health centre lists over 14,000 names and contact details of people who have been a patient at the centre at some time since it began its operation.

Task 1

- What will be your sampling unit for the survey? Are there other options?
- What might you use as your sampling frame? Again, are there other options?
- How will you define your population? In other words:
    - Will you include all patients or only those aged over 18?
    - Will you include all patients, or only those that have used all the health services?
    - Will you have separate populations for each health service?

Task 2

- Devise a sampling strategy to undertake your survey of your patients using:
    - a probability sampling technique
    - a non-probability sampling technique.
- For the probability sampling strategy, ensure you address the following questions:
    - How many cases do you need in your sample?
    - How would you ensure randomness and representativeness of your sample?
- For the non-probability sampling, ensure you address the following questions:
    - What type of non-probability sampling strategy would best suit?
    - How many cases might you want in your sample?
    - How would you ensure that your case selection is not biased?

Voices in the field

Wally Karnilowicz

Wally Karnilowicz is an academic within the School of Social Sciences and Psychology, Victoria University, Melbourne, Victoria. His major area of expertise is in Social Research Methods (quantitative and qualitative) with interests and research activity in Social Psychology, Cross-Cultural Psychology and Cultural Psychology. Wally's early work was in the area of stigma and how it related to notions of disability (behavioural and physical). More recently, his emphasis is on cultural psychology, and in particular examining notions of psychological ownership related to disease state. Consequently, this change in emphasis has resulted in a change in approach. Wally's earlier focus was on quantitative methods and its associated concerns with the determination of the problem, appropriate sampling, identification of groups and statistical modelling. This approach was also reflected in the work of a large number of his honours, masters and PhD students in that period of time. The latter focus on notions of ownership and disease state required a re-examination of appropriate methodologies, given the nature of the problem at hand. Psychological ownership as it relates disease state—such as breast cancer, prostate cancer and hepatitis C—is a unique and often individual experience. It tends to differ significantly in a qualitative sense between individuals, and considers cultural symbols and actions. To 'get at' the problem it is necessary to embed yourself within the experience and to inform and soak in what is happening around you. It seeks a non-critical 'I' and the skill is in informing one of 'what is?' Its primary purpose is not to seek universal truths but rather to assume a relativist stance. As such, it is an approach different to dominant positivist notions and quantitative research in Psychology. This is not to say that Wally has completely abandoned his quantitative roots. In fact, he is heavily and collaboratively involved in survey research with the Department of Human Services, Victoria, in their Neighbourhood Renewal Project. It is more to say that the question at hand drives the research process, and that each question needs to consider the appropriate epistemology and larger theory in harmony with the method.

Bruce Tranter

From method to practice

This next section details the sampling details of two recent Australian research projects, one quantitative, using probability sampling, and the other qualitative, using non-probability sampling processes.

The Australian Survey of Social Attitudes 2007

The 2007 Australian Survey of Social Attitudes (AuSSA) is the third in a biennial series that studies social attitudes and behaviour of Australian citizens for the Australian and international research community. The AuSSA collects cross-sectional data on the social attitudes and behaviour of Australians, repeating a core questionnaire for each cross-section and fielding specific modules relevant to the changing needs of the social research community. The 2007 survey includes questions on attitudes and behaviour organised into thirteen categories: Describing Australia; Role of government; Risk; Culture; Retirement; Private health insurance; Financial future; Aboriginality; Work; Gender; IVF technology and sex selection; Politics and society; and Personal background.

Random sampling of persons on the 2007 Australian Electoral Roll was used to access a sample of potential respondents. This sample was mailed a self-complete questionnaire to be returned by mail. The survey had three different subsamples—A, B and C. The details of sample numbers and outcomes for each of these is detailed in the box below. As can be seen, all three subsamples had similar response rates of around 40 per cent.

Table 5.3: AuSSA response rates and sample sizes

Sent	Subsample	Out of scope	Refusals	Never returned	Completed	Response rate (%)
6,666	A	348	905	2,631	2,782	42
6,666	B	374	837	2,686	2,769	41
6,666	C	348	921	2,814	2,583	39

Source: Australian Survey of Social Attitudes 2007

Action to minimise losses

A five-stage mailout was used. In week 1, potential respondents initially received an introductory letter informing them of the survey objectives and the researchers responsible for the survey. At week 2, respondents were sent a survey package that included a cover letter, information on how to complete the questionnaire, and the processes used to ensure confidentiality, a questionnaire booklet and a reply-paid envelope. The letter also included contact information for the survey administrators and for the Australian National University Ethics Committee, and the number of a toll-free telephone hotline run by trained archive staff for any queries about completing the questionnaire or the survey in general. In the third week, a reminder–thank you postcard was mailed to potential respondents who had not yet replied, encouraging them to complete the survey and reminding them that all responses are confidential. The reminder also included the number of the toll-free telephone hotline. Approximately two weeks after the reminder postcard was sent, a reminder package containing another copy of the questionnaire and a letter were sent out to those who had not responded, then a final reminder card after another week.

Source: Adapted from Phillips et al. 2008
For details of how to access the AuSSA dataset, visit the AuSSA website at <http://aussa.anu.edu.au>

What makes an environmental leader?

This study outlines a qualitative study of environmental leaders in Tasmania (Tranter 2009). As a follow-up study from earlier research on environmental leaders (Tranter 1995), semistructured interviews were conducted with a small sample (n = 13) of environmental leaders in 2002. The author used a form of 'snowball' sampling to identify the most important environmental leaders and to examine changes that had occurred in the Tasmanian environmental movement since the earlier study. Snowball sampling was an appropriate technique in this case, because the aim was not to draw a probability sample, but to select participants for a study where an appropriate sampling frame did not exist.

Several informants or 'gatekeepers' were identified as potential study participants in 2002. Initial contact was made with five 'gatekeepers' consisting of two position holders in environmental organisations, one Tasmanian Green politician, and two staff members who worked for Green politicians. This method of selecting an initial group of influential environmentalists as informants was based upon the assumption that those who occupied organisationsal positions were influential both within and to an extent beyond the environmental movement because of their strategic location in organisations.

The five informants were interviewed and asked to identify other influential Tasmanian environmentalists. Environmentalists who were identified by three or more gatekeepers were subsequently interviewed where possible. Using Green politicians and employees in environmental movement organisations as informants was an attempt to minimise a problem sometimes associated with the selection of snowball samples, where the use of only one or a few gatekeepers can introduce bias into the sampling process.

As a cross-check, the names of the initial 'positional leaders' also emerged consistently in the interviews. The sampling strategy adopted in this research may miss some influential leaders, for example, by oversampling high profile leaders and under-representing less visible but important leaders. Interviewing gatekeepers in environmental organisations, then snowball sampling, may also have resulted in a narrower focus on organisational-based leadership and downplayed the role of other movement leaders, although in the state of Tasmania, with its small population and limited number of influential environmentalists, these potential problems were viewed to be of relatively low risk.

Bruce Tranter

Conclusion

Main points

> For most social science research we use a sample rather than the whole population as our data source.

> Sampling is used because it is not practicable to survey all members of a given group; we can use probability samples to generalise our results back to our whole population; it is not necessary to survey a whole group to gain meaningful results; and for many units of analysis a complete list is not available.

> There are two main sampling methods: probability and non-probability sampling.

> Probability sampling selects our sample in accordance with probability theory. All elements in the population must be known, and each element must have a known chance of being selected.

> Sampling error, confidence levels and confidence intervals allow us to account for the differences between our sample and the whole population in probability sampling.

> Non-probability sampling is used mostly in qualitative research designs.

> Non-probability sampling is a range of sampling techniques, and includes: convenience sampling; purposive sampling; snowball sampling; quota sampling; and self-selected sampling.

> Which method is chosen and what size sample depends on the project.

Further reading

Maisel, R. and Persell, C. (1996). *How Sampling Works*. Thousand Oaks, CA: Pine Forge Press.

References

Australian Election Study (2008). Canberra: Australian National University <http://aes.anu.edu.au> Accessed 10 January 2008.

Babbie, E. (2002). *The Basics of Social Research* (2nd edn). Melbourne: Thomson Wadsworth.

Babbie, E. (2005). *The Basics of Social Research* (3rd edn). Belmont, CA: Thomson Wadsworth.

Barnett, V. (1974). *Elements of Sampling Theory*. London: English Universities Press.

Curtin, R., Presser, S. and Singer, E. (2005). 'Changes in Telephone Survey Nonresponse Over the Past Quarter Century', *Public Opinion Quarterly*, 69 (1): 87–98.

de Vaus, D. (2002). *Surveys in Social Research*. Sydney: Allen & Unwin.

Easthope, G., Beilby, J., Gill, G. and Tranter, B. (1998). 'Acupuncture in Australian General Practice: Practitioner Characteristics', *Medical Journal of Australia*, 169 (4): 197–200.

Gow, D., Bean, C. and McAllister, I. (2000). *Australian Constitutional Referendum Study, 1999*. Canberra: Social Science Data Archives, Australian National University.

McAllister, I. and Clark, J. (2007). *Trends in Australian Political Opinion: Results from the Australian Election Study 1987–2004*. Canberra: Australian National University.

Maisel, R. and Persell, C. (1996). *How Sampling Works*. Thousand Oaks, CA: Pine Forge Press.

Natalier, K, Walter, M., Wulff, M., Reynolds, M. and Hewitt, B. (2008). *Child Support and Housing Outcomes*, AHURI Final Report 113, Melbourne: Australian Housing and Urban Research Institute.

Phillips, T., Mitchell, D., Tranter, B., Clark, J. and Reed, K. (2008). *The Australian Survey of Social Attitudes, 2007*. Canberra: Australian Social Science Data Archive, Australian National University.

Porter, S. (2004). 'Raising Response Rates: What Works?', *New Directions for Institutional Research Special Issue: Overcoming Survey Research Problems*, 121: 5–21.

Tranter, B. (1995), 'Leadership in the Tasmanian Environmental Movement', *Australian and New Zealand Journal of Sociology*, 3: 83–93.

Tranter, B. (2009). 'Leadership and Change in the Tasmanian Environment Movement', *Leadership Quarterly* (forthcoming).

Welch, A., Walter, M. and Ezzy, D. (2009). *Long Term Benefits Study Workers Compensation Research Phase Two Research Report*. Hobart: School of Sociology and Social Work, University of Tasmania.

2

Quantitative Methods and the Power of the Numbers

For those approaching the quantitative methods of social research with trepidation, I need you to ask yourself if you have command of the following complex mathematical processes:

- addition
- subtraction
- division
- multiplication.

If you have, then social research methods involving numbers and statistical techniques are well within your grasp.

This is not to say you will be a master of the statistical universe at the end of these chapters, but that within them and between them, chapters 6 to 9 *will* equip you to collect and analyse quantitative data to a level of practical competence. The module on experiments and the quantitative analysis chapters included on the website <www.oup.com.au/orc/walter> add to this capacity. Combined, these chapters contain enough detail of the theory and practice of quantitative data collection and analysis to allow you to plan, design and implement basic quantitative research projects.

Not only is much of the practice of statistics relatively straightforward, but quality quantitative research can be achieved by the use of such statistical techniques. Complex statistical procedures are not a prerequisite for obtaining insightful and even groundbreaking quantitative results. As the mini-analyses in chapter 8 demonstrate, the basic and easily understood and performed statistical techniques of frequencies, percentages, means and medians, cross-tabular analysis and chi square provide sufficient statistical firepower to answer important social science research questions.

Quantitative data collection and analysis is typically associated with big picture research, and often big research projects. Designing, developing, implementing and analysing a nationally representative survey is not for the fainthearted, or those in a hurry, but there is strength in this approach. Examining trends, perspectives, attitudes, behaviours and knowledge at a national, state, subgroup or perhaps even global level allows us to make strong and often unique claims of associations, if not stronger links between various phenomena. At its heart, quantitative research is about comparisons and connections. For example, if researching loneliness, we not only want to know if people who live alone are lonely, we want to know if they are more likely to experience loneliness than those who live in other household types. And the requisites of meaningful comparison explain why quantitative research methods tend to be highly structured in their process and their practice. To compare the responses of respondents' living on their own with those living in a couple household, we need to be sure the same questions were asked in the same way and under the same (or as similar as possible) circumstances.

As most quantitative data is founded on the content of questionnaires, either collected by the researcher or others, chapter 6 provides an overview of selecting, planning, designing and implementing data collection using a survey. The material in this chapter is important not only from a pragmatic 'how to' of survey implementation, but because understanding the process, format and survey type by which the data were obtained is a crucial aspect of conducting analysis. Valid and robust use of specific techniques, as outlined in chapters 8 and 9, is predicated on understanding a range of factors about the research. These include: what type of data we have; the overarching question of the original research project; the individual question items that make up the survey (and not just the ones we want to use); the way the data were collected; what sampling methods were used to obtain the sample; the representativeness of the final sample; and details such as response rate and timing of data collection. This comprehensive list of necessary knowledge emphasises the key point that all quantitative data have context—social, political, temporal and technical—and this context is an integral part of the analysis. For the datasets we access from other sources, such as those from the Australian Social Science Data archives, most if not all of this information will be contained in the Data Codebook. If we collect our own data we must ensure we record and report all the contextual details.

There is a tendency from non-practitioners to view quantitative methods as essentially variations of the same method. Chapter 7, relating to demographic analysis, demonstrates that this is patently not the case. Population level analysis also uses statistics, but quite differently and on different types of data than outlined in the survey and other data analysis chapters. This chapter demonstrates that not only does quantitative data and analysis come in different types (note that content analysis and evaluation analyses, from part 3, also can involve statistical analysis), but also reminds us of the scope of numerical information to provide meaningful, reliable and rigorous social research results and outcomes. The power of the numbers is indeed significant.

Chapter 6

Surveys

Maggie Walter

Why a survey?

- What are the financial, social and health outcomes for longer-term workers' compensation claimants?
- What are the social attitudes of Australians? How are these changing?
- When do older Australian workers intend to retire, and what motivations might induce them to remain in the labour force for longer?
- What do Aboriginal and Torres Strait Islander children need to have the best start in life to grow up strong?
- How does the paying or receiving of child support have an impact on parents' ability to afford housing suitable for their children?

To answer these and other burning questions, social scientists associated with this text have selected a survey as their research method for data collection.

Sources: Ezzy et al. 2008; Gibson et al. 2003; Walter et al. 2008; FaCS 2004; Natalier et al. 2008

Key terms

closed questions
cross-sectional design
longitudinal studies
one-shot case study
open-ended questions
panel study
quasi-panel study
questionnaire
researcher-administered survey
self-administered survey

Introduction

Surveys are a basic tool in the social researcher's method kit. Technically, surveys are a specific research method distinguished by the structured form of the data collection and by a case-comparative method of analysis (de Vaus 1995). More simply, survey research is the collection and analysis of respondents' (people, organisation or other group who respond to the survey) answers to the same set of structured questions.

Have you ever participated in a survey? Nearly everyone has. Surveys are probably the most widely used research method, and their conduct and results are a familiar backdrop to our social world. An examination of any daily paper will usually yield at least one article based around a survey. This widespread use of surveys is a testament to their value as a research method. The popularity of survey research, however, does not equate to surveys being an easy or generic way of investigating social questions. While a survey will always provide some data, it is relatively easy to conduct a survey that generates results that are misleading or of limited value. An effective survey requires substantial planning and the sequential use of specific skills across all its major phases. In this chapter, we concentrate on the development and implementation phases of a survey-based research project. Analysis and interpretation are discussed in chapter 8.

Choosing a survey as your social research method

Social sciences regularly use surveys as a primary way to gather data for social analysis. A survey can form the major data-collection and research tool of a research project, providing the data to answer the key research questions or as a secondary method, collecting preliminary or base data on the topic of interest. However, before we can decide if a survey is the most appropriate research method to answer our specific research question, we need to have an understanding of both the strengths and weaknesses of this type of research.

Advantages of surveys

Surveys have some distinct advantages as a social research method.

Surveys are versatile

Surveys can be used to investigate a wide array of topics, from varying perspectives and across a range of different respondents. In their structured format, surveys are a good way to collect information on people's characteristics, attitudes, values, beliefs, behaviour and opinions. For example, a survey on employment might ask not only what occupation a respondent holds, but also assess future employment aspirations. Respondents to surveys can be individuals, households, organisations or other social entities.

Surveys are efficient at collecting large-scale data

Surveys can collect a lot of information from a large sample in a relatively short period of time. The set nature of survey questions means that the survey can be conducted using a range of measures that facilitate rapid data collection. Mail or email **questionnaires** can all be posted together, and for telephone or face-to-face surveys, many interviewers can be employed to concurrently collect the data. For example, in the Australian Bureau of Statistics' (ABS) General Social Survey, face-to-face interviews were conducted by what must have been a small army of interviewers, at around 15,500 dwellings between March and July 2002 (ABS 2002).

Questionnaire: Structured set of questions administered (via mail, internet, telephone, personal interview or other method) to a group of survey respondents.

Surveys allow us to study large populations

A key advantage of surveys is that a well-designed random sample survey can provide reliable and valid information on a large population from a comparatively small sample of respondents. Importantly, the results from representative random sample surveys can be generalised to the whole of the population being studied. For example, in the Australian Election Studies (AES) (1987–2007), a stratified random sample of around 2000 provides information on the political attitudes and choices of the whole population of Australian voters.

Survey data is conducive to statistical analysis techniques

The comparative nature of survey data means that relationships between different variables in the data can be identified and analysed using statistical analysis techniques, allowing a wide range of robust results. For example, in a representative survey, if we examined attitudes to gun ownership variables, we would not only be able to assess the predominant Australian gun-use attitudes, we would also be able to explore subgroup variations; for example, do residents from urban regions vary in their attitudes towards gun ownership from those from rural regions?

Surveys facilitate secondary data analysis

The data set generated by a survey can be analysed by researchers other than the original conductor of the survey. This extra use by other researchers of collected survey data is referred to as **secondary data analysis**, and can often provide new and previously unconsidered insights into the survey's basic topic or subject matter. For example, the ABS makes many of its survey data sets available to academic and other researchers in the form of Confidentialised Unit Record Files (CURF). See chapter 9 for more details on secondary data analysis.

Secondary data analysis: The methods and techniques involved in analysing a set of raw survey data to which a researcher has been granted access by a social science data archive.

Maggie Walter

Disadvantages of surveys

The traffic on surveys, however, is not all one way. Surveys, as a social science research method, also have some weaknesses and drawbacks, and these need to be borne in mind during the design, implementation and analysis stages of the survey.

Survey data are (mostly) snapshot, not constant

Most survey data are collected at a specific time and, therefore, are reflective of this time rather than being a fixed phenomenon. For example, the results of a survey that examined the patterns of cohabitation among young Australians in 1975 would probably be very different to a similar survey conducted in 2009. While this means that survey data can become quickly out of date, this moment-in-time factor can also be a strength when comparing panel or repeat cross-sectional survey data. In the example above, the change in the patterns between 1975 and 2009 would itself provide a very interesting analysis.

Survey data are self-report data

Survey data rely on people's perceptions, attitudes or memories, and, therefore, must be viewed as essentially subjective. Questions are also answered within their social context, and sometimes respondents can be influenced by what they want us to hear, or sometimes even what they think we want to hear. For example, responses to a survey asking adolescents about their use of alcohol might be influenced by bravado on the part of some, as well as minimisation on the part of other respondents. Subjectivity does not negate the value of survey data, but neither can survey data be regarded, unambiguously, as 'fact'.

Establishing a relationship does not equal establishing causality

Survey data can establish statistical relationships between variables, but this is not the same as establishing causality. That is, a relationship between two variables, no matter how strong, does not indicate that one is the cause of the other. For example, a survey of car preferences might establish that women are more likely to drive yellow cars and men more likely to drive red cars, but this does not mean that being a man causes you to drive a red car, or that driving a red car causes you to be a man.

Surveys cannot provide adequate answers for all research questions

Not all research questions are amenable to be fully answered by a survey. For example, if we want to find out how the families of disabled children cope with the different stages of childhood, a survey would probably only provide limited insight into this question.

Would we be able to measure 'coping' in any meaningful way? Even if we could measure 'coping', would the data collected be the most effective way of gaining an insight into this issue?

Surveys are a relatively expensive method of data collection

Collecting survey data is relatively expensive in money and time terms (for researchers and respondents). Before selecting a survey, we need to ensure that the data either has not been already collected in other formats or cannot be obtained more cheaply by other research methods. For example, rather than surveying workers' compensation claimants to assess the return-to-work rates, a case-file study could achieve a similar, cheaper, quicker result with less intrusion into workers' lives.

Common types of survey design

Survey designs come in an array of types and levels of complexity. Which design type you select depends on the question your research seeks to answer and the resources available. The range of the most commonly used survey designs is listed below in order of increasing complexity. While the more complex the survey the more expensive in time and money, the increased usability and versatility of the results can make the additional expense worthwhile.

One-shot case study

A **one-shot case study** collects information from one group of respondents at one point in time. An example is data collected from members of a student union at a specific university on their attitudes towards building a new student bar. This method is relatively simple, and will provide information suitable to the purpose of the survey. But because the sample is not representative, broader conclusions cannot be made about the attitudes of student union members.

> **One-shot case study:** A survey that collects information from a specific group of people at one point in time.

Cross-sectional design

Cross-sectional design surveys are the most common survey type. In a cross-sectional design, a randomly drawn representative sample is used to survey a cross-section of the target population being studied. Cross-sectional surveys are 'point in time' data collections; that is, data collected once, from one group of respondents. Therefore, although the results of cross-sectional surveys can often be generalised to a whole population, their data cannot be used to make causal inferences.

> **Cross-sectional design:** A survey of a cross-section of a population conducted at one point in time.

Maggie Walter

Longitudinal studies

Longitudinal study: A study that collects data on the same phenomena over an extended period of time.

Longitudinal studies are designed to collect data on the same phenomena over an extended period of time. They are usually large, expensive and long running, but the quality and the value of the data is often much higher. In some countries, longitudinal studies have been in operation over many years. For example, the New Zealand Christchurch Health and Development Study (2005) has studied the health, education and development of a cohort of 1265 children for the past 25 years. Australia is a relative newcomer in this area, with longitudinal surveys only beginning in the 1990s or later. Australian longitudinal surveys include the Negotiating the Lifecourse Project (NLC) 1996 onwards, the Household, Income and Labour Dynamics (HILDA) survey, 2001 onwards and the Longitudinal Study of Indigenous Children (LSIC) 2008 onwards.

Longitudinal studies also come in a variety of designs.

Panel study

Panel study: A study designed to repeatedly survey the same sample group at set periods of time in order to measure changes in key variables.

A **panel study** surveys the same sample at different periods of time. The major value of this type of study is the ability to use the data collected to observe and measure changes in key variables over time. The HILDA survey is a major Australian panel study. Beginning in 2001 with an initial sample of 13,969 cases, HILDA collects a new wave of data annually.

Quasi-panel study

Quasi-panel study: A study designed to repeatedly survey samples of a target population on the same phenomena over time. Differs from a panel study in that the survey respondents are not from the same sample group each time.

Similar to a panel study, a **quasi-panel study** conducts repeated surveys on the same topic area over time. The difference is that each survey is conducted using a different sample. The approach avoids the problems inherent in maintaining the same sample of survey respondents over an extended period of time and the loss of respondents from the sample group over the life of the study. An example is the Australian Election Study, running since 1988, which surveys around 2000 people at the time of each federal election across a wide variety of electoral and social issues, allowing changes in attitudes and opinions, and their associated demographic and social characteristics, to be tracked.

The process of survey research

As shown in the following diagram, the process of survey research can be conceived of as a set of related, sequential steps, beginning with formulation of the research topic.

Stage 1: Research formulation and method selection
- Develop primary research question(s) first
- Define core concepts
- Check a survey is the best research method to answer your question

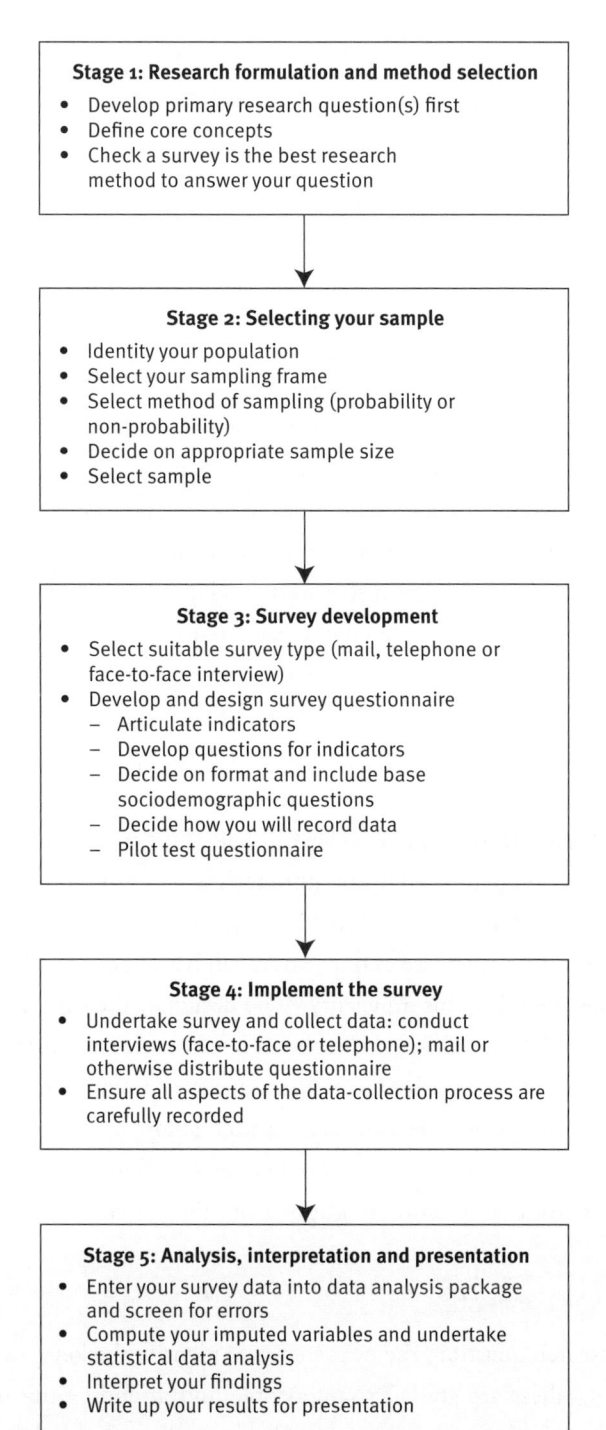

Stage 2: Selecting your sample
- Identity your population
- Select your sampling frame
- Select method of sampling (probability or non-probability)
- Decide on appropriate sample size
- Select sample

Stage 3: Survey development
- Select suitable survey type (mail, telephone or face-to-face interview)
- Develop and design survey questionnaire
    - Articulate indicators
    - Develop questions for indicators
    - Decide on format and include base sociodemographic questions
    - Decide how you will record data
    - Pilot test questionnaire

Stage 4: Implement the survey
- Undertake survey and collect data: conduct interviews (face-to-face or telephone); mail or otherwise distribute questionnaire
- Ensure all aspects of the data-collection process are carefully recorded

Stage 5: Analysis, interpretation and presentation
- Enter your survey data into data analysis package and screen for errors
- Compute your imputed variables and undertake statistical data analysis
- Interpret your findings
- Write up your results for presentation

Figure 6.1: The survey research process

Maggie Walter

Stage 1: Research formulation and method selection

We have already identified our key research area and undertaken our literature review. In stage 1 of the survey process, we need to take these steps:

- develop the primary research question(s) first
- conceptualise our key concepts
- decide if a survey is the most appropriate method to answer the research question(s).

Develop the primary research question(s) first!

A basic, but often disastrous, survey design error is to develop the survey instrument before identifying exactly the research question the survey itself is to answer. Whenever I am asked to review a survey questionnaire I immediately ask for the research question so I can assess whether the survey will do the job for which it has been designed. Amazingly, quite often a research question has not been formulated. Instead, what tends to happen is that once a survey is considered for a topic, the researcher rushes into developing survey questions. But there is an absolutely essential difference between the research question(s) and the survey questions.

To illustrate this difference, and other key aspects of survey development and design, we will use an example around study habits. Imagine that you have noticed that your male and female friends at university tend to study differently and theorise that study habits might have a gendered dimension. You are interested enough in the phenomenon to search for previous research on this topic and also have a look at theories and concepts around 'doing gender' in education (this is your literature review). You find only limited evidence to support your theory, so you decide to research the topic for a survey unit you are taking next semester. You work out that your research question will be: 'Is gender a factor in study habits among young people attending this university?' The design of the survey will therefore focus on providing the data to answer this research question. If you, instead of formulating a research question, had moved straight to writing survey questions from your topic, you are likely to have ended up with a whole lot of data around study habits, but probably not the data to answer with any validity whether or not gender is a factor. You would be left trying to work out what the research question might be from the answers, rather than the other way around.

Conceptualising key concepts

Once you have a research question, the next step is to identify the key concepts. In the example we are using, these are 'study', 'young people' and 'attending this university'. With a defined research question, this is the easy bit. Conceptualising, unambiguously defining what we mean by these concepts for our example research project, as per chapter 2, tends to be bit more work. It is hard to overemphasise the importance of having your core concepts unambiguously defined before moving on. Unless they are absolutely clear, you risk your survey becoming muddled further down the process.

So, to begin, what do you mean by young people? Given that most don't start university until age 18 or 19 and most have completed by age 24, you might restrict the age group to those aged 18–24 years inclusive.

How would you conceptualise 'study'? Do you only mean doing assignments, or other study, such as preparing for tutorials and/or studying for exams? People are likely to have very different study habits across these, so to reduce the complexity of the project, you might restrict study to mean doing assignments only. The next concept, 'attending this university', is fairly clearcut—a person is either attending this university or not—but do you mean only full-time students or include part-time students as well? Do you mean only undergraduates? You decide to conceptualise attending this university to mean students enrolled full time (part-time students may study differently) in an undergraduate degree course, and operationalise 'enrolled' as enrolled at the university census date. This means someone who is enrolled full time in an engineering–commerce degree would be included, but someone completing an honours degree in anthropology would not.

Deciding if a survey is the best research method

The popularity of surveys can sometimes mean that the method is selected without adequate consideration of whether a survey is the best method for a project. Using the method selection model from chapter 2 as a guide, we need to ensure that conducting a survey is the best way to answer the specific research question from a social science, timewise and costwise, and from a feasibility perspective. Referring back to our study habits project, a survey would seem to be the most effective research method, according to all three criteria.

Stage 2: Selecting your sample

- Identify the survey population, sampling frame and type of sampling.
- Decide on an appropriate sample size and select the sample.

In this stage we begin by identifying the survey population. Remember from chapter 5, in this context the survey population is the term used to describe that finite set of cases or elements you wish to study. Using the study habits example, based on your research questions and conceptualisations, your survey population is quickly identified: all full-time students enrolled in an undergraduate degree at this university at census date aged 18 to 24 years. The total undergraduate population fitting these criteria is around 12,000, so you need to select a sample. The sampling frame, listing all cases, is the enrolment records of the

Maggie Walter

university, allowing probability sampling. Assuming that you have permission to access this list (and this is a fairly heroic assumption) and based on the details on sampling sizes from chapter 5, you decide on a sample of 1000 students. The helpful university IT unit will agree to run a random sample of 1000 students for you.

Exercise 6.1: Deciding to use a survey

Research background

As in the example in chapter 5, you work as the manager of a community health centre in town X. The details are repeated for this survey question exercise.

Your service employs two doctors full time and two nurses full time, with one focusing on diabetes and hypertension management and the other on general nursing work. Your service also provides regular access to a range of other services including social work (two days per week), dentistry (one week per month), and podiatry (two days per month). Additionally, there is yourself as manager, one administrative staff member and the receptionist. The hours of the centre are 9 a.m. to 5 p.m. Monday to Friday.

Your service is open to all members of your local community, and has been up and running for three years. The feedback you get from the community is mostly positive, although lately you have heard a few complaints, usually second-hand, about waiting times for some services, attitudes of some staff (but no specific instances) and the location of your service, which is in a suburban setting. You decide to try to evaluate how satisfied your clients are with the health centre so that you can gain a fuller picture of how your services are meeting the health needs of your community. You are considering whether a survey will be the most appropriate research method for this topic.

Your research question

How satisfied are our patients with the health services they receive at the community health centre?

Task

In groups, answer the following questions:
1. Is a survey an appropriate way to answer this research question?
   a. Is it the best method?
   b. Are there alternatives to conducting a survey?
   c. What considerations would you need to take into account?
2. Outline the advantages or disadvantages of using a survey as the key research method in this research situation.

3   What possible subresearch questions (not survey questions) might be added to the overarching research question? What types of survey design could you use to conduct this survey?
4   What would be the advantages or limitations of using each major type of survey data collection outlined in the next segment?
5   For both strategies, what would change depending on the type of survey you select to collect your data:
    a   telephone interview?
    b   face-to-face interview?
    c   mailed questionnaire?

Stage 3: Survey development

Stage 3 of the survey process is where decisions are made about the design of the survey questionnaire and the data-collection format. As per the survey research process diagram, the key steps are:

- Select the most suitable survey type (mail or internet, face-to-face, or telephone interviews).
- Develop the survey questionnaire:
    - Articulate what things you need to know to answer your overall research question(s)
    - Develop indicators that operationalise these dimensions
    - Develop specific questions that directly gather the information on these indicators
    - Select the best question type and format for each question or set of questions
    - Include your base of sociodemographic questions
    - Decide on the best question sequence and layout.
- Plan how to record your data.
- Pilot or pre-test the survey questionnaire, adjusting as necessary.

Select the most suitable survey data collection type

Data collection in surveys falls into three basic types: face-to-face interviews; telephone interviews; or questionnaires delivered (by mail or electronically) for the respondent to complete. The 'best' type depends on the questions you want answered, who you want to answer them, your resources, and your time frame. For your study habits survey, you know that the members of your sample are likely to have good technology skills, and you have their email addresses, so you would probably choose a self-administered survey, delivered and returned electronically.

Maggie Walter

Self-administered surveys

Self-administered survey: A survey where the respondent undertakes the survey without direct interviewer guidance, such as in mail or internet surveys.

Self-administered surveys are where the respondent undertakes the survey without direct interviewer guidance, as in mail or internet surveys. The Australian Election Study (AES) is an example of a nationally representative mail survey. The AES uses a stratified random sample drawn from the Commonwealth electoral roll.

In a self-administered survey, the questionnaire is mailed or delivered in some other way to a potential respondent. A letter of introduction, explanation of the rationale and purpose of the survey, and why the respondent should complete the questionnaire should accompany the survey form. The respondent is asked in the letter to return the completed survey either by mail or, perhaps, to submit online.

Despite the lack of direct interviewer contact, self-administered surveys have relatively high rates of return. For example, in the 2001 AES survey, 4000 questionnaires were mailed to respondents. Of these 215 were 'return to sender', and for 154 more, the sample person was overseas, deceased or otherwise incapable. Of the remaining 3631 questionnaires, 2010 were returned completed; a response rate of 55 per cent (Bean et al. 2001). As noted in chapter 5, the response rate equals the proportion of the total number of surveys delivered minus those who are unreachable or otherwise ineligible.

Self-administered surveys have significant advantages and disadvantages when compared to phone or face-to-face interviews. These are outlined in table 6.1.

Designing a self-administered survey: mail or internet

The question topic, format and construction are all vital aspects of questionnaire design, and there are some tried and true rules for this type of survey design. You need to ensure the questionnaire has a professional, attractive, easy-to-follow and not-too-cramped layout. Design the front cover of the survey to look interesting and to grab the potential respondents' interest. Ensure that each question is accompanied by clear, concise instructions. To encourage completion, you need to make answering the questions as easy as possible. Use multiple choice responses with tick boxes, or other easily answered formats, and keep the number of open-ended questions or those requiring more complex written responses to a minimum. Always provide space for any additional comments your respondents might want to make, and ensure that you thank them for participation.

Maximising mail or internet survey response rates

Response rates can be problematic with self-administered surveys. Engaging respondents is therefore crucial. Asking potential respondents to complete a (usually) unsolicited survey form is a significant request, and you need to be mindful that what may be important to you is not necessarily at all important to the sample group. In a self-administered survey,

Table 6.1: Features of self-administered surveys

Self-administered surveys: Mail, internet, or email questionnaires	
Upsides of self-administered surveys as a data-collection method	Downsides of self-administered surveys as a data-collection method
The cheapest survey data-collection method in time and money.	The lowest response rates of the three main survey data-collection methods.
A high level of respondent anonymity, and may encourage more honest answers around sensitive topics.	Tend to have more missing data, especially on questions requiring open or more detailed responses.
As there is no interviewer, self-administered surveys are not subject to problems of interviewer influence or bias.	Often require up to three mailings of the questionnaire—the original and two follow-up mailings—to achieve a satisfactory response rate.
Can include all major question types, including open-ended questions.	Can be prone to providing a biased sample, as participation is easy to refuse and the less literate or those not confident in English are less likely to complete and return the survey form.
Are easily and relatively rapidly distributed to potential respondents.	Researcher cannot be sure that the respondent has not misinterpreted the questions.
Are less confrontational and less immediate for respondents. Respondents can complete the survey in their own time, taking time to consider their answers or even alter them on further consideration.	Probing is not possible. This means that questions may not be answered as fully as with telephone or face-to-face interviews or that more nuanced responses may be missed.

your contact is usually limited to a letter accompanying the survey form. This letter needs to be short, dated and written on your organisation's letterhead. Long, complex or unofficial-looking letters are less likely to be read.

While short, the letter needs to be very carefully written to encourage maximum respondent interest. The letter should:

- explain the purpose and the value of the survey
- respectfully request the respondent's participation
- guarantee the confidentiality of returned surveys and advise how the survey results will be used
- provide the researcher's contact details
- where applicable, include the contact details for the approving ethics committee
- if at all possible, let respondents know when and how they can access a summary of the survey's results.

By completing and returning the survey form, respondents become important stakeholders and should be a partner in the results of their investment in time and information.

Timing is important. Do not send questionnaires during major holiday periods such as Christmas or Easter. Also, always remember to include a postage-paid, researcher-addressed envelope big enough to easily fit the completed survey form to encourage survey return mailings.

Managing the process and follow-up mailings

Monitoring the return of surveys is part of the data-collection process. Each return should be opened, visually scanned, assigned a sequential identifying number, and the date of return recorded. This allows both the pattern and rate of return to be monitored. It also means that patterns in responses and timing can be identified. For example, if a survey examining attitudes to personal safety and storms had been sent out in the month before the 2006 Asian tsunami, the responses returned prior to that event would likely have been different from those completed after that date.

To achieve acceptable response rates, follow-up mailings are generally required, and Salant and Dillman (1994:138) suggest three mailings of the questionnaire—the original and two follow-ups—as the most efficient practice. If the identity of non-respondents is known, send follow-up questionnaires, accompanied by an encouraging accompanying letter to that group only. If non-respondents cannot be identified, resend a copy of the questionnaire to the entire sample, ensuring that the accompanying letter makes clear that the mailing is only aimed at those who have not already responded.

Researcher-administered surveys

Researcher-administered survey: A survey where the researcher completes the questionnaire from the respondents' answers, as in face-to-face or telephone interviews.

Researcher-administered surveys are those where the researcher completes the questionnaire from the respondents' answers, as in face-to-face or telephone interviews. The Negotiating the Lifecourse (NLC) Project, with an original sample of 2231, is an example of a successful telephone interview-based panel survey. The HILDA survey is a larger panel study, with an initial sample of 13,969 cases, and uses face-to-face interviews to gather the survey data.

Researcher-administered interview surveys have both advantages and disadvantages.

Telephone surveys

Cost and speed of data collection are likely to be the major factor when choosing to interview by phone. Telephone interviewing is comparatively cheap and fast, with interviewers being able to make many phone calls in the time that it takes to set up or conduct one face-to-face interview. The relative anonymity of a telephone interview can also assist surveying on sensitive issues. On the downside, response rates are lower. Telephone interviews are relatively easy to end or avoid, and are likely to miss certain types

Table 6.2: Features of researcher-administered surveys

Researcher-administered surveys: Telephone and face-to-face interviews	
Upsides of researcher-administered surveys as a data-collection method	**Downsides of researcher-administered surveys as a data-collection method**
Flexible in the types of question and the way questions can be asked. Face-to-face interviews offer more question flexibility than phone interviews. For example, visual aids and question surveys are more expensive than telephone surveys.	Requirement for multiple interviewers in larger researcher-administered surveys can both increase time and financial costs. Face-to-face cards are often used in face-to-face interviews.
Less prone to question misinterpretation, as the interviewer can check or correct the respondents' understanding as the interview progresses.	Can be subject to interviewer influence in the respondents' answers or interviewer bias in the recording of responses.
Offer immediate and direct access to potential respondents. This immediacy and proximity operate to increase response rates.	The actual presence of the interviewer on the phone or face to face may reduce response honesty, or produce responses influenced by social desirability.
Allow the researcher–interviewer to address respondents' queries and concerns directly, and thus increase response rate and respondent ease.	The use of multiple interviewers can increase risk of variability in the way the survey interview is conducted and, therefore, the comparability of the data.

of respondents. The rising use of mobile phones to replace, rather than supplement, the traditional household landline, especially among less settled households, means possible sample bias needs to be considered.

Larger phone surveys mostly use **computer assisted telephone interviewing (CATI)**. The CATI system manages the contacting, the conduct and the recording of the responses through the one system, leading to significant efficiencies in time, survey processes and data coding. The interviewer reads the survey questions, including appropriate introductory comments, prompts and contingencies, directly from a computer screen, and then enters the responses straight into the survey database. The CATI system is also used to select a random sample. With random digit dialling, numbers are randomly dialled by the computer in the sequences that make up telephone numbers. This system also overcomes the problem of unlisted numbers, as all numbers have an equal chance of being called.

> **Computer assisted telephone interviewing (CATI):** is widely used in telephone surveys to direct the interviewer's questioning and to allow responses to be directly input into the survey database.

Maximising response rates from telephone interviews

As for maximising all survey responses, the key is in design attention to detail, timing and engaging with the respondent.

The practice of telemarketers cold-calling people, especially around meal times, means many people are suspicious of survey calls and/or resistant to giving up their time to participate. It is therefore important that interviewers introduce themselves and their institution immediately to establish that the call is a legitimate research survey and why it is important. Another worthwhile strategy, if the names and addresses of those to be phoned is known, is to send a letter in advance, telling the respondent about the survey and the approximate time of the call. As an example, in a pilot survey of longer-term workers' compensation claimants in Tasmania, we sent information sheets a week before the survey. Around 20 per cent of those contacted took advantage of the opportunity to decline participation in advance, but the other interviews proceeded, with most of those called being available and willing to be interviewed. Another few respondents contacted the survey phone number in advance to arrange a more suitable time for the survey interview. However, for most telephone surveys, a list of respondents is not available.

Survey research guides usually recommend that each respondent be phoned up to four times, varying the time of the calls. Matching the time of the calls to the survey population is also important. For example, in a recent national survey on retirement intentions, we timed our calls for weekends and week evenings, as all survey respondents needed to be in the labour market. While this limitation on the 'who' of respondents meant that the survey data collection period took longer, the end result—valid, specific survey data—was worth the effort.

Face-to-face interviews

Face-to-face interview surveys have the best reputation for response rates and the quality and flexibility of the data gathered, but are the most expensive in time and money. For large studies, comprising hundreds or thousands of interviews, researchers usually employ and train interviewing staff for the task. In line with the structured comparative nature of survey research, face-to-face surveys should be completed in a standardised way, but this aspect is more difficult for this data collection method, as the context and circumstances of the interview are unlikely to be standard. To minimise interviewer bias, interviewers usually have very strict instructions to follow on how to present themselves and how to administer the questionnaire.

In face-to-face interviewing, observation data can also be gathered. The interviewer is physically present with respondents during the interview, and can note items such as the respondent's housing or interview circumstances. For example, the HILDA survey has a section in its 'Person questionnaire' that the interviewer must complete immediately on leaving the respondent's home. This section asks questions such as:

Computer assisted interviewing (CAI): is used to collect, store and transmit data collected by interviewers in personal (face-to-face) survey interviews.

Were there any other adults present during the interview?
How much do you think they influenced the answers? (HILDA 2001)

Computer assisted interviewing (CAI) is increasingly used in face-to-face interviewing. CAI is similar to CATI, in that the interview questions, including introductory comments, prompts and contingency questions are asked by the interviewer from a portable computer screen, rather than a paper questionnaire, and the responses are recorded directly into the survey database by the interviewer. The General Social Survey conducted by the Australian Bureau of Statistics in 2002 used a CAI system to collect, store and transmit data on the face-to-face interviews conducted with the survey's respondents (ABS 2003). The benefits of CAI are that the sequencing of the survey is performed automatically, and the appropriate wording for the questions is automatically displayed. These features allow greater consistency between interviews.

Technology is also being used to enhance the survey process from the respondents' perspective. Touch pad designs are being used, where respondents can both be asked the question (often in several languages) and record their answers. Such technological aids not only add confidentiality, but can be used to increase accessibility for groups that are often, advertently or inadvertently, excluded from survey collection exercises, such as children and people whose first language is not English.

Maximising response rates for face-to-face interviews

The following strategies help to ensure that the response rates are maximised for face-to-face inteviews (Salant & Dillman 1994; de Vaus 1995; Neuman 2004; Babbie 2005).

- Send an advance letter outlining the details and purpose of the survey and the day and approximate time of your visit.
- Provide a phone number for respondents to call if they do not want to participate.
- Dress neatly and wear an identity card.
- Know your area. Try to anticipate which times would be most effective; for instance, in an outer suburban area, many households will be away at work and school during weekdays.
- If using interviewers, make sure they are well trained and you conduct frequent debriefing sessions.
- Try to discourage the presence of third parties at an interview.
- If the respondent is too busy, try to arrange a more convenient time.
- If the respondent is not at home, call back up to four times, varying the times of your visits, leaving a card so the respondent can contact you to make a more convenient time.

Collecting data electronically

The large-scale nature of much survey data collection and the set structure of the survey questionnaire make survey research highly amenable to computer technology. Nearly

60 per cent of Australian households now have home internet access, so surveys are increasingly completed and submitted completely online. However, it is worth remembering that despite high rates of internet connection, barriers for electronic surveys remain. First, distribution of access is not even, and some types of households are more likely to have internet connection and others less likely. For example, while around 70 per cent of households in the ACT are connected to the internet, the majority with a broadband connection, only just over half of all Tasmanian households are connected, with a higher proportion of these reporting slower dial-up access. Additionally, those from regional areas are considerably less likely to be connected than those living in capital cities, and households with older residents are also underrepresented. Second, unlike the electoral roll, or even the White Pages, full listings of email addresses are not publicly available and, unlike random digit dialing for telephone interviews, it is not yet possible to systematically randomly access a suitably sized sample. Electronic surveying, therefore, is only currently suitable for specific purpose surveying of particular accessible populations.

Develop the survey questionnaire

A good survey instrument requires careful design. To begin this process we need to decide, in a formal way, what things we actually need to know to answer our research question. In the example of exploring gender in relation to student study habits, you obviously need to know what gender the person is and the person's age, but what is it you need to know about their study habits and across what dimensions? This is hard work, and requires a lot of thinking through and reference back to your literature review. For this example, you might decide the dimensions of the topic you need to explore are:

- What is the 'normal' pattern of assignment study behaviour for this student?
- What are the elements of that pattern in terms of:
  - intensity: how intensely do they study? (repeated study periods? all at once?)
  - temporality: what is their pattern of study time use and how much time?
  - resources: what resources do they use (library, internet, lecture recordings)?
  - intentionality: do they have a planned or ad hoc study approach?

Being clear about the sort of information we are seeking allows the systematic development of indicators to measure these dimensions and the specific questions to gather the needed data.

When thinking about the survey questions, we need to consider both their purpose and task. In relation to task, de Vaus (1995) suggests thinking of the questions might include four aspects:

1   **Measures of the dependent variable or the major factor:** questions that measure what it is the survey primarily seeks to explain or explore.
2   **Measures of the independent variables or other key factors:** questions that cover all the key concepts in the research question or problem.
3   **Measures of other relevant variables:** questions on factors that might be associated with the topic's core variables.
4   **Background measures:** questions around basic sociodemographic items such as age, gender and occupation, allowing identification of the patterns among different subgroups of our sample.

You also need to consider the purpose of the question; what sort of data you want to collect. Neuman (2004:162) lists six categories of questions. These are:

1   **Behaviour:** in the last week how many hours did you spend in assignment preparation study?
2   **Attitudes, beliefs and opinions:** for example, what do you think is the most efficient study method: regular, planned periods of study, or one long session before the assignment is due?
3   **Characteristics:** are you in the first year, second year, third year or fourth year of your degree?
4   **Expectations:** what grade do you expect to get for this subject?
5   **Self-classification:** how would you classify your assignment study preparation: very good, good, fair, poor, very poor?
6   **Knowledge:** what does the lecturer recommend for assignment study preparation?

The key point is: every question needs a clear rationale for inclusion and specific indicator outcome. For instance, it is no use asking whether a student ever submits an assignment late, if knowing about late assignments is not a dimension needed to answer your research question. And if you do need to know it, you need to know not just if a student has submitted a late assignment but how often and under what circumstances.

Finally, when putting your survey together you need to decide on the best question sequence and layout to suit this research question, this survey type and this group of respondents.

Framing your research questions

The literature on survey construction regularly includes suggestions on how best to frame or word your survey questions, and these are summarised in the list below (see, for example,

Maggie Walter

Sarantakos 1993:170–1; de Vaus 1995:83–6; Bryman 2004:152–6; Neuman 2004:169). However, as Salant and Dillman (1994:91) point out, there are no perfect rules for writing good questions. This is because survey questions are always developed to address a particular research question for a particular research population at a particular time.

Box 6.1: Guide to framing survey questions

1. **Keep questions short, concise, and use simple wording:** short questions are clearer and less ambiguous. Use a basic vocabulary and avoid jargon or slang. If possible, keep questions under 10 words in length.
2. **Avoid personal questions:** unless you really need the information, avoid asking personal questions or for personal information.
3. **Make sure your subjects have the information you seek:** do not ask a question if you are unsure if your respondents will know the answer. Otherwise, provide a 'don't know' category.
4. **Avoid leading questions:** don't ask: 'How upset are you about rising interest rates?' Ask respondents to rate (across a scale) how much a 1 per cent rise in the interest rate will have an impact on their ability to meet mortgage payments.
5. **Avoid questions loaded with social desirability:** if you ask respondents if they give money to charity, for example, many will say yes, even if they don't, because they want to be seen as generous.
6. **Avoid double-barrelled questions:** if you ask a double-barrelled question such as 'How strongly do you agree/disagree that universities are understaffed and underfunded?', the results will be uninterpretable. You won't know if the respondent is answering the underfunding or the understaffing part of the question, or both.
7. **Limit questions to a minimum, avoiding repetitive questions:** only ask those questions that are absolutely necessary. A long survey form or question session will tire or bore your participants. They may give you unconsidered responses or refuse to answer more questions.
8. **Be aware of response sets:** if the questions share similar answer choices, respondents can get locked into a certain answer. This is a particular problem with Likert-type questions (see below). Avoid by phrasing questions to alter the general pattern of answers.
9. **Don't reinvent the question wheel:** examine and be informed by the questions that other social researchers have developed and successfully used.
10. **Think about coding and analysis:** design your questions with coding and analysis in mind. This will facilitate the coding and analysis processes.

Selecting the question format

The other key part of questionnaire design and development is to decide on the response format. Responses can be either open or closed, and the format for most surveys is a majority of closed questions and a minority of open questions.

Closed questions

Closed questions come in a wide variety of formats, but basically ask participants to select their response from a limited set of options. A number of exhaustive, fixed alternative, usually mutually exclusive responses are provided to a question, from which the respondent can select only one, such as male/female. An 'other' response category must be provided if there is a possibility that a person can answer outside the range of responses listed. Closed questions are the easiest to answer and score, but can be limited by the range of responses given. Another disadvantage is that respondents may resist the fixed alternatives and give half or other ambiguous responses. Examples of commonly used alternative formats for closed questions are as follows:

> **Closed questions:** A type of question that asks respondents to select their response from a number of exhaustive, fixed alternative options. Closed questions are often asked in a structured interview.

Simple multiple-choice

In simple multiple-choice questions, respondents are asked to choose one of a group of fixed alternative, mutually exclusive items.

Example 6.1

Q12
At what kind of educational institution are you currently enrolled?
a	School	1
b	TAFE college	2
c	Higher education	3
d	Other	4

Source: ABS 2003

Likert-type items

A Likert-type scale is used to record the level of a response. Most commonly, this is how strongly the respondent agrees or disagrees with a statement or item. Typically, these are divided into five categories: strongly agree; agree; neither agree nor disagree; disagree; strongly disagree. The same format can test across other measures such as importance or unimportance.

Because it is generally accepted among social scientists that the differences between the levels of response are of the same magnitude, this type of question format can yield interval rather than nominal data. This increases the amenability of data from these items to a wider variety of statistical analysis.

Example 6.2

K9

And now I am going to read out some statements about living in Australia. Using a scale where 1 means strongly disagree and 5 means strongly agree, please tell me the extent to which you agree or disagree with each statement.

	Strongly disagree	Disagree	Neither agree nor disagree	Agree	Strongly agree
You can make what you want of yourself in Australia	1	2	3	4	5
Australia offers a great future for our children	1	2	3	4	5
I am glad to be living in Australia	1	2	3	4	5

Source: Adapted from HILDA 2001, Living in Australia (HILDA) Person Questionnaire

Semantic differential formats: In a semantic differential format survey question, the respondent is asked to select his or her response from between the two extreme values of a continuum.

Semantic differential formats

In this format, respondents are presented with a continuum and asked to select a point between the two extreme values.

Example 6.3

C12

Some people say that no matter who people vote for, it won't make any difference to what happens. Others say that who people vote for can make a big difference to what happens. Using the scale below, where would you place yourself?

1	2	3	4	5
Who people vote for can make a big difference.				Who people vote for won't make any difference.

Source: Bean et al. 2001

Ranking formats

In ranking formats, respondents are asked to rank a set of listed items according to a specified criterion, such as order of preference. As there is no way to measure the intensity with which preference 1 is rated over preference 2, ranking formats yield only ordinal data. But, as in example 5, the ranking of items can be important information itself.

Example 6.4

Q158
We are all part of different groups. Some are more important to us than others when we think of ourselves. In general, which in the following list is the most important to you in describing who you are? And the second most important? And the third most important?

Put the LETTER of the statement in the appropriate box below.
- A   Your current or previous occupation (or being a homemaker)
- B   Your race/ethnic background
- C   Your gender (that is, being male or female)
- D   Your age group (that is, being young, middle-aged, older)
- E   Your religion (or being agnostic or atheist)
- F   Your preferred political party, group, or movement
- G   Your nationality
- H   Your family or marital status
- I   Your social class (that is working, middle or upper class)
- J   The part of Australia that you live in
- [ ]   Most important   [ ]   Second most important   [ ]   Third most important

Source: Adapted from Gibson et al. 2003

Contingency questions

Contingency questions operate as a filter, directing respondents to the questions that are relevant to them. Boxes or arrows highlight the contingency or follow-up questions.

Example 6.5

Q1
Do you think there are any problems from crime or people creating a public nuisance in your neighbourhood?

Maggie Walter

[ ]   No crime problems (go to question 2)
[ ]   Yes
Please circle all that apply:
1a   Housebreaking/burglaries/theft from homes
1b   Car theft
1c   Other theft
1d   Louts/youth gangs
1e   Prowlers/loiterers
1f   Vandalism/graffiti
1g   Dangerous/noisy driving
1h   Illegal drugs
1i   Sexual assault
1j   Other assault
1k   Problems with neighbours/domestic problems

Source: Kelly et al. 1996

Open-ended questions

Open-ended questions are just that, open. They allow respondents freedom in their response and add a richness to the data that is unobtainable from closed questions. They also allow for unexpected, but important, responses. The major disadvantages of open questions are that respondents tend to skip them in mail surveys, and their inclusion may introduce a bias against less literate respondents. Open-ended questions are also hard to record fully in a timely manner in either face-to-face or telephone interviews. Such questions also require a different approach to analysis than closed questions.

> **Open-ended questions:** Questions that are open in that they allow respondents freedom in their response rather than selecting from pre-determined category responses used in closed questions.

Example 6.6

Q66
Why aren't you in paid work at present?

Source: McDonald et al. 1997

Pre-test or pilot the questionnaire

Always conduct a pilot of your questionnaire to eliminate weaknesses and test if the data gathered will actually answer the specific research question(s). Piloting your questionnaire means surveying a small group of people similar to those who will be in your actual sample. Piloting allows us to assess if the questionnaire flows well, if the instructions are adequate, if some items are regularly misunderstood or skipped, and if the time taken to complete the survey is reasonable. As a researcher, it can be very surprising to see how respondents interpret what we considered were completely unambiguous questions or instructions. Adjust the questionnaire according to the insights gained from the piloting exercise.

Voices in the field

Allan Welch

Dr Allan Welch is a Post-Doctoral Fellow at the University of Tasmania, School of Sociology and Social Work, currently working on a three-year research project on the longer-term outcomes for long duration workers' compensation claimants in Tasmania. He writes the following on how he adjusted his way of thinking about analysis and the results that can be obtained from a survey when working on a larger scale social survey.

'Before taking up sociological research, my research background was in education, testing the attitudinal effects of certain educational programs on students' motivation. My research focused on hypothesis testing in control group experiments; that is, whether or not the educational program had the predicted effect, or not, the null hypothesis. As such, my statistical focus was on reporting Type I and Type II statistical errors, relevant effect sizes and their direction. Since my involvement in social survey research I have seen a broader, more predictive role for statistical analysis, which moves beyond the acceptance or rejection of null hypotheses. Social survey analysis has the capacity to discern dominant influences that otherwise might lie undetected in large masses of data. Bivariate and multivariate statistical analyses provide information about the research variables, defining their direction and strength and, importantly, their relationship with other variables in the survey. Hence, while extant knowledge, usually via a literature review, informs the survey, the survey analysis is capable of detecting previously unidentified relationships in the data.

'My experience in both experimental and social survey research leads me to appreciate the symbiotic relationship between hypothesis testing and survey research. Each is necessary and supports the other. Experimental social researchers progress incrementally through hypothesis testing, all the while seeking replication, and minimisation of experimental limitations. Correspondingly, the exploratory nature of survey research may advance knowledge exponentially, but with limited information about the nature of the relationships underpinning that knowledge expansion. Thus, survey research can inform hypothesis testing by revealing questions about relationships between variables that were not apparent initially. Such investigation then turns to hypothesis testing, seeking to verify various interpretations of survey research through confirmation and replication.'

Maggie Walter

From method to practice

In 2005 my colleagues, Associate Professor Natalie Jackson and Dr Bruce Felmingham, and I received a large ARC grant to answer the research question: will older workers be prepared to stay longer in the workforce in response to government encouragement for them to do so? The rationale for this research was the emerging labour market shortages from Australia's ageing population. While the federal government had introduced a number of policy changes, including financial incentives, to encourage later retirement and discourage early retirement, there had been no research into whether these were likely to be effective. A telephone survey was the only way to collect this information, as there is no list of older workers, using random digit dialling to contact potential respondents.

It was my job to develop and implement the survey. I started the process by building a profile of all the surveys I could find that had addressed the topic of retirement. As population ageing labour market issues are of concern throughout the Western world, there were plenty to choose from. This resource allowed me to see what had been done before and what questions had been used. Our research team then held a full-day workshop to decide what we needed to find out to answer our research question and to conceptualise our key concepts. Older workers were conceptualised as Australians aged 40–59 years—essentially the Baby Boom generation—who were actively engaged in the labour market, either working or looking for work. 'Staying in the workforce longer' we conceptualised into two definitions: willing to stay working past their current expected retirement age; and willing to stay working past the age at which the Age Pension can be paid, 65 years. 'Government encouragement' we conceptualised to mean three prominent policies that had been introduced to encourage longer workforce participation: the Pension Bonus Scheme, Transition to Retirement Measures and superannuation access changes. Because our theoretical framework considered that the policy presumption of choice in retirement age may be overestimated, our additional dimensions included:

> how, when and with whom were retirement decisions made
> how firmly retirement decisions were held
> if there was a difference between expected retirement age and preferred retirement age and the reasons for this difference
> health or physical demands of jobs as a factor in retirement decisions
> respondents' views on the sorts of policies that might encourage them to stay longer in the workforce
> sociodemographic details, such as age, occupation, marital status, current age of children and mortgage details

From method to practice

I then designed a set of survey questions to gather the data needed to answer our key questions about intentions and the impact of the particular policies, as well as the additional dimensions, and compiled these into a logically flowing survey instrument. This process was pragmatic as well as creative. It is generally accepted that 25 minutes is the optimum time for a telephone survey. Any longer and respondents tend to lose interest or are unwilling to commit further time. A pilot of our survey found that it ran to just over 28 minutes on average. So, after a team conference we decided to cull several interesting, but not essential, questions on current job satisfaction. The result was the Australian Survey of Retirement Attitudes and Motivation (ASRAM) (I got to make up the name as well), which was conducted between July and November 2006 with a nationally representative sample of 2501 respondents.

Exercise 6.2: Developing survey questions: Computers Red survey

At Computers Red we do our best to bring you top quality stock at the lowest possible prices with a high level of service. To help us improve even further the standards of our stock and service, we ask you to please complete the questionnaire below.

Have you ever bought anything from the Computers Red Shop? _____

Have you shopped at the Computers Red Shop in the last three weeks? (Tick if yes)

What of the following items did you buy?

___ Geforce 6800 card ___ Barracuda 160 GB 8M H ___ DDR 3200 512M chips
___ Computer ___ USB2 card ___ Firewire card ___ Software package

Please rank these items in order of your preference

_____
_____
_____

Are you male or female?_____
What is your favourite subject? _____
Do you study computing? _____
Do you shop at the computer shop often? Yes ___ No ___
Would you recommend shopping at the Computers Red Shop to your friends?
Yes ___ No ___

Maggie Walter

We recently compared our prices in software and computer parts with other computer shops in the area and ours are the cheapest. How do you think our shop compares with other computer shops?

Better _____   Worse _____

Concept: Nardi 2003

Task 1

Examine the Computers Red survey questionnaire and answer the following questions.

- Is the survey, as it stands, capable of providing the data needed to assess customers' opinion of the stock and service in the computer shop?
- Identify as many problems with the survey form as you can.
- Why are these items problematic?
- What difficulties might these problematic items cause for the data collection and the data analysis aspects from this survey?

Task 2

The survey states that its aim is to assess its customers' opinion to improve the quality of the service and the stock (even though it doesn't ask anything about the service).

To provide the computer shop staff with some badly needed assistance, develop a set of 10 questions (five for assessing the quality and range of the stock and five for the service) that will actually assess its customers' opinions on:

- the quality and suitability of the current stock available
- the current quality of the service.

Develop the questions using the major formats for survey questions outlined in this section, ensuring that you have at least one question in each of the main formats:

- simple multiple choice
- Likert-type item
- semantic-differential format
- ranking format
- contingency question
- open-ended question.

Conclusion

Main points

> Survey research is the administration of questionnaires to a sample of respondents who have been selected from a population.

> Surveys are an effective way of finding what people are thinking, feeling or doing, and are especially useful for exploratory studies.

> Surveys can gather a large amount of data from a large group of people more effectively and less expensively than most other methods.

> Before selecting a survey as your method of data collection, ensure it is the appropriate method to answer your research question or problem.

> Know what your research question(s) are before you begin to develop your survey.

> Select your sampling method (probability or non-probability) based on your research question and your practical limitations.

> Appropriate sample size depends on the type of sampling, the size of the population of interest, the homogeneity of the population, and the degree of accuracy you want in your results.

> Self-administered, telephone or personal interview surveys all have their own strengths and weaknesses.

> Select the type and format of your survey questions according to the category of information you are seeking.

> Clear, relevant, concise questions are the key to a good survey.

> The sequencing of questions is an important consideration.

> Survey questionnaires always should be pre-tested or piloted.

Further reading

If you want to learn more about using a survey as social research method, the following books are recommended:

de Vaus, D. (2002). *Surveys in Social Research*, 5th edn. Crows Nest: Allen & Unwin.

Maggie Walter

Nardi, P. M. (2003). *Doing Survey Research: A Guide to Quantitative Methods.* Boston: Pearson Education.

Salant, P. and Dillman, D. A. (1994). *How To Conduct Your Own Survey.* New York: Wiley.

References

Australian Bureau of Statistics (2002). *AusStats: 4159.0.55.001 General Social Survey: Data Reference Package.* Canberra <www.abs.gov.au>. Accessed 20 December 2004.

Australian Bureau of Statistics (2003). *1999–2000 Survey of Income and Housing Costs Australia, Confidentialised Unit Record File (CURF) Technical Paper.* Catalogue 6541.0.30.001.

Australian Institute of Housing and Urban Research (2004). *21st Century Housing Careers and Australia's Housing Future.* CRV2 (Ongoing Research Project).

Babbie, E. (2002). *The Basics of Social Research*, 2nd edn. Southbank: Thomson Wadsworth.

Babbie, E. (2005). *The Basics of Social Research*, 3rd edn. Southbank: Thomson Wadsworth.

Barnett, V. (1974). *Elements of Sampling Theory.* London: English Universities Press.

Baxter, J. (2002). 'Patterns of Change and Stability in the Gender Division of Household Labour in Australia, 1986–1997', *Journal of Sociology*, 38 (4): 399–424.

Bean, C., Gow, D. and McAllister, I. (2001). *Australian Election Study: User's Guide for the Machine-Readable Data File: SSDA Study No 1048.* Canberra: Social Science Data Archive, Australian National University.

Bryman, A. (2004). *Social Research Methods*, 2nd edn. Oxford: Oxford University Press.

Christchurch Health and Development Study (2005). University of Otago, Christchurch <www.chmeds.ac.nz/research/chds/htm>. Accessed 24 April 2005.

de Vaus, D. (1995). *Surveys in Social Research.* St Leonards: Allen & Unwin.

Ezzy, D., Welch, A. and Walter, M. (2008). *Long Term Benefits Study Workers Compensation Research Phase One Research Report.* Hobart: School of Sociology and Social Work, University of Tasmania.

FACS (2004). *Footprints in Time: The Longitudinal Study of Indigenous Children: An Overview of the Study.* Canberra: Longitudinal Surveys Section, Department of Family and Community Services.

Gibson, R., Wilson, S., Denemark, D., Meagher, G. and Western, M. (2003). *The Australian Survey of Social Attitudes: User's Guide.* Canberra: Australian Social Science Data Archive, Research School of Social Sciences, Australian National University.

HILDA (2001). *Living in Australia (HILDA) Person Questionnaire Draft 17 date 10/8/01.* <www.melbourneinstitute.com/hilda/survey-inst/PersonSch.pdf>. Accessed 10 March 2005.

Jackson, N., Felmingham, B. and Walter, M. (2005). Will Older Workers Change Their Retirement Plans? Ongoing research project.

Kelly, J., Bean, C., Evans, M. D. R. and Zagorski, K. (1996). *National Social Science Survey 1993: Inequality II.* Canberra: Australian Social Science Data Archive, Australian National University.

Maisel, R. and Persell, C. H. (1996). *How Sampling Works.* Thousand Oaks, CA: Pine Forge Press.

McDonald, P., Jones, F., Mitchell, D. and Baxter, J. (1996). *Negotiating the Lifecourse: CATI Interview Schedule.* Canberra: Social Sciences Data Archives, Australian National University.

McDonald, P., Jones, F., Mitchell, D. and Baxter, J. (1997). *Negotiating the Lifecourse: User's Guide for the Machine-Readable Data File: SSDA Study No. 1015.* Canberra: Social Sciences Data Archives, Australian National University.

Nardi, P. M. (2003). *Doing Survey Research: A Guide to Quantitative Methods.* Boston: Pearson Education.

Natalier, K., Walter, M., Wulff, M., Reynolds, M. and Hewitt, B. (2008). *Child Support and Housing Outcomes.* AHURI Final Report 113. Melbourne: Australian Housing and Urban Research Institute.

Neuman, W. L. (2004). *Basics of Social Research: Qualitative and Quantitative Approaches.* Boston: Pearson Education.

Robson, C. (1993). *Real World Research: A Resource for Social Scientists and Practitioner-researchers.* Oxford: Blackwell.

Salant, P. and Dillman, D. A. (1994). *How to Conduct Your Own Survey.* New York: Wiley.

Sarantakos, S. (1993). *Social Research.* South Melbourne: Macmillan Education.

Walter, M., Jackson, N. and Felmingham, B. (2008). 'Keeping Australia's Baby Boomers in the Labour Force: A Policy Perspective', *Australian Journal of Social Issues*: 43 (2): 291–301.

Chapter 7
Population-level Analysis

Natalie Jackson

Asking critical questions, seeking evidence-based answers

In 1991, when the high levels of youth unemployment associated with economic restructuring were peaking, the New Zealand government raised the age of eligibility for the adult rate of unemployment benefit. The changes had a disproportionately negative effect on the Māori population, not simply because it had a higher unemployment rate, but because it also had a more youthful age structure than the 'European-origin' population (age structure refers to the proportion of the population that is at each age). Should the New Zealand government have been able to anticipate this effect?

Jackson (2002) argues 'yes'. In 1991, the Māori population had a median age of 21 years, compared with 33 years for the European-origin population. This meant that there were proportionately more than one and a half young Māori for every young 'European'. Unemployment is a characteristic that disproportionately affects young people. The differences in age structure meant that the Māori population in 1991 was disproportionately exposed to the risk of unemployment. Even if the unemployment rates of Māori and European youth had been identical, the policy changes would have had a disproportionate impact on the Māori population by virtue of its age structure alone.

As it was, the labour force unemployment rate of Māori youth at the time was 37 per cent, almost double that of their European counterparts (19 per cent). Incorporating the multiplicative effects of age structure, the relative impact of the above policy on the Māori population would therefore have been around three times greater than that experienced by the European-origin population, not twice as great, as the youth employment rates themselves implied.

While the policy to raise the age of eligibility for the adult rate of unemployment benefit was ostensibly 'ethnically neutral' in that it did not intentionally seek to disadvantage the Māori population, it did in effect have this disparate impact.

Jackson argued that, while the ethnic differences in age structure were generally well known (for example, Pool 1987), there was no acknowledgment by the New Zealand government of the differing impact the policy change would have on each population. Using the simple technique of standardisation (outlined in this chapter), she was able to develop this information. The same techniques can be used to examine an enormous number of issues concerning social inequality, and are especially useful in assessing the disparate impacts of policy.

Source: Jackson 2002

Key terms

administrative collections
age composition
age-specific
aggregated
artefact (of technique)
Census of Population and Housing
composition
cross-sectional analysis
decomposition
demographic data
diachronic

disproportionately	longitudinal analysis	ratio
frequency distributions	median age	standardisation
index of dissimilarity	percentage	summary measure
intercensal estimates	percentage change	synchronic
inter-collection discontinuities	percentage point	vital statistics
intra-collection discontinuities	policy implications	
judgment	proportionately	

Introduction

Population-level data analysis is both simple and complex. It is simple because, if you can add, subtract, multiply and divide, you can do it. It is complex because it is not always straightforward to determine exactly what it is that you should add, subtract, multiply or divide, or how to treat (and describe) the data to tell the most useful story about them.

This chapter simplifies the problem, explaining the two dimensions in detail, and elaborating each with many examples. First, we consider what population-level analysis is all about, where these data typically come from, and how we go about such research by reviewing some related analytical issues and techniques. Relatedly, we consider the complexities involved. For example, if we wish to analyse trends in full-time employment, ethnic group affiliation or any other social category, we need to understand that the definition of what constitutes full-time employment, 'ethnicity' or any other social category typically changes over time. Finally, having deliberated on these complexities, we return to the issue of analytical techniques and outline two highly useful approaches.

Before continuing, a word of qualification is necessary. Most of the examples used in this chapter are 'demographic', in that they pertain to topics conventionally studied by demographers, such as births, deaths and marriages. However, not all population-level data are demographic, while not all **demographic data** are collected at the level of the population. Researchers of all callings regularly collect demographic data, such as age and sex data, at the level of the individual, the focus group and the survey, while many population-level researchers investigate topics that are less obviously demographic, such as income, labour force status, class, car ownership or housing type.

> **Demographic data:** Data that categorise groups of individuals according to such characteristics as their age, sex, marital status and birth and death rates.

What differentiates population-level data from other data is that, with few exceptions:

- they account for all members of the group
- they are typically 'secondary' data, in that they have been collected by someone else: most often an official government agency.

What is population-level data analysis?

Population-level data analysis refers to the analysis of social phenomena as they pertain to entire populations and subpopulations. These populations and subpopulations may exist at the global, national, state/territory or subregional level. They may also be ethnic groups, religious groups, gender or age groups, industrial or occupational groups, or classes.

Typically, population-level data are obtained from national collections, such as:

- The **Census of Population and Housing**, which collects information on a broad variety of demographic and socioeconomic characteristics, and tends to be run in some form or other in most of the world's countries every five to 10 years.
- **Vital statistics**, which are collections that officially record each vital event, of birth, death, marriage, divorce and migration.
- **Intercensal estimates**, which comprise estimates of population numbers by age, sex and geographical location made in the years between census collections, on the basis of recorded changes in vital events.
- **Administrative collections**, such as Australia's Medicare health card registrations, which ostensibly cover most of the population; car registrations, which ostensibly cover most car owners; and income-assistance collections, which cover most of those receiving income assistance, such as pensions or benefits.

Census of Population and Housing: The typically five-yearly official (government) enumeration of the population; the census collects both demographic and social data.

Vital statistics: Data collections pertaining to vital events, such as births and deaths, that typically occur only once. Marriages, divorces and migration are also often considered vital events.

Intercensal (estimates): The period between censuses; estimates made between censuses.

Administrative collections: Data collections like Medicare health card records, unemployment registers and electoral rolls.

Clearly some of the latter sources do not enumerate the entire population, but rather, entire populations having direct experience of something. A further exception to the rule that population-level data enumerates all people occurs in some census counts. While the entire population is counted in Australia and New Zealand, this is sometimes not the case when censuses are undertaken in very large populations, such as China and the USA. In the USA, for example, a sampling process is followed, in which only one in every six households fills out the full census questionnaire, while five in every six fill out a shorter version (Weeks 1999:45). The extreme size of the population means that the data are highly representative, and thus cost savings can be made. Yet another

Natalie Jackson

exception occurs where people are either missed or counted more than once, as a result of errors in the collection process relating to the sampling frame, failure to contact the respondent or incorrectly filled in household forms. Undercounting may be significant for some subpopulations.

Differences between population-level data and survey data

Although both use quantitative techniques in their analysis, population-level data differ fundamentally from survey data (see chapters 9 and 14). Rather than counting entire populations, survey data usually collect data on a relatively small sample of the population of interest, which are then generalised back to the broader population. The contrasting of the two approaches is not meant to suggest that one is superior to the other. In fact, the two are highly complementary, and to a large extent depend on each other.

On the one hand, population-level analysts tend to paint very broad-brush pictures. Without surveys (and of course qualitative research) to put flesh on the bones, much population-level analysis would be meaningless. On the other hand, survey analysis relies on population-level data to demonstrate its representativeness. For example, if the survey is collecting data on attitudes to home ownership by age or education level, it is necessary for the survey sample to be similar in proportion at each age and education level to the total population; that is, be representative of the population being surveyed.

Further, analysts from each side often take their inspiration to investigate something because of the research findings of the other. Who would think of asking (surveying) why people are having fewer children or marrying or partnering later (or not at all) if it were not for population-level data in identifying the trend? Equally, why would those preparing a census think to ask questions on, say, Indigenous subgroup identity if it were not for survey, and also qualitative, researchers drawing their attention to the significance of this issue?

Reflecting these differences, raw population-level data also differ in fundamental ways from survey data. The former tend to be available in primarily numerical but precoded (categorised) and already **aggregated** form, while the latter are typically available in categorical 'unit record' (individual person) and recodable form. This means that population-level data analysts have considerably less flexibility to ask questions of their data than do survey and other analysts. That said, however, there is a veritable treasure trove of population-level data in a great many countries awaiting analysis.

> **Aggregated:** Already added; subtotals and totals; the effects when added.

Uses of population-level analysis

Though population level data may lack flexibility, they possess abundant other invaluable features. Population-level data allow analysts the opportunity to:

- identify and track large-scale and long-term (and emerging) patterns and trends
- compare these patterns and trends internationally, subregionally and categorically
- at least partially explain them by cross-correlating with a wide variety of other social, economic, cultural and political factors.

For example, the decline in the classic Western 'two-parent family with children' can be observed to have occurred systematically throughout all developed (and many developing) countries over a very short period of time. By correlating these trends with other societal characteristics, it has been possible for researchers to make international comparisons of factors that appear to have (and not to have) contributed to this outcome.

What other topics might lend themselves to population-level analysis? As implied above, the list is essentially endless: in short, anything that population-level data has been collected on. Box 7.1 gives an indication of the sorts of data available from a census; in this case, the Australian Census of Population and Housing. Examination of the wide range of variables available from population-level collections, and a little thought as to how they might be used, can facilitate many exciting research projects.

Keep in mind that all such data are available as cross-tabulations, both bivariate—combining two variables, such as income by age—and multivariate, that is, combining more than two variables, such as 'income by age, sex, marital status, employment status, industry and occupation'. It would be feasible, although somewhat impractical, to include every item. You would simply determine the dependent variable of interest, such as 'income' in the example just outlined, and then correlate it with every other relevant variable.

Box 7.1: Population-level data

(Example variables from Australia's census.)
- Age
- Sex
- Ancestry
- Country of birth
- Parents' country of birth
- Language
- English proficiency
- Religion

Natalie Jackson

- Postcode (one year ago; five years ago)
- Marital status (both formal and social)
- Household and family type
- Education level
- Employment status
- Hours of work
- Student status
- Field of study
- Industry, occupation
- Income; pensions or allowances
- Method of travel to work
- Computer usage
- Car ownership
- Home ownership or rental status.

Strengths and weaknesses of population-level analysis

As with all forms of analysis, population-level analysis has both strengths and limitations. Understanding these aspects of the research process is critically important, as is acknowledging them in your study. They are like the 'small print' in legal documents: they provide both authentication for those who might later use or report on your findings, and qualification of any shortcomings. The latter is particularly important to ensure that any future misuse of your findings is not your fault. Box 7.2 highlights the main points.

Box 7.2: Why population-level analysis? Strengths and weaknesses

- Population-level analysis is fun to do; it is often groundbreaking, identifying or discovering new or emerging issues, and indicating where survey analysts and other researchers might usefully look for more detailed answers; it is often involved in collaborative and 'big picture' projects.
- Population level analysis covers the entire population(s) you are interested in. All differences in and between population-level data are therefore 'statistically significant' (although they may not be meaningful; that involves judgment). Accordingly, this form of analysis is relatively easy; there is no need to use inferential statistics (inferential statistics are used to infer things about the general population from the survey population; see chapter 8).

- The data are typically 'secondary' data: they have been collected by someone else. This saves having to get ethics clearance from your institution; a big timesaver for tight research time frames (and small budgets).
- The data have typically been collected by official government bureaus under rigorous collection and reporting procedures. They are thus highly reliable and replicable (although they may not always assure 'validity'; that is, measure what you 'think' you are measuring. To be sure, it is a good idea to check out the original census question—and often those surrounding it).
- Population-level data are relatively inexpensive to access. A broad range of census data for an enormous number of countries—currently around 240—are downloadable free from the web (see box 7.9); access to more detailed collections for individual countries is typically available through your university or polytechnic.
- The data facilitate the undertaking of valuable comparative studies, both between countries and between subpopulation groups (like ethnic and religious groups) within and between countries. Such studies add much to our understanding of social behaviour, patterns and trends.
- Population-level data from census collections are typically available for long periods of time, permitting highly informative **longitudinal analysis**—something that is not always available from surveys, which tend to be single 'snapshots' in time (although advanced survey developers and analysts can develop excellent longitudinal studies from cross-sectional data by asking retrospective questions).

> **Longitudinal analysis:** Analysis over time; time-series analysis.

If these features sound too good to be true, you are well on the way to being a good researcher!

Population-level analysis also has a number of limitations. These include:

- The fact that the questions asked and the data available may not answer your burning question.
- Population-level data are also coded and categorised according to predetermined and dominant classifications, like 'sole parent', 'Indigenous', 'unemployed' or 'not in the labour force', which may offend those who are so categorised.
- These definitions tend to be altered over time, creating intra-collection discontinuities and making longitudinal analysis of the same thing difficult; and/or to differ between collections (inter-collection discontinuities). Intra-collection discontinuities and inter-collection discontinuities make the construction of rates difficult (see the section on analytical complexities for an explanation of these terms).

Natalie Jackson

Analytical issues

To begin the section on how to 'do' population-level analysis, some basic analytical issues need to be clarified. These include:

Synchronic: At one point in time.

Diachronic: Across time.

Frequency distribution: A summary of how cases fall out across the response categories comprising a variable; the numbers or proportions in each subcategory or subgroup comprising the entire category or group.

- when to use absolute numbers or statistics, such as rates or ratios
- what to be aware of when undertaking a 'cross-sectional' (point in time, or **synchronic**), 'longitudinal' (across time, time series, or **diachronic**), or comparative analysis.

Although the questions seem rather simplistic, they raise a number of issues that soon become complex.

Let us imagine that we are interested in the topic of 'education level'. We might begin with a simple **frequency distribution**. A frequency distribution is the number of units or observations within a set (or sets) of data, such as numbers of males and females holding different education levels, as given in table 7.1. Note that the source of these data and other explanatory notes are given as footnotes to the table. Such notes should always accompany tables and graphs.

Table 7.1: Non-school qualification (numerical distribution): Level of education by sex (i), persons aged 15 years or over (excluding overseas visitors), 2006

	Males	Females	Persons
Postgraduate degree	236,072	177,021	413,093
Graduate diploma and graduate certificate	84,685	143,868	228,553
Bachelor degree	826,007	1,014,656	1,840,663
Advanced (undergraduate) diploma and diploma	480,766	649,702	1,130,468
Certificate (vocational) level	1,797,757	865,024	2,662,781
Not stated (ii)	985,758	1,100,504	2,086,262
No post-school qualifications (iii)	3,366,869	4,189,391	7,556,260
Total	7,777,914	8,140,166	15,918,080

i   Excludes schooling up to Year 12.
ii Includes 'inadequately described'.
iii Includes persons who have a qualification out of the scope of the Australian Standard Classification of Education.
Source: ABS 2008

Now, while these absolute numbers are useful for certain purposes, you have to look at them very closely to see what they are telling us, especially when their totals differ. It is much more useful to convert them to percentages (rates per 100), as in table 7.2. This is especially so if you are interested in examining trends over time, or comparing one or more distributions, for example between countries, or ethnic groups or by sex or age groups, all of which may differ substantially in size.

A **percentage** rate is simply the numerator (the phenomenon of interest, in this case education level) divided by the denominator (the population 'at risk' of the phenomenon, in this case the total population aged 15-plus years), and multiplied by 100. For example, in the case of bachelor degree for males the equation is: (826,007/7,777,914) × 100 = 10.6 per cent.

> **Percentage:** A number expressed as a proportion of 100.

With percentages calculated as per table 7.2, we can see that females are less likely than males to hold a postgraduate degree, but more likely to hold a bachelor degree. Also, 47.5 per cent of the Australian population aged 15 years and over does not hold a non-school (post-school) qualification.

Table 7.2: Non-school qualification (percentage distribution): Level of education by sex (i), persons aged 15 years or over (excluding overseas visitors), 2006

	Males	Females	Persons
Postgraduate degree	3.0	2.2	2.6
Graduate diploma and graduate certificate	1.1	1.8	1.4
Bachelor degree	10.6	12.5	11.6
Advanced (undergraduate) diploma and diploma	6.2	8.0	7.1
Certificate (vocational) level	23.1	10.6	16.7
Not stated (ii)	12.7	13.5	13.1
No post-school qualifications (iii)	43.3	51.5	47.5
Total	100.0	100.0	100.0

i Excludes schooling up to Year 12.
ii Includes 'inadequately described'.
iii Includes persons who have a qualification out of the scope of the Australian Standard Classification of Education.

Source: ABS 2008

What if we want to examine these characteristics over time? The Census 'Time Series Profiles' Collection contains data for three observations (1996, 2001 and 2006), and it is a simple matter, in this particular case, to turn our **cross-sectional analysis** for 2006 into a longitudinal one (see the section below on analytical complexities for more discussion; it is not always this straightforward).

> **Cross-sectional analysis:** Analysis of a population at a single point in time; sometimes likened to a 'snapshot' photograph.

Natalie Jackson

Percentage change: The difference between two percentages expressed as a percentage of the first observation.

These data are given as percentages in table 7.3. Note the addition of two columns at the right to show change between 1996 and 2006, given here as **percentage change**, first for males and then for females. Now we are talking about percentages and percentage change. This is where you can encounter some confusion, so we need to work through the steps.

Table 7.3: Non-school qualification (percentage distribution and change): Level of education by sex (i), persons aged 15 years or over (excluding overseas visitors), 1996, 2001, 2006

	Males			Females			Change 1996–2006	
	1996	2001	2006	1996	2001	2006	Males	Females
Postgraduate degree	1.9	2.3	3.0	0.9	1.4	2.2	59.7	141.6
Graduate diploma and graduate certificate	1.0	1.1	1.1	1.6	1.7	1.8	8.9	10.5
Bachelor degree	7.9	9.2	10.6	7.6	10.2	12.5	34.4	64.0
Advanced (undergraduate) diploma and diploma	5.2	5.4	6.2	6.9	6.6	8.0	18.9	15.7
Certificate (vocational) level	20.9	23.1	23.1	6.4	8.8	10.6	10.6	66.0
Not stated (ii)	10.8	10.3	12.7	12.9	12.6	13.5	17.4	4.8
No post-school qualifications (iii)	52.3	48.7	43.3	63.6	58.8	51.5	−17.2	−19.1
Total	100.0	100.0	100.0	100.0	100.0	100.0		

i   Excludes schooling up to Year 12.
ii Includes 'inadequately described'.
iii Includes persons who have a qualification out of the scope of the Australian Standard Classification of Education.
Sources: ABS 2003; ABS 2008

The calculation of percentage change involves two steps:

Percentage point: The difference between two percentage values (for example, the difference between 20 per cent and 30 per cent is 10 percentage points).

- First, the 'raw' difference between two percentage values is calculated, to give the percentage point difference between them. (Note that we have introduced a new term: **percentage point**. The difference between two or more percentage values is always expressed in percentage points.) So, for males with a postgraduate degree, the rate changed from 1.9 per cent to 3.0 per cent between 1996 and 2006: an increase of 1.1 percentage points. Thus: 3.0 − 1.9 = 1.1 percentage points.
- This percentage point difference is then recalculated and expressed as a percentage of the first value, to show percentage change; thus: (1.1/1.9) × 100 = 59.7 per cent.

Social Research Methods

Showing change or difference between two or more sets of data is a conventional presentation technique to aid communication. Now we can readily see that, while females in 2006 continue to have lower rates of holding a postgraduate degree than males, in this area they have advanced at a significantly faster rate than males; while the percentage of the population not holding a non-school qualification has declined. In the first instance, the percentage of males with a postgraduate degree has increased by 59.7 per cent. For females, the increase has been 141.6 per cent, two and a half times the increase for males. In the second instance, 'not holding a post-school qualification' has declined by 17.2 per cent for males and 19.1 per cent for females.

Box 7.3 summarises the basic analytical issues involved in population-level analysis.

Box 7.3: Summary of basic analytical issues

- Population-level data pertain to entire populations, whether they be the global population, or national, subregional, ethnic group, labour force, age group, gender, religious, occupational or 'class' populations. Missing numbers are usually relatively small, and have a minimal effect on the distribution of characteristics. The data are typically collected by official government agencies, and are thus secondary data. An enormous array of unanalysed population-level data exists. The stories it can tell are limited only by your imagination.
- Frequency distributions refer to the units or categories within a single set (or sets) of data, such as age groups or educational qualifications or industries. When comparing two or more frequency distributions, it is conventional to convert absolute numbers to rates (percentages or proportions) or ratios.
- Rates most correctly refer to percentages (per 100), where the numerator (the phenomenon we are interested in) and denominator (the population 'at risk' of the phenomenon) belong to the same 'set' (for example, the unemployed as a percentage of the labour force). By contrast, **ratios** are used to compare aspects of different sets (such as births per woman).

  > **Ratio:** The relativity between two absolute numbers (such as the ratio of 30 and 20 is 1.5 for every 1.0. This ratio would typically be expressed as 1.5).

- Cross-sectional analysis refers to point-in-time 'snapshots' of the population or phenomenon of interest (technically called synchronic analysis), while longitudinal analysis refers to across time (technically called time-series or diachronic analysis).
- Simple indices may be constructed to aid communication, like 'change' between two points in time. The index chosen to illustrate change is a matter of judgment. Sometimes percentage change is appropriate, while at other times it may be just the raw percentage point difference (the difference between two percentages) or another index altogether.

Natalie Jackson

Analytical complexities

When undertaking population-level analysis over time or between populations, a number of data quality issues emerge. Uppermost of these for longitudinal analysis is the issue of data continuity. Data continuity is the extent to which questions (like those in box 7.1) have been asked in each past census or other 'continuous' data collections, and the extent to which each was asked in an identical manner. Periodically, questions are dropped for a census or two (read the same for other data collections) when other more pressing questions need to be asked (note that for practical reasons census-takers endeavour to limit the size of the census). They may also be left off permanently, for example, if they become redundant, as in asking whether or not the household has a telephone. At still other times, they may be rephrased, if and when the previous wording becomes inappropriate or post-census surveys indicate that it is ambiguous.

Intra-collection discontinuities

Intra-collection discontinuities: Gaps or changes in the data categories or criteria within a single collection.

These changes lead to **intra-collection discontinuities**, that is, discontinuities caused by question gaps, or by the introduction of new questions within a single data collection. Those outlined above might be thought of as Type 1 discontinuities. There are two further types of intra-collection discontinuities to be aware of. The first relate to definitional and classificational changes; that is, changes in the criteria used to define something like full-time employment or ethnicity. The second relate to category jumping, the propensity for people to shift (either purposefully or inadvertently) from one ostensibly permanent designation, like ethnic group or sex, to another between observations (see Hout & Goldstein 1994 on how 4.5 million Irish immigrants became 40 million Irish Americans). The definitional changes give rise to what we will term Type 2 discontinuities, and the category jumping to Type 3 discontinuities.

A classic example of a Type 2 discontinuity is one that occurs with labour force data around definitions of what constitutes full-time work, part-time work or unemployment. Throughout the 1960s, full-time work across most of Australia was considered to be 30 hours or more, while since the 1980s that has been 35 hours or more. Accordingly, there is a discontinuity between the 1960s and 1980s that would show up (probably as a decrease in proportions employed full time) if we were endeavouring to graph a trend in full-time work. Similar problems occur with changes in the classification of race and ethnicity. In New Zealand in 1986, for example, there was a shift from 'blood fraction' (the percentage of Māori 'blood'—a 'racial' measure of ancestry) to 'ethnic group affiliation' as the main measure of classifying 'Māori'. The implications of these definitional and classificational changes are similar to, but differ from, the technically different Type 3 discontinuity (category jumping) whereby a child who is perhaps listed in the census (by his or her parents) as Indigenous later self-identifies as non-Indigenous, or vice versa. Both affect our ability to accurately enumerate the size of ethnic groups (Pool 1981; Morrison 1991; Gould 1992).

Let me reiterate that category jumping does not refer to conventional changes in status, say from single to married, or from no post school qualifications to bachelor's degree, but only to changes where the shift occurs in a category that might be considered fixed, like birth origin. However, the term is commonly applied by official statistical bureaus to changes in migrant status where, for example, an international migrant may enter the country on a temporary visa, and later be awarded permanent citizenship. Such changes cause a headache for analysts working with migration data, who must constantly recalculate and revise their publications. Mostly the changes are small and have a reasonably minor effect on trends, but they are nevertheless important to correct. They become more significant when projections, that is scientifically developed estimates of future population size and composition, are made on the basis of them. Small inaccuracies can become large ones when compounded.

Inter-collection discontinuities

We now turn to **inter-collection discontinuities**, which are discontinuities between data collections. These are important for both longitudinal and comparative analysis. Again, there are Type 1, 2 and 3 discontinuities, each reflecting their intra-collection counterparts.

Inter-collection discontinuities: Gaps or changes in the data categories or criteria between different collections.

- Type 1 inter-collection discontinuities arise when the questions asked differ, however slightly, between collections. For example, one collection (such as the Census) may provide a list of options for ethnic affiliation or marital status, while another (such as the Birth Register) may ask the respondent to state these without providing any such prompts. As a result, the proportions listed as one or another ethnic group or marital status may differ between collections, making comparison between and/or combination of the two difficult.
- Type 2 inter-collection discontinuities occur when the criteria that define, for example, unemployment in one collection (such as the Census) differ in another (such as the Unemployment Register).
- Type 3 inter-collection discontinuities occur when people identify (or are identified) differently in different collections. An example would be when a child is registered at birth (in the Vital Registrations Collection) as Indigenous, but later self-identifies

Natalie Jackson

(in the census) as non-Indigenous. This situation differs subtly but importantly from its category jumping intra-collection counterpart. There, the person 'changes identity' over time, within the one collection; here, he or she identifies, or is identified by others, differently in different collections.

Box 7.4 summarises these seemingly convoluted issues. In short, intra-collection discontinuities concern changes within the collection over time, while inter-collection discontinuities concern factors that differ between collections. Note that the latter may also involve changes over time; that is, different collections may contain both intra- and inter-collection discontinuities. The issues are of paramount importance to rigorous (squeaky-clean) quantitative analysis. It is of little utility to track a trend, or make a comparison between populations, if at least part of your finding is corrupted by an artefact of the data.

Box 7.4: Intra- and inter-collection data discontinuities

	Intra-collection discontinuities (within one collection)	Inter-collection discontinuities (different collections)
Type 1	Questions dropped or new questions added	Different ways of eliciting information (questions added, questions—e.g. options provided/not provided—rephrased/changed)
Type 2	Changes to definitional and classification criteria	Different definitional and classification criteria used
Type 3	Category jumping (e.g. changing ethnic identity between observations)	Category jumping (e.g. identifying differently in different collections)

When undertaking secondary data population-level analysis, researchers should therefore, wherever possible, read the underlying questions and definitional notes carefully. Footnotes explaining any disparities should ideally accompany each table or figure, and are typically located immediately beneath the table or figure. Such understandings and annotation are particularly important where data collections are combined to investigate factors that are not all contained within the one collection, such as birth and death rates, especially when these are calculated for ethnic groups. Obviously, people who die do not fill in the census after the event, nor do we wait for the census to register births. It is in these cases that the classic category jumping outlined above occurs. In the case of both births and deaths, someone else provides information to the relevant authorities. In the event of a death, this person may be a relative of the deceased, but equally well may be a medical practitioner or traffic officer. That person may provide incorrect information, especially when it concerns ethnicity. In the case of a birth, the information-giver is typically the parent.

However, while that parent may register the child's ethnicity (and perhaps religion and gender) in accordance with his or her own affiliations, that child may affiliate differently when he or she becomes an adult and provides his or her own information.

These data eventually find their way to (typically) the same official bureau of statistics that has responsibility for the census collection. Then, if we wish to calculate the birth or death rate, we find the numerator in the Vital Registrations collection, and the denominator in the Census. While these data then permit us to construct rates, what we in fact construct are typically ratios, because we are attributing the births and deaths of people defined by someone else as one or another ethnic (or religious or educational) group, to the population that is typically self-defined. If a numerator or denominator is artefactually inflated or deflated, the resulting rate will be affected. For example, an inflated numerator will increase the rate, while an inflated denominator will lower it.

Having now developed an appreciation for the complexities, we can turn to the more interesting application of population-level analysis. As indicated above, a wide range of techniques can be used to elicit very different stories from the same data. In the remaining space of this chapter, we will consider the index of dissimilarity, and standardisation; two of my favourites.

Useful techniques

Index of dissimilarity

The **index of dissimilarity** (ID) was originally designed to measure the degree of residential segregation by race (Duncan & Duncan 1955:493–503). It is a very simple technique for comparing differences (and similarities) between two or more populations. It generates a single-figure index, which is especially useful when tracked over time; that is, to compare whether the populations are becoming more or less (dis)similar. An index of 100 would indicate complete dissimilarity, and one of zero would indicate complete similarity. It would tell you what percentage of one population would need to change categories for the frequency distributions of both populations to be the same.

> **Index of dissimilarity:** A measure of the extent to which one population differs or is similar to another; an index of 100 would indicate complete dissimilarity while an index of 0 would indicate complete similarity. The index expresses the percentage of the population that would need to change categories in order for the two populations to have identical frequency distributions in relation to a specific factor.

The index is most often applied to the comparison of the industrial and occupational distributions of different ethnic and/or gender groups. But it can also be calculated on any relevant frequency distribution data, for example, proportions of the population by marital or educational status. (Note that the ID is also often used to compare distributions from sample survey data; it is not solely used for population-level analysis.) The worked example in box 7.5 applies the index to the educational distributions from table 7.3, and compares the ID for males and females across time.

Box 7.5: Calculating the index of dissimilarity

Step 1

Locate and assemble the data distributions you wish to compare, ensuring that each pertains to identical information (for example, the same qualification categories) and totals 100 per cent. Here we are using the data from table 7.3 above, now retitled table 7.4 (on page 199).

Step 2

Subtract the relevant percentages for each 'category' (in this case, individual educational qualification group) for one group (such as females) from the other (males). Here we subtract the 1996 value for females with a postgraduate degree (0.9 per cent) from the corresponding value for males (1.9 per cent). The result is 1.0 percentage point, as shown in the 1996 column under the heading 'Males – females' (males minus females).

Repeat for each category. Some will result in positive values (as with postgraduate degree) and some, negative (as with graduate diploma). The positive signs are saying that males have higher levels of the qualification, while the negative signs are saying that they have lower levels. When the sign shifts from positive to negative (or vice versa), it is indicating that a crossover has occurred (as with bachelors degree, which shifts from positive to negative between 1996 and 2001, indicating the point at which females began to have higher levels of this qualification than males).

Step 3

Sum the positive signs only (that is, of the answers in your results columns). The overall result for 1996 is 15.7, while that for 1996 is 14.2, and 2001, 11.5. These are percentage point differences.

Step 4

Validate (check) your result by summing the negative signs separately. This time, you should get −15.7, −14.2 and −11.5. You can now ignore these negative answers; they are simply used to check that you have added up correctly. An alternative check is that the overall total of the positive and negative results should sum to zero.

Social Research Methods

Table 7.4: Non-school qualification (percentage distribution and change): Level of education by sex (i), persons aged 15 years or over (excluding overseas visitors), 1996, 2001, 2006

	Males 1996	Males 2001	Males 2006	Females 1996	Females 2001	Females 2006	Males – females 1996	Males – females 2001	Males – females 2006
Postgraduate degree	1.9	2.3	3.0	0.9	1.4	2.2	1.0	0.9	0.8
Graduate diploma and graduate certificate	1.0	1.1	1.1	1.6	1.7	1.8	−0.6	−0.6	−0.7
Bachelor degree	7.9	9.2	10.6	7.6	10.2	12.5	0.3	−1.0	−1.9
Advanced (undergraduate) diploma and diploma	5.2	5.4	6.2	6.9	6.6	8.0	−1.6	−1.2	−1.8
Certificate (vocational) level	20.9	23.1	23.1	6.4	8.8	10.6	14.5	14.3	12.5
Not stated (ii)	10.8	10.2	12.7	13.0	12.5	13.4	−2.2	−2.3	−0.7
No post-school qualifications (iii)	52.3	48.7	43.3	63.6	58.8	51.5	−11.4	−10.1	−8.2
Total/index of dissimilarity	100.0	100.0	100.0	100.0	100.0	100.0	15.8	15.2	13.3
Validate							−15.8	−15.2	−13.5

i   Excludes schooling up to Year 12.
ii   Includes 'inadequately described'.
iii Includes persons who have a qualification out of the scope of the Australian Standard Classification of Education.

Sources: ABS 2003; ABS 2008

Interpreting your results

The results show that the ID for educational qualifications between Australian males and females has been steadily reducing since (at least) 1996. Remembering that complete dissimilarity would be 100, findings of 15.8 and 13.3 show that dissimilarity is approaching relatively low levels. However, it remains that in 2006, 13.3 per cent of females would need to change qualification categories for their educational qualification distribution to equal that of males. At this point, you have to ask yourself what this finding means. It might, for example, be that females simply choose to pursue different qualifications than males, and that they may not wish to 'trade places' with them. We can largely dismiss this proposition, because, as shown above, females have been increasing their acquisition of higher qualifications at greater rates than males.

Natalie Jackson

Limitations of the index of dissimilarity

Judgment: Considered opinion.

So, interpretation of your results also requires an element of **judgment**. You may, for example, believe that females should have lower educational qualifications than males, and be horrified to see the ID reducing. However, we will assume that you are not going to interpret your findings from a value position. Rather, in interpreting them you would be better to consider their limitations. The index of dissimilarity has been argued to have a number of limitations, for example:

- the number of categories within the overall frequency distribution influences the results (Shyrock & Siegel 1976:233; Swanson & Siegel 2004)
- differences in the relative size of categories influence the results, especially when the ID is compared across time, and/or between populations
- it is not always easy to determine exactly what is a 'high' or 'low' result. For example, while it might be considered that an ID of 20 is relatively low, and one of 50 or more is high, that will depend on the number of categories in the distribution being examined (and also on whether the categories are similar in size to each other, but this is a more complicated limitation that can be left for further reading; for example, Gibbs 1965; Karmel & Maclachlan 1988:187–95; Jones 1992).

Artefact of technique: An anomaly that is caused by the technique being used or the data categories chosen.

These limitations can lead to findings that are **'artefacts' (anomalies) of the technique**. Let us then complete our acquaintance with this index by recalculating it with a reduced number of categories, to see the effect. As you can see in table 7.5, the data for all qualifications 'bachelor degree and above' have been aggregated into one category, and that for 'not stated' and 'no post-school qualifications' into another. Although the trend remains the same (the ID reduces over time), the reduced number of categories causes the ID for each observation to reduce slightly in magnitude. It is a good example of the problem of interpretation, because we must now confront the dilemma of what the 'true' level of dissimilarity actually is. There is no real answer for this, except your judgment in terms of the issue being examined and an understanding that a trend tells us much more than does a 'snapshot' (a one-off observation). And it also pays to keep in mind the question of whether the people in those categories would actually wish to be in different ones, and indeed, what would happen (to society, or the labour market etc.) if they were. In short, the ID is not used to say that it is desirable for different populations to have the same educational (or industrial etc.) distribution; it is merely a readily observable index of difference.

Table 7.5: Non-school qualification (percentage distribution and index of dissimilarity): Level of education by sex (i), persons aged 15 years or over (excluding overseas visitors), 1996, 2001, 2006

	Males 1996	Males 2001	Males 2006	Females 1996	Females 2001	Females 2006	Males minus females 1996	Males minus females 2001	Males minus females 2006
Bachelor degree and above	10.8	12.6	14.7	10.1	13.3	16.4	0.7	−0.7	−1.7
Advanced (undergraduate) diploma and diploma	5.2	5.4	6.2	6.9	6.6	8.0	−1.7	−1.2	−1.8
Certificate (vocational) level	20.9	23.1	23.1	6.4	8.8	10.6	14.5	14.3	12.5
Not stated/ No post-school qualifications	63.1	58.9	56.0	76.6	71.3	65.0	−13.5	−12.4	−9.0
Total/Index of dissimilarity	100.0	100.0	100.0	100.0	100.0	100.0	15.2	14.3	12.5
						Validate	−15.2	−14.3	−12.5

Sources: ABS 2003; ABS 2008 (notes as for table 7.4)

Box 7.6: Summarising the index of dissimilarity

- The index of dissimilarity (ID) is a simple statistical technique for comparing differences (or similarities) between two or more populations.
- The ID is calculated by subtracting the percentage distribution for each individual category of any 'frequency distribution' (such as educational qualifications) of one population from another and summing the 'positive' results.
- An ID of zero denotes complete similarity, and an ID of 100 denotes complete dissimilarity. The answer refers to the percentage point difference between the two distributions, and indicates the percentage of one population that would need to change categories in order for it to have the same frequency distribution as the other population.
- The number of categories in an overall distribution (for example, the number of different educational qualifications within the overall distribution for educational qualifications) influences the results.
- Determining whether an ID is 'high' (a high level of dissimilarity) or 'low' (a low level of dissimilarity) involves judgment. An ID of 20 for educational qualifications might be considered relatively high, because it means that 20 per cent of one population (such as females) would have to change categories for it to have the same qualification levels

Natalie Jackson

as the other population (such as males). On the other hand, an ID of 20 for industrial distribution might signify relatively low levels of inequality, because it might simply reflect a highly diverse industrial structure (one with many categories or one in which men and women choose to work in different industries).
- The ID is also not calculated in order to argue that two or more populations 'should' (or 'shouldn't') have identical frequency distributions for any given factor, but simply as a means of expressing the degree of that difference or similarity. It is of most value when examined as a trend rather than a single observation.
- Interpreting the ID thus also involves judgment, first, about the number of subcategories involved; second, about the substantive issue being investigated; and third, about what complete similarity (if achieved) would mean for that society.

The ID is an extremely easy and useful technique to learn. Why not try working through the steps yourself? Exercise 7.1 provides data for the same qualification categories in table 7.4, but this time for Australia's Indigenous and non-Indigenous populations (males and females combined).

Exercise 7.1: Calculating and interpreting the index of dissimilarity

Step 1
Examine the data distributions in table 7.6 (below).

Step 2
Subtract the relevant percentages for each educational qualification category for the Indigenous population from the corresponding category for the non-Indigenous population (that is, non-Indigenous minus Indigenous).

Step 3
Sum the positive signs only (that is, of the answers in your results columns).

Step 4
Validate (check) your result by summing the negative signs separately. (Alternatively check that the overall total of the positive and negative results sum to zero.)

Table 7.6: Non-school qualification: Level of education (i) by Indigenous status (percentage distribution and index of dissimilarity), persons aged 15 years or over, 2006

	Non-Indigenous	Indigenous	Non-Indigenous minus Indigenous
Postgraduate degree	2.8	0.4	
Graduate diploma and graduate certificate	1.5	0.4	
Bachelor degree	12.4	2.9	
Advanced (undergraduate) diploma and diploma	7.6	3.1	
Certificate (vocational) level	17.7	13.2	
Not stated/No post-school qualifications (ii)	58.0	80.0	
Total/Index of dissimilarity	100.0	100.0	
Sum			
Validation			

i   Excludes schooling up to Year 12.
ii   Includes 'inadequately described', persons who do not have a qualification and persons who have a qualification out of scope of the Australian Standard Classification of Education.
Source: ABS 2007

Step 5
Interpret your results.

Answer
The ID is 22.0, which means that 22.0 per cent of the Indigenous population would need to change educational categories for its educational distribution to be the same as that for the non-Indigenous population. The Indigenous population is underrepresented in every category except 'Not stated/No post-school qualifications'.

Standardisation

We now turn to a slightly more sophisticated measure of dissimilarity: the technique of standardisation. This is an extremely useful technique for the social science researcher's toolbox.

The basic premise of **standardisation** is that any **summary measure** (like the total unemployment rate, the suicide rate or the home ownership rate) is always a product of at least two things (see over page).

Standardisation: A statistical technique by which one or more factors are reduced to a common standard or held constant (such as the age structure that occurred in a given year may be applied to each successive year to see what the effect on some factor would be if the age structure had not changed).

Summary measure: The average or mean.

Natalie Jackson

1   the underlying level of the phenomenon of interest (that is, unemployment, suicide, home ownership)

2   the **composition** of the population for which the calculation is being made; that is, the extent to which the population is concentrated in categories like age, sex, marital status or education level where the phenomenon of interest is particularly likely or unlikely to occur.

Composition: The subcategories or subgroups comprising the whole category or group.

Let's say you are interested in whether various government policies on unemployment have had any effect on lowering the unemployment rate. You might begin by comparing the total unemployment rate at various points between 1985 and 2006, and find that it has fallen steadily. However, in 1985, the Australian population was relatively youthful (it had a youthful age structure), while by 2006 it had 'aged' considerably; that is, by 2006 it contained a smaller proportion of young people and a greater proportion of elderly. This seemingly innocuous change will have had an effect on the total unemployment rate (all else remaining equal), because, as noted in the case study opening this chapter, unemployment is something that typically affects young people.

Of course, age structure is not the only factor that will have changed. Others, like the changing educational qualification distributions examined above, will also have had an impact. Ideally then, we need to be able to separate out or 'control for' these effects. Standardisation performs this little miracle for us. It doesn't alter the underlying reality of the situation, but it does tell us what (for example) the unemployment rate in 2006 would have been if there had been no change in the age structure since 1985.

Standardisation is also used to refine comparisons of summary data between different groups, both across time—as with the above example—or at the same point in time. The case study example outlined at the start of the chapter used standardisation to examine the effect of a particular government policy on differences in the **age composition** of the Māori and European-origin populations of New Zealand, as they were in 1991.

Age composition: Distribution of the population by age.

The exercise in box 7.7 similarly applies the technique to the analysis of the gap in the total unemployment rates of the Indigenous and non-Indigenous populations of Australia. We do this because the age structures of the two populations are dramatically different; the Indigenous population has a **median age** of around 21 years, meaning that half of the Indigenous population falls beneath this age, while the non-Indigenous population has a median age of 38 years, similarly meaning that half of the non-Indigenous population is aged less than 38 years.

Median age: The exact age above and below which half the population falls.

When compared with the Indigenous population, the latter also means that only 26 per cent of the non-Indigenous population is aged less than 19 years.

Figure 7.1 shows the profound nature of these differences. Note that, in reality, the Indigenous population accounts for less than 3 per cent of the total Australian population. The two populations appear the same size here because the numbers at each age have been converted to percentages (rates). It is conventional to do this so that we can compare apples with apples. As noted earlier, numbers have their uses, but for comparative purposes we nearly always need to convert them to rates.

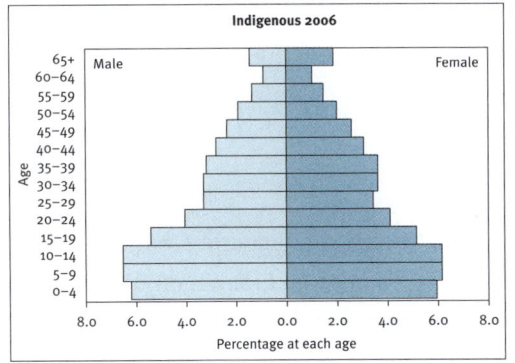

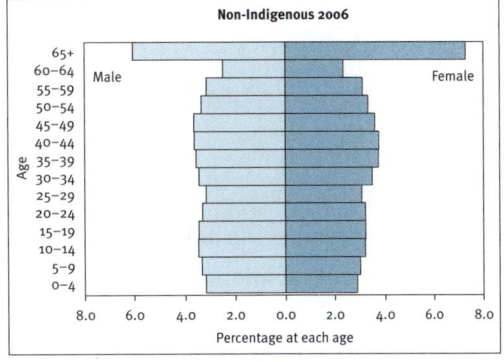

Figure 7.1: **Age–sex structures** of the Indigenous and non-Indigenous populations of Australia, 2006

Source: ABS 2007

Having converted numbers at each age to percentages, we find that at ages 15 to 24, where the risk of unemployment is greatest, the proportions of the Indigenous and non-Indigenous populations are around 18.9 and 13.5 per cent respectively. This disparity means that there are **proportionately** 1.4 young Indigenous people for every young non-Indigenous person. To calculate this ratio, you simply divide the percentage for the former population by the percentage for the latter (18.9/13.5 = 1.4). As a result of this difference, the Indigenous population is **disproportionately** exposed to the risk of being unemployed.

Age–sex structure: Distribution of the population by age and sex.

Proportionately: Relative proportions or percentages, as opposed to numbers.

Disproportionately: Unequal proportions, such as of two populations in the same age group.

Age-specific: Pertaining to a specific age group.

Comparing the proportions of each population at each individual age like this is very useful to get an overview of how they differ, and therefore how they might interact with a particular policy. However, standardisation permits us to examine the overall effect of the differences for all of the age groups at once. Box 7.7 provides a worked example. In short, you multiply each **age-specific** unemployment rate—that is, the

Natalie Jackson

unemployment rate for each individual age group for one population by the corresponding proportion of the other population at each age—and sum the results. The process weights the total unemployment rate for the first population by the age structure of the second, to tell us what the rate would be if the first population did actually have the age structure of the second.

Let's work through the process together. Note that, in this exercise (box 7.7), population age structure refers to 'labour force population', because, technically speaking, this is the population that is at risk of unemployment, not the population as a whole. People who are past retirement age or those still of school age are not at current risk of unemployment.

Box 7.7: Doing standardisation

Step 1

Locate and assemble the data distributions you wish to compare, ensuring that each pertains to identical information (for example, the exact same age groupings). Table 7.7 provides age-specific unemployment data for the Indigenous male labour force (column 1), and the corresponding proportion at each age of the non-Indigenous male labour force (column 2).

Step 2

Multiply (in column 3) the unemployment rates at each age for the Indigenous labour force by the corresponding proportion of the non-Indigenous labour force at those ages. (Do not multiply the total unemployment rate, 15.7 per cent, by anything.)

Step 3

Sum the results. The answer tells us what the total unemployment rate for the Indigenous labour force would be if it had the same age structure as the non-Indigenous labour force. The answer is 13.7 per cent, indicating that if the relatively youthful Indigenous labour force had the same age structure as the 'older' non-Indigenous labour force, it could expect to have lower overall unemployment.

Note that each age-specific answer you get in column 3 is meaningless in and of itself; it is the sum of the age-weighted rates you are seeking to determine.

Social Research Methods

Table 7.7: Standardisation: Indigenous male unemployment rates to non-Indigenous male age structure 2006

Age	Indigenous males age-specific unemployment rates	Non-Indigenous males age structure (of the labour force)	Indigenous unemployment rate with non-Indigenous age structure	Explanation: age-specific results are meaningless in and of themselves; only their sum is relevant
15–24	22.3	0.16	3.6	
25–34	15.9	0.21	3.3	
35–44	13.7	0.24	3.3	
45–54	9.7	0.22	2.1	
55–64	8.5	0.14	1.2	
65+	7.2	0.03	0.2	
Total	15.7	1.00	13.7	

Source: Calculated from Australian Bureau of Statistics (2007) Basic Community Profiles (Indigenous), Catalogue 2002.0, Table I30, and Time Series Profiles, Australia, Catalogue 2003.0

Step 4

Calculate the magnitude of the effect. First, deduct the 'old' unstandardised rate (15.7 per cent) from the 'new' age-standardised rate (13.7 per cent). The answer is −2.0 percentage points (a reduction of 2.0 percentage points). Then convert this result to its percentage effect, by dividing the −2.0 percentage point difference by the original value of 15.7 per cent, and multiplying by 100. That is:

- Standardised rate − Unstandardised rate = 13.7 − 15.7 = −2.0 percentage points
- Change as a percentage = (−2.0/15.7)*100 = −12.5 per cent

The result indicates that, if the Indigenous male labour force had the older age structure of the non-Indigenous male labour force, its total unemployment rate would be around 12.5 per cent lower.

Step 5

You can validate (check) your answer by multiplying the age-specific unemployment rates for the Indigenous labour force by the corresponding proportion of its own labour force population at each age, given in column 2 of table 7.8, below (see exercise 7.2). The answer should be identical to the original total unemployment rate for the Indigenous population, because it has simply been 'weighted' by its own age structure.

Natalie Jackson

Let's work through the exercise again, this time using unemployment data for the non-Indigenous labour force, and age structure data for the Indigenous labour force (see table 7.8 in exercise 7.2). This time, you will observe the opposite effect.

Exercise 7.2: Trying out standardisation

Step 1
Examine the data in table 7.8. Table 7.8 provides age-specific unemployment data for the non-Indigenous male labour force (column 1), and the corresponding proportion at each age of the Indigenous male labour force (column 2).

Step 2
Multiply (in column 3) the unemployment rates at each age for the non-Indigenous labour force by the corresponding proportion of the Indigenous labour force at those ages. (Do not multiply the total unemployment rate—5.0 per cent—by anything.)

Step 3
Sum the results. The answer tells us what the total unemployment rate for the non-Indigenous labour force would be if it had the same age structure as the Indigenous labour force.

Remember that each age-specific answer you get in column 3 is meaningless in and of itself; it is the sum of the weighted rates you are seeking to determine.

Table 7.8: Standardisation: Non-Indigenous male unemployment rates to Indigenous male age structure

Age	Non-Indigenous males age-specific unemployment rates	Indigenous males age structure (of the labour force)	Non-Indigenous unemployment rate with Indigenous age structure	Explanation: age-specific results are meaningless and of themselves; only their sum is relevant
15–24	10.4	0.29		
25–34	4.9	0.25		
35–44	3.7	0.23		
45–54	3.5	0.16		
55–64	4.4	0.06		
65+	1.9	0.01		
Total	5.0	1.00		

Source: Calculated from Australian Bureau of Statistics (2007) Basic Community Profiles (Indigenous), Catalogue 2002.0, Table I30 and Time Series Profiles, Catalogue 2003.0

Step 4

Calculate the magnitude of the effect. First, deduct the old unstandardised rate (5.0 per cent) from the new age-standardised rate (..... per cent). Then convert the percentage point answer (.....) to percentage effect, by dividing it by the original value of 5.0 per cent and multiplying by 100. Or:

- Standardised rate – Unstandardised rate = (...... – 5.0) = ... percentage points
- Change as a percentage = (...... percentage points/5.0)*100 = ... per cent

Step 5

You can validate (check) your answer by multiplying the age-specific unemployment rates for the non-Indigenous labour force by the corresponding proportion of its own labour force population at each age, given in column 2 of table 7.7 (see box 7.7). The answer should be identical to the original total unemployment rate for the non-Indigenous population, because it has simply been 'weighted' by its own age structure.

Answer

This time the answer at Step 3 is 5.9 per cent, which is 0.9 percentage points higher than the original (crude) total unemployment rate for the non-Indigenous labour force. It tells us that if the older non-Indigenous labour force had the more youthful age structure of the Indigenous labour force, it could expect to have higher total unemployment.

When the 0.9 percentage point difference is expressed as a percentage of the original unemployment rate (0.9/5.09)*100), at step 4 we find that, if the non-Indigenous male labour force had the younger age structure of the Indigenous male labour force, its total unemployment rate would be around 18.7 per cent higher.

The findings from the exercise you have just worked through are not merely academic. They have hugely important **policy implications**, because they indicate that at least some of the difference between Indigenous and non-Indigenous Australians (and many other subpopulations) across both unemployment and a range of other social phenomena is attributable to differences in age structure. More awareness of this information would undoubtedly assist in the development of more appropriate (and probably more efficacious) policy interventions, and ensure that existing disadvantages, and advantages, were not further compounded.

> **Policy implications**: Policy-related consequences of an issue or research finding.

As noted earlier, you can also standardise your analysis by a range of other factors that have an impact on the phenomenon you are interested in, such as differences in educational composition and marital status. With a little practice (and a little thought) these factors can be readily controlled for simultaneously. A classic example would be in the examination of

Natalie Jackson

suicide rates, where both age structure and the marital status of the population are known to be risk factors.

Finally, it is worth noting that standardisation is the first step in a further data refinement technique called **decomposition**, sometimes called 'component analysis'. Again, we are not exploring this technique in this book, but it is worth being aware of, because now that you can do standardisation, you are well on the way to doing many exciting projects. The value of decomposition is that it takes the results from standardisation and splits them into their component parts. The impact of each can then be quantified, so that, for example, instead of having two rather lengthy answers for our standardisation exercise (7.2), we would be able to state that '13.6 per cent of the difference in the crude unemployment rates of Indigenous and non-Indigenous males is accounted for by differences in age structure'. It is only a little step, but one that makes your results that much more refined, and also easier to write up.

> **Decomposition:** Sometimes called component analysis: the breaking down of the outcome into its contributing components.

Box 7.8: Summarising standardisation

- The basic premise behind standardisation is that any summary measure such as the total unemployment rate, the suicide rate and the home ownership rate is always a product of at least two things: (a) the underlying level of the phenomenon of interest; and (b) the composition of the population for which the calculation is being made. By composition is meant the population age structure, marital status and educational distribution, where the phenomenon of interest is particularly likely or unlikely to occur.
- Standardisation is a statistical technique that controls for the compositional differences in populations, whether viewed at a single point in time, or across time. In short, it converts each population to a standard base so that we can compare apples with apples.
- The technique doesn't alter the reality of the situation, but it does allow us to observe what the situation regarding the phenomenon of interest would be if the two (or more) populations had the same composition.
- Standardisation has a wide variety of applications. As outlined in this chapter, it can be used to compare populations at a single point in time, or across time. It can also be used to project (forward or backwards) many social phenomena.
- Standardisation is the first step of a further data refinement technique of which you should be aware. This is the technique of decomposition (sometimes called component analysis), which splits the phenomenon of interest into its various components, and quantifies their impact.

For further reading, see Swanson and Siegel 2004.

Voices in the field

Honours student to practitioner

Several of the author's honours students used the above techniques in their thesis projects, and have since found their way into fantastic jobs in a range of government departments and statistical agencies across Australia and Britain.

In 2001, Britany Thompson undertook an analysis of future demand for education in three Australian states. By holding age-specific rates constant at their 1999 levels and applying them to projected numbers at each age (an indirect application of standardisation), she was able to show that demand for education (or alternatively, the supply of students) would soon diminish, and would do so at different rates in each state—as indeed it has. The work was instrumental in getting the issue of declining school populations in Tasmania on the agenda of the Tasmanian government.

In 2003, Cassandra Eaves used the index of dissimilarity to examine differences in educational attainment in Tasmania's three major regions, and in 2004 Katie Hutt used it to examine differences in labour market participation by region.

In 2007, Alice Reid revisited the issue of declining school populations in Tasmania. She extended her study to calculate how many teachers and schools the declining numbers of students would need in the future, and further added in the age structure of teachers themselves. To calculate future teacher demand, she used standardisation to hold the ratio of teachers to students constant at its 2005 level, and applied it to projected student numbers. By then incorporating the age structure of teachers into her interpretation, she was able to show that, while natural attrition from teacher retirements will cause the numbers of teachers and students to decline at similar rates, there will be a brief period where student numbers will increase slightly (because of a recent increase in birth numbers) while teacher numbers will continue to decline, resulting in a shortfall of teachers for that period.

In 2008, Lisa Taylor used the index of dissimilarity to examine the extent to which women with the same qualifications and of the same partner and child status as men would have to change their level of labour market attachment for their labour force status to be the same as that of men. She also used the index to compare the extent to which men and women with the same qualifications were being employed in the same occupations. She found that women were not being utilised in the labour market to the same degree as men. However, the issue was not their participation rates—which have in fact increased substantially over the years—but rather that their qualifications were not being equally utilised because of being a parent and/or

Natalie Jackson

being partnered. She showed that these two factors raise labour market attachment for similarly qualified males, but reduce it for females. She argued that policy intervention aimed at increasing the utilisation of women's qualifications (perhaps via the provision of more appropriate or targeted child care support) may be a more effective strategy in raising their productivity than attempting to raise participation rates per se.

It is work like this that sees students with population-level analytical skills snapped up by employers.

From method to practice

The above techniques are typically used by practitioners who wish to gain a more refined insight into the population-level issue they are investigating, and contribute to more appropriate policy development. For example, as indicated at the outset of this chapter, in 2002 I used a combination of the two techniques to show how a change in the age of access for the adult rate of unemployment benefit (from 20 to 25 years) had markedly different effects on Māori and European-origin New Zealanders, simply because of their differing age structures. The combination involved age-standardising the index of dissimilarity to make it free of age structural effects (a practice I would strongly encourage). More recently (2008 in press), I have used the same approach to examine the impact on educational attainment of the differing age structures of Australia's Indigenous and non-Indigenous populations, and to consider the implications of these findings for the policy of closing the gaps (between the two populations). Using the age-standardised index of dissimilarity, I show first that crude gaps in educational attainment increased across the period 1981–2006, after first declining slightly between 1981 and 1991. Examining each qualification category in turn, I then show how differences in age structure conceal what would otherwise be greater or smaller gaps in attainment. However, most importantly, I was able to illustrate how the Indigenous age structure is becoming increasingly optimal for the gaining of higher qualifications, and to argue that these differences must be explicitly acknowledged and built into all 'closing the gap' policy interventions.

Box 7.9: Where to access population-level data

- www.abs.gov.au (Australia)
- www.stats.govt.nz (New Zealand)
- www.census.gov/ipc/www/idbnew.html (US Census Bureau International Database)
- www.prb.org/databycountry (US Population Reference Bureau)
- www.census.gov/population/www/socdemo/age.html (US data on age groups)
- www.statcan.ca (Canada)

- www.statistics.gov.uk/census2001/default.asp (UK)
- www.oecd.org/home (OECD country data)
- www.stat.go.jp/english/index.htm (Japan plus statistical agencies, worldwide)
- www.nidi.nl (Netherlands Interdisciplinary Demographic Institute)
- www.demogr.mpg.de (Max Planck Demographic Institute, Germany)
- www.demography.anu.edu.au/VirtualLibrary (Population links, worldwide)
- www.bubl.ac.uk/link/w/worldpopulation.htm (24,000 time-series for 196 countries)
- www.un.org/esa/population/unpop.htm (United Nations Population Division)
- www.un.org/Pubs/CyberSchoolBus/res.html (United Nations general database)
- PopPlanet.org/PopPlanet (country profiles on population, health, environment)
- www.un.org/popin (United Nations population information network).

Natalie Jackson

Conclusion

Population-level analysis is both simple and fun to do. It provides evidence-based answers to many critical questions. It also paints the big picture that provides the context and often the rationale for much other research, like that carried out by qualitative researchers. An enormous array of unanalysed data awaits the skills of population-level data analysts. If you have enjoyed this chapter, you are well on your way to being one.

To help get you started, box 7.9 lists some useful sites for accessing (mainly) population-level data on the web. This list is by no means exhaustive of what is available.

Main points

> Population-level analysis means analysis that is undertaken on whole populations, be they global, national or regional populations, ethnic or gender groups, labour force, industrial, occupational or educational distributions.

> Because whole populations are being analysed, all findings are statistically significant: there is no need to be concerned with confidence levels and sampling errors.

> Nevertheless, population-level analyses are subject to limitations. In particular, there are intra- and inter-collection data discontinuities to be aware of, the former meaning discontinuities (and disparities) within the same data collection, and the latter meaning discontinuities (and disparities) between data collections. Such information should always be included somewhere in the report, especially at the base of any tabular or graphical illustrations.

> Like other analysts, population-level analysts must employ judgment in their choice of unit(s) of analysis, and when or whether to use absolute numbers, rates, ratios, percentages or proportions.

> An extremely useful and simple measure for assessing similarity or difference between two or more populations is the index of dissimilarity (ID), which measures the proportion of one or other population that would need to shift categories in order for the two (or more) distributions to be the same. An index of 100 would indicate complete dissimilarity; one of zero would indicate complete similarity.

> Judgment is also important in interpreting a study's findings. What may appear to be a strong or weak, high or low finding may be an artefact of the particular technique, such as the number of categories in the analysis.

> A more refined and slightly more complex technique for assessing similarity (or difference) between populations at either a single point in time, or across time, is standardisation. This process holds one factor, such as age (or marital or industrial) structure, constant in order to see what the situation would be if the two (or more) populations had the same age (or marital or industrial) structure.

> Both of the techniques illustrated in this chapter are particularly useful for assessing the impact of policy interventions, the timing of which can be annotated on graphs and analysed for their impact(s).

Acknowledgment

ABS data included in this chapter is used with the permission of the Australian Bureau of Statistics. <www.abs.gov.au>.

Further reading

If you want to learn more about using population-level analysis as a social research method, the following books and articles are particularly recommended:

Glen, N. (1975). *Cohort Analysis*. London: Sage.

Swanson, D. A. and Siegel, J. S. (2004). *The Methods and Materials of Demography*, 2nd edn. California and London: Elsevier.

References

Australian Bureau of Statistics (2003). *Time Series Profiles 1991–2001 Australia*. Catalogue 2003.0, Table 11.

Australian Bureau of Statistics (2007). Non-School Qualification: Level of Education by Indigenous Status and Age, customised database. Available from author.

Australian Bureau of Statistics (2008).Unpublished time series data for 2006 provided by ABS. Available from author.

Duncan, O. D. and Duncan, B. (1955). 'A Methodological Analysis of Segregation Indices', *American Sociological Review*, 20: 210–17.

Gibbs, J. (1965). 'Occupational Differentiation of Negroes and Whites in the United States', *Social Forces*, 44 (2): 159–65.

Glen, N. (1975). *Cohort Analysis*. London: Sage.

Natalie Jackson

Gould, J. D. (1992). '"Māori" in the Population Census, 1971–1991', *New Zealand Population Review*, 18 (1,2): 36–67.

Hout, M. and Goldstein, J. R. (1994). 'How 4.5 Million Irish Immigrants Became 40 Million Irish Americans: Demographic and Substantive Aspects of the Ethnic Composition of White Americans', *American Sociological Review*, 59 (1): 64–82.

Jackson, N. O. (2002). 'The Doubly-Structural Nature of Indigenous Disadvantage. Indigenous Age Structures and the Notion of Disparate Impact', *New Zealand Population Review*, 28 (1): 55–68.

Jackson, N. O. (2008 in press). 'Educational Attainment and the (Growing) Importance of Age Structure: Indigenous and non-Indigenous Australians', *Journal of Population Research*, 25 (2).

Jones, F. L. (1992). 'Segregation Indices: An Historical and Conceptual Note', *Australian and New Zealand Journal of Sociology*, 28 (1): 105–10.

Karmel, T. and Maclachlan, M. (1988). 'Occupational Sex Segregation: Increasing or Decreasing?', *Economic Record*, 64 (186): 187–95.

Morrison, P. (1991). 'Change or Continuity in the Census? Problems of Comparability in the New Zealand Census', *New Zealand Population Review*, 17 (1): 4–40.

Pool, D. I. (1981). 'New Zealand: Ethnic Questions in the Census and Other Official Data', *New Community*, ix (1): 91–7.

Pool, I. (1987). Implications of Changes in the Cohort/Age Structure of the New Zealand Population. Paper presented to the Biennial Conference of the Population Association of New Zealand, Auckland.

Shyrock, H. S. and Siegel, J. S. (1976). *The Methods and Materials of Demography*. New York: Academic Press.

Swanson, D. A. and Siegel, J. S. (2004). *The Methods and Materials of Demography*, 2nd edn. California and London: Elsevier.

Weeks, J. R. (1999). *Population: An Introduction to Concepts and Issues*, 7th edn. Belmont: Wadsworth.

Chapter 8

Analysing Quantitative Data

Tim Phillips

What do people in Australia think about capitalism?

Mark Western (1999) conducted a secondary data analysis examining the question of individual attitudes to capitalism in Australia. Using national social survey data, the research examined how class location influences opinions about key economic institutions within capitalist society.

However, to investigate this interesting question, Western was not compelled to undertake an expensive and time-consuming new national survey of his own. This was because a national social survey had recently been conducted, which happened to include subsets of survey questions that connected directly with his topic of interest. The survey was the National Social Science Survey (1995), a mail survey of a national random sample of 2338 Australians. The raw data and questionnaire associated with the survey was available for public access through the Australian Social Science Data Archive (ASSDA). Western applied for and was granted access to the survey data and related documentation. Western proceeded to undertake a process of quantitative data analysis, which involved examining associations between the variables from the survey that were of particular interest to his research question. Western wrote up the findings of his quantitative data analysis in a research paper.

Results: The article was subsequently published in the *Journal of Sociology*, the official journal of the Australian Sociological Association.

Key terms

association
chi square
cross-tabular analysis
data
data set
dependent variable
independent variable
mean
median
mode
nationally based general social surveys
population
primary data collection
probability sampling
process of iteration
quantitative data
secondary data analysis
social science data archives
SPSS (Statistical Product and Service Solutions)
standard deviation
statistical analysis
variance

Introduction: The lure of quantitative data and analysis

When we first discover social science, we will invariably find ourselves immersed in an exciting and dynamic world of key theorists and abstract ideas. The new ways of seeing the social world we are exposed to can seem profound. They might challenge our established patterns of thinking about social life, or open up new possibilities we may not have previously been aware of. In essence, a sociological perspective can appear relevant and authoritative. It seems to matter for making sense of the rapidly changing social world we live in. Furthermore, the interpretations it proffers feel persuasive to us. They may perhaps even resonate closely with our own experiences and perceptions.

Yet, no matter how important and believable they seem, social theory is just that, theory. A sociological explanation that may seem significant or plausible to us in the first instance can often turn out in the cold light of day to be wrong. As social scientists, we need to open ourselves up to this possibility. This involves establishing scepticism (or doubt) as a default style of thinking with respect to theoretical, or 'commonsense' claims about the nature of social life.

Scepticism alone, however, is not helpful. We need a way of clarifying the veracity of such claims, theoretical or everyday. A key way of holding such 'accounts to account' is quantitative social science research. Based on principles of systematic observation, the collection and analysis of **quantitative social science data** is an effective and powerful way of testing, verifying, rejecting or proffering revised or different explanations of social life.

Quantitative data: A set of observations of the social world recorded in numeric form.

Population: The collection of all the units that we want to study.

Quantitative social research studies can be carried out in a variety of different ways. Running a survey (see chapter 6), performing an experiment (see online module), undertaking systematic social observation and undertaking **population** level analysis (see chapter 7) are all popular approaches to doing quantitative research. What they all share is a central concern with the collection and analysis of quantitative data. Social researchers do quantitative data analysis for the purpose of producing reliable evidence that can be used to clarify and refine understanding of the social world. This chapter introduces you to both the practice and the purposes of quantitative data analysis in a social research context.

What is quantitative data, and why do we analyse it?

In social research projects, **data** is something we first 'collect' and then 'analyse'. More precisely, it is the actual record of the full set of observations of the social world that we undertake within a research project. In effect, this record can be envisaged as a container, holding the entire collection of observations carried out for a study. This receptacle of recorded information is known as the data. Data represents the tangible outcome of the data collection process. Furthermore, data constitutes the raw information to be examined in the data analysis phase of the project. The **data set** is the social researcher's record of his or her observations. In any one study, this data set will be either qualitative (a collection of texts) or quantitative (a set of sequenced numbers). Whether a social researcher compiles a data set comprised of documents or digits primarily reflects the type of information sought about the social world.

> **Data**: The information we collect and analyse to answer our research question. Data come in all manner of forms, such as survey forms, documents and secondary data.
>
> **Data set**: The entire set of observations recorded in the course of data collection.

As detailed in chapter 1, the questions social researchers ask about social life fall into two broad methodological categories. Questions of the first kind are concerned with uncovering key meanings, themes and processes in social life. What does it feel like to be depressed? What is the experience of driving a taxi? How do you get involved in Witchcraft? Researchers working along these lines of enquiry aim to provide a rich and vibrant portrayal of a specific filament of social life. They seek to reveal the intricacies and complexities of particular experiences or events. In social research, it is usual to generate such detailed accounts out of the analysis of qualitative data. As outlined in the chapters on qualitative methods, the data that qualitative researchers typically base their studies upon is made up of a small number of cases. Each case is carefully selected as a way of capturing a key social quality of interest to the research, and the details of each case are often recorded verbatim in the form of a distinct narrative or story.

Questions of the second type are quite different. They focus on finding out things about the social world such as: the degree to which a particular social quality is in existence (such as fear of crime); or 'What is the nature of the relationship between two or more different social qualities?' (such as crime victimisation and age). It is common for research in this style to seek to develop answers to such questions with respect to a particular population. 'Is fear of crime at a high, moderate or low level in Australia?' Another aim of studies of this kind is to clarify whether social subgroups within a specific population are

Tim Phillips

different in the degree to which they possess a certain social quality. For example, 'Do older and younger people in Australia diverge in how likely they are to be victims of crime?'

Social researchers conventionally rely upon the results of the analysis of quantitative data to generate answers to these second kinds of questions. What do such quantitative data sources look like? In short, a grid of numbers. This grid is typically comprised of a massive array of numbers crisscrossing in columns and rows. The numbers in each row represent the sequence of answers connected to a specific respondent in the data collection process. The numbers running down each column capture the pattern of answers linked with particular questions. Using techniques of quantitative analysis, such weighty collections of numeric information can be condensed, providing us with meaningful information for reflecting on the research questions driving our study.

How to do quantitative data analysis

Tools for getting started with quantitative data analysis: a PC and SPSS

The actual task of quantitative data analysis is invariably done on a personal computer. Computers provide the social researcher with a powerful tool for processing quantitative data. Computers enable us to perform complex operations in an exacting, efficient and rapid-fire manner, and enable us to generate accurate and succinct information about our data set extremely quickly. To put a computer to work on your data in such dynamic ways, you first need access to a software program designed to perform **statistical analysis**. There is a range of such programs on the market. Some of the better known packages are SAS (Statistical Analysis System) and Stata (Statistical Software for Professionals).

Statistical analysis: A means for revealing patterns and regularities within a quantitative data set.

SPSS (Statistical Product and Service Solutions): the most popular computer program in the social sciences for managing and analysing quantitative data.

The most popular program among social researchers is **SPSS (Statistical Product and Service Solutions)**. SPSS finds commonplace use in sociology, political science, psychology and communications.

In this book the next chapter covers the basics of quantitative analysis using SPSS. The widespread deployment of SPSS among social researchers is a result of the program being originally developed especially for social scientists. In fact, SPSS originally stood for Statistical Package for the Social Sciences. While used more broadly these days, it remains well liked by social researchers because it includes the kinds of statistical techniques, both introductory and advanced, that are used as a matter of convention in the social sciences.

Statistical analysis programs with a Windows user interface such as SPSS help new social scientists overcome initial self-doubts about their potential to understand quantitatively based social research, let alone do it on a personal computer. Once you begin, you will quickly realise that you are more than up to it.

Accessing data: The promise of secondary data analysis

Quantitative social researchers usually have two options with respect to accessing data.

Primary data collection

The first option is that they collect the data themselves. This is known as **primary data collection**. Yet, while the idea of designing our own data collection instrument and taking it to the field is clearly very attractive, it is often not a feasible option. As detailed in chapter 6 on surveys, collecting high-quality data that will render meaningful results requires resources, time and specialist knowledge. While primary data collection might be the ideal, its use is usually constrained to circumstances where you have secured the appropriate time, money and expert advice needed to produce high-quality data. However, if no current, relevant data on our topic are available, then collecting our own data, and all that entails in relation to design and implementation, is the only option.

Primary data collection: The process of administering a data-collection instrument to a sample of cases and recording the pattern of observations that arise in numeric form.

Secondary data analysis

The second option for accessing data is locating secondary data. Research that involves bypassing the primary data collection process, and working directly on data that have been gathered by other social researchers, is known as **secondary data analysis**. In essence, this method involves the reanalysis, or perhaps more accurately additional analysis, of publicly available survey data.

As detailed in chapter 6, one of the key advantages of surveys is that the data generated by a survey can be analysed by researchers other than the original conductor of the research. The validity of this mode of analysis means that it is increasingly routine practice for researchers to deposit the primary data they have collected from their survey with a **social science data archive**. Once archived, the raw survey data is made available to other researchers. As social researchers, making data available to others is part of the shared scientific method standards of professionalism, transparency and integrity, as outlined in chapter 1. Case study 8.1 is an example of secondary data analysis.

Secondary data analysis: The methods and techniques involved in analysing a set of raw survey data to which a researcher has been granted access by a social science data archive.

Social science data archive: An organisation responsible for the storage and dissemination of social science data.

Accessing secondary data

Social science data archives are great places for anyone interested in doing quantitative social research. All that is usually required to gain access to any particular data set is completion

Tim Phillips

of a user form and payment of a modest service fee. The most established social science data archive in Australia is in Canberra at the Australian National University (Breusch & Holloway 2004). You can visit the Australian Social Science Data Archive (ASSDA) online by going to <http://assda.anu.edu.au>.

Social science data archives such as the ASSDA typically contain a wealth of high-quality social research data on a wide cross-section of topics. While some of these studies are small-scale and specialised, many are general social science surveys, which are wide-ranging surveys conducted on a large scale. They will have information from hundreds or thousands of respondents collected on a diverse range of topics of social research interest. Typically, they are based on samples designed to achieve consistency with the social mix of the national population or **nationally based general social surveys**.

> **Nationally based general social surveys:** These are key sources of data used for undertaking secondary analysis in the social sciences.

A common misunderstanding of secondary data analysis is that it limits researchers' ability to undertake original social research. This misguided thinking is based on the notion that you need always collect your own data to conduct original research. As the range of excellent studies based on secondary data analysis attest, this assumption is incorrect. Nationally based general social surveys are excellent resources for doing your own research, and allow plenty of opportunity to do original analysis. Rather, what is important to consider is the kind of data that have been gathered. Some data do not lend themselves easily to secondary data analysis. Here we are talking about small-scale studies, local community research or projects on very narrow or specialised topics. However, increasingly, large-scale nationally representative survey data are being gathered for the explicit purpose of secondary analysis. Such data sources are the product of studies undertaken by teams of social research experts. They are typically based upon the administration of vast batteries of general questions on a wide range of topics to a **large representative national sample** of respondents of between 1500 and 2000 participants.

> **Large representative national sample:** A kind of sample that allows researchers to produce findings that enable them to more confidently make claims about the condition of any particular social phenomenon within the confines of a specific national population.

Furthermore, there is an increasingly minimal time lag between the collection of such data and its release for public access. The Australian Survey of Social Attitudes (AuSSA), used extensively throughout this text, was available to interested researchers almost immediately after it was collected.

Box 8.1: Accessing data for secondary data analysis

The following list is just a small sample of the titles of the many studies that have been deposited with the ASSDA since the 1960s.

- D0948: Survey of the Military Profession: Australian, 1994
- D0954: Migration in Australia: A Study of the Gold Coast, 1994
- D0961: Union Membership in South Australia, 1993
- D0963: Children's Attitudes to Television, 1993
- D0967: National Policy Custody Survey, August 1992
- D0992: New Zealand Election Survey, 1996
- D1057: Survey of Retirement Village Residents and Managers, 2000
- D1069: The Mental Health of Young People in Australia: Child and Adolescent Component of the National Survey of Mental Health and Well-being, 1998
- D1079: Australian Election Study 2004.

To explore the full list, go to ‹http://assda.anu.edu.au/studies/titlelisting.html›. Clicking on an individual title will give you more details about the data, including:

- an abstract of what the survey was about
- the principal investigators (the social researchers who designed and implemented the survey)
- the universe sampled (the target population)
- the sampling procedure used to select the sample
- the method of data collection
- the dimensions of the data set; that is, the number of cases and the number of variables per case
- a list of publications emanating from the survey
- the accessibility of the data set.

In summary, secondary analysis of data provides excellent possibilities for the imaginative and devoted student of quantitative social research. Working from the robust foundations provided by such data, you are able to undertake quantitative research on topics of interest to you that may otherwise simply not be possible. A study developed using such a source may be based upon the careful analysis of respondents' answers to just one or two modules of questions. While this may seem a small amount of data to base a project upon, let me assure you that it is not. Examining the pattern of relationships between responses to even a small subset of questions can be a detailed and exacting process. Properly done, it offers the potential reward of a new and insightful study of social life.

A mini-quantitative analysis

This section provides an illustration of how quantitative data analysis is actually done. We conduct a mini-analysis of a selection of variables from the AuSSA data subset available online

Tim Phillips

at this text's website <www.oup.com.au/orc/walter>. In the process of this mini-analysis, we introduce a number of basic techniques for conducting statistical analysis. How to undertake these using SPSS is developed in chapter 9. Two quantitative analysis extension modules—one detailing how to undertake correlations using SPSS and the other looking at the statistical techniques involved in comparison of means, again using SPSS—are also available on this website. The topic of our mini-quantitative analysis is 'Are attitudes towards the relevant importance of national issues influenced by age?'

Before proceeding with the analysis, it is important to reflect a little on the research topic we will bring the AuSSA data to bear on. How individuals feel about important issues for the nation is a question of growing sociological interest. While we all want our governments and societal institutions to tackle the pressing social issues, just what those issues are, and in what priority order they should be placed for access to scarce public resources in time and financial terms, is a more contentious topic. This is especially important, because the issues affecting or of concern to one age cohort might end up the fiscal or problem responsibility of another. This potential for a clash of interests or disparate access to societal wealth or resources might highlight clashes between the generations. Additionally, different age groups may have different priorities of what is important to them. On the basis of these understandings, the research question we ask in this mini-analysis is: 'Do differences in age play out in attitudes towards what are the most pressing social issues?'

Factor analysis: A useful statistical method that helps the researcher to validate a proposed **multiple indicator** measure of a concept.

Multiple indicators: Different measures of the one concept; often combined to generate a more valid and reliable measure.

A central concern in this section is to demonstrate how the application of even simple statistics to relevant quantitative data can provide significant social insights. While multivariate techniques, such as ordinary least squares regression and **factor analysis**, offer quantitative social researchers access to more advanced statistical analysis, valid, rigorous and socially important research is very possible using relatively straightforward univariate and bivariate techniques such as those outlined in this section.

The results from our mini-analysis are reported in a series of tables from results generated using SPSS. However, it is important to note that the tables are not reproduced in the same format as that produced by SPSS. This is because social researchers need to produce their own tables, rather than transpose directly from their SPSS output into their research results. While SPSS and other statistical software programs will turn out a wealth of statistical results, the tables produced by social scientists to illustrate their findings need to be more straightforward. The aim is to highlight the results of principal interest rather than including all possible information. Rather than just reproducing computer-generated statistical output, a key skill for quantitative social researchers is to be able to distil what is important from this myriad of information, and to present these data in a table, graph or figure that conveys the findings in a simple and efficient form.

Beginning the analysis: Locating appropriate data

Our research topic—the relative ranking of social issues by perceived importance—were of interest to the AuSSA researchers. Of particular interest to our analysis is a subset of two questions that gauged respondents' ranking of issues. Question A1a asked respondents to nominate which of a set of 18 issues they regarded as most important. Question A1b asked respondents to nominate the issue from the same list that they considered the next most important. This is how the question appeared in the AuSSA questionnaire:

Section A—Describing Australia

A1. Here is a list of issues facing Australia. Which of the following do you see as most important? And the next most important?

A   An ageing population
B   Lack of affordable housing
C   Crime
D   Environmental damage
E   Taxes too high on ordinary Australians
F   Inadequate public transport
G   Lack of moral values in the community
H   Terrorism
I   Not enough progress towards Aboriginal reconciliation
J   Corruption in government
K   Gap between rich and poor
L   Australian jobs going to other countries
M   Drugs
N   Minorities having too much say in politics
O   Health care and hospitals
P   Too much 'red tape' holding business back
Q   Refugees and asylum seekers
R   Australian involvement in military conflicts overseas

Put the letter of the statement in the appropriate box below.

☐ First choice
☐ Second choice

Source: AuSSA Version A <http://aussa.anu.edu.au/questionnaires/questionnaireA2007.pdf>

Tim Phillips

The survey also included a series of questions tapping sociodemographic characteristics of the sample. These included the age of each respondent, which for our analysis has been recoded (see chapter 9) from age in years into four age groups: 18–34; 35–49; 50–64; and 65 years and over.

Exercise 8.2: Where do you stand?

At this point, it is a good idea to answer these questions yourself.

1. Which issue do you consider the most important? Write down your answer.
2. Which issue do you consider second in importance? Again write down your answer.
3. What age group do you fit into?

Now see how your answers compare with those of the AuSSA respondents.

Univariate analysis

The first concern in our mini-analysis is to describe what the pattern of answers to each of these questions looks like. To do this, we turn to univariate statistics. Univariate analysis means one variable at a time. In quantitative data analysis, univariate statistics are used for the purpose of describing the pattern of responses to discrete questions. Among the most popular univariate statistics used by social researchers are frequency distributions, measures of central tendency and measures of dispersion.

Frequency distributions

Frequency distributions display in tabular form the number of responses that fall into each category of our variable of interest. At its most basic, the table will report the number of cases associated with each category. Frequency distributions will also usually tell us the percentage of answers found in each category. In other words, they give us information about the proportion of responses that fall into any one category, allowing us to see more precisely what share of cases is connected with different response options. Table 8.1 displays the frequency distribution for social issue items in rank order by first choice. While there is considerable variation in what Australians see as the most important issue, a pattern is evident. As you can see, health care and hospitals is ranked most important by the largest proportion of respondents, followed by environmental damage; population ageing; and lack of affordable housing. Taxes, lack of moral values, the gap between rich and poor, the export of Australian jobs and crime follow in order. The other listed issues all have fewer than 4 per cent of the respondents nominating them as their number one priority.

On the respondents' age variable, the frequency distribution shows that the respondents are distributed through the age brackets, with the lowest proportion aged 18–34 at nearly

Table 8.1: Important issues facing Australia: Most important

Issue	Frequency nominated most important	Percentage who nominated as most important %
Health care and hospitals	378	14.3
Environmental damage	338	12.8
An ageing population	283	10.7
Lack of affordable housing	264	10.0
Taxes too high on ordinary Australians	236	8.9
Lack of moral values in the community	236	8.9
Gap between rich and poor	185	7.0
Australian jobs going to other countries	181	6.9
Crime	158	6.0
Drugs	88	3.3
Terrorism	77	2.9
Minorities having too much say in politics	43	1.6
Australian involvement in military conflicts overseas	41	1.6
Corruption in government	36	1.4
Refugees and asylum seekers	28	1.1
Inadequate public transport	24	.9
Not enough progress towards Aboriginal reconciliation	22	.8
Too much 'red tape' holding business back	19	.7
Total	2637	100.0
Missing	144	

Source: The Australian Survey of Social Attitudes 2003, N = 2183

20 per cent and the largest number falling into the 50–64 age group. As per the population distribution patterns outlined in chapter 7, these figures appear representative of age group patterns in Australia.

The frequency distributions displayed in tables 8.1 and 8.2 give us a good initial feel for how responses are distributed across the response categories. However, on top of this information, we also want to know how the age groups are more generally configured. To find this out, we use the information generated within frequency distributions to calculate summary statistics; in this case measures of **central tendency** and measures of **dispersion**.

Central tendency measures: A descriptive statistic related to the central measures such as the mean, median or mode.

Dispersion measures: Statistics that describe how data are patterned around the mean.

Tim Phillips

Table 8.2: Respondents: ages by four categories

Age group	Numbers in each age group	Percentage in each age group
18–34	512	18.7
35–49	790	28.9
50–64	850	31.1
65 and over	585	21.4
Total	2737	100.0
Missing	44	
N = 2781		

Source: The Australian Survey of Social Attitudes 2003

Measures of central tendency

Measures of central tendency are valuable, because they give us an indication of the typical response.

The measures of central tendency most commonly used in social research are the mean, the median and the mode (see box 8.3). Which of these measures we decide to use will depend on the level at which the variable is measured. As detailed in chapter 9, individual variable data is measured at different levels, building in complexity from nominal data, through ordinal data and interval data to ratio data.

Box 8.3: Definitions of key summary statistics

Measures of central tendency

- **Mean:** the average of the scores. To calculate the mean, you add up the values for each case and divide the total by the number of cases.
- **Median:** the middle score or measurement in a set of ranked scores of measurements; the score that divides a distribution into two equal halves.
- **Mode:** the most common (most frequent) score in a set of scores.

Measures of dispersion

- **Standard deviation:** a statistic that shows the spread, variability or dispersion of scores in a distribution of scores around the mean.
- **Variance:** a measure of the spread of scores in a distribution of scores; that is, a measure of dispersion.

Source: Adapted from Vogt 1999

Social scientists tend to use:

- the mean when variables are measured at interval or ratio level
- the median for ordinal level variables
- the mode with nominal level variables.

The question format for the variables laid out in table 8.1 is by rank (see chapter 6). We cannot determine a mean or median for these data; only respondents' first choices are recorded. Neither can we use measures of dispersion on these data.

The use of these measures is restricted to interval or ratio level and therefore not suitable for our issues data, but is applicable to our age data in years. Measure of dispersion statistics provide an indication of how widely, or narrowly, spread out a set of scores are around the average score. They tell us whether the scores are tightly clustered or widely dispersed. Using the ungrouped age data we can ascertain the following statistics:

- the mean age of the respondents is 50.5 years
- the median age of the respondents is 51 years
- the youngest respondent is 18 years and the oldest is 97 years
- the standard deviation is 16.65 years.

For nominal data, the best way to get a feel for the degree of dispersion among the scores is to use a frequency distribution or graph to display the spread of cases. Details about standard deviations are to be found in box 8.4.

Box 8.4: Illustrating dispersion: Standard deviation: Years of education and gender

AuSSA includes a subset of questions measuring educational attainment. One of these questions asks about total number of years of education completed by the respondent. A frequency distribution for this question shows that respondents report having undertaken between 0 and 30 years of education at the time of completing the survey. The mean score is 13.07 years and standard deviation 3.98 years.

Having calculated these descriptive statistics for all respondents in the sample (N = 2162), it is interesting to relook at them by gender and see what differences exist.

The first thing to note is that men on average have completed marginally more years of education than women. Whereas the mean was 13.28 years for men, it was 12.96 years for women. We can see a difference between the two subgroups here of 0.29 years (which converts to an average discrepancy of between three and four months).

Now, how were the scores for each group spread around these means?

Tim Phillips

> The standard deviation calculated for each subgroup shows a slightly greater degree of dispersion among the men. The standard deviation for men was 4.10 years and for women 3.86 years. So, this tells us that the women's scores were a little more likely to be clustered around the mean for their subgroup (12.96) than was the case for the men's scores. Men's scores were more widely spread out around the subgroup mean (13.28).

Cross-tabular analysis

So far in the mini-analysis, we have displayed, summarised and discussed the configuration of responses in AuSSA to: (a) a question gauging how Australians rank issues of national importance; and (b) the demographic characteristic of age. In effect, we have examined patterns of variation in response sets. We now need to bring them together in a way that will shed light on our research topic 'Is age group connected to a respondent's ranking of issues in order of importance? And if so, what is the nature of the link'?

Association: The extent to which the pattern of observations within one variable align with the pattern of observations within a second variable.

This task requires us to go beyond looking at (a) and (b) in isolation to looking at the relationships between them. More particularly, we need to examine the **associations** between categories in each variable. Reducing the items on the first question to those ranked in the top six captures the most highly ranked items and reduces the complexity of the analysis. It also reduces the sample size, but includes roughly two-thirds or all first choice responses. These items are:

- ageing population
- lack of affordable housing
- environmental damage
- taxes too high on ordinary Australians
- health care and hospitals
- lack of moral values in the community.

Because all the items are categories of the one variable, and we only want to examine six of them, we need to do a little more analytical preparation. We want to separate out the data to create a separate variable for each item. Each of these new variables will have two categories, one for if the item were the respondent's first choice, and the other the responses of those who selected another item as their first choice. Thus, for the ageing population item, we divide our respondents into those who nominated an ageing population as their first choice and those who nominated another item as first choice. This operation can be done by recoding (see the next chapter for how to undertake this in SPSS). We can now examine the relationship between our variables, ascertaining if there is 'a tendency for a change in one variable to be associated with a change in the other' (Weisberg et al. 1996:177). In other words, is the ranking of first choice items differently patterned among older, younger or middle age respondents? The technique we use is **cross-tabular analysis**. This technique is commonly used within the social sciences to illustrate the nature of association between two variables. In cross-tabular analysis, it is important to distinguish which variable is dependent and which is independent. In our example, this distinction is clearly implied by our research question, which indicates that we are looking for the influence of age (the **independent variable**) on ranking national issues by level of importance (the **dependent variable**). That is, we expect that ranking will be dependent on age.

> **Cross-tabular analysis:** A simple form of statistical analysis that usually represents the relationship between two (or sometimes three) variables.
>
> **Independent variable:** The independent variable is a variable that has an effect on another variable; a quality hypothesised to account for variation in a dependent variable.
>
> **Dependent variable:** The dependent variable is the variable that is dependent on or affected by another variable; what the researcher treats as a quality to be explained.

What cross-tabular analysis does is provide us with frequency distributions within the categories of the independent variable. So, in our mini-analysis, it provides a picture of the different ranking preferences of people from different age groups. The findings from our cross-tabular analyses are presented in table 8.3. Please note that the percentages do not add up to 100. This is because of our data subdivision, which only includes the proportion of each age group who nominated that particular item as their first choice. Thus, while 69.2 per cent of those aged 18–34 nominated one of our six items as their first choice, the other 30.8 per cent of respondents in this age group nominated one of the other 12 items not included here or were coded as missing data.

In table 8.3, by reading across the three rows, one at a time, we can get an immediate sense of whether age influences attitudes to issues of national importance. Read through these now for yourself.

These results indicate substantial differences across first choice of national importance issue by age group. In particular, look down the 18–34 year old column at the percentage who nominated an ageing population compared to those aged 50–64 years. Older people rated population ageing as their first choice, at triple the rate younger people did. However, the opposite is true for the items relating to affordable housing and the environment, which younger people were substantially more likely to rate as their first choice. Theoretically this makes sense; the impact of ageing population and health services is more likely to be on the priority radar of older Australians, just as the environment and high housing costs are more likely to directly affect younger people (although younger people might have to pay for the ageing population). The item on tax is first choice for the peak employment age group of

Table 8.3: First choice item of most importance cross-tabulated by respondent's age group

	Respondent age group				Total
	18–34 %	35–49 %	50–64 %	65+ %	%
• Ageing population***	4.9	8.5	14.1	14.1	10.7
• Lack of affordable housing***	16.8	10.4	8.1	6.4	10.1
• Environmental damage***	18.1	14.7	10.6	8.6	12.8
• Taxes too high on ordinary Australians***	8.7	12.2	8.5	5.5	9.0
• Health care and hospitals**	11.8	13.2	14.3	18.8	14.4
• Lack of moral values in the community	8.9	9.5	8.1	9.4	8.9
Total %	69.2	68.5	63.7	62.8	65.9

p<.05:*, p<.01: **; p<.001: ***

Source: The Australian Survey of Social Attitudes 2007

those aged 35–49 but falls for others, especially those aged 65 and over, who are unlikely to still be paying tax. The result on concern about lack of moral values in the community is interesting, in that it is even across the age groups, with roughly 9 per cent of each group rating it their number one choice.

Statistical inference

Our cross-tabular analysis outlined in table 8.3 documents some interesting associations between our variables, but a key question remains. How much confidence can we have that the relationships observed capture what is going on in Australia more generally? As discussed in chapter 5, **probability sampling** is a powerful feature of quantitative data analysis because it allows for inference. The AuSSA survey was administered to a large national sample of Australians using random sampling techniques for the very purpose of providing a safe foundation on which to make such statistical judgments. To gauge if a relationship observed in a sample is sustained in the broader population, we use tests of statistical significance.

The best known **test of significance** for ordinal or nominal data is the **chi square** (χ^2) test. Basically, a chi square tests that 'there is no relationship between the variables in the population … and whether the observed data justify rejecting the null hypothesis'

Probability sampling: Samples selected in accordance with probability theory. Probability sampling relies on (a) that we have a list of all elements or cases in the population we are studying; and (b) that we are able to randomly select elements or cases from this list and that all cases or elements have an equal chance of being selected.

Test of significance: A statistical test used to determine if the result observed can be regarded statistically significant; that is, not due to chance. See *chi square* or *Pearson chi square*.

Chi square: A test of significance used for nominal data to test the ability to generalise from the sample to the general population.

(Weisberg et al. 1996:277). As a general rule, if the chi-square value required for attaining statistical significance at the p<.05 level (that the probability that this result is just a matter of chance is 5 or less chances in 100) is attained (typically represented by *), then we can feel confident that there is a relationship between the variables in the broader Australian population. The achievement of even lower significance levels (p<.01: **; p<.001: ***; that is, 1 or less chances in 100, or 1 or less chances in 1000 respectively of the result being merely chance) indicates that we are justified in asserting an association exists with an even greater level of certainty.

Re-engaging with the findings in table 8.3, if we apply a chi-square (χ^2) test of significance to each of six first-choice items cross-tabulated separately against the age group variable, we find that the differences by age group are indeed significant for the majority of items. The probability, that the null hypothesis, that there is no relationship, can be rejected for each item noted by the relative * symbol in the format noted above. Therefore, looking back at table 8.3, the null hypothesis that there is no relationship can be rejected for the items relating to population ageing, the environment, taxes, health and hospitals, and housing affordability signifies that a statistically significant relationship between the variables exists. The chi square test of the relationship between the item on moral values and age group however does not achieve statistical significance (p = .769), and therefore the null hypothesis cannot be rejected.

Exercise 8.2: Following up on the findings from the mini-analysis

Reflecting on the results

So, in sum, did the results of this mini-analysis surprise you? Or were they what you expected? To find out more about the influence of age on attitudes, go to the library to see what you can discover about the topic. Write a paragraph summarising what you discover.

Doing your own mini-analysis

What role do social factors play in predisposing how people rank the importance of various social issues? To find this out for yourself, you need to access the subset of data from AuSSA. This data set is available from the following URL: <www.oup.com.au/orc/walter>.

The data set includes the variables used in the mini-analysis we have just concluded, plus a subset of additional variables that include variables we might expect to play a part in giving rise to feelings about national issues.

Tim Phillips

These include the respondent's:

- gender
- marital status
- background: urban or rural.

Now, under the guidance of your lecturer, see if you can do two things:

- Replicate the mini-analysis that has been undertaken here.
- Extend the analysis by looking at whether men or women, the partnered or the single, city dwellers or rural residents, are distinguished by different patterns of first choice items of importance.

If you find doing this mini-analysis interesting and enjoyable, you might like to eventually consider undertaking your own larger-scale research study using the complete AuSSA data set.

The thesis component of an honours degree would be an excellent place to do this. To find out more about accessing the full AuSSA dataset, go to the AuSSA website at ‹http://aussa.anu.edu.au›.

Choosing appropriate techniques in quantitative data analysis

A key issue in any quantitative data analysis is selecting the most appropriate statistical techniques. By choosing suitable methods, we configure the data to speak to the research questions of interest to us. Yet, the challenge often faced by the social researcher is to know which techniques enable us to do this with confidence. Fortunately, within social research there are established conventions on this issue.

The value of any particular quantitative analysis technique is its ability to enable social researchers to clearly and directly connect their data to their key research questions.

A detailed examination of all the major statistical techniques is beyond the scope of this chapter. For this level of explanation, you need to refer to a text that focuses specifically on teaching quantitative techniques. But a good way of learning which techniques work best with which questions is to read a range of social science quantitative-based journal articles. Look at what techniques the researcher has used and for what purpose. Look also at how clearly the results using that technique address the key research questions (see exercise 8.4).

In a typical quantitative research project, social researchers will seek to bring their data to bear on a series of research questions. To this end, a corresponding sequence of techniques will be mobilised. In a top-quality piece of quantitative social research, just as there is a logical flow between the set of research questions to be addressed, so too are there chains of interconnection between consecutive phases in the data analysis process.

Exercise 8.3: Selecting statistical techniques for use in quantitative data analysis

Go back to the results of the mini-analysis in the preceding section of the chapter. Five kinds of statistical technique were used: frequency distribution; measures of central tendency; measures of dispersion; cross tabulation; and chi square.

Your task

For each type of technique, write a sentence describing what purpose it served in answering the research question.

Quantitative data analysis at its strongest and weakest

In this chapter, we have pointed to the unique and valuable qualities that quantitative data analysis can bring to the social research enterprise. Yet, like all methods quantitative analysis has strengths and limitations.

Quantitative data analysis is at its strongest when it emphasises what it continues to be able to do confidently. This includes: examining complex associations between concepts of interest; working with samples that enable inferences to be drawn about wider populations; subjecting propositions derived from social theory to empirical scrutiny; identifying the circumstances under which theories hold up (and do not), and running competing theories off against each other to see which provide a better explanation. Like all research methods, however, quantitative analysis needs to be sensitive to the wider ongoing discussion about social research methodology (see the discussion in chapters 1 & 2). More critically, when done in this limiting way, quantitative data analysis runs the risk of becoming disconnected from 'where the action is' in the broader social research field. This can happen when: the variables that are used in the analysis to measure key concepts lack validity and reliability; analysis proceeds on the basis of an arbitrary vision of causal relations between the relevant concepts; highly complex statistical techniques are applied in analysis leading us to lose sight of the human individuals we are actually studying; and data analysis is unbound from theoretical guidance and proceeds as if how to do it is simply a matter of impulse or common sense. Under these conditions, quantitative data analysis is at its weakest. To summarise, when quantitative methods fail to recognise the implications of the interpretivist and postmodern challenges for routine research practices, the validity of the research itself is liable to be significantly weakened. The specific conditions under which quantitative data analysis is at its strongest and weakest are summarised in box 8.5.

Tim Phillips

Box 8.5: Problems and prospects within quantitative data analysis

Quantitative data analysis is at is strongest when:

- looking at complex relationships
- making inferences from samples to populations
- examining grand claims within social theory and specifying the conditions under which they hold up
- adjudicating between competing theories.

Quantitative data analysis is at its weakest when:

- variables are poor measures of concepts
- the status of variables in causal chains is determined arbitrarily
- statistical methods are used that place too many demands on the data
- it is done in the absence of theory.

Exercise 8.4: Evaluating the quality of quantitative data analysis

Locate the collection of holdings for the *Journal of Sociology* (the official research journal of the Australian Sociological Association) in your university library. It will most likely be held in either hard copy or electronically.

Now, identify all issues of the Journal for the last five years (which will be 20 issues: five volumes comprising four issues a year). Pick up one issue at a time (or volume if it is hardbound in this way on the shelf of the library), and locate a paper on a topic of interest to you that uses techniques of quantitative data analysis. Find five different articles.

Once you have found an article, your job is to read it carefully, then reflect upon the strengths and weaknesses of the quantitative data analysis contained therein. Using the criteria laid out in box 8.5 as a guide, evaluate the quality of the quantitative data analysis undertaken in the article in a paragraph or two.

Compare your ideas with the other members of your class. See if you came up with similar or different kinds of general observations.

Doing quantitative data analysis well: Imagination and devotion

To be a proficient quantitative data analyst, you do not need to be a computing expert, a statistical wizard, a 'quant jock', or even a 'number-crunching maniac'. While doing quantitative analysis involves using a computer and putting statistics to work, a specialty background in either of these areas is not required. Instead, if you already undertake such commonplace tasks on a computer as emailing, web browsing, and word-processing, and want to find out more about how statistics can help social researchers get answers to their research questions, you have a solid platform in place on which to develop new skills in quantitative data analysis. What will determine how far you go will be your orientation to analysing quantitative data. By orientation, I essentially mean the way you approach any particular thing you happen to be involved in, how you think about it, and how you do it.

People who are good at quantitative data analysis tend to bring two important qualities to the activity.

Quantitative analysis as imaginative practice

First, they exercise imagination. A common stereotype is the notion of quantitative data analysis as a mechanical exercise, something simply done by technicians in a formulaic or predetermined manner. Nothing could be further from the truth. To do a top piece of quantitative data analysis requires approaching the task in a creative and dynamic manner. This is because there is never simply 'one right way' to analyse a quantitative data set to derive an answer to a research question (Becker 1986). In fact, different researchers will often highlight divergent aspects of the same set of data (see Jones 1997 in comparison to Pakulski & Tranter 2000, for example). So the one set of data may potentially be configured in different ways to address any particular research problem. What is important for the researcher is figuring out a persuasive and compelling analytic strategy. To do this, you need to unleash your inner 'sociological imagination' (Mills 2000).

Working out how best to mobilise the data to engage with the research question is often a case of balancing convention and innovation. Sometimes you may feel that established ways of proceeding with quantitative data analysis on a particular research question are reasonable and compelling. On such grounds, there may be little reason to depart from a customary approach. Yet on other occasions you might find that conventional approaches engender a sense of doubt within you (Bauman & May 2001). Under these conditions, you might feel it is time to posit what you believe to be a better strategy for unravelling the data. When you proceed down this pathway, imagination and intuition come to the fore as vital qualities for 'steering' your data analysis (Giddens 1990).

Quantitative analysis as devoted practice

Besides exhibiting imagination, people who are masters of quantitative data analysis in the social sciences also tend to be persistent about what they do. They exhibit devotion. Let's confront another stereotype here. A familiar mistaken assumption about quantitative sociology is the notion of an instant solution. This notion works around the idea that the

Tim Phillips

computer is a 'magic numbers machine' that will provide an immediate 'right' answer. The image here is that of a passive researcher sitting back while the computer (through application of a statistical software program to the relevant data) does the work of finding an on-the-spot solution. This way of imagining quantitative data analysis is false. High-quality quantitative data analysis always takes places through a **process of iteration**. Further, it is always steered by the researcher. Approaching data analysis in this way will greatly increase your chances of coming up with a clear window into whatever salient patterns may be lying dormant within the data you are working on.

> **Process of iteration:** The step-by-step practice by which relevant patterns in a quantitative data set are progressively revealed.

Voices in the field

Joanna Sikora and Lawrence J. Saha

Joanna Sikora and Lawrence J. Saha teach sociology at the Australian National University, and together they have been researching adolescent career plans using cross-national survey data and multilevel modelling.

Previously sociologists had doubts whether early career plans were important for the later attainments of young adults. However, recent research shows that early goal-setting can make a difference. The socioeconomic background of students is an important determinant in this process. Adolescents whose parents are in professional jobs or who do very well at school are more likely to formulate their plans for specialised professional careers and tailor their educational plans accordingly.

In contrast, those who come from lower-status backgrounds often do not make clear plans for the future, or do not acquire the education necessary to realise them.

Recently some sociologists, including Joanna and Larry, have been working with data collected through the Program for International Students Assessment <www.oecd.org/PISA> to find out how the characteristics of schools, and also country-level institutional settings, may affect students' career plans. Large surveys involving thousands of students, hundreds of schools and dozens of countries make possible the empirical assessment of macrosocial factors affecting students' career plans. This involves comparing how strongly these factors influence students' job expectations, relative to individual and family characteristics. Larry and Joanna found that many high school students in countries with lower levels of economic inequality have less ambitious plans than their peers living in nations with higher levels of inequality where fewer students obtain secondary education.

The significance of this research is that it provides evidence that social selectivity that affects individual chances for upward mobility operates at many levels. Social disadvantage dampens career plans at the individual and school levels. At the country level, students who live in more unequal countries and make it to high school, despite barriers typical for less accessible secondary education systems, feel very optimistic about their career prospects. It is important to recognise these multilevel social structural factors, because many believe that individual decisions and characteristics are the only factors which determine career attainment and intra-generational mobility.

From method to practice

Consider the following example. I, with another researcher, have recently completed a large-scale survey of a nationally representative sample of Australians. The survey is designed to document Australians' everyday experiences of 'rude strangers'. Before going to the field, we carried out various background preparations. Three key areas of activity were involved:

1. spending sustained periods of time over many months designing the survey
2. attaining a large research grant to pay for the survey's administration over the telephone to people across the country
3. acquiring advice from different experts about the best way to undertake particular steps in the survey's implementation and sample selection.

At the outset of the research project, we made a conscious decision to undertake these preparatory tasks in an extremely careful and systematic manner. We knew the prospects for the assemblage of a top-quality data set would be significantly diminished if we proceeded into the field against a background of less 'thinking' time, fewer resources and an absence of specialist advice. Poor data quality is anathema to good social research, because there is little prospect for deriving meaningful results from such data. This is a critical issue because, in the absence of meaningful findings, your research is heavily compromised. In the absence of high-quality data, it is unlikely that the findings from a research project will be taken seriously.

The result of our work was the *Everyday Life Incivility in Australia* survey. This was a random national sample survey collecting systematic narrative information on interpersonal encounters involving a rude stranger. The analysis of our data on urban incivility used univariate, bivariate and multivariate analysis to produce results that challenged received wisdom about the corrosive effects of urban incivility on society. Our interpretation was that a new agenda, one that explores how everyday life incivility is experienced by the broader population in the course of daily routine, is needed (Phillips and Smith 2006).

Tim Phillips

Conclusion

This chapter provides an introduction to quantitative data analysis in the social sciences. In particular, it has emphasised the importance of 'thinking sociologically' or using our 'sociological imagination' in the process of quantitative data analysis. While being familiar with the great variety of statistical techniques and the associated software programs that can be used to apply them is an important part of quantitative data analysis, we need to be careful not to fall into the trap of treating these activities as ends in themselves. To avoid this pitfall, it is important to keep reminding ourselves that the reason we undertake quantitative data analysis is to bring reliable evidence to bear on the wider ongoing discussion about how social life works, and what kind of society we would like to live in.

The best quantitative social science studies evince a workmanlike level of statistical competence. However, what sets them apart from the pack is their genuine capacity to illuminate the social world. This is invariably done by bringing quantitative data to sociological life through a process of active engagement with the abstraction and generality of social theory and analysis. Quantitative data analysis is powerful in that it enables us to clarify if, and how, the complex relationships about any 'society of individuals' (Elias 1991), posited within social theory, do in fact work when subjected to test via systematic empirical observation. The dynamic world of sociological ideas holds abundant promise for 'sensitising' the understanding and insight generated by any concrete empirical study (Giddens 1984). However, the linchpin is to make the links. This, as I stated earlier, is a matter of imagination and devotion.

Main points

> - Quantitative data is the actual record of the full set of observations of the social world in a social research project stipulated in numeric form.

> - Based on principles of cool detachment and systematic observation, the collection and analysis of quantitative sociological data works in the discipline as a way of 'balancing out' the potential problems arising from excessive theoreticism.

> - The actual task of carrying out quantitative data analysis in the social sciences is invariably done on a personal computer, often using SPSS statistical software.

> - Much quantitative social science research takes on the form of secondary analysis. Rather than researchers collecting their own primary data, secondary analysis involves re-analysis of publicly available survey data. Such data sources are commonly large national sample surveys covering a wide range of topics of social science interest.

> Recognising the implicit links between common kinds of research questions in quantitative social science and the statistical techniques regularly used to address them is a key skill in doing quantitative social science research and analysis.

> Quantitative data analysis is at its strongest when it is attuned with the broader ongoing dialogue about social research methodology, and at its weakest when disengaged from this conversation.

> Doing good quantitative social science research requires imagination and devotion.

> Bringing quantitative data to sociological life involves a process of active engagement with and reflection around key ideas in social theory and analysis.

Further reading

Bryman, A. and Cramer, D. (2005). *Quantitative Data Analysis with SPSS for Windows*. Hove: Routledge.

Babbie, E., Halley, F. and Zaino, J. (2003). *Adventures in Social Research: Data Analysis Using SPSS for Windows*, 5th edn. London: Sage.

de Vaus, D. (2002). *Surveys in Social Research*, 5th edn. Sydney: Allen & Unwin.

Phillips, T. and Aarons, H. (2005). 'Choosing Buddhism in Australia: Towards a Traditional Style of Reflexive Spiritual Engagement', *British Journal of Sociology*, 56 (2): 215–32.

Rojek, C. and Turner, B. (2000). 'Decorative Sociology: Towards a Critique of the Cultural Turn', *Sociological Review*, 48 (4): 629–48.

References

Adams, P. and Burton, L. (1997). *Talkback: Emperors of the Air*. St Leonards: Allen & Unwin.

Babbie, E., Halley, F. and Zaino, J. (2003). *Adventures in Social Research: Data Analysis Using SPSS for Windows*, 5th edn. London: Sage.

Bauman, Z. and May, T. (2001). *Thinking Sociologically*, 2nd edn. Oxford: Blackwell.

Beck, U. (2004). 'Cosmopolitan Realism: On the Distinction between Cosmopolitanism in Philosophy and the Social Sciences', *Global Networks*, 4 (2): 131–56.

Becker, H. (1986). *Writing for Social Scientists*. Chicago: University of Chicago Press.

Breusch, T. and Holloway, S. (2004). 'Data Surveys: Australian Social Science Data Archive', *Australian Economic Review*, 37 (2): 222–9.

Tim Phillips

de Vaus, D. (2002). *Surveys in Social Research*, 5th edn. Sydney: Allen & Unwin.

Elias, N. (1991). *The Society of Individuals*. Oxford: Blackwell.

Gibson, R., Wilson, S., Denemark, D., Meagher, G. and Western, M. (2004). *The Australian Survey of Social Attitudes*, 2007 [data file]. Canberra: Australia Social Science Data Archive, Research School of Social Sciences, Australian National University.

Giddens, A. (1984). *The Constitution of Society*. Cambridge: Polity.

Giddens, A. (1990). *The Consequences of Modernity*. Stanford, CA: Stanford University Press.

Holton, R. and Phillips, T. (2001). 'Popular Attitudes to Globalisation', *Policy, Organisation and Society* (Special Issue: 'Different Globalisations'), 20 (2): 5–21.

Jones, F. (1997). 'Ethnic Diversity and National Identity', *Journal of Sociology*, 33 (3): 285–305.

Mills, C. W. (2000). *The Sociological Imagination*. 40th Anniversary Edition. Oxford: Oxford University Press.

Pakulski, J. and Tranter, B. (2000). 'Civic, National and Denizen Identity in Australia', *Journal of Sociology*, 36 (2): 205–22.

Phillips, T. (2001). 'Positivist Research', in Michie, J. (ed.), *Reader's Guide to the Social Sciences*, Vol. 2. London: Fitzroy Dearborn: 1272–3.

Phillips, T. and Aarons, H. (2005). 'Choosing Buddhism in Australia: Towards a Traditional Style of Reflexive Spiritual Engagement', *British Journal of Sociology*, 56 (2): 215–32.

Phillips, T. and Smith, P. (2006). 'Rethinking Urban Incivility Research: Strangers, Bodies and Circulations', *Urban Studies*, 43 (5–6): 879–901.

Rojek, C. and Turner, B. (2000). 'Decorative Sociology: Towards a Critique of the Cultural Turn', *Sociological Review*, 48 (4): 629–48.

Skrbis, Z., Kendall, G. and Woodward, I. (2004). 'Locating Cosmopolitanism: Between Humanist Ideal and Grounded Social Category', *Theory Culture and Society*, 21 (6): 115–36.

Travers, M. (2005). 'Review of the Practice of Research in Criminology and Criminal Justice (2nd edn)', *Australian and New Zealand Journal of Criminology*, 38 (1): 161–3.

Vogt, P. W. (1999). *Dictionary of Statistics and Methodology*, 2nd edn. London: Sage.

Weisberg, H., Krosnick, J. and Bowen, B. (1996). *An Introduction to Survey Research, Polling, and Data Analysis*, 3rd edn. London: Sage.

Western, M. (1999). 'Who Thinks What about Capitalism? Class Consciousness and Attitudes to Economic Institutions', *Journal of Sociology*, 35 (3): 351–70.

Chapter 9
Using SPSS for Quantitative Analysis

Phillip Patman

SPSS and quantitative analysis

This chapter is an introduction to the basics of SPSS (Statistical Product and Service Solutions), and builds practically on the quantitative analysis covered in chapter 8. It will get you started, but does not cover statistical theory or assumptions in any detail. To take your statistical analysis skills further you will need a dedicated statistics text. The version of SPSS used in this chapter is Version 16. Earlier packages will have a slightly different interface, but are functionally the same.

SPSS is probably the most commonly used of the quantitative data analysis software packages in academic and industry settings. Its main benefits are its ease of use and the ability to analyse large data sets. The Windows environment of SPSS allows users to undertake sophisticated analysis with a few clicks of the mouse, using the menu items and dialogue boxes, and provides easily readable output results. The researcher can use SPSS to generate descriptive and inferential statistics as well as high-level simulations and model-building from their data. Advanced users can still use syntax files, a written set of instructions that enables SPSS to analyse data, and it is this automatically generated syntax file that we see at the top of the output screen.

It is worthwhile re-emphasising a key message from chapter 8 at this point: SPSS is the tool, it does not 'do' the analysis. The researcher is the driver of the statistical analysis, and quality quantitative analysis requires a thorough grounding in your topic area, the ability and creativity to translate these into statistical questions, and the theoretical knowledge and insight to interpret what the results of these questions mean in relation to your research question.

Key terms

Analyze menu
Australian Survey of Social Attitudes (AuSSA)
bivariate analysis
chi square
coding
compute variable function
cross-tabulation
cumulative per cent

Data view
descriptive statistics
dialogue box
frequencies
frequency table
interval data
longitudinal quasi-panel study
nominal data
ordinal data

Output window
ratio data
Recode function
SPSS file
transform tool
univariate analysis
valid per cent
Variable view

Introduction: Our SPSS dataset

Australian Survey of Social Attitudes (AuSSA): A nationally representative longitudinal quasi-panel study conducted in 2003, 2005 and 2007, collecting data on respondents, social attitudes, opinions and behaviours.

Longitudinal study: A study that collects data on the same phenomena over an extended period of time.

The data used in this chapter are from the **Australian Survey of Social Attitudes (AuSSA).** As discussed in previous chapters, AuSSA is a representative **longitudinal quasi-panel study** of Australians, covering social opinions, behaviours and attitudes across a diverse range of topics, such as government spending, crime and families. AuSSA is a mail out, mail back survey. It began its first data collection in 2003 and collected further sets of data in 2005 and in 2007. This chapter uses data from the 2007 survey and the specific question (question B6) about government spending, relating health, education, law enforcement and defence, to demonstrate basic quantitative analysis techniques using SPSS. To provide focus for our analysis we have posed the research question: 'Do Australians respond differently to day-to-day life issues of health and education than they do to less personally impacting issues of law enforcement and defence?'

To do the tutorial questions in this chapter, you will need to access the AuSSA data subset included on the text's website at <www.oup.com.au/orc/walter>. Question B6, as asked in the AuSSA survey, is outlined below.

Table 9.1: AuSSA survey, question B6

Listed below are various areas of government spending. Please show whether you would like to see more or less government spending in each area. Remember that if you say 'much more', it might require a tax increase to pay for it.

		Spend much more	Spend more	Spend the same as now	Spend less	Spend much less	Can't choose
a	Health						
b	The police and law enforcement						
c	Education						
d	Military and defence						

Coding your data into the SPSS file

Within the social sciences, our data are typically contained in returns from a survey questionnaire. Before we can begin any analysis, we need to code the information contained within each individual response into the SPSS datafile. Coding in quantitative analysis is essentially summarising the data into a **format** amenable to statistical analysis.

The data takes the form of numbers rather than text, and if the information is not numeric (an actual quantity such as height, weight or dollars), the information needs to be changed to a numeric format. This does not mean we turn non-number information into numbers; rather we allocate numbers to represent the different variable categories. This process, which is known as **coding**, ensures consistency in developing the data set and consistency of data entry.

> **Format**: The format of data or other information to suit different social research software analysis software packages, such as Excel, SPSS and Stata.
>
> **Coding**: The process by which data are organised for analysis.

The example below is the coding structure of some of the variables in the AuSSA 2007 data set. What numbers we allocate to represent different variable categories (such as male and female) is arbitrary, but the convention is to use running numbers from 1, 2, 3 … etc. Zero (0) is also used for some coding, but tends to be reserved for variables that need dichotomous (only two) variables for specific statistical techniques. As we can see from the chart below, minus numbers, such as −1, in this case, tend to be reserved to indicate missing data.

Table 9.2: Variable coding example

Variable	SPSS Name	Coding information
Sex	Sex	−1 = Missing
		1 = Female
		2 = Male
Govt spending a. Health	B6a	−1 = Missing
		1 = Spend much more
		2 = Spend more
		3 = Spend the same as now
		4 = Spend less
		5 = Spend much less
		6 = Can't choose
Govt responsibility d. To keep prices under control	B6d	−1 = Missing
		1 = Spend much more
		2 = Spend more
		3 = Spend the same as now
		4 = Spend less
		5 = Spend much less
		6 = Can't choose

Phillip Patman

Missing data is where a survey was completed but the respondent either skipped that question or the response is not usable. How to signify a value as 'Missing' is covered later in the chapter.

The practice of coding goes back to the early days of computing, where memory was expensive and small. Instead of typing in 'Male' or 'Female' for each response, a number that represents that piece of data was entered to represent that piece of information. So if the respondent ticked 'Male', a '2' would go into the data set, and for a 'Female' a '1' in the data set. This practice is continued, because data entry is faster and has fewer errors if a number is typed instead of an actual word, and coding into numbers is necessary for some statistical analysis.

> **SPSS file**: One of many SPPS data files that can hold data (.sav), output (.spo) or syntax (.sps).
>
> **Variable view**: The SPSS screen that contains definitive information on each variable.
>
> **Dialogue box**: A window, or series of windows, that open up from via the menu and allow commands to be performed. It uses arrows and buttons to select SPSS functions without having to write a syntax or command file.

Opening up a blank SPSS file

To code in our data we need to open a new **SPSS file**. Figure 9.1 shows what we see when we open the SPSS program. It consists of a blank SPSS file in **Variable view** mode, and the **dialogue box** that asks what type of task is needed.

Box 9.1: SPSS opening options

- **Run the tutorial**: a tutorial that takes you through a variety of SPSS topics and can be run through the Help menu item; this is covered later in the chapter.
- **Type in data**: opens a blank data file.
- **Run an existing query**: runs an existing query.
- **Create a new query using Database Wizard**: allows SPSS to import non-SPSS data and modify it before putting the data into an SPSS file.
- **Open an existing data source**: allows the user to open an existing data file from the list of recently used files or browse and find a file.

To begin coding and creating a new SPSS dataset, we choose the 'Type in data' option. Once we have started, named and saved this dataset, we need to choose the 'Open an existing data source option' to go back to our file, either to enter more data or begin analysis. As shown in Figure 9.2, SPSS will even give us a list of our most recently used data files to speed up our access.

SPSS screens: Variable, Data and Output views

SPSS uses three main screens, each with a specific purpose. When using SPSS either to input or analyse our data we need to toggle through these screens to complete our analysis tasks. The major features and purposes of each of these are explained in this section.

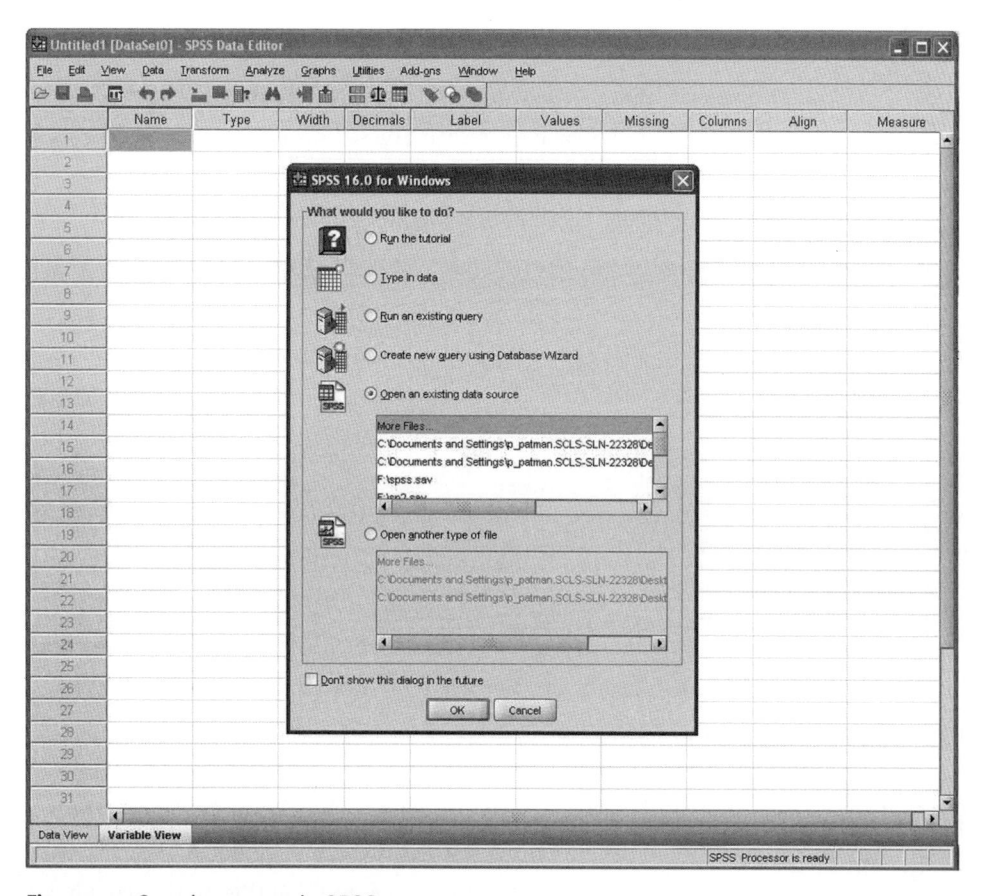

Chapter 9: Using SPSS for Quantitative Analysis

Figure 9.1: Opening screen in SPSS

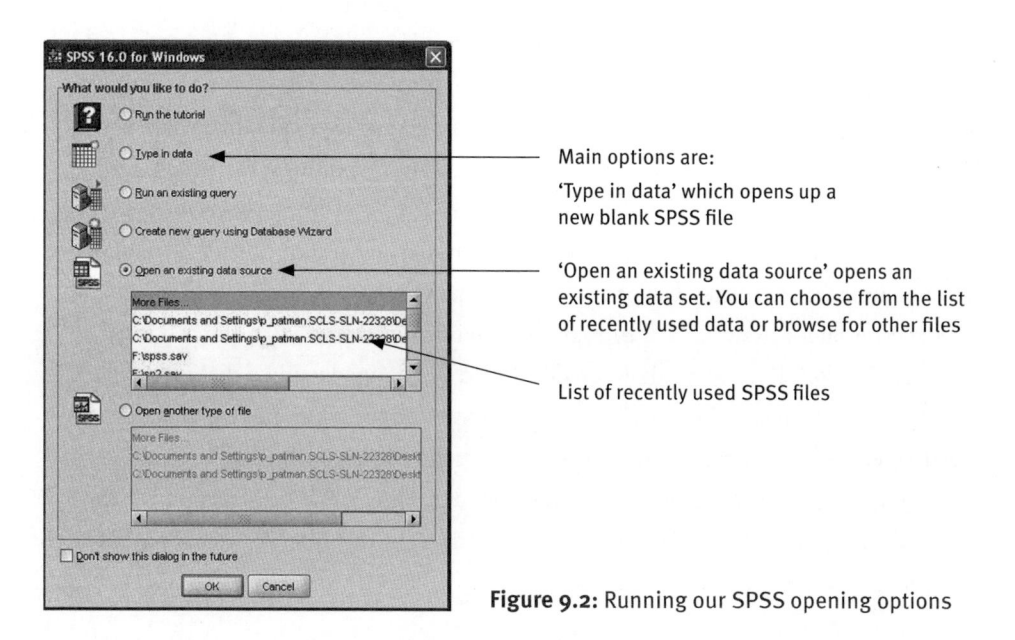

Figure 9.2: Running our SPSS opening options

Main options are:

'Type in data' which opens up a new blank SPSS file

'Open an existing data source' opens an existing data set. You can choose from the list of recently used data or browse for other files

List of recently used SPSS files

Phillip Patman

Variable view: The SPSS screen that contains definitive information on each variable.

Variable view

A blank SPSS file usually opens up in **Variable view**, which holds information about each of our variables. This information is especially important when we are coding. This is where we outline the specifications of each of our variables. We also use this screen when recoding or generating new analytical variables.

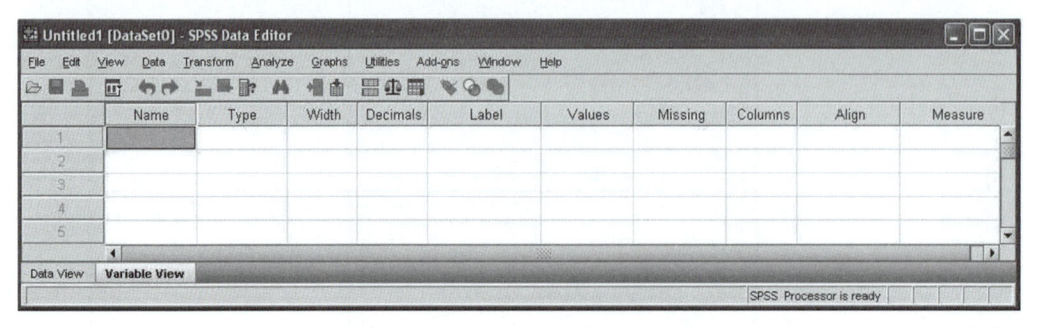

Figure 9.3: The SPSS variable screen

- The first column, *Name*, is a brief descriptor of the variable. In older versions of SPSS this descriptor could be only 8 characters, but from Version 12 the column can take a larger number of characters. Each variable must be unique, and must start with a letter and cannot contain spaces or symbols.
- *Type* is the assigned value of the data, and is assumed to be a number. *Number* is the default setting. You can choose other options through the dialogue box.
- The *Width* of the column is 8 characters wide. It is usual to leave this on the default setting, but it can be changed using the up and down arrows.
- The number of *Decimal* places is 2 decimal places. It is usual to leave this on the default setting but can be changed using the up and down arrows.
- A *Label* is a user-defined description of the variable that allows us to overcome the limitations of *Name* protocol by giving more information about the variable. *Labels* are are also printed as part of any analysis undertaken.
- *Value* allows us to make sense of the codes and numbering system. In the *Value* dialogue box, the numbers are turned back to words that make sense to us, as they replicate the original criteria; for example, for the variable 'Gender', if the value in the cell is a 2, then 'Male' is the value. The values are developed or changed using a dialogue box.
- *Missing* allows the researcher to allocate a specific value for when there is no code or measurement for a particular cell. This is usually when a person has not responded to a question in a survey. It is not a requirement that a missing value be placed in the data set, as SPSS assumes that a blank cell is missing data. In the AuSSA survey −1 has been allocated as a *Missing* value.

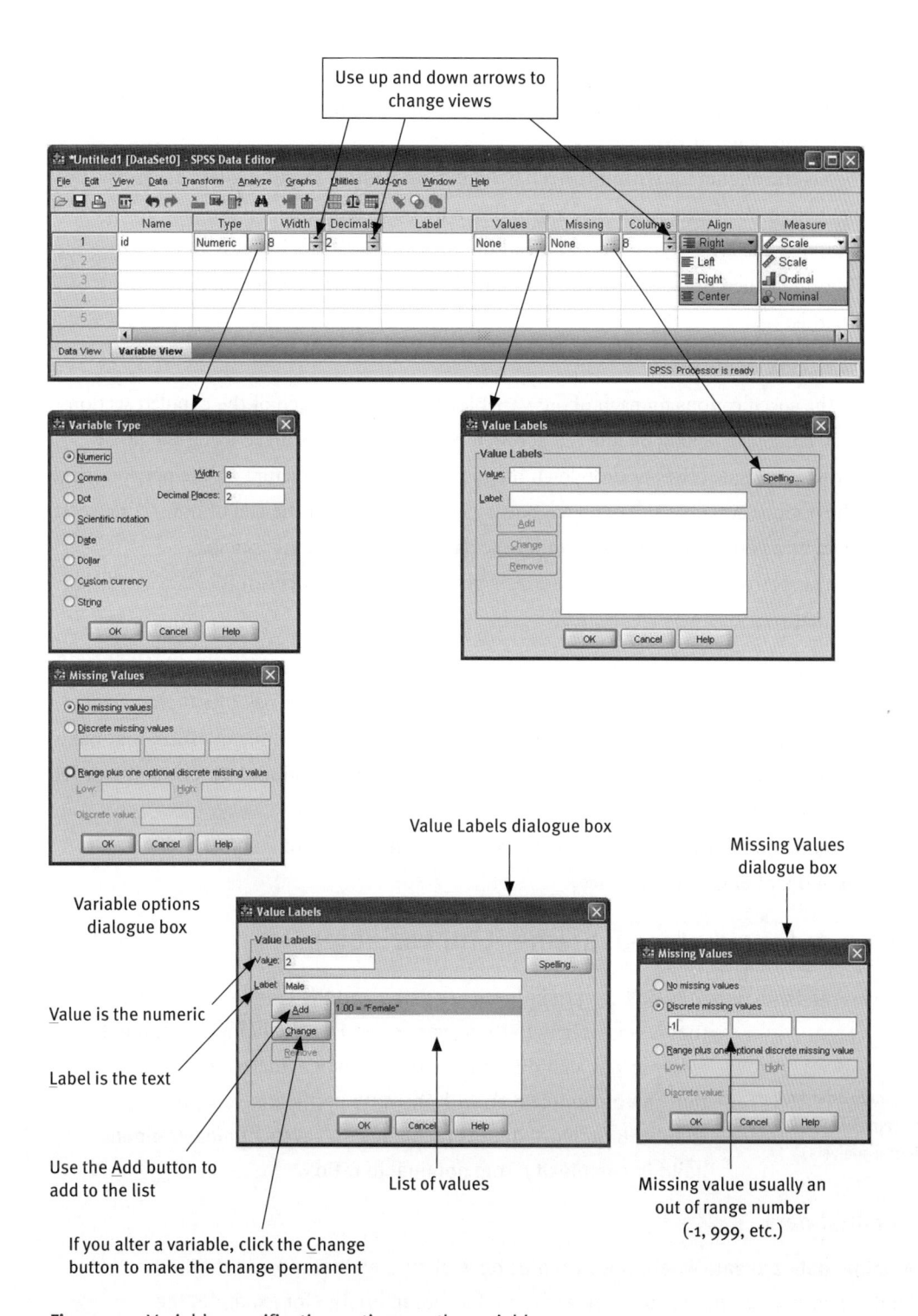

Chapter 9: Using SPSS for Quantitative Analysis

Figure 9.4: Variable specification options on the variable screen

Phillip Patman

- *Column* is the number of characters that can be viewed within the cell. The default is 8 characters. It is usual to leave this on the default setting, but it can be changed using the up and down arrows.
- *Align* is the alignment within the cell, where the default is 'right'. Unless necessary, do not change this, but you can use a dropdown menu to alter this.
- *Measure* is the type of data, as discussed in box 9.2. For SPSS, interval and ratio are the same, and called *Scale*. The default measure is *Scale*, and you use a dropdown menu to alter this.

Entering the data

To enter the specifications for each of our variables, we complete each of the detailed sections about that variable. Clicking on any cell allows the defaults to be changed using the up or down arrows, dialogue boxes or dropdown menus. The composite picture on the previous page shows the options available and dialogue box options. To really get the feel of how these work, now would be a good time to work through the data-entering tutorial exercise.

Each survey respondent or data source is given a unique number in the data set. There are three main reasons why we do this:

- Data entry is easier using numbers: there is less likelihood of making a mistake if a number is used rather than a complete word with its attendant risk of a typing error.
- If an error is made in the entry stage (for example, there is a 33 in a question that has a 1 to 5 response set), it allows the analyst to return to the questionnaire, check the actual response and correct the entry.
- A unique number for each questionnaire reduces the chance of data from that respondent being entered twice.

Box 9.2: Levels of measurement for variables

How we measure depends on the variables we are using and the **level of measurement** that is possible with those variables. The level of measurement is important as it determines the statistical techniques and tests that can be undertaken with the data in the analysis phase (see chapter 8 for more details on analysis). Levels of measurement build in complexity from nominal to ratio.

Level of measurement: How a variable is measured (nominal, ordinal or interval–ratio); determines its subsequent treatment in the process of statistical analysis.

Nominal data

Nominal data are data where the variables have attributes that represent different kinds of characteristics rather than amount of a characteristic; for example, the variable gender has the attributes of male and female.

Ordinal data

Ordinal data are data where the attributes of the variables represent more or less of a variable, and can be placed in a logical ranked order, but the difference between the rank intervals is not determined. For example, in the variable 'highest level of qualification', an undergraduate degree can be ranked above a diploma, but not by a clearly defined amount.

Interval data

Interval data are data where the attributes of the variable can be meaningfully rank ordered and the intervals between the ranks is equal but there is no zero point. For example, Person A with an IQ score of 110 has a higher IQ score than Person B with an IQ score of 100, but because you cannot have an IQ score of zero, you cannot say that Person A has 10 per cent more intelligence than Person B.

Ratio data

Ratio data can be found where the attributes of a variable have the same rank-ordered features as those in interval data, but where the variable being measured has a true zero point. This allows us to compare our data observations by the ratio of one to the other. For example, a person earning $40,000 per annum earns twice as much as a person earning $20,000 per annum.

Exercise 9.1: Entering data in SPSS

The following is a list of variables that you have collected in a survey examining the household circumstances of Australian families. You need to enter them into a database on SPSS to begin your analysis. But before you can do this you need to set up your SPSS database.

- Open your SPSS program
- Click on **SPSS** *Enter new data*
- Switch to **Variable view** (at bottom of screen) and
- Using the set of data below, enter your variables and their specifications across each of the variable view dimensions (note you are not entering the actual data on this screen).
- Save the data set and give it a name.

Phillip Patman

Your data

ID number	Sex	Age in years	Annual respondent income	Years in education	Partnered status	Colour of car	Housing tenure
1	Male	18	$ 6000	12	Single	Green	Private rental
2	Male	24	$19000	15	De facto	Blue	Private rental
3	Female	18	$23000	11	Single	Red	Private rental
4	Female	57	$28000	15	Divorced	Red	Public rental
5	Male	62	$72000	16	Married	White	Home owner
6	Female	33		16	Separated	Yellow	Public rental
7	Female	37	$30000	12	Married	Blue	Home purchaser
8	Male	19	$28000	10	De facto	Green	Board and rent
9	Male	47	$52000	12	Married	White	Home purchaser
10	Female	45	$18000	15	Married	Blue	Home owner

Questions

1. What *Type* is your *Sex* variable?
2. How does your variable name differ from your variable label on the *Housing tenure* variable?
3. Do you have any missing data? How did you deal with them?
4. What measure is your variable for *Partnered status*?
5. What value labels did you give the variable categories in your *Colour of car* variable?

Check with others around you to see if your variable view for this data is the same as theirs. Now read the new section about the Data view screen, then enter your data into that screen.

Data view

Data view: The SPSS screen that holds the raw data, and indicates where columns are variables and rows are cases, and where all data on individual respondents are entered and displayed.

Switch into **Data view** (toggle at the bottom of your screen). A blank data view screen is shown in figure 9.5. It is in this window that the data is entered, using the codes or measures we have set out in our Variable view. Figures 9.5, 9.6 and 9.7 focus on the major attributes of the Data view screen. Figure 9.6 shows that each cell holds an individual observation—for your 'sex variable' you would enter whether the respondent for this row is male or female by the variable of gender's numeric category codes. In Figure 9.7 we can see that each variable column holds all data from all respondents on that particular variable, and in Figure 9.7 we can see that each row contains all the responses from one individual respondent.

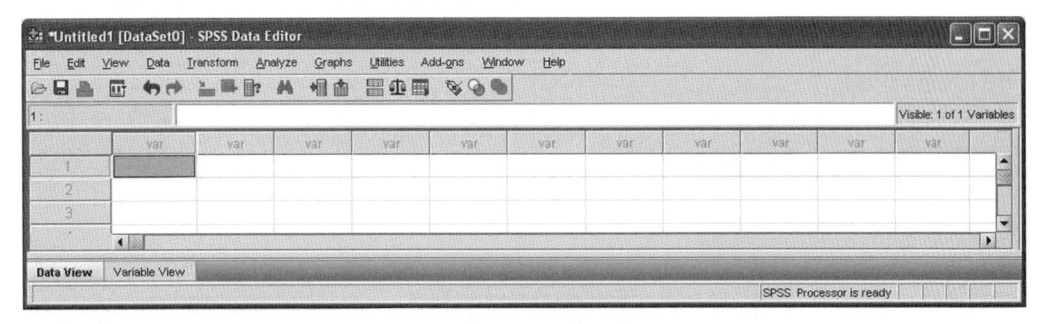

Figure 9.5: Data view screen

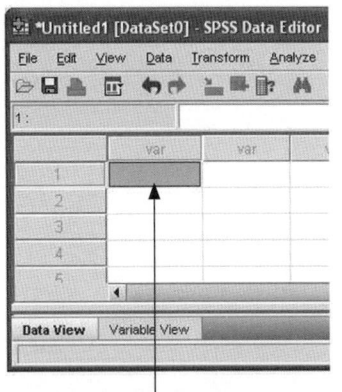

Each cell holds an individual observation variable.

Figure 9.6: Data view variable cell

Each column represents a single variable.

Figure 9.7: Data view variable column

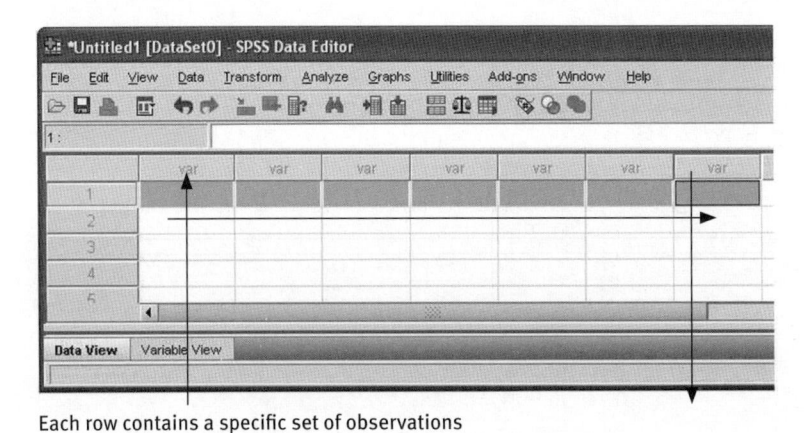

Each row contains a specific set of observations

Figure 9.8: Data view variable rows

Phillip Patman

Variable view and Data view

The relationship between the Variable view and Data view is demonstrated below, where Variable view contains information about the variable, including the Name specification, and Data view is where data is entered for each response, and with the *Name* specification as variable headings.

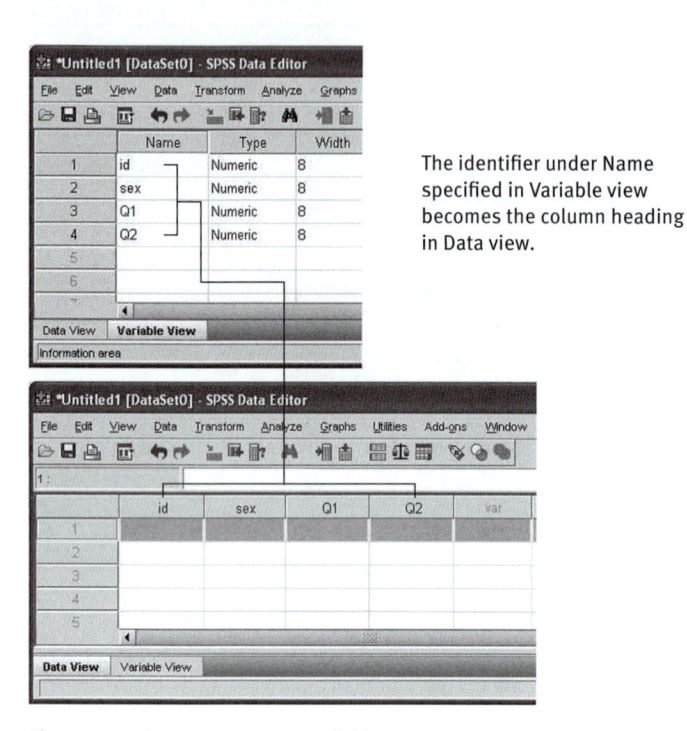

Figure 9.9: Data view name variable

Figure 9.10: Data view screen of Data set

Figure 9.9 shows what an entered data set in Variable view will look like. Now go back to exercise 9.1 and, if you haven't already done so, enter your data.

Another useful feature of the Data view screen is the *Label* button. As shown in figure 9.11, we use the *Label* button to change the data view from numbers to labels. It is a toggle system, and can be turned from numbers to words and back again by clicking the icon. Changing our data from the variable category to its numeric representation is useful to remind us of our variable categories while we are trying to decide what analysis to undertake, and also to screen the data; that is, checking that our data is entered correctly.

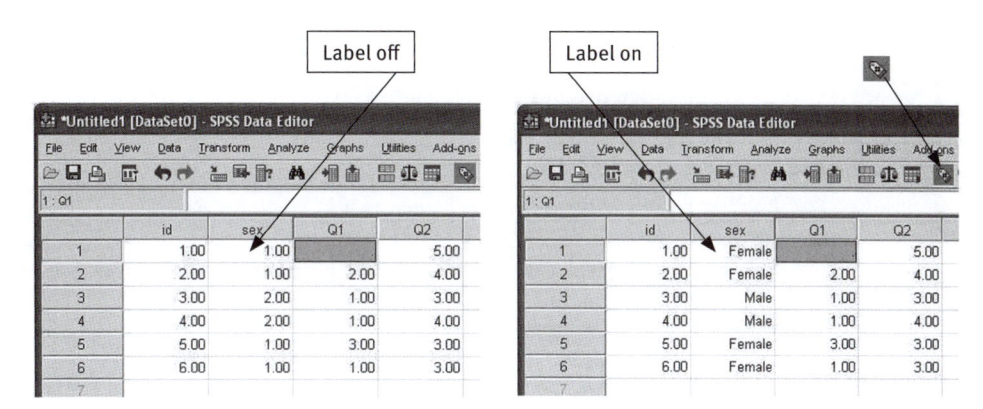

Figure 9.11: Using the Label button

Output window

The **Output window** is where the results of our analysis are set out. Before we start generating some results, it is important to be familiar with this window's format. Basically, for each analysis performed using SPSS we are provided with three pieces of information: the **syntax file**; the case summary of the data; and the statistical task results table. In the example below, it is a **cross-tabulation** of the variable of Australians' attitudes towards government spending on health and the variable of gender. While we might be most interested in the actual results table, the case-processing summary is also important. For example, if your analysis has a large percentage of **missing data** we need to take this into account in interpreting the results table. These facets of the Output window are detailed in figure 9.12.

Output window: The SPSS window where the results (output) of our analysis are displayed.

Syntax file: The SPSS coding that can be used to generate analysis instead of the windows interface, and which in newer SPSS packages appears at the top of all Output windows.

Cross-tabulation: A table of rows and columns where one variable in the column is crossed (compared) with another variable in the row. This produces a matrix where each cell is a case that has characteristics of both the row and column elements.

Missing data: The number of cases in a quantitative analysis defined as not valid.

Phillip Patman

Missing case: A missing case in an observation that does not have a value or valid response.

A Syntax file is automatically generated in newer versions of SPSS; in older versions you use the Paste function in dialogue boxes to generate a syntax file.

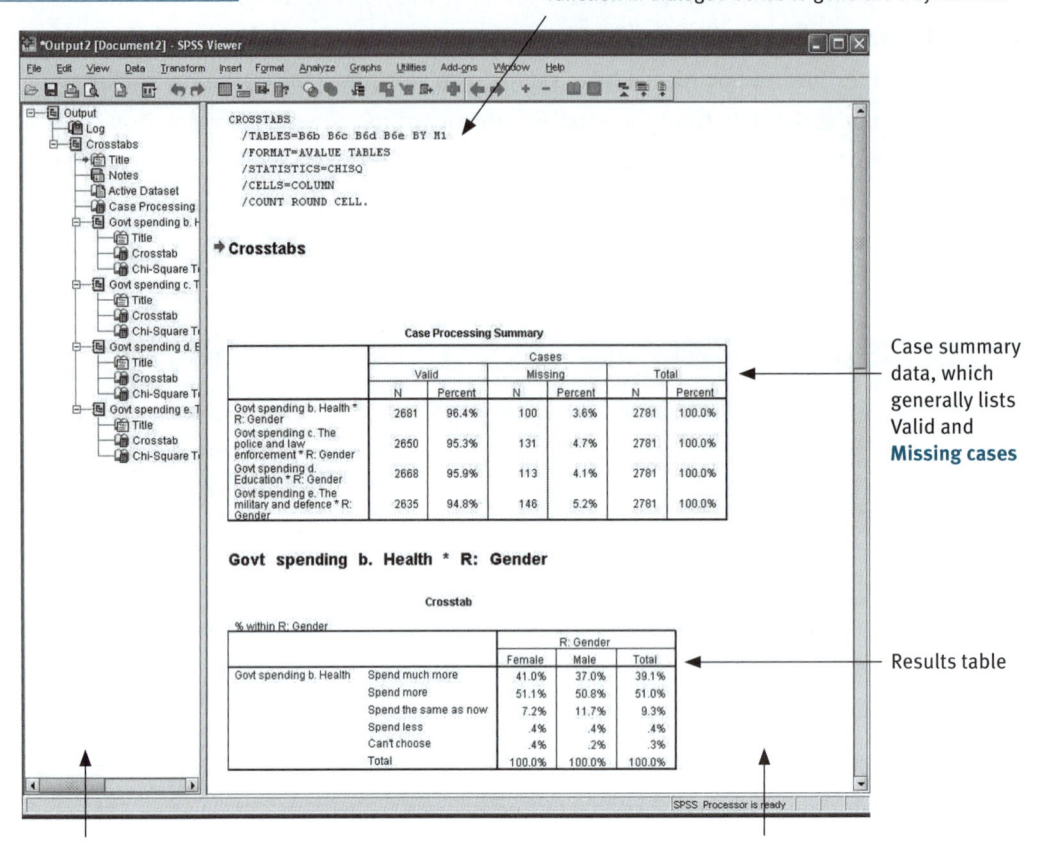

Case summary data, which generally lists Valid and **Missing cases**

Results table

The left-hand panel is a navigation window, and clicking on any element will take you to the relevant table.

The right-hand panel presents the results of any analysis, in this case a cross-tabulation.

Figure 9.12: Typical Output window

Data analysis in SPSS

To analyse our data statistically in SPSS we use dialogue boxes. There are different dialogue boxes for the different types of statistical analysis tasks. In the typical SPSS dialogue box, the left-hand window shows the complete list of variables and the right-hand window is the working area in which variables are moved in or out, using the arrows. Also on the right are buttons that bring up other dialogue boxes for generating statistics, criteria for analysis and display or formatting options. The example below is a Frequencies dialogue box.

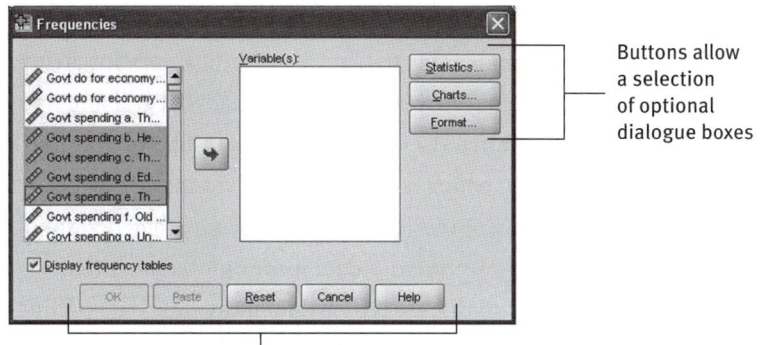

Chapter 9: Using SPSS for Quantitative Analysis

[Frequencies dialog box screenshot with callouts: "Buttons allow a selection of optional dialogue boxes" and "Standard operating buttons"]

Arrows allow the movement of variables into and out of the Variable(s) window and change direction depending on which area you are in, either the List or Variable(s) section.

As in the example above, the OK will remain grey until a minimum set of conditions is set, and this is contingent on the type of analysis that you are undertaking. If the button remains grey it is probable that you have not set up the analysis correctly. The change is demonstrated below.

You can use the Shift and Control keys to select multiple variables for analysis. Click on the first variable and then hold down either the Shift or Control key and select the variables.

Figure 9.13: Frequencies dialogue box

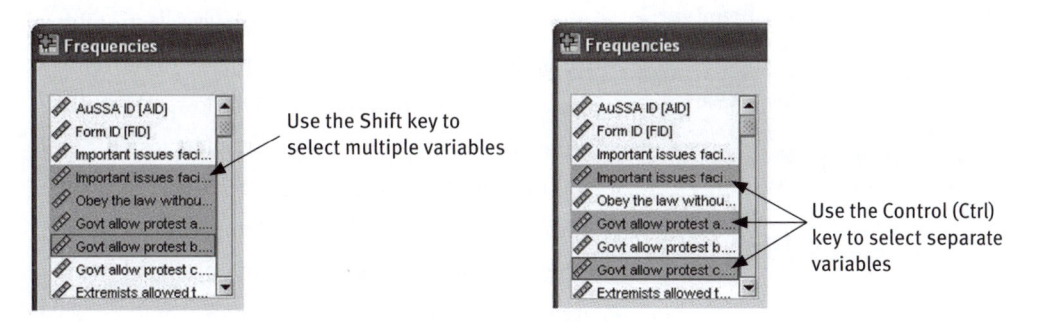

[Two Frequencies dialogue screenshots with callouts: "Use the Shift key to select multiple variables" and "Use the Control (Ctrl) key to select separate variables"]

Figure 9.14: Frequencies dialogue variable selection panels

Univariate analysis

Analysing our data is a sequential process, and it is a good idea to start with the most straightforward statistics and move through gradually to the more complex statistics. We need to get to know our data. It is only by knowing our data that we can understand our results and interpret them. When deciphering the Output window we need to know enough about the

Phillip Patman

Univariate analysis: Quantitative analysis that examines one variable at a time.

Descriptive statistics: Quantitative statistics that describe the data or summarise the data (such as the average or mean).

Central tendency measures: A descriptive statistic related to the central measures such as the mean, median or mode.

Dispersion measures: Statistics that describe how data are patterned around the mean.

Frequency: The number or counts for each category of a variable.

Analyze menu: The SPSS tool outlining statistical analysis techniques using a menu system and submenu options.

characteristics of our dataset to tell whether they make sense. Have we used the right variables, and is this statistical test or task appropriate to the data and our research question? SPSS doesn't know; it will attempt any statistical task we command, even ones that are invalid or pointless.

Univariate analysis, which is one variable at a time, is a good place to start. **Descriptive statistics** are what they say; they describe our data. They allow us to summarise data into some value(s) that make available a statistic to discuss rather than individual data points. As noted in chapter 8, common descriptives include measures of **central tendency** (such as mode, median and mean) and **measures of dispersion** (such as range, variance and standard deviation) and **frequencies**. The **Analyze menu** contains the list of analysis techniques, using a menu and submenu lists.

Producing frequencies

Frequencies are one statistic routinely used in the research process to describe data, and can be used to make comparative statements across variables. The output produces a count of responses to that variable and percentages of the counts. To produce a Frequencies output, go to the Analyze and *Descriptive statistics*, and open the dialogue window.

Frequencies dialogue box allows selection of variables for analysis using the arrows to move the variables in and out of the windows. As well, there are other options in the Frequencies task that you may need. Looking at figure 9.16, locate the buttons on the right. These buttons control the other analysis options. The main options of interest are *Statistics* and *Charts*.

For *Charts*, the default is *None*, and options are for *Bar*, *Pie* and *Histograms*. Click your preference if you want your frequency displayed in a chart as well as a table. You can also add more statistical detail by using the *Statistics* option to indicate that you want *Percentiles*, *Central tendency*, *Dispersion* and/or *Distribution* statistics added to

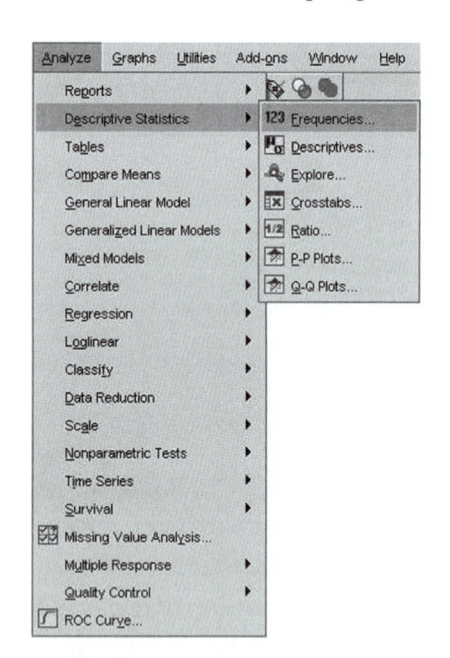

Figure 9.15: Analyze menu options

the analysis. After adding each option, click the *Continue* button to take you back to the Frequencies dialogue box.

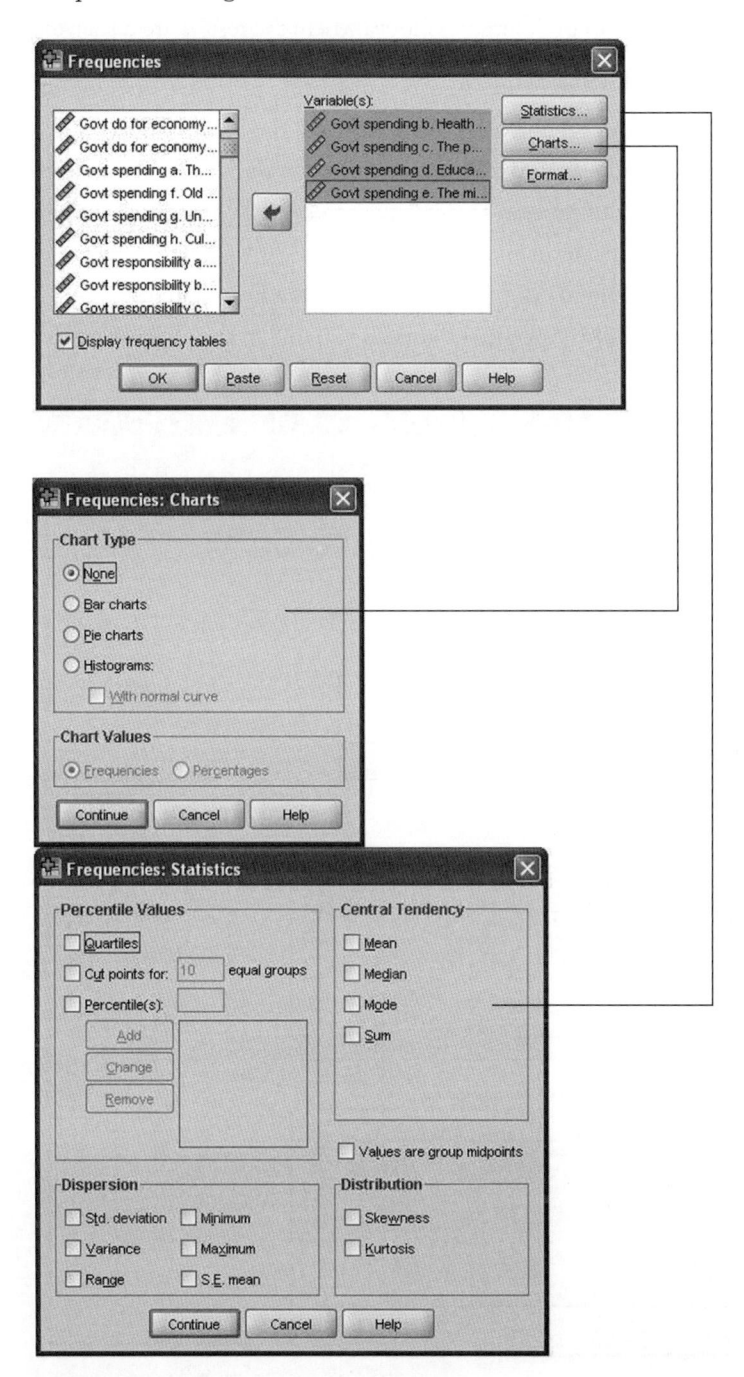

Figure 9.16: Frequencies dialogue box options

Part 2: Quantitative Methods and the Power of the Numbers

Once we have selected our frequency variable and decided if we want charts or additional statistics, we click the *OK* button. The SPSS program will now run the analysis we have requested, and will automatically take us to the Output window, where the results are displayed.

Frequencies output window

Frequency table: A table that displays the number and percentage of each instance or category of a variable.

Statistics table: The SPSS output table that reports the number of missing and valid cases in the analysis.

The first few lines on our Output window are the SPSS syntax commands for this analysis. This is useful if we want to record exactly what was done, and to gain familiarity with syntax coding for when we move to higher-level analysis.

The first table in our output window is the **Frequencies statistics table.** This table looks at each variable in the analysis and

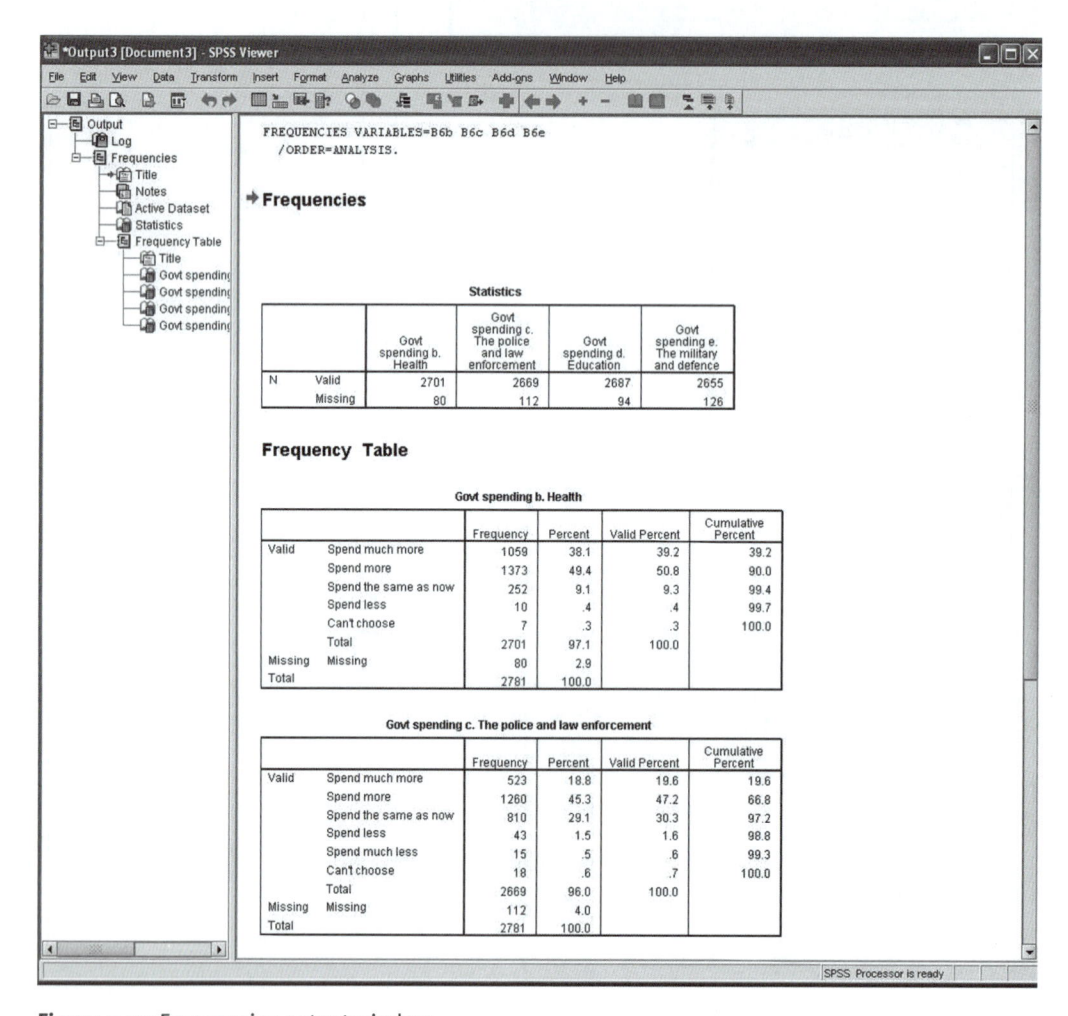

Figure 9.17: Frequencies output window

Social Research Methods

reports the number of Valid and Missing. *Valid* is only those cases where a response has been coded and those who do not are reported as a non-response or a *Missing* value. From this table we are able to see that the number of cases with no data varies from 80 for the question on government spending on health to 126 for the question relating to defence spending. Can you think of any reason why there are 46 more completed cases on the health question than on the defence question?

The next two tables are the frequencies for two of our four variables (the others are not included in this figure for reasons of space). As we can see the number of cases (1059) and the proportion of cases (39.2 per cent) who think the government should spend much more on health is considerably higher than the number (523) and the proportion (19.6 per cent) of those who think the government should be spending much more on police and law enforcement.

Reading the results table requires an understanding of the differences between frequencies, per cent, **valid per cent** and **cumulative per cent**. In table 9.3 the different elements of the table are named and explained.

> **Valid per cent:** The third column of a Frequencies output in SPSS, showing the percentages of only those instances where there is response; that is, do not contain missing data.
>
> **Cumulative per cent:** A calculation of the valid responses that adds each individual percentage value to the previous value and totals to 100 per cent.

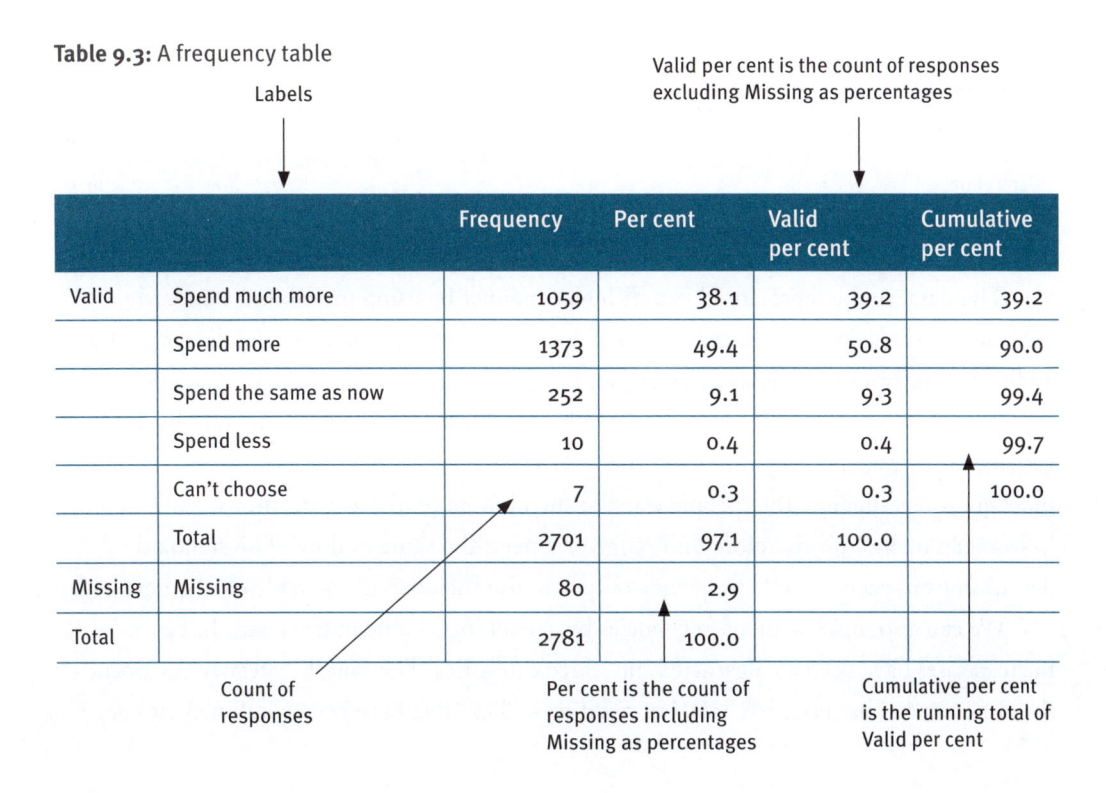

Table 9.3: A frequency table

Labels

Valid per cent is the count of responses excluding Missing as percentages

		Frequency	Per cent	Valid per cent	Cumulative per cent
Valid	Spend much more	1059	38.1	39.2	39.2
	Spend more	1373	49.4	50.8	90.0
	Spend the same as now	252	9.1	9.3	99.4
	Spend less	10	0.4	0.4	99.7
	Can't choose	7	0.3	0.3	100.0
	Total	2701	97.1	100.0	
Missing	Missing		80	2.9	
Total			2781	100.0	

Count of responses

Per cent is the count of responses including Missing as percentages

Cumulative per cent is the running total of Valid per cent

Phillip Patman

The frequency table (table 9.4) presents the frequency distribution for the four questions about health, law enforcement, education and defence. Note that we have used the *Valid per cent* figures. The results show that people do have different attitudes to the four questions, with respondents more supportive of spending more on health than they are on defence. For health, around 90 per cent of people replied 'Spend much more' or 'Spend more'. For law enforcement it is around 67 per cent; education, around 80 per cent; and defence, the combined total for 'Spend much more' or 'Spend more' is only 25 per cent. In relation to our research question, 'Do Australians respond differently to day-to-day life issues of health and education than they do to less personally impacting issues of law enforcement and defence?', we can make an initial answer. The pattern of responses confirms that day-to-day impact issues are more likely to be considered to require more or much more funding.

Table 9.4: Comparing the frequency results across variables

	Health	The police and law enforcement	Education	The military and defence
Spend much more	39.2	19.6	31.1	4.6
Spend more	50.8	47.2	48.3	20.2
Spend the same as now	9.3	30.3	19.6	52.8
Spend less	.4	1.6	.5	15.1
Spend much less	.0	.6	.1	5.9
Can't choose	.3	.7	.4	1.4
Total	**100.0**	**100.0**	**100.0**	**100.0**

The data can be represented in a different manner by using means and standard deviations to explain differences in opinion across the four questions. Using data from the additional statistics options we selected, we know that because the original scale in the coding of these responses (if we can't remember these are listed against this variable in variable view) was '1 = Spend much more' to '5 = Spend much less', a mean of around 2 for most questions suggests that people want to spend more on these institutions, while defence has a mean of 3 and is therefore mid range or 'Spend the same as now'. The standard deviation from each variable frequency output is also included in the table on the next page.

We can also make sense of frequencies by generating a comparative chart. In figure 9.18, the responses have been amalgamated into three categories. The middle category '3 = Spend the same as now' has been left as is, but first two and last two have been combined into one

Table 9.5: Mean and standard deviation results

	Health	The police and law enforcement	Education	The military and defence
Mean	1.72	2.18	1.91	3.01
Standard deviation	0.68	0.83	0.77	0.95

category (we can do this using the **Recode function** outlined later in this chapter). Reading the graph, we can see that the first three questions have small differences overall, but are similar in having a high 'Spend more' response. The last question on the military is different with most people in the middle 'Spend the same as now' category. Because we never just get results, but need to interpret them in line with our theoretical and conceptual framework, using what you know about attitudes to government spending, why do you think far fewer people are likely to think the government needs to spend much more on the military and defence than on health?

> **Recode function:** Recoding allows the user to collapse variables that have numerous values into more discrete values (such as collapsing respondents' age into categories)

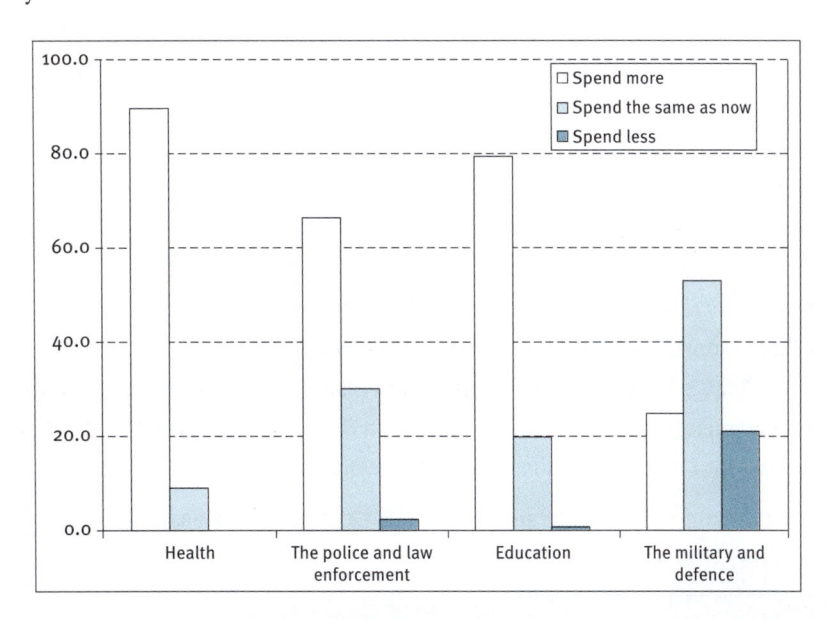

Figure 9.18: Charting comparative frequencies

Collapsing categories, as done here, reduces the amount of information a reader needs to focus on, but does lose some of the detail. This is an issue for researchers, where the reduction of information to increase readership leads to a reduction of the variability of information.

Phillip Patman

Exercise 9.2: Frequency distributions

Analyses and questions

Run frequency distributions for the following AuSSA variables and answer the associated questions. Hint: the variables are listed in coded alphabetical order, so M1 Gender will be a bit over halfway down and come just after the L coded variables.

1. (M1) Gender
   a. What percentage of the AuSSA sample is female?
   b. What are the differences and similarities between the results found under the headings of 'Frequency', 'Per cent', 'Valid per cent' and 'Cumulative per cent'?
2. (Age 4) R: Age (4 categories)—towards bottom of listing
   a. What percentage (valid per cent) of the sample is aged 65 and over?
   b. How many cases of missing data are there on this item?
   c. Is the level of missing data on this item likely to influence your results in a meaningful way?
   d. At what level might missing data become problematic, and what explanations can you think of to explain why some variables would have more missing data than others?
3. (M30) How often do you attend religious services?
   - Use the 'Cumulative per cent' column to find what proportion of Australians attend a religious service at least once a month.
4. (M4) R: What is the highest level of education you have completed?
   a. How many cases in the sample hold a bachelor degree or above?
   b. What proportion of Australians hold a bachelor degree or above?
5. Redo the analysis for R: Age (4 categories), but also click the *Charts* button at the bottom of the **Frequencies** box. Within this box, click on *Bar graph* and then click *Continue*. Finally click on *OK*. Your bar graph is displayed below your frequency distribution.

Do you think the comparison between the variable categories is easier to make when the data is presented in chart format? Why?

Bivariate analysis

From the information generated by our univariate analysis, it is now possible to pose other statistical questions. In this section we will specifically focus on the defence question. Given the overall response to the defence item, we might then ask would different groups, such as men and women, respond in a different manner? Soldiering has been until recently mostly a male occupation—it is still mostly men who go off to war—so do males have a different attitude to defence spending than females? To test how one variable associates or relates to another we need to move into **bivariate analysis**, which basically means analysing two variables against each other. The most common statistical technique for comparing one variable's responses with those of another is by cross-tabulation, often referred to as a crosstab.

> **Bivariate analysis**: Analysis of the relationship between two variables.

To undertake this task in SPSS:

- Go to the Analyze tool
- Select Descriptive statistics
- From this dropdown menu select Crosstab.

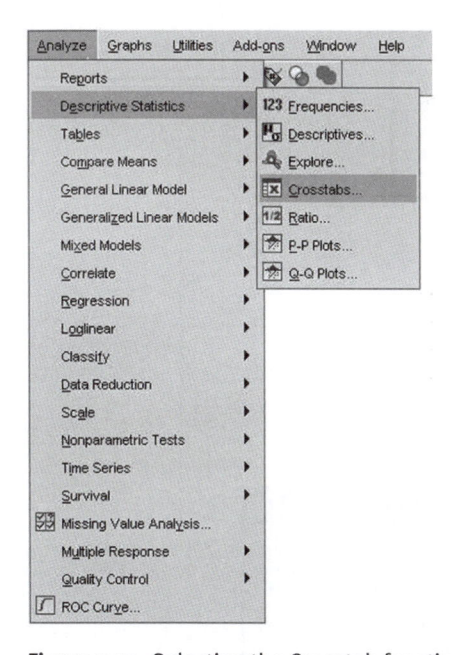

Figure 9.19: Selecting the Crosstab function

The Crosstab function is very useful, because it can test the non-mathematical nominal or ordinal variables, and it also allows us to also conduct significance tests within the Crosstab analysis. The test of significance is the **chi square** (χ^2) test of significance: the chi (pronounced 'ky') square test. For more discussion about chi square, refer back to chapter 8. A test of significance (and there are others besides chi square) looks at the results and, using various statistical methods, tells whether those results are in fact significant or possibly a result of chance. If the sample is representative (see chapter 5) and the results are significant,

> **Chi square**: A test of significance used for nominal data to test the ability to generalise from the sample to the general population.

Phillip Patman

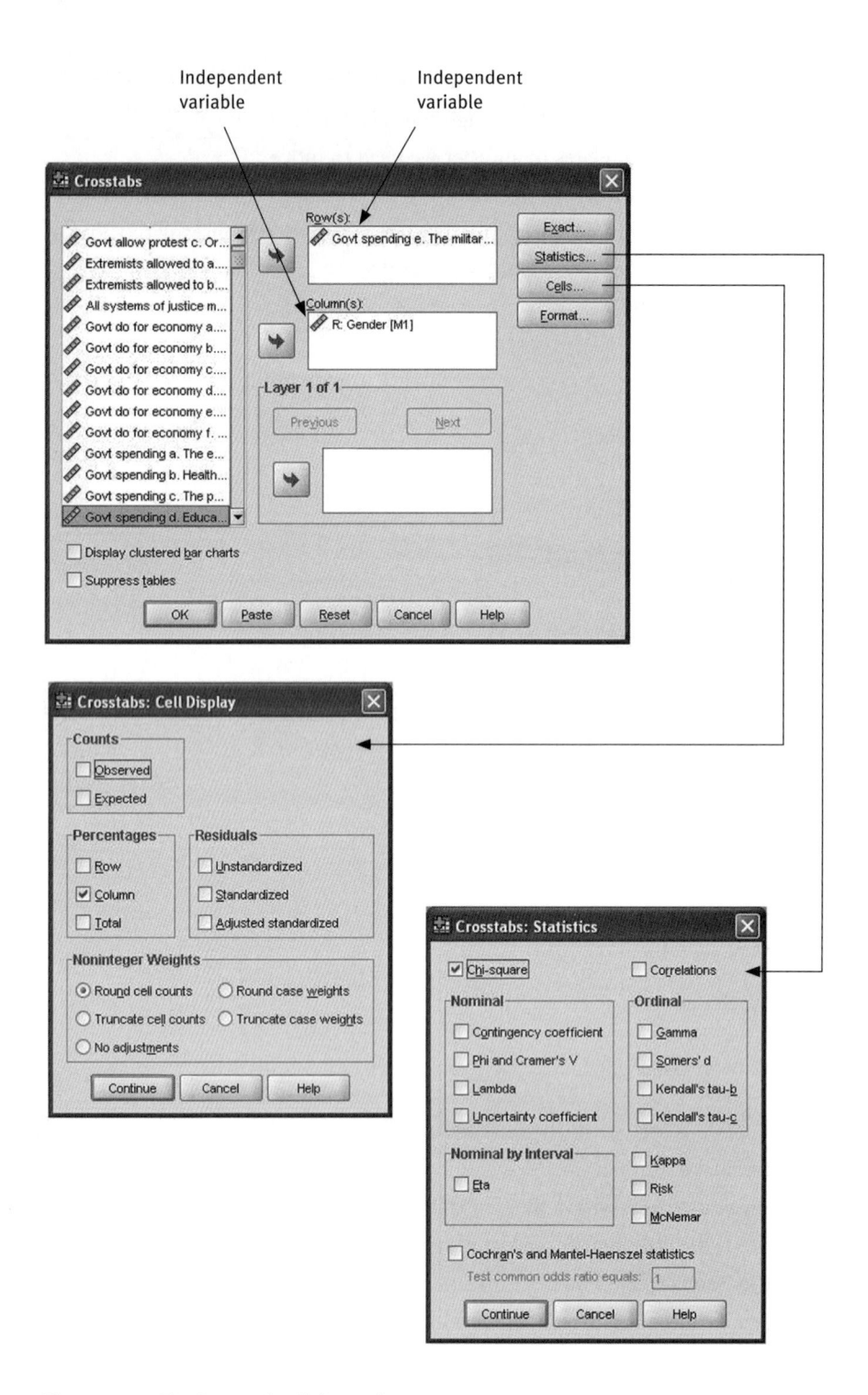

Figure 9.20: The Crosstabs dialogue box

then we are able to generalise the results back to the population from which the sample has been drawn. In this instance, we can say whether indeed Australian men and Australian women differ in their attitudes to government spending on defence and the military.

In setting up a Crosstab, there are two variables. One of these goes in the *Row(s)* window, and the other in the *Column(s)* window. The general rule is that the dependent variable—that is, the variable that is dependent on the other variable, in this case, attitude to government spending on defence—goes in the *Row* window.

The default setting for a Crosstab is *Counts*. If we want to not only have the numbers of men and women in each category, but also the percentages in each group, we need to open the *Cells* table on the right-hand side of the dialogue box and tick percentages by *Columns*; that is, by the independent variable, *Gender*. Then click *Continue*, and return to the Crosstab dialogue box and click *OK*.

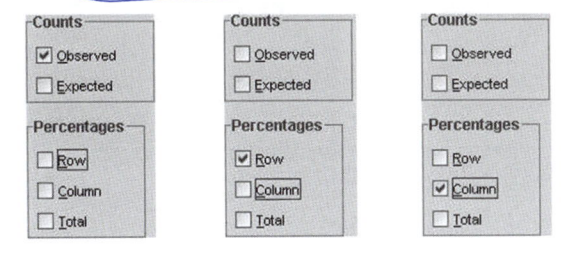

Figure 9.21: Crosstab cells options

The results output for our Crosstab is in four parts. The first, as usual, is the syntax (not shown here). Next is the Case summary, which again is the number of people who have answered the question and the level of missing data. This is important in bivariate analysis, as one of our variables may have a lot more missing data than the other, possibly skewing the results.

Table 9.6: Case processing summary

	Cases					
	Valid		Missing		Total	
	N	Per cent	N	Per cent	N	Per cent
Government spending and defence* R: Gender	2635	94.8%	146	5.2%	2781	100.0%

Next is the Cross-tabulation table, giving us the results by gender, including column percentages. As you can see, there is not a lot of difference to the question about spending on defence. Only 4.1 per cent of women, compared to 5.2 per cent of men, think there should be much more spending, and 4 per cent of women compared to 7.4 per cent of men think there should be much less spending. Most of each group (54.3 per cent for women, 51.2 per cent of men) think spending should stay about the same as now. Is this enough difference to point to a gender influence on attitude, or is it just the chance of how the numbers come out?

Table 9.7: Cross-tabulation Government spending e. The military and defence • R: Gender crosstabulation

% within R: Gender

DV	Categories	R: Gender		
		Female	Male	Total
Government spending e.g. the military and defence	Spend much more	4.1%	5.2%	4.6%
	Spend more	20.2%	20.1%	20.2%
	Spend the same as now	54.3%	51.2%	52.8%
	Spend less	15.0%	15.3%	15.1%
	Spend much less	4.4%	7.4%	5.8%
	Can't choose	2.0%	0.7%	1.4%
	Total	100.0%	100.0%	100.0%

Because we have included a chi square test of significance in our analysis we are able to see, statistically, whether those few percentage point differences mean men's and women's attitudes are actually different. The chi square table below tells us that indeed the differences between men and women's attitudes are significant, and there is only 1 chance in 1000 that the null hypothesis can not be rejected.

How did I read the table? The chi square test compares the frequency of cases in each cell (observed) with what the frequency would be (expected) if there were no differences between the two groups. The comparison between these two is then assessed on its level statistical significance. As you can see in the *chi square test* output on the next page, there are many numbers, including value, *df* (means *degrees of freedom*) and *Asymp. sig. (2 sided)*. There are also results for tests other than Pearson chi square.

The format of these numbers goes back to the days when this type of analysis was done by hand. For some disciplines these numbers still need to be reported, so they remain in the output. But the line that is most important to us is the top one relating to Pearson chi square, and the number that is most important is the last figure on the top line *Asymp. sig. (2 sided)*, which is the significance value. For most social science purposes, a value below .05 is significant, and above .05 is not significant. The .05 relates to how many chances in 100 there are that these results are not significant. As we can see, our number .001 (1 in 1000) is well below the 0.05 level. But use this .05 figure with some caution. It is not a magic number, and .04 or .06 are not much different.

Table 9.8: Chi square test of significance output

Chi square tests (Pearson chi square)

	Value	df	Asymp. sig. (2-sided)
Pearson chi square	21.378[a]	5	0.001 ← Significant value
Likelihood ratio	21.827	5	0.001
Linear-by-linear association	0.019	1	0.891
N of **valid** cases	2635		

a 0 cells (0.0%) have expected count less than 5. The minimum expected count is 17.24.

Also note the comment below the *chi square significance table*. This states that 0 cells (0 per cent) have counts less than 5. For chi square to be useful, this percentage should not be more than 20 per cent, if it is above 20 per cent, chi square is not an appropriate test of significance (see Kinnear & Gray 2006:385; Pallant 2007:216).

Valid data: A result using only cases defined as valid in the quantitative analysis.

The other limitation of chi square is that the numbers in the *Value* column are not easily interpreted, as the size of this number is directly influenced by the number of cells (degrees of freedom) in each cross-tabulation.

Exercise 9.3: Bivariate analysis: cross-tabulation and chi square

Analyses and questions

Cross-tabulate the variable *Gender (M1)* (in the *Columns* box) with the variable *(J5a)). Agree: I always take care of the way I dress and look* (in the *Rows* box).

1. From this table, see if you can tell if men and women differ on how much they agree or disagree with the statement about taking care of appearance. Write your interpretation down.
2. We can increase the readability of our analysis by adding percentages to the data on the frequency of responses in our cross-tabulation. Run the same analysis, but this time with column percentages added.
3. How do the percentages add to your interpretation? Where are the results for each group similar and where are they different?

Phillip Patman

4   If you add the percentages of *Strongly agree* and *Agree* together, what percentage of men agreed overall with the statement compared to what percentage of women?

5   Using your data write a brief (social science-related) paragraph to explain Australian men and women's attitudes towards the care they take on the way they dress and look.

6   Pick three other attitudinal variables from the dataset, and cross-tabulate them with gender. Which ones show a difference in attitudes by gender?

Optional analyses and questions

Add a chi square test of significance to your cross-tabulation to see if the difference between men's and women's responses on this variable is statistically significant.

7   From these results, are the differences in the data significant?

8   How do you know?

9   Given the significance level of the chi square test, what are the chances that the result you have is just a result of chance?

Recoding data

In the graph produced from the outcome of the frequencies analysis, the number of categories for each of the items was collapsed from five to three. That is, we combined the variable categories 'Spend much more' and 'Spend more' into just the one 'Spend more' category, and did the same for the 'Spend less' and 'Spend much less' categories at the other end of the scale. This function is useful if we want to summarise our data further, or we want to use a chi square test of significance but have too many cells with counts less than 5 for validity. In SPSS, we use the Recode function (in the Transform tool menu) to achieve this outcome.

Figure 9.22 shows how this function looks in SPSS. You will note that there are two Recode functions: one into the same variable and the other into different variables. Mostly we would always use the *Recode into different variables* function in preference, because this creates a new variable while leaving the original source variable in its current form. We retain this variable with five

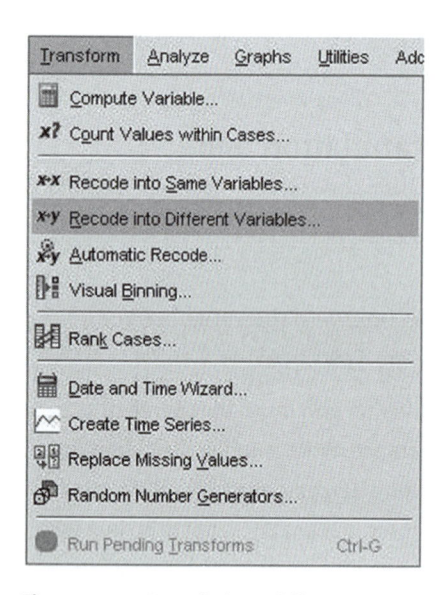

Figure 9.22: Recode into different variables function

categories for other analysis. The *Recode into same variables* will alter our original variable, and is usually only used when we want to adjust this variable in some way.

Figure 9.23 shows the *Recode into Different Variables* dialogue box. We start by shifting, via the arrow, the variable we want to recode into the right-hand box. We then have to give the new variable a unique name and label in the *Output variable* spots, and click the *Change* button. We can then move to setting out the criteria for our new variable by clicking the *Old and new values* button. This takes us through to the next screen, which is shown in figure 9.24.

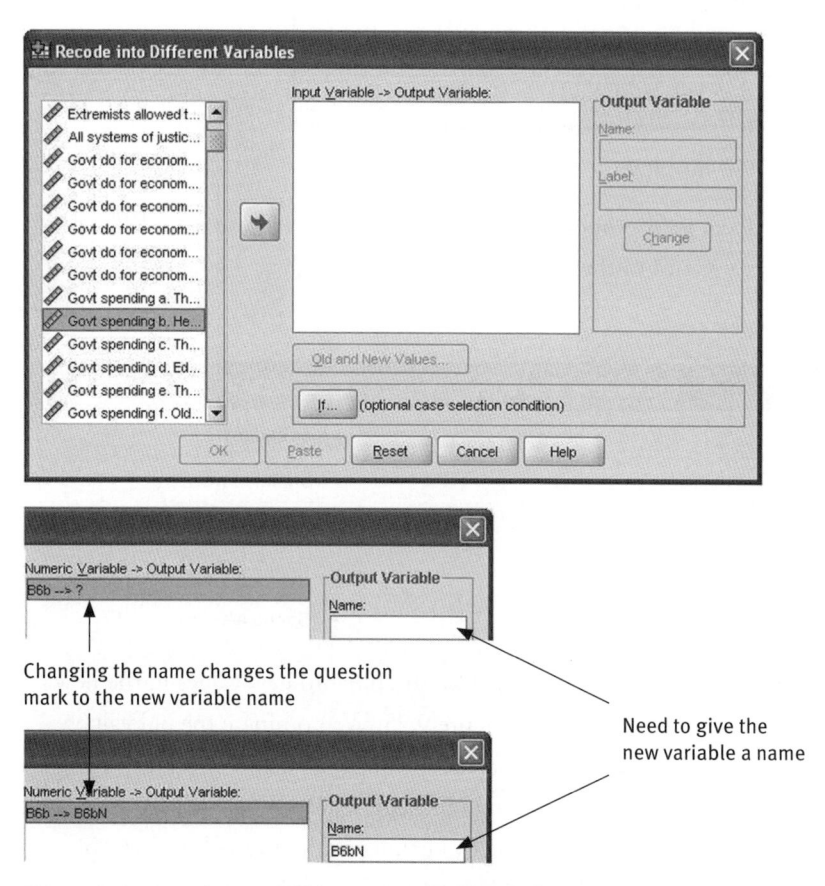

Figure 9.23: Recode into different variables dialogue box

Table 9.9 below also indicates the logic of changing our variable by altering the scale to a three-category variable on attitudes towards government spending. We need to change the old codes of 1 and 2 to now equal *1*, change the old value of 3 to now equal *2*, and the old values of 4 and 5 into the new value of *3*. If this seems confusing, it sometimes can be, and

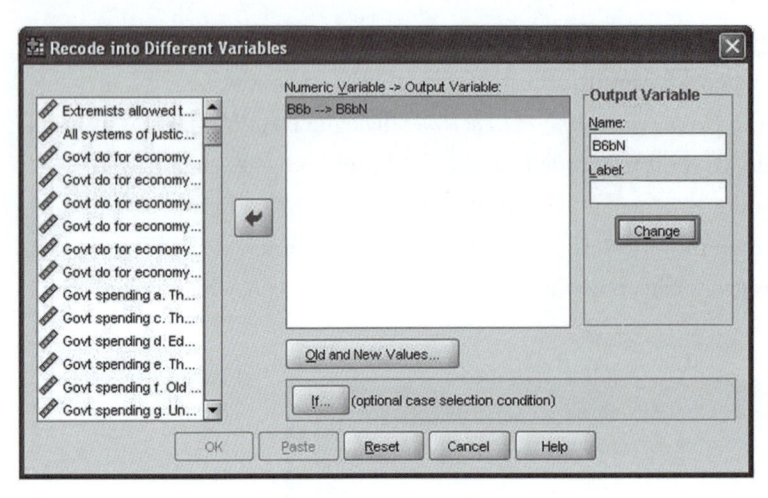

Figure 9.24: Recode values dialogue box

it is a good idea to write down your proposed changes, not only to give you a guide for the actual recoding but also as a record of the variables you have created.

Table 9.9: Collapsing categories

Old scale	Old code = New code	New scale
1 = Spend much more	1 = 1	1 = Spend more
2 = Spend more	2 = 1	1 = Spend more
3 = Spend the same as now	3 = 2	2 = Spend the same as now
4 = Spend less	4 = 3	3 = Spend less
5 = Spend much less	5 = 3	3 = Spend less

The process of changing the old values in the old variable into new values in the new variable is straightforward, and demonstrated in figure 9.25. We nominate the old value and what we want the new value to be on each side of the dialogue box. We can use a single value, a range of values, range from *lowest* and range through *highest*. We can also just change one value and keep all the others the same by clicking in the *Copy old value(s)* box on the left-hand side to the list. The final step, when all values have been recategorised, is to click the *Continue* button to take us back to the first Recode into different variables dialogue box, and then click *OK* to run the recode.

Always run a frequency of your new variable and your old variable to see if the recoding is correct (the numbers should add up), then go back to the Variable view screen to complete the details of your new variable, such as specifying what your new codes mean: 1 = 'Spend more'. You can now use your new variable in your analysis.

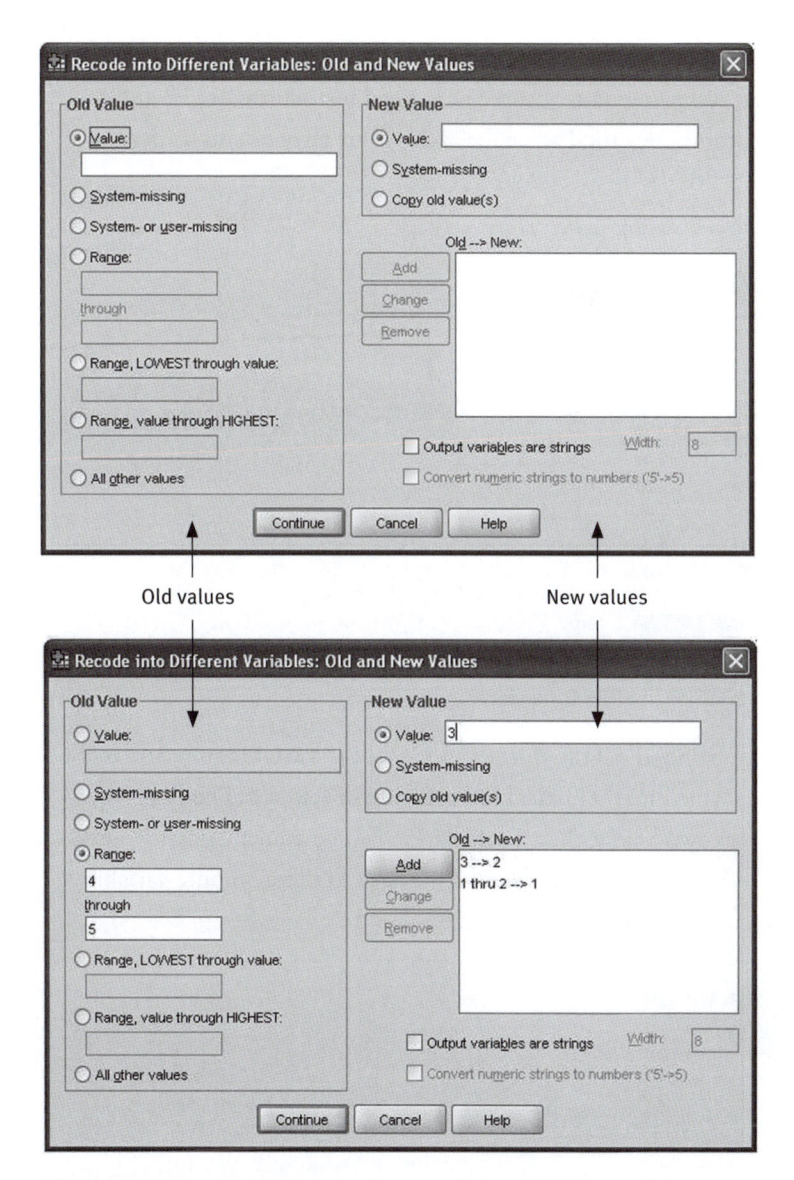

Figure 9.25: Changing values in the Recode into different variables

Transforming data

Another data manipulation that we might want to undertake is to transform our data from one form to another. An example of such a transformation is if we want create a total score for each respondent over each of the government spending areas to see if there are differences in sociodemographic characteristics, such as marital status or age, in their general attitude to government spending. This example is not easy to demonstrate in SPSS screens

Transform tool: SPSS menu of functions related to the transforming of data or variables within the data set transform data: a method of changing variables using the Recode or Compute functions.

(although the principles are the same) so we have used a simpler format of having data of three individual test scores T1, T2 and T3 to compute a total score for each of our respondents as per figure 9.26.

	T1	T2	T3
1	9.00	8.00	8.00
2	5.00	8.00	6.00
3	6.00	7.00	5.00
4	7.00	6.00	6.00
5	8.00	5.00	8.00
6	6.00	6.00	7.00

Figure 9.26: Three test score variables in SPSS Data view screen

Compute variable function: SPSS function that allows calculations to be performed or criteria to be set on one or more variable.

In SPSS, the **Transform** and **Compute variable function** is the way in which mathematical formulas are developed. The data is set out as shown below, then a calculation can be made. Clicking on the *Compute variable* option takes us through to the Compute variable dialogue box shown in figure 9.28.

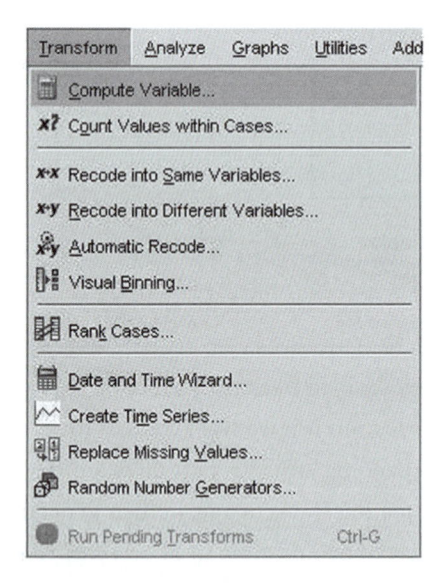

Figure 9.27: Transform tool with Compute variable function option

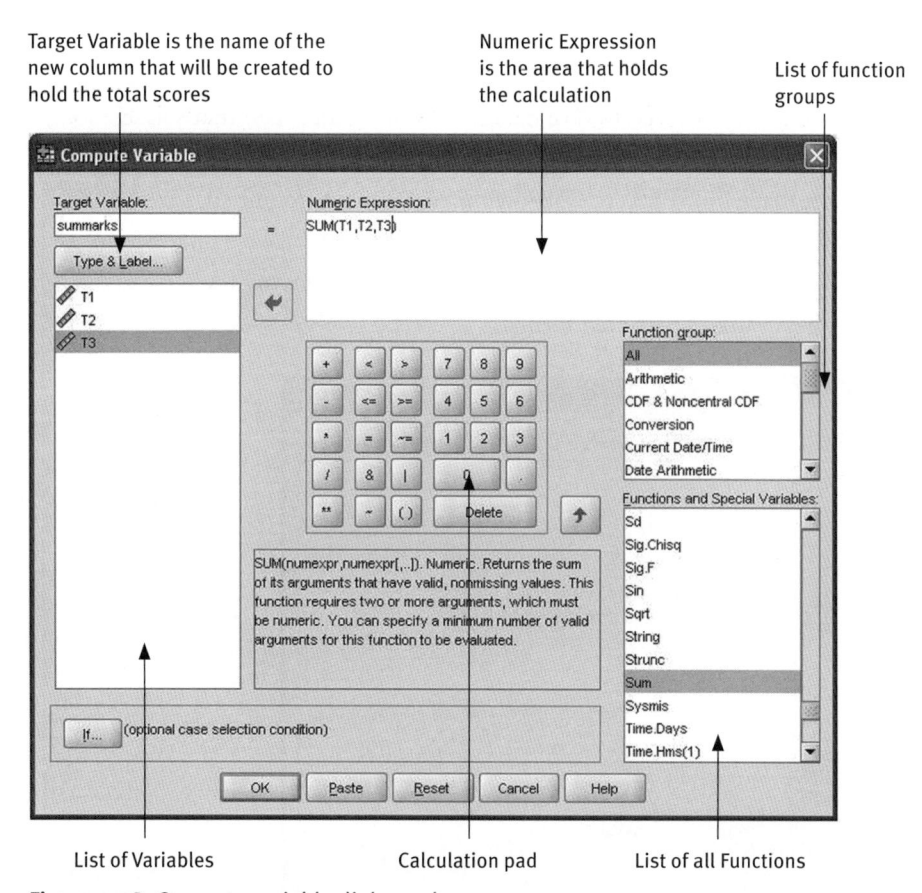

Chapter 9: Using SPSS for Quantitative Analysis

Figure 9.28: Compute variable dialogue box

Figure 9.29: Computed variable in Data view screen

Our new variable will now appear in the Data view screen, as shown in figure 9.29. Don't forget to run a frequency comparison check, record the new variable created, and complete the new variable's details in the Variable view screen. Also make sure to save the data set so you don't lose all your hard work when you close your SPSS session.

Phillip Patman

Saving data

There are times when we might need to save data in a format other than that suitable for SPSS; for example, to use the data in another statistical package, such as Stata or Excel. The alternative formats available in SPSS are: Tab-delimited; Comma-delimited; Fixed ASCII; Excel; Lotus 1-2-3 spreadsheet; SYLK (*.slk); and Stata. Using the Save data function, as shown in figure 9.30, we can alter the format of the data set by changing the *Save as type* from the default of SPSS to our preferred format.

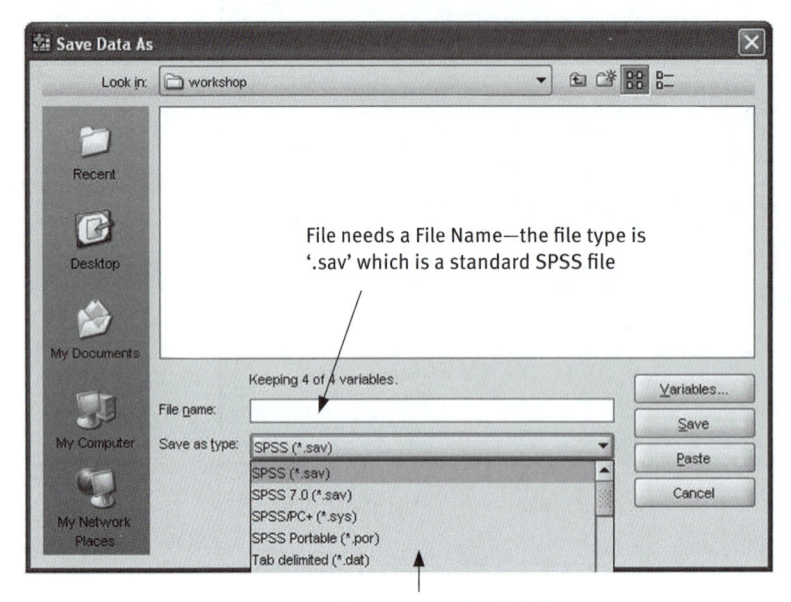

Figure 9.30: Saving data in alternative formats

Exporting data

We can also use the data or results from our workings in SPSS in other documents or formats. For example, if we want to copy a frequency table in another document, this is fairly easily done. Remember from chapter 8 that SPSS output is usually not suitable for direct use as the presentation of our results in our research write-up, but it can still be useful for working documents.

To export from Output view, click on the table, as shown in figure 9.31, so that there is a red arrow shown. This arrow indicates we can *Copy* and *Paste* this item. Then go to *File* and *Export*, which will open up a dialogue window. Use *Browse* to indicate where to place the file and *Type* to change the format that the file will be in.

Chapter 9: Using SPSS for Quantitative Analysis

Frequencies

Statistics

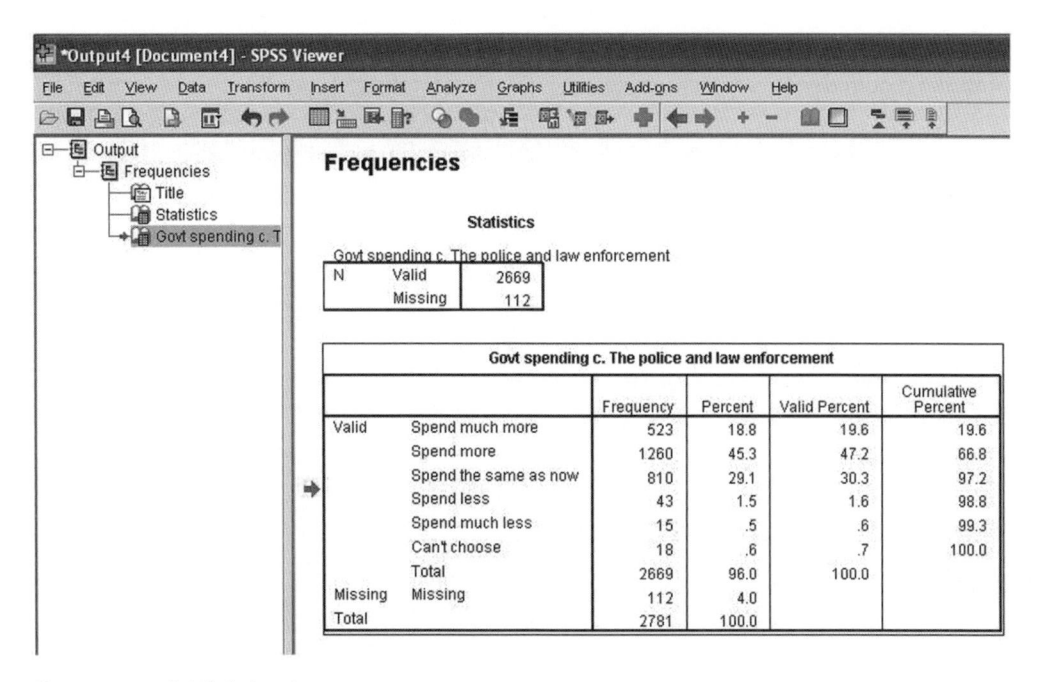

Govt spending c. The police and law enforcement

N	Valid	2669
	Missing	112

Govt spending c. The police and law enforcement

		Frequency	Percent	Valid Percent	Cumulative Percent
Valid	Spend much more	523	18.8	19.6	19.6
	Spend more	1260	45.3	47.2	66.8
	Spend the same as now	810	29.1	30.3	97.2
	Spend less	43	1.5	1.6	98.8
	Spend much less	15	.5	.6	99.3
	Can't choose	18	.6	.7	100.0
	Total	2669	96.0	100.0	
Missing	Missing	112	4.0		
Total		2781	100.0		

Figure 9.31: Highlighting Output to export

If you have conducted a series of analyses and want to place the entire analysis in another document or format, you can *Export* the output.

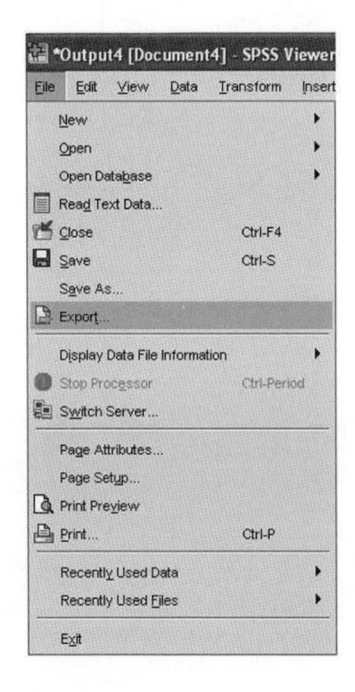

Figure 9.32: Export function under File tool

Phillip Patman

Click on *Type* and arrow to the format to bring up the dropdown list and change the type of file required.

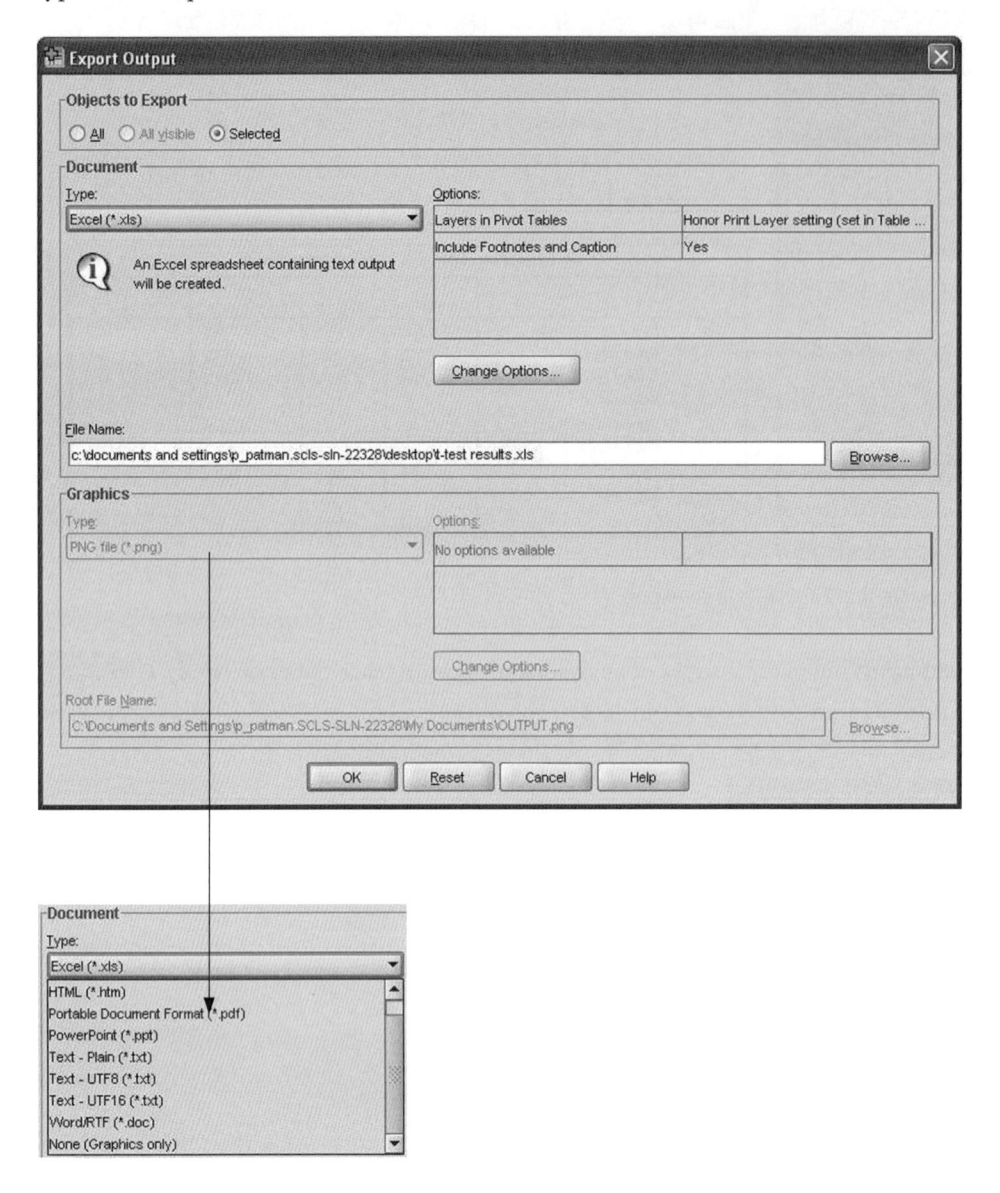

Figure 9.33: Changing format

Voices in the field

Kate Warner

Kate Warner is Professor of Law at the University of Tasmania, where she teaches and researches in the fields of Criminal Law, Criminology, Sentencing and Evidence. The paragraphs below describe Kate's use of SPSS in her current research.

'As a legal academic my research until recently has been primarily doctrinal and reform-orientated work. Only occasionally have I embarked (very tentatively) on quantitative empirical research, and this has involved very simple calculations—nothing beyond percentages and means. More recently I have embarked on a research project that has required a much more sophisticated method of managing and analysing the data we are collecting. With the help of Maggie Walter, our research team (Julia Davis, Rebecca Bradfield and Rachel Vermey) of rather innumerate lawyers has been introduced to the wonders of SPSS. We are enormously excited by the capacity and potential of SPSS to support what we believe will be robust and ground-breaking research findings. The project, which is by the Criminology Research Council, has two central aims. First, it explores the possibility of using jurors as a means of ascertaining informed public opinion about sentencing by surveying jury members about sentencing issues in general and in the case they have tried. Second, it seeks to investigate the usefulness of using the jury as a means of better informing the public about crime and sentencing issues. To achieve these aims, the study recruits jurors from trials delivering guilty verdicts (around 100–150 trials over the two years of the study). For the quantitative phase of the study, the project surveys the attitudes of participants at two stages. Stage 1 surveys jurors for their initial opinion based on their knowledge of the facts of the case before the sentence is imposed. The stage 2 survey occurs after the judge has imposed sentence, the jurors have read the judge's reasons for sentence, and they have received a package of information about the process of sentencing, crime patterns and other contextual matters. Questionnaire responses are then entered into an SPSS database, with jurors' responses and their demographic details matched to case details (type of offence, sentence, age of offender and so on). At this stage of the project, SPSS has been used to generate univariate and bivariate analysis on mid-project responses. These analyses reveal that: if jurors are given knowledge of a case, their sentencing opinion is not as punitive

Phillip Patman

as public opinion polls suggest, and that there is a dichotomy between jurors' views about sentencing in the abstract and jurors' views about the sentencing in the particular case they have been involved in. As the data collection is finalised, we will conduct more in-depth and multivariate analysis of what will by then be a very rich set of data.'

From method to practice

In 2006, as a Sociology honours student, Thomas Walter was interested in the influence of 9/11-related terrorism upon Australian attitudes towards immigration and migrants, and whether these acts of terrorism, and the increased feelings of fear and uncertainty they produced, had resulted in an increase in negativity. To investigate this topic he decided to explore whether attitudes to migrants had changed in recent decades, using sequential quasi-panel data sets from the Australian Election Studies. These surveys had been conducted each election year from 1987 onwards, and all had asked a series of questions around attitudes to migrants, providing running sets of data covering nearly a twenty-year period.

To undertake his analysis, Thomas needed to learn more about statistical quantitative analysis and how to conduct these analyses in SPSS than he had learned from his Sociology course units. With the help and guidance of his supervisor, statistical texts, the SPSS online tutorials (see below) and many hours in the computer lab, he developed these skills. His eventual analysis of his data within SPSS encompassed univariate, bivariate and multivariate techniques, varying from basic descriptive and frequency statistics through to an ordinary least squares regression analysis, to show the existence and level of influence of different sociodemographic characteristics on attitudes towards migrants. His results demonstrated that attitudes had actually changed little between 1987 and 2004, but where levels of negativity had spiked, these levels coincided with dates, like 1996, that had little to do with terrorism. Thomas theorised, based on his conceptual framework of 'othering' (see Hage 1998), that this change could be attributed to the influence of Pauline Hanson and the One Nation Party, which had a strong political and social presence at the time, and that terrorism, despite media portrayals of high risk, had not unduly influenced Australian attitudes towards immigration and migrants.

Postscript: Thomas was awarded upper first class honours and now works for the Department of Foreign Affairs and Trade in Canberra.

Conclusion

This chapter has detailed the basics of analysing quantitative data using SPSS. There is a lot more to learn, and you will need to take an SPSS course to really bring your skills up to a high level. But you can develop your skills from this base by working through the inbuilt SPSS tutorial package. The tutorial is available on opening SPSS, or can be opened through the *Help* section, and has several sections that people can work through at their own pace.

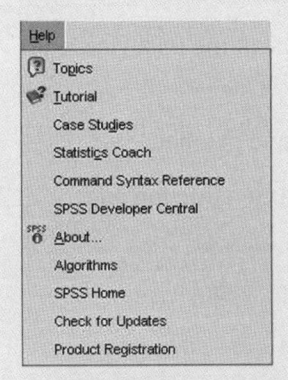

There are also two quantitative extension modules available on this text's website at <www.oup.com.au/orc/walter>. These are: how to undertake correlations using SPSS; and comparison of means, again using SPSS.

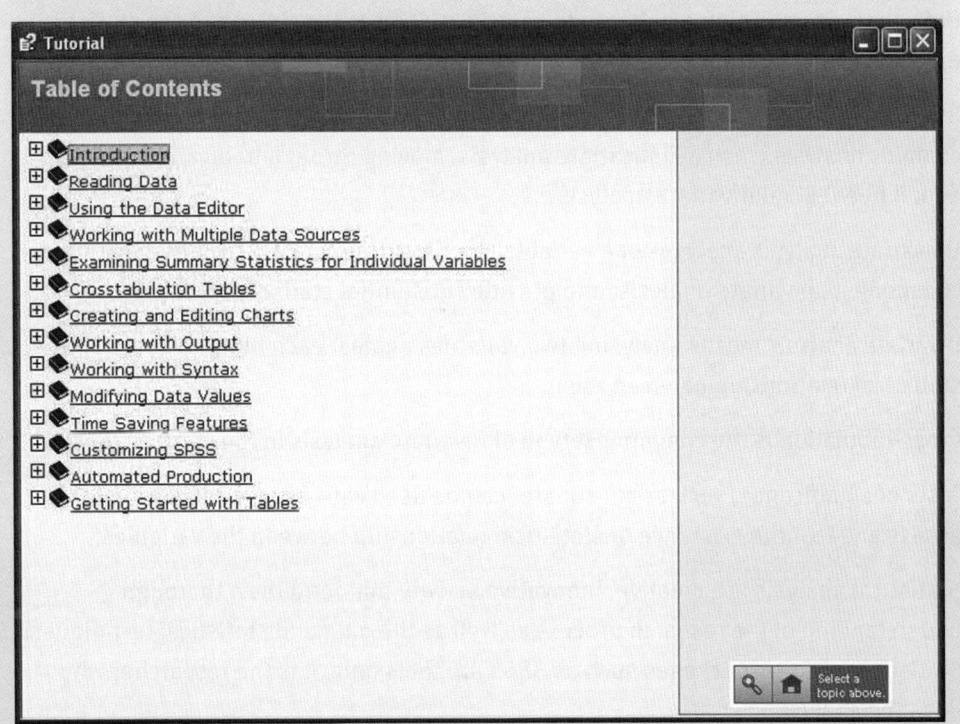

Figures 9.34 and 9.35

Phillip Patman

Main points

> SPSS (Statistical Product and Service Solutions) is a commonly used quantitative data analysis software package that is comparatively easy to use because of its Windows interface.

> Quality statistical analysis depends on quality variable construction and data entry.

> SPSS uses three screens for its major functions: the Variable view; the Data view and the Output window.

> The Variable view shows where the variables are constructed and detailed.

> Different levels of data measurement require different variable construction and layout.

> The Data view is where the data are entered and cases are displayed.

> The Output window is where results generated from the analysis are displayed.

> Data analysis uses dialogue boxes to select variables for analysis and the statistical techniques and functions required.

> It is important to analyse data thoroughly and sequentially, beginning with the least complex analysis, such as univariate analysis, moving through to bivariate analysis, and, if needed, multivariate analysis.

> Univariate analysis analyses one variable at a time; frequency distributions are the commonest univariate analysis, and provide substantial statistical results.

> Bivariate analysis means analysing two variables against each other to assess the statistical relationship between them.

> Cross-tabulation is the commonest type of bivariate analysis in the social sciences.

> Tests of significance, such as chi square, can be used with a cross-tabulation to assess and test the existence of statistical relationship between the variables.

> Statistical analysis is a creative, innovative activity that requires a thorough understanding of the research process as well as the data and statistical techniques. Statistical analysis packages such as SPSS are tools only. It is the researcher who does the analysis.

Further reading

Allen, P. and Bennett, K. (2008). *SPSS for the Health and Behavioural Sciences*. Melbourne: Thomson.

AuSSA (2007). *The Australian Survey of Social Attitudes: AuSSA Data*. Canberra: Australian Demographic and Social Research Institute (ADSRI), Australian National University, College of Arts and Social Sciences <http://aussa.anu.edu.au/data.php>. Accessed 11 November 2008.

Bryman, A. and Cramer, D. (2005). *Quantitative Data Analysis with SPSS 12 and 13: A Guide for Social Scientists*. Hove: Routledge.

Coakes, S. J. and Steed, L. G. (2001). *SPSS: Analysis Without Anguish: Version 10.0 for Windows*. Brisbane: Wiley.

de Vaus, D. A. (2002). *Social Surveys*. London: Sage.

Field, A. (2005). *Discovering Statistics Using SPSS*. London: Sage.

Francis, G. (2004). *Introduction to SPSS for Windows: Versions 12.0 and 11.0*. Frenchs Forest, NSW: Pearson Education Australia.

Ho, R. (2000). *Handbook of Univariate and Multivariate Data Analysis and Interpretation: An SPSS Approach*. Rockhampton: Central Queensland University Publishing Unit.

Tabachnick, B. G. and Fidell, L. S. (2007). *Using Multivariate Statistics* (5th edn). Boston: Pearson.
This is a statistical book that covers more about the statistical nature of the tests and is cited/referenced in many of the books above. It is not SPSS specific, and does use other programs in demonstrating techniques. If you want a good general statistical reference book, this would be useful.

Websites

http://www2.chass.ncsu.edu/garson/PA765/statnote.htm

http://home.ubalt.edu/ntsbarsh/Business-stat/opre504.htm

http://www.statsoft.com/textbook/stathome.html

http://www.socialresearchmethods.net/selstat/ssstart.htm

http://www.statsoft.com/textbook/stathome.html

http://www.sas.com

Phillip Patman

http://www.spss.com

http://www.surveysystem.com

References

Babbie, E. R., Halley, F. and Zaino, J. (2007). *Adventures in Social Research: Data Analysis Using SPSS 11.0/11.5 for Windows*. Thousand Oaks: Pine Forge Press.

Hage, G. (1998). *White Nation: Fantasies of White Supremacy in a Multicultural Society*. North Melbourne: Pluto Press.

Kinnear, P. K. and Gray, C. D. (2006). *SPSS 14 Made Simple*. Hove: Psychology Press.

Pallant, J. (2007). *SPSS Survival Manual* (3rd edn). Crows Nest: Allen & Unwin.

Walter, T. (2006) An Excuse for Prejudice? The Influence of Terrorism upon Australian Attitudes towards Immigration. Unpublished honours thesis, Hobart: School of Sociology and Social Work, University of Tasmania.

3
Qualitative Methods and Meaning-making

Many new social researchers who view quantitative methods as 'hard and technical' often hold a paired tendency to presume that qualitative research will be 'easier'. This is an error. Yes, the shape and practice of qualitative research may align more closely with such researchers' own worldview and standpoint. But the rigorous attention to detail, theoretical understanding of underpinning methodologies and theoretical frames, the essential design and practice process, ethical dimensions and technical skills related to method and analysis required for qualitative research are on a par with those required for quantitative work.

There can also be a tendency to regard qualitative methods as essentially about in-depth interviewing. This indeed is the first topic in this section. But as the other methods outlined here—content analysis, discourse analysis and evaluation research—as well as those included in the online chapters on conversational analysis, participatory action research, ethnographic research and case study methods, memory work and life histories make evident, qualitative research is a very broad and, at times even, a divergent area.

Regardless of type, however, the essential categorising of a method as qualitative is based on its core task of meaning-making. All the methods detailed in this section have at their centre an emphasis on collecting and analysing data that are deep and rich in the understandings that they bring to the social. They are concerned not with structured comparisons, as with quantitative data, but with the specific, and often unique, meanings and perspective that individuals and/or groups attach to the social, whether it be situations, behaviour, experiences or social or political phenomena. Qualitative research is also a more subjective approach, whereby the researcher aims to understand and interpret the experiences of the individuals or groups involved in the research. Also, qualitative research mostly (but not always) has as its focus the smaller units of people and society.

All the methods detailed in this section provide the ingredients for an illumination on how our social world operates. All also provide social insights, but the level and the dimensions along which these are garnered differ significantly between qualitative methods. This variation in how and what social meaning is made is a key strength of qualitative methods. Using only the methods detailed in this section—and there are many more not covered here—the breadth and depth of the analyses available are apparent. In in-depth interviews, the focus is on the individual, with the researcher trying to understand the view of the world through the eyes of their respondents. In focus groups, it is again the individual understandings that are sought, but these insights are harnessed through the power of group interaction and group dynamics. Content analysis moves away from direct analysis of members of society, to gather social understandings and interpretations by analysing societal artefacts of written or recorded communication. Discourse analysis moves one step further again, with its central task of uncovering the implicit meanings of language and its deployment to achieve specific ideological or political objectives. It uncovers the hidden use of power. And evaluation research draws on the range of qualitative methods (and often includes quantitative methods) to construct a critically astute and independent evaluation of the efficacy, efficiency or success of specific programs or practices. The qualitative online modules—that outline the core components of narrative research, conversation analysis, action research, ethnographic research, memory work and sensory and visual methods (available at ‹www.oup.com.au/orc/walter›)—also form part of this section.

So, enjoy this introduction to key qualitative methods. You will be amazed at the social research perspectives and power that they offer.

Chapter 10

Qualitative Interviewing Methods

Max Travers

Uncovering social meaning through interviews

In the summer of 1998 in Sydney, a series of violent assaults took place, committed by what the newspapers described as 'gangs' of Lebanese youths. These incidents received a great deal of attention from politicians during the state election, and led to targeted initiatives designed to stamp out ethnic crime. Young people in the Lebanese community were portrayed as naturally violent, and incapable of being integrated into Australian life.

The public alarm generated by these incidents led a group of researchers at the University of Western Sydney to address this issue (Collins et al. 2000). Like many social scientists, they started by analysing media reports, and attending political meetings. However, the most interesting research data came from interviewing Lebanese youth, and also Sydney police officers, about their experiences on the street and perceptions of the problem. Without taking sides, their study shows how a group of youths can become alienated, but also how the police response to a difficult situation can breed a cycle of distrust and violence.

Like most social science research studies, the study by Collins and colleagues (2000) attempts to challenge the way we normally think, in this case by addressing the experience of groups we rarely meet face to face, although there are often negative reports about them in the media. In this research project, as in many others, in-depth interviews with participants of the particular social phenomenon being investigated provided rich, quality and insightful data.

Key terms

closed questions
conversation analysis
ethnographic fieldwork
focus group
follow-up question
in-depth interview

interpretive perspective
interview guide
open-ended questions
probes
rapport
relativism

social desirability effect
structured interview
transcription
unstructured interview
verstehen

Introduction

In-depth interview: In-depth interviews are guided by general themes rather than pre-set questions. They are also less formal than structured interviews, exploring issues as the interviewee raises them.

The **in-depth interview** is one of the most common research methods employed within the social sciences. Interviewing, as a method of social research, was first used in the late nineteenth century by British social policy researchers to understand the problems of the poor. Anthropologists also used interviews during the same period in their studies of non-Western societies. However, the major type of interviewing used by social scientists today, the in-depth interview, was developed in America during the 1920s by sociologists at the University of Chicago, who have become known as the Chicago School. Robert Park famously encouraged his students to spend less time in dusty libraries, and instead go out and investigate the world around them. The in-depth interview was used, alongside other methods, as a means to investigate groups or social worlds, and also to obtain life histories.

Qualitative interviewing, especially the in-depth interview, is now used extensively as a key way of exploring social meaning within social science research. The easy availability of portable recording equipment since the 1970s has revolutionised the use of interviewing as a social research method. Rather than taking notes or employing a stenographer who sat behind a curtain, so as not to disturb the interview, social researchers can now, easily and cheaply, record the full interview. The resultant increase in the accessibility of interviewing to researchers is one reason some commentators believe we live in an 'interview society' (Silverman 1997).

This chapter details the practical considerations and tasks needed to conduct qualitative social science research interviews. How to analyse and interpret qualitative data, such as that obtained from in-depth interviews, is covered in chapter 14.

Box 10.1: Using qualitative interviewing for social research

One of the strengths of qualitative interviewing as a research method and technique is flexibility in how and with whom it can be used. Consider the variability of both topic and subjects group in the following four research briefs of projects which used qualitative interviewing as their predominant method. Also see how the meanings and understandings that the respondents bring to the topics are the central aspect of the research.

Understanding masculinities

Sociologist Tony Coles (2008) used qualitative interviewing in collecting data from 41 men to investigate meaning and understanding of their lives. Focusing on how men make sense of and live a 'masculine' life, he found that men are able to negotiate masculinities over the life course in a number of ways that allow them to support a range of different ways of being masculine.

Emotional attachment when home is in a caravan park

Social researcher Janice Newton (2008) sought to understand whether, and how, permanent residents of caravan parks could achieve security in their homes. The small exploratory study interviewed 12 permanent caravan park residents and 10 caravan park managers in Melbourne around concepts such as belonging to home and community and place. She found that, despite the challenges of their tenure, safety and security were of central significance to respondents.

Public lived street experience of being an Aboriginal paint sniffer

Three researchers—a social anthropologist, a community health manager and a health researcher—used qualitative individual interviews to uncover the lived experience of 16 homeless Indigenous young people. This group was, at the time, the target of a media furore and indignation in Brisbane because of their paint sniffing in public places. But from the sniffers' perspective, their lives were a chaotic mix of resistance and rejection of White cultural authority and norms and the regular experience of verbal and physical violence perpetrated against them (Ogwang et al. 2006).

Investigation of post-social relationships among financial traders

Social scientist Margery Mayall (2007) was interested in the *post-social relationship*, a concept that reflects the increased presence and relevance of non-human objects in contemporary life. She chose to qualitatively interview a group of share traders from a number of Australia's major cities to gain an understanding of how they used computer imagery of patterns of trade analysis in their interaction with the share market. She found that, while traders were personally attached and interacting with their flow of electronic information, they also used the knowledge gained in their human interactions, such as in share trader forums, to make their decisions.

What is a qualitative interview?

There are a number of ways of conducting interview studies, and the method you choose will reflect two basic research decisions. These are:

- the question your research asks
- the theoretical framework of your research project.

Max Travers

> **Structured interview:** An interview that asks mostly closed questions. It is often used in projects where many people are interviewed, such as in a survey.

As discussed in chapter 6, for many projects the **structured interview**, such as those used in surveys, will be appropriate. Structured interviews involve asking the same set of questions, in the same way, to a number of interview respondents, and are often employed in projects where a team of researchers conducts a large number of interviews. The emphasis is on obtaining comparative data from a sample (often a large, randomly selected representative sample of the population of interest) so that social patterns and relationships between key variables can be identified and statistically analysed. The comparability of each respondent's answers is important, so care is taken, usually through a guide or set of rules given to each interviewer, to ensure that each structured interview is conducted in basically the same way. As discussed in chapter 1, the theoretical framework that guides the structured interview is quantitative, and the focus is on answering the research question by statistically measuring and exploring the social patterns revealed by the collected data.

The focus of this chapter, the in-depth interview, also involves talking with a participant about the topic of research, but rather than using pre-set questions, the interviewer and the interview are guided by a set of general themes. There is also flexibility in how the interview is conducted. The interviewer can ask additional questions, express his or her opinions where appropriate, and explore issues as the interviewee raises them. In short, rather than a structured question-and-answer process, the in-depth interview is more like an open-ended conversation between the interviewee and the interviewer. In-depth interview projects also tend to be smaller in scale than those using structured interviews, often with most interviews conducted and analysed by the researcher. These core differences between a structured and an in-depth interview reflect the different purposes for which they are used within social science research. While the structured interview mostly seeks to obtain large-scale comparative data, the in-depth interview seeks to answer social questions through the subjective meanings and understandings people bring to their interpretation of the social world.

The importance of meaning

At the centre of the theoretical frame that informs the in-depth interview is the importance of meaning and subjectivity. The in-depth interview, as a social research method, is developed from an interpretivist perspective that sees that social research needs to address the complex ways in which people understand their lives. How we act in any social encounter, including an interview, necessarily involves interpretation and judgment.

The theorist most associated with this position in social research is Max Weber. He argued that one advantage social researchers have over scientists studying the natural world is that we can communicate with our objects of study. We are able to do this using the method of **verstehen**, or understanding. This means, first, that we can recognise many of the actions of others immediately through sharing a common culture. Weber used the example of coming across a woodcutter working in the forest and being able to make sense of what we would see (Weber 1978). Weber also suggested that there may be complex subjective meanings attached to this apparently simple act of cutting wood. The woodcutter could be engaged in earning his daily bread, or perhaps chopping wood for pleasure, or even to work off anger. The objective of interpretative enquiry is to address this level of meaning. We can, for example, interview our research subjects about their motives and purposes, or observe their behaviour over a longer period of time.

> **Verstehen**: Interpretive method through which we understand other people's actions.

While, in today's world, we would be unlikely to come across a woodcutter, Weber's example still makes clear how subjective meaning is vital to gaining social understanding. Weber believed that meaning, in all its complexity, was a difficult thing to study. In his example of the woodcutter, we can see how there might be a mixture of motives involved, or different interpretations of the same event. This might seem to lead in the direction of **relativism**, the philosophical position associated with postmodernism. Despite these complexities, however, Weber did not believe that it was impossible to study meaning. This is amply demonstrated in his famous study, *The Protestant Ethic and the Spirit of Capitalism* (Weber 1992), which describes the religious beliefs of Protestant religious groups through analysing extracts from diaries and other historical documents. We can, however, understand Weber's point as indicating that, in focusing on the subjective, there is likely to be variety and richness, possibly even conflicting accounts or versions, in any set of interviews. A single interview might reveal multiple meanings, or different meanings found between two or more interviews with a single interviewee.

> **Relativism**: Philosophical position suggesting that it is not possible to obtain objective knowledge, and that there are only different views and opinions.

How to conduct an in-depth interview

In-depth interviewing is an exciting and challenging activity. For many, the appeal of social research is that it involves going out into society and investigating social processes, the activities of different groups, or what happens in different social settings at first hand. The individual approach of in-depth interviewing means that research using this method will often bring you into direct, face-to-face contact with people who have very different life experiences to your own. This section directly addresses a range of the practical considerations involved in conducting an in-depth interview. Effective in-depth interviewing, while requiring a specific set of skills, is within the grasp of all budding social researchers. My own experience in teaching interviewing skills to undergraduate students has confirmed that all who apply themselves to the task find, despite their initial hesitation, that they can interview effectively. Conversely, a quality in-depth interview is not just having a conversation. In-depth interviewing is hard work, and good listening and reflective skills, in particular, are important to conducting a good in-depth interview.

Case study 10.1: Reporting interview data

This extract from Claire Williams's study *Open Cut* illustrates how extracts from interviews can be used to support a theoretical argument (Williams 1981:139–40). She is describing the relationship between husbands and wives in an Australian mining town:

'Because of the sex segregation of roles in a place like Open Cut ... and the absence of relatives for 70 per cent of the couples, there is a need for some tolerance on the part of each partner toward listening to conversations concerned with the other's sphere of life. Most men ... accepted that they had to listen at least to some details of their wife's day and many, immediately they returned from work, helped with a task usually taking the children 'off their wife's hands' for a few hours. Others listened to wives' worries or feelings of hurt engendered through interactions with other people. For their part, wives listened often daily to their husbands' descriptions of workplace events. A happily married couple describe their attempts to communicate. Even with this couple, there are some areas of reserve. (She said that she usually told her husband her troubles.)'

> You feel you've got to tell someone. He listens and doesn't comment. He lays in bed till I calm down, most bad days I just let off steam ... Occasionally I wish I could talk about some things. There's been times when I felt we could have talked over things and didn't. [Interviewer asked, 'Why not?'.] It was a mixture of both; couldn't bring ourselves to. I don't talk about feelings of hurt. I can get hurt in funny little irrational ways. You know you're being irrational at times. You're shy to confess it to your husband. He agreed that sometimes he wished they would talk more ...

'She described an earlier period of marital tension before they moved ... when the inability to fully communicate raised the level of tension.'

> We were four people in twenty-three feet. There was no privacy in the caravan park. He couldn't sit still; he had no shed to potter; he nearly drove himself mad. He kept it bottled up. We never had arguments in our lives till we went there. It affected our sex life. I used to cry when I was by myself. Nobody ever knew about that and we didn't talk about it between ourselves.
>
> These extracts vividly convey a sense of the hardships experienced by families in this community in a way that would not be possible through summarising reported speech.

Choosing a topic

The social research topics amenable to research using in-depth interview techniques are endless. Any social topic that can be researched through an exploration of subjective understanding can make use of in-depth interviewing as the research method. Many researchers select topics that are of particular interest to them, because they relate to their own life experience. This personal perspective can add to the depth of understanding the researcher brings to the topic and, in many circumstances, a familiarity with the subject enhances the richness of the study. For example, a research student recently completed a qualitative study using in-depth interviewing on the nature of spiritual experiences. This study drew on the researcher's own interest in alternative religions. In another example, a female student who was a part-time police officer used in-depth interviews with other female officers to develop understandings of the way women experience the police service.

Alternatively, selecting a social research topic and question of which you have little personal experience can also lead to unique insights. Although as a researcher you would always investigate the topic through relevant literature before embarking on any interviews, being unfettered by pre-existing experiences, attitudes, or beliefs can be an advantage, and reduce the risk of your own experiences influencing your interpretation of your interview data. Examining a social process from the outside can also bring unique understandings and perspectives. For example, a study on how new migrants make sense of their lives and experiences in their new social settings, conducted by someone who was not a migrant, would be likely to produce very different, but equally viable, insights from one conducted by a researcher with personal experience of migration.

Regardless of how a topic is selected and the dimensions of that topic, in each case a sociological imagination is needed to develop a clear research question. At its simplest, this means relating the experiences of a particular group of people to changes taking place in wider society. A study about spiritual experiences might, for example, need to consider debates about

Max Travers

the place of religion in the modern world. A study about female police officers might want to consider the much broader issue of how women are treated in society. In each case, the interviews can be used as a case study to explore themes in the relevant academic literature. It is, of course, impossible to read everything written about any area of social life, but you should, at a minimum, read the major studies cited in textbooks, and also look for any recent journal articles. This should give you some ideas and arguments that help to develop or shape a research question. The most exciting and important findings, however, will come from what you discover through conducting empirical research. You may find that previous studies are mistaken or have not adequately addressed the experiences of your interviewees. If this happens, you will have added something to the existing literature on your topic.

How many interviews?

There are no pre-set rules on the number of interviews that are needed for a qualitative project. As discussed earlier, the question of how many interviews depends on the purpose and the aim of the project as well as the research question. In practice, the numbers of actual in-depth interviews conducted varies enormously among research projects. Some qualitative interviewing research projects will conduct in-depth interviews with a relatively large group of interviewees. For example, Catherine Garrett's (1998) study on eating disorders was based on interviews with 64 people. However, it is also possible to obtain interesting and valuable research findings through conducting only a few interviews. For example, Collins and colleagues' (2000) study about moral panics surrounding Lebanese youths in Sydney includes an analysis, in the case of the Lebanese youth, of interviews with only four young people.

In another example, a research student recently conducted an excellent qualitative research project that was based on only two in-depth interviews. The researcher examined the success of a government initiative to reduce youth offending through creating multi-agency partnerships. Careful analysis of the two interviews, one with a police officer and another with a community safety officer, on their view of the policy drew out not only the practical difficulties involved in making partnerships work, but also the different values of these two occupational groups. The key issue is, in a qualitative project, not the number of interviews, but what you do with the interview material you have collected.

Some American traditions take this a step further by suggesting that one can only achieve an adequate understanding by conducting repeat interviews with the same person (Spradley 1979). The objective is to get to know the interviewee and, in doing so, attempt to understand the circumstances of his or her life. Gubrium and Holstein (1997) also make the point that depth of understanding can only be achieved by being open to different experiences and perspectives, and treating the interviewee as a unique and valuable human being.

The question of how many interviews, however, can be a problem if the number of interviews needed becomes confused with philosophical debates about the scientific basis of a research project. Despite the different aims and perspectives of qualitative and quantitative research, there sometimes appears to be a lurking feeling at the back of every qualitative researcher's mind that more is better. Qualitative research data can sometimes be analysed using quantitative techniques, such as the percentage of interviewees who expressed one view as opposed to another (as indeed qualitative analysis techniques are sometimes applied to data from primarily quantitative projects). However, qualitative findings cannot be generalised to findings about the broader population. For example, although 6 of the 10 people you have interviewed might believe X, you cannot claim, from these results, that a majority of people believe X. Your findings are specific to your particular research project and a particular sample of interviewees.

More pragmatically, the number of in-depth interviews you conduct is also a product of the resources that are available in terms of time and money. Each in-depth interview is unique, and often involves the researcher travelling to meet with the respondent. In-depth interviewing is also a personally demanding process. It would be unusual for a researcher to be able to complete more than three or four in-depth interviews in a day, without exhaustion. It can take a lot of time arranging interviews, and it is important to take these aspects into account and be realistic about what can feasibly be achieved when designing a research project. You also need to allow time, and money, for the analysis part of the research process. If sound-recorded, each in-depth interview needs to be transcribed. This is an important and enjoyable part of the research process, in that it allows you to review what happened in the interview, identify the most useful sections, and develop themes that will be used in organising and presenting extracts from the interviews. However, it is also labour intensive. Allow at least two hours for **transcription** for every hour of recorded interview.

> **Transcription**: A full written record of interview data.

Case study 10.2: Experiencing the transition from welfare to work

Social researchers Maureen Baker and David Tippin (2002) examined the experiences of New Zealand sole mothers of the work-to-welfare programs that are part of the restructuring of the welfare state in that country. Based on data from 120 in-depth interviews with sole mothers currently on work-tested social benefits in three regions of New Zealand's North Island, Baker and Tippin found that the work-to-welfare transition presented the sole mothers with complex dilemmas.

Some mothers struggled with the problem of how to improve their family's economic position, meet the workfare demands of the state, and also meet their own and society's expectations and images of a good mother. As one Māori mother working full time noted:

> The school does not accept children before 8 a.m. so my children are actually at the gate at 8 a.m. That is something that is a bit hard during the winter period, but I have no choice ... [School] starts at 8.30 a.m. (Baker & Tippin 2002:352).

The lack of flexibility in the labour market also proved difficult for many of the sole mothers. The comments of this mother demonstrate this problem:

> I have been working at a supermarket ... and was made redundant again because they wanted me to start earlier or finish later. With my daughter, I can't start at 6.40 in the morning ... They want people who can work shifts and start early and finish at 3 p.m. or start later and work late nights. They don't even want to look at you if you can't work those hours ... I am honest and work hard ... but because of the hours they would rather let you go! (2002:354).

The in-depth interviews in Baker and Tippin's study provide insights into the lived experience of women who now must move from a relatively flexible welfare system to the less flexible labour market. As the researchers note in their conclusion, for sole mothers to achieve economic independence through paid work requires 'resolving issues related to maintenance of personal identity, a sense of well-being and family relationships' (2002:357–8).

Recruiting interviewees

Recruiting suitable and willing interviewees can be a difficult part of the qualitative research process. Participation by interviewees in social science research projects is, of course, totally voluntary, and the path to participation can be relatively complex. Recruiting interviewees is reliant on all the following four criteria being present for prospective interviewees:

1. they must learn about the research project and its need for participants
2. they must be interested enough in the topic or the project to agree to participate
3. participation must be practically feasible
4. they must be motivated enough to take the time and trouble to follow through with the interview.

Obtaining access to a suitable number of interviewees can, therefore, take a significant period of time, without assured results. In some cases, the difficulties can even mean that the whole project has to be dropped or substantially redesigned. To give an example, a researcher I know plans to interview women who have undergone, or are about to undergo, cosmetic surgery. To obtain access to potential interviewees, she has approached plastic surgeons, and asked if they could recommend patients or if she could leave advertising cards in their surgery. The outcome is that, while at this stage it looks like she will obtain sufficient interviews, this cannot be guaranteed. The problem here, as you can probably guess, is that, although undergoing cosmetic surgery is becoming a relatively common experience, admitting to such surgery still retains a social stigma. As a result, many people who have undergone cosmetic surgery do not want anyone to know they have had surgery, let alone be interviewed about their decision.

Case study 10.3: Finding interviewees

For her study *Beyond Anorexia*, about the experience of recovering from this illness, Catherine Garrett interviewed 33 people, most of whom were women from upper-middle-class backgrounds (Garrett 1998). In recruiting interviewees, as well as conducting the interviews, it undoubtedly helped that Garrett herself had suffered from anorexia. Most of the study is an autobiographical account supplemented by the stories told by her interviewees.

Garrett made contact with the interviewees through approaching a journalist on the *Sydney Morning Herald* who wrote a column 'designed to appeal to people over forty'.

At the journalist's suggestion, the piece was about her personal story, rather than presenting her as simply having an academic interest in the topic. In the following passage, she describes the response:

> Fifty people responded. Some were journalists and publishers interested in my research. Others had questions about anorexic friends and family members or about recovery from other kinds of suffering. Some (like 'Lesley', a doctor) offered to speak to me anonymously because they believed that revealing their past would compromise their present lives. Others (like 'Meredith', a food writer who subsequently told her own recovery story to the press) were inspired by [the article] to 'come out' publicly (Meredith's words). Some lived too far away for us to meet and a few did not respond to my letters after their initial contact. Of these potential participants, I eventually interviewed thirty. Three of these were men. In addition, three of my friends (Kate, Simone and Miranda) also agreed to participate. Counting myself, the stories of thirty-four people were included in my research (Garrett 1998:19).

Ironically, the most sensitive topics, dealing with difficult personal issues, can sometimes be the easiest to research. This is because, as in Garrett's study, some

Max Travers

people in the group welcome the opportunity to tell their stories to a sympathetic listener. Garrett notes that:

> these people chose to participate in part for their own benefit; they saw participation as an opportunity to discover, develop and create deeper understandings of their lives, outside a clinical setting; many of them made copious notes, re-read diaries and brought out photographs in the weeks leading up to my visit ... Above all, however, they wanted their stories to be of value to others. In telling them, they hoped to correct some of the misconceptions about anorexia and recovery they had encountered in media reports and in the general public (Garrett 1998:22).

In a smaller project, you may be able to recruit sufficient numbers of suitable participants by using your personal contacts. Often, if your topic area is one in which you have some personal experience, you will know other people who also have similar experiences. Even if you do not know prospective interviewees yourself, other people you know probably will. In a criminology program I taught, students were required to complete a project on a relevant topic. It was remarkable how many students had a relative who was a magistrate, or police officer, or a psychologist working in a prison. Admittedly, one interview will not usually be sufficient, but this one contact can often help secure other interviews. Using the snowball method of sampling outlined in chapter 5, one suitable participant may be willing to assist you to locate other prospective interviewees. This method of recruitment is especially useful when you are researching a topic that is sensitive and potential interviewees are hard to locate by conventional methods.

Approaching the interview

The question 'How do I conduct an interview?' has some similarities to asking someone how to ride a bicycle: almost everyone has acquired the basic skills needed. This is not to say, however, that it makes no sense to talk of a 'good' or 'bad' interview, or a 'good' or 'bad' interviewer. While almost all new social researchers will have the skills necessary to conduct a good interview, you need to know how to use those skills to best advantage during the interview process.

The importance of preparation

The best way to learn how to be an effective in-depth interviewer is to practise interviewing. Working through exercise 10.2 will give you some experience of what it feels like, both to conduct an in-depth interview and to be interviewed. As the objective of this exercise is not data analysis, recording the interview is not required. Rather, the emphasis is on thinking about what happens during an interview, how the interview process works in actuality, and the effectiveness of different kinds of questions and questioning. For example, almost all new interviewers ask too many **closed questions**, which lead the interviewee to give a 'yes' or 'no' answer. Or you may find that your questions were too long and detailed, and did not give the interviewee enough space or time to respond thoroughly. A little silence works wonders. Or you might find that you were not sufficiently concentrating on the interviewee's answers and so did not think of **follow-up questions**, or even that the interviewee headed off on a tangent from the interview topic and you ended up talking about things that were of little relevance to the research topic. Or, the commonest mistake new interviewees make, you responded to the interviewee's statements rather than encouraging him or her to speak more, and ended up with a conversation, not an interview. If you are able to interview someone for an hour (which is not possible in a classroom exercise), you will begin to see first, how the in-depth interviewing process makes it possible to explore a research question in much greater depth than a structured questionnaire, but second, the difficulties involved in keeping the interviewee on track, or maintaining your own concentration.

> **Closed questions:** A type of question that asks respondents to select their response from a number of exhaustive, fixed alternative options. Closed questions are often asked in a structured interview.
>
> **Follow-up question:** A question used during an interview that encourages interviewees to explain, clarify or expand on a previous answer. It might be worth trying out follow-up questions such as 'What do you mean by that?' in a practice interview.

For any topic, it should be possible to come up with a general set of open questions or themes that are of interest to you. It is also important to recognise, however, that all qualitative research is, to some extent, exploratory or inductive. For example, you may think you know what is involved in being a member of a religious community, or the problems faced by female police officers. Once you interview a few people, however, you will inevitably obtain a much richer account of different experiences and perspectives, and these will raise questions you did not originally consider. Even in a single interview, it is possible to generate many new questions or themes, simply by asking the interviewee to expand or explain their answers. The themes you develop at the start of a project should not, therefore, be regarded as fixed. Rather, you should expect new themes to emerge and develop through the process of interviewing your participants.

Box 10.2: Using different kinds of questions to get different kinds of answers

Questions suitable for in-depth interviews come in all shapes and sizes, and you should vary your question technique, depending on the sorts of answers you are seeking. In the following list, the examples are framed around the hypothetical case of an in-depth interview with a homeless young person, living on the streets.

Max Travers

Descriptive questions

Asks about descriptions of places, people or experiences. Often used as beginning questions. For example: 'Where do you spend most of your day?'

Contrast questioning

Asks interviewees to make comparisons of situations or events, and then discuss the meanings of the situations. For example: 'You say you get hassled by the police and by other people living on the street. Which is the hardest for you to deal with?'

Opinion or value questions

Aimed at gaining access to or understanding what people think about an event or issue. For example: 'What do you think about the idea of opening up a youth shelter in the city?'

Feeling questions

Aimed at understanding emotional responses. For example: 'You say you got woken up and moved on by the police last week. How did you feel when that was happening?'

Knowledge questions

Aimed at finding out what factual knowledge the interviewee has. For example: 'Do you know of anywhere you could go if you needed medicine or were sick?'

Devil's advocate questions

Poses the opposite view as an abstraction so it is less confronting. For example: 'What would you say to people who see what you are doing when you take food from the supermarket as just stealing?'

Hypothetical questions

Where a scenario is presented and the interviewee is asked to comment on how they would react to it or deal with it; for example, 'If there were a hostel set up in the city for young people only, would you make use of it?'

Posing the ideal questions

Ask the interviewee to outline what he or she sees as the ideal situation. For example: 'You tell me you are not happy having nowhere to live, but don't want to return to your parents' home. If you could choose any type of housing, what would it look like?'

Reflecting questions

Questions that reflect the answers back to the interviewee to clarify or verify that you have understood. For example: 'So, you didn't think the way you were treated at home was fair?'

Summary questions

Questions that summarise and can allow clarification of the main things the interviewee has said. For example: 'So, you feel that the police deliberately target you and want to force you out of the area?'

Interview guide

While an in-depth interview is a far more unstructured way to collect data than a survey interview, you still need to develop an **interview guide** before the interview. An interview guide is just a short list of the main topics or themes you want to address during the interview. The point of the guide is to ensure that you cover all the key areas. It is very easy to become so engrossed in what the interviewee is saying that you can forget to ask about some of the core issues. The guide ensures that, if you get diverted into an unforeseen area, you are reminded to come back to the original themes before ending the interview.

The interview guide is initially developed from your literature review and the topics that are important in your specific research question. It is worth remembering, however, that in the **unstructured interview**, the aim is to explore the topic fully from the perspective of the participant, and your interview should retain significant room for flexibility. The objective is to explore topics in greater depth through **probes**, or asking for explanation or clarification of answers. Also, consulting notes too frequently, or sticking too rigidly to your topic list, may prevent you from having a free-flowing conversation with the interviewee. Additionally, new topics that emerge as important from earlier in-depth interviews can be added to your interview guide as you progress through the research project.

Interview guide: A list of themes and questions prepared before the interview.

Unstructured interview: An interview that asks mostly open questions. It is often used in projects where one researcher conducts interviews with a small number of people, and informed by interpretivist assumptions.

Probe: Another term for a follow-up question.

Case study 10.4: An interview guide

Catherine Garrett provides an example of the interview guide she used in interviewing people who suffered from anorexia. Interestingly, there is a dimension to the study that Garrett never revealed to the participants: her interest in recovery as a spiritual experience. She was hoping, and it proved to be the case, that the interviewee's religious or spiritual beliefs, and how these helped during recovery, would emerge during the interview without explicit questioning. Here are some of the questions she asked about the process of recovery. They give an idea of how to draw out different aspects of a topic even before conducting an interview:

- 'How long did it take?'
- 'When did the recovery begin?' 'Were there turning points? stages? key factors?'
- 'What do you think you were recovering from?' (in other words, 'What do you now, in retrospect, think anorexia was about for you?')
- 'Would you describe it as recovery, or would you use another word?'
- 'Do you think there are degrees of recovery?'
- 'Perhaps you feel that you never fully recovered?'
- 'How do you know/would you know that you had recovered?' (that is, 'What are your criteria for recovery?')
- 'Why did you need to be anorexic? And why don't you need it now?'
- 'What has changed since you were anorexic? Do symptoms recur? Do you expect them to?'
- 'Do you feel like the same person you were when anorexic? Before anorexia?' (Garrett 1998:198–9).

The set of questions you might ask someone about their experiences at work, or their leisure activities will, of course, be quite different to asking someone about recovery from an illness. It is also interesting to consider the many questions that Garrett did not ask. There are no questions in her interview guide, for example, asking for details about the physical symptoms of anorexia and the treatment received from doctors. This is because she was most interested in the process of recovery.

If you were examining this topic, what issues would you ask about?

Exercise 10.1: Preparing an interview guide

This exercise will help you think about developing general question areas to help you explore a specific topic using in-depth interviews to collect your data. You will need to work with another student.

Task

1   Imagine that you have been asked to conduct research about the problems students experience in writing essays and taking examinations. Pick a specific topic from this general area of interest; that is, the amount of time involved, the difficulties involved in obtaining books, problems in knowing what is expected, or exam nerves.

2. Spend 20 minutes preparing a list of 10 questions, covering the main themes and subthemes you wish to address in an interview.
3. Try to ensure that most are **open-ended questions** that will encourage interviewees to give long, reflective answers.
4. Compare your interview guides, and discuss the different ways you have approached the exercise:
   – Is there a difference in focus between the two lists?
   – Is one more likely to result in good answers, and if so, why?
   – Compare the techniques used in designing open questions.

> **Open-ended questions**: Questions that are open in that they allow respondents freedom in their response rather than selecting from pre-determined category responses used in closed questions.

Interviewing techniques

An in-depth interview is based on talk between two people, the interviewer and the interviewee, with the interviewer asking about the interviewee's views, experiences and understandings of a particular topic. However, the in-depth interview differs significantly from everyday conversations. To help you and your interviewee achieve the best results, there are a number of tried-and-tested interviewing techniques you can use (for example, see Rubin and Rubin 2004 for more detail on these techniques). The following techniques outline also makes clear that the in-depth interview has a process to its practice and is made up of specific phases.

Beginning interviews

- Each interview should be preceded by a preparatory period where you are just chatting generally with the interviewee. This time helps develop a relationship and helps the interviewee feel more relaxed about the interview.
- The first formal stage involves explaining the purpose of the interview, how the information will be used, how confidentiality will be protected and the voluntary nature of participation. If the interviewee has reservations, you should be sensitive to his or her concerns, and address these where possible.
- Explaining the general purpose will, like the other questions you ask, shape the answers. You must also explain who you are, your own role in the research project and your objectives for the interview.

Getting good answers

According to Rubin and Rubin (2004:129), in an in-depth interview you should be looking for 'depth and detail, vivid and nuanced answer, rich with thematic material'. 'Nuanced' means answers in which interviewees do not just describe their own activities in simple terms, but convey a deeper level of complexity.

Similarly, in asking people for their political views, the aim is to get beyond the options you might find offered in a structured interview. Ideally, your interviewees will supply vivid examples or stories to illustrate their meanings or experiences. By contrast, a bad interview will contain short, uninformative answers, and you may feel that you have learnt little from the interview.

Some techniques

If you are not getting 'good' answers, there can be a number of reasons.

- The interviewee may be a shy person and not comfortable discussing the particular topic. You need to work hard to make the interviewee as relaxed as possible.
- You may also need to refine your interview technique. Are you asking too many closed questions? Or perhaps you have approached a sensitive area too directly rather than approaching the topic more generally, so that the area arises naturally during the interview.
- Another key technique is to use prompts that encourage the interviewee to give longer answers. This can include knowing when to say nothing. Alternatively, nodding or providing encouraging prompts such as 'I see' or 'tell me more' reflect your interest and that you have heard and understood what the interviewee is saying.
- The ability to ask relevant follow-up questions, identifying and exploring an interviewee's responses, is also important. One way to assist in this process is to ask yourself mental questions as the interview proceeds, such as 'What is the central idea that is being conveyed at the moment?', or 'Do I fully understand what the interviewee means?' This inner dialogue also helps you retain your concentration.
- Observing and listening are very important. Observing means watching the interviewee's body language and facial expressions, and listening to tones of voice for additional cues about how they feel about the topic. Listening means much more than hearing the words. Listening is about concentrating very hard, and trying to understand exactly and fully what they are trying to communicate. Good listening is tiring work.

Fortunately, with some practice, most social researchers can conduct a good in-depth interview. Importantly, an interview that does not go as well as you would have liked is an important learning opportunity. There is usually no need for anguish or self-recrimination. Instead, after each interview it is important to reflect on the process: 'Where did it go wrong? What parts worked? What parts didn't? Was there anything I could have done or should have done differently?' Similarly, reflections on interviews that you feel have gone well can also reveal important information and help you to improve your technique.

See box 10.3 for a summation of the sorts of things you need to reflexively ask yourself after an interview.

Achieving rapport

Establishing trust is, arguably, more important than perfecting technique in achieving good results from interviews. This is particularly the case if you are interviewing someone from a different background, or where you are asking about a personal or private issue. Another term for this is achieving **rapport**. Rapport is basically about trust and ease between the interviewee and interviewer. Achieving rapport is also about trying to gain an understanding of another person's model of the world and being able to communicate this understanding. In a good interview, this means that you feel that you are really getting an insight into someone else's life.

> **Rapport:** The relationship of trust that is required to conduct a good interview.

Conversely, sometimes you can achieve too much rapport. This may mean that you start to share experiences or opinions, so that the interview becomes what Rubin and Rubin (2004) call a 'conversational partnership' rather than an in-depth interview. Too much rapport can also mean that you lose your ability to be objective or ask difficult questions, or that the interviewee tries to give you the answers he or she thinks you want rather than what the person really thinks. How much rapport is too much rapport? This can depend on your theoretical frame. In some feminist research, for example, interviewers are encouraged to share their own experiences with interviewees, and to understand this politically (see Travers 2001, chapter 7). Only you can judge if you have enough, but not too little or too much rapport, and having enough rapport will change depending on the topic and the interviewee.

One problem you might encounter in achieving rapport is that your first task as interviewer is often to explain the risks involved in a project and obtain the signature of the interviewee on a consent form. As explained in chapter 4, qualitative research projects, like all social research involving research with people, require clearance from a human research ethics committee (HREC) before they can proceed. Under the current system, interviewees have to be advised that they can withdraw from an interview at any time, be told of their right to complain if there is unethical conduct, and are usually required to sign a consent form to indicate their willingness to participate. This can create problems if you are interviewing someone who, for whatever reason, is uncomfortable about signing a form—see Hannah Graham's discussion of the problem of needing written permission before interviewing respondents with a mental illness (chapter 4). Rubin and Rubin (2004:105) note that 'with its flavour of medical experiments and hospital informed-consent rules, the form suggests a much more manipulative kind of research in which the interviewee is the passive recipient of some kind of treatment rather than an active partner'. One way around this, is while emphasising the importance of ethical behaviour in research, you can also explain that consent forms are an ethical requirement in nearly all research projects.

Box 10.3: Reflectively evaluating an interview

Rubin and Rubin (2004:127) note that, sometimes, when reviewing your interview data, you will notice that your questions did not get the hoped-for depth. To determine why this might have happened, and to improve your technique, they suggest reflectively reviewing your interview transcripts. Questions to pose include:

- Did you miss key opportunities to ask second or third questions?
- Did you discourage the interviewee expanding on their answers by interrupting a long reply?
- Did you miss opportunities to follow up incomplete answers?
- Did you accept a generalisation that should have been questioned?
- Did you use too many closed questions?
- If the interviewee was cautious or timid, did you then encourage them to speak his or her mind?
- Did you express your own opinions too strongly or too often?
- If the interviewees contradicted you, were you defensive rather than curious and supportive?
- Was the pace of the interview right for the interviewee, or too slow or too fast?
- If your interviewee seemed tense, did you ask difficult and stressful questions at the right place in the interview or did you approach the topic too quickly?
- Did you recognise when your questions provoked stress and back away quickly enough to restore the interviewee's comfort?

You might feel after reading this extract that a lot depends on developing your interviewing skills through practice. There is no correct or incorrect way to interview!

Sensitive interviews

Conducting social research, by its nature, often involves researching topics that are sensitive. Social research topics frequently encompass issues that are intensely personal, or address questions that can arouse strong feelings either on political, moral or ideological grounds. For example, the focus of Claire Williams's (1981) study (see case study 10.1) was the relationship between couples, and how this was affected by isolation and harsh working conditions. And in studying the experience of recovery from anorexia, Catherine Garrett (1998) sought to draw out deeply personal experiences, and investigate religious beliefs.

Conducting in-depth interviews around personal experiences or controversial issues can be an emotionally fraught experience for both the interviewee and the researcher. To minimise the risk of harm to participants who may find the process disturbing, most social research projects that address sensitive topics include access to support for interviewees. Indeed, such support is likely to be a prerequisite for approval from the human research ethics committee (see chapter 3). However, it is important for researchers to also consider their own emotional reactions to being exposed to disturbing information and, sometimes, tragic personal stories. While all in-depth interviewing is an intensive experience in itself, conducting research on sensitive topics can be even more physically and psychologically demanding. As shown in case study 10.5, the intensity of the in-depth interviewing process and the limited nature of the research relationship between the interviewee and the interviewer can feel incongruous.

Case study 10.5: Interviewing on sensitive topics

Doug Ezzy interviewed 33 people in Melbourne about their experience of becoming unemployed. Some of the interviewees viewed this as a positive experience, but in other cases, experienced feelings of depression and anxiety, or bitterness towards previous employers.

Ezzy reports that interviewees were happy to be interviewed. However, as an interviewer, he sometimes felt uncomfortable hearing about their personal feelings, while not having the time to establish a proper relationship:

> None of the interviewees indicated feeling threatened or compromised by the interview process. One of the ambiguities I experienced whilst conducting long intensive interviews was that the mutual trust developed during the interview had no place in an ongoing relationship. Interviewees often revealed quite personal feelings about their experiences and some cried as they discussed particularly painful events in their past. My feelings of incongruence were sometimes exacerbated by the isolation and distress that some people described as their experience of unemployment. Similarly, at the end of the interview, I left 'with the data' and the interviewee was left with the memory of a conversation (Ezzy 2001:155).

Recording your data

The objective of interviewing is to come away with data that can be analysed to illustrate the key themes and theoretical frame of your research topic. For this reason, interviews should, wherever possible, be sound-recorded. Sound-recording your interviews, as opposed to the older technique of note-taking, makes it easier to concentrate on the interview and to give the interviewee your full attention. Against this, sound-recording can make some interviewees uncomfortable, and they may deny permission.

Alternatively, asking for permission can sometimes risk damaging the relationship with an interviewee. I have experienced this phenomenon when interviewing civil servants in the United Kingdom: they were often prepared to reveal considerably more without a sound-recorder. Sometimes, even in a sound-recorded interview, the most revealing answers or discussion can often take place after the sound-recorder has been switched off. In situations where sound-recording is not feasible or suitable, you will require good note-taking and memory skills. To maximise the quality of your interview data, you need to write up your notes as comprehensively and as immediately after the interview as you can.

Also, always check before finishing that the recording equipment has, indeed, recorded. One of my honours students experienced the nightmare of all new researchers, an interview where the recording equipment failed. But by sitting down immediately after the interview and writing down everything she could remember she had enough notes and details to make the data usable in her project.

Exercise 10.2: Interviewing

This exercise gives some experience of interviewing, and designing questions or topic themes. You will need to conduct this with another student.

1. Each decide on a topic for an interview. This should address something the interviewee knows about, such as being a student. Two examples are: how students relate to the feedback forms that are given out at the end of units, or their experiences of sport at school and university.
2. Each interviewer should write down 5 general questions relating to their topic.
3. You should each conduct a 15-minute interview without using a sound recorder, instead taking brief notes. These will not be used in an analysis, but will help you review the interview and deciding whether particular questions or interview techniques worked.
4. Remember to start by chatting about unrelated matters, so the interviewee feels at ease, but that you should then introduce the interview formally. Make sure you explain who you are and why you are conducting this interview. You will not need to use a consent form for this interview, but should be able to see the problems it might create for achieving rapport.
5. During the interview, try to use probes and different kinds of questions. You should also think of follow-up questions that develop themes or ideas suggested by the interviewee on your topic.

6   At the end of the two interviews, compare notes about interviewing technique (see also box 10.3). How far did you succeed in obtaining rich information about this topic? If you were unsuccessful, how can this be explained? Remember that in a real research project you will be interviewing a few people about the same topic, or even conducting repeat interviews. How would you do things differently in the next interview?

7   In your discussion, consider how it felt to be interviewed, and what questions or interview techniques encouraged fuller answers. Did any questions or parts of the interview disrupt rapport or make the interview more difficult?

8   Finally, it is worth considering the issues that might arise if you interviewed someone from a different background to yourself, or were asking questions about a sensitive topic. The best qualitative studies usually tell us something about unfamiliar social worlds. For example, Mitchell Duneier's (1999) *Sidewalk* provides an insight into the lives of street people trying to survive by selling secondhand books and magazines in Greenwich Village, New York.

Beyond interviewing

Good social science research is reflective and self-critical, and you should be aware of the possible weaknesses of in-depth interviewing as a research method as well as its strengths. In-depth interviewing can be contrasted not only with survey methods, but also with **ethnographic fieldwork** and **conversation analysis** (see the online chapters for more details on these two methods).

> **Ethnographic fieldwork:** Spending a long period of time observing some group or social setting.
>
> **Conversation analysis:** Conversation analysis uses a special type of transcription system to analyse audio- or video-recordings of naturally occurring conversation. It is usually used when the research interest lies in what participants do outside a formal research setting.

Common criticisms

From the perspective of survey research, the main weakness of in-depth interviewing is that it only addresses the experiences of a small group of people. There is no concern with obtaining a representative sample from a larger population. For this reason, quantitative researchers choose to conduct structured interviews with larger samples. There is also the worry, from this perspective, that the freedom given to the interviewer in asking questions or talking about his or her own experiences during the interview means that the findings are shaped or produced by the interviewer (the problem of interviewer influence).

Concerns have also been raised about interviewing by researchers who conduct ethnographic fieldwork. This method of research involves spending long periods of time observing people engaging in their day-to-day activities. While in-depth interviewing will certainly provide a richer and more nuanced picture than available from a structured interview,

Max Travers

such as in a survey, how do we know if it is a true picture? In their observational study of medical students, Howard Becker and Blanche Geer (1967) were struck by the different information obtainable through observation (that is, spending a lot of time accompanying students to classes) and interviewing. The interviews suggested that students were diligent and serious-minded, liked their lecturers and respected the dignity of patients. However, the observation revealed a very different picture of their preparation for assignments, and what they said about lecturers and patients among themselves. In the observational study, the medical students referred to some patients as 'crocks': meaning a patient who took up time that they felt could be used to learn about more interesting and examinable illnesses. Or, in another example, while interviews with voters on their voting intentions for the 2004 Australian federal election consistently indicated a close result, the actual outcome was a clear victory for the Coalition parties. How can we explain such anomalies?

Becker and Geer (1967) suggests two explanations. The first is that interviewees, like all of us, can be reluctant to reveal highly personal information. The result is that interviewees will sometimes self-censor what they reveal, keeping back information they consider to be too personal or controversial. There can also be a **social desirability effect**, where interviewees slant what they reveal about themselves to give one impression or another. In Becker and Geer's study, the medical students' interview version of their study habits may have been more about what they believed they should be doing, rather than what they were doing.

> **Social desirability effect**: The tendency of interviewees to present themselves in a good light by concealing damaging or controversial information.

The second is that an interviewee may be unable to remember information that is relevant to the research topic. In this situation, interviewees might sometimes, consciously or unconsciously, fill in the missing details in their discussion. It is also possible that something important that happens in their daily life is never mentioned: Becker and Geer only learnt about the significance of the term 'crock' through spending time with the students. From this perspective, the in-depth interview is not simply potentially misleading, but gives only a shallow insight into what actually happens in different social worlds, and how people understand their own activities.

Box 10.4: Strengths and weaknesses of in-depth interviews

The strengths of in-depth interviews

In-depth interviews

- allow the researcher to address meaning in depth, and with more attention to complexity, than structured interviews

- make it possible to address the experience or perspective of people in a variety of social settings
- can deal with a wide range of topics, from life histories to experiences at work
- require less time than conducting ethnographic fieldwork
- are less intrusive and impose fewer demands on research subjects than ethnographic fieldwork
- are socially acceptable; we live in an 'interview society' (Silverman 1997).

The weaknesses of in-depth interviews

In-depth interviews

- address the experience of a small group of people only, so the results cannot be used to make generalisations about larger populations
- may allow interviewees to give, deliberately or inadvertently, misleading or incorrect information
- may make it difficult to address taken-for-granted or routine activities
- cannot achieve the depth of understanding of one social setting that is possible through extended periods of ethnographic fieldwork
- encourage the assumption that the interview is a window into the mind of the interviewee. Rather, the interview is produced collaboratively through the interaction between the interviewer and interviewee.

In defence of interviewing

Most researchers who use in-depth interviews are not unduly troubled by criticisms from these different perspectives. This is because of the unique properties and strengths that the in-depth interview can bring to social research. The interview is a remarkably effective means of collecting information about a wide range of topics quickly and cheaply. It requires a considerable amount of time and effort to design and administer a survey, conduct ethnographic fieldwork or transcribe a short piece of talk employing the method of transcription used in conversation analysis. Interviewing is relatively easy to do, and is normally less intrusive than ethnographic fieldwork. Most people enjoy being interviewed, and are familiar with this method of research. It allows people to talk about themselves, and to share their experiences with wider audiences.

It can also be argued that the in-depth interview has many advantages over alternative methods of investigation in addressing lived experience. Structured interviews are good at obtaining quantifiable information about large numbers of people, but there is no opportunity to explore what interviewees mean by their answers in any depth.

Ethnographies often depend on interviewing, in addition to observation, in understanding what happens in a social setting; in practice, the two methods are often used together, and share the same strengths and weaknesses. In any interview project, it should be possible to do some ethnographic fieldwork, by describing the setting in which the interview takes place, and what it reveals about the interviewee. The interview is also a particularly useful tool for investigating what happens in a range of settings. Ethnographers produce detailed studies about particular social settings, whereas an interview study, based for example on 30 interviews, allows researchers to engage in comparative analysis, or simply to address a wider range of experiences.

From method to practice

The best way to learn about qualitative interviewing, especially in-depth interviewing, is actually to do some. While you will have gained some experience from exercise 10.2, interviewing a tutorial classmate is not the same as the real thing. Not only is the physical and social environment (the crowded classroom) very different from a live, purpose-driven interview, so is the context and the situation. A one-off interview with a easily available subject (your classmate) is also very different from conducting a series of focused interviews with a range of interviewees you have recruited and organised the interview with yourself.

How to move from method to practice? If you are lucky enough to be working in an organisation that has the capacity, it might be possible to negotiate with your manager to undertake a series of work-based interviews with organisational staff on a topic that would be useful to management. If you take this path, remember that informed consent, confidentiality and other ethical issues must be taken into consideration. If you don't have access to a more professional field and context, perhaps you might want to think about interviewing amenable friends or family members. As an example, one student was able to hone her interviewing skills by interviewing five older family members about their family memories around Christmas, and brought the insights and perceptions to life in a family book.

Whatever route you take, it will be helpful to look at the transcripts of the five interviews on the nature of Australian identity and the accompanying interviewing guide that are available on the website for this text (see the introduction), along with the interviewing guide ‹www.oup.com.au/orc/walter›. The interviewees for this small project are all university students who volunteered to participate after the topic was raised in a first-year tutorial. All were of a similar age, around 20, and all had grown up in Australia. It was decided for this project that it was important for the interviewees to have similar backgrounds and ages to provide a comparable base point. In practical terms, while it was easy to recruit the respondents for 15-minute interviews, organising and carrying out those interviews was less straightforward.

Some students, who were happy to volunteer, forgot their prearranged interview appointments and had to be rescheduled for another time (one student forgot three times). The need to reschedule or to make other times is a normal aspect of being a qualitative interviewer. We must always be aware that the interviewee is the focus of the process and it is his or her schedule that must be prioritised. However, if an interviewee misses a number of times, it is wise to recheck with them whether they are still happy to be a part of the process; missing appointments may be a way of refusing participation without being put in the position of having to say so.

When looking at the interview transcripts on the website, you can see how the researcher followed the interview guide, but also asked probing questions as they arose. The interview guide really helps to avoid getting diverted onto other topics, but allows flexibility to follow up on important aspects. The transcripts also show how the researchers shared experiences to explore the topic and build rapport. What you should also note from the transcripts is that even conducting a few short interviews results in a set of rich data about what it means to be an Australian.

Voices in the field

Margaret Alston

Margaret Alston is Professor of Social Work at Monash University. A significant component of her research activity focuses on issues affecting women in rural areas and, because of her feminist orientation, she uses qualitative research techniques extensively. While qualitative research is time and labour intensive, requiring significant time in the field and critical attention to data capture, storage and analysis, its use is important because it allows an engagement with the lived experience of rural women. Professor Alston's research brings her into contact with rural women and their families across Australia, and she has used qualitative interviewing methods to delve into rural women's understandings of issues of health, mental health, work roles, service delivery, drought, violence and agriculture and rural development.

The research Professor Alston undertakes has a significant impact on social policy in the area of rural social issues and services, and in gender issues, both in Australia and internationally. For example, in 2008 she was appointed to the Australian delegation

Max Travers

to the United Nations Commission for the Status of Women meeting in New York, where she represented not only the views of rural women, but of all Australian women.

She has also been invited on two occasions under the visiting expert program to the Gender Division of the United Nations Food and Agriculture Organization.

Focus groups

Focus groups are a form of in-depth interviewing, but conducted with a group of people rather than an individual participant. This grouping is not just about doing lots of interviews at once, but also harnesses group dynamics and group processes into the process. The term **focus group** defines itself: 'focus' refers to the fact that a focus group, while relatively unstructured, usually has only a limited number of related issues it discusses.

Focus group: A research method that involves encouraging a group of people to discuss some social or political issue.

'Group' refers to the fact that the people being interviewed usually have something in common in relationship to the focus group topic. A focus group makes use of the strengths of in-depth interviews to gain rich and detailed insights into people's understandings of a topic, but within a group setting. The aim is to generate a wide range of opinions and insights, which are informed by the interaction of people in the focus group. Conducting a focus group, therefore, involves guiding a discussion about an issue with a small group of people. The discussion is sound-recorded, or in some cases, filmed to record facial expressions and body language.

Focus groups are not suitable for all social research topics. First, for a good focus group, the participants must share an interest or common experiences around the topic. They are useful in exploring reactions to some political initiative, views on a consumer product or perceptions of some social problem. Second, focus groups, again because of their group nature, are not normally suitable to discuss sensitive or controversial topics. Not only are participants likely to be reticent when asked to discuss sensitive or controversial topics within a group setting, but as a researcher, you are not able to guarantee the confidentiality of any deeply personal information that is revealed. It is, however, possible to generate a lively conversation in a focus group, and the interaction between people with different perspectives can produce insights in a way that is not possible in an interview.

A key requirement for a successful focus group is a skilled moderator. This is someone who can put participants at ease, and direct a guided discussion, starting with general questions and then addressing more specific issues. Stewart and Shamdasani (1990) suggest that it is more difficult moderating a focus group than conducting an interview. It requires being able to monitor body language and facial expressions, and ensure that everyone has the opportunity to speak. It can also help knowing how to use humour to defuse tension or conflict, and encourage participants to relax and share personal experiences.

Box 10.5: Pros and cons of focus groups

Focus groups, like all research methods, have both strengths and weaknesses, and their selection should be entirely based on your view that using a focus group is the best method available to you to answer your research questions.

Strengths of focus groups

Focus groups

- can produce concentrated amounts of data exploring opinions about social issues
- are relatively efficient and inexpensive in time and money terms
- generate group interaction and group synergy, which can produce data that cannot be obtained through individual in-depth interviews
- usually result in a lively and relevant discussion.

Weaknesses of focus groups

Focus groups

- require a skilled moderator
- can be dominated by members with strong personalities or opinions
- have a greater social desirability effect than individual interviews
- are not suitable for sensitive topics or investigating personal experiences or views in depth
- are not suitable unless the participants share a common relationship to the topic.

Focus groups have been extensively used in Australian research as an alternative means of collecting representative data about large populations to structured interviews. Michael Pusey's (2003) study about attitudes among the Australian middle class is a good example. Careful sampling techniques were employed to select 'a stratified random sample of 400 respondents in five Australian capital cities'. Four focus groups were held 'to define major themes' that were later explored in more detail through a self-administered questionnaire and interview with the whole sample. In addition, six 'exit' focus groups were held to clarify issues raised by responses to the questionnaires and interviews. Pusey's focus groups form part of a study intended to demonstrate that a significant proportion of middle-class Australians experience anxieties, particularly about possible job losses, but also rising crime and the breakdown of communities. This is caused, in his view, by economic reform intended 'to make us less dependent on states and governments and more dependent on economies, markets, prices, money, and more directly upon ourselves' (Pusey 2003:1).

The focus group can also be understood from an **interpretive perspective**. Here there is less emphasis on making general statements about a larger population, or quantifying responses, but instead the aim is to examine how a particular group of people respond to some issue and the interaction between them. Kevin McDonald (1999) brought together young people with different backgrounds and experiences, and was particularly interested in the contradictions and different versions that emerged. Conversation analysis offers an additional tool for use in analysing interaction and language use during these often fraught encounters (Bloor et al. 2001). If you want to know more about conversational analysis, go to the online segment on this research method.

> **Interpretive perspective:** A way of understanding the process of conducting research promoted by Max Weber, among other social theorists. It emphasises the importance of addressing meaning and interpretation in social life.

Voices in the field

Tim Marjoribanks

Tim Marjoribanks is a sociologist in the School of Social and Political Sciences at the University of Melbourne. Through his research in areas including medicine, media and sport, he has used a diverse range of qualitative research approaches, including interviews, observations, textual analysis and focus groups.

In a research project with colleagues at the University of Melbourne, Associate Professor Jenny Lewis (Political Science) and Dr Marie Pirotta (General Practice), Tim used focus groups to explore how general practitioners felt about the impact of policy reform on their professional autonomy. The research project was funded by the Commonwealth Government General Practice Evaluation Program grant scheme, established to evaluate and inform general practice in Australia. Bringing together general practitioners in focus groups ranging in size from four to eight, the research team hoped that participants who were going through similar experiences would be able to discuss autonomy by listening to, and engaging with, the opinions and experiences of their colleagues. This indeed was what happened, and the focus groups provided rich insights into the challenges confronted by general practitioners. Tim and his colleagues also used an open format, with questions seen as discussion starters, meaning that groups were able to raise issues of importance that had not been asked about by the researchers.

The research also highlighted specific challenges of focus groups. It was important to ensure that all participants were able to talk, which involved the researcher directly asking individuals for their views. It was also important not to ask too many questions. With several participants engaging with each other, the time goes by very quickly.

Overall, this project revealed the importance of focus groups as a qualitative interviewing technique for allowing people with a shared professional background to come together to share their views and experiences. In particular, while individual voices remain important, the insights provided by interaction among participants made the focus groups in this case a valuable tool for the research team.

Case study 10.6: Struggles for subjectivity

Kevin McDonald's (1999) study *Struggles for Subjectivity* used 'a sociological intervention, a research strategy developed by Touraine (1982) for the study of social movements' (McDonald 1999:19). This strategy involved focus groups and research sessions to explore the experience of young people in Melbourne. The research is an engaged political study that examines issues such as unemployment, growing up in a deprived neighbourhood, youth crime and racism.

This study illustrates the kind of issues that arise in studying a political topic where interviewees might have very different views. McDonald's study involved Asian young people who complained about discrimination and racist attacks, as well as young, working-class Anglo-Australians (both male and female) who expressed racist views towards Asians. While McDonald mostly kept the groups separate, there were some mixed groups, and in one group he brought together white working-class youths with a police liaison officer responsible for reducing youth crime in that area. McDonald tells us that 'twice during the research, the sessions almost went out of control because of the anger of the young people' (1999:66).

The following extract describes the participants in one group, and suggests how they differ in their understanding of social reality. You should not expect to find any simple answers to your research questions in any project involving interviews!

The young people are aged between 15 and 25. They are all unemployed, and are of mixed ethnicity. Most are Anglo-Australians, Mandy is Koori, Elsa is Egyptian, and Rima's family is from Lebanon. Almost all left school early, a number before the minimum age of 16, with Beccy (the youngest) leaving school at 14. Stereotypes suggest that these young people would not have much to say.

Max Travers

But once they realise that we are here to listen to them, and that they can use the research process to get others to listen to them as well, they have a great deal to say …

> From the beginning, the picture is one of tensions rather than coherence, between opposing dimensions of their reality … What becomes clear in these first sessions are the powerful tensions confronting and at times threatening these young people. They emerge with compelling clarity and great urgency' (McDonald 1999:23).

Conclusion

Although there are a variety of interviewing methods, including the unstructured interview and focus groups, this chapter has concentrated on explaining how social researchers use in-depth interviews. It is again worth noting that this is easily the most popular method used in social research. The great strength of interviewing as a research method is that anyone can interview, and collect rich and informative data about a range of people or social settings quickly, without needing specialist training. This is not to suggest that everyone can achieve the same standard, and it may take time developing confidence and skills through learning from mistakes and reflecting on practice. There are also, as in the case of other research methods, many technical debates about particular types of interviewing, and theoretical and philosophical debates about the nature and purpose of research. Many traditions are reviewed in Gubrium and Holstein (2002). After reading this chapter, and working through the exercises, you should already be in a good position to design a small interview project, and collect the data. You might also want to read some of the studies summarised in the chapter, and refer to these along with discussions of interviewing in texts like Rubin and Rubin (2004) when writing about why you have chosen this method in research reports. To broaden your knowledge of qualitative methods read the online modules on narrative research, conversation analysis, action research, ethnographic research, memory work and sensory and visual methods; these are available at <www.oup.com.au/orc/walter>.

Main points

> Interviewing was first developed as a method of social research by British social policy researchers and anthropologists during the late nineteenth century, and by sociologists at the University of Chicago during the 1920s.

> Interview studies usually present extracts from the answers given by interviewees, so the reader gets a sense of what the interviewee said in his or her own words.

> Structured interviews use closed questions, whereas unstructured interviews are like free-flowing conversations. A focus group involves conducting a guided discussion about an issue with a small number of people.

> Interviewing does not require great technical skills, but it is possible to become a better interviewer through reflecting on your experience of using the research method.

> Preparation is important, and it may help to use an interview guide.

Max Travers

> You should be aware of ethical issues relating to collecting research data, and the effects of written consent forms on achieving rapport.

> Common criticisms of the interview include the fact that an interviewee may wish to conceal what he or she really feels about some issue. The strength of interviewing is that it allows you to produce rich and interesting findings quickly without having to undertake long periods of ethnographic fieldwork.

Further reading

Gubrium, J. and Holstein, J. (2002). *The Handbook of Interview Research: Context and Method.* Thousand Oaks, CA: Sage.

Rubin, H. and Rubin, I. (2004). *Qualitative Interviewing: The Art of Hearing Data.* Thousand Oaks, CA: Sage.

References

Baker, M. and Tippin, D. (2002). '"When Flexibility Meets Rigidity": Sole Mothers' Experiences in the Transition from Welfare to Work', *Journal of Sociology,* 30 (4): 345–60.

Becker, H. and Geer, B. (1967). 'Participant Observation and Interviewing: A Comparison', in Manis, J. and Meltzer, B. (eds), *Symbolic Interaction: A Reader.* Boston: Allyn & Bacon.

Bloor, M., Frankland, J., Thomas, M. and Robson, K. (eds) (2001). *Focus Groups in Social Research.* London: Sage.

Coles, T. (2008). 'Finding Spaces in the Field of Masculinity: Lived Experiences of Men's Masculinities', *Journal of Sociology,* 44 (3): 233–48.

Collins, J., Nobel, G., Poynting, S. and Tabar, P. (2000). *Kebabs, Kids, Cops and Crime.* Annandale, NSW: Pluto Press.

Duneier, M. (1999). *Sidewalk.* New York: Farrar, Straus & Giroux.

Ezzy, D. (2001). *Narrating Unemployment.* Aldershot: Ashgate.

Garrett, C. (1998). *Beyond Anorexia: Narrative, Spirituality and Recovery.* Cambridge: Cambridge University Press.

Gubrium, J. and Holstein, J. (1997). 'Active Interviewing', in Silverman, D. (ed.), *Qualitative Research: Theory, Method and Practice.* London: Sage: 113–29.

Gubrium, J. and Holstein, J. (2002). *The Handbook of Interview Research: Context and Method.* Thousand Oaks, CA: Sage.

McDonald, K. (1999). *Struggles for Subjectivity: Identity, Action and Youth Experience.* Cambridge: Cambridge University Press.

Mayall, M. (2007). 'Attached to their Style: Traders, Technical Analysis and Postsocial Relationships', *Journal of Sociology*, 43 (4): 421–38.

Newton, J. (2008). 'Emotional Attachment to Home and Security for Permanent Residents in Caravan Parks in Melbourne', *Journal of Sociology*, 44 (3): 219–32.

Ogwang, T., Cox, L. and Saldanha, J. (2006). 'Paint on their Lips: Paint-sniffers, Good Citizens and Public Space in Brisbane', *Journal of Sociology*, 42 (4): 412–28.

Prus, R. (1996). *Symbolic Interaction and Ethnographic Research: Intersubjectivity and the Study of Human Lived Experience.* New York: State University of New York Press.

Pusey, M. (2003). *The Experience of Middle Australia: The Dark Side of Economic Reform.* Cambridge: Cambridge University Press.

Rubin, H. and Rubin, I. (2004). *Qualitative Interviewing: The Art of Hearing Data.* Thousand Oaks, CA: Sage.

Silverman, D. (1997). 'Towards an Aesthetics of Research', in Silverman, D. (ed.), *Qualitative Research: Theory, Method and Practice.* London: Sage: 239–53.

Spradley, J. (1979). *The Ethnographic Interview.* New York: Holt, Rhinehart & Winston.

Stewart, D. and Shamdasani, P. (1990). *Focus Groups: Theory and Practice.* London: Sage.

Travers, M. (2001). *Qualitative Research Through Case Studies.* London: Sage.

Weber, M. (1978). *Economy and Society.* Berkeley: University of California Press.

Weber, M. (1992). *The Protestant Ethic and the Spirit of Capitalism.* London: Routledge.

Williams, C. (1981). *Open Cut: The Working Class in an Australian Mining Town.* Sydney: Allen & Unwin.

Chapter 11
Content Analysis

Warren Sproule

Study of suicide notes

Ever since Durkheim's groundbreaking study of 1897, the act of suicide has exerted a strong hold over the sociological imagination. Content analysis can be a useful way of exploring this social phenomenon through documentation such as coroner's or police reports. In 1967, Jerry Jacobs used content analysis as his research method when exploring the motives of those who commit suicide. He used as his raw data the contents of 112 suicide notes of adults and adolescents who succeeded in suicide in the Los Angeles area. He coded these into six categories:

- first form notes, that is, notes that beg forgiveness or indulgence on the part of survivors
- illness notes, broken into two subcategories ('sorry'/'not sorry')
- notes of direct accusation
- last will and testament and notes of instruction
- precautions taken to exclude this world's problems from the next world
- an 'other' category, to include the notes whose contents were not covered by the coding scheme (10 out of 112).

Therefore, instead of having 112 different accounts of why people chose to end their lives, Jacobs was able to show certain specific patterns within the documents. By analysing the content of the notes and categorising that content, he was able to demonstrate their common threads: the essential underpinning of content analysis.

Source: Jacobs 1976

Key terms

codebook	inter-coder reliability	specialised dictionary
coding	level of implication	strength of relationship
concept	operationalisation	text
direction of relationship	ratio	translation rules
explicit coding	selective reduction	unit of analysis
implicit coding	sign of a relationship	

Introduction

Content analysis: A research method that detects, records and analyses the presence of words or concepts in forms of communication.

Concepts: Concepts are components of theories that can be drawn from theory, or developed through induction from the data. They describe key aspects of the processes or patterns examined in the research.

Text: Any form of written communication; or any cultural artefact bearing messages that can be analysed in the same fashion as texts (such as films, fashion, photographs or sports events). Often associated with *content analysis* and *discourse analysis*. The requirement is that every aspect of the data with which the research is concerned must be covered by one category.

Content analysis is defined by Berelson (1952:18) as 'a research technique for the objective, systematic and quantitative description of the manifest content of communication'. More simply, content analysis is a research method that detects, records and analyses the presence of specified words or **concepts** in a sample of forms of communication. Content analysis researchers count and analyse the presence, meanings and relationships of these words and concepts. They then make inferences about the messages within the texts, the writer(s), the audience, and the time, place and the 'wider cultural context of which they are a part' (Rose 2001:55).

Content refers to the words, phrases, pictures or photos, symbols, themes or other communicative devices within a form of communication. The communication forms that are the subject of content analysis are usually referred to as **texts**. These can be books or book chapters, essays, historical documents, newspaper headlines or articles, and transcriptions of speeches, interviews or discussions. However, the term 'text' also includes other forms of communication, such as informal conversation, imagery, theatre and advertising. Virtually any form of communicative language can be subject to content analysis.

Since any piece of writing or specimen of recorded communication is open to content analysis, this research method is widely used in academic disciplines such as literature, cultural studies, psychology, sociology and political science. Content analysis is also used within the cognitive sciences, rhetoric studies, marketing, ethnography and the media. Additionally, it is closely linked with socio- and psycholinguistics, and continues to play a key role in the development of artificial intelligence.

What is content analysis?

The major purposes of content analysis are summarised in the following list, adapted from Berelson (1952). Content analysis can be used to:

- identify the intentions, focus or communication trends of an individual, group or institution
- reveal international differences in communication content
- describe attitudinal and behavioural responses to communications

- detect the existence of propaganda
- determine psychological or emotional states of persons or groups.

In the basic process of content analysis, the text is first coded, or broken down, into manageable categories. This **coding** or breakdown of the text occurs on a variety of levels. For example, the text can be broken down from a word or word sense perspective, or by phrase, sentence or theme. Coding is essentially a process of **selective reduction**. By reducing the text to a set of categories consisting of a word, set of words or phrases, the content analyst can concentrate on, and code for, specific words or patterns that are important and relevant to the research question. In the introductory box, Jacobs categorised a selection of suicide notes into six different categories. Each of these categories reflects what Jacobs perceived as the overall intention of the person in writing the note. These categories then provided the analytical framework for Jacobs to interpret his data.

Coding: The process by which data are organised for analysis.

Selective reduction: The central tenet of content analysis: text is reduced to categories consisting of a word, a set of words or phrases, on which the researcher can focus. The resultant patterns inform the research question, and determine levels of analysis and generalisation.

Explicit and implicit coding

Although Berelson's earlier cited definition of content analysis only mentions manifest content, the implicit content of the text is also important. While it is relatively easy to identify explicit or manifest terms, coding for implicit terms (and assessing their **level of implication**) is more problematic. Implicit coding relies on judgment calls based on a more overtly subjective system. Coding of texts into categories within content analysis, therefore, can occur on two levels: the explicit, or manifest, level; and the implicit, or latent, level:

- **Explicit coding** is coding for the visible, easily identified content of the text. For example, if we were interested in how much reporting of sport, as opposed to other news items, is included within Australia's newspapers, we might identify and count the number of articles that include either the word 'sport' or include the name of a specific sport such as 'tennis'. Explicit coding is a highly reliable way of coding the data. Because the rules by which content is categorised can be made so clear, a researcher can be reasonably certain that other researchers using the same coding guidelines would also code the data in the same way.

Level of implication: Determining whether to code simply for explicit appearances of concepts, or for implied concepts as well; for example, deciding whether to code 'unmarried' as an entity in and of itself or, if coding for 'unmarried' references in general, to code 'single' as implicitly meaning 'unmarried'. Thus, by determining that the meaning 'unmarried' is implicit in the words 'single', any time the words 'single' or 'unmarried' appear in the text, they will be coded under the same category of 'unmarried'.

Explicit coding: Term used in content analysis to signify coding for the visible, easily identified content of the text.

Warren Sproule

- **Implicit coding** is coding for the underlying and implicit meaning of the content of the text. This type of coding is far more subjective than explicit coding, but allows for a greater depth of analysis. Using again the comparative coverage of sport, if we conceptualised news articles to be current events of social significance, then an article about riots by fans from different ethnic backgrounds at soccer matches in Melbourne might be coded as a news item, rather than a sports item. We might also be interested in the page—sports or news—where the article appeared in the newspaper.

> **Implicit coding:** Term used in content analysis to signify coding for the underlying and implicit meaning of the content of the text.

The coding process is research project dependent. It depends on the text being examined, the theoretical framework of the researcher and the question the researcher is seeking to answer. However, within this complexity, the basic guideline for establishing codes is that the codes must be exhaustive, exclusive and, importantly, enlightening. These basic coding rules are outlined in box 11.1.

Box 11.1: Coding: The three 'golden rules'

When coding, the categories selected must fulfil three core content analysis requirements. They must be:

1. **exhaustive:** every aspect of the data with which the research is concerned must be covered by one category
2. **exclusive:** categories must not overlap, or ambiguities must at least be minimised
3. **enlightening:** categories must produce a breakdown of content that will be analytically interesting and coherent.

> **Exhaustive categories:** The requirement that every aspect of the data with which the research is concerned must be covered by one category.
>
> **Exclusive categories:** The requirement that categories must not overlap, or ambiguities must at least be minimised.
>
> **Enlightening categories:** The requirement that categories must produce a breakdown of content that will be analytically interesting and coherent.

Once coded, the selected text(s) is then examined using one of two basic content-analysis methods:

1. conceptual (thematic) analysis
2. relational (semantic) analysis.

An overview of these two methods is developed in the following section. However, it is important to understand that conceptual and relational analysis can also be understood as 'variations on a theme', rather than necessarily exclusive (sub)categories. Although sometimes treated as distinct, their commonalities outweigh their differences, which largely hinge on a change of focus rather than any issues of substance.

Types of content analysis

Conceptual analysis

Conceptual analysis was originally, and in some research quarters still is, regarded as the only form of content analysis. Sometimes also referred to as thematic analysis, conceptual analysis chooses a concept, or related concepts, for examination. The role of the analysis is to quantify and tally the presence of the concept within the text.

The focus of conceptual analysis is to identify any occurrences of the concepts (both explicit and implicit) within the selected text or texts. In trying to limit subjectivity, as well as to satisfy universal analytical standards of reliability and validity, coding for concepts usually involves the development and use of:

- a **codebook:** essentially the conceptualisation of all the concepts to be measured in the analysis. The development of a set of full explanations of the key concepts guides the researcher through the coding task. In computer-based text content analysis, a **specialised dictionary** performs this task. Essentially another term for category system, this dictionary consists of all search patterns that form the categories.
- **translation rules:** to further guide the researcher, a set of rules for the coding process is developed. This involves the researcher deciding how concepts will be both identified and translated in their allocation into the different categories. This constructed translation rule then instructs the researcher to code for the concept in a certain way throughout the text.
- **inter-coder reliability:** allowed for by the development of explicit translation rules, which therefore confer reliability of data and analysis. As noted in chapter 1, reliability is the consistency of our data or results. Inter-coder reliability is the extent to which two or more independent individuals agree on coding, categories and assignation of concepts to categories. The coding can be regarded as consistent, and categories operational to the degree that all the researchers assign the same texts to the same categories.

> **Codebook:** A category system in which all variable measures are fully explained.
>
> **Specialised dictionary:** In computer text content analysis, another term for category system: a dictionary consists of all search patterns that form the categories.
>
> **Translation rules:** A protocol whereby less general concepts will be translated into more general ones; a researcher must make this distinction; that is, make an implicit concept explicit, then code for the frequency of its occurrence, resulting in the construction of a translation rule that instructs the researcher to code for the concept in a certain way.
>
> **Inter-coder reliability:** The extent to which two or more independent individuals agree on coding, categories and assignation of concepts to categories; the research is reliable, coding consistent and categories operational to the degree that all the researchers assign the same texts to the same categories.

The basic research process of conceptual analysis is similar to that of most social research, as outlined in chapter 2. After the topic has been selected, the content analyst

Warren Sproule

identifies and articulates a specific research question. The most appropriate method of data collection is then chosen and the sample is selected, although, in the case of content analysis, this sample will be a text or selection of texts. The text(s) must be coded into manageable bite-sized content categories. The following case study of research using a conceptual analysis technique demonstrates the practical ways this method is used by social scientists.

Case study 11.1: Changing attitudes to animals

Adrian Franklin and Bob White (2001) used content analysis to examine changing attitudes to animals. Their unit of analysis was newspaper articles about animals and their sampling frame was articles that appeared in the Hobart *Mercury* in the 50 years from 1949 to 1998 inclusive. To sample, Franklin and White took every twenty-fifth issue of the paper over the period, looking at the first five pages of the selected issues only, and only at stories about Tasmania. As part of their theoretical assumptions, they expected that changes in attitudes to animals would be consistent with Ulrich Beck's concept of 'risk' (see Beck 1992). So, in one phase of the study, they coded every story for whether it was about 'risk', and, if so, whether the story was about animals posing a risk (such as a savage dog or a charging bull) or animals being at risk (such as dumped pets or endangered species). Breaking the 50-year period into 10 five-year periods, they then counted the number of stories from these two categories in each period, and expressed them as a **ratio**. They expected that there would be a gradual increase in that ratio. And this is in fact, although slightly raggedly in its pattern, was what they found. Articles about animals at risk rose over time compared to those about animals posing a risk. As this example demonstrates, what looks like a fairly simple method of analysis can produce theoretically and empirically interesting results.

Source: Franklin & White 2001

Ratio: The relativity between two absolute numbers (such as the ratio of 30 and 20 is 1.5 for every 1.0. This ratio would typically be expressed as 1.5).

Relational analysis

As with conceptual analysis, relational analysis begins with the act of identifying concepts present in a given text or set of texts. However, relational analysis seeks to go beyond presence by exploring the relationships between the concepts identified. In a relational analysis, the focus is on the discovery of semantic, or meaningful, relationships. These meanings emerge as a product of the relationships among the concepts in a text.

In relational analysis, once the words or phrases are coded, the text can be analysed for the relationships among the concepts. Palmquist and colleagues (1997) define three relational aspects that play a central role in exploring the relations among concepts:

- **Strength of relationship**: the strength of the relationship refers to the degree to which two or more concepts are related. These are easiest to analyse and compare when all relationships between concepts are considered to be equal. Assigning a strength to relationships between concepts also retains a greater degree of the detail found in the original text.
- **Sign of a relationship**: the sign of the relationship refers to whether or not the concepts are positively or negatively related. To illustrate, the concept 'factional' is negatively related to the concept 'political party', in the same sense as the concept 'unified' is positively related. Thus, 'it's a factional political party' could be coded to show a negative relationship between 'factional' and 'political party'. Another approach to coding for the sign of the relationship entails the creation of separate categories for binary oppositions. Defining the sign of a relationship between concepts, that is, defining whether the words under observation were used adversely or in favour of the concepts, is important to establishing meaning within relationships.
- **Direction of the relationship**: the direction of the relationship refers to the type of the relationship between the categories. Coding for this sort of information can be useful in establishing whether some concepts influence or precede other concepts. For example, in a content analysis of text that analyses the emergence of new trends or social phenomena, direction of the relationship coding can help reveal the level of influence of different concepts identified as important in the analysis. For example, in what sort of order do the concepts appear within the text over time? Does concept X always or generally precede concept Y in the sample?

> **Strength of relationship**: The degree to which two or more concepts are related.
>
> **Sign of a relationship**: Whether or not the concepts are positively or negatively related.
>
> **Direction of relationship**: The type of relationship that categories exhibit.

Case study 11.2 is based on research that draws primarily on relational analysis methods. It not only draws out the major concepts inherent in the content of the newspaper analysis of this particular media scandal, but demonstrates the relationships, first, between the key concepts; and second, between the concepts and the wider social context of the scandal.

Warren Sproule

Case study 11.2: Exploring a media scandal

From inter-city bidding to closing ceremony, the Olympic Games are persistently dogged by media-fuelled controversy, the latest being incidents of pro-Tibet activism in the Torch run leading up to the 2008 Beijing Olympics. To examine the topic of the social significance and patterns of media scandals, McKay and colleagues (2000) selected an earlier case: that of Kevan Gosper and Australia's own Olympic Torch scandal. This occurred in the lead-up to the 2000 Sydney Olympics, when Gosper, as chairman of the Australian Olympic Committee, attempted to replace a nominated torchbearer (of Greek descent) with his own daughter. The researchers wanted to see how the scandal unfolded, and then draw conclusions about the political significance of both the case study and the phenomenon of media scandals.

Their interests were semiotic: analysing the cultural codes, especially the mythologies and narrative devices that determined how the stories were told, and the way meanings are put together to produce discourse.

Because of the focused nature of the study, the sample selected was a straightforward matter. The scandal broke on 10 May and died out 10 days later. The researchers selected three large-circulation Australian newspapers (the *Age*, the *Sydney Morning Herald* and the *Daily Telegraph*) as their unit of analysis, and sampled and analysed reports, editorials and readers' letters on the issue over the 10-day period.

Rather than trying to see if the data would fit into a pre-existing theoretical framework, they opted for a 'grounded' approach, which grouped items into extant themes. This allowed for the specificities of the Australian context to emerge rather than fitting the specific events onto a pre-given template. Their analysis identified the following three central themes: betrayal of the Olympic ideals; abuse of family privileges; and Gosper as 'the Ugly Australian'.

The researchers then related these themes to the state of the international Olympic movement, and the politically conservative function of media scandals. This approach helped in making connections between the particular features of the Gosper scandal, and the character and functioning of media scandals more generally.

Source: McKay et al. 2000

Note that, in this particular case study, the authors have combined content analysis with other methods: notably discourse analysis (for a thorough treatment of the latter, see chapter 12). We can see with this exercise that there is a 'fit' between content analysis and discourse analysis. The two methods, in this case, are used in a complementary manner.

Two points are worth noting here. First, content analysis and discourse analysis share similarities in their interest in recorded communication and the content of these. Relational analysis is closer to discourse analysis than conceptual analysis. However, there are also key distinctions to be made between the two research methods. As its name implies, discourse analysis is directly involved in making explicit the way discourse is expressed and deployed within communication. Content analysis, in contrast, treats texts as potential generators of concepts rather than reflections of dominant ideologies.

Exercise 11.1: Analysing the content of popular culture

Comic books have long been regarded as bearers of heavily symbolic messages aimed at peculiarly impressionable audiences (see, for example, Dorfman & Mattelart 1975; Reynolds 1992). The recent box office success of comic book heroes, in cinema adaptations such as *Iron Man*, the *Dark Knight* or the *X-Men* franchise, testify to the genre's durability. In this exercise, select a small sample of action hero or heroine comic books.

Construct a research question around the social values associated with the depiction of the different characters and how these vary according to the role of the character; for example, good guy, bad guy major or bad guy minor, or love interest. Coding categories you might include:

Physical characteristics of characters

- colour of hair
- age
- colour of eyes
- body structure
- height
- sex
- weight
- race/ethnicity.

Social aspects of characters

- occupation
- status
- education
- role
- religion

Warren Sproule

- nationality
- socioeconomic class.

Emotional nature of characters

- warm or cold
- powerful or weak
- anxious or calm
- loving or hateful
- stable or unstable
- individualist or conformist
- authoritarian or dependent
- vivacious or apathetic
- friendly or hostile.

Conducting a content analysis

To provide a practical demonstration of how a content analysis is done, the next section works through the different stages of an analysis. This hypothetical content analysis provides examples of how we would proceed in both conceptual and relational analysis mode.

As with all research, the content analysis process begins with the selection of a topic. The topic used here as an example is the impact of globalisation on local, state and national issue representation in the Australian print media. This issue is chosen for its social relevance. Various literatures provide a theoretical suggestion that, despite the predicted impacts of globalisation, which include increasing internationalism, the decline of the centrality of the nation-state, and an increasing irrelevance of the local, as in other countries, Australian attitudes and issues retain their prominence in Australian media and public debate.

The specific research question for content analysis example is: 'Has the level and prominence of local and national issues in Australia declined during the era of globalisation?'

Stage 1: Decide the rationale for the study and its level of analysis

The first decisions to be made concern what content is to be examined and why. There is no doubt that we live in a far more globalised world than did our grandparents, and there is little in our daily lives that does not have a global component.

Theorists alternatively define globalisation across a number of criteria. For example, Robertson (1992:8) explains that globalisation as a concept refers to both the compression of the world and the intensification of consciousness of the world as a whole. Waters (2001) provides a more direct definition, arguing that globalisation refers to the social processes in which the constraints of geography on economic, political, social and cultural arrangements recede, in which people become increasingly aware that they are receding and which people act accordingly (cited in Kivisto 2004:159). 'Are these changes affecting our media content and focus?' With scholars such as Anthony Giddens (2003) arguing that, in this era of globalisation, global rather than national forces shape social phenomena, we might expect that national and local perspectives would be increasingly overshadowed by those with a global focus. Therefore, we will assess this theoretical concept deductively by using content analysis to research the topic empirically. We conceptualise the era of globalisation as beginning in the period of most recent dramatic change, economically, industrially and politically, post Second World War.

Stage 2: Identify appropriate texts, sample, and specify the units of analysis

Next we have to select the unit of analysis and the sample. This process is similar for conceptual and relational content analysis. The key aspect of sampling is to be systematic in our selection. For example, in case study 11.1, Franklin and White selected every twenty-fifth issue of the Hobart *Mercury* in the period 1949 to 1998. They further limited their sampling frame to only the first five pages of the selected issues, and only stories about Tasmania. Whatever our decisions about sampling, we need to be able to justify why we have selected the sample that we have, how we have selected it and how it relates to our research question.

With the sampling process, we must specify our units of analysis. As outlined in chapter 3, the unit of analysis is the specific 'what' of our examination. In content analysis, the unit of analysis is a form of communication, so the question is: 'What form of communication will we examine?'

For our example, we select editorials from the leading papers (judged by circulation figures) in our home states—such as the *Mercury* in Tasmania, or the *Sydney Morning Herald*, or the *Age* in Melbourne. The sample is designed like a core drilled in a geological survey. Starting in 1949 and proceeding in five-year steps to 1999, we will take editorials from the first ten week days in June for each chosen year. The choice of June is arbitrary, and successive days should reveal any connections between themes. Weekend editions of the paper are excluded, because they are published under somewhat different constraints. We will therefore end up with 110 editorials covering a 50-year period. The assumption is that the topics covered will reflect the conventions of public discourse in each of our time periods.

Warren Sproule

To access our sample, we need to access archived or electronic copies of the editorials from the specific newspaper for each of the 11 strata identified across the 50-year period. The next decision is to include all editorials in our sample, or to perhaps restrict our 50-year time span, and provide an alternative rationale for that selection. Our decision will depend on the number of stories identified and our time resources. We also need to be clear about the difference between the **unit of analysis** and the unit of observation. While the unit of analysis is the selected state newspaper, the unit of observation will be the editorials, insofar as they relate to local, state, national and international issues over the specified period.

> **Unit of analysis:** A particular instance of what or who we are researching. A unit of analysis can include individuals, groups, social artefacts such as newspaper articles or policy documents, or anything related to social life that can be investigated.

Stage 3: Decide on the parameters of the analysis

This stage is where we decide on our key concepts and coding categories. We also need to decide if we will code for all phrases and terms in the text, or only code for a set of concepts that we feel are most relevant to our topic and question. Complete coding of the text is extremely time-consuming, but results in a thorough analysis, while coding for only selected concepts can deliver a highly relevant analysis, but risks overlooking some important concepts.

Often, based on our literature review and understanding of the topic, we will have developed a predefined set of concepts and categories. Even with such a set, however, we must still decide how much flexibility to allow when coding. Do we code only from this set, or do we add in relevant categories not included in the set as we find them in the text?

Coding parameters for conceptual content analysis

For the conceptual analysis we first scan the editorials, then count electronically the frequency of words selected to show attention to local, state, national and international issues. We index the first three of these simply by the occurrence of the selected capital city (such as 'Hobart'), chosen state (such as 'Tasmania') and 'Australia'. For a global focus, we derive a global repertoire, comprising all uses of 'foreign', 'international', 'offshore', 'overseas' and 'world'. For detail within attention to international affairs, we select countries and/or regions that have been of particular importance to Australia. Given Australia's history of looking to the UK and the USA as great and powerful friends, we count all explicit uses of these terms. Given the importance of the former Soviet Union as a great and powerful other in the postwar world, we repeat this process for it, and do the same for 'China' and 'Asia'. In each case we need to include variants under the same count, taking, for example, 'Australia', 'Australian' and 'Australians' as instances of the same term. We then standardise the frequencies as occurrences per thousand words, and average the scores for each of the strata.

Coding parameters for relational content analysis

In the relational analysis, our interest is in the topics or issues treated in the editorials. The number of topics in any one editorial column will typically shift over time, varying between one and three. The 110 editorials should yield approximately 200 topics, each of which can be coded by the following schema:

1. Purely international events
2. International events with an Australian involvement
3. Purely national events
4. National events involving our selected state and/or other states
5. Purely selected-state events
6. Selected-state events with a local involvement
7. Purely local events.

We can then express the number of editorials in each category as a percentage of the total number of events in the relevant stratum.

Determining a certain number and set of concepts keeps us on task, and allows us to examine a text for very specific things; but introducing a level of coding flexibility permits new, important material to be incorporated into the coding process that can have a significant impact on our results.

Stage 4: Decide how to measure our codes

Deciding how to code for a certain concept for either conceptual or relational content analysis is a key question, because it alters the coding process. This decision is about how we will **operationalise** our key concepts. When coding for existence, we only count a word once, no matter how many times it appears. This is a very basic coding process, which only gives us a limited take on the text. Coding for frequency (the number of times that particular word appears) may be a better gauge of importance. For instance, finding that the word 'aggressive' or its variants, such as 'hostile' or 'invasive', appeared five times in an article, compared to one appearance of the term 'foreign policy', might suggest that the leader writer is concentrating on a country's image or national characteristics at the expense of its political agenda (what it does). Knowing that 'aggressive' and its variants appeared, but not how frequently, wouldn't allow us to draw this inference, regardless of its validity.

> **Operationalisation:** The process of defining how concepts will be measured.

This is not to say, however, that simplicity of procedure leads to simplistic results. Many studies have successfully employed the coding for existence strategy; see, for example, case study 11.3 later in this chapter.

Warren Sproule

On the other hand, the requirement of a research question will often need deeper levels of coding to preserve greater detail for analysis. We might, for example, code for how often ambiguous words were used, or for words that hold double meanings, such as 'patriotism', with its gamut of meaning running from 'selfless devotion to one's country' to 'xenophobia'. Also problematic are words or phrases that have an ambiguous nature when taken in context of the information directly related to those words. In a given editorial, phrases like 'national mourning' or 'outpourings of grief' might be perceived either as a positive or negative statement, depending on whether they are interpolated in an item dealing with a Holocaust memorial or a Tiananmen Square massacre, the assassination of Mahatma Gandhi or the death of Josef Stalin.

Stage 5: Decide how to distinguish among concepts

The next task in content analysis is to decide on the level of generalisation; that is, are concepts to be coded verbatim, exactly as they appear, or can they be recorded as the same when they appear in different forms? Generalising means we gather all the instances into the one category, but may mean we lose nuanced detail; for example, should the terms 'foreign corporations' and 'international corporations' be considered the same or different? The terms included in our global repertoire at stage 3 are a relatively unproblematic instance. We would need to determine whether different words that are related to the one concept are so similar that they can be coded as being the same thing, or if they actually mean different things. Again, we need to bring our own judgment to bear and, importantly, record our decision (see translation rules below).

Likewise, we need to determine the level of implication we are going to allow in our coding. By including implicit concepts, we can code not only for the word 'international', but also for words that imply 'international' or 'world' or 'worldwide'. Phrases such as 'leading global player' imply international and worldwide. Absences can also be implicit concepts. For example, if an editorial noted the award of an Oscar to an Australian actor, but was silent on the international standing of the Australian movie industry, we might decide to code this article as implicitly comparing global impact and status in a given field.

Stage 6: Develop rules for coding texts

Having taken the generalisation of concepts into consideration, we need next to create translation rules. These rules help in organising and streamlining the coding process so that we are coding for exactly what we want to code for. Developing this set of rules helps guarantee consistency of coding throughout the text, and allows the same coder to code different material repeatedly in the same way, or multiple coders to code the same material in the same way. For instance, if we coded 'tariff barrier' as a separate category from 'import duty' in one paragraph, then coded it under the umbrella of 'tariff barrier' when it occurred in the next paragraph, the validity of our data would be threatened. Consequently, the validity of the interpretations drawn from that data would also be reduced. Translation rules act as an insurance policy against this, giving the coding process a crucial level of reliability and coherence. It is important to be meticulous when assigning value to the different concepts.

Stage 7: Decide what to do with surplus information

We now need to decide whether surplus information—that is, information that does not fit into the predetermined categories—should be ignored, or used to reexamine and/or alter the coding scheme. Our options are either skipping over, or removing, unwanted material; or seeing all information as relevant and important, and using it to re-examine and reassess, and possibly even change, our coding scheme. For example, words like 'not yet' or 'still', trivial by themselves, carry a certain suggestive weight when coupled directly with the words 'independent' and 'parochial'.

Stage 8: Code the texts and perform statistical analysis

Our next step is to code the text. The coding is usually a manual task, but, as with other forms of qualitative analysis, there are now computer programs available to automate the process of coding. While, on the one hand, computerised coding has been a boon to content analysis, in that it facilitates the examination of large amounts of data quickly and efficiently, on the other hand, the success of the process is entirely dependent on thorough preparation and category construction. Computer programs are remarkably 'dumb beasts' in many ways, only capable of responding to the exact information they are fed. The human brain, on the other hand, has the capacity to make sense of, and render sensible, information that in itself may be illogical, incomplete and/or incorrect (McHoul 1982).

Although more tedious and labour intensive, coding by hand allows flexibility in the coding process, and can make spotting errors easier. Problems related to automation are more evident when coding for implicit information, and where thorough category preparation is essential for accurate coding. Also, as noted in chapter 14 on qualitative data analysis, it is worth remembering that computer programs can organise and manage the data, but they do not interpret it; that is the job of the researcher.

The statistical analysis of our coded data will depend on how we operationalised our concepts in stage 4. If we decided to count the frequency of a concept (both explicit and implicit frequencies), our analysis here may be just a matter of tallying the figures and comparisons of

Warren Sproule

the different concept tallies. Alternatively, if we decided to code for the existence of a concept, we may need to compare how the concepts were associated with the different categories. Also note that chapter 10 includes a section on analysing content analysis data.

Stage 9: Interpret the results

The analysis now needs to be interpreted and presented. What trends are evident, and how do these patterns and trends fit with the theoretical framework? For example, does the content analysis indicate that, over a 50-year period, the local and national issues have receded, persisted or re-emerged in a different form? Has the presentation of such issues changed, and if so—and how—might the differences be related to globalisation? If our research concentrated on a conceptual content analysis, we would be able to determine the relative pattern of frequency of local, national or international foci in the editorials over the time period, and assess if that frequency had altered in the last 50 years and in what direction: more global focus, less or about the same.

If our research were more interested in the implicit globalisation-related content of editorials, our analysis would provide us with a more complex picture of the way national, state, local and global events and attitudes to the global–local nexus have changed or not changed over our 50-year examination period.

In exercise 11.2, you can work through these stages yourself in an examination of the content of a sample of personal ads.

Exercise 11.2: Are you lonesome tonight?

The exercise is probably best completed in a group setting. Use the seven questions provided to interrogate the content of the selected material.

Some years ago, Australian sociologist Mark Western devised this exercise for his upper-year undergraduate methods students at the University of Tasmania. He was interested in the ways people represented themselves in 'lonely hearts'/dating service columns in newspapers. Sampling from the 'miscellaneous' section in the classified index of the three leading newspapers in the state (Launceston *Examiner,* Hobart *Mercury* and *Sunday Tasmanian*), he provided students with examples of these advertisements (see figure 11.1), and sought answers to the following questions:

1. Are there some common characteristics of ads placed by men and women?
2. Comparing the ads placed by men and women, how do members of each describe themselves?
3. What sorts of features do men emphasise, and how do they compare with women's emphasis?

4   Which advertisements are longer?
5   Are men more or less likely than women to indicate what they are looking for in a partner?
6   Are there differences in the 'tone' of the ads placed by men and women? Of what type?
7   Do ads placed by agencies differ from ads placed by individuals?
8   Think about issues of sampling, conceptualisation, and operationalisation in these ads. Do you think that some of your findings might differ if you sampled different kinds of newspapers or magazines?

A 60 YO MALE would like contact with fit and healthy self-sufficient female without baggage, any age or nationality with personality. Good SOH who likes travel, adventure and who thinks she missed out so far. Photo would be great. Reply to Box H0##, *Mercury*.

LADY 27 would like to meet slim, unattached, good looking guy with no children 25–33 yrs only in view of relationship. Phone/text 04## ### ###. Strictly genuine replies.

Perfect Match

A LOCAL business with HUNDREDS of L'ton people joining — nice people trying a new way to meet others.

Oblig-free appts.

PHONE 01# ### ###

Mon-Fri 9–6 pm, Sat. 9–12 pm

32 YO Lawrence is a real softie — romantic and a bit shy, he wants to meet a girl who likes country life. Children fine.

47 YO Bert is a tall hardworking man who also enjoys being a full-time dad, but he longs for the company of a warm, straightforward lady who enjoys the simple things in life.

Call Miriam (BA Psychology)
PHONE 019 ### ###
707 Elizabeth St, Launceston.

PETITE blue-eyed lady early forties, enjoys walks, dining, nature looking to meet intelligent good-natured n/s gent 35 plus. Reply to Box H0##, *Mercury*.

LOVE ON THE INTERNET

Easy safe exciting way to find romance in Tasmania.
www.spiceoflife.com.au

GORGEOUS GEMINI
All of us just want to meet someone special to enrich our lives. That's all 49 yo Marilyn wants. Petite brunette who loves country living. A woman of her word. Don't you deserve happiness? Don't be alone any more. Call now on (03) #### ####. Quote 39N7.

LONELY Christian man, 55, no ties, would like to meet a lonely lady in the same position for friendship and outings. Very genuine. *Examiner* Box J##.

YOUNG man seeks lady 30–37 for Guys and Dolls and friendship and outings. *Mercury*, Box H0##.

LADIES SEEKING LOVE (LAUNCESTON) AREA
SONIA, single, 21, pretty, slim, long brown hair, a quiet girl who likes the outdoors and nature, own car, dislikes the pub scene, seeks genuine guy 21–30 for close friendship/relationship.
LIZ, 35, divorced, no kids, nice looking, full shapely figure, very lonely, enjoys keeping fit, outdoors, animals, seeks genuine man 35–46 who is also lonely and ready for a close, steady friendship based on trust.
HAYLEY, 28, single, very petite and lively, blonde hair, green eyes, dresses stylishly, very genuine, seeks guy 28–40, any status for outings, to share weekends together, view something serious, in time.
EVE, Asian girl 30, never married, very sweet and attractive, long hair, slim and shapely, a lovely nature, reliable and sincere, looking for gent 35–55, mature, trustworthy and genuine, any nat. who wants friendship, leading to marriage.
TO MEET ANY OF THESE LADIES PHONE 039 ### ###.

THE GENTLEMAN who likes the Dandenongs and Mocha Kenya coffee (met on the Spirit of Tasmania). Please contact me on (03) #### ####.

Humorous Romantic
Ron is a single 36 y.o., loveable chap who wants to meet a lass of her word. Country gent who is open-minded and willing to meet a lady with children. Men like Ron are hard to find: he has so much to give. Free to meet. So what are you waiting for? CALL TODAY ON #### ####. QUOTE 34EX#

YOUNG TOWN BEAUTY
Sun-kissed skin, flowing hair, captivating hazel eyes, personality plus ... the list is never-ending with so many fine qualities. 28 yo Shelley is a single country girl who wants to enrich her life with a gent up to 45. A man who believes in being faithful and honest. Is that you? Call now (03) #### #### Quote26N8.

---

22 YEAR-OLD guy seeking ladies 18–30 years old for friendship and discreet meetings. Reply *Examiner* Box 0##

SOULMATE
42 yo appealing blonde with smiling brown eyes, Jan is upmarket and enjoys the finer side of life, music sport, art and gardening. Don't hesitate. Phone (03) #### #### to meet. Quote 6G22.

WANTED to meet, female, 40–46 yrs for long-term friendship with working male. No objection to 1 child. Reply to PO Box ### Claremont 7011.

SELF MADE MILLIONAIRE seeks his Lady-in-Waiting Phone (03) #### ####. J5.

Figure 11.1: Lonely hearts newspaper adertisments

Warren Sproule

Box 11:2 Content analysis: Some pros and cons

Content analysis can be distinguished from other social scientific methods by three key features:

- the simplicity of its components: it is a relatively easy method to explain and to use
- the modesty of its claims: practitioners acknowledge its limitations
- the length of the tradition from which it draws: as shown in the example opening this chapter, forms of content analysis research have existed for a very long time.

These features of content analysis also contribute to some of the identified strengths and weaknesses of content analysis as a social research method.

On the strengths side, content analysis is a relatively cheap method of social research in terms of financial costs. The material and raw data of content analysis are, as forms of recorded communication text, both cheap and easy to access. The development of communication technologies such as the internet has dramatically widened the availability and variety of text available to researchers for analysis. Content analysis is also a relatively secure research method. If we make a mistake, such as poorly conceptualising our key concepts, we can simply go back to our text sample and revise them. Such a mistake in survey or field research can jeopardise the validity of the entire research project.

Despite its relative simplicity as a research method, content analysis can provide sophisticated analysis of the both explicit and implicit content of communication texts. These texts are important conveyors and reflectors of our cultural and social values. Also, as demonstrated by case study 11.2, content analysis can provide this analysis of cultural and social phenomena over time, allowing researchers to identify and pinpoint changing patterns and trends. Also, as case study 11.4 demonstrates, a relatively simple coding and counting of categories of content can produce quite powerful results.

Case study 11.3: Media representations of ethnic groups

Van Krieken and colleagues (2000: 546–7) report David Triggers' (1995) investigations of representations of different ethnic groups within the media. Trigger looked at 2408 items in the *West Australian* and five rural newspapers from 1984 and 1988. He coded the items according to whether stories featuring ethnic groups or members of ethnic groups had a generally positive or negative message. Criteria for coding a story in a positive way included 'the attractive features of a group or individual'. This might include stories about sporting or cultural achievement, community development or community leadership. Negatively coded stories usually referred to criminal activity and, in the case of Aborigines, the 'threat' presented by land rights claims.

The results shown in (the table below) indicate that Aboriginal and Asian groups received far more negative coverage than other groups.

Table 11.1: Frequencies of newspaper records presenting positive and negative content, *West Australian*, 1984 and 1988 (column percentages)

	Aboriginal (N=1453)	Asian (N=390)	British (N=80)	Western European (N=106)	Eastern European (N=73)	General (N=207)	Total (N=2408)
Positive	8.4	9.2	11.3	22.5	13.7	13.0	10.0
Negative	20.5	35.6	15.0	18.9	13.7	7.7	22.2

Source: van Krieken et al. 2000

A particular strength of content analysis is the method's unobtrusiveness. By using existing communication texts in various forms as its data source, content analysis avoids many of the ethical problems of research methods that conduct their research directly with people. Many of the ethical dilemmas outlined in chapter 3, such as imbalance of power between the researcher and the researched, are not an issue with content analysis. Content analysts such as Krippendorf (1980) also point out that using text rather than people as its observation method avoids problems such as the Hawthorne effect (see chapter 1), where the research subjects' own awareness of being studied can influence behaviour and reduce the validity of the research.

The very unobtrusiveness of content analysis is also sometimes seen as a weakness. Its use of text-based data and secondary sources over research methods that directly observe social phenomena on the ground is seen as removing the researcher from the social phenomena he or she seeks to research. For example, Elton Mayo argued that text-based research causes social science researchers to take refuge in the library, and 'dwell apart from humanity in certain cities of the mind—remote, intellectual, preoccupied with highly articulate thinking' (Mayo 1945:20–1). Becker (1960:809) similarly maintained that a method such as content analysis is 'no substitute for remaining in close touch with the empirical evidence, with "the damned facts"'.

Other critics point to the already mediated and secondary nature of the texts, such as print, audiovisual or electronic documents, that content analysis uses as its data source.

Warren Sproule

For example, Platt (1981) suggests that using such mediated secondary data is at best a severe handicap to any worthwhile form of scientific analysis. By studying only communication text, content analysis is limited to recorded communications. Content analysis cannot analyse those communications that are not recorded or published in some way. This is important because the people who set up communications, write reports or make speeches are conscious social beings. They can and do make choices about what communications they choose to have recorded, and those they do not.

However, on the positive side, using text and documents as their data source was the main research tool of the classical sociologists. As Scott (1990:1) notes:

> Marx made extensive use of the reports of factory inspectors, Weber utilised religious tracts and pamphlets, and Durkheim employed official statistics on suicide. The bulk of the historical and comparative work that is undertaken in contemporary sociology involves the use of documentary materials, as does much work on contemporary societies. But textbooks on research methods have generally failed to recognise this, and have given most of their space to discussions of questionnaires, interviews and participant observation.

Perhaps the strongest criticism of content analysis is to point to the limitations of the method. While a content analysis exploring television violence, such as that by Baker and Ball (1969), can meticulously count, code and analyse instances of violence on television, it is beyond the scope of content analysis to do more than infer the motives of the producers of such material. Additionally, such counts, even if high, cannot assume the actual effects of such violent items on the audience.

Critics of content analysis as a research method in the social sciences also argue that content analysis is too subjective in its coding and interpretation. Like all data, text comes in all shades of grey, rather than strictly black and white. Even with translation rules in place, how communications are conceptualised can be a very subjective decision. For example, in David Trigger's study of media representation of different ethnic groups, defining an article as negative or positive is, in much of his sample, unlikely to have been a clearcut decision. While content analysis is sometimes criticised for its categorising of concepts, analysts such as Thomas (1994:691) argue that the placement of human behaviour into articulated categories reflects what happens 'each and every day, from birth to death' by 'people in social interaction'.

Conversely, content analysis has also been criticised for being too empirical. Critics such as Slater (1998) argue that content analysis tends to be fairly mechanistic in both its readings of text and its conclusions; that it is essentially a word count, and in reducing the analysis of text to counts of categorised content or concepts, the method reduces complex phenomena and concepts to rudimentary counts and inappropriate codes. The respective strengths and weaknesses of content analysis are summed up in box 11.2.

Box 11.3: Advantages and disadvantages of content analysis

Advantages of content analysis

- Content analysis looks directly at communication via texts or transcripts, a central aspect of social interaction.
- Content analysis is inexpensive.
- Content analysis can allow for both quantitative and qualitative analysis.
- Content analysis can provide valuable historical and cultural insights through analysis of texts over time. It can deal with current events, past events or both.
- Content analysis can be used to interpret texts for a variety of purposes.
- Content analysis relies on raw data that are relatively easy to obtain.
- Content analysis is an unobtrusive means of analysing interactions, and therefore has fewer ethical dimensions than many other forms of social research.

Disadvantages of content analysis

- Content analysis can be extremely time-consuming.
- It is hard to be certain that the sample studied is representative.
- Content analysis can be very subjective in its interpretation. This is especially so with relational analysis, which has a high level of inference.
- It is not always easy to find a measurable unit such as a frame in a comic strip. What does one do about films or magazine articles?
- Content analysis is inherently reductive, particularly when dealing with complex texts.
- Content analysis tends too often to simply consist of word counts.
- Content analysis does not always allow sufficiently for the social context that produced the text, or the state of things after the text is produced.
- It is not possible to prove that the inferences made on the basis of a content analysis alone are correct.

Warren Sproule

Voices in the field

Adrian Franklin

Professor Adrian Franklin trained as an anthropologist in the UK, and is best known for his work on the relationships between humans and the natural world. His books include *Animal Nation: The True Story of Animals and Australia*, *Animals and Modern Cultures*, *Nature and Social Theory* and *Tourism*. Adrian Franklin's work has focused on social and cultural change in modernity, and this includes work on city life, the sociology of nature and environments, our relationships with animals, and the orderings of travel, mobility and tourism, and he has written extensively on travel and tourism theory and the impact that modern mobilities have had on everyday life and the ordering of global modernity. His research work encompasses a variety of methods and methodologies, and he creatively used content analysis of newspaper articles from 1945 to 1995 in a research project (with R. White) to assess if and how attitudes towards animals had altered in the half-century. As outlined in case study 11.1, this research demonstrated that articles about animals at risk rose over time compared those about animals posing a risk. His new research is inspired both by relational materialism and posthumanism, and current projects include work on the social life of bushfires, acclimatisation landscapes, the anthropology of the effervescent city and the relationship between individualism, freedom and loneliness.

From method to practice

The example used to outline the key steps in undertaking a content analysis amply indicates both the value and signficance of the method. The following description of a content analysis undertaken by a sociology honours student adds to this by demonstrating the level of theoretical and empirical validity that can be garnered by this deceptively simple method.

In 2006, Rebecca Dance began her honours year in sociology. She had noted that the recently introduced Maternity Payment (dubbed the baby bonus) of $3000 per child, designed to help parents cope with the considerable costs of a new baby, was attracting much interest from current affairs shows and media articles. The focus of this media attention was a concern that the baby bonus would encourage young unpartnered women, especially teenagers, to have babies for the bonus. Rebecca was interested in finding out if this claim of baby bonus-inspired births was a legitimate social problem, or whether it might be an overreaction: in sociological terms, a moral panic. Therefore the aim of the research was to analyse the validity of the media's reaction to the Maternity Payment, using the theoretical framework of objective social problems and moral panics as outlined by Cohen (1987) and Goode and Ben-Yehuda (1994). Her research question was: 'Does the media's reaction to the Maternity Payment policy in relation to teenage births constitute a moral panic or an appropriate response to an objective social problem?' She chose a content analysis as the best method for conducting a research project that would answer this question.

In her literature review, Rebecca noted that most media on the topic were typically anecdotal, referring usually to a particular young woman, rather than establishing any pattern of baby bonus-inspired pregnancies. She also examined empirical data from the Australian Bureau of Statistics relating to the pattern and level of teenage births over the previous few decades. These data indicated that the level of teenage births had been actually declining steadily over the last few decades.

Rebecca's sampling frame was all newspaper articles published in four large circulation newspapers, two broadsheets and two tabloids, between 11 April 2004 and 11 May 2006. She sampled all articles that mentioned the terms 'Maternity Payment' or 'baby bonus' in this period, then filtered these to those that contained mention of the social, economic and/or sociodemographic implications of the policy. Her final sample consisted of 67 articles.

Goode and Ben-Yehuda (1994) outline five criteria that must be met for a reaction to a social phenomenon to be classified as a moral panic. These are: a heightened level of concern regarding the behaviour; the reaction must comprise an increased level of hostility towards the group perceived as engaging in the behaviour; there must be widespread consensus that the concern is real; the reaction must also be volatile, erupting fairly suddenly and then subsiding; and finally, as the key element, the reaction must be disproportionate to the level of actual threat posed by the behaviour. Using the risk of unpartnered, especially teenage women, having babies to access baby bonus funds as the behaviour, Rebecca coded her sample of articles using these five criteria as her categories for analysis. The phrases and sentences that pertained to these categories were the recording units, and all were recorded in a research codebook.

Her content analysis detected all five moral panic categories in the sample articles. For example, an analysis of articles by date showed that indeed the reaction was highly volatile, rising in all newspapers examined sharply after the announcement of the Maternity Payment in April 2004, but then falling away two months later to almost nothing, before rising sharply again in March 2005, again only for a two-month period. Hostility towards unmarried teenage mothers was also evident in many of the articles, as was the level of concern about the depth of the problem.

Warren Sproule

From method to practice

There was virtually no mention of the fact that less than 5 per cent of the births in 2004 were to teenagers, and that current teenage fertility was the lowest ever recorded in Australia, indicating that the media's reaction was disproportionate to the actual level of the behavior occurring.

These findings led Rebecca to conclude that the media's reaction to the Maternity Payment did, indeed, constitute a moral panic. Using Cohen's (1987) theories around moral panics to interpret her results, she theorised that teenage mothers had been labelled 'folk devils', and that such labelling helped strengthen society's moral boundaries, in this case around unwed, young parenting. As an already stigmatised group, it was impossible for young women to counter the portrayals of their deviance, or the threat they were deemed to pose to two-parent traditional families. Finally, at the end of her study, statistics from Centrelink established that over the period that the baby bonus had been paid, the birth rate had indeed increased, but that most of this increase was among 35–39-year-old mothers, and the number of claims from teenagers had only increased marginally.

Conclusion

This chapter has demonstrated the use of content analysis as a research method within the social sciences. Content analysis is basically about the study of communications. Communication for content analysis includes all forms of recorded communication, whether they be written texts, such as newspaper articles or novels, spoken communications, such as speeches, or audiovisual and electronic communications, such as internet sites and film and television. The aim of researchers undertaking a content analysis study is to analyse the data, develop categories to make sense of these data, then analyse these categories to interpret the analysis. The particular unique value of content analysis as a social research method lies in its unobtrusiveness and ability to identify trends and patterns over time. To broaden your knowledge of qualitative methods read the on-line modules on narrative research, conversation analysis, action research, ethnographic research, memory work and sensory and visual methods; these are available at <www.oup.com.au/orc/walter>.

Main points

> Content analysis is a research method that detects, records, and analyses concepts within some form of communication.

> Content analysis texts can include any form of recorded communication. These include books, essays, historical documents, newspaper articles, imagery, theatre, advertising, and electronic media.

> Conceptual and relational analysis are both forms of content analysis.

> The research process for content analysis is similar to that of other social research, with the exception of the unit of analysis. In content analysis, the unit of analysis is some form of communication text.

> The process of content analysis involves coding and (often) counting the presence, meanings and relationships of words and concepts.

> The concepts coded and counted can be both explicit and implicit concepts.

> The data are interpreted to make meaning of the content of the communication.

> The strengths of content analysis include its unobtrusiveness and its ability to provide social, cultural and historical insights over time.

> The weaknesses of content analysis include that it is too often simply a word count and it can be inherently reductive.

Warren Sproule

Further reading

Ball, M. and Smith, G. (1992). *Analysing Visual Data*. Newbury Park, CA: Sage.

Berger, A. A. (1991). *Media Analysis Techniques*. London: Sage.

Krippendorf, K. (1980). *Content Analysis: An Introduction to its Methodology*. London: Sage.

Thomas, S. (1994). 'Artifactual study in the Analysis of Culture: A Defense of Content Analysis in a Postmodern Age', *Communication Research*, 21 (6): 683–97.

References

Allard, T. (2000) 'Howard Hails Death of the Cultural Cringe', *Sydney Morning Herald*, 30 December 2000: 1.

Baker, R. K. and Ball, S. J. (1969). *Mass Media and Violence: Report to the National Commission on the Causes and Prevention of Violence*. Toronto: Bantam.

Ball, M. and Smith, G. (1992). *Analysing Visual Data*. Newbury Park, CA: Sage.

Beck, U. (1992). *Risk Society: Towards a New Modernity*. London: Sage.

Becker, H. P. (1960). 'Normative Reactions to Normlessness', *American Sociological Review*, 25: 803–10.

Berelson, B. (1952). *Content Analysis in Communication Research*. New York: Free Press.

Britain, I. (1998). *Once An Australian* Sydney: Oxford University Press.

Cohen, S. (1987). *Folk Devils and Moral Panics: The Creation of the Mods and Rockers*. Oxford: Basil Blackwell.

Dance, R. (2006). The Baby Bonus Encourages the 'Wrong' Women to have Babies: Social Problem or Moral Panic? Unpublished Honours thesis. Hobart: School of Sociology and Social Work, University of Tasmania.

Dorfman, A. and Mattelart, A. (1975). *How to Read Donald Duck: Imperialist Ideology in the Disney Comic*. New York: International General.

Franklin, A. (2006). *Animal Nation: The True Story of Animals and Australia*. Sydney: University of New South Wales Press.

Franklin, A. and White, R. (2001). 'Animals and Modernity: Changing Human–Animal Relations in Tasmania', *Journal of Sociology*, 37 (3): 219–38.

Giddens, A. (2003). *Runaway World: How Globalisation Is Reshaping Our Lives*. New York: Routledge.

Goode, E. and Ben-Yehuda, N. (1994). *Moral Panics: The Social Construction of Deviance*. Oxford: Blackwell.

Henderson, G. (1990) *Australia Answers*. Sydney: Random House.

Jacobs, J. (1976) 'A Phenomenological Study of Suicide Notes', in Sanders, W. B. (ed.), *The Sociologist as Detective*. New York: Praeger Press: 247–66.

Kivisto, P. (2004). *Key Ideas in Sociology*. Thousand Oaks, CA: Pine Forge Press.

Krippendorf, K. (1980). *Content Analysis: An Introduction to its Methodology*. London: Sage.

Malouf, D. (1998). *A Spirit of Play: The Making of Australian Consciousness*. Sydney: ABC Books.

Mayo, E. (1945). *The Social Problems of an Industrial Civilization*. Andover, MA: Andover Press.

McHoul, A. W. (1982). *Telling How Texts Talk*. London: Routledge & Kegan Paul.

McKay, J., Hutchins, B. and Mikosza, J. (2000). 'Shame and Scandal in the Family: Australian Media Narratives of the IOC/SOCOG Scandal Spiral', *Olympika: The International Journal of Olympic Studies*, 9: 25–48.

Palmquist, M. E., Carley, K. M. and Dale, T. A. (1997). 'Two Applications of Automated Text Analysis: Analysing Literary and Non-literary Texts', in Roberts, C. (ed.), *Text Analysis for the Social Sciences: Methods for Drawing Statistical Inferences from Texts and Transcripts*. Hillsdale, NJ: Lawrence Erlbaum Associates.

Phillips, A. A. (1950). 'The Cultural Cringe'. *Meanjin*, 9: 299–302.

Platt, J. (1981). 'Evidence and Proof in Documentary Research', *Sociological Review*, 29 (1): 31–66.

Reynolds, R. (1992). *Super Heroes: A Modern Mythology*. London: Batsford.

Robertson, I. (1992). *Sociology* (5th edn). New York: Worth Publishers.

Rose, G. (2001). *Visual Methodologies: An Introduction to the Interpretation of Visual Materials*. London: Sage.

Scott, J. (1990). *A Matter of Record*. Cambridge: Polity Press.

Slater, D. (1998). 'Analysing Cultural Objects: Content Analysis and Semiotics', in Searle, C. (ed.), *Researching Society and Culture*. London: Sage.

Stratton, J. (2000). 'Not Just Another Multicultural Story', *Journal of Australian Studies*, September: 23–47.

Studdert, D. (1999). 'Bondi, Baywatch and the Struggle for Community', *Arena*, August: 28–33.

Thomas, S. (1994). 'Artifactual Study in the Analysis of Culture: A Defense of Content Analysis in a Postmodern Age', *Communication Research*, 21 (6): 683–97.

Warren Sproule

Trigger, D. (1995). 'Everyone's Agreed, the West Is All You Need', *Media Information Australia*, 75: 102–22.

van Krieken, R., Smith, P., Habibis, D., Hutchins, B., Haralambos, M. and Holborn, M. (2000). *Sociology: Themes and Perspectives* (3nd edn). Frenchs Forest, NSW: Pearson Education.

Chapter 12

Discourse Analysis

Keith Jacobs

Why discourse analysis?

A defining feature of the contemporary world is our reliance on texts as the basis of communication. In our everyday lives, most of us encounter newspaper reports, notices in corridors, emails, telephone text messages, books and magazines, advertisement billboards, and of course the internet. Since the world we live in is constituted by texts, social scientists have sought to develop methods to understand its functions and assess its wider influence. Discourse analysis is generally regarded as an influential method, and is now widely accepted as an important tool for social science research. Some of the questions that discourse analysis seeks to address are:

- How are texts used to advance social and political change?
- What is the relationship between language and power?
- How are texts understood?
- How does discourse affect our views and understanding of the social world?

In practice, discourse analysis is fundamentally concerned with the analysis of language. This analysis, however, is more than an examination. It entails a critical reading of text in order to make explicit its meaning and significance.

Key terms

active style	discursive practice	metaphor
ambiguity	dispositive analysis	modality
archaeological discourse	Foucauldian-inspired analysis	order of discourse
analysis	framing	passive style
audience	genealogy	regimes of truth
cohesion	genre	self-technology
context	ideology	social practice
critical discourse analysis	intertextuality	textual analysis
discourse	language	validity (discourse analysis)

Introduction

Discourse analysis is generally understood to be a method of research that highlights the importance of language. Though there are different ways of conducting a discourse analysis, the key aim is to provide a critical understanding of how language is deployed. Discourse analysis does this by making explicit the social and political context in which texts are situated. In this respect, discourse analysis is best viewed as an interpretative method. However, to make effective use of discourse analysis, it is essential to understand the theoretical tradition that has informed the method.

Discourse analysis is a broad field, and researchers engage in discourse analysis in a variety of ways. For example, the linguistic and ethnomethodological strands are widely used by social psychologists. Particularly prominent in this stream of discourse analysis is the work of academics associated with the Discourse and Rhetoric Group in the Department of Social Sciences at Loughborough University in the United Kingdom (see, for example, Billig 1995; Potter 1996, 2003, 2004; Edwards 1997; Antaki et al. 2003) alongside the work of Wetherell and colleagues (2001a). Their mode of discourse analysis is often referred to as discursive psychology to demarcate it from other approaches (Potter 2004). The methods of discursive psychology pay particular attention to how actors interpret the world and how these interpretations are produced in discourse. This mode of discourse analysis has been used effectively to analyse transcriptions of conversations, but unlike some modes of content analysis (see chapter 5), it eschews counting and coding, on the basis that these can obscure the activities that entail talking and text production (Potter 2004). In theoretical terms, the work of discursive psychologists links closely to the work of ethnomethodologists and sociologists such as Garfinkel (1967) and Sacks (1992). Australian work that has been informed by these studies includes Augostinos and Walker (1995), McHoul (1996) and McHoul and Rapley (2001). Students interested in learning more about this method of research should read Potter (2004) and the introductory chapter in Rapley (2004).

This chapter provides an introduction to discourse-inspired methods used by social scientists, and includes the insights that can be gained from this mode of analysis as well as some of the pitfalls. It is, therefore, not possible to include examples of all the different traditions of discourse analysis. We have opted to discuss two approaches in some detail that have been particularly influential in recent years: critical discourse analysis and Foucauldian-inspired discourse analysis.

The background to discourse analysis

Theoretical origins

The origins of discourse analysis stem from a number of sources, but the work of the Cambridge-based philosopher Ludwig Wittgenstein (1889–1951) is especially influential. One of Wittgenstein's primary philosophical arguments was that the view of language as a neutral or transparent medium was mistaken. Instead, Wittgenstein (1974) stressed the active component of language use, suggesting that the meaning of words is inseparable from practice. He argued that there is no intrinsic meaning in any of the words we use. Instead, meaning is derived by reference to the wider social context and interaction. Wittgenstein's impact has been considerable in the fields of linguistics, psychology, anthropology, literary criticism and sociology. For example, in sociology, Wittgenstein's insights have encouraged researchers to adopt a more politicised perspective of language, viewing it as a 'performative activity', with a dynamic and ideological component. In practice, this has meant paying more attention to the role of language in all aspects of everyday life.

Emergence as a social science method

Insights of the performative aspects to language help explain the interest in discourse analysis among social scientists. However, discourse analysis was fundamentally propelled into the mainstream by:

- changes in communication technologies
- the desire by many social scientists to adopt more qualitative modes of enquiry.

Technological innovation has affected the ways that information and texts (including advertising) are produced and consumed. In turn, these changes have bolstered the development of academic subdisciplines, such as cultural and media studies, both of which make use of discourse analysis. Discourse analysis has also been taken up by many researchers in the area of applied social science interested in more critical and innovative research techniques. This interest stems from a concern that applied social science is sometimes too closely aligned to the interests of government and policy-makers. The attraction of discourse analysis is its capacity to provide nuanced insights relating to the production and consumption of texts.

Discourse analysis also fits with a changing public awareness and increasingly sophisticated understanding of the performative role of language in areas such as advertising and the media. Consider the way in which government elections are viewed. We are much more aware of the ways in which politicians put in place discursive strategies to secure an agenda in their own interests. New terms such as 'sound bites' and 'spin' are frequently used

Keith Jacobs

by journalists to describe the ways in which politicians seek to use language for specific effects. And, in a general way, we are much more critical of, some would say cynical about, the ways in which language is organised in the public realm of politics and governance. For example, how often do politicians seek to display their commitment to popular causes (such as, protecting the 'environment', tackling 'poverty') without necessarily setting out in detail what measures they will enact?

Advantages of discourse analysis as a method of social research

The key advantage of discourse analysis is that it provides a useful tool for researchers interested in understanding the ways in which power is exercised in organisational and social settings. The specific focus on text can provide significant insights that are not always discernible when using other methods. As shown in case study 12.1 and exercise 12.1, discourse analysis enables a close scrutiny of the ways in which texts are utilised to promote a specific ideological agenda.

For social scientists, discourse analysis also offers a method of uncovering some of the ways in which people or groups (or 'actors' or 'agents', as they are often termed in discourse analysis) seek to represent their actions in texts and language. As Fairclough (2003:4) argues, 'people not only act and organize in particular ways, they also represent their ways of acting and organizing, and produce imaginary projections of new or alternative ways, in particular discourses'.

In other words, all forms of social activity have a representation in discourse. For this reason, discourse analysis is often used to provide a political critique of different modes of government policy-making and organisational decision-making processes.

Key terms and concepts in discourse analysis

It is important to understand how concepts such as language and 'discourse' are used within discourse analysis. For example, although linguists usually use the term 'discourse' to denote a single or group of utterances or texts, Van Dijk (1997:3) provides two straightforward working definitions, suggesting that:

- **discourse** could be defined as 'language use', and
- **discourse analysis** as the 'study of talk and text in context'.

Incorporating these definitions, the term 'discourse' is often used within social theory to make the connection between power and language use. As Sharp and Richardson (2001:194) write, discourse in this sense 'is a complex entity that extends into the realms of ideology, strategy, language and practice, and is shaped by the relations between power and knowledge'.

The following table sets out some of the key terms commonly used in a discourse analysis. It should be referred to when you are working through exercise 12.1 at the end of the chapter.

Table 12.1: Key terms in discourse analysis

Active and passive styles	Sentences that are **passive** usually entail the author placing the object in the subject position; for example, 'Home ownership policies to be reviewed by the Commonwealth government' is an example of a passive phrase. The normal **active** phrase would be 'The Commonwealth government to review home ownership policies'. In academic and policy contexts, authors frequently deploy passive writing styles to convey a sense of objectivity.
Ambiguity	Vague or imprecise terms are often used deliberately to convey multiple meanings. For example, in policy writing, it is quite common for the word 'community' to be used. The term has no precise meaning, so it is difficult to take exception to its deployment.
Audience	The audience of any text can differ quite markedly. For example, in academic texts, there is an internal audience of other academics and an external audience made up of students and general readers. Very often, the producer of texts will target particular audiences.
Cohesion	The way certain words or terms are linked together to elicit a particular response. For example, terms such as 'objectives', 'targets' and 'planning' are often deployed in government policy reports to signal to the reader a commitment to service delivery.
Context	In discourse analysis, researchers try to show how texts are situated in wider contexts. The contextual effects of texts include how they are interpreted by the reader or audience and the context in which texts are produced by the author. For these reasons, discourse analysts pay a great deal of attention to the production and interpretation of texts.
Discourse	A generic term to denote language in use. It usually means the written or spoken word, but also can be used to cover any activity in which individuals seek to convey meaning.
Framing	This term is used to show how political messages are regulated and controlled. For example, in articles written by journalists, the authors usually seek to frame their work as being objective and unbiased.
Genre	The style in which texts are produced and consumed; for example, there are a number of different genres in policy publications. Informational reports tend to adopt a neutral style of writing and polemical texts seek to persuade the reader.
Ideology	Ideology is a key concept, since discourse analysis seeks to uncover the ideological values that inform the production of a text. Ideology is best understood as the shared values held by groups and societies. Dominant ideologies, such as a belief in the efficacy of the market (capitalism), are referred to as hegemonic.

Intertextuality	Very often, texts contain linkages to other sources. Examples might include direct quotations or references to other works. The presence of other works is used to reinforce arguments.
Language	Language is seen as a performative activity encompassing words, texts and other expressive behaviour.
Metaphor	The figurative use of terms. Often used by authors to make a point by using an example, which, while not strictly relevant, nonetheless helps make a point; for example, 'The government minister has been forced to make a U-turn'.
Modality	A term to signify the author's or speaker's level of 'commitment' to the claim being made within a sentence. Usually, claims are made in terms of obligation or truth. An obligation modality is a statement about what ought to be. An example of obligation modality is the following sentence: 'It is important in politics to have a clear agenda and not get sidetracked by events.' A truth modality is a statement about what is (which is ideologically informed rather than objective). An example of a truth-modality claim is the sentence: 'Australia's education system is in crisis'.
Order of discourse	The power relationship between authors and readers or consumers of text is rarely equal. In most cases, texts exhibit (albeit subtly) unequal power relationships between authors and readers. In some cases, this power relationship is more explicit; for example, academic publications are 'positioned' unambiguously to convey to the reader that the author has detailed knowledge and expertise that the reader is seeking to acquire.

Sources: Fairclough 2000, 2003; adapted from Campsall 2004

Critical discourse analysis

Critical discourse analysis: Research methods associated with the work of Norman Fairclough.

Critical discourse analysis is one of the most influential approaches to discourse analysis in applied social science (areas such as social policy, social geography and politics). The method is associated with Norman Fairclough (1989, 1992, 2000, 2003), and draws on the insights associated with political economy. In particular, critical discourse analysis emphasises the importance of ideology and the discursive strategies that are employed by actors to shape political outcomes. Fairclough's most influential work, *Discourse and Social Change* (Fairclough 1992), sets out a three-dimensional framework of analysis that brings together three analytical traditions on the connections between policy texts and broader political change. His analytical frame includes:

- the micro concerns evident in linguistics
- the meso interpretation on the social production of texts
- the macro analysis associated with social theory.

At the micro and meso levels, text and statements can be studied in specific detail:

- **Textual analysis** examines vocabulary, grammar cohesion and text structure. Text analysis can, for example, reveal how alternative wordings have entered into political language.
- **Discursive practice** requires the researcher to examine the strategic devices used by the author to reinforce argument (for example, rhetoric, exaggeration and irony).
- **Social practice** analyses the discourse by making reference to the wider context and explicit theories of hegemony and power; in particular, the ideological components (explicit or implicit) in texts are discussed within this wider frame.

> **Textual analysis**: Analysis of the vocabulary, grammar cohesion and structure within a text.
>
> **Discursive practice**: A critical discourse analysis method that focuses on rhetorical strategies within a text.
>
> **Social practice**: Method associated with critical discourse analysis to highlight ideology and power relations.

Critical discourse analysis is a common method of discourse analysis in the social sciences, as it provides a clear sequential methodological framework. A model conceptualising Fairclough's three-dimensional framework is set out below.

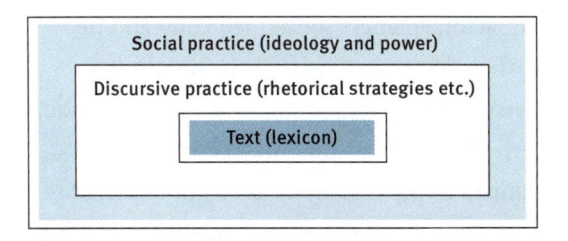

Figure 12.1: Conceptual framework for discourse analysis

Source: Adapted from Fairclough 1992

Foucauldian-inspired analysis

Also influential is the discourse analysis inspired by the writings of Michel Foucault (1971, 1974, 1977, 1980, 1986). Foucault's key argument is that discourses are contested, and that the key task is to identify how discourses exemplify conflicts over meaning that are linked to power. For Foucault, discourse plays a pivotal role in establishing what he calls **regimes of truth**. Regimes of truth are the basis from which we assert our understandings of the social world. From a Foucauldian perspective, our understandings are subject to historical shifts, depending on the ways in which power is exercised. Foucault's understanding of power can be difficult to grasp. In his view, power is not reducible to individual(s), but is instead constituent of a network of relations. In other words, power is contingent on the relationships between individuals.

> **Regimes of truth**: Term used in Foucauldian discourse analysis to denote the basis from which understandings of the social world are asserted.

Keith Jacobs

> **Foucauldian-inspired analysis:** Generic term used in discourse analysis to denote methods associated with the work of Michel Foucault.

In practice, **Foucauldian-inspired analysis** concentrates on making explicit the historical context in which discourse is situated. In contrast to critical discourse analysis, Foucauldian research is less systematic. This is partly because Foucault did not provide any detailed explanation as to how a discourse analysis should proceed (Hastings 1998). Academics who have sought to develop a Foucauldian-based discourse analysis of the policy process, for example Sharp and Richardson (2001:196), interpret discourses 'as a multiple and competing set of ideas and metaphors embracing both text and practices'. Changes in discourse are not viewed as a rational deliberative set of events, but rather as the outcome of power conflicts in which different groups vie to impose their agenda.

A practical example can help make this point clear. In social policy discourse, different interest groups, such as welfare lobbyists, government agencies, industry pressure groups and academics, have sought to impose interpretations of concepts such as 'poverty'. The meanings of these concepts are never static, but change over time, depending on the capacity of interest groups to impose their definition. In the 1960s and 1970s, an understanding of poverty was generally attributed to structural factors, namely social inequality and the impact of government policies. In recent years, there has been a shift in the dominant understanding of poverty to the extent that nowadays it is quite common to stress individual failure and fecklessness as a reason people experience poverty. The shift in common understandings of poverty is viewed by Foucauldian-inspired analysts as symptomatic of the power of neoliberal and conservative pressure groups and the relative weakness of those aligned with social democratic and left-wing politics seeking to establish a more structurally informed conception of poverty.

Foucault's ideas on discourses and power are developed in his books. His most influential work, *Discipline and Punish* (1977), though ostensibly a book about prisons, seeks to show how discipline and surveillance discourses enter into other more generalised discourses in public policy, including education, health and organisational working practices. In *The Order of Things* (1974), he examines the emergence of structuralism as an academic discourse in areas such as psychoanalysis, anthropology and literary criticism, while in *Madness and Civilisation* (1971) he charts how discourses relating to madness and reason are inextricably bound up together. In this work, Foucault sets out to show how understandings of madness are historically contingent. For example, in the Middle Ages madness was viewed more sympathetically and as less threatening. Those deemed mad were assumed to have insights and close access to religion. Only in the seventeenth and eighteenth centuries was madness portrayed as an illness and something that required scientific medical intervention (Andersen 2003:4).

Attempts have recently been made to map out more precisely the different approaches adopted by Foucault over the course of his writing. For example, Andersen (2003:32) argues that Foucault had four different analytical strategies. The most widely known, **archaeological discourse analysis**, seeks to clarify the emergence of different paradigms or truth regimes; **genealogy** seeks to highlight how different disciplinary discourses are superseded at certain historical junctures; **self-technology** highlights the ways in which new discursive practices are ordered; and finally there is **dispositive analysis**, a complementary mode of analysis that seeks to reveal the logic of different practices, institutions and new technologies, and how these combine.

> **Archaeological discourse analysis**: Discourse analysis method based on the writings of Foucault aimed at providing a historical context.
>
> **Genealogy**: Discourse analysis method, associated with Foucault, to show how different discourses are superseded at certain historical junctures.
>
> **Self-technology**: Term used in Foucauldian discourse analysis to denote how new discursive practices are ordered.
>
> **Dispositive analysis**: Used within discourse analysis to denote a Foucauldian mode of analysis that seeks to reveal the logic of different practices.

Analysts who have drawn upon the work of Foucault tend to emphasise the historical context in which a text is situated. This is because discourse, for Foucault, is a particular knowledge about the world, which shapes how the world is understood and how things are done in it (Rose 2001:136). Unlike other forms of discourse analysis, a Foucauldian approach does not attempt to excavate the surface meaning in order to penetrate deeper meanings. Rather, he was interested in the way in which power is exercised and the ways in which texts are discursively produced (Rose 2001). The aim of a Foucauldian-inspired discourse analysis is, therefore, to reveal the power relationships within any text. Those writers who have used Foucault's work (e.g. Dean 1999) have sought to show how neoliberal (laissez-faire) free market ideology has incorporated aspects of welfare-orientated language as a means of securing greater legitimacy. This appropriation of more social forms of governance is characteristic of contemporary politics. For Foucault, discourses establish regimes of truth that to a large extent determine the acceptable formulations of problems and their solution. Texts are construed as representing a body of statements that perform a number of functions (such as rhetorical, legitimising and synthesising). Later in this chapter, an excerpt from a parliamentary speech illustrates the ways in which welfare-orientated language is now used to justify new policies to regulate the behaviour of tenants residing in public housing (see exercise 12.1).

A key task for the researcher wishing to use Foucault's arguments is to show how regimes of truth are articulated and to reveal evidence of contradictions in the text. A Foucauldian-inspired discourse analysis requires the researcher to pay particular attention to the way meanings are produced, to assess the way the text is organised and to reveal how themes are articulated. As Tonkiss (1998:258) writes, this 'requires the researcher to adopt a rather "split" approach to the text'. Tonkiss means by this that it is important to explore not

Keith Jacobs

only how meanings are produced but also to read critically, identifying the connections with other texts, the underlying ideology of the text and the rhetorical strategies used within it.

Table 12.2 provides a summary of how the two different methods of discourse analysis compare.

Table 12.2: Critical discourse analysis and Foucauldian-inspired analysis compared

Critical discourse analysis	Foucauldian-inspired analysis
Detailed critique of text to highlight the connections to ideology and the exercise of power	Seeks to make explicit the connections between text and wider social practice
Three-tier approach: 1 textual analysis 2 discursive practice 3 social practice	Historical and archival, identifying different 'regimes of truth' and how these find expression in text
Popular in the social sciences, especially social policy	Cultural studies, literary and visual criticism, and, to a lesser extent, social policy

Challenges associated with discourse analysis

Discourse analysis, as a social science method, is subject to a number of criticisms. Four common criticisms are explained below.

The selection of texts

Critics point out that discourse analysis-based research is not always clear in setting out its methods. One of the biggest challenges here is the way in which texts are selected. Since any analysis entails the selection of texts and the exclusion of others, it is essential that researchers are open about the ways in which they choose material. In practice, only relatively small pieces of text can be analysed, so the discourse analysis research is potentially always open to allegations of partiality or bias.

Reductionism

Discourse analysis has also been criticised as reducing all aspects of social life to language. Critics argue that, because its focus is primarily linguistic, it falls into the trap of entangling linguistic ideas and concepts with social and spatial practices. Social and spatial practices, however, have a material existence that is independent of their discursive element. In defence, discourse analysts point out that discourse—whether the spoken word or written text—has a material component, and is part of a complex set of social events (Van Dijk 1997; McKenna 2004). Discourse analysts are therefore not seeking to claim that there is no distinction between the material and discursive realm; rather, they are asserting that our access to the material world is mediated through the prism of language and discourse.

The privileging of agency

Another criticism is that discourse analysis privileges individual actors and subjectivity, and understates structural factors that arise from both institutional practices and economic inequalities (Jessop 1991; Badcock 1996). Doing so, it is argued, reduces what are complex phenomena into simplistic categories. In response to this criticism, discourse analysts contextualise individual agency by making clear the wider social and political milieu. In practice, texts are not studied in isolation but are linked to historical and other sources. Text and wider social processes are connected.

Validity issues

Discourse analysis is also portrayed by some critics as obscure and 'unscientific'. A way to counter this criticism is for those using discourse analysis to be as open as possible about the research process and the ways in which texts are selected and analysed. Writing in a style that is clear and accessible is also important. In practice, this requires the researcher to write about his or her own role and the objectives of the research so that others can judge the merits of his or her research and its findings. Another way of testing the **validity** of discourse analysis is to assess how the interpretations put forward accord with other sociological interpretations, and assess the plausibility of the arguments advanced by discourse analysts.

> **Validity (discourse analysis):** The degree to which arguments are coherent and accepted within the text.

Undertaking a discourse analysis

The best way to understand discourse analysis is to see how it operates in practice. The next section of this chapter is practical in focus, working through a critical discourse analysis of a recent article on housing affordability by Bob Day. The major elements of a Foucauldian analysis of the same article are also included. For another exercise based on discourse analysis, see exercise 12.6.

Box 12.1: Using critical discourse analysis to study housing affordability

Background

In recent years, there has been considerable debate in Australia about addressing the shortage of housing for low-income households. Recent data estimate that nearly a million low-income households are paying more than a third of their income on housing-related costs. The issue is widely contested, with interest and pressure groups all trying to influence the government as to the best policy prescription. Critical

Keith Jacobs

discourse analysis offers a methodological framework for looking at the links between the text and wider social debates and ideology, and the textual strategies authors adopt in order to position themselves in key debates to influence the policy agenda.

The excerpt below is from a speech by the former national president of the Housing Industry Association Bob Day, that was reported in the *Australian* in April 2008.

To make the most of this example, first read through the article as a general reader; then work through the article again, following the four tasks of critical discourse analysis detailed on the following pages.

See how discourse analysis reveals and critiques the political arguments that are advanced in the text. Has the way you view the text (note whether you agree with the author or not) changed in reading the discourse analysis of its content?

How to plan for a fiasco

Paragraph 1: For more than 50 years the average Australian was able to buy their first home on the average wage. Traditionally, the median house price was about three times the median household income. Today, in Adelaide, Melbourne and Brisbane, the median house price is more than six times the median income; in Sydney and Perth, it is more than eight times.

Paragraph 2: In 2006 former Reserve Bank of Australia governor Ian Macfarlane asked: 'Why has the price of an entry-level new home gone up as much as it has? Why is it not like it was in 1951 when my parents moved to East Bentleigh, which was the fringe of Melbourne at that stage, and were able to buy a block of land very cheaply and put a house on it very cheaply? I think it is pretty apparent now that reluctance to release new land, plus the new approach whereby the purchaser has to pay for all the services up-front—the sewerage, the roads, the footpaths and all that sort of stuff—has enormously increased the price of the new, entry-level home'.

Paragraph 3: Until the 1970s, land was abundant and affordable, and the development of new suburbs was largely left to the private sector. Our pre- '70s leafy suburbs of large allotments and wide streets are an enduring testimony to the private sector approach.

Paragraph 4: Enter state and territory government land management agencies which, since their inception, have been responsible for astronomical rises in land prices, leading to astronomical mortgage costs. This escalation in land prices, in turn, has pushed up the cost of rental accommodation, road widening and key infrastructure projects, establishing schools, community centres and health services, and so on.

Paragraph 5: State and territory governments were spurred on by an urban planning cheer squad obsessed with curbing the size of our cities and pushing a policy of urban consolidation. The case for urban consolidation was that it was good for the environment, stemmed the loss of agricultural land, encouraged people on to public transport, saved water, led to a reduction in car use and saved on infrastructure costs for government.

Paragraph 6: None of this is true. By promoting urban consolidation while demonising growth, planners have inflicted enormous damage on the economy and society, and politicians and public servants should stop listening to them.

Paragraph 7: The economic consequences have been as profound as they have been damaging. The capital structure of our economy has been distorted to the tune of many hundreds of billions of dollars and getting it back into alignment will take time.

Paragraph 8: California, birthplace of the sub-prime mortgage industry, is paying the highest price of any US state as the housing meltdown there persists. By the end of the year, property values in that state alone will have fallen by $US600 billion. California also has one of the strictest urban planning regimes in the world. It and Florida, another highly regulated urban planning regime, account for about 70 per cent to 80 per cent of all sub-prime losses in the US. Foreclosure losses, however, are significantly lower in low urban planning states such as Texas and Georgia. Like most epidemics, the US sub-prime mortgage housing crisis can be traced back to this one source: urban planning laws. The credit crisis is the direct result of unprecedented house price inflation caused by urban planning policies.

Paragraph 9: In Australia, the housing affordability problem, mortgage stress and the rental crisis are all caused by the same thing.

Source: Bob Day is the former national president of the Housing Industry Association. This is an edited version of a speech he gave to the Adam Smith Club. *Australian*, 22 April 2008 <www.theaustralian.news.com.au>

Undertaking a critical discourse analysis

Task 1: Selection of the text

A primary task before commencing any discourse analysis is to explain why and how a selection of text(s) has been chosen for analysis. This is especially important, as it provides evidence for the reader about the rationale for the analysis. In this case, Day's article was chosen because it is a succinct work of journalism setting out an unambiguous ideological subject position about housing policy in Australia.

Task 2: Social practice: Setting out the political and ideological context

A second task is to provide the reader with the political context in which the article was produced, what Fairclough terms 'social practice'. Day's article attempts to influence a

Keith Jacobs

debate within social policy about how governments should respond to the difficulties experienced by low-income households. On the one side of this debate are the welfare pressure groups such as Shelter and the Australian Council for Social Services (ACOSS), alongside state governments that are calling for more resources to increase the supply of public housing. On the other side, there are those calling for a reduction in planning controls and fewer taxes on speculative property development. Day's article is very much from this latter perspective. He advocates the removal of bureaucratic constraints, and seeks to question interpretations of the housing affordability problem that connect the lack of affordability to poverty. Instead Day argues that all the major housing problems stem from bureaucratic regulation.

As is made clear in the source line of the article, Day is a former president of the Housing Industry Association (a lobby group representing house builders) and that the article is a shortened version of speech he gave to the Adam Smith Club, a society that promotes the free market. The article, and speech, attributed blame for the lack of low-cost housing in Australia on planners and state and territory land management agencies.

Task 3: Textual analysis

The main component of critical discourse analysis is a study of the text itself. The analysis that follows selects some key sentences to show how the author has carefully sought to elicit a response from readers about the causes of the housing affordability problem and the most appropriate modes of intervention.

The author uses various devices in the text to denigrate oppositional discourses and to extol the credibility of his own arguments. First, consider sentences of paragraph 1 and 2 in which Day makes the claim that the high cost of housing is only a recent phenomenon, and cites the governor of the Reserve Bank of Australia as evidence to reinforce his conceptualisation of the problem. In making reference to the past and the governor of the Reserve Bank, Day is seeking to demonstrate the legitimacy of his argument. It is evidence of what is known as **intertextuality**, for Day is making reference to other accounts to buttress his subject position.

Intertextuality: Term used in discourse analysis to denote how texts contain linkages to other sources.

Genre: A particular form of expression, with its own established structural and stylistic conventions; the style in which texts are produced and consumed.

A critical discourse analysis also needs to make plain the **genre** of the text. In this selected text, the genre is an opinion piece published in the broadsheet newspaper, the *Australian*. These opinion pieces are a common feature of newspapers, providing space for prominent individuals to argue from a particular perspective. For example, though the *Australian* includes writers from a left-wing perspective, as part of the News International stable of newspapers owned by Rupert Murdoch, it is widely viewed as politically neoliberal. The article by Day is therefore not atypical of the newspaper's opinion pieces, in that it unambiguously adopts a free market approach to social policy problems and, by implication, is dismissive of welfare-orientated perspectives.

Further on in the article, in paragraph 6, Day claims 'by promoting urban consolidation while demonising growth, planners have inflicted enormous damage on the economy and society'. The above quotation is an example of what is known as **cohesion**; that is, the way in which certain words are arranged and linked together to elicit a particular response. In this extract, 'planners' are linked to a 'enormous damage'. The **order of discourse** is used to disparage alternative interpretations that do not concord with the argument advanced by Day.

> **Cohesion**: Denotes how terms are used to elicit a particular response.
>
> **Orders of discourse**: Power relationships that exist between readers and producers of texts. These are rarely equal.

Task 4: Discursive practice

In overall terms, Day has framed his article to advance a controversial policy diagnosis as a set of self-evident truths. The style and frame of the article is purposefully constructed to make the diagnosis appear rational and commonsensical. One of the techniques is to insert what are known as truth modality claims. For example, consider paragraph 4, in which the author asserts: 'State and territory government land agencies, since their inception, have been responsible for astronomical rises in land prices, leading to astronomical mortgage costs.' This assertion is ideologically loaded and unambiguous, leaving the reader in no doubt about the general political perspective being adopted. To reinforce the argument, paragraph 8 makes reference to the economic problems in the US, which have been attributed to the sub-prime mortgage industry. A sentence in paragraph 8 asserts that 'like most epidemics, the US sub-prime mortgage housing crisis can be traced back to this one source: urban planning laws'. In making this assertion, the author is inviting the reader to understand the 'housing crisis' is a consequence of excessive planning restrictions limiting the amount of land available for property construction.

The text is part of a persuasive strategy to convince readers of the negative consequences of urban planning controls. Day has carefully provided a policy scenario to make it appear that all housing problems can be traced back to this one source. For example, at the end of the article (paragraph 9), Day writes that 'in Australia, the housing affordability problem, mortgage stress and the rental crisis are all caused by the same thing'. This text is a strategic ploy to substantiate his argument in paragraphs 6 and 7 on the role of planners and their efforts to limit urban sprawl.

Keith Jacobs

There are also some interesting sentences that seek to belittle planning-based approaches through carefully selected words. For example, in the first sentence of paragraph 5, Day writes 'state and territory governments were spurred on by an urban policy cheer squad obsessed with curbing the size of our cities'. The use of the words 'cheer squad' is intended to cast aspersion on the credentials of those who might take an alternative view. The belittling of alternative perspectives is the central part of his argument, as there is little evidence to show why planning controls are the cause of house price inflation. The ideological assumptions rest on a version of politics that eschews government regulation in the housing market, and instead advances prescriptions that would limit the capacity of local and state governments to manage the development process. This brief analysis of Day's article provides an indication of what critical discourse analysis can achieve in highlighting the way in which texts are purposefully constructed. An important point to remember is that the analysis can be more or less extensive, depending on the level of detail required.

Foucauldian-inspired analysis

A Foucauldian-inspired analysis of the newspaper article written by Day would be less systematic, but in practice would cover similar territory. The emphasis of the analysis would be primarily historical and archival; that is, making connections between the arguments presented by Day and other wider discourses prevalent in social policy. A characteristic of Foucauldian-inspired discourse analysis is the attention paid to the silences in the text, that is, value statements that are omitted from the text but nevertheless can be imputed from a reading of the text as a whole. A discussion of any text's significance is always one of interpretation. In this text, Day assumes the case for the free market, not by making detailed arguments to support his view, but by castigating alternative interpretations. His article can be read as an attempt to undermine current Australian urban planning controls. Day dismisses the value of planning agencies and castigates their urban land management approach.

The ideology that Day draws upon is one implicit in most neoliberal discourses, namely the valorisation of market-based mechanisms and denigration of regulatory modes of governance that seek to limit the negative impact of free markets. A Foucauldian analysis would almost certainly draw on other textual sources to corroborate arguments and also seek to contextualise the text historically. Those writers who use Foucault seek to both interpret the rhetorical and legitimising narratives of the text and, if possible, provide examples of contradictions or ruptures within the narrative. It should be clear from this brief discussion that a Foucauldian analysis seeks to build up as much information as possible on the social and political debates in which a text is located, and places less emphasis on making any inferences specifically from the text itself.

Exercise 12.1: The example of antisocial behaviour

Exercise 12.1 contains an extract from a speech by Matthew Morris, a Labor member of the Legislative Assembly in the New South Wales Parliament representing Charlestown (New South Wales Parliament 2008). The speech, delivered 7 December 2007, presents arguments for the introduction of 'antisocial behaviour contracts' for public housing tenants deemed to be perpetuators of antisocial behaviour. Read the passage carefully and then answer the questions at the end of the extract. These are typical of some of the issues explored by researchers engaged in a discourse analysis. The passage has been selected because it provides an example of how politicians are keen to support policies that reprimand individuals who are viewed as transgressing 'normal' standards of behaviour. The attempt by governments to address 'antisocial behaviour' can be viewed as part of a wider attempt to tackle some of the issues commonly associated with poverty. In contrast to previous government policies in the 1960s and 1970s, which stressed social inequality as a causal factor to explain crime and poverty, government agencies, in countries like Australia, the United Kingdom, and the USA, frequently connect antisocial behaviour with individual fecklessness and moral ineptitude. In practice, policy recommendations emphasise individual responsibility rather than increased government intervention to address structural inequality.

Antisocial behaviour programs

Background

Over the last 20 years, there is a perception that the problems of antisocial behaviour (such as vandalism, crime, and neighbourhood conflicts) have intensified, and there has been pressure on politicians to develop new policies to tackle these perceptions. In the extract below, NSW politician Matthew Morris (New South Wales Parliament 2008) makes the case for the antisocial behaviour contracts used in the UK to penalise individuals who engage in 'antisocial behaviour practices'.

Private members statements

Paragraph 1: Mr MATTHEW MORRIS (Charlestown) [12.49 p.m.]: Along with all developed countries, Australia still faces difficult challenges from drug addiction, violent crime and antisocial behaviour. The result of that is over time a minority of small groups or individuals responsible for it have come to think that they are untouchable and above the law. These challenges need to be overcome if we are to create and advance to a safer, secure and progressive society. I have listened to my community, to police officers, to lead agency staff, councils and courts about what the problems are and what could be done to rectify them.

Keith Jacobs

Paragraph 2: My conclusion is that a that a package of measures is required to give the police, housing officers, local authorities and courts the powers to tip the balance firmly in favour of the law-abiding majority. I recently had the pleasure of hosting guests from the United Kingdom, including Sergeant Paul Dunn MBE, a member of the Metropolitan Police Service Anti-social Behaviour Team; Mr Edmund Hall, Crown Prosecution Service, London, Antisocial Behaviour Order Specialist Prosecutor; and Mr Steve Waggott, the Charlton Athletic Club Trust Chief Executive. These gentlemen gave of their time in visiting the Charlestown electorate and participating in a local community forum.

Paragraph 3: Leading agencies, community organisations and not-for-profit service providers attended the forum. I thank them sincerely for sharing their knowledge and experience, which they introduced to my constituency of Charlestown. I want to introduce into the House programs that are currently United Kingdom based, that is, acceptable behaviour contracts and antisocial behaviour orders. An acceptable behaviour contract is a written, voluntary agreement between a person who has been involved in antisocial behaviour and one or more local agencies whose role it is to prevent such behaviour. The contracts save thousands of hours in court and police time, enabling officers to be in their communities deterring and catching criminals.

Paragraph 4: Antisocial behaviour contracts are useful for stopping low levels of antisocial behaviour and nipping it in the bud. Their flexibility means they can also be used effectively in other more serious or problematic situations. Contracts are agreed to and signed at meetings with the individual and the lead agencies. The contract specifies a list of antisocial acts that the person can be shown to have been involved with and which they agree not to continue. The contract can also include positives, such as activities that will help prevent recurrence, such as attending school. The flexible nature of antisocial behaviour contracts means that they can be used incrementally. This means that very minor misdemeanours are dealt with quickly, requiring nothing more than a simple contract with one agency.

Paragraph 5: Where behaviour is more problematic—either because it is persistent or because it is serious—support to address the underlying causes of the behaviour should be offered in parallel with the contract. This may include diversionary activities, such as attendance at a youth project, counselling or support for the family. It is therefore vital to establish which agencies are already involved in the case so as to maximise the opportunities for cooperation and to minimise the risk of duplication or inconsistency. An antisocial behaviour order is only stated on the acceptable behaviour contract where there is potential that the individual will break the contract and that breach then leads to a legal consequence. The prospect of a more formal, legal intervention can provide an added incentive to adhere to the contract.

Paragraph 6: Antisocial behaviour contracts have been used in the United Kingdom to address a wide range of antisocial behaviour with great success. That behaviour includes harassment of residents or passers-by, criminal damage, vandalism, noise nuisance, graffiti, substance abuse and joy riding. Australia has assessed the United Kingdom-based programs, where results continue to be achieved in and around London. Clearly looking at what is achievable within the United Kingdom, there is potential to consider implementation of the programs in New South Wales.

Paragraph 7: I have undertaken discussions with the Attorney General's Department, which is currently considering a range of similar contracts and orders to be implemented in New South Wales. Those programs will be tailored to suit our particular needs, given the range of issues that we deal with. Visits by the United Kingdom guests clearly demonstrated that other options are available to deal with antisocial behaviour, particularly juvenile crime. I hope that in future appropriate orders and contracts will be in place, not too dissimilar to the United Kingdom models, that can be used to deal with issues that are vitally important to local communities.

Task

Read through the text of this speech and then answer the questions at the end of the exercise, analysing the speech from a discourse analysis framework.

Questions for discussion

1. What ideological discourses, or positions, are being drawn upon in the argument made by Matthew Morris to support the introduction of new antisocial behaviour contracts? How could these arguments be critiqued? Are there alternative perspectives? Can you spot different policy rationales within the text?
2. Identify instances where the speaker has deployed rhetorical strategies (a device to persuade the audience that the arguments presented are valid and coherent).
3. What is the political context that has made the arguments to introduce contracts appear plausible?
4. What does the text tell us about contemporary Australian society? In particular, what is the dynamic of power relations that enables politicians to frame issues of crime and disorder in this way?

Keith Jacobs

Voices in the field

Brendan Churchill

Brendan Churchill is a research higher degree candidate in his first year, and the broad subject of his research is Generation Y and the labour market. In the paragraphs below he discusses using discourse analysis (along with content analysis) in his honours research.

'For my honours thesis, I wanted to research a topic within the field of Indigenous issues, but it was not until the emergence of sexual abuse claims in the Northern Territory and the media attention they afforded did I narrow my topic down to representations of Indigenous family violence. My research question was primarily informed by the availability, or unavailability in my case, of data on Indigenous family violence. So I decided to look at how Indigenous family violence was presented in the media. The Nanette Rogers exposé and ensuing media onslaught was current and accessible. To achieve my research aims, I utilised two research methods: a quantitative content analysis of all available newspaper articles on Indigenous family violence over a 12-month period and a critical discourse analysis of Louis Nowra's *Bad Dreaming: Aboriginal Men's Violence Against Women and Children*.

'My critical discourse analysis of Nowra's extended essay followed Fairclough's three-dimensional model and sought to look at the text's language, syntax and the wider sociocultural themes. The critical discourse analysis found that Indigenous family violence was overwhelmingly portrayed as cultural—an integral part of Indigenous life itself. Within Nowra's text, he explicitly and implicitly treats Indigenous family violence as 'other', different from ordinary everyday family violence, positing that the explanation for this differentness is to be found in the Indigene. For example, he always refers to the people in his case studies as Aboriginal—an Aboriginal man or an Aboriginal girl, rather than as a man or a girl—even though his work is entirely about Indigenous people. As such, this device emphasises and re-emphasises the Indigeneity of the victims and the perpetrators.

'This finding of the positioning of Indigenous family violence as specifically Indigenous in nature and explanation was not only at odds with my review of literature surrounding this topic, but clearly demonstrated the divide between the media's perception and other understandings.

'To further interpret my results, I discussed these findings alongside my theoretical framework based on the works of social theorists Edward Said and Michel

Foucault. Against my theoretical framework, I determined that Indigenous family violence was portrayed as cultural and traditional to reinforce the idea of Indigenous Australians as the "Other".

'The research process was instrumental to the success of my honours thesis and has become an invaluable tool for not only my PhD thesis, but also a cornerstone for my research skills.'

From method to practice

Discourse analysis is often used as a method to explore the politics and media interface; for example, the reporting of the Australian 2007 election and the portrayal of Aboriginal people in the national media. By reading this chapter and working through the exercise, you will have acquired an understanding of discourse analysis, its rationale and the insights that it offers for understanding the social world. However, to develop the analytical skills to use discourse analysis effectively in your research will also require you to read examples of work that has deployed this method and acquire knowledge about the pitfalls of this approach. It is also helpful to adopt a critical approach when reading texts you encounter on a day-to-day basis, such as newspapers and magazines, noting for example the strategies deployed by the author to convey authority and the way in which the text draws from ideological arguments. It is also a good idea to talk about articles you have read with friends and colleagues: these conversations will help you develop a more critical line of argument—an essential attribute for using discourse analysis as a tool. Finally, make the effort to read some of the articles that appear in journals such as *Critical Discourse Studies* and key books listed at the end of this chapter.

Keith Jacobs

Conclusion

Discourse analysis provides a useful methodology for the social science researcher seeking to explore the significance of language and the way in which it is deployed to secure ideological and political objectives. However, some caution is required when using a discourse approach so as not to imbue too much significance into text, thereby overlooking wider social and material practices. Discourse analysis is most successful when used as a method to supplement other qualitative research techniques, such as in-depth interviews and participant observation. At its best, a discourse analysis provides opportunities to engage in an informed analysis that can help shed light on the ways in which power is exercised in society. Though this chapter has focused on the production of written texts, there is scope to use the methods of discourse analysis in other areas, including visual representation and other texts. To broaden your knowledge of qualitative methods read the on-line modules on narrative research, conversation analysis, action research, ethnographic research, memory work and sensory and visual methods; these are available at <www.oup.com.au/orc/walter>.

Main points

> There are different ways to engage in a discourse analysis. Some of the most influential in social sciences are the methods associated with Norman Fairclough (known as critical discourse analysis), Michel Foucault (Foucauldian analysis), and Jonathan Potter, Margaret Wetherell and others (discursive psychology).

> Discourse analysis is a method of research to highlight the importance of language in particular texts.

> The aim of discourse analysis is to provide a critical understanding of how language is deployed by making explicit the political context in which texts are situated.

> Discourse analysis entails asking clear and insightful questions about the text and its significance.

> Discourse analysis views language not as a neutral or transparent medium, but as a performative act, and hence inseparable from practice.

> A critical discourse analysis entails a number of tasks (social practice, discursive practice, and textual analysis).

> A Foucauldian-inspired analysis adopts a more historical approach and seeks to make connections between text and wider social practices. There is less of an attempt to make inferences specifically from the text itself.

> Be aware of the criticisms that are frequently made against discourse analysis (selecting texts, reductionism, privileging agency, and validity issues).

> When undertaking a discourse analysis, aim to be both systematic and explicit when developing your arguments, and be careful not to infer too much significance into the text.

> Discourse analysis is often best used as a supplementary method alongside other qualitative research techniques.

> It is a critical mode of analysis and is best suited to research that is seeking to highlight the political significance of text (that is, policy documents and political statements).

Further reading

There are some excellent introductory articles and books on the methods associated with discourse analysis.

For a brief summary, see the work of Tonkiss (1998), and for a more extensive introduction, see the books by Fairclough (2003), Wodak and Meyer (2001), Wooffit (2005), Fairclough et al. (2007) and Widdowson (2007). A reader that includes some of the seminal texts is Wetherell et al. (2001b). Students interested in the discourse analysis approach popular with psychologists should consult Wetherell et al. (2001a) and Potter (2004). For a review of discourse analysis in the field of urban policy, see Jacobs (2006).

An Australian-based research from a Foucauldian perspective can be found in Lee and Poynton's (2000) edited collection. Other recent Australian examples are Marston (2003, 2004) and Mee (2004). Marston's analysis of public housing in Queensland draws principally on critical discourse methods, and is notable for its accessible style and clarity of argument. Mee's (2004) study provides an extensive discourse analysis of newspaper texts to identify discursive shifts in Australian housing policy in New South Wales. A useful book that provides an overview of Foucault's methods is Kendall and Wickham (1999).

Critical Discourse Studies, a journal published by Routledge <www.tandf.co.uk/journals/titles/17405904.asp>, explores some of the key debates surrounding discourse analysis. Finally, students interested in the application of discourse analysis to visual production should make use of the excellent book by Rose (2001).

Keith Jacobs

References

Andersen, N. (2003). *Discursive Analytical Strategies.* Bristol: Policy Press.

Antaki, C., Billig, M., Edwards, D. and Potter, J. (2003). 'Discourse Analysis Means Doing Analysis: A Critique of Six Analytical Shortcomings', *Discourse Analysis Online,* 1 <www.shu.ac.uk/daol/previous/v1/n1/index.htm>.

Ashmore, M. (1989). *The Reflexive Thesis: Wrighting Sociology of Scientific Knowledge.* Chicago and London: University of Chicago Press.

Augostinos, M. and Reynolds, K. (eds) (2001). *Understanding Prejudice, Racism and Social Conflict.* London: Sage.

Augostinos, M. and Walker, I. (1995). *Social Cognition: An Integrated Introduction.* London: Sage.

Badcock, B. (1996). '"Looking glass" Views of the City', *Progress in Geography,* 20: 91–9.

Billig, M. (1995). *Banal Nationalism.* London: Sage.

Campsall, S. (2004). *Glossary of Linguistic Terms* <www.englishbiz.co.uk/grammar/index.htm>. Accessed 10 March 2005.

Day, B. (2008) 'How to Plan for a Fiasco', *Australian,* 22 April. <www.theaustralian.news.com.au/story/0,25197,23576957-7583,00.html>. Accessed 28 April 2008.

Dean, M. (1999). *Governmentality: Power and Rule in Modern Society.* London: Sage.

Edwards, D. (1997). *Discourse and Cognition.* London and Beverly Hills, CA: Sage.

Fairclough, N. (1989). *Language and Power.* London: Longman.

Fairclough, N. (1992). *Discourse and Social Change.* Cambridge: Polity Press.

Fairclough, N. (1995). *Critical Discourse Analysis.* London: Longman.

Fairclough, N. (2000). *New Labour, New Language?* London: Routledge.

Fairclough, N. (2003). *Analysing Discourse: Textual Analysis for Social Research.* London: Routledge.

Fairclough, N., Graham, P., Lemke, J. and Wodak, R. (2004). 'Introduction', *Critical Discourse Studies,* 1 (1): 1–7.

Fairclough, N., Cortese, G. and Ardizzone, P. (eds) (2007). *Discourse in Contemporary Social Change.* Bern: Peter Lang.

Foucault, M. (1971). *Madness and Civilisation.* London: Routledge.

Foucault, M. (1974). *The Order of Things: An Archaeology of the Human Sciences.* London: Tavistock.

Foucault, M. (1977). *Discipline and Punish.* London: Penguin.

Foucault, M. (1980). *Power/Knowledge: Selected Interviews and Other Writings 1972–1977.* Brighton: Harvester.

Foucault, M. (1986). *The Archaeology of Knowledge.* London: Tavistock.

Foucault, M. (1991). 'Governmentality', in Burchell, G., Gordon, C. and Miller, P. (eds), *The Foucault Effect: Studies in Governmentality.* Hemel Hempstead: Harvester: 87–104.

Garfinkel, H. (1967). S*tudies in Ethnomethodology.* Englewood Cliffs, NJ: Prentice Hall.

Hastings, A. (1998). 'Connecting Linguistic Structures and Social Practices: A Discursive Approach to Social Policy Analysis', *Journal of Social Policy*, 27 (2): 191–211.

Hastings, A. (1999). 'Introduction: Special Issue: Discourse and Urban Change', *Urban Studies*, 36 (1): 7–12.

Hastings, A. (2000). 'Discourse Analysis: What Does It Offer Housing Studies?', *Housing, Theory and Society*, 17 (3): 131–9 <www.englishbiz.co.uk/grammar/main_files/definitionsa-m.htm#Discourse>.

Jacobs, K. (2006) 'Discourse Analysis and Its Utility for Urban Policy Research', *Urban Policy and Research*, 24 (1): 39–52.

Jessop, B. (1991). 'Foreword', in Bertramsen, R., Peter, J., Thomsen, F. and Torfing, J. (eds), *State, Economy and Society.* London: Allen & Unwin: xiv–xxvii.

Kendall, G. and Wickham, G. (1999). *Using Foucault's Methods.* London: Sage.

Lee, A. and Poynton, C. (eds) (2000). *Culture and Text: Discourse and Methodology in Social Research and Cultural Studies.* St Leonards: Allen & Unwin.

Marston, G. (2003). 'Metaphor, Morality and Myth: A Critical Discourse Analysis of Public Housing Policy in Queensland', *Critical Social Policy*, 20 (3): 349–73.

Marston, G. (2004). *Social Policy and Discourse Analysis.* Aldershot: Ashgate Press.

McHoul, A. (1996). *Semiotic Investigations: Towards an Effective Semiotics.* Lincoln: University of Nebraska Press.

McHoul, A. and Rapley, M. (eds) (2001). *How to Analyse Talk in Institutional Settings: A Casebook of Methods.* London and New York: Continuum.

McKenna, B. (2004). 'Critical Discourse Analysis: Where To From Here?', *Critical Discourse Studies*, 1 (1): 9–39.

Mee, K. (2004). 'Necessary Welfare Measure or Policy Failure: Media Reports of Public Housing in Sydney in the 1990s', in Jacobs, K., Kemeny, J. and Manzi, T. (eds), *Social Constructionism in Housing Research.* Aldershot: Ashgate Press.

Keith Jacobs

New South Wales Parliament (2008). *Proceedings from the Legislative Assembly Hansard*, <www.parliament.nsw.gov.au/prod/PARLMENT/hansArt.nsf/V3Key/LA20071207018>.

Potter, J. (1996). *Representing Reality: Discourse, Rhetoric and Social Constructionism.* London: Sage.

Potter, J. (2003). 'Discourse Analysis and Discursive Psychology', in Camic, P., Rhodes, J. and Yardley, L. (eds), *Qualitative Research in Psychology: Expanding Perspectives in Methodology and Design.* Washington: American Psychological Association: 73–94.

Potter, J. (2004). 'Discourse Analysis as a Way of Analysing Naturally Occurring Talk', in Silverman, D. (ed.), *Qualitative Research: Theory, Method and Practice*, 2nd edn. London: Sage: 200–21.

Rapley, M. (2004). *The Social Construction of Intellectual Disability.* Cambridge: Cambridge University Press.

Rose, G. (2001). *Visual Methodologies.* London: Sage.

Sacks, H. (1992). *Lectures on Conversation, Vols. I and II.* Jefferson, G. (ed.) Oxford: Blackwell.

Sharp, L. and Richardson, T. (2001). 'Reflections on Foucauldian Discourse Analysis in Planning and Environmental Policy Research', *Journal of Environmental Policy and Planning*, 3 (3): 103–209.

Tonkiss, F. (1998). 'Analysing Discourse', in Seale, C. (ed.), *Researching Culture and Society.* London: Sage: 245–60.

Van Dijk, T. (ed.) (1997). *Discourse Studies: A Multidisciplinary Introduction. Vol. 1: Discourse as Structure and Process. Vol. 2: Discourse as Social Interaction.* London: Sage.

Wetherell, M., Taylor, S. and Yates, S. (eds) (2001a). *Discourse as Data: A Guide For Analysis.* London: Sage.

Wetherell, M., Taylor, S. and Yates, S. (eds) (2001b). *Discourse Theory and Practice: A Reader.* London: Sage.

Widdowson, G. (2007). *Discourse Analysis*, Oxford: Oxford University Press.

Wittgenstein, L. (1974). *Philosophical Investigations.* Oxford: Blackwell.

Wodak, R. and Meyer, M. (2001). *Methods of Critical Discourse Analysis.* London: Sage.

Wooffit, R. (2005). *Conversation Analysis and Discourse Analysis : A Comparative and Critical Introduction.* London: Sage.

Chapter 13

Doing Evaluation Research

Rob White

Evaluating the Inside-Out Prison Program

The Inside-Out Program is directed at providing material and non-material support to prisoners and their families, with the aim of preventing suicide and self-harm among prisoners. An evaluation of the program at Risdon Prison was commissioned by Corrective Services Tasmania in 2003. The terms of reference for the evaluation of the Inside-Out Program were:

Appropriateness, efficiency and effectiveness
- whether Inside-Out has a relevant role in the Tasmanian prison system in reducing reoffending
- whether Inside-Out has relevant roles to play other than in reducing reoffending
- whether Inside-Out is an efficient means by which to achieve collaboration and progress both inside and outside the Tasmanian prison system in line with established core values and principles.

Processes
- whether alternative mechanisms could have been adopted to better deliver on the aims of reducing stresses on prisoners and detainees as well as reducing recidivism when the program was initially being scoped
- whether it would be desirable to change any current practices to ensure alignment and consistency of process in order to better distinguish Inside-Out from other prisoner support programs

Management and administration
- whether allocation resources, including budgets, lines of accountability and authorisation are appropriate and effective, and if not, what changes should be made to increase performance and better measure progress into the future
- whether the current administrative structure is adequate.

Source: White & Mason 2003

Key terms

benchmarks	implementation	primary sources
contextual analysis	limitations	process
environment assessment	multi-agency cooperation	scoping
evaluation	naturalistic	secondary sources
experimental methods	outcomes	social mapping
formative evaluation	performance indicators	strategic partnerships
impact	performance targets	summative evaluation

Introduction

Evaluation: A process of assessing what we are doing, valuing why we are doing it and understanding how we can make improvements in the future.

Evaluation is basically about assessing what we are doing, evaluating why we are doing it and understanding how we can make improvements in the future. Evaluation research, therefore, is basically about determining how a particular initiative is working, and what might be done to improve its chances of success or, indeed, to stop it altogether. This chapter explores the ways in which we might actually 'do' evaluation, but is not a blueprint. Rather, the chapter is more akin to an evaluation toolbox, containing the various understandings and methods used by evaluation researchers. The practical framework for these is demonstrated through the case study of the phases of the Inside-Out prison program evaluation. In the case study above, this program is outlined, along with the terms of reference for the evaluation project.

Evaluation is a social enterprise. Like most social research methods, it directly involves people. As such, an evaluation can never be simply a technical exercise, or something for which there is a recipe. Evaluation research requires open reflection about aims and objectives; an acknowledgment of the diverse reasons for undertaking evaluation; recognition of the moral and ethical responsibilities associated with evaluation; conscious thinking about **outcomes** and **processes** of the program; a professional approach to the gathering of information; clarity in presentation of findings; and a culture of constant appraisal.

Outcomes: The specific consequences of a particular course of action.

Process: Progressive changes over time, which may include actions directed towards a particular result.

The unique aspects of evaluation research

Evaluation research also differs from other social research methods.

First, evaluation research tends to revolve around specific projects (such as a youth project that involves teaching young offenders about car maintenance and safety issues), specific programs (such as a school program designed to reduce truancy among students) or specific intervention strategies (such as the use of juvenile conferencing as an alternative to court or to detention).

Second, the impetus for evaluation research does not usually originate with the researcher. In most cases, evaluation will be commissioned by a state agency, a business organisation or a professional body. This means that the terms of reference—what is being evaluated and how—are frequently predetermined by those funding the evaluation (see above). This can influence the evaluation process in terms of budgets, who is consulted and the potential outcomes of the evaluation.

Third, evaluation research is inherently political. Because evaluation is ultimately about making judgments, and these in turn may have significant consequences for the actors involved in the evaluation, such research also tends to be more overtly politicised than other types of social research. The institutional environment within which agencies or businesses operate will shape how they construct and how they respond to the evaluation. In the light of this, it is vital that evaluators be vigilant in protecting the integrity of their work, and that they be clear about their independence. From an evaluator's perspective, the success or otherwise of any particular strategy or specific project cannot be taken for granted, no matter how good the intentions of the people involved or how laudable the goals and objectives.

Purposes of evaluation

The actual purpose of an evaluation must be clearly identified if we are to establish what it is we in fact wish to measure. These include:

- **impact** or outcomes: as a means to check or audit progress towards specified ends
- process and **implementation**: as a means to investigate the scope, reach and interactions associated with an intervention
- program management and administration: as a means to gauge competency of performance
- identification of needs: as a means of opening up areas for further investigation, defining whether or not something is a problem, and instigating possible program development.

Impact: The effect of a particular course of action.

Implementation: Putting something into practice.

Underlying these, however, is the primary purpose of most evaluation research: a need to know concretely whether or not something is making a difference.

Another major driver of evaluation research is that projects, programs or interventions are not static, but are in a continual state of flux or change (e.g. changes in personnel, changes in methods of service delivery). Process or continuous evaluation, therefore, is important to monitor such changes over time.

Ideally, evaluation should be an integral part of any initiative rather than a discrete post-program option. The timeframe of evaluation should be continuous, in the sense of monitoring the social processes associated with conceptualisation and implementation of specific initiatives, and time specific, in the sense of providing snapshots of impacts and outcomes at any point in time.

Rob White

Undertaking an evaluation

Evaluation can take a number of different forms, approaches and methods, and the model used is a matter of design. From the very beginning, evaluation is about making decisions. Clarification of aims and objectives, processes and responsibilities and intended outcomes is vital to maximise efficient use of resources and to minimise potential misunderstandings about the purposes and uses of the evaluation. This process takes place over three discrete stages: planning, methods and techniques. The essential questions the evaluator needs to ask themselves and others as a guide through these stages are summarised in box 13.1.

Box 13.1: Central planning questions

What?

- What precisely is to be evaluated? What is its focus in relation to agency, community, process, and outcome?
- What values underlie the evaluation's intended outcomes? Are these participatory, administrative, proving efficiency and effectiveness, social empowerment or continuous improvement?
- What are the potential conflicts? Might conflict occur between participants in the evaluation group, or between the evaluation group and other members of the community?
- What are the intended outcomes? Is the evaluation to measure competence of a funded agency, to determine community perceptions, or to identify where to go to from here?
- What is the intended product? Is it a written report, an oral briefing and/or recommendations, or all three?

Why?

- Why is the evaluation taking place? Is it the result of community pressure; for example, an initiative of the council to enhance service provisions?
- Why do these questions need to be answered? Are the reasons for evaluation in relation to existing uses of resources, effects of a program and so on?

Who?

- For whom is the evaluation being undertaken?
- Who will be part of the evaluation team?
- Who are the key stakeholders involved in, or affected by, the evaluation; for example, agency personnel, police, community groups and possible interview subjects?

How?

- How are the main sources of information or data collected to be identified, and how will the method be determined? What resources can be drawn upon in this process (including both information sources and agency resources)?
- How will the criteria that will be used to serve as benchmarks for the assessment be determined? How do we ensure that they relate to the object and purposes of the evaluation?

When?

- When is the evaluation to take place? What are the completion timelines, and when do specific tasks need to be carried out and by whom?

Stage 1: Planning

Effective evaluation research relies on solid and thorough pre-project planning. The evaluation must relate to the specific principles and objectives of a particular program or project, making reference to the broad social vision that underpins any initiatives, programs or projects, and their specific intent and focus. The environment, internal and external, of the evaluation project, the setting up of administrative structures to support and define the evaluation and working out the resources available and needed are also all important aspects.

Scoping the project framework

The first step is to examine the nature of the project or policy to be evaluated. We need to gain a sense of the history of the initiative and its current assumptions and values. The idea of **scoping** refers to the review of the specific aims, targets and strategies of a particular program or project. The kind of information we need at this stage includes:

> **Scoping**: The review of specific aims, targets and strategies of a particular program or project.

- What is the problem, and why is it perceived to be a problem?
- Which interest groups are associated with or affected by the problem, and how do they perceive the nature of the problem?
- Who or what is affected by the problem?
- What is the extent and seriousness of the problem?
- What kind of 'needs analysis' (including literature review) was undertaken in determining the nature of the problem?
- What sort of data (quantitative and qualitative) has already been collected (if any) in relation to the specific problem the project is trying to address?
- Who instigated the project and why?

- What assumptions and values underlie the project aims and objectives?
- What specific interventions or strategies have been adopted by the project and why?

Environment assessment

Environment assessment: Analysis of the context within which research or evaluation is to occur, such as auditing the human and material resources needed for a project and examining the policies that might affect its development.

Limitations: Limits or weaknesses of a project or a particular form of data collection, that ought to be acknowledged in undertaking social research and in interpreting the findings of social and evaluation research.

Another essential precondition is to undertake an **environmental assessment**, or a preliminary analysis of the context within which the evaluation will take place. This has a number of dimensions.

Internal focus

Evaluation requires human and material resources and we need to be aware of the strengths and **limitations** of the agency or body funding and/or undertaking the evaluation. Key questions and issues here include:

- available resources, such as computers, paper and telephones
- budget, especially the relationship of financial resources to the kind and extent of evaluation required or desired
- culture of the workplace, and specific values and principles that might underlie the evaluation process, such as perspectives on aims and objectives
- staff skills, such as technical expertise, in areas such as interviewing, telephone contacting, computer analysis and report writing
- staff morale; for example, evaluation as adding to stress or as means of relieving tensions
- availability of outside financial assistance and human resources, either via direct funding bodies or other sources
- timing of evaluation relative to agency peak periods of activity or service provision, and to grant application deadlines.

External focus

Evaluation also must make reference to, and be undertaken in the light of, developments outside the specific agency context. Background information could be sought on questions and issues such as:

- national and state policy initiatives and programs relevant to the specific activity of the agency; such as specific initiatives and demonstration projects from elsewhere
- policy changes at the national, state and local level that may have a bearing on agency work and the evaluation process, such as funding allocations and priority projects

- social and community issues in the local area, such as those based on events, media reports and statistical trends
- literature on activities related to the initiative, such as needs studies, consultation reports, other evaluation reports and research articles
- identification of main opportunities raised, and threats posed by the evaluation process and potential findings to funding bodies, government agencies and community groups
- **social mapping** of local conditions and factors that may influence specific project development, and evaluation processes, such as the physical environment, **demographic data**, and the role and activity of authority figures such as the police.

Social mapping: A description of local social conditions, key players and social factors that may influence specific project development and evaluation processes.

Demographic data: Data that categorise groups of individuals according to such characteristics as their age, sex, marital status and birth and death rates.

Once an assessment is made of the context, and what may be required to be done before, or as part of, the evaluation process, then the planning process can begin in earnest.

Administrative structures

Evaluation can be a relatively simple or a complicated process, depending upon its aims and the number of people involved as both participants and organisers. To maximise the climate for effective evaluation practice, there are a number of administrative issues that need to be worked out before evaluation begins.

Conflicts over purposes

It is essential to define the aims and objectives of the evaluation in relation to particular conceptions of the program, project or strategy at hand, and, if need be, to establish a hierarchy of aims and objectives in cases where there are multiple aims. In commissioned work, it is particularly important to clarify the evaluation brief by negotiating matters relating to purposes, costs, methods and deliverable outcomes early in the process.

Nature of multi-agency relationships

The nature of any multi-agency partnerships or relationships also require clarity. These relationships may be construed: as **strategic partnerships** involving a formalised relationship between parties built on group decision-making and adherence to the decisions by the group as a whole; or **multi-agency cooperation**, where the emphasis is on communication with interested parties, in a consultative manner, but decision-making is largely restricted to the core evaluation group.

Strategic partnerships: Formalised relationships between parties, which are built upon group decision-making and adherence to the decisions of the group as a whole.

Multi-agency cooperation: An emphasis on communication with interested parties, in a consultative manner, such that decision-making is by and large restricted to the core research or evaluation group.

Rob White

Being flexible and responding to change

The possibility and likelihood of changing details and scope of the evaluation needs to be acknowledged from the beginning. The coordinating group needs to consider ahead of time what kinds of contingency plans may be required. It is important, as well, to be flexible in terms of delegated authority. For example, a steering committee or evaluation coordinating group may wish to set broad parameters on the scope and aim of evaluation, but leave the details and process aspects up to the direct evaluators or project coordinators.

Evaluation resources

While good evaluation is not determined by its resources, it is nevertheless bounded by the resources at its disposal. Evaluation can only proceed according to the limits and possibilities offered by resources available. Before adopting a particular evaluation method, it is essential to audit the resources available, and the resources needed, to undertake the evaluation. Consideration needs to be given to:

- the resources associated with the values underlying the evaluation and the cost implications of particular evaluation methods
- the money and overall funding allocated to the evaluation process, including final evaluation reports by the personnel who are to carry out the evaluation, and which agencies will be contributing which people
- the kinds of work needed to be carried out, and by whom
- the timeline for the evaluation, and how this relates to staff time, financial support and preparation of reports
- the use of experts and/or external consultants to assist with the evaluation process, and how this might impact on budgets, timelines and staff participation
- the equipment needed in order to carry out the evaluation, including, for example, computers, sound recorders, paper and telephones
- the cost associated with particular evaluation needs, such as renting of community halls, payment for statistical records or data analysis
- the gathering of examples of experiences related to the type of evaluation you wish to undertake or in gathering information about existing model approaches.

Stage 2: Methods and techniques

Evaluation methods

Evaluation uses a broad field of methods. These different methods serve to provide different kinds of information about the social world. This section outlines three: **experimental** or quasi-experimental, **naturalistic** and **contextual analysis** methods. Importantly, while each method tends to be identified with certain types of data collection (such as reliance on questionnaires or use of interviews), and certain sorts of conceptual concerns (such as 'cause and effect', 'meaning and process', 'context and decision-making'), each method may use a variety of data-collection techniques. Also, an evaluation project often uses a combination of number of methods in its execution. Any of the methods included in this text—either within the book or in the on-line modules available at <www.oup.com.au/orc/walter>—could conceivably be used as part of an evaluation. As detailed in chapter 2, the selection of the best method and technique for the evaluation is determined by the evaluation research question/s. The 'how' of evaluation is inseparable from the 'why' of evaluation.

> **Experimental:** A research method in which pre-test measurements are taken of a target group or area, before the implementation of an experimental intervention (introduction of a particular program, strategy or project), followed by post-test measurements after the intervention has had time to take effect.
>
> **Naturalistic:** A research method in which information is gained by asking people directly about specific features of their lives, and how particular innovations and initiatives affect their daily routines.
>
> **Contextual analysis:** An evaluation research method concerned with how an initiative was implemented, through examination of its structure and decision-making processes, the nature and extent of community and interagency involvement and the extent of implementation.

Experimental and quasi-experimental methods

Sometimes characterised as before-and-after surveys, these quantitative methods evaluate the effectiveness of a policy or program intervention. That is, has the intervention made a difference, and if so, in what ways?

Pre-test measurements are usually taken from a target group or area before the intervention (a particular program, strategy or project) is implemented. Post-test measurements are then taken after the intervention has had time to take effect. Pre-test and post-test measurements are also taken for a control group or area, where no intervention has occurred, so if there are differences between the program or strategy group or area and the control group or area, these can be attributed to the intervention. The emphasis is on cause and effect, based on group comparisons using quantitative data, including large-scale surveys, as well as official statistical records. For example, crime and victimisation rates in a specific locale before and after a crime prevention initiative evaluate the effectiveness of this initiative.

A major drawback with this method is that it is extremely difficult to have full control over the conditions in which trial programs or strategies are being conducted. People are dynamic. Areas are dynamic. Change is a constant feature of human and urban life. Complicating factors can include changes that occur in the area between the pre-test and post-test measures (such as new housing developments, or a change in police numbers or police strategies) and ensuring that respondents are representative of the target population (which itself may change over time), or being able to compare groups over time (because of changing demographics of an area, such as an influx of older or younger people). Distinguishing between the impact of the intervention and the natural fluctuations in social phenomena over time (such as burglary rates) and the use of different measurement methods in the pre-test and post-test phases (such as changes in how the police record offences) can also raise challenges.

Naturalistic methods

This evaluation-related method emphasises actors speaking for themselves in their natural surroundings. It is a means of gaining people's perceptions through asking them directly about features of their community or work life, and how specific innovations and initiatives affect their daily routines, and is particularly appropriate for obtaining information about program or project context, processes and outcomes. The emphasis on meaning and process is based on gathering qualitative data, usually through in-depth interviews and observation. As shown in the 'Method to practice' section of this chapter, in the Inside-Out evaluation the views of all the actors in the prison system were canvassed, from prisoners and guards through to family members and service providers.

A major difficulty with a naturalistic method lies with the range of sources of information needed to gain a comprehensive understanding. This is partly a question of adequate resources, as well as efficiently selecting who to talk with, and why. Some of the specific problems include:

- the restrictions or biases in the selection of people who are to be interviewed, because of lack of resources, interpreters or trained interviewers (sample issues)
- the refusal to be interviewed by those most negatively affected by, or who have the most critical views of, a particular program or project (thus skewing the findings in a positive direction)
- differing interpretations of what was 'observed' in a local area, because of varying assumptions, philosophies and values held by participants, including researchers and evaluators (issues of consistency and reliability)
- difficulties in interpreting the findings, insofar as the accounts given by participants are, in turn, subject to reinterpretation and repackaging in written form by the evaluator (reflexive selection of what is or is not important in any specific account).

Contextual analysis methods

This method is orientated towards process evaluation, but is also useful in examining an initiative retrospectively, or after the fact. The main concerns include how an initiative was implemented, whether implementation went as planned, and the ways in which the context in which the initiative was set encouraged or undermined its impact. Specific areas include the structure and decision-making processes of an initiative, the nature and extent of community and inter-agency involvement, and the extent of implementation.

The emphasis is on 'context and decision-making'. Contextual analysis evaluations are based on documentary evidence (such as meeting records or newsletters), and interviews with planners, participants and (for comparison purposes) non-participants.

Some of the problems associated with this method can include:

- difficulties in gaining a full picture of the informal, as well as formal, ways in which people interact, which has a major bearing on implementation processes (issues of personality and shared interests)
- differing interpretations among participants as to the meaning of concepts such as 'inter-agency cooperation' or 'community consultation' (which requires sensitivity to multiple meanings of key terms)
- an emphasis on 'context' may imply that the lessons learned from the evaluation may not be transferable to other local areas (thereby limiting its applicability to other projects and regions)
- the political sensitivity of information gathered about implementation may result in efforts to censor the findings or to criticise the evaluator (protecting one's own turf or sectoral interests).

Countering method limitations

The problems and difficulties associated with each method are not insurmountable. In many cases, they simply require the researcher/evaluator to be conscious of them, and to make sure that this is reflected in the evaluation report. The three methods outlined above are also not mutually exclusive, and limitations in one method can be overcome by including aspects of another. It is possible, and sometimes desirable, to use a mix of methods and a variety of data-collection techniques, in undertaking evaluation. As noted in chapter 1, triangulation of methods can result in increased research richness and validity of results.

Establishing benchmarks

The point of an intervention is to make a difference. In order to assess this we need to know what the situation was like before, and after, the specific project or strategy was introduced. **Benchmarks** make the data collected through various methods meaningful, providing the baseline used to evaluate the performance of the project or strategy. In establishing benchmarks, emphasis may be put on **summative evaluation**, **formative evaluation** or a combination of the two.

Summative evaluation is about results. It takes place after a project or strategy has been in place for some time. The purpose

> **Benchmarks:** Data that are collected at a particular point in time and in relation to which future comparisons are made.
>
> **Summative evaluation:** Concerned with results, this type of evaluation is backward looking, and is used to assess performances and outcomes up to a certain point in time.
>
> **Formative evaluation:** Forward-looking evaluation, the purpose of which is to identify needs, clarify rationales and improve implementation into the future.

Rob White

is to monitor performance and outcomes up to a certain point in time. In this sense, it is retrospective (or backward looking), and concerned with learning from experience in determining the impact of an initiative.

Formative evaluation is about processes. It takes place at the beginning and during the implementation phase of an initiative. The purpose is to identify needs, clarify rationales and improve implementation. In this sense, it is prospective (or forward looking), and concerned with continuous assessment and ongoing feedback as a means to guide further developments.

Designing performance indicators

Performance indicators: Measures designed to indicate present performance in relation to stated goals.

Performance targets: Identification of the end point goals of a particular program or project.

The evaluation criteria or **performance indicators** are the measures used to evaluate whether something is 'successful' or 'unsuccessful', 'valuable' or 'not valuable', 'working' or 'not working'. They can be aligned with the conceptualisation and operationalisation processes outlined in chapter 2, and are concrete ways in which performance is measured. Measurement can be by processes or outcomes, and provides signs by which we can determine whether a project is doing what its objectives and goals say it is, or should be, doing. To be measurable, performance indicators are generally descriptive and quantitative in nature; that is, they refer to actual developments, such as the holding of a meeting to discuss community safety, and quantifiable units of measurement, such as the number of meetings or number of participants. Performance indicators indicate present performance, and should not be confused with **performance targets**, which refer to the endpoint goals of a particular program or project.

Performance indicators serve different purposes, and reflect the agendas of those involved in the evaluation. For example, they may reflect the immediate concerns of community residents or service users, who might be interested in how a program or service is meeting their perceived needs. Alternatively, the administrative concerns of government and community agencies might be whether or not their program is reaching its target and its cost effectiveness. It is important, therefore, when designing performance indicators that agreement is reached with the body commissioning the evaluation on the desired goals and outcomes, and how these will be expressed in objective terms via the indicators. Meaning and measurement criteria must be clear *and* agreed upon before the evaluation begins.

Developing performance indicators always takes place in the context of the evaluation's objectives. It is essential to identify the specific need or goal, conceptualise its particular meaning (as per this project), and operationalise the best way to measure whether or not progress is being made relative to the goal. For example, if the goal of the project is to reduce the number of assaults outside certain licensed establishments, then there is a need to first define what is meant by 'reduce', 'assaults', which type of establishment, and also how a reduction is to be measured. In this case, a reduction in the number of arrests, police attendance or the number of ambulance callouts may operate as appropriate measurements of a reduction.

Performance indicators have a number of possible dimensions. These are summarised in box 13.2.

Box 13.2: Dimensions of performance indicators

Quantity
Measuring performance in terms of 'how many', 'how often' or 'how much' (numbers of, frequency of, rate of).

Quality
Measuring performance in terms of 'how well' (opinions of, feedback from, continued participation of).

Time frame
Measuring performance in terms of 'how long' (time taken, changes over time).

Cost
Measuring performance in terms of 'how expensive' (money spent, equipment purchased, staff wages).

Resources
Measuring performance in terms of 'how much' and 'what was contributed by whom' (agency contributions, cash or in-kind contributions, use of volunteers, funding base).

Participation
Measuring performance in terms of 'who was involved' (members of target group, project organisers, funding agency, community residents).

The choice of, and emphasis placed upon, different performance indicators is partly a matter of what the evaluation is intended to do. The aims of evaluation will determine the nature of the performance measures to be used.

Data collection

Data collection is how evaluation researchers gain the needed information about a project, strategy, community or agency. There are many different types of information that might be collected, and many different ways of collecting it. Any evaluation project needs to consider from whom information will be sought, and for what purposes.

Quantitative: Numeric evidence

This type of data collection is concerned with measurement and often provides broad statistical trends:

- numbers of people using a service: examples are a simple numerical count of who actually walks in through the door; or who uses which specific types of service provision, such as counsellors, doctors or youth workers
- extent of service use in particular geographical areas: for example, the linking of numbers with particular locations, or expressed as a proportion of possible user population, such as the total youth population in a region
- rate of service use: these data can be expressed in relation to time, fluctuations in numbers of users per week or month or year, and/or expressed in relation to total populations, such as relative to youth population in a region
- trends in service use: examples can include broad changes in rate over specified time periods, downwards or upwards.

Quantitative evidence can be collected using formal preset questionnaires or surveys, as well as drawing upon formal records (such as the use of official police statistics or local area data from the ABS) or data derived from experiments. Quantitative data lends itself to large-scale studies and to statistical analysis of numeric data. See chapters 6, 7, 8 and 9 for more details on quantitative methods and analysis.

Qualitative: Interviews and participant observation

This type of data collection is concerned with people's views, perceptions and understandings of particular issues. It provides an in-depth appreciation of how people make sense of their lives, emphasising their own accounts. Qualitative methods used to collect this kind of data generally involve a combination of description (based upon observation) and unstructured or in-depth interviews (based around certain core questions or themes) (see chapter 10). The point is to gain information around the social contexts and social processes that inform how people feel about themselves, their neighbourhoods and their issues of concern. As such, qualitative methods for data collection tend to be orientated towards small-scale research, involving interactions with small groups and in local contexts.

Qualitative: Documentary analysis and critical interpretation

This type of data collection is basically concerned with critical analysis. It allows a reflection on the social meaning of official documents, existing statistical collections, policy statements, media reports and citizen attitudes (see chapters 11 and 12 on content and discourse analysis). This form of evaluation identifies the perspectives that underlie the issues and attempts to expose the assumptions, discourses and ideological propositions embodied in particular policies, programs and strategies. The data collected are, in effect, the meanings assigned to particular forms and kinds of information, and the theories that are implicit in the language used, and concepts employed, in documentation of an issue or trend.

The contribution of this form of data collection, therefore, is to provide critical appraisal of taken-for-granted assumptions, opening the door for alternative explanations, programs for action or suggestions for reform.

Box 13.3: Methods of data collection

- Document analysis: for example, files, agency reports, maps, correspondence, budgets.
- Media accounts: for example, cartoons, newspaper editorials, articles, letters, films.
- Statistical records: for example, police statistics, Australian Bureau of Statistics, or local council surveys.
- Internet and computer records: for example, internet sites, home pages, computer games.
- Record-keeping: for example, referral records, diaries, daily contact sheets, attendance records.
- Literature reviews: for example, journals, government reports, community research.
- Surveys: for example, use of questionnaires, telephone surveys, suggestion boxes.
- Group discussions: for example, invited respondents, public meetings, teleconferences.
- Focus groups: for example, specific sample groups, briefing and debriefing sessions.
- Life histories: for example, selective in-depth discussions, storytelling.
- Observation: for example, closed-circuit cameras, field visits, participant observation.
- Peer research: for example, exploring friendship and family networks.

Stage 3: Evaluation outcomes

The concern of this stage of evaluation is with the processing, analysis and communication of evaluation findings. It is also concerned with the question of what to do once an evaluation has been completed.

Data organisation

Once information is collected it needs to be organised. How evaluation data are organised depends on the sources of information and the kinds of information collected.

Focus of study

First, reidentify the specific purposes for which the data have been collected. The information will likely cover a wide range of issues and concerns, so collate different types of information into different files. These can be organised according to broad categories of focus. For example, as shown below, you might arrange your information according to key emphasis.

Rob White

Process data

Materials relating to the extent and nature of participation by various people, including project staff, in the initiative; budget papers and administrative records; policy statements and media reports; involvement of diverse sections of the community.

Impact data

Materials relating to measuring changes in an agency or local community as a result of the initiative, such as external statistical indicators; changes in community perceptions; movement in how different groups or individuals view the issues.

Information that is relevant to both process and impact assessment and should be filed in both of these two areas.

Grouping of information

Beyond clarifying where and how the information is to be used (in terms of process and impact analysis), the biggest task is to group the information according to substantive issues covered and/or sources of information. For example, the grouping of information might take the following form:

Quantitative information

Filing all materials that provide a statistical picture of an area or project in separate folders. This is material that basically consists of numbers.

Qualitative information

Filing all material that may not lend itself to quantitative grouping of information, but which nevertheless provides important insights into the issues. This is material that basically consists of interview records or observations.

It is important that evaluators keep track of where specific items of information have come from; that is, the sources of various data that has been collected.

Another way in which to group the data is to divide it into primary and secondary sources:

Primary sources: Information that you have directly collected yourself (such as undertaking your own survey).

Secondary sources: Information that you have not directly collected yourself, but which is available through other means (such as Australian Bureau of Statistics information).

Primary sources

Primary sources include information that you have directly collected yourself, and which needs to be processed by you according to questions and answers, topic areas, issues raised and descriptions of the sample (who participated).

Secondary sources

Secondary sources include information that you have not directly collected yourself, but which is available through other means (such as ABS statistics and media reports). These likewise can be grouped according to topic areas and issues raised (such as community profile in terms of levels of unemployment, crime statistics and number of users of community services).

The key to data processing is to establish which questions you are trying to answer, and to develop separate files that allow you to group the information that will answer that question as it becomes available.

Data analysis

Data analysis identifies the patterns and issues relating to process and impact assessment. This is an interpretative process. Following are some of the analysis techniques commonly used by evaluation researchers (see also chapters 8 and 14 on qualitative and quantitative data analysis).

Issue mapping

The mapping of issues will vary by data type. For example, quantitative data can provide an indication of trends over time, changes according to locale or particular social group and correlations between certain groups and particular perceptions or types of activities. The data can be presented in the form of tables and graphs, which basically provide a numerical summary of the information collected. Qualitative data, such as records of interviews and observations, can be used to illuminate key conceptual understandings and insights. The usual mode of presentation is through quotations, in the case of interview material, or word pictures, drawings or photographs for observation material, to provide an interpretative summary of the information.

Reliability and cross-checks

Where possible, it is important to cross-check data. To assess the reliability, or potential differences in the picture emerging from various types of data, it is useful to test this information against other data (triangulation of data). More generally, comparing and contrasting different types of information provides a rounded perspective on a particular issue, and indicates potential differences in interpretation for each type of data collected.

Omissions and inclusions

Data must be analysed and collected as objectively as possible. The evaluator must be prepared to put aside his or her own assumptions and preconceptions regarding any particular project or policy initiative, and allow the data to speak for themselves without conscious or inadvertent censoring by the evaluator. What the data actually tell us, however, does require active interpretation. We need to be clear as to what the data are saying, given the ways in which they were collected, and the specific questions we ask

Rob White

of them. Any interpretation must be framed in terms of the data they relate to, and it is unwise to extrapolate or infer meaning from data collected for specific purposes. For example, data on elderly people's fear of crime should not be used to explain fear of crime more generally.

Alternatively, it is useful to also explore the 'silences' in the data. We want to know what is omitted as well as what is included. For instance, reviews of fear of crime in public spaces may include material on how adults see the issues, but not include young people's perspectives. The omission of young people from such studies then becomes a significant issue in its own right (especially if young people are a main source of fear for the adult population).

Preparing the report

Writing up our research is discussed in detail in chapter 15, but the process has particular aspects related to evaluation. The output requirements for the evaluation need clarification at the very beginning of the process. For example, if the evaluation findings are to be widely distributed—to participants, funding bodies or to members of wider communities—then funding provisions must be made for the production of appropriate feedback mechanisms such as pamphlets, booklets or bound copies. Reporting the findings costs money, and we need to know who is going to pay for the final report.

Another issue is who, precisely, is going to write the report? Report writing by 'committee' is extremely difficult and time-consuming, and may lead to constant debates over minor (or major) matters regarding style, content and presentation. Alternatively, leaving the report writing to one person may privilege that person's interpretation of the process and of the findings. It is vital, therefore, to discuss thoroughly the processes involved in writing the report, to assess the skills and possible contributions of different members of the evaluation team, and to ensure that everyone gets a chance to comment on the drafts of the evaluation report.

It is also vital to keep in mind the audience for the final report. In other words, the issue of communication is central to the report-writing process. The best policy is to keep it simple in language, format and structure. A report should explain, in plain and clear language:

- why the evaluation was undertaken
- how it was done
- what the findings were
- how we might interpret the findings in terms of future activity.

If appropriate, an executive summary can be included, which provides a snapshot of the key findings. Likewise, a list of evaluation recommendations might be included in order to suggest future directions, including comments on the evaluation processes themselves.

The evaluation report should provide a fair and balanced response to the terms of reference of the evaluation, and reflect the findings as accurately and comprehensively as possible. It is important to be honest, and to be seen to be honest, in the presentation of findings. This means including both negative and positive material; but doing so in ways that do not artificially presume that there will necessarily be a 'balance' between good and bad features of a project or program. Be reflective, critical and constructive.

It is also important to be up front about how the findings have been interpreted. This is crucial, since different types of information can be interpreted in quite different, and even opposing, ways. For example, boxing may be seen as a positive 'recreational outlet', or it may be seen negatively as reinforcing 'male aggression'.

In presenting the findings, care has to be taken to identify who is saying what: a participant, a quote from a government report or the evaluator. Respect the anonymity of respondents, but do identify that it is a participant response rather than an evaluator comment. Keep editorialising to a minimum; for example, 'this person obviously did not have a clue what they were talking about' is both inappropriate and judgmental.

Limitations of evaluation

It is important to be aware of the limitations of evaluation, particularly in relation to issues of community safety. Some of the common difficulties include:

Methodological issues

- Limitations associated with level and quality of resources available to undertake a comprehensive evaluation process.
- Inherent difficulties in attempts to measure change in a social environment, given that such environments are in a constant process of change in their own right. Factors such as the movement of people into and out of a neighbourhood, and new residential and business developments, all affect the social environment.
- The problems associated with trying to measure a non-event, such as a decline in the rate of crime, rather than something that offers a concrete measurable outcome, such as increased community participation.
- The time frame of evaluation may not be sufficient to record any substantive change.
- There may be difficulties in ascertaining whether the apparent success or failure of a project lies in the implementation of a particular initiative, or whether it is associated

Rob White

with the evaluation measurement process itself and the criteria used to determine success or failure.
- The complication of multiple aims for any specified project or strategy, the variable emphasis placed by different people on different aims, and the fact that some aims may be met while others may not be met.

Values issues

- Differences in the commitment of evaluation partners to the evaluation, and in the respondents to which, and for whom, the evaluation is intended, can skew the results.
- Conflicts can also arise relating to the overall rationale for evaluation, in particular between concerns with cost–benefit accountability and concerns with community enhancement and capacity building.
- Differences in the philosophical perspective underlying project or program development can affect how processes and outcomes will be assessed. For example, issues of inequality, deprivation and injustice can only be addressed in ways that are long term and diffuse. Because of this, interventions that deal with these as the key focus are not amenable to short-term cost–benefit analysis.
- Different emphases on process evaluation and impact evaluation can create conflict and confusion over what the evaluation is meant to convey.

Consequence issues

- An evaluation of a project, event or group may demonstrate that it performs well within its particular terms of reference and performance criteria, yet evaluation solely in these terms may fail to recognise unintended consequences that have negative impacts on individuals and communities. For example, a crime-prevention project may decrease a particular type of crime, but the community safety measures adopted as part of the project may heighten the fear of crime in a local community by their very existence.
- Further unintended consequences include such things as an increase in the stigmatisation of particular groups as being deviant (or even criminal) because they have been targeted in the evaluation process. Evaluations dealing with mental illness, youth drug use and sexuality are particularly prone to issues of stigmatisation.
- The evaluation may be constructed in, or seen to be constructed in, self-serving terms. For example, if the evaluation is seen as too positive, it might be viewed as simply a justification for, and defence of, a particular project, or as something that has been instrumentally designed to increase funding.

- The evaluation may be perceived as too negative or critical. There is a need, therefore, to be specific in what is criticised, and to critique the parts that need to be criticised, without necessarily criticising the total project or program or its participants.
- Evaluations cannot please everyone, in terms of how they are carried out, and by whom, and in relation to the evaluation findings.

Exercise 13.1: Evaluating student disability services

The issue

Universities say that they are committed to ensuring that students with disabilities are accorded complete and equitable access to all facets of university life, as far as circumstances reasonably allow. However, questions can be asked regarding how disability is defined, who makes the key decisions in regard to assessment of student situation and needs, and how academic and support staff within the university ought to assist students with varying types of disability. To address these issues requires answers to a series of pertinent questions relating to principles, procedures, practices and people.

The key question

What are the strengths, limitations and issues surrounding student disability services within a university environment?

The evaluation project

The task of the class is to prepare an evaluation scoping document that:

- sets out the nature and purposes of the evaluation
- identifies potential ethical issues
- examines the resources and expertise required for the evaluation
- decides on the evaluation method(s) to be used
- determines the types of data to be collected
- sets out the intended outcomes and outputs of the evaluation.

1 **In preparing the document, divide the class into two groups.**

Each group has a specific task (25-minute discussion and note-taking session).

Group 1: Your task

Prepare responses to the following questions:

- Is the evaluation needed or relevant? How do we know this?
- Who will be affected by the evaluation, and how?

Rob White

- What is the key purpose of the evaluation?
- What internal and external factors will influence the evaluation process?
- What resources are available or needed to undertake the evaluation?

Group 2: Your task

Prepare responses to the following questions:

- How and who defines 'disability'?
- How are we going to quantify and measure performance of disability services?
- What are the main sources of information we wish to use?
- Where can we gain specific information relevant to this evaluation?
- How can we convey the findings to different audiences?

2   Class discussion (15 minutes)

Each group is to report back to the class on how it answered their specific questions, leaving time for comment on the findings and opinions of each group.

Handy hints

Some general questions with which you might wish to start:
- What evidence, apart from self-report, is required in identifying students with disabilities?
- Who interprets or adjudicates claims for special treatment or entitlements?
- How is the form and amount of assistance determined?
- What are current university policies?
- Is information on disability policy and practice readily available to students, and to all staff?
- What is the thrust of university policy? Is it to assist students to study under fair conditions, or to give special concessions to students unable to complete their studies at the same standard as their peers?
- What protocols and policies does the university have, and are staff aware of these?
- Who provides the resources needed to implement policy?
- Should resources be prioritised according to type of disability and level of assistance required?
- Who enforces policy, and who evaluates this?

Voices in the field

Diane Heckenberg

Diane Heckenberg is a PhD candidate in Criminology at the University of Tasmania, who also undertakes evaluation research projects outside her postgraduate study. Below she describes how she recently undertook the often difficult task of negotiating the relationship between the evaluators and the stakeholders of the project. The key was through the establishment of clear and agreed roles and purposes.

'My colleague and I have been involved in a "continuous evaluation" project that is to last three years. The project involves a non-government agency and several government agencies, and deals with services for vulnerable clients. One of the first things we did was to develop a one-page statement in order to defuse initial suspicion and fears about the evaluation process. The document was intended to place clear boundaries around our role as evaluators, as distinct from that of project management and performance management of individual staff and to emphasise that we were evaluators, not performance police or data collectors for the project. The key elements of the document are outlined below:

- 'We "own" the evaluation ... you "own" the project
- 'Our role as evaluators is to:
  — develop the evaluation strategy
  — describe what you are doing
  — raise and discuss barriers to the evaluation
  — direct the evaluation
  — collect, store and analyse the data
  — prepare and conduct interviews
  — build trust by surfacing, discussing and resolving conflict
  — meet regularly with the core group throughout the project
  — meet with the Reference Group, on request
  — give and receive feedback
  — report in a timely manner.

'In the early phases of the project we spent a lot of time discussing aims and objectives with diverse stakeholders, and describing what we needed from them in order for us (as evaluators) to contribute to improvements in their particular work practices and client interventions.'

Rob White

From method to practice

The translation of evaluation methods into practice very often hinges upon one key element: the human factor. That is, the success or otherwise depends to a great extent upon the human resources available, the quality of the individual contributions to the evaluation, and the level of conflict or cooperation associated with a particular project. The evaluation of the Inside-Out prison program provides an example of an evaluation in working practice.

The conduct of this evaluation was complex, in that it concerned a wide range of stakeholders, who had different views, perceptions, values and interests in the program. It was essential that time was spent at the very beginning of the project on extensive discussions with stakeholders about the evaluation. These preliminary discussions were directed at clarifying the key purpose of the evaluation, roles, perspectives, key players and the specific tasks of the evaluators. For example, the collection of what data and for what purposes (data was collected from prisoners and prison staff) had to be negotiated, and data-sharing procedures had to be put into place. Based on these negotiations and discussions, a comprehensive evaluation plan was developed, including the crucial data-collection plan identifying the kind of data collected, and by whom, and for what purposes.

The data-collection process was directly and explicitly tied into the evaluation criteria. The Inside-Out program objective—to reduce rates of recidivism among prisoners by providing intensive transitional support—and the processes put in place and in pursuit of this goal were assessed via series of performance indicators (for example, number of prisoners recruited into the program, level of recidivism rate, source of referrals, type of referrals and extent of consultation in the referral process). The data-collection plan also specified the kinds of data required to gauge the performance of the program (such as monthly statistics on number of prisoners involved in the program), and the methods needed to gather the data (such as agency records in regards to number of prisoners recruited; interviews with prisoners and their families on the extent of consultation in the referral process). In summary, for the Inside-Out program two primary questions were central to the evaluation. These were:

> What are the benefits and strengths of the program?
> What are the limitations and shortcomings of the program?
> Information for the evaluation was derived from two main sources. These were:
> analysis of documentation held by various agencies, such as Attorney-General's Department, Department of Justice (Corporate Office), Corrective Services, Care and Communication Concern (CCC), and the Inside-Out service
> interviews with major stakeholders.

Individual semistructured interviews were conducted with the following people:
- prisoners
  - 12 prisoners ranging from age 18–57 years
  - 10 male prisoners (9 from maximum, 1 from medium security)
  - 2 female prisoners.
- prison officers
  - Director of Prisons
  - General Manager, Maximum Security
  - Manager, Custodial Services, Maximum Security
  - Manager, Accommodation Services, Maximum Security
  - Manager, Medium Security
  - Manager, Women's Prison
  - 2 staff members Prisoner Support Unit
- service providers
  - Program Manager Inside-Out
  - support worker Inside-Out
- family members
  - 2 families from the north of the state
  - 2 families from the south of the state.

The evaluators engaged in this assessment needed to maintain their independence and to 'play with a straight bat' when it came to critical observations of process, detailing problems in project management, identifying problems in data collection and more generally acknowledging the strengths *and* limitations of project development. Given the possibility of competing interests between different stakeholders, such as the prison bureaucracy, the prison staff and prisoners, such independence not only had to exist, but explicitly be seen to be in operation. The relationship between evaluators and evaluees can sometimes be close, and involve individuals who know each other quite well. But negotiating personal relationships is part of the challenge of providing evaluation that is fair, objective and constructive.

The key findings of the Inside-Out program evaluation were:

- Prisoners valued the Inside-Out program, and thought it provided a useful non-institutional avenue for inmates to reduce or relieve the stresses associated with incarceration by providing someone to talk to and communicate with. It also enabled them to better liaise with their families and loved ones.

Rob White

> Prison authorities had mixed attitudes towards the program, because of:
>   — problems with how it was introduced and implemented
>   — how funding was established and subsequently allocated for the program
>   — differing perceptions regarding the status and role of a lay worker within the prison environment
>   — the perceived lack of reporting and accountability of a prison-funded program.
> From a service provision perspective, while the Inside-Out Support Worker was highly committed to assisting prisoners and their families, there were serious shortcomings in the support available to the worker, both from prison authorities (such as provision of adequate space, or suitable report-back and consultative mechanisms) and the funded organisation (in the form of a locally based support network and constructive administrative and supervisory support).
> The support worker was placed in an ambiguous position. On the one hand, to do the job effectively required certain personal qualities and task-related attributes. On the other hand, these very qualities and attributes may be seen as inappropriate in secure punishment facilities. This was a Catch 22 situation, which could only be resolved by careful consideration of the philosophical rationale guiding prison management and prison programs.

As a result of these findings, the following recommendations were made:

> That there be regular consultation between prison authorities and the Attorney-General's office, and that no program be approved or implemented without full analysis of costs and benefits, and assessment of the program background and history.
> That for any prison program, internally or externally run, there be a comprehensive and detailed description of the program, including aims, strategies and performance measures, and that this be circulated to all relevant parties (including inmates and prison staff).
> That for each prison support worker there be a position description, which provides an outline of key tasks and responsibilities, including reporting obligations and the responsibilities of prison authorities to each worker.
> That there should be clarification of specified target groups for particular programs, and that performance indicators (such as specific tasks) and administrative protocols (such as information from prison authorities) be developed in relation to these target groups.
> That there be development of improved reporting mechanisms and procedures (for example, through the use of a reporting pro forma) that provide user-friendly mechanisms for reporting, and that there be structured opportunity for regular consultations between program staff and prisoner support services.

> That tensions arising from diverse interpretations of prison programs and prison priorities (such as security versus services) be addressed via pre-service and in-service training and education programs that reflect best practice contemporary penology.
> That issues of service provision, as they relate to recidivism, suicidal behaviour and self-harm, prisoner and family support and post release, be evaluated in the context of an assessment of the whole-of-prison environment and the constellation of services and programs on offer. Such an evaluation could also consider diverse programs' aims and goals, and the direct and indirect influences of each on any of the above concerns.

In summary, it was found that while the program provided an invaluable service to prisoners, there were aspects of the program, particularly relating to reporting mechanisms and procedures, that required attention. Overall, however, the program represented excellent value for money, given the time, energy and resources put into direct service provision by the key support worker, and the positive response from prisoners and their families to the service.

Source: White & Mason 2003

Rob White

Conclusion

This chapter has provided an outline of the key issues and methods of evaluation, and included examples of the evaluation process. The crucial thing about evaluation is that it lets us know 'how we have gone' and 'where we are going'. It is a positive and constructive process. In the end, however, there is one major lesson that experience has taught us: the best way to learn about evaluation is simply to do it. The doing of evaluation is a hands-on exercise—and it is this that will most assist you in making sense of, and finding a use for, the material presented in this chapter.

Main points

> Evaluation is a method of gauging performance in relation to a specific project, program or strategy.

> There are multiple purposes of evaluation, and these include assessment of outcomes, processes and management issues, and identification of current and future needs.

> Evaluation takes planning: this requires a scoping of relevant issues, problems, information, resources, administrative structures and environments.

> It is crucial to ask the right questions beforehand if evaluation planning is to succeed.

> Evaluation research involves a wide range of methods and techniques, ranging from experimental to naturalistic to forms of contextual analysis, each of which has its own strengths and weaknesses.

> A key aspect of evaluation is that it frequently focuses on performance, and thus there is a need to establish benchmarks and performance indicators as a means to assess what a specific project, program or strategy is actually doing.

> There are many different types of data collection associated with evaluation research, and wide-ranging sources of information, and these need to be tailored to the purposes of each specific evaluation project.

> Processing of evaluation data requires careful scrutiny of patterns according to the aims of the evaluation project, and appreciation of the limitations of the data, as well as the limitations of evaluation research generally.

Further reading

Australasian Evaluation Society (1998). *Guidelines for the Ethical Conduct of Evaluations*. Canberra: Australian Evaluation Society.

Australian Youth Foundation and Sharp, C. (1996). *START: Do-It-Yourself Evaluation Manual*. Sydney: Australian Youth Foundation.

Murray, G., Homel, R., Wimshurst, K., Prenzler, T. and O'Connor, I. (1993). *A Framework for Evaluating Community-Based Juvenile Crime Prevention Programs*. Research and Policy Paper No 4. Brisbane: Centre for Crime Policy and Public Safety, Griffith University.

Wadsworth, Y. (1991). *Everyday Evaluation on the Run*. Melbourne: Action Research Issues Association (Incorporated).

White, R. and Coventry, G. (2000). *Evaluating Community Safety: A Guide*. Melbourne: Crime Prevention Victoria, Department of Justice.

White, R. and Mason, R. (2003). *An Evaluation of the 'Inside-Out' Prison Program, Occasional Paper No. 2*. Hobart: Criminology Research Unit, School of Sociology and Social Work, University of Tasmania.

Wilson, G. and Wright, M. (1993). *Evaluation Framework: Women's Health Services and Centres Against Sexual Assault*. Melbourne: Centre for Development and Innovation in Health.

References

White, R. and Mason, R. (2003). *An Evaluation of the 'Inside-Out' Prison Program, Occasional Paper No. 2*. Hobart: Criminology Research Unit, School of Sociology and Social Work, University of Tasmania.

Chapter 14
Analysing Qualitative Data

Karen Willis

Drowning in the data?

The story so far...

It was a fantastic idea for her research project. Jill had read the literature, and talked with her friends, and found that little was known about how encounters with UFOs influenced everyday understandings of the social world. Her supervisor was enthusiastic and ethics approval to undertake in-depth interviews was obtained. Fifteen people agreed to be interviewed. Jill loved talking to people about their experiences—they were so interesting and varied, all having lots to say on the topic.

Each interview lasted for at least one-and-a-half hours. After five interviews, there was a small and growing pile of recordings containing 'the data'. Even though she had addressed issues of analysis in her research proposal, she realised with a sinking feeling that there was much more to the research process than she had originally envisaged ...

Key terms

a priori codes	inductive codes	thematic analysis
coding	life histories	themes
deviant cases	narrative analysis	theoretical sampling
field notes	open coding	theoretical saturation
focus groups	reflective memos	theoretical sensitivity
grounded theory	reflexivity	transcription
immersion	selective coding	

Introduction

A key issue confronting social science students is that their first encounter with data analysis often does not occur until they are actually engaged in a project. While considerable energy goes into research design and undertaking data collection such as interviews, it may not be until confronted with the data itself that the analysis process is fully considered. As with Jill, the realisation that data collection is only a part in a much larger process can be daunting. This chapter provides a guide on the 'how to' of qualitative data analysis, as well as exploring some of the main analytical methods.

At the core of qualitative data analysis are the ways in which qualitative researchers make meaning from their data. In qualitative research, the practices of analysis and interpretation are not linear stages that occur after data collection. Rather, initial analysis should occur as we enter the field. It is therefore essential that we have clear ideas around what we intend to do with our data at the project's commencement, and can put in place strategies to maximise the richness of the data collected.

Qualitative data are collected using a myriad of methods and sources. These may be obtrusive in the case of individual or group interviews and some forms of observation. The degree of obtrusiveness will vary: from anonymous interviews on the internet, to note-taking in participant observation, or to audio- or video-recorded research interviews. Or they may be unobtrusive, drawing on existing texts, such as case or file notes, observation of social phenomena (manually or video-recorded), media (including newspapers, television and film), and collection of data from sources such as the internet.

The ultimate aim of most social science research is the development of theory that will contribute to our understanding of the social world. And whatever the source, the qualitative researcher usually has a large volume of material that needs to be described and summarised without losing the intrinsic meaning. Qualitative analysis, therefore, cannot begin without an understanding of the methodological underpinnings of the research project (see chapter 1). Our method of analysis is dependent on the theoretical framework adopted for the project, as well as the research questions, alongside the questions we ask of our data. There is, for example, a difference between naturalistic interpretation, where the focus is on understanding through rich description of the social world, and social constructivist interpretation, which attempts to uncover how experiences and processes in telling a story are socially constructed. Our methodological approach will also shape our view on what is 'truth' within our research. Many interpretative and postmodern researchers couch their research within a framework of competing claims—thus all one can do is to re-present the views that emerge from the research, rather than definitive results.

Whatever methodological approach or specific research method is adopted, however, the analysis of qualitative data contributes to the development of knowledge in our society. In this chapter we make use of the transcripts of the example qualitative in-depth interviews on the topic of national identity (previously discussed in chapter 10) to demonstrate the basics of qualitative analysis, and also in one of the exercises. You can access these transcripts at <www.oup.com.au/orc/walter>.

Creating meaning: The vital ingredients

The task of qualitative data analysis is meaning-making. Exactly how to *do* qualitative analysis, however, tends to be limited to texts that focus on qualitative data analysis (Ezzy 2002; Silverman 2002) or to those that relate to a specific methodological approach such as grounded theory (Glaser & Strauss 1967; Strauss & Corbin 1990). Most general research texts include little on the actual process of qualitative data analysis, perhaps because the interpretive and contextual emphasis makes prescription a complex task. However, all analysis, qualitative and quantitative, requires creativity, theoretically informed interpretation and an understanding of research context. So, while acknowledging these elements, it is also important to ensure that qualitative research processes are rigorous and, in some cases, replicable. As such, certain ingredients and processes are integral to qualitative data analysis.

Reflexivity

Qualitative methods make specific demands for the active engagement of the researcher. The need for **reflexivity**—a self-conscious awareness by the researcher of his or her position in the research process—has resulted from methods in which the researcher plays an overt and explicit role in the research process. Reflexivity emerged out of concerns with the dimensions of power in research, and is the key to qualitative methods such as ethnographic research, feminist research and participatory action research (see the online segments on ethnographic and participatory action research). Reflexivity does not just comprise reflection on individual interviews. It is a whole-of-research approach that commences with clear understanding of one's self in the research process, and concludes with a clear explication of research method when writing up the research results. The reflexive researcher is one who acknowledges the ways in which power may be constituted and enacted during the research encounter and beyond into analysis of the data. Reflexivity can therefore be aligned with the standpoint aspect of methodology discussed in chapter 1. As with acknowledging and understanding our standpoint, reflexivity acknowledges that

> **Reflexivity:** A self-conscious awareness by the researcher of their impact on the research and research process.

Karen Willis

the researcher is integrally bound up in the data collected, the way they are collected and the ways data are analysed. The researcher is the research instrument, the conduit through which the data are collected. In this way, the sensitivity of the research instrument becomes an important factor in understanding the findings that result from the data. It is therefore important to contextualise the interview process as representing an interaction between researcher and researched, acknowledging both as social actors within this research setting. The researcher should pay close scrutiny to the way that he or she approaches and conducts the interview, and reflect on how this may affect the interview as a process.

Reflective memos: An ongoing process by which the researcher notes process issues associated with the research.

One way that we can consciously focus on reflexivity in the research process is the writing of **reflective memos** during the project. (The advantages of doing so are not limited to an awareness of reflexivity.) Short reflections after each interview can contribute to the richness of the research in a variety of ways. They may be particularly important in improving interview techniques, in reflecting on questions that work best, as well as considering the role of the researcher in facilitating the research process. In terms of reflexivity, consider the way that the interview impacted on you emotionally. Consider:

- How did it make you feel and how did this make you respond to the participant?
- Did the participant respond emotionally to the interview? What were the indicators of this?
- How did you respond to their feelings?

Case study 14.1: Using memos to reflect

Following is an excerpt from Dr Kristin Natalier's PhD thesis on share housing, where she reflected on the role of memos as an integral part of her research method:

In order to analytically engage with the implications of my positioning as share householder and researcher I decided to use a reflexive journal in which I recorded my experiences in the household in which I was then living. I wrote the journal for three months. I recorded events, interactions and my responses, and later subjected them to the same analysis as that directed towards the interview data. This was also to help sensitise myself to the processes of group living that might be of more general significance to the study. The diary was a means of tracking experiences and pointing to their potential effects on research and interpretative processes. A decision from the outset that the journal would not be incorporated as data that others might read (and judge) freed my expression—any pettiness, nastiness and foolishness would be subject only to my analytic eye at a later date. Having said this, it is also important to note that an entry made 'honestly' does not equate to one that is free of bias.

Reading back over the diary, I gained a sense of the issues and actions that were of most concern to me. When writing the entries I had felt dispassionate, recording rather than making sense of my own and others' actions and feelings. On re-reading I was reminded of how false claims to objectivity can be: annoyances, misunderstandings and resentments loop their way through what I had written. Studying the text encouraged a more sensitive approach to my attempts to pursue what was of concern to me, rather than the respondents. For example, the household in which I lived was initially friendly, but over the course of the three months became increasingly tense. This undermined my confidence to broach the issue of what I considered to be an unfair division of labour. Considering interview transcripts with reference to these diaries, I became aware of my attempts to steer the discussion in the direction of tensions in the home, an emphasis I now believe reflected a continuing resentment over my own situation. This had its advantages—I did not accept the initial protestations of pure goodwill in the homes of participants—but the motivation was not as theoretically pure as I might have otherwise imagined it to be.

Through the months of interviewing I supplemented the journal with field notes and reflections on my interactions with the people in the study. These held the same value as the journal, sensitising me to biases and possible misreading of the data. Re-reading these sections could at times make me aware of the negative feelings that showed through in my response to and analysis of what subjects said (although this was by no means foolproof and other readers have sometimes been more sensitive to my tone than I). The entries were also used for initial analysis (intuitive rather than systematic) and identifying the questions that 'worked' and those that seemed irrelevant to the householders. Overall, these strategies were helpful in organising and articulating, in a reflexive way, my relationship to the research process. Thus, during the course of the study the journal/field notes came to document a personal and emotional context to the study, and rendered transparent the interconnections between data collection, analysis and researcher subjectivity.

Source: Natalier 2003

As can be seen from case study 14.1, self-consciously reflecting on our role within the research process, the shaping role that we have within the interview or data-collection phase of the project, and our stance when it comes to interpreting our data are all important aspects of the research process and practice. They also form an aspect of another integral requirement of qualitative research; that is, of immersing one's self in the data.

Karen Willis

Exercise 14.1: Reflexivity

Consider the following quotes about reflexivity and research practice: they make three key points about the role of the researcher:

- first, the impact of the researcher on the research process
- second, the importance of understanding the subject position of the researcher
- third, the impact of research on people's lives and the ways that research can be used in the wider social and political sphere.

Quote 1

It is an ability to locate yourself in the picture, to understand, and factor in, how what you see is influenced by your own way of seeing, and how your very presence and act of research influences the situation in which you are researching (Fook 1999:12).

Quote 2

Focusing on the lives of 'other people' obscures the researcher's own experiences and concerns ... The primacy of other people's concerns is established by the diminishment of one's own. Although covert, this practice reflects the view that the researcher is merely a technician who records, documents and publishes the material of others. However well meaning, this practice is far from neutral (Seymour 2001:122).

Quote 3

Recognising the social context of research requires critical thinking. In many academic disciplines, critical thinking is used merely to assess the extent to which the rules of scientific inquiry have been followed, in order to ensure scientific validity and analyse the data. In the social sciences, critical thinking should go further, to incorporate careful assessment of the effect that our research has on the lives of our research participants. We should also be alert to the purposes our research may serve in the social and political debates surrounding a particular ... issue (Pyett 2001:107).

Task

Briefly note the ways in which the insights from the three quotes may shape the way in which you conduct and analyse your research. Discuss your notes with another class member.

Immersion and incubation

In order to reach depth in our analysis, we need to saturate ourselves in the interview material we are analysing. Repeated reading of text, watching of audio-visual material or listening to recordings is the first requirement of undertaking analysis. We need to keep reading the material, listening to the recordings or watching videos, thinking about what participants say, or the documents we are analysing, and try to obtain some form of pattern. Sometimes this can happen when we least expect it. For example, after a day of reading and rereading transcripts and coding, when we feel like we haven't achieved anything, we will suddenly make a connection. These breakthroughs often happen at unlikely times: while driving; in the shower; or even at 3 o'clock in the morning. Keep a pad and pen handy to write such breakthrough thoughts down as soon as they occur, or otherwise you might lose them!

A critical first step in **immersion** in the data is **transcription** of audio or video recordings. As noted in chapter 10, while it is undoubtedly a time-consuming and sometimes tedious part of the process, it is a key point at which we develop insights into our data. A transcription of the whole research encounter is essential; it cannot be reduced to the parts of the interview that we think are the most important. What we judge as important at the early stage of analysis may not be the case when we are developing theoretical insights from interviews. It is much more tedious to have to go back to the original recordings and transcribe when it is apparent we have missed an important factor. If possible, particularly when we have small numbers, we should undertake the transcription. It forces us to pay attention to the detail of the interview.

Immersion: A process in which the researcher becomes familiar with data.

Transcription: A full written record of interview data.

A transcribing machine is an essential data analysis tool. In particular, digital audio-recorders and accompanying computer transcription programs have increased the ease of recording and transcribing our data. Rather than manually stopping and starting the audio-recording, transcribers have controls (operated as foot or keyboard controls) that allow us to minimise the interruptions caused by taking our fingers off the keyboard. Transcribing machines (whether manual or digital) allow us to slow down the recording and to return to specific points to check the audio accuracy. We need to take into account the availability and type of transcribing machines when we commence data collection, as this will determine the type of audio-recording we will make.

We also need to determine the form of our transcription. This will be dictated by the type of research we are undertaking. For example, we may need to transcribe only the spoken word or, as in the case of conversation analysis (see the online segment on this method at <www.oup.com.au/orc/walter>) or focus groups (see chapter 10), we will also need to transcribe non-verbal material. Some topics may require us to understand and contextualise the long pauses that occur in responses to topics. These are important, because pauses can indicate discomfort or embarrassment, or may simply be a pause to recall a detail within the story being told. Laughter may signify that the verbal response is sarcastic or witty (remember that these nuances are lost on the written page). Words such as 'well

Karen Willis

'... er ... I suppose ...' may also be important. The minimum we need to transcribe are the questions as asked, and the verbal responses of the participants.

If we employ someone to do the transcription, we need to provide the person with strict guidelines on how to transcribe. It is a mistake to assume that the transcriber will automatically know not to summarise some parts of the material, or to include or exclude laughter and pauses. If we are getting focus groups transcribed, we will need to provide information that will help the transcriber to identify the participants. The extra time for the task needs to be considered also when outsourcing the transcribing process.

Exercise 14.2: Transcription

Ask a member of your family, or a close friend, to participate in a 10-minute interview with you. Start with a broad question and then probe for additional information. In line with our example interview transcripts, as per chapter 10, you might want to ask your interviewee what constitutes 'being Australian'. Make sure you probe for information about the activities he or she considers important in 'being an Australian'. Audio-record the interview, then transcribe it as fully as possible. Now consider the following:

1. How long did the transcription take, compared with the original interview?
2. Highlight the non-verbal communication you are able to include. What does it tell you in addition to the words you have recorded?
3. Consider the questions you asked, and any comments you gave. How did these contribute to the participant's responses?
4. Listen to the recording again, with the transcript in front of you. Did you change any words (perhaps to make it more grammatically correct)? Did you transcribe everything accurately?

This exercise should help you gain some understanding of the intricacies of transcription: the length of time transcription takes, the importance of non-verbal cues in contextualising the information being provided, the role of the researcher within the interview and the ways in which editing may inadvertently change the participant's intended meaning.

Source: Lacey & Luff 2001

The second, and even more vital, aspect to immersion is what some writers have called incubation (Hunter et al. 2002). It occurs alongside and after the initial immersion in the data and the focus is analytical interpretation. It is here that we make sense of what the data are telling us. Time dedicated to this stage is critical to undertaking analysis, but these time needs are often not fully appreciated in the planning process. Qualitative research project timelines (see chapter 2) are often drawn, with data collection as the most time-consuming aspect of the research, and only a brief period is allocated to analysis, as if the insights will automatically emerge from the data. The essential component of meaning-making—that is, interpretation—is scarcely accorded a mention. In the incubation stage, the researcher must mull over the insights from the data and try to make sense of them. It is at this point that analytical rigour meets creativity. We may find concept maps, models and diagrams useful in this conceptual phase of meaning-making, but the essential ingredient is dedicated time.

Organising our data
Using word processing for data organisation

You will have already gathered that an in-depth interview results in a significant physical quantity of data. Transcripts of interviews can amount to hundreds of pages. For example, interviewing 18 people involved in the women's health policy area in 2001 produced nearly 800 pages of data. To make sense of so much data it must be organised, and word-processing packages can dramatically increase the ease of that organisation. Setting out our transcript in a user-friendly way is important. Minimise the formatting is an important hint: we may want to cut and paste sections of the interview. We can also use line numbers to assist in identifying segments of text. I find that five-line intervals work best, assisting in tracking and sorting the data and enabling the identification of specific ideas in the transcript as well as the length of particular segments of data (see box 14.2 for an example of how is used in practice).

Microsoft Word also has useful search functions that assist in the management of data. Full transcripts are an essential part of interview analysis, and at the time of transcription we need to give each transcript an identifying name. Assign either a name or a code that can be attached to any segment of the data that we will use. This is also useful if we wish to create cases in computer-assisted data management programs such as NVivo (see box 14.1 below). For example, in my women's health policy research, I interviewed three key groups of informants. My transcripts were identified with pseudonyms and categorised as A (activist); B (bureaucrat); and SP (service provider). This enabled quick and easy identification of the transcript from which a particular quote or idea originated. It also meant I could readily identify if a particular theme related to all groups interviewed or specifically to one group. Another benefit was that the assigning of pseudonyms and categories enabled me to identify if a particular participant or group had been silent on various aspects of the topic. However, before speculating on why this may be the case, I also checked the transcripts to ensure that the participants had had the opportunity to speak on these aspects, an important point if we are using semistructured or unstructured interviews.

Karen Willis

Computer-assisted data management

Purpose-developed computer programs are also available to help manage and organise our qualitative data. These programs are especially useful when we have large amounts of data. They can assist with storing and coding data, the creation of classification systems, enumeration of specific categories, attaching memos to data, finding relationships between concepts and producing graphics of these relationships. But it is important to remember that these qualitative data programs essentially assist in the sorting and managing of the data. They do not analyse; that is the role of the researcher.

Computer data management has been the source of contention in qualitative research. In the debate, some researchers claim that to use computers in the coding of qualitative data takes away the creative element, and mechanises a process that relies on the researchers' understanding of context in interpretation. Others have taken to electronic assistance with enthusiasm, as a way of making the process easier, and with a fond regard for the 'coded inscriptions' that are produced as capturing the reality of the data. However, these are two extreme views. There is also debate about the ways in which computer programs might serve to fragment rich data. Indeed, overreliance on the coding reports as representing the story being told must be avoided. Rather, as in all coding, the researcher must constantly move between the original transcripts and the coded categories, questioning how the categories capture the meanings conveyed by research participants, and how useful the segments are in the analytic process.

The computer packages used in social science qualitative research can broadly be categorised as two types. The first are those used to generate theory (ostensibly modelled on grounded theory); for example, NVivo (now in NVivo8) and its predecessor NUD*IST. The second are those that assist in thematic analysis by providing a code and retrieve function, such as the Ethnograph. Such code-and-retrieve packages require the development of a codebook, and then the application of this codebook to chunks of text. This enables the marking out of chunks of text (often overlapping) and easy retrieval of all text that relates to a particular code. Programs that focus on theory generation, as in the first type, allow the development of codes throughout the data analysis process. Once data are entered and coded, the relationship between coded categories can be explored.

To use such packages effectively, we need to have a clear appreciation of their specific capacity, and a good understanding of our data. For the former, we need some skills and training in the software program, and for the latter we need immersion in our data. The decision about whether we will use computer-assisted data management needs to be made at the time of transcription, at the latest, as there are implications for the way in which we will format and save our data.

As a general rule of thumb, and remembering that this will depend on our methodological approach, I would suggest that any less than 15 in-depth interviews are easier to manage manually. Between 15 and 25, there is potential for software to assist in data management, but it may be a better use of time to work manually with the data than to spend time learning a program. With more than 25 interviews, there is probably benefit in learning the intricacies of a relevant software package.

Ezzy (2002) provides an extensive summary of issues surrounding computer-assisted programs. Similarly, Liamputtong and Ezzy (2005: 274–82) discuss the use of these programs in qualitative research including their advantages and disadvantages.

Box 14.1: Using NVivo

NVivo8 is a commonly used computer assisted data management package. Using this package it is possible to import a wide range of documents that may comprise data, code large amounts of text data and sort data into categories.

It is beyond the scope of this chapter to fully describe the program. However, a brief summary of coding may familiarise you with its key elements. Once we have set up a project, we need to save your project into the Documents part of the menu. When we are moving to coding, we start with the creation of *nodes*. These enable coded material to be saved under representative headings.

Those categories that can be linked together are coded as *tree nodes*. In our study of national identity, it may be useful to have a tree node called Lifestyle, and linked to this tree node may be subcategories where we code positive or negative statements about lifestyle, feelings about lifestyle, or lifestyle activities that are mentioned by participants. Those categories for which the links are not immediately obvious may be categorised as *free nodes*. We may be uncertain about where the ideas about difference fit, and code these initially as free nodes.

NVivo8 also allows other documents to comprise the data set. For example, pdf documents, visual images, media files or web pages can be imported into the project file to be coded and analysed.

Exercise 14.3: NVivo

Go to <www.qsrinternational.com/products_nvivo.aspx> and click on Play tutorial. After you have watched the tutorial, consider the following:

1   Of the features described, which do you think are most useful to approaching data analysis?

Karen Willis

2. How would use of this program shape the way that you think about how to interpret and report on your data?
3. What are the advantages of using a program like NVivo to organise your data?
4. What are the disadvantages of using a program like NVivo to organise your data?

Approaches to analysis

Thematic analysis: Analysis of qualitative data that explores the presence of themes, both predetermined and those that emerge, within the data.

Narrative analysis: The making sense of data by focusing on the story that the participant tells. This analysis explores how participants tell their stories and how these stories link to a broader social or structural context.

Many qualitative researchers use interview studies as their major method, and this section provides information and exercises on **thematic analysis** and **narrative analysis** to assist in understanding differing ways of approaching interview data. It is important to be clear about the analytical approach you will adopt in your study. However, there are many other types of qualitative data, and ways of conducting research and information on approaches to content and discourse analysis are discussed in chapters 11 and 12.

Thematic analysis

Thematic analysis is the most commonly used form of analysis in qualitative research, particularly research involving interviews. In essence, a theme is a central idea that emerges from the data. In some cases, where substantial reading has been done on the topic, themes may be predetermined, and analysis involves the exploration of those themes within the data collected. More commonly, use of a thematic analysis approach means that the research is concerned to identify themes that emerge from within the data. A close reading and coding of the data, sensitivity to what participants are expressing in their encounters with the researcher, and the capacity to move beyond description of participant accounts to interpretation of how these accounts fit within the research topic are the hallmarks of a thematic analysis.

Commencing analysis

Memos and fieldnotes

Writing memos or fieldnotes is an important part of the research process. As stated, the reflexive researcher needs to consider their impact on the research process, and memoing is a good way of thinking through the issues and decisions that are taken during the research process. Memos also help to contextualise the data and assist in the development of theoretical insights into our data. Through our reflections on the data, we start to make connections between the experience being recounted and broader ideas. It is important to note these as we are undertaking our analysis.

Coding

An integral first part of qualitative analysis is **coding**. At first glance, coding may appear to be the antithesis of qualitative analysis. It may be argued that coding serves to fragment rich data, and the task at hand is to regain the wholeness of meaning. However, coding provides an important way of organising the material, and it is the task of the qualitative researcher to ensure that the richness of the meanings in the material remains. Coding works particularly well in identifying similarities in experience between participants; the challenge for the qualitative researcher is to recognise these, but at the same time, retain the unique aspects of individual cases.

> **Coding:** The process by which data are organised for analysis.

Coding is the marking of segments of data with symbols, descriptive words or category names. To begin the coding process, carefully read the transcribed data, line by line, and divide the data into meaningful analytical units. As we locate meaningful segments, we code them, ensuring that we record the code and its rationale. We need to keep a master list to reapply the codes (which may change or be amended) throughout our analysis. Some people use card indexes or coloured pens to organise the categories that emerge. Trial coding categories allow us to test whether they will capture the ideas we want to code, before settling on categories and subcategories. Always keep a category for 'Other' data. These are data we suspect are relevant, but are unsure how, at this early stage, they fit within the analysis. The data listed in our Other category can be reviewed later to see if they do fit within one of our identified categories or subcategories. Sometimes it will become apparent that some of the Other data actually form a category of their own.

We may already have a set of existing codes. **A priori codes** are those that we either develop through our understanding of the literature, or that we have already deemed as significant. For example, in content analysis, as per chapter 11, much of the coding is undertaken on this basis. Our method may require that we alternatively, or also, develop the codes through the coding process; these are **inductive codes**, emerging from the data that we are analysing. In practice, much research is a combination of both a priori and inductive coding. We also may code particular segments with more than one code, because the concepts may partially or completely overlap. If examining the recurrence of particular codes or concepts, we need to be aware of the importance of contextualisation: a particular code may occur frequently throughout all

> **A priori codes:** The coding of themes that are determined prior to the data analysis.
>
> **Inductive codes:** The coding of themes that emerge from the data.

Karen Willis

text documents; however, it may also be that it may occur frequently because one participant used the concept many times rather than it occurring across our sample.

Box 14.2 gives an example of coding, using the transcript from the example interview on national identity with Anna, to be found on this text's website <www.oup.com.au/orc/walter>. Although this example only shows Anna's transcript, it is vital to remember that the researcher needs to read all five transcripts before beginning the analysis of any individual transcript. Having read all five transcripts and then returned to the transcript of Anna's interview, it is possible to identify some beginning codes. At this initial stage of inductive coding, it is hard to be sure what will be important in the final analysis, so code more, rather than less.

Box 14.2: Coding our data

Initial Coding of Anna's transcript

Line	Transcript	Notes	Code
23	ANNA: I was born in Hobart and I've lived here my whole life and both my parents were born in Tasmania as well.	Personal Whole life	History History/time
	INTERVIEWER: And grandparents, just out of interest?	Family	
29	ANNA: I think, um, they definitely did on my mum's side and I think one of my dad's parents did—was born in Tasmania as well but one wasn't.	Family	History
37	ANNA: I suppose because I've lived here my whole life it's familiar and I've just turned 18 so when I go out I mix, like, a lot—most of the people out I know and I'm friends with and the kind of social networks are quite dense. Does that make sense?	Whole life Age Familiarity	History/time Activities Social networks
43	INTERVIEWER: Yes. ANNA: Oh, and I like the environment as well. I spend a lot of time, like, at the beach and bushwalking and things like that. So it's ideal for that kind of thing.	Environment Lot of time Place ideal	Environment Time Activities Env Positive
49	INTERVIEWER: It is. If I said what do you like about Australia, is it the same question for you? ANNA: No. I don't think it is.	Difference	Identity—Aus or State

Initial coding of the first page of Anna's transcript points to possibilities to consider as the coding continues in this and the other interviews. The beginnings of themes important in understanding the relevance of the concept of 'national identity' are emerging. These are:

- whether personal and family history in a particular location creates a stronger sense of national or state identity

- the concept of lifestyle and how it is described as creating a positive sense of place attachment. In particular, the components of lifestyle that are described may be important here. Do they occur throughout the other interviews? They may need to be elaborated on as various aspects of lifestyle are defined and discussed by participants
- the extent to which identity is tied to place, state or nation.

As this process continues, consider how participants' views of three events—Anzac Day, Australia Day and the Olympics—may inform our analysis of what it means to be Australian. How do statements about these events link to the beginning ideas identified above? Similarly, consider how these interviewees from Tasmania see themselves as separate from, different from or the same as people from mainland Australian states, and how this may impact on their views about what it means to be Australian.

Exploring relationships between categories

Having sorted through our data and coded them into categories, the task of analysis is to explore the relationships between codes. Do some categories relate to other categories? For example, how are the perceptions about Australia Day linked with what participants say they like about living in Tasmania? What might be the reasons for this? We may develop a hierarchy wherein all coded information is sorted according to where it fits within the various categories. As further categories are developed, we start to get an understanding of those that are stand-alone, and those that overlap with other categories. At this stage, we need to be constantly checking our interpretations against the transcripts, to ensure the veracity of our claims about the data.

Discrepancies and deviant cases

The initial analysis may reveal some inconsistencies in the data. We may find that our sample throws up discrepancies that we haven't anticipated or that there are some issues that remain unclear. At this stage, we need to consider whether these inconsistencies indicate evidence that does not fit within our conceptual framework. While there may be clear patterns across the group we are studying, there may be one or two that do not seem to fit within the framework we are developing. The analysis of these **deviant cases** can be useful in two ways. First, such cases can challenge the way in which we are thinking about

Deviant cases: Data that do not appear to fit within the analytical categories being developed.

Karen Willis

our data and demand we interpret it in a different way. Second, the information gained may indicate that we should re-enter the field. Perhaps our sampling strategy needed to be better defined, or maybe there were complexities in the field settings we had not fully anticipated. In the case of national identity, how would we code an interview with a young Australian of Aboriginal heritage? Would the themes starting to emerge from the analysis of Anna's transcript be likely to be repeated in this transcript?

Explaining what is going on: Themes

Having spent time immersed in our data, coding the transcripts and exploring how codes fit together into categories, we will find particular ideas or concepts that assist in the interpretation or explanation of the data. These ideas or concepts are called themes. As Green and colleagues (2007:549) state: 'A theme is more than a category. The generation of themes requires moving beyond a *description* of a range of categories; it involves shifting to an *explanation*, or even better, an *interpretation* of the issue under investigation.' In the sample of transcripts on national identity, the codes may relate to activities that people associate with being Australian, the pace of life in Australia, and values and beliefs about the importance of being laid back, thus suggesting an overall theme of an Australian lifestyle. The task of the analyst is to use the data to explore why this theme has emerged as a significant component of national identity.

Exercise 14.4: Thematic analysis

You have previously undertaken some coding of the interview on national identity undertaken with Anna. This exercise takes your analysis further.

Your task

1. In groups, or separately, take the other four transcripts located on the textbook website. Start with an open coding approach, developing a range of codes to cover the key ideas and concepts in these interviews.
2. When you have developed your master list of codes, review all the codes to see what codes link together throughout and between the transcripts.
3. See if you can identify themes that pertain to the idea of national identity as expressed by the five participants in this exercise. Remember, themes are not codes; they are conceptual ideas that emerge from a consideration of what the codes and categories mean. Check your themes with another class or group member; can you account for differences?

4   As a final task, locate four media reports that identify attributes of being Australian, and identify the key themes to be found in these. Are they the same as those you found in the personal stories? Can you theorise why these themes are the same, or may be different?

Grounded theory

Closely aligned with thematic analysis is grounded theory. Developed in 1967 by Anselm Strauss and Barney Glaser, grounded theory is a body of thought about analysis, with the aim of generating theory rather than simply providing mechanistic processes to undertake analysis. It is most often utilised for its approach to thematic analysis and coding. A process of inductive analysis drives this methodological approach, from selection of participants to interviewing, and an ongoing approach to analysis of interview data.

In grounded theory, coding commences with the collection of data. While in-depth interviews may be the key source, other data sources are also important. Grounded theory emphasises the importance of writing memos throughout the research process; in addition, other sources of information, such as newsletters, contemporary media items and observational notes, may also become part of the data to be analysed. The heart of grounded theory is theoretical sampling. Theoretical sampling requires that we continually analyse as we collect data in order to guide our sampling process. Data collection ceases when no new information on any particular code is emerging (this is called theoretical saturation). In this way, data collection is controlled by the emerging theory. In terms of meaning-making, grounded theory has an insistence on theoretical sensitivity; that is, the ability 'to see the research situation and its associated data in new ways, and to explore the data's potential for developing theory' (Strauss & Corbin 1990:44).

Using grounded theory, **open coding** is the first part of the coding process. The aim is to generate an emergent set of categories and their properties; usually through line-by-line analysis of data, alongside theoretical memos that are written at the time of data collection. Here the emphasis is on looking for similarities and differences, and the grouping of information into categories. **Axial coding** is the process by which the codes that are developed are more rigorously specified and elaborated, most commonly through the development of subcategories. Selective coding is the process by which all categories are unified around a core category (for example, in the earliest work by Strauss on illness patterns, the core category became 'trajectories of illness'). 'The core category can be identified by its centrality, frequent occurrence, good connections to other categories and

> **Open coding**: Initial line-by-line examination for themes from data.
>
> **Axial coding**: The coding process used in grounded theory in which codes are rigorously specified and elaborated to reflect theoretical core categories.

Karen Willis

implications for a more general theory' (Grbich 1999:177). This enables the development of theory.

Narrative analysis and life histories

Life history: A life history approach uses the 'stories' that people tell of their lives as a source of data. In-depth interviews are usually used to solicit data, although letters, diaries, photographs and so on can also be used. Also see *narrative analysis*.

Life histories are quite simply 'an account of one person's life in his or her own words' (Plummer 2001:18). Grounded originally in symbolic interactionism, and more recently in postmodernism, this approach is concerned with people as social actors and active social agents, and a sense that the narrative of a life conveys the essence of this in meaningful ways. The focus in narrative analysis is less on gaining 'the truth' about an event or social situation than in understanding people's interpretation of the event. Thus, the narratives or stories that people tell of their lives, and the way they construct their narratives, are rich sources of data that can be used to explore social life. This approach is also known variously as: narrative, documents of life, self stories or 'my-stories', oral histories or personal testaments. In sociology, often the aim of a life history or narrative approach is to reveal how individuals' actions and interpretation coexist with broader social structures and patterns. The stories people tell contain the following elements:

- stories and plots;
- characters and story lines;
- genre and tropes; and
- life patterns (Plummer 2001:196).

In short, a life history approach aims to reveal the inner life of the person. Life histories or narratives are usually solicited through in-depth, open-ended interviews, although social researchers can also use a variety of different sources. The guided interview requires gentle probes, and can last anywhere from half an hour to several hours. A well-formed story needs to answer the following kinds of questions: 'What was done?' (act); 'When or where was it done' (scene)'; 'Who did it?' (agent); 'How did he or she do it?' (agency); and 'Why?' (purpose) (Burke 1945:xv in Plummer 2001:196).

Narrative analysis is also explicit about the role of the interviewer in the construction of the narrative. As Atkinson describes: 'In a life story interview, the interviewee is a storyteller, the narrator of the story being told, whereas the interviewer is a guide, or director, in this process. The two together are collaborators, composing, constructing a story the teller can be pleased with' (1998:9).

There are different frameworks for undertaking a narrative analysis. Riessman (2008), a leading exponent of narrative analysis, points to the way that narratives can be analysed thematically or structurally. Grbich (2007) provides a concise discussion of these differences, distinguishing between sociolinguistic and sociocultural approaches. Sociolinguistic approaches to narrative focus on the structure of the telling of the narrative, usually containing an orientation to the story, the explication of a particular issue or event and then a resolution of the event. The interest is in how structure and language are used to convey the information. In contrast, the sociocultural approach locates narratives within a broader social and political context; the interest for the analyst is in how the telling of the story relates to broader social forces in interaction with the researcher.

When analysing a narrative interview, it is important to retain the structure of the narrative as a whole. It is important not to fragment the story into discrete thematic categories, as is the case in more traditional forms of qualitative data analysis; rather, narrative analysis needs to search for larger units of discourse and code their structure and thematic content (Rice & Ezzy 1999:125).

Box 14.3 provides some points on how to analyse narratives.

Box 14.3: Narrative analysis

When writing life histories, it is important to provide:

1. **A sense of ordering of events**
   Events are usually presented in a linear fashion, although not always, because it is difficult to understand the sequence of events with no time frame.
2. **A sense of a person behind the text**
   It is difficult to cope with people who are mere fragments and lack any sense of predictability, so the people in the life narrative need to have a kind of stability of identity and continuity.
3. **A sense of voice and perspective belonging to the narrator**
   Someone has to tell the story and that someone needs to be identifiable.
4. **A sense of causality**
   Plot matters—if this, then that. People are motivated to do things, there are reasons things happen, even if sometimes the reason becomes 'chance', so a clear plot structure needs to be included.

Source: Adapted from Plummer 2001:196

Karen Willis

Case study 14.2: Stories of infertility

Kirkman's (1999) research on infertility used narrative analysis. She researched the stories of 33 women, one of whom was herself. On acknowledging the partiality of the research encounter, Kirkman comments that 'I could also see that the stories I told of myself gave only a partial view of me. This must also have been true of the other participants in the research. Including myself as a participant helped to avoid the pitfalls of believing that one knows all about another person' (Kirkman 1999:35).

She was interested in women's constructions of their lives, and particularly in the way that their lives intersected with a feminism that was often unsupportive of reproductive technologies. She argues that there are four features of narrative research:

- the recognition of the individual person
- the recognition of the subjective dimension of lives and the importance of meaning
- the recognition of the contribution of context to meaning
- the recognition of the collaborative construction of autobiographical narratives.

Kirkman's analytical strategy with the interview data was to derive coherent narratives by condensing the transcripts. She omitted her own comments and queries, and material not relevant to infertility. Where possible, she used women's own words, using summaries only when space demanded it. She constructed the narratives with a view to ensuring that women themselves 'owned' their narratives. She returned the constructed narrative to individual participants, along with her own narrative. She claims that this process of narrative construction enabled her to work with the documents as 'comparable data'. Kirkman's account is interesting, not only for the details about the use of narrative analysis, but for the explicit ways in which reflexivity is embedded in her research process (Kirkman 1999).

Exercise 14.5: Narrative analysis

Interview a class member about his or her experiences at university so far. Consider carefully what sort of questions you would ask in order to elicit the story of their life as a university student.

1. How important is your role as a university student in getting the person to respond to you?
2. How do you 'tell the story' of being a student?
3. Can you discern the dimensions of narrative that are pointed to in case study 14.2?

Extending the analytical challenge: Analysing focus groups

So far we have discussed two ways of approaching analysis of one-on-one interviews. The work of the qualitative researcher is further challenged when interviews are conducted in a group setting. In this section we will explore the importance of analysing both the content and interaction of focus group interviews. The following discussion (taken from Willis et al. 2009) points to these challenges.

Focus groups attempt to gain understanding of an issue through examination of perceptions, values and beliefs of group participants. As outlined in chapter 10, it is the interaction between participants that is the defining feature of a focus group, and the interview structure needs to take account of inclusion of multiple voices in the research encounter. Focus groups are useful because they enable exploration of personally held values and beliefs and how these may be articulated in, and intersect with, publicly held values, beliefs and attitudes. This requires skilful interviewing by the researcher (often referred to as the facilitator). Focus groups can provide deep understanding of how and why people's views differ, the strength of attitudes, beliefs and opinions held, and the factors influencing particular perspectives. Researchers can analyse how social ideas and values shape individual behaviour through attention to the processes of group discussion.

> **Focus group:** A research method that involves encouraging a group of people to discuss some social or political issue.

Focus group discussion cannot be analysed in the same way as one-on-one interviews, even though many analytic procedures may be similar (such as developing codes, categories and themes). With three layers of data—the individual, the group and the group interaction—analysis requires attention to the dynamics of the discussion, the type and range of speech acts (verbal and non-verbal), the context within which discussion occurs and the group production of content. This has implications for recording data—audio-recordings must be comprehensive enough to include nuances in expression, and the data generally also consists of **field notes** by trained co-facilitators.

> **Field notes:** Field notes provide a record of the participant observations made by an ethnographer. Field notes take the form of notes or sound recordings, and record not only what the researcher has seen but also his or her feelings and perceptions of the events. Also see *ethnographic approach*; *participant observation*.

The dynamics of the discussion can inform not only the strength of views held, and the level of consensus, but the way that consensus or disagreement may be achieved. Views may change, moderate or perhaps be strengthened during the group encounter. For this reason, it is important to consider the sequence of discussion that occurs within the group. This assists in understanding the variation in perceptions, and enables

Karen Willis

the researcher to make sense of what may appear to be contradictory statements in the unfolding of the discussion.

Further, the interaction in a well-facilitated focus group can push the boundaries of discussion beyond what can be achieved in a one-on-one interview (Warr 2005). Kitzinger and Farquhar (1999) point to the way that sensitive moments in focus groups may deepen understanding of public health issues that are viewed as private, sensitive and controversial. Data analysis should, therefore, comprise examining verbal and non-verbal expressions, discontinuities in interaction, the strategic use of humour, and discord between participants. In research on sexual behaviour, Wellings and colleagues (2000), for example, illustrate the use of humour by a participant who acknowledges to the group that his behaviour goes against the social norm by the tone he uses and specific language (the word 'information'):

> Yeah it was a one night job [said jokingly] (group laughter) and erm … you see that's why I was really a bit worried you know, because I didn't know her. So … a friend knew her too. So I got information (laughter). Sorry—I know that's bad innit? But … (p. 260).

In the same project, they also witnessed discord about safe sex practices through the following exchange between a male and female participant: a challenge to a participant perspective not achievable in a one-on-one interview situation, and opening up the discussion to exploration of gendered responses about safe sex:

> Male: I had unprotected sex with her and she really had a go at me because she had to go and get the morning after pill. She really, really dug the knife in, saying that I was a real bastard and everything even though she was just as up for it as me, you know?
>
> Female: Yeah, but it's different the next day when one of you has got to take a pill that makes you vomit for three days and the other one hasn't (p. 262).

Recurrence of ideas may be only one indicator of the strength of evidence when analysing focus group data. Brief intense discussion of an issue may be as, or more, important as lengthy, negotiated but superficial coverage. Frequency of discussion of specific topics may not be as relevant as diversity of opinions. The task of the analyst is to question constantly how interaction may indicate consensus, negotiated understanding or disagreement. For example, did the participants have clear views that were consistently held throughout the discussion, or did their views change as a result of listening to others?

Analysis of focus group interactions requires attention to the following:

- Was robust discussion evident or was the discussion mainly directed by the facilitator?
- How did the group members signal consensus or disagreement?

- Did the group refuse to discuss some aspects of the topic or some viewpoints?
- Were non-verbal signs or behaviours evident, and did they affect the discussion?
- Did all group members participate in the discussion?

The analyst is, therefore, less concerned with whether the information presented by participants is 'objectively true', and more interested in the way that such information is presented and received within the group and how group interaction may challenge or confirm people's stated views. As Silverman states, 'By analysing how people talk to one another, one is directly gaining access to a cultural universe and its content of moral assumptions' (2002:113).

Voices in the field

Jane Maree Maher

Jane Maree Maher is an academic at Monash University and currently Director of the Centre for Women's Studies and Gender Research. In the following paragraphs she describes her research practice, especially around the use of semistructured in-depth interviews

'Over the past decade, my research has focused on Australian experiences of contemporary mothering, how couples divide the domestic work, and how women with children make decisions about employment. I have been interested in how well common social and media accounts of these decisions match what people actually say about their experiences. These projects have all been qualitative ones undertaken in collaborative research teams, using semistructured interviews with very open questions. This approach has proven vital in allowing people to talk about their decisions and experiences in their own terms; the research findings have often been very different to outcomes of surveys of women's family experiences, where people can only choose from a set number of responses to predetermined questions. While broad survey data is important to reveal trends, qualitative research allows insights into people's lives and stories that is crucial to understand our society.

'My research has found that women's views and decisions about employment and motherhood are shaped by many different social factors and pressures. Concepts such as 'motherguilt' which are often used to describe women's anxious feelings about balancing work and family, don't capture the complex

Karen Willis

negotiations in family life, and views about what children need that really shape mothers' employment decisions. Commitment to mothering and commitment to work are often presented as mutually exclusive, whereas most women seek out opportunities to combine both successfully. One of the most rewarding opportunities to use this research has been in contributions to policy forums such as the Human Rights and Equal Opportunity Commission review in 2007, *It's About Time: Women, Men, Work and Family*. It is so important that real voices and experiences can inform the decisions that we make as a society.'

Voices in the field

Fiona Gill

'I am currently working as a lecturer in the Department of Sociology and Social Policy at the University of Sydney. My research interests have been in the development, management and performance of identities in changing or ambiguous contexts. Recently I have been engaged in researching the Australian dairy industry, and the ways farmers are managing change and environmental challenges in Sydney's urban fringes. Understanding how people are managing the structural and social changes, as well as their motivations for continuing to farm, is an important part of Australia's continuing economic well-being in addition to contributing to our understanding of family dynamics and identity performance. This research was carried out using an in-depth case study of three family farms. The farms exhibit characteristic multigenerational management structures of a farmer, in his late forties or fifties, running the farm with his wife, overseen by his (semi-) retired father. Over 15 months in 2006 and 2007, three semi-structured interviews were conducted with each member of the three 'active' couples and of two 'retired' couples. Each interview covered a different temporal period: the past, present and future; and lasted between 45 minutes to an hour. In addition, I spent time socially with members of each couple and assisted at a local show in the dairy ring. This use of repeated qualitative interviews is relatively underutilised in social research, but has significant benefits. Repeated interviews facilitate the development of a strong relationship between researcher and the participants, resulting in rich data in the form of on-going life narratives. As participants reflect on the previous interviews, and the different stages of their lives, a clearer picture of changing identities and relationships emerges. Repeated interviews move away from the snapshot of life provided by the use of standardised or semi-structured interviewing. Instead, a more complete understanding of a social context is developed because we see the context over a period of time—we gain a more complete perspective, which is otherwise limited to either ethnographies or longitudinal studies.'

From method to practice

In 2007, Madeleine Smart used in-depth interviewing as one of her two methods in her triangulated honours research project into the division of domestic labour in Australia. By conducting in-depth interviews with four couples who hire a house cleaner, Madeleine aimed to gain a clearer understanding of the motivations behind the decisions to outsource (at least some anyway) domestic housework. Her conceptual frame was developed from social theories on the role of gender in unpaid work allocation and the ideologies associated with gendered divisions of labour. This broad frame allowed her to interpret her analysis against the conflicting theoretical approaches of Catherine Hakim's (2000) view that mothers now have full choice in their decisions to undertake a primary domestic or primary worker role, against Hoschschild's (1989) concept of the stalled revolution of continuing gender inequality. She used the a priori codes of 'gender strategies', 'power relations', 'class' and 'changing gender roles', which were garnered from her literature review to begin her thematic analysis of her transcripts. During the coding process she added others that emerged from the data. These included 'managing relationship tensions'; 'notions of inegalitarianism'; and 'gendered socioeconomic status'.

Madeleine's study concluded that, while couples hire cleaners to relieve family pressures relating to combining work and young children and clashes over the division of domestic roles, the households of higher educated women are more likely to hire a cleaner. Most couples also felt somewhat ill at ease at the inegalitarian connotations of employing someone to do household tasks. However, her key finding was that gender roles do not really change as a result of hiring a household cleaner. The women interviewed were still primarily responsible for running the household, regardless of their own ideologies around the household division of labour. Regardless of the expressed opinion of both adult members of the household, hiring a cleaner was still seen in terms of relieving the woman's workload. Mostly a reduction in cleaning work just allowed other unpaid, mainly female-allocated tasks, such as caring for children, to achieve a higher prominence.

Madeleine Smart is now employed in a policy position with a state governement department.

Karen Willis

Conclusion

Analysing and interpreting qualitative data is, on the one hand, hard work, and on the other, extremely rewarding. Particularly in interview studies, qualitative researchers are privileged in being able to enter people's lives and obtain material that can lead to important insights. Our love of social interaction and fascination with the insights gained into the lives of others, as well as the amount of work required to recruit and conduct interviews, means that often the interview becomes the focal point in our relationship with the research. But, as novice researchers such as Jill, in the opening to this chapter, find out, there is much more to the process than the interview. Indeed, the analytical components of research are often more exciting and fascinating than the data-collection phase. In qualitative analysis, the art of interpretation and the rigour of analysis must come together to produce a coherent, well-thought-through research product. The processes outlined in this chapter should be used as a guide only. While undertaking the exercises is far from the 'authentic' analysis of our own carefully gathered data, they should provide some understanding of the different ways in which qualitative researchers work to create meaning in their research. To explore a range of other qualitative methods and their key modes of analysis, read the on-line modules available at <www.oup.com.au/orc/walter>. This site contains modules on conversation analysis, action research, ethnographic research, narrative research, memory work and sensory and visual methods.

Main points

> - The task of qualitative analysis is to make meaning from a rich source of texts: individual interviews, focus group interviews or unobtrusive methods, such as observation or content analysis.
> - Essential ingredients in the task of analysis include: dedicated time, reflexivity and immersion in the data.
> - The reflexive researcher is one who actively acknowledges, and engages with, the ways in which the researcher influences the process and outcome of the research.
> - Immersion in the data requires saturation in the texts being analysed.
> - Transcription is a vital part of the research process: full transcriptions of interview data must be undertaken, and where possible transcription should be undertaken by the researcher.
> - Computer programs available to assist in the management of data are useful research tools, but should not be seen as more than this.

› Coding is the process of organising our data for analysis.

› Management of data requires attention to such details as code names for transcripts, appropriate formatting of transcripts, and the capacity to code in a way that provides a clear understanding of the meanings conveyed by participants.

› Memos and field notes are important in documenting the research process. They can assist in developing a reflexive approach to the research, as well as providing useful analytical information.

› Approaches to analysis for interview data include thematic and grounded theory analysis, and narrative analysis.

› Focus group data add a dimension of complexity to analysis, because the task is to understand the group interaction as well as the individual views of participants.

› Understanding approaches to analysis, as well as the time commitment required to undertake analysis, must be an integral part of research design.

Further reading

Ezzy, D. (2002). *Qualitative Analysis: Practice and Innovation*. Crows Nest: Allen & Unwin.

Grbich, C. (2007). *Qualitative Data Analysis: An Introduction*. London: Sage.

Liamputtong, P. and Ezzy, D. (2005). *Qualitative Research Methods*. 2nd edn. South Melbourne: Oxford University Press.

Riessman, C. K. (2008). *Narrative Methods for the Human Sciences*. Los Angeles: Sage.

Silverman, D. (ed.) (2004). *Qualitative Research: Theory, Method and Practice*. 2nd edn. London: Sage.

Strauss, A. and Corbin, J. (1990). *Basics of Qualitative Research: Grounded Theory Procedures and Techniques*. London: Sage.

References

Atkinson, R. (1998). *The Life Story Interview*. London: Sage.

Ezzy, D. (2002). *Qualitative Analysis: Practice and Innovation*. Crows Nest: Allen & Unwin.

Fook, J. (1999). 'Reflexivity as Method', *Annual Review of Health Social Sciences*, 9: 11–20.

Fraser, H. (2004). 'Doing Narrative Research: Analysing Personal Stories Line by Line', *Qualitative Social Work*, 3 (2): 179–201.

Karen Willis

Glaser, B. G. and Strauss, A. M. (1967). *Discovery of Grounded Theory: Strategies for Qualitative Research*. Chicago: Aldine.

Grbich, C. (1999). *Qualitative Research in Health: An Introduction*. St Leonards: Allen & Unwin.

Grbich, C. (2007). *Qualitative Data Analysis: An Introduction*. London: Sage.

Green, J., Willis, K., Hughes, E., Small, R., Welch, N., Gibbs, L. and Daly, J. (2007). 'Generating Best Evidence from Qualitative Research: The Role of Data Analysis', *Australian and New Zealand Journal of Public Health*, 31 (6): 545–50.

Hakim, C. (2000). *Work–Lifestyle Choices in the 21st Century*. New York: Oxford University Press.

Hochschild, A. (1989). *The Second Shift*. New York: Avon Books.

Hunter, A., Lusardi, P., Zucker, D., Jacelon, D. and Chandler, G. (2002). 'Making Meaning: The Creative Component in Qualitative Research', *Qualitative Health Research*, 12 (3): 388–98.

Kirkman, M. (1999). 'I Didn't Interview Myself: The Researcher as Participant in Narrative Research', *Annual Review of Health Social Sciences*, 9: 32–41.

Kitzinger, J. and Farquhar, C. (1999) 'The Analytic Potential of "Sensitive Moments" in Focus Group Discussions', in Barbour, R. S. and Kitzinger, J. (eds), *Developing Focus Group Research: Politics, Theory and Practice*. London: Sage: 156–73.

Lacey, A. and Luff, D. (2001). *Trent Focus for Research and Development in Primary Health Care: An Introduction to Qualitative Analysis*. UK: Trent Focus.

Liamputtong, P. and Ezzy, D. (2005). *Qualitative Research Methods*. 2nd edn. South Melbourne: Oxford University Press.

Natalier, K. (2003). I'm Not His Wife: Doing Gender in Share Households. PhD thesis, Brisbane: School of Social Science, University of Queensland.

Plummer, K. (2001). *Documents of Life 2: An Invitation to a Critical Humanism*. London: Sage.

Pyett, P. (2001). 'Innovation and Compromise: Responsibility and Reflexivity in Research with Vulnerable Groups', in Daly, J., Guillemin, M. and Hill, S. (eds), *Technologies and Health: Critical Compromises*. South Melbourne: Oxford University Press.

Rice, P.L. & Ezzy, D. (1999). *Qualitative Research Methods: A Health Focus*. South Melbourne: Oxford University Press.

Riessman, C. K. (2008). *Narrative Methods for the Human Sciences*. Los Angeles: Sage.

Seymour, W. (2001). 'Putting Myself in the Picture: Researching Disability and Technology', in Daly, J., Guillemin, M., and Hill, S. (eds), *Technologies and Health: Critical Compromises*. South Melbourne: Oxford University Press.

Silverman, D. (2002). *Interpreting Qualitative Data: Methods for Analysing Talk, Text and Interaction*. 2nd edn. London: Sage.

Silverman, D. (ed.) (2004). *Qualitative Research: Theory, Method and Practice*, 2nd edn. London: Sage.

Smart, M. (2007). Changing Ideologies? Why Families Hire Domestic Cleaners. Unpublished honours thesis. Hobart: School of Sociology and Social Work, University of Tasmania.

Strauss, A. and Corbin, J. (1990). *Basics of Qualitative Research: Grounded Theory Procedures and Techniques*. London: Sage.

Warr, D. (2005) '"It Was Fun … But We Don't Usually Talk About These Things": Analyzing Sociable Interaction in Focus Groups', *Qualitative Inquiry*, 11 (2): 200–25.

Wellings, K., Branigan, P. and Mitchell, K. (2000). 'Discomfort, Discord and Discontinuity as Data: Using Focus Groups to Research Sensitive Topics', *Culture, Health and Sexuality*, 2 (3): 255–67.

Willis, K., Green, J., Daly, J., Williamson, L. and Bandyopadhyay, M. (2009). 'Perils and Possibilities: Achieving Best Evidence from Focus Groups in Public Health Research', *Australian and New Zealand Journal of Public Health*, 32(2): 131–6.

Karen Willis

4
Writing Up Our Research for Dissemination

Writing up is the cumulative aspect of the social science research process. Regardless of whether our project is qualitative or quantitative in approach, developed using theoretical frameworks from a feminist or Indigenous paradigm, funded by a competitive grant or undertaken as part of an undergraduate, honours or postgraduate course, writing up this research is generally a non-negotiable aspect of the task. It is in the writing-up stage that all other phases of the research process come together. As a reemphasised message of this book, the research project itself is built on a thorough grounding and understanding of its methodological underpinnings, a strong design, adherence to the research process and ethical practice, rigorous data collection, careful analysis and theoretically informed interpretation. The writing up of the research project, in all its phases, provides the capstone, completing the process.

Writing up has twin purposes. First and most obviously, it is the process by which we record the theoretical foundations, data and analysis and the results of our research, but this process is more than just a recording. As discussed in the following chapter, writing up is an essential aspect of the conceptual and interpretive process of research itself. While this text has emphasised the need for preparation and having key phases such as the research question and theoretical framework solidly in place before proceeding to collection, analyses and interpretation, it is a rare researcher who does not have a eureka moment during the writing-up stage. Struggling to articulate our process, practice and results on paper in a coherent and structured way often leads to insights that were not apparent during the individual phases.

The second, and less discussed, purpose of writing up is dissemination. Dissemination is not only about releasing our findings into our disciplinary and/or public realm, but also opening up our research process and practice to disciplinary and/or public scrutiny. Here we come full circle back to chapter 1, where we discussed what makes social science research scientific. As argued there, the scientific method includes professionalism, ethical integrity in how we go about the social research process, plus ensuring that the social research we conduct is rigorous and transparent in method, techniques and interpretation. In the writing-up process this transparency and rigour of all stages is made explicit. Opening up our research by writing up its processes and practice, as well as the analysis, results and interpretations of our findings, to public and peer inspection ensures that social science research is professional, integrity bounded and transparent.

It is also important to remember that the research is not really 'ours'. There are many stakeholders with a legitimate claim to at least some ownership of the research. Not only do we have disciplinary obligations, to our peers or to our examiners, but the input of our respondents entitles them to an ownership stake in the research project. The writing-up process allows all these disparate groups to assess how 'their' research project has been conducted and to judge its merits, from a variety of perspectives.

Additionally, most research is funded in one way or another. And while many student projects are not funded as explicitly as those receiving full funding via a grant or a consultancy, the receipt of a scholarship, the use of university facilities and resources, and even the time of our supervisors are all publicly supported. As such, we also have a moral obligation to write up the research we have undertaken and to write it up in a way that makes it as accessible and as clear as possible.

Finally, the writing-up process, which always takes longer than anticipated (often much longer), varies throughout from being a tedious slog to a brain-aching challenge. Completing the writing-up phase requires not only dedication and inspiration but also a dogged perseverance. But such perseverance is also a key trait of a successful researcher. And as noted in Michelle Gabriel's chapter, the reward at completion of writing up—the pleasure of holding your research report, thesis or article in your hand and knowing it is a job well done—is worth the effort.

Chapter 15

Writing Up Research

Michelle Gabriel

On writing

Writing is ... a way of 'knowing'—a method of discovery and analysis. By writing in different ways, we discover new aspects of our topic and our relationship to it.

Laurel Richardson (1994:516)

Writing about a subject forces one to study in an organised way and with a focused aim; to read all the important literature about it; to cover the whole ground, not leaving material gaps; and it gives one a powerful motive to get even the most trivial details right, not to let errors creep in. Most important of all, it forces one to think about the subject—and to organise one's thoughts as well as one's material, into coherent structures.

Bryan Magee (1997:33)

Key terms

annotated bibliography
audience
authorial voice
bibliography
constitutive role of writing
genre
generative view of writing
narrative
stream of consciousness

Introduction

Writing is an integral part of research. How we write about our research project will shape the way we and others come to understand the topic. As a new researcher, you may have given little thought to the write-up stage, believing that such issues can be faced when you are further into the research process; that it is something for later on. Nothing could be further from the truth. For the social science researcher, the writing task should begin on day one. Research also demands an active involvement by the social researcher in the multiple writing tasks that occur at different phases of the research process.

New researchers often approach the task of writing with trepidation. Writing up your research is seen as a daunting and difficult task. While undertaking the research itself may seem manageable, producing a 4000- or 8000-word report on your research project at the end of the process can be a significant barrier for many students.

Fortunately, there are many practical strategies to help with the task of research writing. To give a head start on the research writing and writing-up process, this chapter provides:

- an insight into current understandings of the relationship between research and writing
- an overview of academic writing styles
- a guide to writing research plans and reports
- tips on writing and editing.

Discovery through writing

Researchers are involved in many diverse written tasks. For example, sketching out our early visions of what it is we plan to research, preparing a grant proposal to attract research funds, writing letters to potential interviewees, keeping a diary of our experiences when conducting fieldwork, and writing a polished report or article about what we have discovered are all research writing tasks. Accordingly, the when and where and how of writing up the research to the research process is the subject of debate in the social sciences (see, for example, Wason 1985; Becker 1986; Richardson 1990, 1994; Richardson & St Pierre 2005). While writing up has traditionally been viewed as the final stage in the research process—something that social scientists do when they finish data collection and analysis, or return from the field—the **iterative** approach to writing is now more prominent. By iterative we mean a process of writing and rewriting, revising as we go, throughout the entire research process. The researcher starts writing from day one and continues to move between writing-based and non-writing-based research tasks until project completion.

> **Iterative research practice**: Research that occurs in the process of moving between writing-based and non-writing-based research tasks.

Preference for an iterative approach reflects a growing recognition of the pitfalls associated with the traditional two-step model of doing research first and writing up later, as well as the benefits of writing early and writing regularly. Experienced researchers argue that not only does the traditional two-step model create an unrealistic impression of the research process, it also fails new researchers in a number of important ways.

First, researchers who follow a two-step strategy run the following risks:

- without the aid of a clear and comprehensive written plan, which others can read and comment on, we could proceed down a wrong-headed path
- we might lose material we've collected along the way
- we might underestimate how much time is required to edit and fine-tune a major report or dissertation.

Second, a research-now-write-later model underplays the role of writing as a tool of discovery and the role of writing in crafting reality.

This idea of writing as a tool of discovery is sometimes referred to as a **generative view of writing**. For those who usually only write in response to institutional demands or obligations—'I have to write this essay to pass my exam'; 'I have to write and thank her for the gift'—the idea of writing as a tool of discovery might sound strange. And yet, most people would agree that when they sit down to write a letter, they do not know exactly what they want to say. After a first draft, however, the writer may decide that the letter is too brief and dismissive, or too long and personal. Indeed, it may take several drafts until the writer is satisfied with the tone and content. When undertaking research, the process is similar. We may have talked at length with a friend about what we plan to research, but when we get the chance to sit down in front of the keyboard and write out the plan, brainstorm the ideas and sort these themes into different groups, the direction and scope of the research may have changed. A revision to what we have written the next day or so will usually result in even more insights and ideas.

> **Generative view of writing**: Writing is recognised as a tool of discovery.

The potential of writing to stimulate new questions and to help clarify the project is why experienced researchers encourage new researchers to start writing from the start, and to continue to write regularly throughout the research process.

Another reason researchers emphasise the importance of writing is that how we write about the research can also influence how others come to understand that topic. In this sense, writing is viewed by social scientists as **constitutive**. According to this view, social scientists don't only tell a story about what they've found; they are also actively involved in crafting a particular view of reality (Richardson & St Pierre 2005). As per chapter 1, writing

> **Constitutive role of writing**: How you write about an issue influences the way that issue is understood.

Michelle Gabriel

has ontological dimensions, with different writing approaches perhaps creating different visions of the reality of a particular social phenomenon. Similar arguments are advanced by academics working in media studies. They recognise that media producers and journalists don't just report the news, but play a key role in framing news items through the use of sensationalist headlines, perspectives and approaches, or familiar **narrative** structures.

Narrative: A story of events, experiences or the like.

An appreciation of the role that writing plays in the construction of knowledge helps in the formulation of a realistic research plan. When most new researchers say that they are keen to 'get on' with the research, they are usually referring to getting out in the field, observing some interactions, interviewing participants and wading through archives. However, as with the other more fundamental tasks of the research process such as research design, literature review or concept delineation, as outlined in chapters 2 and 3, once we have recognised that writing is a critical part of doing research, we can boast that we have spent a hard day on the job while sitting in front of the keyboard at home or scribbling notes at the pub.

Writing style

When social scientists write, we are usually doing two things. First, we are exploring and explaining the social world; and second, we are trying to convince our **audience** that our claims about the social world are valid and should be taken seriously. In undertaking research, social scientists spend extended periods of time observing phenomena, listening to the views and perspectives of others and collating statistical data. As such, they believe that their research allows them to validly espouse a view, theory or particular perspective about the social world. Within the social sciences, a high value is placed on the capacity of the researcher to examine a particular social phenomenon in a way that sheds new light on the topic. Consequently, the style of writing social researchers employ tends to be persuasive and assertive. The use of this **authorial voice** stems from a breadth of knowledge about the discipline and the command of the research topic. Although this persuasive style is evident in most social science research, when we start reading literature in the field, we will discover that there is a wide range of authorial voices and writing styles.

Audience: The reader or consumer of a text.

Authorial voice: The author's voice or style in written words, which is influenced by their selection and usage of words.

As well as authorial voice, there are generally agreed principles regarding what constitutes 'good writing' (Watson 2003; Renton 2004). All researchers, no matter what our particular writing style, should adhere to these basic tenets. These are summed by Australian author Don Watson (2003) in his spirited defence of the use of clear and persuasive prose.

Don Watson warns against:

- the use of clichés and management-speak; for example, phrases such as 'going forwards'
- the tendency towards extra padding in phrasing: for example, employing the phrase 'in terms of' when a simple 'to' or 'on' is required
- the underuse of verbs in public language; on this topic, Watson states (2003:156): 'Verbs are doing words. Give them up for long enough and chances are you will stop doing anything.'
- He is cautious, however, about installing prescriptive rules regarding language:

> The injunction 'write plainly' can be taken to mean 'write lifelessly'. To write clearly is not to think shallowly. It can be useful to pare away extraneous words and eschew the flourish in the interests of clarity, but there must be something at the end of it, at least something with a point.
>
> Watson (2003:45)

In addition to clear language, researchers also need to understand the audience we are writing for. Obviously, if writing for an examiner, we need to use a more formal register than if writing a research note for ourselves. In addition, we need to give some thought to the level of assumed knowledge of the audience. Do we need to explain key terms in the research? For example, 'Do I need to explain what ethnography is?' The answer will depend on the audience for the writing. Basically, if in doubt, it is better to explain terms than presume knowledge.

When developing an authorial voice, it is important to note that writing style preferences within the research community change over time. For instance, there is now a greater acceptance of the use of personal pronouns in academic writing than in the past. For example, 'I will' is now more often used in place of the impersonal phrase 'This study will'. This development stems from the belief that researchers need to take responsibility for the claims that they make (Haraway 1991; Rose 1997). The use of personal pronouns and naming those responsible for particular ideas and actions ensures that readers are not tricked into thinking that these arguments are universally accepted. Using terms such as 'I propose' makes it clear that the views being put forward are shared by one or several researchers, and that such 'truth claims' are historically and culturally situated (see chapter 12 on discourse analysis). In line with the idea of standpoint as part of our research methodology, as per chapter 1, the use of 'I' acknowledges that we understand that we are part of the research process, and that our approach to the research is fundamentally influenced by who we are and how we see ourselves in relation to the social world.

Another shift in academic writing is the increasing preference among researchers for 'active' rather than 'passive' language. Active language means placing the subject or the

Michelle Gabriel

actor at the start of the sentence, followed by the verb or action, and then the object or description. A comparison of passive and active grammatical constructions is provided in box 15.1. While research and report writing do not always lend themselves to active language, using active language where possible livens up the writing style and reduces the level of ambiguity within the piece of writing.

Box 15.1: Active and passive constructions

The main focus of a sentence is on its first component—typically its subject—as in the following two examples:

- The participant signed the ethics consent form prior to the interview [active].
- The ethics consent form was signed prior to the interview by the participant [passive].

The first example is in the active voice, with the subject ('the participant') undertaking the action. The second sentence is in the passive, where the subject (the 'ethics consent form') is being acted upon.

Source: Adapted from Snooks & Co. 2002:54–5

Exercise 15.1: Tuning in to style and voice

Task 1

Exposure to a range of authorial voices is the first step in sharpening your critical faculties, as you are then able to compare one voice with another.

1. Locate a recent edition of the *Journal of Sociology*, either in the library or online.
2. Read through three articles and observe any differences or similarities in the various authors' writing styles.
3. When you have finished browsing, choose one of the articles and write down, from a writing style perspective, why that article appealed to you or annoyed you. What are its strengths and weaknesses? In particular, consider the style and tone of the writing. What adjectives would you use to describe this author's voice: exciting, even-handed, dense, ironic, passionate, cynical, learned or tedious?
4. Has the author used personal 'I propose'-type language or more remote 'this article will'-type language? How does the use of the type of language affect how you read and understand the research outlined?

Task 2

Now that you're more familiar with different authorial voices within the research community, you might want to critically reflect on your own writing.

1. Locate one of your completed essays.
2. Read your essay with a critical eye. Once again, ask yourself, from a writing perspective, what are its strengths and weaknesses? What adjectives would you use to describe your own written voice? Reflecting on what you have learnt so far in this chapter, are you satisfied with your writing style or do you see room for change?

Task 3

Finally, it is a good idea to gain some insight into what style of writing appeals to different people, particularly experienced researchers. Ask your lecturer, tutor or supervisor to nominate some examples of what they consider to be excellent research writing, and then search them out.

Writing a research plan or proposal

As detailed in chapter 2, the first major writing task of the research process is to produce a research plan. This research plan should outline what the researcher proposes to investigate and how he or she plans to investigate it. Developing a comprehensive research plan is time consuming, but important in clarifying the project objective and methods, and communicating to others the significance of the research and the potential benefits of conducting the research. This is especially so if we are seeking financial support for our research. A comprehensive research plan needs to convince the funding agency that the project is of merit and worth supporting.

While the length and detail of the research plan will depend on the scale of the project, all research plans should include:

- the research objective and the key research question(s)
- a statement of the significance of the research (that is, the project's potential contribution to current public policy or theoretical debates)
- a discussion of existing research and any gaps within this research
- the scale and location of the study
- the major data sources and methods for obtaining relevant data
- how we propose to analyse the data
- time schedule
- budget
- proposed outputs (such as research reports, public seminar, journal article).

Michelle Gabriel

To prepare a research plan, we need to have first conducted a literature review in our chosen topic area. This review forms the basis of the second stage, designing a viable research program. These two major tasks are now discussed.

Literature review

Writing a high-quality research plan needs time spent becoming familiar with existing research in our topic area. The next step is to review the material collected from the literature search. As per the section on the literature review in chapter 2, this means not just reading, but taking notes, and writing about the literature in the light of your own project. Remember that reviewing literature is a critical process, and involves us evaluating the literature critically in light of our research question and our methodology. This process can be summarised into three core steps:

1 **Describe:** We need to describe the research that has been conducted in the area we propose to investigate: the theoretical approach, the size of the study, the location of the study, the type of analysis conducted.
2 **Compare:** We also need to compare studies and assess the quality of the research. Did the researchers encounter any problems collecting their data, and did this affect their results? Are the findings generalisable? How valuable is this literature in informing our thinking, theoretically and/or empirically, about our research topic?
3 **Identify the gaps:** In particular, we need to identify any gaps within the literature. For example, we might find that much of the research in the proposed area is based on qualitative interviews, and therefore there is a need for some further research that might be able to quantify the issues.

Research design

Also a detailed in chapter 2, the research design is the formalised plan of how we intend to conduct the research. This design is primarily influenced by the research question and the methodological approach that the researcher will use in his or her approach to this question in particular, and the topic more generally. The research design is also influenced by the pragmatic concerns of the amount of time available to conduct the research, the amount of resources available, the availability of particular data sets and the feasibility of different approaches. Writing a formal research plan therefore underpins the research project and is integral to the validity and coherence of the research itself.

A research design should also include details of any potential limitations or difficulties that we envisage we may encounter in conducting the proposed research. Here we need to specify any strategies for minimising anticipated problems.

Exercise 15.2: Ready, set, write

Task 1

Team up with a partner and decide on a research topic. Then, independently, conduct an online search for relevant literature. When you've compiled your reference list, you should compare references with your partner. Have you obtained similar results? If not, did you approach the task differently? Compare the databases you have searched, as well as the search terms you have used to locate particular references.

Task 2

Choose two papers that you located during your online literature search, and write a short summary and critique of these papers. If you have access to a bibliographic software package, then compile the notes (about 200 words) you have made as an annotated **bibliography**.

> **Bibliography**: A complete or selective list of literature on a particular subject or by a given author.

Task 3

Write a first draft of your research plan. Start by jotting down some dot points or notes under each of the headings below:

1. aim of research
2. significance of research
3. literature review
4. research design
5. time schedule
6. budget.

Writing a research report

Typically, the end product of the research project will be a research report or journal article or, for those enrolled in honours or postgraduate programs, a research thesis or dissertation. Although it is the finale of the project, deciding the approach or format such writing up will take is a task for the research design phase. While there are alternative forums to communicate findings, such as presenting at a community forum, these are usually in addition to, not a replacement for the research report or journal article. The report or article details each step of the research process, enabling others to judge the validity of the research process and research outcomes, an important part of the social science process (see chapter 1). The report or article also allows other researchers to build on the original research, by replicating or extending the research program. Finally, insights derived from the research are more

Michelle Gabriel

durable or more lasting when written than delivered verbally. For social scientists, the research report or journal article is a vital means of participating in the collective process of constructing knowledge within our fields.

Report structure

Genre: A particular form of expression, with its own established structural and stylistic conventions; the style in which texts are produced and consumed.

Research writing is also a **genre** with its own established structural and stylistic conventions. Those who read research hold expectations about what should be included and in what order. For example, Howard Becker (1986:52) makes the serious point that research reports are not detective novels in which clues are littered throughout the text and the murderer revealed at the end. Rather, the aims and central argument need to be clearly articulated in the opening chapter. While there are differences in authorial voice and approaches to the writing-up process, research reports and dissertations also typically conform to a basic broad structure. This structure is outlined in table 15.1. In the 'typical' research project, the researcher introduces the topic and provides some background information on the topic in the early part, including a critical analysis of the literature. The details of the research approach are then explained, followed by presentation of the data and its analysis and results in the middle. Finally, the researcher interprets these results and draws some conclusions based on a synthesis between existing knowledge and what the research has revealed. Of course, in reading table 15.1, keep in mind that we will need more specific titles than those listed under 'report sections'. For example, if we are conducting a comprehensive literature review on the housing careers of young people in rural areas, we might use the title 'Section 2: Rural youth housing careers: International and national evidence', rather than 'Literature review'. See the 'Method to practice' section at the end of this chapter for an example of the headings of an honours thesis.

There is also some flexibility in the way this structure might be executed. Although a conventional structure is recommended as an effective means of organising the research, we can adapt the layout of report sections. For example, some researchers prefer to synthesise existing research findings with their own research from the outset, while others are keen to emphasise how theoretical debates have shaped their research design. Alternatively, the report sections could be organised thematically. Choosing to adapt the framework in line with the demands of your own research program, however, does not negate the need to address the questions concerning content detailed in the third column of table 15.1. This is not all new work. We can adapt aspects of our research plan (see chapter 2), and incorporate these into the report. Our literature review can be included, although it will need to be fine-tuned, especially if the research has shifted direction and the methods section of the research plan repeated with more detail added of what we actually did. For example, we may have had to use an alternative way of recruiting participants if the proposed strategy had been unsuccessful. We will also need to discuss any problems or limitations that we encountered in trying to execute our proposed research program.

But most of the report will be new material and, of course, the data, analysis, results and interpretation, will have been generated since writing the research proposal. Much of the new writing in the research report will entail presenting the research results and discussing the theoretical and empirical significance of these results.

Table 15.1: Conventional report framework

Broad structure	Report sections	Content
Introduction	Title page	
	Abstract	
	Table of contents	
	Introduction	What is the research question/objective?
		Why is it important?
		What knowledge have we gained or produced through the process of doing our research?
Background	Literature review	What have others said about our topic?
		What aspects of this topic have not been granted much research attention?
Own work	Methods	What methods have we used to answer our research question?
		Why did we choose that strategy?
	Results	What evidence have we uncovered?
Synthesis	Discussion	How does the evidence we've collected answer our question?
		How does the evidence we've collected support our central claims?
	Conclusion	What knowledge have we gained/produced through the process of doing our research?
		What future research questions need to be answered?
	Appendices	
	References	

Note: Table adapted from O'Leary (2004); Evans & Gruba (2002).

Michelle Gabriel

Presentation of data and findings

When presenting our data, analysis and subsequent results, the aim is to communicate clearly what we have found and to make an impact on our audience. These aims are supported by:

- clear language
- logical, well-supported arguments
- effective ordering of material
- use of charts and tables to present complex data
- use of examples, including quotations and visual images.

Writing software

Tools available in word-processing programs such as Microsoft Word can greatly assist in the production of a polished document. For most students, writing on the computer screen is second nature. We open up a new document, type away, play around with the fonts, run the spell-checker and word count, and then print out the document. Easy! While this cursory understanding is certainly enough to get through an essay, there are many more resources available to assist. The advanced tools within word processors are a key resource. Table 15.2 lists a range of useful word-processing applications, and outlines how they might make the report writing process easier. If we are unsure how to access these tools, use the Help button on the program menu for instructions. It's amazing what is actually available within these programs. Additionally, the university library or student support service will often offer excellent courses on making the most of standard software packages such as Microsoft Word and Excel.

Saves time and avoids errors

As a writing researcher, you also need to be familiar with programs that assist in the production of charts, figures, graphs and tables, such as spreadsheet programs or SPSS (see chapter 9). Although not essential for research students, those who produce research for companies or government agencies might also use desktop publishing packages to enhance the look of their product.

Some researchers use an **annotated bibliography** to keep track of their notes on particular research articles. An annotated bibliography includes a list of relevant citations, a summary of each paper and any additional notes on the paper. Most bibliographic software packages now provide the option of writing extended commentaries on each of the articles stored in the reference library.

> **Annotated bibliography:** A bibliography in which each citation is followed by an annotation containing a brief descriptive and/or evaluative summary synopsis.

Table 15.2: Essential word-processing tools for large documents

Tool	Purpose	Benefits
Templates	A template is a blueprint for the text, graphics and formatting of a document. You can modify this format to reflect your preferences.	It can save you a lot of time when editing your document if you can change the formatting of text that has been allocated styles (i.e. 'heading 1' or 'body text') simultaneously.
Master document	A master document helps you organise a long report that is comprised of numerous chapters or parts.	You can work on short, manageable chapters, while also being able to cross-reference between documents and create tables of contents or indexes for the report as a whole.
Document map	The document map displays a list of the text that you have ascribed as 'headings' in a separate window.	It highlights the structure of the report or chapter. You can use it to navigate through a large document quickly.
Numbering	You can format headings and table captions so that they are numbered sequentially and cross-referenced with text (e.g. 'see table 2 below' is linked to the caption 'table 2').	Chapter headings, table numbers and references to these numbers in the text are updated automatically when the layout of the document is reordered.
Table of contents	Tables of contents and figures can be created automatically on completion of your document if you have used 'Heading styles' and 'Captions' in your text.	Saves time and avoids errors.
Track changes	Marks changes in the current document and keeps track of each change by reviewer name.	The document is returned to you with editorial suggestions already inserted in the text. These are clearly visible and you can choose to accept or reject them.

Compiling a reference list is made easier by the wide availability of electronic resources. Bibliographic software packages (or a reference management database), such as Biblioscape, ProCite or Endnote, are also very useful in assisting the sorting, recording and management of the research literature. Most library catalogues and databases enable us to 'mark' the publications that we think might be useful to the project, and then download this marked list of references into our own reference library in these programs. The main advantages of these bibliographic programs is that they:

- allow downloading of references found through online searches directly into the database
- automatically create a database of references so that we can search and retrieve particular types of references: we can create a 'keyword' index and link the references by subject themes

Michelle Gabriel

- insert references from the database directly into the text of a report, then use the program to create a bibliography
- easily modify the citation style to suit our needs; for example, change the style of referencing from Harvard to Oxford.

Presentation of quantitative data

As outlined in part 2 of this text, quantitative research is concerned with measuring the comparative scale and extent of the social phenomenon under study. In particular, quantitative research is concerned with the associations and relationships between variables, and the scale and extent of the influence of these variables on the social phenomenon. There are different types of quantitative analysis, and the choice of approach will vary, depending on the purposes of the research and the nature of the data themselves. The essential task of presenting quantitative analysis within the writing-up process is to provide an accurate description of the data and data collection methods, so that the reader can judge the veracity of the results obtained and the researcher's interpretation of them.

Researchers working with quantitative data sets typically present their data and findings in tables, graphs or plots, and there are standard conventions to ensure the information is presented in a clear and succinct fashion. The first relates to the nature of the information; the second relates to style and layout.

As the primary aim is to provide an accurate and comprehensive view of research, tables and figures should be used judiciously. The point is to summarise the major findings, not to present every permutation of the analysis process. We need to decide which findings are the most important in terms of answering the research question(s) and be creative in presenting these to ensure simultaneously that important findings are clear, while also minimising the number of tables and charts. We want to ensure that the reader can follow the logic of the discussion, but does not feel swamped by reams of data. Crucially, results also only need to be presented once. Do not present the same data in different formats, such as a table and again as a bar chart.

The layout and format of tables and figures must also be standardised throughout the report. This is easily be achieved by creating a template based on our preferred style. This template maximises the visual impact of the tables and figures by attending to size, colour and layout, while at the same time maximising readability. Consistency in numbering and labelling also helps the reader to easily locate the tables and graphs referred to in the discussion. Finally, if the researcher is drawing on secondary data, the source of that data needs to be referenced at the base of the figure; such as ABS Summary Tables and Trends 2007. As much a courtesy to the original author or data collector, referencing work this way helps the reader to source further information relevant to the argument.

Example 15.1: Presentation of quantitative data

The following example uses a report on a quantitative (survey) research project on the how and why of what influences medical students' decisions about where to practise once qualified. In short, the results indicated that, while medical students who grew up in rural areas were generally more positive about working in a rural location than those who grew up in urban areas, urban origin students did indicate that they would be willing to work in a rural location for a short period of time or on a flexible basis. As table 15.3 shows, 81.3 per cent of urban origin students envisaged working in a rural area for at least part of their career, and 47.9 per cent envisaged working in a remote area for at least part of their career. Note how the table provides a concise summary of a number of aspects of the research. We can see the question that was asked in the survey, how many urban origin students' results are included (n = 123), and the comparative proportions of the career plans of these students in relation to rural and remote areas.

Table 15.3: Career plans of urban origin students

I believe I will work in a:	Rural area (%)	Remote area (%)
Almost all of my career	4.9	1.6
Most of my career	8.9	0.8
About half of my career	9.8	0.8
Part of my career	57.7	44.7
Almost none of my career	18.7	52.0
Total (n = 123)	100.0	99.9

Source: Orpin & Gabriel 2005

Presentation of qualitative data

As detailed in chapter 14, the analysis of qualitative data is primarily concerned with drawing out the nuanced understanding of the study's respondents and the elaboration of meaning. Participants' understandings of situations, and how they make sense of social phenomena within the context of their own lives, are important. Qualitative analysis interpretations, especially those based on in-depth interviews, therefore, rest heavily on other people's actual words, and the write-up of qualitative data tends to quote extensively from the interview transcripts, and provide a commentary of the context in which particular statements are made.

Michelle Gabriel

When writing up their data analysis, qualitative researchers will also describe the life-worlds of the interviewees, to give the audience a sense of who the interviewees are, the challenges they face in their everyday lives, and why they might hold particular views about the world. This combination of rich description and the use of people's own words is not only important in terms of providing insight into the interviewees' lives specifically, and the social phenomenon of the research question more generally, but the use of respondents' words enables the reader to decide whether or not the interpretations and conclusions offered are reliable and valid. For this reason, direct quotations are always better than paraphrasing of other people's words. Paraphrasing always involves some variation on words used, which can intentionally or unintentionally result in misunderstanding or loss of original meaning.

A quick look through existing qualitative research provides an insight into how to present data. Generally, qualitative researchers will arrange their data with a view to telling a story, weaving together the relevant literature, extracts from their primary data, and their own thoughts and interpretations of that data. Often the analysis section will be divided into a number of themes. These themes are based on theoretical considerations, or may reflect the major issues and priorities identified in the analysis. For example, if studying medical students' career pathways, the reporting of the results might be divided into the themes of 'practice intentions', 'practice location' and 'work–life balance'. Under each heading, the researcher will provide a general statement and then present primary data to illustrate this point (see example 15.2).

To ensure the reader can distinguish between the researcher's words and the interviewee's words, quotations are also usually indented and a different font used or the size of the font reduced.

A descriptor section is usually provided in parenthesis so the reader has insight into the basic characteristics of the interviewee such as age and sex. If the research is based on the interpretations of a small number of people interviewed at length, and/or on multiple occasions, a pseudonym to enable the reader to identify a particular interviewee throughout the text will usually be used. Under no circumstances would the person's actual name be used, or any information that could lead to the participant being identified be included.

A major consideration in presenting qualitative data is deciding what to include and what to omit. As in quantitative research, qualitative researchers are unable to present all their data within a report, journal article or thesis. As noted in chapters 10 and 14, interviews produce many pages of transcribed data, and only a small portion can ever make it into the final write-up. This can be frustrating, as the research process can uncover many unique and interesting stories. However the research's key purpose needs to be kept in mind, and good presentation of data as they relate to this depends on the development of a coherent and focused narrative. Select extracts that respond to the major research questions, especially those that either challenge or confirm the original assumptions. Usually, qualitative researchers provide extended quotations (two or three sentences) from one or two interviewees to illustrate a particular point, rather than short soundbites from lots of interviewees. This meets the essential qualitative aim of exploring the meanings people ascribe to particular things or situations, rather than to show how many people hold the same attitudes. They also juxtapose extracts that demonstrate conflicting views on a subject to illustrate the range of potential meanings and interpretations. The question of how much is also constrained by institutional demands. For example, many journals restrict the size of articles to 7000 words or less. For students, your lecturer will likely set a word limit for the task of writing a research report, perhaps of around 4000 words, and for honours students the limit is usually around 12,000 words. While this seems like a lot of words before you start the writing process, most honours students struggle to get their thesis into the allotted word limit.

Example 15.2: Presentation of qualitative data

Work–life balance

In focus group discussions, final year medical students spoke about their future career directions largely in terms of the lifestyle that accompanied being a general practitioner or medical specialist, and also in terms of the impact of different life-stages on their workload and their work location. Students emphasised that keeping a balance between work and their personal lives was a major factor in making decisions about their future careers, including choices about practice location. The following quotes reflect these key concerns:

> I think it's important to always keep the balance between your own personal life and your career. I mean I don't think there's any point ... in completely putting aside your social life for your career even if it is just for the first five years. I mean you should keep the balance, and never give it up, even if you sacrifice it a bit (Male, 24).

> I'd probably put family first and have medicine just as a career. And you don't let it rule your life. You put your life first and then it's just your occupation. But at the same time it is part of your lifestyle because you are obviously doing it because you enjoy it. So it is part of your lifestyle but it's not the most important thing (Female, 27).

Source: Orpin & Gabriel 2005

Michelle Gabriel

Exercise 15.3: Visual impact

Task

For this task you need a SPSS output from a cross-tabular relationship. You can use those you generated in chapter 8 or 9.

Use the information in this output to generate a bar chart. You can do this using Excel, SPSS or another spreadsheet program.

Show the bar chart to others, and ask for feedback on its visual impact:

- Is the chart easy to read?
- Are the colours and shading appropriate?
- Are the titles informative?

Final statement

The final chapter or section or your research report is the most important, but also the one where least writing attention is given. Tight deadlines can mean the report needs to be rushed to completion, yet for most readers the 'hook' or interest in any research are the results, and what they mean for the field and wider society. A key mistake by many new researchers is to undervalue the broader significance of their work, often just summarising or re-stating the key findings. But a final statement or chapter is where the research's major conclusions are drawn; it is where it all comes together. A strong conclusion has five core elements:

- First, the researcher returns to the overarching research question and explains how effectively the research has been able to respond to this question. This may entail simply answering the research question or explaining why the initial research question was qualified or extended in the light of information gained through the research process.
- Second, the researcher explains how the key results confirm or challenge existing research in this field. The researcher should ask, 'What knowledge have I gained or produced through the process of doing my research?'
- Third, the researcher reflects on the significance of the research methods and or methodology, and their strengths or limitations in relation to this research and the particular research field.
- Fourth, the researcher makes explicit the implications of the research findings in the political or public domain, such as for future policy development.
- Fifth, the researcher highlights new research questions, and topics emerging from the research that require further attention.

Writing strategies

Many researchers experience trouble getting started writing up their project, because the research process itself is at times unpredictable. But as one aspect of how research is judged is the quality of the story woven by the researcher, researchers need to overcome fears or doubts about their own capacity to begin writing as soon as possible. For new researchers, it is important to remember that, although still at the research apprenticeship stage, they are already a skilled and able writer. They have written letters, assignments, job applications and possibly far too many undergraduate essays—all of which demonstrate a preparedness for the task of writing up research results into a comprehensive report or dissertation. This section offers practical strategies to build on this writing experience.

First sentence

Writing is a bit like bungy-jumping: delaying the process only heightens anxiety. That said, writing is not nearly as terrifying as jumping off a 50 metre platform, nor is the ordeal likely to be over in under a minute. Instead, writing a major report takes a lot of time, far more time than most students anticipate. Writing can also be a fairly mundane and repetitive process. The best strategy overcoming apprehensions is to open a new document on the first day of the research project and save it as 'First draft'. Even from day one, it should be possible to type a potential title, identify a (draft) central research question, sketch out aims and document hypotheses or hunches about the direction of the research.

Don't worry what the first efforts look like; there is plenty of time to adjust, edit, rewrite and reorder as you go along. The important thing is to make a start. Delaying making a start is usually a form of procrastination, and the longer we allow the delay to go on, the harder the final task will be. As per an early point in this chapter, an evolving, working draft develops with the research process, aiding discussions about the research with supervisors or peers and stimulating thinking about the project itself.

Maintaining momentum

Once started, there are a number of useful strategies for maintaining a writing momentum.

Prioritise the task of writing

First, prioritise writing during the research. As obvious as it sounds, making writing a priority is not so easy. Writing tends to be put on the back burner because it can be difficult and slow, and the rewards not immediately clear. Also, many researchers are convinced that they need to know more before they can start. While there is some truth in this—we cannot write a literature review without having read the literature—we can write

Michelle Gabriel

down a plan of the literature review and its coverage. Will the review encompass national or international studies? Will the review be limited to studies from 1990 onwards, or will we seek out earlier material?

We also need to make notes about the literature as we go, and write provisional analyses for later revision in the light of new material. Experienced researchers generally advocate setting aside a regular time in which to write. While a routine results in some writing sessions that are more productive than others, generally even half a day at the desk will move the project along. In contrast, waiting to be struck by inspiration or the right mood can be a recipe for inaction.

Break up the writing task

It is also helpful to break up a large project into bite-size, manageable pieces. Preparing for an afternoon at the keyboard might involve a target of three things to do. The aim is to be specific and focused. If your proposed writing task list is not achievable in the time available, then limit the task further or strike it out: the idea is to achieve a goal, not set yourself up for failure.

When faced with a particularly difficult writing challenge, we might also employ Evans and Gruba's (2002) strategy of breaking the writing process into two parts. For example, in writing a one-page synopsis of the literature, they recommend first setting aside an hour in the early morning to write down as much as possible about what you have been reading over the past week. The aim is to write in a **stream of consciousness** style, without stopping to think about whether the order of the ideas is logical. Then, later in the day, print this text out and focus solely on identifying the key issues raised, sorting these into major themes, then setting the themes in a logical order. The aim is to avoid the paralysis of trying to achieve simultaneous competing tasks, such as exploring themes, writing creatively, logically ordering the points and critically reviewing the writing.

> **Stream of consciousness:** A style of writing that reflects the flow of a person's continuous thoughts and conscious reactions to an issue or event.

Wolcott (2001:18) outlines a variation on this stream-of-consciousness approach, proposing that the researcher start in the opposite direction by preparing a table of contents. The first session is spent creating simple headings and subheadings that capture the key issues we plan to address, then organising these headings into a table so that a reader can follow the logical progression of the project. The second session involves jotting down the material we plan to cover in dot points under each heading. The third session involves turning these dot points into coherent sentences. Neither approach is 'correct'. The point is to find a writing strategy that works for us.

Go easy on yourself

Finally, be aware of perfectionist tendencies, and go easy on yourself. When in doubt about the priority of writing tasks, always tackle what seem the least daunting. As sociologist Howard Becker advises, 'do whatever is easiest first' (1986:60), acknowledge the wins and regularly reward yourself for achievements. The tougher the writing challenge, the higher the reward! Remember also that breaks are an essential in any working routine; taking time out enables us to see things in a different light and to be more objective about our written work.

While these strategies might often encourage the sentences to flow, there are also times when you simply 'hit a wall' and are struck by writer's block. When stumped or you find yourself organising and reorganising material without discernible progress, it is time to search out your supervisor or associate. Most blocks stem from confusion about the research process (sometimes we can get in too deep for our own good), and conversation (probably combined with caffeine) is an effective option to resolve these. Often the best way of clarifying your own thoughts is to try to explain them to someone else.

Box 15.2: Recommended writing strategies

1. Draft today, revise tomorrow.
2. Make writing a priority.
3. Break the project into a set of specific writing tasks.
4. Shift between different modes of writing: creative and rational.
5. Write table of contents and/or titles, then fill in each section.
6. Do the easiest tasks first.
7. Reward yourself when you've completed sentences, paragraphs and essays.
8. Seek company and help.

Editing and revising

Editing is the key to writing research reports or articles that read with verve and impact. Taking the time to reflect critically on the written notes and to revise and proofread the text is critical to the production of a polished and coherent research report. It is important that new researchers recognise that editing and revision are essential steps in writing effectively about their chosen topic, rather than evidence that they are not good writers.

Asking for feedback

Gaining feedback from others is a vital step in clarifying your thoughts and improving the writing style. In most instances, your research supervisor will provide general editorial

Michelle Gabriel

advice on your work. However, the best strategy is to find a range of people who can provide feedback on drafts. As well as getting a selection of views that we can weigh up, it is valuable to show your work to someone not familiar with the field. Such people are usually quick to identify whether the information we are presenting is confusing or too dense.

When scouting around for an editor, be aware that there are many different types of editing tasks, and that not everyone is uniformly brilliant at all. While some people are great at engaging with the broad topic area, and will be keen to give big-picture advice on the direction of the project, others will have an under-the-microscope approach, grabbing a red pen and scratching away at the split infinitives and dangling participles. There are also some people who can be overly critical. True, we want critical feedback, but if it is not constructive, then it may just dampen our enthusiasm and lead to paralysis. When people raise objections to our work, push them to clarify their concerns and also find out if they can suggest any practical strategies for addressing the problem.

Also, when we ask someone to read and review our work, we need to communicate clearly what it is we want him or her to do. First, take responsibility for explaining what type of feedback you are seeking. Table 15.4 provides a general guide as to the levels of editing that we might expect an editor to undertake. Second, if we are asking for big-picture or middle-range

Table 15.4: Levels of editing

Level	Advice sought
Big picture	The soundness of argument
	The general narrative structure
	The coherence of the document
Middle range	The flow of the discussion
	Clarity of concepts
	What information to include or exclude
	The structure of paragraphs
Under the microscope	Spelling
	Grammar
	References
	Titles, charts, footnotes; links back to text
	Page numbers

feedback, we need to describe the intended audience so that our editor can assess whether we have presented the material in an appropriate way. In contrast, if we are asking someone to use an under-the-microscope approach and proofread the report, we will need to discuss:

- formatting preferences: for example, the font used on headings and body text, the spacing between sections and use of numbering
- stylistic preference: for example, consistent use of quotation marks, italics for foreign words, hyphens, capital letters and spelling
- the form of the editing: for example, do you prefer the editor to edit on the screen, making use of the tracking mechanism within your word processor, which marks the suggested changes in a different colour to distinguish them from the text, or do we prefer suggested changes made on paper?
- timeframe: when do you need your edited work returned, and is this a reasonable request?

Most editors will welcome feedback on how their work has contributed to the production of the final report. If we are relying on one person to do most of our editing, then it is important that his or her efforts are acknowledged in the report, dissertation or article.

Using editing skills

If the research project involves a research team, sharing the work of editing will provide an opportunity to hone our editing skills and to reflect on our own writing style. While editing occurs at all stages of the research process, the type of editing required at each stage shifts. Early editing tends to be general structural revisions, and later editing involves a much more detailed proofreading. Big- and middle-picture editing requires detecting inconsistencies in the logic of theoretical arguments or data interpretation, while under-the-microscope editing requires recognising sound grammar and appropriate word usage. As few people excel at both, it is important to be aware of our own editing strengths and weaknesses. We will also need guidance from the wide selection of editing manuals and style guides that are available (see the references listed in box 15.3). Also, as an editor of someone else's work, we need to show respect for the writer's voice and his or her research objectives, and provide constructive advice within the parameters the writer has specified.

1. The first step in editing is to read through the draft document in one uninterrupted session to get a sense of the coherence and flow. Decide whether the overall document is sound and ready for a more detailed proofread, or whether it needs to be returned to the author with suggestions relating to the document structure.
2. If we and the author are satisfied with the outline of the report, the next step is to focus on middle-range editing. This entails a second, much closer reading of the

Michelle Gabriel

draft document, ensuring that the report reads well. For example, are there are plenty of transitional phrases to help the reader move from one idea to the next, and good signposting to enable the reader to follow the central narrative? Or does the text need cutting back so that the main ideas are not lost? Here, the editor will focus on pruning repetitive and unnecessary sentences that do not develop the central argument, clarifying ambiguous phrases and concepts and removing excess adjectives and redundancies (such as 'my personal opinion' and 'our future plans').

3   In the final stages of proofreading, editors need to read through the text thoroughly and identify grammatical or typological errors. This form of editing is best undertaken in short sessions, as it is difficult to maintain the level of concentration required to pick up minor errors. While some editors rely on their memories to ensure that the corrections they propose are consistent, most editors make use of a style sheet. Style sheets, created by the editor in the process of editing the document, provide a summary of the grammatical rules and spelling preferences already applied within the document. In making stylistic decisions, the editor should consult:
   — the style guide that is provided by the university department or any other organisation for which the dissertation or report is being prepared
   — the author, who may have personal preferences for particular stylistic conventions
   — up-to-date style manuals (such as Hudson 1997; Snooks & Co. 2002).

Box 15.3: Essential references for Australian and New Zealand editors

Flann, E. and Hill, B. (2004). *The Australian Editing Handbook*, 2nd edn. Milton, QLD: John Wiley & Sons.

Hudson, N. (1997). *Modern Australian Usage*. Melbourne: Oxford University Press.

Orsman, H. (ed.) (1998). *Dictionary of New Zealand English*. Oxford: Oxford University Press.

Renton, N. E. (2004). *Compendium of Good Writing*. Milton: John Wiley & Sons.

Ritter, R. M. (2000). *The Oxford Dictionary for Writers and Editors*. Oxford: Oxford University Press.

Snooks and Co. (2002). *Style Manual for Authors, Editors and Printers*, 6th edn. Milton, Qld: John Wiley & Sons.

Watson, D. (2003). *Death Sentence: The Decay of Public Language*. Milsons Point, NSW: Random House.

Exercise 15.4: Writing as a collaborative task

Task 1

Showing others your writing is an essential step in improvement.

1. Draft a short summary of your research project. It should be around 500 words in length.
2. Pass this summary to a friend or fellow student, and request big-picture feedback on your project and how you've represented it in this summary.
3. Rewrite your summary, and pass it again to the same friend or fellow student, and request an under-the-microscope feedback.
4. Compare the latest version with your original summary.

Task 2

Writing creatively about your research has its own personal rewards; however, many people also find writing at times isolating and frustrating. One way to tap into regular collegial support and motivation is to form your own writing group.

Writing groups work best when comprised of three to five committed people who are willing to meet around once a month to exchange drafts of their work. The members of the group provide each other with support and information about writing opportunities, and they are enthusiastic editors of each other's work. Through working closely on various research topics, the group may also eventually become co-authors. For example, they may write an article together on a particular methodological issue they've all encountered, despite working on quite diverse topics.

Voices in the field

Evan Willis

Evan Willis is Professor of Sociology at La Trobe University in Melbourne. His main area of interest is in the sociology of health and illness. For more than three decades he has investigated the theme of how ill health mediates social relations. With this broad question in mind, he has studied such topics as demarcation disputes between health professions, occupational health and safety, complementary and alternative medicine, chronic illness and the quality of life, the social implications of the Human Genome Project and, most recently, the health implications of climate change. He teaches Introductory

Michelle Gabriel

Sociology and Medical Sociology, as well as research methods within the BA and MPH (Master of Public Health) programs on a number of La Trobe's campuses.

Most of his published work might broadly be called sociologically informed social policy analysis using the unobtrusive research techniques of content and thematic analysis. But he has also done historical research and in-depth interviewing. One of the latter studies was in the chronic illness and quality-of-life area. With colleagues, he studied the transition to adulthood for young people with the genetic disease cystic fibrosis (Willis et al. 2001). They interviewed as many of the young people aged 15–19 with the disease in the state of Victoria as would talk to them (about 40). The sociological problem was the differential life expectancy of young men as compared to young women. In most parts of the world, although there have been huge increases in life expectancy for all young people, there remains a differential with young men living on average about five years longer than women. This has also been a (minor) medical mystery for some time, with medical researchers unable to locate any biophysiological explanation for the difference. The explanation posed by Evan and his colleagues was that the difference can be explained socially in the gendered practices of masculinity and femininity.

Dissemination

'Social research deserves public discussion; indeed, an ethical obligation exists for it, given the large Australian public investment in social research' (Pocock 2005:136).

Dissemination of results is an important aspect of social research. Researchers must make their results available in the form of a research report, a thesis, a peer-reviewed journal article or a monograph. This enables other researchers to access the work and make assessments of its validity in regard to process, theoretical understandings and ethics in relation to existing literature. Especially for social research aimed at facilitating social change, such as that relating directly to public policy, it is critical that the findings circulate quickly and beyond a disciplinary audience to policy-makers and the general public. Accordingly, dissemination of results also often entails presentations at conferences and public meetings, written media releases or extended articles for print or web-based media, and radio and television interviews.

Typically, social research will generate new understandings of an existing problem and bring to light aspects of human behaviour that have previously been taken for granted or gone unnoticed. In addition, such findings might be considered controversial, in that they challenge established assumptions and beliefs about social relations and the organisation of society. These are all important factors in considering how we might engage a broader public beyond the researchers in your chosen field.

The findings of social research often meet key criteria applied by journalists and editors when considering what is newsworthy, including topicality, significance and human interest (Mahoney 2008:75–7). While having an interesting story is a critical first step in attracting media attention, researchers also need to engage effectively with media to ensure that their research findings are reported in an honest, accurate and comprehensive manner. But there are potential hazards for aspiring researchers, who may not be used to the interrogative style of journalistic reporting. Dealing with media is a skill that must be learned, and your university's media unit may run media awareness training or offer written guidelines to research students and academics. When dealing with politically sensitive or controversial research findings, it is essential that researchers take time to write down their key findings and messages in plain English responses to anticipated questions. (For further information on handling the media, see Tymson and Lazar 2006).

A write-up of an honours thesis

This example of a report contents page is taken from an honours thesis from 2006 described in chapter 10. The word count of the thesis was 11,986, 14 under the limit of 12,000, indicating just how tight Rebecca and her supervisor's editing was of the writing up of her research project. The headings and sub-headings used by Rebecca in her thesis provide an outline of how she structured her write-up, from background and research question in the first chapter to the interpretation and discussion of her results in the final chapter.

'The baby bonus encourages the "wrong" women to have babies: Social problem or moral panic?' by Rebecca Dance, BA

Submitted in partial fulfilment of the requirements for the Degree of Bachelor of Arts with Honours in the School of Sociology and Social Work, University of Tasmania

Contents

Chapter 1: Introduction
The introduction of the maternity payment
Research question and aims
Justification for research
Thesis structure

Chapter 2: Literature review and theoretical framework
Literature review
Media reaction to the maternity payment

Michelle Gabriel

Other public reaction
Teenage birth trends
Ex-nuptial birth trends
Characteristics of teenage mothers
Do policies such as the maternity payment affect fertility?
Teenage and sole mothers: Why they are the 'wrong' women to have babies
Theoretical framework
Moral panics
Social problems
Summary
Chapter 3: Methods
Content analysis
Units of analysis
Data analysis
Secondary data analysis
The HILDA survey
Ethical concerns
Summary
Chapter 4: Content analysis results: Was the print media's reaction a moral panic?
Primary moral panic element analysis
Concern
Who are the 'wrong' women?
Other moral panic elements analysis
Volatility
Hostility
Consensus
Disproportionality
Summary
Chapter 5: HILDA analysis results: Who had babies in 2004?
Demographic characteristics
Socioeconomic characteristics
SEIFA deciles
Summary
The 2004 mothers: The 'right' women
The 2004 teen mothers: The 'wrong' women but not a social problem

Chapter 6: Discussion and conclusion: Pulling it all together
Connecting the content and HILDA data analyses
The reaction in terms of the moral panic/social problem framework
Why did the moral panic occur?
Postscript
Limitations of this study and suggestions for further research
Conclusion
References
Appendix A: Content analysis recording scheme
Appendix B: Content analysis codebook (reduced to examples)

Michelle Gabriel

Conclusion

In conclusion, this chapter has provided an introduction to some of the central concerns that confront researchers when writing up their research projects, and some tips on how to maintain your writing momentum. While I have set down some general principles to help induct new researchers into the art of academic writing, it is important to remember that the social scientific literature is comprised of many different academic voices, and that ultimately writing is a creative process.

Finally, and importantly, writing your research can be an enjoyable experience. Although we may spend unreasonably long hours at the keyboard crafting and polishing, the production of a well-written research report can bring considerable rewards. These rewards should not be underestimated. First, producing a paper or a report that details in a clear and scholarly way the research that we have conceptualised, implemented and created ourselves is intensely satisfying. Second, the completed report or article is also a very tangible outcome for all your research endeavours. The experience of seeing in print or holding the finished product in your hands is hard proof that you are, after all your hard work, a social researcher. Finally, your article or report provides you, as a researcher, with an opportunity to participate in a robust dialogue with others—researchers, policy-makers, journalists and neighbours—on the extraordinary thing that is our social world.

Main points

> Writing is a method of discovery and analysis.

> Research is an iterative process, whereby the researcher moves between collecting data, interpreting data and writing about their topic.

> Writing is constitutive: it shapes how you and your audience understand your topic.

> In general, social scientists employ a persuasive authorial voice.

> The key to writing effectively is to know your audience. This will help you make decisions about what material you should cover and what tone is appropriate.

> There is a lot of variation in academic writing styles, and writing style preferences within the research community change over time.

> The development of a research plan is an important step in clarifying the project objective and methods, and demonstrating the significance of the project.

> A literature search can be conducted efficiently and effectively via online library catalogues, websites and databases, with the assistance of a bibliographic software package.

> Research writing is a genre with its own established structural and stylistic conventions.

> When writing up a research report, researchers should make use of the advanced tools within the word processor.

> Researchers are unable to present all the data they have collected; instead, they need to decide which of their findings are the most important in terms of answering their original research questions.

> Researchers need to prioritise writing. Set aside a specific time to write, and don't let other tasks distract you.

> Writing is not a solitary task; instead, researchers are advised to seek feedback and support.

> Be prepared to edit and redraft your work—again and again and again.

Further reading

If you want to learn more about writing up your research, the following books (in addition to the references provided in the text) are recommended:

Back, L. (1998). 'Reading and Writing Research', in Seale, C. (ed.), *Researching Society and Culture*. London: Sage: 285–96.

Creme, P. and Lea, M. (2003). *Writing At University*. Maidenhead: Open University Press.

Cryer, P. (2000). *The Research Student's Guide To Success*. Buckingham: Open University Press.

Fairbairn, G. and Winch, C. (1993). *Reading, Writing and Reasoning*. Buckingham: Society for Research into Higher Education and Open University Press.

Forester, J. (1984). *Learning the Craft of Writing* <http://people.cornell.edu/pages/jff1/learningacadwrtg.htm>. Accessed January 2005.

Glasser, J. (1999). *Understanding Style: Practical Ways to Improve Your Writing*. New York and Oxford: Oxford University Press.

Mills, C. (1959). *The Sociological Imagination*. Harmondsworth: Penguin.

Michelle Gabriel

Pirie, F. D. (1991). *How to Write Critical Essays*. London: Routledge.

Pryke, M., Rose, G. and Whatmore, S. (eds) (2003). *Using Social Theory: Thinking Through Research*. London: Sage: 125–82.

Sociology Writing Group (1998). *A Guide to Writing Sociology Papers*, 4th edn. New York: St Martin's Press.

References

Becker, H. (1986). *Writing for Social Scientists: How to Start and Finish Your Thesis, Book, or Article*. Chicago: University of Chicago Press.

Dance, R. (2006). The Baby Bonus Encourages the 'Wrong' Women to Have Babies: Social Problem or Moral Panic? Unpublished honours thesis. Hobart: School of Sociology and Social Work, University of Tasmania.

Evans, D. and Gruba, P. (2002). *How to Write a Better Thesis*, 2nd edn. Melbourne: Melbourne University Press.

Haraway, D. (1991). 'Situated Knowledges: The Science Question in Feminism and the Privilege of Partial Perspective', in Haraway, D. (ed.), *Simians, Cyborgs and Women: The Reinvention of Nature*. New York: Routledge: 183–202.

Hudson, N. (1997). *Modern Australian Usage*. Melbourne: Oxford University Press.

Magee, B. (1997). *Confessions of a Philosopher: A Personal Journey Through Western Philosophy from Plato to Popper*. London: Weidenfeld & Nicolson.

Mahoney, J. (2008) *Public Relations Writing in Australia*. Melbourne: Oxford University Press.

O'Leary, Z. (2004). *The Essential Guide to Doing Research*. London: Sage.

Orpin, P. and Gabriel, M. (2005). 'Recruiting Undergraduates to Rural Practice: What The Students Can Tell Us', *Rural and Remote Health: International Journal of Rural and Remote Health Research, Education, Practice and Policy*, 5 (412).

Pocock, B. (2005) 'Work, Family and the Shy Social Scientist', in Saunders, P. and Walter, J. (eds), *Ideas and Influence: Social Science and Public Policy in Australia*. Sydney: UNSW Press.

Renton, N. E. (2004). *Compendium of Good Writing*. Milton: John Wiley & Sons.

Richardson, L. (1990). *Writing Strategies: Reaching Diverse Audiences*. Newbury Park, CA: Sage.

Richardson, L. (1994). 'Writing: A Method of Inquiry', in Denzin, N. and Lincoln, Y. (eds), *The Handbook of Qualitative Research*. Thousand Oaks, CA: Sage: 516–44.

Richardson, L. and St Pierre, E. A. (2005). 'Writing: A Method of Inquiry', in Denzin, N. and Lincoln, Y. (eds), *The Handbook of Qualitative Research*. Thousand Oaks, CA: Sage: 959–78.

Rose, G. (1997). 'Situating Knowledges: Positionality, Reflexivities and Other Tactics', *Progress in Human Geography*, 21 (3): 305–20.

Snooks and Co. (2002). *Style Manual for Authors, Editors and Printers*, 6th edn. Milton, Qld: John Wiley & Sons.

Tymson, C. and Lazar, R. (2006).'Media Relations and Publicity', in *The New Australian and New Zealand Public Relations Manual*. Sydney: Tymson Communications: 280–313.

Wason, P. C. (1985). 'How to Write an Essay', *The New Psychologist*, May 1985:15–19.

Watson, D. (2003). *Death Sentence: The Decay of Public Language*. Milsons Point, NSW: Random House.

Willis, E., Miller, R. and Wyn, J. (2001). 'Gendered Embodiment and Survival for Young People with Cystic Fibrosis', *Social Science and Medicine*, 53 (9): 1163–74.

Wolcott, H. (2001). *Writing Up Qualitative Research*, 2nd edn. Thousand Oaks, CA: Sage.

Databases

Multidisciplinary databases

Web of Science

Current Contents Connect

ProQuest

Ingenta

Australia/New Zealand Reference Centre

Social scientific databases

IBSS: International Bibliography of the Social Sciences

Project Muse

FAMILY: Australian Family and Society abstracts

APAIS: Australian Public Affairs Information Service

ATSIhealth: Aboriginal and Torres Strait Islander Health bibliography

Gender Studies Database

Michelle Gabriel

Glossary

a priori codes
The coding of themes that are determined prior to the data analysis.

academic fraud
The misrepresentation or falsification of research findings by the researcher.

active style
Style of written text that entails the author placing the subject in the active position. The opposite of the passive style.

administrative collections
Data collections like Medicare health card records, unemployment registers and electoral rolls.

age composition
Distribution of the population by age.

age–sex structure
Distribution of the population by age and sex.

age-specific
Pertaining to a specific age group.

aggregated
Already added; subtotals and totals; the effects when added.

aims
What we want to achieve by our research; for example, an understanding of how year 8 students use mobile phones.

ambiguity
Vague or imprecise terms that have more than one meaning.

Analyze menu
The SPSS tool outlining statistical analyses techniques using a menu system and submenu options.

annotated bibliography
A bibliography in which each citation is followed by an annotation containing a brief descriptive and/or evaluative summary synopsis.

anonymity
The protection of respondents from identification as participants in the research.

archaeological discourse analysis
Discourse analysis method based on the writings of Foucault aimed at providing a historical context.

artefact of technique
An anomaly that is caused by the technique being used or the data categories chosen.

association
The extent to which the pattern of observations within one variable align with the pattern of observations within a second variable.

Australian Survey of Social Attitudes (AuSSA)
A nationally representative longitudinal quasi-panel study conducted in 2003, 2005 and 2007, collecting data on respondents, social attitudes, opinions and behaviours.

audience
The reader or consumer of a text.

authorial voice
The author's voice or style in written words, which is influenced by their selection and usage of words.

autoethnography
A type of ethnography, usually written in the first person, in which the researcher includes him- or herself in the research to make the writing up of the research more personal and interactive.

Axial coding
The coding process used in grounded theory in which codes are rigorously specified and elaborated to reflect theoretical core categories.

axiology
The theory of values that informs how we see the world and the value judgments we make within our research.

benchmarks
Data that are collected at a particular point in time and in relation to which future comparisons are made.

bibliography
A complete or selective list of literature on a particular subject or by a given author.

bivariate analysis
Analysis of the relationship between two variables.

CAI
Computer Assisted Interviewing (CAI) is used to collect, store and transmit data collected by interviewers in personal (face-to-face) survey interviews.

case study approach
A case study approach focuses on individual instances rather than on a broad spectrum by using just one instance (or a few instances) of the thing that is being researched. Multiple research methods are usually used to produce an in-depth study.

categories of a variable
The subgroups into which observations within a variable are allocated.

category jumping
Where people shift, purposefully or inadvertently, from one ostensibly permanent designation, like ethnic group or sex, to another between observations.

CATI
Computer Assisted Telephone Interviewing (CATI) is widely used in telephone surveys to direct the interviewer's questioning and to allow responses to be directly input into the survey database.

Census of Population and Housing
The typically five-yearly official (government) enumeration of the population; the census collects both demographic and social data.

central tendency measures
A descriptive statistic related to the central measures such as the mean, median or mode.

chi square
A test of significance used for nominal data to test the ability to generalise from the sample to the general population.

closed questions
A type of question that asks respondents to select their response from a number of exhaustive, fixed alternative options. Closed questions are often asked in a structured interview.

codebook
A category system in which all variable measures are fully explained.

coding
The process by which data are organised for analysis.

cohesion
Denotes how terms are used to elicit a particular response.

composition
The subcategories or subgroups comprising the whole category or group.

computer assisted interviewing (CAI)
CAI, or computer aided interviewing system, is where the interview questions, including introductory comments, prompts and contingency questions are asked by the interviewer from a portable computer screen and responses recorded directly into the survey database.

computer assisted telephone interviewing (CATI)
Using a CATI system the interviewer reads the survey questions, including introductory comments, prompts and contingencies, directly from a computer screen, and then enters the responses straight into the survey database. The CATI system is can also be used to select a random sample.

compute variable function
SPSS function that allows calculations to be performed or criteria to be set on one or more variable.

concepts
Concepts are components of theories that can be drawn from theory, or developed through induction from the data. They describe key aspects of the processes or patterns examined in the research.

conceptual analysis
Analysis which examines communication for the explicit or implicit presence of selected concept, or related concepts.

conceptual framework
The theoretical frame that we use to conceptualise the collection, analysis and interpretation of our data.

conceptualisation
The process of developing concepts that focus on the research question.

confidence
The quantitative researcher is, more often than not, very interested in specifying the level of certainty with which a relationship between variables within a data set can be generalised beyond the confines of a specific sample to some wider population.

confidence level
Tells us how confident we can be that our population parameter lies within a given confidence interval.

confidence interval
The statistical range (interval) of our results within which we estimate the true population figure lies.

confidentiality
The principle of ensuring that the specific contribution of respondents cannot be identified.

consent form
A short, written statement that respondents are asked to read and sign before participation in an investigation. It states that respondents have been fully informed about the study and that their participation is voluntary.

constitutive role of writing
How you write about an issue influences the way that issue is understood.

context
The settings in which texts are situated.

content analysis
A research method that detects, records and analyses the presence of words or concepts in forms of communication.

contextual analysis
An evaluation research method concerned with how an initiative was implemented, through examination of its structure and decision-making processes, the nature and extent of community and interagency involvement and the extent of implementation.

convenience sampling
Convenience sampling is making up your sample of respondents from people who are easy to locate, such as your friends, family, students or classmates.

conversation analysis
Conversation analysis uses a special type of transcription system to analyse audio- or video-recordings of naturally occurring conversation. It is usually used when the research interest lies in what participants do outside a formal research setting.

covert research
The inclusion of respondents in a research project without their awareness and/or agreement to their participation.

critical discourse analysis
Research methods associated with the work of Norman Fairclough.

cross-sectional analysis
Analysis of a population at a single point in time; sometimes likened to a 'snapshot' photograph.

cross-sectional design
A survey of a cross-section of a population conducted at one point in time.

cross-tabular analysis
A simple form of statistical analysis that usually represents the relationship between two (or sometimes three) variables.

cross-tabulation
A table of rows and columns where one variable in the column is crossed (compared) with another variable in the row. This produces a matrix where each cell is a case that has characteristics of both the row and column elements.

cumulative per cent
A calculation of the valid responses that adds each individual percentage value to the previous value and totals to 100 per cent.

data
The information we collect and analyse to answer our research question. Data come in all manner of forms, such as survey forms, documents and secondary data.

data continuity
The extent to which questions have been asked in continuous data collections (like the census) and asked in an identical manner.

data set
The entire set of observations recorded in the course of data collection.

data view
The SPSS screen that holds the raw data, and indicates where columns are variables and rows are cases, and where all data on individual respondents are entered and displayed.

decomposition
Sometimes called component analysis: the breaking down of the outcome into its contributing components.

deductive research
Research in which the questions asked by the social researcher are primarily shaped by reading through previous theory and research.

deductive theory
Deductive theory is a way of developing theory that begins with the idea (theory) and proceeds to collect data to test the validity of the theory.

demographic data
Data that categorise groups of individuals according to such characteristics as their age, sex, marital status and birth and death rates.

dependent variable
The dependent variable is the variable that is dependent on or affected by another variable; what the researcher treats as a quality to be explained.

descriptive research
Research that has as its major purpose to describe social phenomena.

descriptive statistics
Quantitative statistics that describe the data or summarise the data (such as the average or mean).

deviant cases
Data that do not appear to fit within the analytical categories being developed.

diachronic
Across time.

diachronic analysis/time-series analysis
Analysis undertaken using longitudinal or time series datasets.

dialogue box
A window, or series of windows, that open up from via the menu and allow commands to be performed. It uses arrows and buttons to select SPSS functions without having to write a syntax or command file.

direction of relationship
The type of relationship that categories exhibit.

dispersion measures
Statistics that describe how data are patterned around the mean.

discourse
Generic term to denote language in use.

discourse analysis
Research process that critically analyses how language is deployed within communication.

discursive practice
A critical discourse analysis method that focuses on rhetorical strategies within a text.

disparate impact
Unequal impact or outcome (as of a policy) that is typically unintended, as opposed to intended.

dispositive analysis
Used within discourse analysis to denote a Foucauldian mode of analysis that seeks to reveal the logic of different practices.

disproportionately
Unequal proportions, such as of two populations in the same age group.

ecological fallacy
An ecological fallacy occurs when we incorrectly draw conclusions about one unit of analysis from research conducted using a different unit of analysis. This often occurs if results from an aggregate unit of analysis, such as a group or an organisation, are applied to a disaggregated unit of analysis such as an individual.

empirical data
Pieces of information that are the result of observing and/or measuring social phenomena.

enlightening categories
The requirement that categories must produce a breakdown of content that will be analytically interesting and coherent.

environment assessment
Analysis of the context within which research or evaluation is to occur, such as auditing the human and material resources needed for a project and examining the policies that might affect its development.

epistemology
Theory of knowledge concerned with understanding how knowledge is defined, valued and prioritised.

ethical research
Ensuring that ethical principles and values always govern research involving humans.

ethics
The establishment of a set of moral standards that govern behaviour in a particular setting or for a particular group.

ethnographic approach
An ethnographic approach explores a particular social or cultural setting with the aim of understanding the phenomenon from an insider's point of view. The ethnographer is usually an active participant in the research setting. Also see *field notes*; *participant observation*.

ethnographic fieldwork
Spending a long period of time observing some group or social setting.

ethnography
A research method that involves conducting ethnographic fieldwork.

evaluation
A process of assessing what we are doing, valuing why we are doing it and understanding how we can make improvements in the future.

exclusive categories
The requirement that categories must not overlap, or ambiguities must at least be minimised.

exhaustive categories
The requirement that every aspect of the data with which the research is concerned must be covered by one category.

experimental
A research method in which pre-test measurements are taken of a target group or area, before the implementation of an experimental intervention (introduction of a particular program, strategy or project), followed by post-test measurements after the intervention has had time to take effect.

explanatory research
Research that seeks to provide or develop explanation of the social world or social phenomena.

explicit coding
Term used in content analysis to signify coding for the visible, easily identified content of the text.

exploratory research
Research undertaken to explore or open up new areas of social enquiry.

factor analysis
A useful statistical method that helps the researcher to validate a proposed multiple indicator measure of a concept.

field notes
Field notes provide a record of the participant observations made by an ethnographer. Field notes take the form of notes or sound recordings, and record not only what the researcher has seen but also his or her feelings and perceptions of the events. Also see *ethnographic approach*; *participant observation*.

focus group
A research method that involves encouraging a group of people to discuss some social or political issue.

follow-up question
A question used during an interview that encourages interviewees to explain, clarify or expand on a previous answer. It might be worth trying out follow-up questions such as 'What do you mean by that?' in a practice interview.

format
The format of data or other information to suit different social research software analysis software packages, such as Excel, SPSS and Stata.

formative evaluation
Forward-looking evaluation, the purpose of which is to identify needs, clarify rationales and improve implementation into the future.

Foucauldian-inspired analysis
Generic term used in discourse analysis to denote methods associated with the work of Michel Foucault.

framing
Term used in discourse analysis to show how political messages are regulated and controlled.

frequency
The number or counts for each category of a variable.

frequency table
A table that displays the number and percentage of each instance or category of a variable.

frequency distribution
A summary of how cases fall out across the response categories comprising a variable; the numbers or proportions in each subcategory or subgroup comprising the entire category or group.

genealogy
Discourse analysis method, associated with Foucault, to show how different discourses are superseded at certain historical junctures.

generalisation
Quantitative researchers will conventionally seek to generate a sample that will enable them to extrapolate survey results with a good level of certainty to a population of concern.

generative view of writing
Writing is recognised as a tool of discovery.

genre
A particular form of expression, with its own established structural and stylistic conventions; the style in which texts are produced and consumed.

grounded theory
Analysis that has the aim of generating theory.

human research ethics committee (HREC)
A committee established by an institution or organisation for the task of viewing research proposals and monitoring ongoing investigations with the aim of protecting the welfare and rights of participants in research.

hypothesis
Hypotheses are prescriptive forms of research question that state a particular scenario that the research will confirm or refute.

ideology
Shared values held by groups and societies.

immersion
A process in which the researcher becomes familiar with data.

impact
The effect of a particular course of action.

implementation
Putting something into practice.

implicit coding
Term used in content analysis to signify coding for the underlying and implicit meaning of the content of the text.

in-depth interview
In-depth interviews are guided by general themes rather than pre-set questions. They are also less formal than structured interviews, exploring issues as the interviewee raises them.

independent variable
The independent variable is a variable that has an effect on another variable; a quality hypothesised to account for variation in a dependent variable.

index of dissimilarity
A measure of the extent to which one population differs or is similar to another; an index of 100 would indicate complete dissimilarity while an index of 0 would indicate complete similarity. The index expresses the percentage of the population that would need to change categories in order for the two populations to have identical frequency distributions in relation to a specific factor.

inductive codes
The coding of themes that emerge from the data.

inductive research
Research that begins with the data. Patterns and processes are identified by observing and noticing these as they occur in the data.

inductive theory
Inductive theory is a way of developing theory that begins with the identification of a pattern in a social phenomenon and then proceeds to the development of a theory to explain that pattern.

inference
Inference is where we can infer that the statistical results from our sample can be sustained within the whole of our population of research interest.

information sheet
A short written document that provides respondents with a summary of key aspects of the research for the purposes of informed consent. This includes what the research is about, what participation involves and any potential risks arising from participation.

informed consent
A document or agreement that ensures, first, that research respondents are fully informed about what the research is about and what participation will involve, and second, that they make the decision to participate without any formal or informal coercion.

intercensal (estimates)
The period between censuses; estimates made between censuses.

inter-coder reliability
The extent to which two or more independent individuals agree on coding, categories and assignation of concepts to categories; the research is reliable, coding consistent and categories operational to the degree that all the researchers assign the same texts to the same categories.

inter-collection discontinuities
Gaps or changes in the data categories or criteria between different collections.

interpretation
Data analysis results must be interpreted in light of our conceptual frame; that is, not only what our results indicate, but what they mean in the context of our topic.

interpretations
Interpretations are how people make sense of their social situations and circumstances.

interpretive data collection
Data collection concerned with critical analysis and reflection, through examination of the social meanings reflected in documents, policy statements, theoretical statements and other sources of secondary data.

interpretive perspective
A way of understanding the process of conducting research promoted by Max Weber, among other social theorists. It emphasises the importance of addressing meaning and interpretation in social life.

intertextuality
Term used in discourse analysis to denote how texts contain linkages to other sources.

interview guide
A list of themes and questions prepared before the interview.

interval data
Interval data are data where the attributes of the variable can be meaningfully rank ordered and the intervals between the ranks is equal but there is no zero point.

intra-collection discontinuities
Gaps or changes in the data categories or criteria within a single collection.

iterative research practice
Research that occurs in the process of moving between writing-based and non-writing-based research tasks.

judgment
Considered opinion.

language
A performative activity encompassing words, texts and other expressive behaviours.

large representative national sample
A kind of sample that allows researchers to produce findings that enable them to more confidently make claims about the condition of any particular social phenomenon within the confines of a specific national population.

latent structure
An emergent pattern of association between a subset of variables able to be revealed by a statistical technique such as factor analysis.

level of implication
Determining whether to code simply for explicit appearances of concepts, or for implied concepts as well; for example, deciding whether to code 'unmarried' as an entity in and of itself or, if coding for 'unmarried' references in general, to code 'single' as implicitly meaning 'unmarried'. Thus, by determining that the meaning 'unmarried' is implicit in the words 'single', any time the words 'single' or 'unmarried' appear in the text, they will be coded under the same category of 'unmarried'.

level of measurement
How a variable is measured (nominal, ordinal or interval–ratio); determines its subsequent treatment in the process of statistical analysis.

life history
A life history approach uses the 'stories' that people tell of their lives as a source of data. In-depth interviews are usually used to solicit data, although letters, diaries, photographs and so on can also be used. Also see *narrative analysis*.

limitations
Limits or weaknesses of a project or a particular form of data collection, that ought to be acknowledged in undertaking social research and in interpreting the findings of social and evaluation research.

literature review
A critical analysis of the existing research literature, theoretical and empirical, related to our research topic. It informs us of what is known and not known about our topic.

longitudinal analysis
Analysis over time; time-series analysis.

longitudinal study
A study that collects data on the same phenomena over an extended period of time.

low-risk research
Research where the only foreseeable risk to respondents is one of discomfort. Low-risk research may involve a lower level of scrutiny by HRECs.

mean
The average score for a set of cases.

measurement
How we are going to measure our key concepts. How we measure and what we measure differs between quantitative and qualitative methodologies.

median
The middle score or measurement in a set of ranked scores; the score that divides a distribution into two equal halves.

median age
The exact age above and below which half the population falls.

memory work
Memory work is a collaborative technique used to generate stories that are based on personal memories among a group of co-researchers. Also see *triggers*.

metaphor
Used in discourse analysis to denote the figurative use of terms.

method
The research technique or practice used to gather and analyse the research data.

methodology
Methodology is the theoretical lens through which the research is designed and conducted.

missing case
A missing case is an observation that does not have a value or valid response.

missing data
The number of cases in a quantitative analysis defined as not valid.

modality
Term used in discourse analysis to denote the level of commitment made by the speaker to claims within a sentence.

mode
The most common, or most frequent, score in a set of scores.

multi-agency cooperation
An emphasis on communication with interested parties, in a consultative manner, such that decision-making is by and large restricted to the core research or evaluation group.

multiple indicators
Different measures of the one concept; often combined to generate a more valid and reliable measure.

multiple regression analysis
An advanced statistical technique that enables the researcher to examine the impact of a range of independent variables on a dependent variable simultaneously.

narrative
A story of events, experiences or the like.

narrative analysis
The making sense of data by focusing on the story that the participant tells. This analysis explores how participants tell their stories and how these stories link to a broader social or structural context.

narrative devices
Language or other communication facets that determines how stories are told and the way meanings are put together.

nationally based general social surveys
These are key sources of data used for undertaking secondary analysis in the social sciences.

naturalistic
A research method in which information is gained by asking people directly about specific features of their lives, and how particular innovations and initiatives affect their daily routines.

negligible risk research
Research that carries no foreseeable risk of harm or discomfort to respondents.

nominal data
Data where the variables attributes represent different kinds of characteristics rather than an amount of a characteristic i.e. attributes of male and female in gender.

nominal definition
A definition of exactly what we mean by the particular concepts we are using.

non-probability sampling
A sampling process that does not use probability sampling techniques to select a sample. Examples include convenience sampling, snowball sampling and self-selected sampling.

official collections
Data collections typically carried out by government agencies.

one-shot case study
A survey that collects information from a specific group of people at one point in time.

ontology
The understandings of reality and the nature of being that inform our view of the world.

open coding
Initial line-by-line examination for themes from data.

open-ended questions
Questions that are open in that they allow respondents freedom in their response rather than selecting from pre-determined category responses used in closed questions.

open questions (or open-ended questions)
Questions that are designed to elicit an open response rather than a yes/no or other closed response set i.e. 'how did you feel when that happened?

operational definition
A definition of how we will measure our defined concepts.

operationalisation
The process of defining how concepts will be measured.

orders of discourse
Power relationships that exist between readers and producers of texts. These are rarely equal.

ordinal data
Data where the attributes of the variables represent more or less of a variable, and can be ranked ordered, but the difference between the rank intervals is not determined.

outcomes
The specific consequences of a particular course of action.

output window
The SPSS window where the results (output) of our analysis are displayed.

panel study
A study designed to repeatedly survey the same sample group at set periods of time in order to measure changes in key variables.

paradigm
A shared framework of viewing and approaching the investigation and research of social phenomena.

paradigm shift
When a dominant paradigm is successfully challenged for dominance by a competing paradigm.

participant observation
The main data-collecting technique used by ethnographers. It involves the researcher observing first hand in the research setting. The researcher is free to be an active participant in the normal routines of the research.

participatory action research
A cyclical research process aimed at providing feedback into a cycle for problem solving. It is a practical research method that requires an equal and open collaboration between the researcher and the research community.

passive style
Style of written text that usually entails the author placing the object in the subject position. Sometimes deployed to convey a sense of objectivity.

Pearson chi square
A statistical technique used to precisely gauge the likelihood of any particular association between a pair of variables being reproduced within a larger population. See *chi square*.

percentage
A number expressed as a proportion of 100.

percentage change
The difference between two percentages expressed as a percentage of the first observation.

percentage point
The difference between two percentage values (for example, the difference between 20 per cent and 30 per cent is 10 percentage points).

performance indicators
Measures designed to indicate present performance in relation to stated goals.

performance targets
Identification of the end point goals of a particular program or project.

plagiarism
The unacknowledged use of the work of another person so that the ideas or information appear to be one's own.

planning
Making decisions in a systematic manner about what to do in the future.

policy implications
Policy-related consequences of an issue or research finding.

population
The collection of all the units that we want to study.

primary data collection
The process of administering a data-collection instrument to a sample of cases and recording the pattern of observations that arise in numeric form.

primary sources
Information that you have directly collected yourself (such as by undertaking your own survey).

probability sampling
Samples selected in accordance with probability theory. Probability sampling relies on (a) that we have a list of all elements or cases in the population we are studying; and (b) that we are able to randomly select elements or cases from this list and that all cases or elements have an equal chance of being selected.

probability theory
The mathematical theory used within probability sampling that allows us to determine how accurately our sample characteristics (sample statistics) estimate our population characteristics (population parameters) by quantifying the degree of sampling error.

probe
Another term for a follow-up question.

process
Progressive changes over time, which may include actions directed towards a particular result.

process of iteration
The step-by-step practice by which relevant patterns in a quantitative data set are progressively revealed.

proportionate ratio
The relativity between two proportions or percentages (such as the proportionate ratio of 30 per cent and 20 per cent is 30 for every 20, or 3 for every 2, or 1.5 for every 1.0. This ratio would typically be expressed as 1.5).

proportionately
Relative proportions or percentages, as opposed to numbers.

purposive sampling
Purposive sampling is selecting a sample in a systematic or purposive way, based on what we know about our target population and the purpose of our study.

qualitative data collection
Data collection concerned with the views and understandings of actors and the observation of people and events.

qualitative information
Takes the form of direct quotations or descriptions of social phenomena.

qualitative research
Qualitative research is concerned with exploring the understandings, meanings and interpretations that people or other groups attribute to their social world. Major qualitative methods include participant observation studies and in-depth interviews.

quantitative data
A set of observations of the social world recorded in numeric form.

quantitative data collection
Data collection concerned with counting and measurement; that is, data expressed in numbers, rates and trends.

quantitative information
A statistical profile of social phenomena.

quantitative research
The study of social processes through the collection of data that is amenable to statistical analysis. Quantitative research is often used to identify and establish relationships between research variables. Major quantitative social research methods include surveys, structured interviewing and secondary data analysis.

quantitative–qualitative debate
Debate in which sides are taken by researchers as to whether quantitative methods (that is, methods that produce data relating to social phenomena that are amenable to statistical analysis) or qualitative methods (that is, methods that concentrate on drawing on the detail and social meaning of social phenomena) are 'superior'.

quasi-panel study
A study designed to repeatedly survey samples of a target population on the same phenomena over time. Differs from a panel study in that the survey respondents are not from the same sample group each time.

questionnaire
Structured set of questions administered (via mail, Internet, telephone, personal interview or other method) to a group of survey respondents.

quota sampling
The development of a sample that is representative of a population by drawing a sample on the bases of population estimations of factors such as gender, age and education level.

rapport
The relationship of trust that is required to conduct a good interview.

ratio
The relativity between two absolute numbers (such as the ratio of 30 and 20 is 1.5 for every 1.0. This ratio would typically be expressed as 1.5).

ratio data
Data where the attributes of a variable have the same rank-ordered features as those in interval data, but where the variable being measured has a true zero point.

raw data
Numeric data in a crude, unanalysed form.

recode function
Recoding allows the user to collapse variables that have numerous values into more discrete values (such as collapsing respondents' age into categories).

reductionism
Reducing complex arguments to simplistic assertions.

relational analysis
A form of content analysis where the focus is on the discovery of semantic, or meaningful, relationships among concepts in a communication.

reflexivity
A self-conscious awareness by the researcher of their impact on the research and research process.

reflective memos
An ongoing process by which the researcher notes process issues associated with the research.

regimes of truth
Term used in Foucauldian discourse analysis to denote the basis from which understandings of the social world are asserted.

relativism
Philosophical position suggesting that it is not possible to obtain objective knowledge, and that there are only different views and opinions.

reliability
Reliability is the consistency of our data or results. If we repeated the data collection or analysis, will we consistently get the same results?

representativeness
What quantitative researchers want their sample to achieve with respect to a population of interest.

research design
The thorough planning process that develops an outline of all aspects of the research project and how they will fit together to result in rigorous research.

research methodology
The overall approach to the research process, justified in terms of pre-existing theories about how to do research.

research proposal
A formal written document that fully details all aspects of the research we intend to undertake. A research proposal is usually required before academic research can proceed.

research question
Research questions state the major aim of the research in question form, specifying the key idea that the research seeks to investigate and/or explain and also identifying the key concepts of the research.

researcher-administered survey
A survey where the researcher completes the questionnaire from the respondents' answers, as in face-to-face or telephone interviews.

rigour
Rigour is how researchers ensure that qualitative research faithfully represents the stories and experiences of the people being studied. Rigour includes close scrutiny of the detail of participants' lives, 'thick description', a focus on process and subjective meanings, and a tolerance for complex and nuanced explanations.

sample
A sample is a set of cases or elements that are selected from a population.

sample non-response
The number of sample respondents who do not participate in the research.

sample statistic
The estimate of the population (real) result generated from analysis of sample data.

sampling
Sampling is the process of selecting a sample of our research population of interest. In quantitative social research, sampling usually uses probability sampling techniques, and non-probability sampling techniques for qualitative research.

sampling error
The error in sampling statistics caused by the difference between a sample and its population.

sampling frame
A list that represents as closely as possible an abstract population; the researcher uses this list to draw a probability sample.

scientific method
Planned methodical research based around observing, analysing and interpreting our research data, conducted with professionalism and ethical integrity, and transparent and rigorous in its approach.

scoping
The review of specific aims, targets and strategies of a particular program or project.

secondary data analysis
The methods and techniques involved in analysing a set of raw survey data to which a researcher has been granted access by a social science data archive.

secondary sources
Information that you have not directly collected yourself, but which is available through other means (such as Australian Bureau of Statistics information).

selective coding
The qualitative analytical process by which coding categories are unified around a 'core' category. The core category can be identified by its centrality to other categories and implications for a more general theory.

selective reduction
The central tenet of content analysis: text is reduced to categories consisting of a word, or a set of words or phrases, on which the researcher can focus. The resultant patterns inform the research question, and determine levels of analysis and generalisation.

self-administered survey
A survey where the respondent undertakes the survey without direct interviewer guidance, such as in mail or internet surveys.

self-selected sampling
Where people self-select into a survey or study by making contact with a researcher or by choosing to respond to questions, such as in television programs or newspaper polls that ask people to register their opinion or vote.

self-technology
Term used in Foucauldian discourse analysis to denote how new discursive practices are ordered.

semantic differential formats
In a semantic differential format survey question, the respondent is asked to select his or her response from between the two extreme values of a continuum.

sign of a relationship
Whether or not the concepts are positively or negatively related.

simple random sampling
Sampling randomly using probability, but with no additional techniques such as stratification.

snowball sampling
Used to access respondents from hard-to-reach groups by asking respondents to suggest other prospective respondents to the researcher.

social aggregates
The collective, aggregate social outcomes or circumstances of individuals or groups.

social attitudes and actions
The kinds of phenomena the quantitative social researcher usually seeks to account for or explain.

social desirability effect
The tendency of interviewees to present themselves in a good light by concealing damaging or controversial information.

social mapping
A description of local social conditions, key players and social factors that may influence specific project development and evaluation processes.

social meanings
How people(s) make sense of aspects of their social lives and the understandings that they develop of these.

social patterns
Persistent patterns in social phenomena that occur repeatedly in the social world.

social practice
Method associated with critical discourse analysis to highlight ideology and power relations.

social research
The systematic study of society, the patterns in it and the processes that shape what people do.

social science data archive
An organisation responsible for the storage and dissemination of social science data.

social theory
An idea or a set of ideas that explain social phenomena.

specialised dictionary
In computer text content analysis, another term for category system: a dictionary consists of all search patterns that form the categories.

SPSS
Statistical Product and Service Solutions: the most popular computer program in the social sciences for managing and analysing quantitative data.

SPSS file
One of many SPPS data files that can hold data (.sav), output (.spo) or syntax (.sps).

standpoint
The way we see the world and our position in it in relation to others and society. Our standpoint recognises the filters and frames that have an impact on our approach to our research.

standard deviation
Provides an indication of how cases are spread across the categories of an ordinal or interval-ratio level variable.

standardisation
A statistical technique by which one or more factors are reduced to a common standard or held constant (such as the age structure that occurred in a given year may be applied to each successive year to see what the effect on some factor would be if the age structure had not changed).

statistical analysis
A means for revealing patterns and regularities within a quantitative data set.

statistics table
The SPSS output table that reports the number of missing and valid cases in the analysis.

strategic partnerships
Formalised relationships between parties, which are built upon group decision-making and adherence to the decisions of the group as a whole.

strategic plan
An outline of key aims, intended outcomes, and strategies and methods of a project or strategy.

stratified sampling
Often used with probability sampling to ensure that certain subgroups (such as an equal number from each state) are included at an appropriate level within the sample.

stream of consciousness
A style of writing that reflects the flow of a person's continuous thoughts and conscious reactions to an issue or event.

strength of relationship
The degree to which two or more concepts are related.

structured interview
An interview that asks mostly closed questions. It is often used in projects where many people are interviewed, such as in a survey.

summary measure
The average or mean.

summative evaluation
Concerned with results, this type of evaluation is backward looking, and is used to assess performances and outcomes up to a certain point in time.

synchronic
At one point in time.

synchronic analysis
Analysis undertaken using a one point in time dataset.

syntax file
The SPSS coding that can be used to generate analysis instead of the windows interface, and which in newer SPSS packages appears at the top of all Output windows.

systematic sampling
A probability sampling approach that uses a sampling fraction to determine the system of drawing a random sample.

test of significance
A statistical test used to determine if the result observed can be regarded statistically significant; that is, not due to chance. See *chi square* or *Pearson chi square*.

text
Any form of written communication; or any cultural artefact bearing messages that can be analysed in the same fashion as texts (such as films, fashion, photographs or sports events). Often associated with content analysis and discourse analysis. The requirement is that every aspect of the data with which the research is concerned must be covered by one category.

textual analysis
Analysis of the vocabulary, grammar, cohesion and structure within a text.

thematic analysis
Analysis of qualitative data that explores the presence of themes, both predetermined and those that emerge, within the data.

themes
In qualitative analysis a theme is a central idea that emerges from the data.

theory
Social theory is already defined in Chapter 1 as: An idea or a set of ideas that explain social phenomena. If you think we need the term 'theory' separate we should use the same definition but remove the term 'social'—an idea or a set of ideas that explain phenomena.

theoretical sampling
The process using in qualitative research where the data is continually analysed as it is collected to guide the further sampling process.

theoretical saturation
The point in qualitative data collection when no new information on any particular code is emerging.

theoretical sensitivity
The ability to perceive the research situation and the data in new ways, especially as they relate to the development of theory.

transcription
A full written record of interview data.

transform tool
SPSS menu of functions related to the transforming of data or variables within the data set.

transform data
Where quantitative data is transformed from one format to another, such as age data in years into age data in age groups.

translation rules
A protocol whereby less general concepts will be translated into more general ones; a researcher must make this distinction; that is, make an implicit concept explicit, then code for the frequency of its occurrence, resulting in the construction of a translation rule that instructs the researcher to code for the concept in a certain way.

triangulation
Triangulation describes the combining of different research methods. The value of this practice is that the researcher can gain the advantages of each method used while also reducing the limitations of a single method.

triggers
Triggers or themes are used in memory work to solicit memories. Triggers are usually collectively determined by the group. Care needs to be taken when selecting triggers, as less obvious triggers have often been found to be more effective in soliciting rich memories than more obvious triggers. Also see *memory work*.

unit of analysis
A particular instance of what or who we are researching. A unit of analysis can include

individuals, groups, social artefacts such as newspaper articles or policy documents, or anything related to social life that can be investigated.

unit of observation
The disaggregated research item i.e. in content analysis the unit of analysis might be the newspaper but the unit of observation is the article selected for specific examination.

univariate analysis
Quantitative analysis that examines one variable at a time.

unstructured interview
An interview that asks mostly open questions. It is often used in projects where one researcher conducts interviews with a small number of people, and is informed by interpretivist assumptions.

valid cases
The acceptance of only those instances where there is response; that is, do not contain missing data.

valid data
A result using only cases defined as valid in the quantitative analysis.

valid per cent
The third column of a Frequencies output in SPSS, showing the percentages of only those instances where there is response; that is, do not contain missing data.

validity
Validity is the extent our data or results measure what we intended them to measure.

validity (discourse analysis)
The degree to which arguments are coherent and accepted within the text.

variable
A characteristic of data that has more than one category. A variable varies between different values, and is measured in social research; for example, the variable gender has two categories: male and female.

variable view
The SPSS screen that contains definitive information on each variable.

variance
A measure of the spread of scores in a distribution of scores.

verstehen

Interpretive method through which we understand other people's actions.

vital statistics

Data collections pertaining to vital events, such as births and deaths, that typically occur only once. Marriages, divorces and migration are also often considered vital events.

Index

a priori codes 419
Aboriginal and Torres Strait Islander people
   and census 17–18
   ethical research guidelines 106–7
   family violence 370–1
academic fraud 109
active style (discourse analysis) 355
administrative collections 185
age composition (populations) 204
age–sex structures 205
age-specific (populations) 205
aggregated data 186
Alston, Margaret 313–14
ambiguity, defined 11
annotated bibliographies 450
anonymity 101–2
antisocial behaviour 367–9
archaeological discourse analysis 359
artefacts (anomalies) of techniques 200
association (cross-tabular analysis) 230
audience (discourse analysis) 355, 442
Australian Association of Social Workers (AASW),
   ethical standards 95
Australian Bureau of Statistics (ABS) 40
Australian Election Study, response rates 136–7
Australian Housing and Urban Research Institute 41
Australian Institute of Criminology 40
Australian Institute of Family Studies 40
Australian Institute of Health and Welfare 40
Australian Policy Online 40
Australian Social Science Data Archive (ASSDA) 217, 222
Australian Sociological Association (TASA), *Code of Ethics* 94, 108
Australian Survey of Social Attitudes 2007 (AuSSA) 144–5, 227, 244
authorial voice 442
authorship, acknowledgement of 109–10
axiology 15–16

Baker, Maureen 295–6
Baudrillard, Jean 22
Baxter, Janeen 79–80
benchmarks 387
Beyond Anorexia 297–8
bivariate analysis 264–9

CAI (Computer Assisted Interviewing) 166–7
capitalism, attitudes to 217
CATI (Computer Assisted Telephone Interviewing) 165

causality, and survey data 154
Census of Population and Housing 17–18, 185, 187–8
central tendency measures 227, 228–9, 258
Centre for Independent Studies (CIS) 8
chi square test 22, 265
child support, and housing 140
Churchill, Brendan 370–1
closed questions 171, 299
codebooks 327
coding (data)
   defined 245, 325
   golden rules 326
cohesion (discourse analysis) 355, 365
composition (populations) 204
concepts
   defined 70, 324
   operationalising 71
   specification of 70
conceptual content analysis
   coding parameters 334
   nature of 327–8
conceptual frameworks
   defined 13
   in social research 19
conceptualisation
   defined 32, 47
   and definition of key concepts 47–8
conference proceedings 39
confidence interval (sampling) 130
confidence level (sampling) 130
confidence sampling 124, 137
confidentiality 102–3
conflict perspective 20–1
constitutive role of writing 441
content analysis
   advantages 343
   coding parameters 334–5
   coding texts and statistical analysis 337–8
   conceptual analysis 327–8
   conducting 332–8
   deciding on parameters of analysis 334
   deciding rationale for study and its level of analysis 332–3
   defined 324
   disadvantages 343
   distinguishing among concepts 336
   explicit coding 325
   identifying appropriate texts, sample, units of analysis 333–4
   implicit coding 326

Social Research Methods

interpreting results 338
measuring codes 335–6
rational analysis 328–31
rules for coding texts 336–7
selective reduction 325
strengths and weaknesses 340–3
surplus information 337
types of 327–32
uses of 324–5
context
    defined 15
    in discourse analysis 355
contextual analysis 385, 386–7
contrast questioning 300
conversation analysis 309
covert research 95, 113–14
critical discourse analysis
    discursive practice 365–6
    explained 356–7
    selection of text 363
    social practice 363–4
    textual analysis 364–5
    undertaking 363–6
cross-sectional analysis 191
cross-sectional design surveys 155
cross-tabular analysis 230–2, 265–9
cultural differences, impact on social research 6, 17–18
cyber porn study 89

Dance, Rebecca 344–6
data
    defined 5, 219
    reliability 71
    validity 71
data analysis, in research process 74
data collection
    in evaluation research 389–91
    primary data 221
    secondary data 221–3
    in surveys 161–8
data management 103
data quality, impact of cultural differences 17–18
data sets 219
data storage 103–4
Declaration of Helsinki 94
decomposition (component analysis) 210
deductive theory, defined 50
deductive theory development 49–50
demographic data 184, 383
dependent variables 231
descriptive questions 300
descriptive research 11
descriptive statistics 258
deviant cases 422
devil's advocate questions 300
diachronic analysis 190

direction of relationship (concepts) 329
discourse, defined 354
discourse analysis
    advantages of 354
    challenges 360–3
    critical approach 356–7, 360
    defined 354
    emergence as social science method 353–4
    example study of housing affordability 361–3
    explained 352
    Foucauldian-inspired analysis 357–60, 366
    key terms and concepts 354–6
    privileging of agency 361
    racism in newspapers 83–4
    reductionism 360
    selection of texts 360
    theoretical origins 353
    validity issues 361
discursive practice 357, 365–6
dispersion measures 227, 228, 258
dispositive analysis 359
documentary sources 39–41
domestic labour 431
Durkheim, Emile 20, 323

Eaves, Cassandra 211
ecological fallacy 76
edited books, as sources 39
electronic surveying 167–8
empirical data, defined 18
employment, and motherhood 429–30
enlightening categories (coding) 326
environment assessment (evaluation) 382
environmental leaders 145
epistemology 14–15
ethical research
    acknowledgement of authorship 109–10
    anonymity of participants 101–2
    in Australia 94–5
    basic principles for human experimentation 92–4
    and beneficence 97
    confidentiality 102–3
    covert research 95, 113–14
    disclosure of funding sources 110–11
    distributive and procedural justice 96–7
    governing values 96–7
    and informed consent 96, 98–101
    nature and importance of 90–2
    payments to research subjects 112
    principles of 97
    relationship between researchers and research participants 91, 97
    research merit and integrity 96, 105
    and respect for human beings 97
    safety of participants 104–5
    safety of researchers 108

ethical research (cont.)
    truthful reporting   108–9
    volunteer participants   111–12
    vulnerable participant groups   105–7, 114
ethical research guidelines
    for Aboriginal and Torres Strait Islander peoples   106–7
    Australian Health Ethics Committee   94
    for Maori people   107
    National Statement on Ethical Conduct in Research Involving Humans   94, 96–8
    Nuremberg Code   93–4
    professional codes of ethics   94–5
    for vulnerable groups   105–6
ethical review, need for   95–6
ethics
    and covert research   95
    defined   5, 90
    and the organisation   110–11
    and research   74, 90–2
    and the researcher   108–10
ethnic groups, media representations of   340–1
ethnographic fieldwork   309
ethnography   21, 103
evaluation, defined   378
evaluation methods and techniques
    contextual analysis   385, 386–7
    countering limitations   387
    data collection   389–91
    designing performance indicators   388–9
    documentary analysis & critical interpretation   390–1
    establishing benchmarks   387–8
    experimental and quasi-experimental methods   385–6
    interviews and participant observation   390
    numeric evidence   390
    range of   384–5
evaluation research
    administrative structures   383–4
    central planning questions   380–1
    commissioning of   378
    consequences issues   396–7
    data analysis   393–4
    data organisation   391
    environment assessment   382
    establishing benchmarks   387–8
    evaluation resources   384
    external focus   382–3
    focus of study   391
    impact data   392
    internal focus   382
    issue mapping   393
    limitations of   395–7
    methodological issues   395–6
    methods and techniques   384–91
    omissions and inclusions   393–4

outcomes   391–4
planning   381–4
political nature of   379
primary sources   392
process data   392
purposes of   379
qualitative information   392
quantitative information   392
reliability and cross-checks   393
report preparation   394–5
scoping the project framework   381–2
secondary sources   393
undertaking   380–1
unique aspects   378–9
values issues   396
Everyday Life Incivility in Australia   239
exclusive categories (coding)   326
exhaustive categories (coding)   326
experimental methods   385
experiments, defined   93
explanatory research   11
explicit coding   325
exploratory research   11
Ezzy, Doug   307

face-to-face interviews   166–7
factor analysis   224
Fairclough, Norman   356
family violence   370–1
feeling questions   300
feminist paradigms   21
field notes   427
Financial Disadvantage in Australia: 1990–2000   7–8
focus groups   5
    analysing   427–9
    defined   314
    role of moderator   314–15
    strengths and weaknesses   315
    uses of   314, 315–18
follow-up questions   299
Footsteps in Time   4
format (data)   245
formative evaluation   387–8
Foucauldian-inspired analysis (discourse analysis)   357–60, 366
Foucault, Michel   357
framing (discourse analysis)   355
Franklin, Adrian   344
fraud   109
frequencies
    defined   258
    producing in SPSS   258–60
frequency distributions   190, 226–7
functionalism   20
functionalist perspective   20

Garrett, Catherine 297–8, 301–2
genealogy (discourse analysis) 359
Generation Y 370–1
generative view of writing 441
genres (discourse analysis) 355, 364
Gill, Fiona 430–1
Glaser, Barney 423
grounded theory 423–4

Hawthorne effect 6–7
Heckenberg, Diane 399
housework 79–81, 431
housing, and child support 140
housing affordability 361–3
human experimentation, and ethical research 92–4
human research ethics committees (HRECs), role of 5, 94–5
hypotheses, defined 22
hypothetical advocate questions 300

ideology
    defined 76
    as a key concept in discourse analysis 355
immersion
    defined 413
    and incubation 412–15
impact (evaluation) 379
implementation (evaluation) 379
implicit coding 326
in-depth interviews 5
    choosing a topic 293–4
    common criticisms of 309–10
    conducting 291–2
    in defence of 311–12
    and importance of meaning and subjectivity 290–1
    interview guides 301–3
    interviewing techniques 303–7
    nature of 288
    number needed 294–5
    preparation for interviews 298–9
    recording data 307–8
    recruiting interviewees 296–8
    reflectively evaluating an interview 306
    reporting interview data 292–3
    social desirability effect 310
    strengths of 310–11
    transcription 295
    types of questions 299–301
    weaknesses of 311
independent variables 231
index of dissimilarity (ID)
    calculating 198–9
    defined 197–8
    interpreting results 199–201
    limitations of 200–1
    summarising 201–2
Indigenist research methodology, development of 23
Indigenous paradigm 21–2
inductive codes 420
inductive theory, defined 50
inductive theory development 50
informed consent 96, 98–101
Inside-Out Program 377, 400–3
inter-coder reliability 327
inter-collection discontinuities 195–7
intercensal estimates 185
internet sites
    research-orientated sites 40–1
    as sources 40
interpretations, data analysis 71
interpretive perspective 316
interpretivist paradigm 21
intertextuality (discourse analysis) 356, 364
interval data 251
interview guides 301–3
interviewing techniques
    achieving rapport 305–6
    beginning interviews 303
    getting good answers 303–4
    reasons for poor answers 304
    reflectively evaluating an interview 306
    for sensitive topics 306–7
intra-collection discontinuities 194–5, 196

journal articles (peer reviewed) 39
judgement, defined 200

Karnilowicz, Wallym 143
knowledge questions 300

language
    defined 4
    in discourse analysis 356
large representative national sample 222
level of implication (coding) 325
level of measurement (variables) 250
life histories 424
Likert-type scale 171–2
limitations (evaluation) 382
literature reviews
    defined 43
    evaluating sources 38–41
    key social science databases 38
    locating right literature 37–8
    managing 42–3
    nature and purpose of 36
    process of reviewing literature 36–7
    writing 43–4, 446
longitudinal analysis 189

longitudinal quasi-panel studies   244
longitudinal studies
    defined   102, 156, 244
    nature of   156
low-risk research   96
Lyotard, Jean-Francois   22

McDonald, Kevin   317–18
Maher, Jane Maree   429–30
Maori people, ethical research guidelines   107
Marjoribanks, Tim   316–17
Martin, Karen   23
Marx, Karl   20
Maternity Payment, media reaction to   344–6
mean, defined   8
meaning, importance of   290–1
measurement, process of   32
media items, as sources   40
median age (populations)   204
memory work, defined   21
mental illness, role of spirituality in recovery   98–101
metaphor (discourse analysis)   356
method
    defined   12
    as part of methodology   22–3
    see also research methods
methodology
    defined   12
    difference from method   12–13
    elements of   13–23
    method   22–3
    quantitative and qualitative   24, 25–6
    standpoint   13–18
    theoretical foundations   18–22
mini-quantitative analysis   223–4
modality (discourse analysis)   356
monographs   39
motherhood, and employment   429–30
multi-agency cooperation (evaluation)   383
multidisciplinary databases   38
multiple indicators   224
multiple-choice questions   171

narrative analysis   418, 424–6
National Health and Medical Research Council (NHMRC), research ethics   94–5
National Statement on Ethical Conduct in Research Involving Humans   94, 96–8
nationally based general social surveys   222
naturalistic methods   385, 386
negligible risk research   95
nominal data   250
nominal definition, defined   47
non-probability sampling
    case study: child support and housing   140
    defined   124
    methods   137–9
    selecting sample size   140–2
    uses of   137
NUD*IST software   416
Nuremberg Code   92–4
NVivo software   416, 417–18

one-shot case studies   155
ontology   16–17
open coding   423
Open Cut   292
open-ended questions   174, 303
operationalisation
    defined   32, 335
    and measuring or identifying concepts   48–9
opinion questions   300
order of discourse (discourse analysis)   356, 365
ordinal data   251
outcomes, defined   22, 378

panel studies   156
paradigms, defined   13
Parsons, Talcott   20
participant observation   103
participant safety
    ethical research   104–5
    protection of vulnerable participant groups   105–7
participatory action research   22
passive style (discourse analysis)   355
payments, to research subjects   112
peer reviewed articles in scholarly journals   39
percentage change   192
percentage points   192
percentages   191
performance indicators (evaluation)   388–9
performance targets (evaluation)   388
plagiarism   108
policy implications, defined   209
population parameters   126
population studies   123
population-level data
    accessing   212–13
    available from Census of Population and Housing   187–8
    differences to survey data   186
    sources of   185–6
population-level data analysis
    analytical complexities   194
    analytical issues   190–3
    defined   185
    index of dissimilarity   197–203
    inter-collection discontinuities   195–7
    intra-collection discontinuities   194–5, 196
    nature of   184–5
    standardisation   203–10

strengths and weaknesses 188–9
techniques 197–203
uses of 187
populations
defined 72
defining 124–5
posing the ideal questions 300
postmodernism 22
poverty, measurement of 7–8
primary data collection 221
prisoner suicide prevention 377, 400–3
probability sampling
core assumptions 126
deciding sample size 133–4
defined 124, 232
and inference 232
methods of 126–9
sampling errors, confidence levels and confidence intervals 129–32
probes 301
process, defined 378
process of iteration 238
purposive sampling 138

qualitative data analysis
analysing focus groups 427–9
approaches to analysis 418
coding data 419–21
commencing 419–21
computer-assisted data management 416–18
creating meaning 409–15
data organisation using word processing 415
discrepancies and deviant cases 421–2
fieldnotes 419
grounded theory 423–4
immersion and incubation 412–15
introduction 408–9
life histories 424–6
memos 419
narrative analysis 418, 424–6
reflective memos 410–11
reflexivity 409–12
relationships between categories 421
thematic analysis 418, 422
transcription 413–14
written presentation 453–5
qualitative interpretive research 68
qualitative interview studies
environmental leaders in Tasmania 145
teenage witchcraft 81–3
using for social research 288–9
qualitative interviewing
and exploring social meaning 288
nature of 280–1
qualitative methodology 25–6
qualitative research 68

qualitative-quantitative debate 26
quantitative data analysis
accessing secondary data 221–3
choosing techniques 234–6
cross-tabular analysis 230–2
as devoted practice 237–8
example mini-quantitative analysis 223–34
as imaginative practice 237
locating appropriate data 225–6
lure of 218
secondary data analysis 221
skills and approach 236–7
statistical inference 232–3
strengths and weaknesses 235–6
tools for 220–1
univariate analysis 226–30
uses of 219–20
written presentation of 452–3
see also SPSS
quantitative methodology 24, 25, 105
quantitative research 67
quantitative social science data
defined 218, 219
primary data collection 221
quantitative statistical research 67–8
Australian Survey of Social Attitudes 2007 (AuSSA) 144–5
quasi-experimental methods 385
quasi-panel studies 156
questionnaires 153
quota sampling 139

racism, in newspapers 83–4
ratio data 251
ratios 193, 328
raw data 103
reductionism 76, 360
reflecting questions 301
reflective memos 410–11
reflexivity 409–12
regimes of truth 357
Reid, Alice 211
relational content analysis
coding parameters 335
nature of 328–31
relativism 291
reliability (data) 71
representativeness (sampling) 124
research aims 35–6
research design
defined 32
writing up 446
research methodology
defined 4
developing 67–8
see also methodology

research methods
   deciding on   32
   selecting   44–6
research plans, writing   445–7
research process
   analysis of data   74–5
   defining, measuring and observing   70–1
   delineating main variables or processes   69–70
   developing research methodology   67–8
   focusing on a research question   65–6
   identifying the topic   65
   interpretation of results   75
   political and ethical dimensions of research   74
   and role of social research   62
   selecting a research sample   72–4
   specifying theoretical framework   66–7
   ten key issues   64
   writing up results   77
research proposals
   general principles   53–4
   getting started   53
   nature and purpose of   32, 52–3
   structure of   55–6
   writing   445–7
research questions   13, 31
   defined   32
   generating   33–5, 65–6
   importance of   32–3
   and selection of research method   45–6
research reports
   annotated bibliographies   450
   conventional framework   449
   final statement   456
   presentation of data and findings   450
   presentation of qualitative data   453–5
   presentation of quantitative data   452–3
   as sources   39–40
   writing   447–52
researcher safety   108
researcher-administered surveys
   defined   164
   face-to-face interviews   166–7
   features of   165
   maximising response rates to telephone interviews   165–6
   telephone surveys   164–5
resources   52
results
   interpretation of   71, 75
   truthful reporting   108–9

Saha, Lawrence J.   238–9
sample non-response
   calculating response rates   134
   case study: Australian Election Study (1987–2007)   136–7
   defined   134
   weighting to adjust for   134–5
sample statistic, defined   126
samples
   defined   11, 72
   selecting   72–4
sampling
   defining the population   124–5
   key definitions   125–6
   reasons for   124
sampling errors   129
   calculating standard errors   132
   example   130–1
sampling frames, defined   72, 126
sampling methods, selecting   125
scientific method, and social science   8–9
scoping (evaluation)   381
secondary data analysis
   accessing data   221–3
   defined   153
   promise of   221
secondary sources   392–3
selective reduction   325
self-administered surveys
   defined   162
   designing   162
   features of   163
   managing process   164
   maximising response rates   162–4
self-report data   154
self-selected sampling   139
self-technology   359
semantic differential formats   172
shoplifting study   70
Short, Trisch   46
sign of a relationship (concepts)   329
Sikora, Joanna   238–9
simple random sampling (SRS)   127
Smart, Madeleine   431
Smith Family   7–8
snowball sampling   138
social aggregates   10
social desirability effect   310
social mapping   383
social meanings   9–10
social movements, study of   317–18
social patterns   9–10
social practice (discourse analysis)   357, 363–4
social research
   aim of   10–11
   complexity of   5–7
   core levels of   10–11
   cultural factors and assumptions   6
   and Hawthorne effect   6–7
   and human ambiguity, irrationality and social awareness   5–6

nature of   4
   process of   63
   researching the social   4–7
   role of   62
   and social and personal change   6
   and the social context   7
social science
   language of   12
   and scientific method   8–9
social science data archive   221
social science databases   38
social theory
   conceptual frameworks   19
   defined   10, 18
   theoretical paradigms   19–22
Sociological Association of Aotearoa New Zealand
      (SAANZ), ethical standards   94–5
software packages
   bibliographic   451
   for qualitative research   416, 417–18
   word-processing   450–2
   see also SPSS
sources
   evaluation of   38–41
   on internet   40–1
   reference works for editors   462
specialised dictionaries   327
spirituality, and recovery from mental illness   98–101
SPSS (Statistical Product and Service Solutions)
      software   220–1
   bivariate analysis   264–9
   charting comparative frequencies   263
   coding data   244–6
   comparing frequency results across variables   262
   compute variable function   274
   cross-tabulation   255, 265–9
   crosstabs dialogue box   266
   cumulative per cent column   261
   data analysis   256–7
   data view screen   252–4
   dialogue boxes   246
   entering data   250–2
   exporting data   276–8
   frequencies output window   260–3
   frequencies statistics table   260
   missing data   255
   opening a blank file   246
   output window   255–6
   and quantitative analysis   243
   recode function   263
   recoding data   270–3
   relationship between variable view and data view
         screens   254–5
   saving data   276
   screens   246–50
   syntax files   255

   transform tool   274
   transforming data   273–5
   univariate analysis   257–63
   valid cases   269
   valid per cent column   261
   variable view screen   246, 248–50
standard deviation   229–30
standardisation
   basic premise   203–4
   defined   203
   process of   206–8
   summary   210
   uses of   204–6
standpoint
   axiological framework   15–16
   defined   13
   epistemological framework   14–15
   ontological framework   16–17
statistical analysis, defined   220
statistical inference   232–3
strategic partnerships (evaluation)   383
stratified sampling
   defined   128
   disproportionate and proportionate   128–9
Strauss, Anselm   423
strength of relationship (concepts)   329
structured interviews   290
Struggles for Subjectivity   317–18
study populations, defined   125
suicide notes   323
suicide prevention, prisoners   377, 400–3
summary measure   203
summary questions   301
summative evaluation   387–8
survey data
   differences from population-level data   186
   and secondary data analysis   153
   snapshot nature of   154
   and statistical analysis techniques   153
survey data collection
   electronic surveying   167–8
   researcher-administered surveys   164–7
   selecting best method   161
   self-administered surveys   162–4
survey design, types of   155–6
survey questionnaires
   developing   168–9
   pre-testing or piloting   174–5
survey questions
   closed questions   171
   contingency questions   173–4
   framing   169–70
   Likert-type items   171–2
   open-ended questions   174
   ranking formats   173
   rationale for   71, 168–9

survey questions (cont.)
    selecting question format 171–4
    semantic differential formats 172
    simple multiple-choice questions 171
survey research process 156–7
    research formulation and method selection 158–9
    sample selection 159–60
    survey development 161–75
surveys
    advantages of 152–3
    disadvantages of 154–5
    as a research method 152, 160–1
    study of housework in Australia 79–81
    uses of 151, 152
synchronic analysis 190
systematic sampling 127–8

Taylor, Lisa 211
teenage witchcraft study 81–3
telephone interviews 164–6
test of significance 232
textbooks as sources 39
texts, defined 3
textual analysis 78, 357, 364–5
thematic analysis 418, 422–3
theoretical paradigms 19–22
Thomas, Walter 280
Thompson, Britany 211
timelines 50–2
Tippin, David 295–6
transcription 413–14
translation rules 327
triangualtion 26

unemployment 307
units of analysis 72, 75–6
univariate analysis
    defined 226, 258
    frequency distributions 226–7
    measures of central tendency 228–9
    uses of 226
    using SPSS software 257–63
unstructured interviews 301

validity (data) 71
validity (discourse analysis) 361
value questions 300
variables, levels of measurement 250–1
verstehen 291

vital statistics 185
volunteer participation 111–12
vulnerable populations 105–6

Walter, Maggie 71–2
Warner, Kate 279–80
Watson, Virginia 24
web sites *see* internet sites
Weber, Max 21
Welch, Allan 175–7
Wendt, Sarah 77–8
Western, Mark 217
Williams, Claire 292
Willis, Evan 463–4
Wittgenstein, Ludwig 353
working sole mothers 71–2, 295–6
writing
    constitutive role 441
    dissemination 464–5
    editing and revising 459–62
    editing skills 461–2
    example contents page from honours thesis 465–7
    final statement 456
    gaining feedback 459–61
    generative view of 441
    as an integral part of research 440
    iterative approach 440–1
    levels of editing 460
    narrative structures 442
    presentation of quantitative data 452–3
    qualitative data 453–5
    references for editors 462
    as a tool of discovery 440–2
    two-step strategy 440–1
    useful software 450
    and word processing software 450–2
writing strategies
    breaking up writing task 458
    first sentence 457
    maintaining momentum 457–8
    overcoming blocks 459
    prioritising task of writing 457–8
    recommended strategies 459
    stream of consciousness 458
writing style
    active versus passive language 443–4
    authorial voice 442
    changes over time 443
    principles for 'good writing' 442–3